THE NEW
TESTAMENT
EXPLORER

ALSO BY MARK L. BAILEY

To Follow Him: The Seven Marks of a Disciple

———————————————

ALSO BY TOM L. CONSTABLE

Talking to God

SWINDOLL
LEADERSHIP
LIBRARY

THE NEW TESTAMENT EXPLORER

*Discovering the Essence,
Background, and Meaning
of Every Book in the
New Testament*

MARK BAILEY AND TOM CONSTABLE

CHARLES R. SWINDOLL, *General Editor*

ROY B. ZUCK, *Managing Editor*

WORD PUBLISHING

NASHVILLE

A Thomas Nelson Company

THE NEW TESTAMENT EXPLORER
Swindoll Leadership Library

Unless otherwise indicated, Scripture quotations used in this book are from
the *Holy Bible: New International Version,* copyright © 1978
by the New York International Bible Society.
Used by permission of Zondervan Bible Publishers.

Scripture quotations identified NKJV are from the *New King James Version* of the Bible.
Copyright © 1979, 1980, 1982,
by Thomas Nelson, Inc. Used by permission.

Scripture quotations identified KJV are from the *King James Version* of the Bible.

Scripture quotations identified NASB are from the *New American Standard Bible,*
copyright © 1960, 1962, 1963, 1971, 1972, 1973, 1975, 1977, 1999
by the Lockman Foundation. Used by permission.

Published in association with Dallas Theological Seminary (DTS):
General Editor: Charles R. Swindoll
Managing Editor: Roy B. Zuck
The theological opinions expressed by the authors are not necessarily the official
position of Dallas Theological Seminary.

Library of Congress Cataloging in Publication Data:

Bailey, Mark (Mark L.)
The New Testament explorer / Mark L. Bailey, Tom L. Constable
p.   cm.—(Swindoll Leadership Library)

ISBN 0-8499-1448-5
1. Bible. N.T.—Commentaries. I. Constable, Thomas L., 1939– II. Title. III. Series

BS234.1.2.B35   1999   99-39608
225.7–dc21   CIP

Printed in the United States of America
00 01 02 03 04 05 06 BVG 9 8 7 6 5 4 3 2

CONTENTS

Foreword VII

Preface XI

Acknowledgments XIII

Matthew: Jesus, King of the Jews and the Nations 1

Mark: Jesus, Model of Faithful Service 65

Luke: Jesus, Perfect and Innocent Savior 101

John: Jesus, the Wonderful Word of Life 153

Acts: The Beginnings of Christianity 195

Romans: The Righteousness of God 249

1 Corinthians: The Spiritual Viewpoint on the Church 293

2 Corinthians: The Christian Ministry 341

Galatians: Liberty in Christ 375

Ephesians: The Mystery of the Church 395

Philippians: The Mind of Christ 411

Colossians: The Supremacy of Christ 423

1 Thessalonians: The Return of the Lord 435

2 Thessalonians: The Day of the Lord 447

1 Timothy: Effective Church Life 457

2 Timothy: Effective Church Leadership 477

Titus: Effective Church Organization 489

Philemon: Christian Ethics in Action 497

Hebrews: The Superiority of Christianity 503

James: Faith at Work 537

1 Peter: Living as an Alien 555

2 Peter: Heresy in the Last Days 569

1 John: Fellowship and Eternal Life 579

2 John: The Importance of Truth 593

3 John: The Importance of Love 597

Jude: False Teachers 601

Revelation: The Culmination of History 607

   Endnotes 663

   Bibliography 675

FOREWORD

*E*ver heard of spelunking? I have friends who do it, but I'm not so wild about the idea. A layman's phrase for this strange word would be "cave crawling."

Spelunkers love lowering themselves into the earth's deep, dark crevices and poking around. When they reach the point where they can no longer walk (the point where most of us would announce, "Hey, nice cave, think I've seen enough!") spelunkers are just warming to the task. At this point they crawl and slide into the narrowest and deepest of areas. Once I warned a friend, " There are bats in those caves!" To which he responded, "Oh, we love bats!" It's all part of the lure of the labyrinth. One soon learns spelunking is not for the fainthearted.

Studying the Bible at the deepest levels can similarly be viewed as a daunting task. Certain books and passages appear as deep, dark caves, seemingly unexplored. Yet they need not appear as such. Some eager students, brimming with enthusiasm, have plunged headlong into the exegetical task, only to find they have bumped into individual trees in their rush into the forest.

I remember when one of my mentors, Dr. Howard Hendricks, began teaching a group of us young seminarians how to study the Bible for ourselves. The mood that day in the lecture room was, as usual, electric. Many of us shared the sense that we were embarking on an exciting, lifelong journey. None of us was certain where we were headed, but we shared the feeling we were acquiring a skill we would never stop using, especially with a seasoned guide named Hendricks in the lead.

Even at that level, however, we were introduced to other tools we were told we would need. Dr. Hendricks spoke of "handbooks" that provided the groundwork for our intense individual studies. He mentioned works that provided material covering such essentials as authorship, date, geography, as well as the general argument of each biblical book. These, however, were not to be the end results of our study. Our own individual study was to include careful interpretation, and the all-important ingredient of practical application. The volume you're holding in your hands is the type of handbook Hendricks spoke about.

Produced by my colleagues at Dallas Seminary, Dr. Mark Bailey and Dr. Tom Constable, this work provides a powerful launching platform for your own personal in-depth Bible study. All the New Testament books are included. Having a tough time figuring out to whom the Book of James was written? Want to know when the Gospel of John was penned? Struggling with finding the thread that holds Hebrews together? *The New Testament Explorer* will take you there—and further. Much further.

As you may know, I love books. Where else, someone has asked, can you have a group of professors at your fingertips? In this book Bailey and Constable guide you through the New Testament as they clear away the confusion and lay down the groundwork for your own individual study. Because it is so resourceful, you will refer back to this fine book again and again. While sitting at your desk, you will find yourself reaching over to grab this work, much as you do with other well-worn reference tools in your study.

Through the years people have wondered how I find sermon material. Some have even asked if there is a particular trick or shortcut to producing sound expositional stock. Early on in my Christian walk I harbored the assumption, like others, that a good preacher was a man with a head full of ideas and theories who went looking into Scripture for validation. Foolishly, I thought those with the greatest number of clever ideas must make the best preachers. Once I got to Dallas Seminary I learned otherwise. Through Hendricks and other competent teachers of the Word, I learned the process employed is just exactly the opposite. A good preacher goes into the Bible *and stays there, studying intently* until he comes out not only with something to say, but also with something he must declare with passion. *The New Testament Explorer* will become a tremendous help while you are "in there" studying intently.

You might want to think of the process as spiritual spelunking! Bailey and Constable have their headlighted helmets on. They're strapped in and ready to guide you into the depths of a cave called "Personal Bible Study." For those of you still unsure about being lowered in, allow me to let you in on a vital secret that will encourage you to crawl in—*the gold is at the bottom of the cave!*

—CHARLES R. SWINDOLL
General Editor

PREFACE

*M*arco Polo
Christopher Columbus
Ferdinand Magellan
Lewis and Clark
Edmund Hillary

What do these men have in common?

Each one was an explorer!

Whether crossing the wastelands of central Asia, sailing around the world, climbing over the Rocky Mountains to the Pacific Ocean, or scaling the world's highest mountain, each of these adventurers was driven by the urge to discover, to explore something he had never seen before.

Studying the Scriptures can be an exhilarating adventure too. Exploring, discovering, traversing, analyzing, and probing—that's the essence not only of famous world explorers of previous years, but also of pondering the Bible.

Marco Polo, Columbus, and Lewis and Clark may have often puzzled over their surroundings. Where were they? What was the significance of what they saw? How unique were the marvels they discovered?

Similarly in Bible study we are often perplexed by what we read in God's Word. What does this phrase mean? How does this group of verses fit the verses around it? How does this chapter relate to the flow of the book? What is the uniqueness of this Bible book in relationship to other Bible books?

These are some of the questions *The New Testament Explorer* seeks to answer for you. Whether you are preparing a Sunday school lesson, putting together a sermon for Sunday morning, or reading the Bible devotionally for your own soul's edification, the *Explorer* can help guide you as you study the New Testament.

Not a detailed word-by-word commentary, nor a concise Bible hand-book, the *Explorer* discusses each paragraph of each New Testament book, showing how each human author, guided by the Holy Spirit, developed a single purpose in his book point by point. The introductory pages on each Bible book include material on the author, date, purpose, theological emphases and/or special characteristics, and an outline. Along the way biblical principles and points of application are highlighted, helping you see how the Scriptures relate to life.

A bibliography at the end of the volume lists books recommended for further study in each New Testament book.

Mark Bailey and Tom Constable are long-time faculty members at Dallas Theological Seminary, experienced expositors of the Bible. Dr. Bailey wrote the *Explorer* material on the four Gospels, and Dr. Constable wrote on Acts through Revelation.

Like a compass to a hunter or a map to a traveler, may this volume help guide you as you explore the Scriptures, God's inerrant—and richly relevant—Word.

—ROY B. ZUCK
Managing Editor

ACKNOWLEDGMENTS

Mark L. Bailey

I am grateful for the privilege of contributing to this project and appreciate the leadership of Dr. Charles R. Swindoll and his encouraging friendship.

I continually thank God for the loving support of my wife, Barby, and our two sons, Josh and Jeremy. Together with the Lord, they help make any ministry in which I serve possible and pleasurable.

Dr. Roy Zuck has served with grace as a consummate editor. His advice on this project as on others is always appreciated.

To my parents, who helped create a thirst for the Word of God early in my life, I dedicate my portion of this book.

Tom L. Constable

I would like to thank Dr. Charles Swindoll for the opportunity to write this exposition and Dr. Roy Zuck for his editorial oversight through the stages of its production.

Mary, my faithful and loving wife, guarded my study times and provided an atmosphere conducive to thinking and writing. Thank you, Sweetheart.

To my father, Robert L. Constable, now with the Lord, I owe my initial love for the Word of God. He also gave me much encouragement to continue studying it. And to my mother, Mildred B. Constable, now in her ninety-fifth year, I wish to express my deepest thanks for her prayers and her example of servanthood.

MATTHEW
Jesus, King of the Jews and the Nations

AUTHOR

In his list of the twelve disciples' names, Matthew referred to himself as a "tax collector" (Matt. 10:3), whereas Mark and Luke referred to him simply as Matthew (Mark 3:18; Luke 6:15). Matthew wrote that he was sitting at the tax collector's booth when Jesus called him to follow Him (Matt. 9:9). Matthew held a feast "in his own house" (Mark 2:19; Luke 5:29), whereas Matthew wrote that it was "in the house" (Matt. 9:10, literal translation). These observations support the fact that Matthew was the author of the Gospel that bears his name. Also the fact that he used nine words for money (three of which are found nowhere else in Scripture) reflects his background as a tax collector. Therefore it is not surprising that he is the only one of the Gospel writers who included the account of the payment of the temple tax (17:24–27).

Matthew was the son of Alphaeus, and he also bore the surname of Levi (Mark 2:14; Luke 5:27). Jesus chose him as one of the twelve disciples, and the last record of his name is in Acts 1:13.

DATE

We know Matthew wrote his Gospel before the destruction of Jerusalem in A.D. 70 because he referred to the city numerous times as though it was still standing, even calling it "the holy city" (4:5; 27:53). Therefore Matthew must have written his Gospel sometime between A.D. 50 and 60. The phrases "unto this day" (27:8, KJV) and "until this day" (28:15) imply that Matthew wrote his book sometime after Jesus' resurrection and ascension. The year A.D. 50 would be appropriate if Matthew was the first of the four Gospels, or A.D. 60 would seem appropriate if Mark was the first of the four Gospels.

HISTORICAL BACKGROUND

Did Matthew write in Aramaic or Greek? Those who say Aramaic point to the statement of Papias, quoted by Eusebius, that Matthew wrote in the Hebrew dialect and then translated it. Those who say Matthew's Gospel was written in Greek point out that he explained words and certain Palestinian customs, which would not seem to be necessary if he had written in Aramaic.

Did Matthew write this book in Palestine or Antioch of Syria? Those who say he wrote in Aramaic believe the place where he wrote his Gospel was Palestine. Or if he wrote in Greek, then he may have written outside Palestine where many Greek-speaking Jews resided. Syria seems a likely place since there were large numbers of Jewish Christians living in the area (Acts 11:19, 27). Antioch of Syria is favored by many since this was the second major center for Christianity, and the other Gospels are also associated with prominent centers.

Church fathers Irenaeus and Origen said the Gospel of Matthew was addressed to early Jewish converts. Many references in the book to Jewish customs and concerns suggest a Jewish audience. Commissioned by Christ (Acts 1:8), the early church expanded geographically from Jerusalem to Rome, and many Jews accepted Jesus Christ as their Messiah.

PURPOSE

Matthew recorded selected events from the life and ministry of Jesus Christ in order to confirm to a Jewish audience that Jesus is indeed the Messiah and to explain God's kingdom program for the present age in light of Israel's rejection of her King.

CHARACTERISTICS

Several features are characteristic of the Gospel of Matthew.

First, eschatology is emphasized in the parables and discourses in the book.

Second, Jesus' teaching on the kingdom is prominent.

Third, the royal majesty and authority of Jesus Christ is set forth (Matt. 25:31–46; 28:18–20), as well as His superiority over Israel's prized institutions: the Law (5:21–22, 27–28), the Sabbath (12:8), the prophets (12:41), the temple (12:6), and the king (12:42).

Fourth, Matthew is a bridge between the Old and New Testaments, viewing Jesus' ministry as the fulfillment of the prophetic past and the hope of the prophetic future. Precise, detailed references to fulfilled prophecy distinguish the presentation of Matthew from the other Gospel writers.

Fifth, Matthew is the only Gospel of the four that mentions the church (16:18; 18:11).

Sixth, the teaching ministry of Christ is highlighted. Five of Jesus' discourses are recorded, each of which ends with the statement "when Jesus had finished" (5:3–7:27; 10:5–42; 13:13–52; 18:3–35; 24:4–25:46).

Seventh, the Book of Matthew demonstrates Jesus' notable concern for Gentiles (see 8:11–12; 15:24; 21:43; 28:19).

OUTLINE

I. The Person of the King (chapters 1–4)
   A. The Birth and Infancy of Jesus (chapters 1–2)
   B. The Ministry of John the Baptist (3:1–12)
   C. The Inaugural Ministry of Jesus (3:13–4:25)

II. The Platform of the King (chapters 5–7)
   A. The Beatitudes (5:1–12)
   B. The Influences of Salt and Light (5:13–16)

    C. The Relationship of Righteousness and Law (5:17–48)

    D. The Relationship of Righteousness to Life (6:1–7:12)

    E. The Invitations and Applications (7:13–29)

III. The Power of the King (chapters 8–10)

    A. Miracles of Healing (8:1–17)

    B. Calls to Discipleship (8:18–22)

    C. Miracles of Power (8:23–9:8)

    D. Challenges of Discipleship (9:9–17)

    E. Miracles of Restoration (9:18–34)

    F. Commissions to Discipleship (chapter 10)

IV. The Pivotal Rejection of the King (chapters 11–12)

    A. Clarification about John the Baptist and the Kingdom (11:1–19)

    B. An Indictment and an Invitation (11:20–30)

    C. Controversies and Signs (chapter 12)

V. The Parables of the Kingdom (13:1–52)

    A. The Parable of the Sower and the Soils (13:1–9)

    B. The Reasons for the Parables (13:10–17)

    C. The Interpretation of the Sower (13:18–23)

    D. The Seven Other Parables (13:24–52)

VI. The Progressive Rejection of the King (13:53–18:35)

    A. A Series of Reactions to Jesus (13:53–16:12)

    B. A Series of Revelations by Jesus (16:13–18:35)

VII. The Presentation of the King (chapters 19–25)

    A. Teachings en Route to Jerusalem (chapters 19–20)

    B. Controversies in Jerusalem (chapters 21–22)

    C. Further Denunciations of Israel's Leaders (chapter 23)

    D. The Olivet Discourse (chapters 24–25)

VIII. The Passion of the King (chapters 26–28)

    A. The Preparation for the Passover (26:1–16)

    B. The Inauguration of the Lord's Supper (26:17–30)

    C. Gethsemane and the Arrest of Jesus (26:31–56)

    D. The Trials (26:57–27:26)

    E. The Crucifixion (27:27–56)

    F. The Burial (27:57–66)

    G. The Resurrection and the Great Commission (chapter 28)

I. THE PERSON OF THE KING (CHAPTERS 1–4)

A. The Birth and Infancy of Jesus (chapters 1–2)

The covenantal heritage of the Messiah (1:1). The title in the opening verse of the Book of Matthew points back through Jesus' Davidic ancestry to His Abrahamic origins. The opening assertion that Jesus is the Messiah is bold—an assertion that no doubt Mattthew knew needed to be supported before it would be acceptable to a Jewish audience. The opening lines link Jesus as the Messiah to the Abrahamic and Davidic covenant expectations of the Old Testament.

The genealogy of Jesus the Messiah (1:2–17). After looking backward to the Jewish roots of the Messiah in Abraham, Matthew made a U-turn and marched forward through three sets of fourteen names to trace the ancestry of the Messiah. Three distinct periods are delineated: Abraham to David, David to the Babylonian Captivity, and the Captivity to Christ (see 1:17). The first period shows the rise of the Jewish monarchy; the second demonstrates the fall of the Davidic kingdom; and the third anticipates the restoration of the kingdom under the Messiah's sovereign rule. The outworking of the Abrahamic, Davidic, and New Covenants can be anticipated through this overview of Hebrew history.

Noteworthy in the genealogy is the mention of five women. God's grace is thus highlighted in this opening page of the New Testament. The lives of these women reveal secret closets in the family of Israel, opened for everyone to see. Through the Incarnation the messianic line is identified with real family histories of major spiritual failures. Represented in the lives of these five women are immorality with an in-law (Tamar, 1:3), prostitution (Rahab, 1:5), origin from a nation (Moab) that began with father-daughter incest (Ruth, 1:5; see Gen. 19:36–37), adultery with a murderous cover-up (Bathsheba, Uriah's wife, 1:6), and out-of-wedlock pregnancies (Tamar, Bathsheba, and Mary, 1:3,

> *The plan of God to establish His kingdom through Jesus will transcend the barriers of race, gender, and spiritual failure.*

6, 16). Through the Incarnation God was willing to identify His Son with sinful humanity.

The virgin birth of the Messiah (1:18–25). The birth of Jesus through the Virgin Mary proves that Jesus is the Son of God. In distinction from Luke's account, the experience of Joseph is highlighted. While Jesus is not the physical son of Joseph, He is the legal Heir to the throne through Joseph, a godly descendant of David. Joseph's righteous character is seen in his desire to separate from what appears to be sexual infidelity. His plan to do it privately shows that he was not interested in protecting his own reputation at the expense of Mary's. The fact that he explicitly followed the angel's instructions also demonstrates his righteous obedience.

Jesus' birth fulfilled Old Testament prophecy, as seen in the quotation of Isaiah 7:14 in Matthew 1:23. Both passages, Matthew 1:21–23 and Isaiah 7:14, mention the supernatural sign of a virgin getting pregnant, the anticipation of a son, and the expectation of salvation. In Isaiah we are not told how the virgin conceived, whereas in Matthew we are told it was by means of the Holy Spirit, apart from any involvement with a man. In both passages the son is named Immanuel. In Isaiah, the son was a sign that God would be with Israel in a special protective way. In Matthew the Son is in reality the Son of God. In a literal sense God had come to be with humanity through the physical presence of Jesus on the earth. The "salvation" Isaiah referred to was the deliverance of Judah from the threats of the Israel-Syria coalition. Isaiah wrote of the timing of the salvation, which he said would be before the promised Son would be weaned. In Matthew, however, salvation is the deliverance from sin that Jesus would provide.

Jesus' names reinforce the theology of the entire section. He is called "the Christ," which means He is the "Anointed One" or the "Appointed One" of God, the One who is the promised Messiah. The name "Jesus" (which means "Yahweh saves") is significant in that it is He who would become the Savior from sin. "Immanuel," which means "God with us," rightly introduces us to the Son of God who became flesh. The Messiah who has come to be the Savior is God in the flesh. The conception, a miracle wrought by the Holy

> *Wholehearted obedience is evidence of a righteous heart.*

Spirit, and the fact that Jesus was born while Mary was still a virgin testify again to the obedience of Joseph and the purity of his relationship with Mary.

The worshipful visit of the wise men (2:1–12). The visit and worship of the wise men were recorded by Matthew to authenticate the kingship of Jesus. The star and the gifts associated with royalty (gold), sacrifice (frankincense), and death (myrrh) may have been anticipated in Old Testament prophecy. In Baalam's fourth oracle (Num. 24:17) the expectation of the star as a symbol of Judaic royalty is revealed (and to a seer from the east!). The death of the Messiah was revealed by Daniel (Dan. 9:24–27), who interestingly had been put in command of the Magi of the Babylonian region (2:48). Possibly both of these passages could account for the expectation and anticipation of the Magi who came to Bethlehem. How ironic that the Jewish leaders were out of step with what God was doing in history through His Son, whereas Gentiles from beyond the borders of Israel came to worship the King of the Jews.

When the Magi asked the religious leaders where the Messiah was to be born, the leaders said, "In Bethlehem of Judea." The fulfillment formula (2:5) was used again by Matthew (see 1:22), this time as a direct messianic prophecy connecting Jesus' birthplace with the prophetic anticipation of Micah. The quotation from the Old Testament is a combination of Micah 5:2 and 2 Samuel 5:2. The One born in Bethlehem would be the King of Israel, who would rule with a shepherd's heart. Not mentioned by Matthew, but significant for the theology of the Incarnation, is the unquoted portion of Micah 5:2, "whose origins are from of old, from ancient times." While Jesus became flesh through the virgin birth at Bethlehem, His preexistence demonstrates His deity. Jesus is the eternal Son of God who existed prior to the Incarnation.

The series of angelic appearances in this infancy narrative attest to divine activity throughout these events. Joseph and Mary's obedience to the angel by escaping to Egypt is further testimony to their righteous character. In Matthew 2:15 a third fulfillment formula is used, this time with reference to Hosea. Just as Israel as a nation was called as a "son" of God from Egypt, so Jesus, *the* Son of God, would come out of Egypt (Hos. 11:1). The same God who was working with Israel was now preparing to work through His Son, Jesus.

> God is sovereign in history and can be trusted to fulfill His promises through Jesus the Messiah.

The threat against Jesus (2:13–23). Herod's threat showed he was intimidated by the thought of a future king of Israel. His decree to destroy all newborn sons in the environs of Bethlehem was dictated by the timing of the appearance of the star. By this edict he attempted to eliminate all challengers to his kingship. Even this argues for Jesus' kingship. A fourth fulfillment citation (2:18) is from Jeremiah 31:15. Rachel was the wife of Jacob, whose name was changed to Israel. Ramah was a town north of Jerusalem. By speaking of Ramah, Jeremiah referred to all the wives and mothers of Israel who were grieving over the loss of their families at the time of the Babylonian captivity.

Matthew may have cited Jeremiah 31:15 to highlight several points. First, in both Jeremiah 31:15 and Matthew 2:13 a gentile king was threatening the future of the nation. Second, whereas Jeremiah's reference to children metaphorically referred to the descendants of Israel in general, the loss recorded in Matthew pertained literally to children. The fact that both Ramah and Bethlehem are near Jerusalem allowed Matthew to link the locations. Third, anyone familiar with Jeremiah 31 would know that while Israel was facing the threat of exile to Babylonia, the future restoration and preservation of Israel were guaranteed by the promises of the New Covenant (Jer. 31:30–37), a covenant God established through the death of Jesus.

The final event in the infancy narrative is Jesus' return to Nazareth. Matthew's reference to Jesus as a "Nazarene" (Matt. 2:23) is probably a wordplay on the Hebrew *nāzîr*, a small twig of insignificant size, and Nazareth, a town with a less than desirable reputation. The combination of these two words speaks of the humble beginnings of the Messiah.

B. The Ministry of John the Baptist (3:1–12)

John the Baptist's message called for repentance in light of the coming kingdom of God.

> ### "The Kingdom of Heaven" and "The Kingdom of God"
>
> The term "the kingdom of heaven" is used exclusively by Matthew in place of the more customary term "the kingdom of God." Parallel passages in the Synoptic Gospels suggest that the two phrases speak of the same reality. Matthew revealed that righteousness (5:20), doing the will of the Father (7:21), and having childlike faith (18:3) are required in order for anyone to enter the kingdom of heaven. All three speak of faith in response to the revelation of God that qualifies a person to enter that sphere over which God rules in sovereign authority. Matthew likely employed the phrase "the kingdom of heaven" as an allusion to the prophecy in Daniel 7:13–14, which states that one like the Son of Man will come from the heavens on God's behalf to establish His kingdom on earth.

John's wilderness-based ministry is linked with Isaiah's call for readiness for the arrival of the Lord (Isa. 40:3). His clothing and diet were similar to that of Elijah the prophet (2 Kings 1:8). Confessing one's sins and being baptized symbolized faith in what only God could provide. John's warning of coming judgment (Matt. 3:7–10) was designed to alert the Jews that neither race nor religious traditions guarantee salvation. Without genuine repentance, whose fruit distinguishes it from empty religious profession and its dead works, there is no assurance of salvation. Works-based religion, which has acceptance as its goal, differs greatly from a faith-based righteousness, which has righteous works as its fruit. Like a herald announcing the presence of a king, John introduced Jesus as the One who can save and the One who will judge. The fact that Jesus can baptize people with the Holy Spirit is another evidence of His deity.

> Repentance is the change of mind and heart in response to the grace of God whereby a person recognizes the futility of his or her human condition apart from God and therefore places faith and trust in God alone for salvation.

C. The Inaugural Ministry of Jesus (3:13–4:25)

> *Since Jesus was willing to identify with us, we should be willing to identify with Him.*

The baptism of Jesus (3:13–17). John's baptizing of Jesus underscored Jesus' superiority over John and demonstrated Jesus' messianic identity. John was reluctant to baptize Jesus because he knew that He did not need to repent and that he, John, needed, instead, to be baptized by Jesus. Jesus countered John's resistance by a statement that identified John's work as a work of righteousness (3:15) with which He was identifying Himself. The baptism of Jesus identified Him with the righteous remnant, inaugurated His public ministry, and enabled the Holy Spirit to be identified with Him. The presence and descent of the Spirit, along with the statement of the Father from heaven, link Psalm 2:7 and Isaiah 42:1. This too shows that Jesus is both the Son of God and the promised Messiah, who came from God the Father and with the anointed power of the Spirit.

The temptations of Jesus (4:1–11). Jesus' temptations demonstrate His impeccable character. When Satan said, "If you are the Son of God," the Greek word for "if" means "since," thus showing that Satan knew He is the Son of God. Each of the temptations assumes His dual nature as both God and man. He was tempted as the God-Man and not just in the realm of His humanity. That is, the temptations to perform miracles and manifest Himself as the Messiah are not the normal fare of human temptations.

Satan's first approach was to tempt Jesus to act independently of the Spirit to satisfy His personal needs. Jesus' response, based on Deuteronomy 8:13, shows that direction for life is to come from the Word of God.

Satan's second temptation—that Jesus jump from the pinnacle of the temple—may well have Malachi 3:1 as a background, which anticipated the sudden arrival of the Messiah. Satan's misuse of Psalm 91:11–12 was an appeal to the pride of life in Jesus' relationship to Israel. The response from Deuteronomy 6:16 forbids putting God to the test by improperly depending on Him for sensational deliverance rather than trusting Him for the future.

The third temptation appropriately relates to Jesus' right to rule in the kingdom of God. Satan offered the kingdoms of the ages if Jesus would worship him. This, however, would clearly violate Exodus 20:3, 14. Jesus' response from Deuteronomy 6:13 points out that nothing should be an object of worship or service in place of God. All three temptations show that it is wrong to attempt to find satisfaction in life apart from God and His will.

> *Temptation is the seduction by the world and Satan to find meaning and fulfillment apart from the will and Word of God.*

The initial ministry of Jesus (4:12–25). Matthew did not include the early Judean ministry of Jesus, which is recorded in John 1:19–42 and 2:13–3:36. Following the reaction of the leaders of the synagogue in Nazareth, Jesus took up residence in Capernaum, making it the center of His Galilean ministry in fulfillment of Isaiah 9:1. Various reasons have been suggested as to why Jesus spent so much time in Galilee and especially around the northern shore of the Sea of Galilee. Many Gentiles (as well as Jews) lived there. Two major highways intersected there. Tiberias attracted many of the sick who hoped the spas there could help. In Galilee Jesus could attract a group of disciples while avoiding a premature reaction from the leaders of Jerusalem. Jesus' message echoed John the Baptist's message of repentant faith as the only way to enter the coming kingdom.

The use of the phrase "from that time on" in Matthew 4:17 introduces the Lord's message of the kingdom, and in 16:21 it introduces the necessity of the Cross. Jesus' ministry included teaching, preaching, and healing (4:23). The use of these three words here and in 9:35 serve as an *inclusio* or framing statement around the words and works of Jesus. Matthew's emphasis on the Jewish aspect of Jesus' ministry is seen in his reference to the synagogue, the message of the kingdom and its imminence, and the authenticating manifestation of the miracles.

II. THE PLATFORM OF THE KING (CHAPTERS 5–7)

The Sermon on the Mount (Matthew 5–7), which clarifies the difference between inner righteousness and outer ritual, presents the platform of the King. These are the principles of kingdom living that should characterize one who is waiting for the Messiah to establish the kingdom. This is His way of life. The message is addressed to a mixed crowd of both disciples and multitudes. Some of His words were addressed to those who were already related to their heavenly Father and others were addressed to those who had not yet decided to go through the narrow gate that leads to eternal life. Such a mixed audience is not unlike a crowded church or arena today. In Matthew 5:20, Jesus declared opposition against the Pharisaic perversions of Judaism. The Jewish leaders had so twisted the Mosaic Law for their own traditional benefits that it was necessary for the Lord to clarify the meaning of genuine righteousness.

A. The Beatitudes (5:1–12)

The beatitudes are attitudes that reflect the kind of righteousness that befits kingdom citizenship. The first and last beatitudes (5:6, 10) assume a righteous heart on the part of believers. The other beatitudes describe attitudes of obedience for which there is the promise of future rewards. The blessings of the beatitudes are the divine favor of God which rests on the righteous whether now or in the age to come.

B. The Influences of Salt and Light (5:13–16)

The metaphors of salt and light describe the effect that the righteous can have in our fallen world. Light dispels darkness, and salt helps prevent decay. The righteousness of a believer's life witnesses to the glory and grace of God.

C. The Relationship of Righteousness and Law (5:17–48)

It is important to distinguish the law of God in general from the Mosaic Law in particular. The latter codified the law of God for a specific period of time in God's economy. Christ came to fulfill the predictions about Himself in both portions of the Old Testament, the Law and the Prophets. In contrast to the Jewish leaders' inconsistent application of the law, Jesus took His stand as the Revealer, Interpreter, and Fulfiller of the Old Testament, and He showed its intended spiritual application in contrast to mere external conformity to traditional regulations.

> *Christians are called to influence the world through godly character and conduct.*

The six antitheses Jesus selected from the Old Testament (5:21–48)- are all classic examples of how righteous attitudes are foundational for the practical expressions of righteousness in relationship to God and others. In translating attitude into action, root issues cannot be ignored. The "root" of murder is anger, and so reconciliation at all costs is required. The root of adultery is lust, and so removal of improper stimuli is the heart-level solution. The root issue in divorce is selfishness on the part of at least one member of the relationship. In taking oaths, the root issue is to refrain from swearing by what is beyond one's control. Retaliation is never an option for the individual. Going the "extra mile" in order to solve a conflict is the righteous alternative to the root problem of personal retaliation. Believers are to live up to the family likeness of the Father's godliness by mercifully extending love and prayer and mercy even to their enemies. This will help one avoid the root problem of reciprocity, the opposite of grace and mercy.

D. The Relationship of Righteousness to Life (6:1–7:12)

Doing religion with righteousness (6:1–18). Jesus gave three examples of doing the right thing in the wrong way. The three are introduced with the warning against practicing one's faith to be seen by other people, since that is a sure way to lose one's reward in heaven (6:1–3, 16). The three examples are giving, fasting, and prayer. Twelve times "the Father" is mentioned in this chapter, reinforcing the theme that one's heart disposition toward God is more important than any outward display, however much it might impress other people.

> *A person's heart is revealed by the values and treasures he or she esteems.*

Religious activities should be motivated by one's personal relationship with God rather than one's public reputation before others.

Avoiding the extremes in handling wealth (6:19–34). The danger of having too much is that it divides the devotion of one's heart, whereas the danger of having too little is that it can lead to the distracting worry of the heart. The first is a problem of love; the second is a problem of priority. Kingdom priorities and perspectives help guard a person against anxiety.

Righteousness in relationships (7:1–12). Believers are not to be judgmental, especially in their expectations of unbelievers. Self-righteousness is the biggest blinder to objectivity in one's relationships. Dogs and pigs symbolize the unregenerate (see 2 Pet. 2:22). Grace in one's relationships is modeled by God, who answers the prayers of those who persistently seek Him and His will. The "golden rule" (Matt. 7:12) continues to be the best summary of the righteous life in relation to others. This central section of the message on the mountain begins and ends with a reference to the Law and the Prophets in 5:17 and 7:12.

E. The Invitations and Applications (7:13–29)

This final section of the Sermon on the Mount calls Jesus' hearers to apply His message to themselves. He invited those who had not yet come to God through His message to go through a gate different from the one the majority of the crowd were entering and thus to find the "path of life." Jesus used three illustrations to show the contrasts between those who are considered righteous and those who are not. The illustration of the two roads teaches the unfortunate fact that the majority of people will not be willing to receive the eternal life God provides. The two trees show that the lifestyle of a preacher is the test of whether his message is true. The two houses show that mere religious profession is both unwise and worthless in withstanding the tests and judgments of life. Hearing and doing what Jesus said determines whether one is a success or failure in his or her earthly walk.

III. THE POWER OF THE KING (CHAPTERS 8–10)

The Alternating Pattern of Matthew 8–10

Three Miracles (8:1–17)	Discipleship (8:18–22)	Three Miracles (8:23–9:8)	Discipleship (9:9–17)	Three Miracles (9:18–34)	Discipleship (chapter 10)

A. Miracles of Healing (8:1–17)

Those whom the Lord healed were among the physically contaminated, the culturally estranged, and those marginalized because of marital or gender discrimination. Leprosy often illustrated the defilement of sin (see Leviticus 13–14). Jesus' healing of the leper showed that He is the Messiah, since in Judaism leprosy was considered incurable. The dialogue between Jesus and the centurion about authority shows that Jesus was under the authority of His Father and thus could speak for God in the affairs of humanity. The people of Israel (and anyone, by application) will forfeit their place in the kingdom by failing to believe what the gentile centurion believed about Jesus (8:12–13). Even non-Jews who express faith in Jesus will find their place in the kingdom with the patriarchs (8:11).

Entrance into the kingdom of heaven is determined by one's positive response to the message of Jesus.

The healing of Peter's mother-in-law shows that humility of service should always be the response of those touched by the gracious hand of God. Matthew's quotation of Isaiah 53:4 shows that the Atonement is the basis for all that God will ultimately restore through redemption. Not all healing will take place this side of eternity. The healing of a Jew (a leper), a Gentile (the centurion), and a Jew (Peter's mother-in-law) portrays God's plan to offer salvation to both Jews and Gentiles.

B. Calls to Discipleship (8:18–22)

Two truths in this passage address the level of commitment Jesus desires from those who would be His disciples. First, commitment should not be

THE NEW TESTAMENT EXPLORER

> Discipleship
> demands
> wholehearted
> commitment
> to Christ and
> His
> kingdom.

based on the "possibilities of the good life" of serving God. This world holds no permanent resources for His disciples. Second, commitment should also be without delay and without regard for family or personal convenience. The call of God comes in the midst of real life. Jesus as the Son of man modeled a simple life. The man's excuse about needing to go bury his father was probably a lame excuse. A person was usually buried the day he or she died; so the man's father probably was not yet dead. Buying this kind of time before committing oneself to the Lord is actually a refusal to be committed. "Son of man" (8:20) is the title Jesus most often used for Himself as He progressively revealed His person and purpose to Israel and His disciples.

C. Miracles of Power (8:23–9:8)

In this set of miracles selected by Matthew, Jesus is shown to have power over disaster, demons, and disease. Both the humanity and deity of Jesus are seen in the miracle on the storming sea. He rose from sleep (in His humanity) to command creation (in His deity) within a moment of time. The miracle of exorcism shows that even the demons understand His judgmental authority. Ironically, the Jewish community did not. The dangerous effects of demonic powers can be conquered only through the Lord's authoritative power. The cleansing of the paralytic and the accompanying dialogue show that as the Son of man Jesus has authority to forgive sin. Doing the apparently more difficult proves that Jesus can do the apparently easier. He healed a man from paralysis to show He can do the most difficult task of all, namely, forgive an individual's sins.

D. Challenges of Discipleship (9:9–17)

Jesus' call of Matthew, the challenge of the Pharisees, and the controversy over fasting all serve as a call to salvation and discipleship. That Matthew, a tax collector, responded is a fitting introduction to the fact that Jesus "did not come to call the righteous but sinners to repentance." The principle of mercy over sacrifice quoted from Hosea 6:6 shows that to God the heart is more important than ritual.

The discussion of fasting revealed both Jesus' identity and the problem Israel had with Him. By the bridegroom metaphor Jesus affirmed His identity as the Messiah, who would be violently removed. The illustrations of the wineskin and

> *Nothing compares to the newness of life which can come only through Christ.*

the shrunken garment show that Israel was too inflexible and irreparable, because it could not handle the new revelation of God in Christ. Jesus was new in time and new in kind, but Israel missed the significance of who He is.

E. Miracles of Restoration (9:18–34)

In these verses four miracles are couched within three narratives. The first set revolves around the number twelve: the number of years the woman with the issue of blood had suffered and the age of Jairus's daughter. Matthew seems to have telescoped the account of Jairus, recording nothing about his daughter's sickness in order to get to the fact that she died. The account of the woman on the way yields the principle that the basis of her healing was her faith in Jesus, not the fabric of His robe. By raising Jairus's daughter Jesus revealed that death is no worse than sleep when the Messiah is present. The first of these two miracles was done in public, and the second was intentionally private. In the first, faith was the basis. In the second, the disciples were the private audience of the truth that Jesus has the power to bring back the dead. Neither disease nor death are a problem for Him.

In the account of the healing of the blind men the irony is that they who were blind "saw" Jesus as the Son of David, who had the power and mercy to help them, whereas those who should have been able to "see" seemed to be blind to who He is. The title "Son of David" is quite appropriate for Jesus as the rightful Heir to David's throne and kingdom. The

> *Prayer is the key to a good harvest of workers, and workers are essential to reach people for God.*

response to the exorcism miracle that "nothing like this has ever been seen in Israel" (9:33) serves as the climactic testimony of the ten miracles selected and arranged by Matthew (in chapters 8 and 9) for his Jewish audience. This is placed in contrast to the countercharge of the Pharisees that Jesus, as the prince of demons, got His power from Satan.

Matthew concluded this symmetrical presentation of the ministry of the words and works of Jesus by repeating the pattern of His ministry and the continuing plight of the people under the failing leadership of the Jews. Teaching in the synagogues, preaching the kingdom, and healing summarize Jesus' threefold ministry in Israel. The people were harassed and afflicted by the ungodly shepherding of the leaders, and therefore the need is for prayer for more workers who will lead those people to the true Shepherd.

F. Commissions to Discipleship (chapter 10)

The appointment of the twelve (10:1–4). The list of Jesus' twelve disciples is given four times in the New Testament (Matt. 10:2–4; Mark 3:16–19; Luke 6:14–16; Acts 1:13). Each time they seem to be divided into groups of four each, possibly indicating small-group structure for the purpose of better discipleship. Simon, Philip, and James the son of Alphaeus head those three groups.

Simon	Philip	James son of Alphaeus
Andrew	Bartholomew	Thaddaeus
James son of Zebedee	Thomas	Simon the Zealot
John son of Zebedee	Matthew	Judas Iscariot

The instructions for the mission (10:5–15). The recipients of the message of the Twelve were to be exclusively Jewish. This message was the same as that of John and Jesus: "Repent for the kingdom of heaven is at hand." They went with a delegated power, and their miracles would serve to authenticate their message. The response of the people to the messengers would indicate whether they received or rejected the message. In each of the cities the disciples would give either a blessing of peace or a warning of judgment, based on the people's response.

> *A supreme and incomparable love for Jesus is the first requirement of those who would follow Him.*

The warnings for the Twelve (10:16–23). Jesus warned the disciples that they would face religious, civil, familial, and international persecution for being identified with Him and His message. Looking ahead to the return of Christ to the earth at the end of the age gives encouragement to endure in the face of persecution. Jesus speaks of the importance of reaching the Jewish cities at the time of the Lord's return, thus affirming a future for the nation of Israel and its distinct place in God's plans for that day.

The prerequisites for all disciples (10:24–42). Jesus broadened the discussion of discipleship to describe what it will take to be a committed follower of His in a hostile environment where He is not readily accepted. He exposed one of the most formidable hurdles that keep people from discipleship, namely, fear—fear of being misunderstood, fear of being persecuted by the crowd, and fear of being alienated from one's own family. These fears are countered with the assurance of being identified with Christ, the truth of having the hope of heaven, and the promise of a better, rewarding relationship with Jesus. Thus Jesus prepared His own for the daunting responsibilities of representing Him on earth as His disciples. If one ever hopes to make disciples of others, he or she needs to know first how to be a disciple. Jesus must mean more to the Christian than all other relationships.

IV. THE PIVOTAL REJECTION OF THE KING (CHAPTERS 11–12)

A. John the Baptist and the Kingdom (11:1–19)

Like a president's press secretary who is in jail simply because he represented the policies of the president, John asked whether Jesus has the power to rule or whether he had been mistaken in his identification of Jesus and

> *Wisdom is demonstrated when one makes the right decision about God and His Son, Jesus Christ.*

should therefore expect another. To confirm His messianic identity, Jesus called John's attention to His many miracles.

Jesus clarified the role of John as the herald of Isaiah 40:3. John the Baptist straddled the line with one foot in the old era of the Law and the Prophets and the other in the new era of the preaching of the imminent kingdom of heaven. In announcing the arrival of the King, he fulfilled the office of "another Elijah" whose ministry was in preparation for the day of the Lord (Mal. 4:5–6). The paragraph closes by contrasting John's ministry with that of Jesus. One was likened to a funeral; the other to a party. The children's chorus from the street taught the counterbalancing themes of the gospel. John was the thundering prophet of doom, and Jesus was the gentle Bearer of good news. One had a message of judgment, the other a message of joy. A person can receive judgment or experience the grace of God through Jesus Christ. If one is not won over by the themes preached by John and Jesus, there are no other alternatives. The wisdom of the approach of both John and Jesus would be seen in the results, the fact that many would be brought into the kingdom.

B. An Indictment and an Invitation (11:20–30)

The indictment of the cities of Galilee (11:20–24). Three cities make up what some refer to as "the gospel triangle" of the Galilean ministry of Jesus. Capernaum, Korazin, and Bethsaida were three privileged cities in which Jesus performed many miracles. The principle stressed in this context is a lesson to all: the greater the revelation, the greater the responsibility. Judgment is said to be proportional. The generation who had the privilege of seeing Jesus and His works will be held more accountable for their rejection of Him than the cities of Tyre, Sidon, or Sodom.

The invitation to the oppressed (11:25–30). The interlocking relationship of the Father and the Son is a marvelous mystery. The message of Jesus and His Father is for humble hearts, not for the proud and self-righteous. To those burdened by the weariness of the world or the load of religious legalism Jesus offered the experience of communion with Him in which there is rest for the soul. The character of the teacher is a key to the quality of the instruction. The imagery of a well-tamed and trained ox being yoked to one that is untamed and untrained is a powerful metaphor. Jesus, the

> *Being linked with Jesus facilitates a gentle rest in the midst of the stresses of life and ministry.*

Master Trainer, invites the weary and burdened to be yoked with Him in a harness of service in which He carries the weight and guides the life. The load is thus easy and light. Rest can be found even in the midst of service!

C. Controversies and Signs (chapter 12)

The Sabbath controversy (12:1–13). Complaints against the disciples for eating grain on the Sabbath show how much the traditional interpretation of the Law created such a bias against Jesus. Israel's religious leaders developed thirty-nine prohibitions to protect the people from violating the command against breaking the Sabbath (Exod. 20:9–11). Among those forbidden activities were reaping, winnowing, threshing, and preparing meals. According to this tradition the disciples were guilty of all four.

Two illustrations from the Old Testament were advanced to rebuke the accusers. When David was suffering rejection, he and his men were hungry and entered the tabernacle and ate the consecrated bread (1 Sam. 21:1–6). Jesus aligned Himself with the rejected David and intimated that the action of His men were no more reprehensible than that of David's men. Jesus' second defense came from the actions of the priests themselves, who undoubtedly worked their hardest on the Sabbath. Jesus excused the actions of the disciples by appealing to Hosea 6:6. God desires the exercise of mercy toward people in need more than He desires the rituals of sacrifice. Jesus affirmed the innocence of the disciples and claimed that He is the Lord of the Sabbath.

Healing of the man with the withered hand (12:9–13). Another Sabbath event continued the controversy between Jesus and the Jewish leaders.

> *The life of a person is of more value to God than all religious rituals and regulations.*

They used a man with a withered hand in the synagogue at Capernaum as a test case for Jesus. Jesus confounded them with a convincing question about the value of a person in comparison to a sheep. They would rescue their animals on the Sabbath before they would rejoice that one of their own people was healed. Jesus asserted it was lawful to do good on the Sabbath. If they could do good to an animal, He could do good to a person. His logic was impeccable.

The wisdom behind the plot to kill the Messiah (12:14–21). In rejecting Jesus the Pharisees even plotted to kill Him. As a result Jesus withdrew from them, and even this proved His identity by His fulfilling a portion of Isaiah 42:1–4, one of the songs of the suffering Servant. He is the Spirit–appointed Messiah who, through His humility and patient endurance in the face of suffering, fulfilled God's will for Him. In Him and especially through His rejection, even Gentiles find a place of refuge.

The controversy over the signs (12:22–30). The healing of a demonized man caused the most divided reaction yet to Jesus' miraculous works. The crowds wondered whether He was in fact the Messiah, and the Pharisees assigned His work to Beelzebub. Beelzebub was the name of a Philistine deity who, because of the national conflicts and competition for supremacy between Israel and the Philistines, became a derogatory name used for Satan himself. Jesus refuted the charge by a series of logical arguments and by the warning against committing blasphemy against the Holy Spirit. Divided kingdoms cannot last long. If Satan were involved in exorcisms, he would be on a path toward self-destruction. But if Jesus were indeed casting out demons, then that showed that He is stronger than the devil, which in turn demonstrated His deity. The fact that the Spirit was the source of power behind Jesus' miracles meant that the kingdom was present in the person of Jesus. Blasphemy against the Holy Spirit was the sin of attributing to Satan the works of the Holy Spirit performed by Christ in His earthly ministry. To deny such an irrefutable witness has eternal consequences for which there is no forgiveness. Mark 3:30 explains this sin with the phrase, "because they were saying, 'He has a demon.'"

V. THE PARABLES OF THE KINGDOM (13:1–52)

The fact that the events of chapter 13 happened on the same day as those of chapter 12 is not to be overlooked. A boat off the shore of the Sea of Galilee served as Jesus' pulpit, and the parables became His method. A parable is a fictitious though true-to-life narrative that conveys through analogy some spiritual truth, usually relative (in Jesus' teachings) to God's kingdom program. Jesus taught these parables because the Jewish leaders had blasphemously rejected Him. These parables took on a judicial as well as an instructive purpose. The parables introduced a "mysterious" phase of the kingdom which was not anticipated in the Old Testament. The period of time they reveal extends from the point of rejection in the earthly ministry of Christ to the time when He will return again to earth and will judge the nations.

THE PARABLES OF JESUS

		Matthew	Mark	Luke
1.	Physician, heal Yourself!	4:23		
2.	Fasting and the Bridegroom	9:14–15	2:18–20	5:34–35
3.	New Patch on Old Garment	9:16	2:21	5:36
4.	New Wine in Old Wineskins	9:17	2:22	5:37
5.	Blind Leading the Blind	15:12–14		6:39
6.	A Pupil Is Not above His Master	10:24–25		6:40
7.	Good and Bad Fruit and Trees	7:15–23		6:43–45
8.	Wise and Foolish Builders	7:24–29		6:46–49
9.	Children in the Marketplace	11:16–19		7:31–35
10.	Two Debtors			7:36–50
11.	The Divided Kingdom	12:25–29	3:22–30	11:17–20
12.	The Empty House	12:43–45		11:24–26
13.	The Sower and the Soils	13:3–9, 18–23	4:3–25	8:4–15
14.	The Growing Seed		4:26–29	
15.	The Wheat and the Weeds	13:24–30, 36–43		
16.	The Mustard Seed	13:31–32	4:30–33	13:18–19
17.	The Leavening Process	13:33		13:20–21

		Matthew	Mark	Luke
18.	The Hidden Treasure	13:44		
19.	The Pearl Merchant	13:45–46		
20.	The Dragnet	13:47–50		
21.	The Householder	13:51–52		
22.	The Unforgiving Servant	18:21–35		
23.	The Good Samaritan			10:30–37
24.	The Friend at Midnight			11:5–13
25.	The Rich Fool			12:13–21
26.	The Faithful Servants			12:35–48
27.	The Fig Tree			13:6–9
28.	The Seats of Honor			14:7–14
29.	The Great Supper			14:16–24
30.	Counting the Cost			14:25–35
31.	The Lost Sheep	18:12–14		15:1–7
32.	The Lost Coin			15:8–10
33.	The Lost Sons			15:11–32
34.	The Unjust Steward			16:1–13
35.	The Rich Man and Lazarus			16:19–31
36.	The Unprofitable Servant			17:5–10
37.	The Importunate Widow			18:1–8
38.	The Pharisee and the Publican			18:9–14
39.	The Laborers in the Vineyard	20:1–16		
40.	The Ten Pounds			19:11–27
41.	The Two Sons	21:28–32		
42.	The Rejected Son	21:33–46	12:1–12	20:9–18
43.	The Marriage Feast	22:1–14		
44.	The Fig Tree Reviewed	24:32–34	13:28–32	21:29–33
45.	The Watchful Doorkeeper		13:33–37	
46.	The Watchful Owner	24:42–44		
47.	The Wise Servant	24:45–51		
48.	The Ten Virgins	25:1–13		
49.	The Talents	25:14–30		
50.	The Sheep and the Goats	25:31–46		

A. The Parable of the Sower and the Soils (13:1–9)

This first parable teaches through the imagery of sowing and harvest the relationship of hearing and responding to Jesus' teaching about the kingdom. In the parable three soils produced no fruit, and there are three levels of fruitfulness from the fourth soil. The four soils represent the kinds of heart conditions in those who are confronted with the message of the kingdom. The wayside soil illustrates the problem of satanic interruption in the preaching process. The rocky soil represents the external pressures that might keep one from following Jesus. The thorny soil conveys the internal distractions of the heart and mind. The well-cultivated soil represents the responsive heart that responds to the kingdom message with faith. This fourth soil cautions us not to expect identical levels of fruitfulness in all people, since believers grow spiritually at different rates.

B. The Reasons for the Parables (13:10–17)

In answer to a question by the disciples, Jesus said His parables had two purposes. To those with receptive hearts the parables were designed to reveal new truths about God's kingdom program. Concealing truth from the unresponsive was also a purpose of the parables. The truth is hidden from those who reject His teaching. The "secrets" ("mysteries," NASB) of the kingdom are those truths about that kingdom that God was revealing through the ministry and message of Jesus. The expected kingdom was delayed and the mystery element was added because the people were not ready to respond. The inverted parallel structure (called a chiasm) of 13:13–17 on the next page shows contrasts between the response of the disciples and the response of Israel's leaders.

Jesus quoted Isaiah 6:9–10 from the Septuagint (the Greek translation of the Old Testament) to show that the stubbornness of Israel of old was repeated by the Jews in Jesus' day. Those like the disciples who did respond were said to have receptive and understanding hearts and were therefore candidates for the new revelation that would come in Jesus' parables. A comparison of Matthew and Mark shows that as a result of the rejection there would be a judicial spiritual blinding. Blindness was both the result of rejection and a purpose in another phase of God's kingdom program.

This is why I speak to them in parables:

1   Though seeing, they do not see; though hearing, they do not hear or understand.
   2   In them is fulfilled the prophecy of Isaiah:
      3   You will be ever hearing but never understanding;
         4   You will be ever seeing but never perceiving.
            5   for this people's heart has become calloused;
               6   they hardly hear with their ears,
                  7   and they have closed their eyes.
                  7'   Otherwise they might see with the eyes,
               6'   hear with the ears,
            5'   understand with the hearts and turn,
                      and I would heal them.
         4'   But blessed are your eyes because they see,
       3'   and your ears because they hear.
    2'   For I tell you the truth, many prophets and righteous men
1'   longed to see what you see but did not see it, and to hear what you hear but did not hear it.

The parables were used to hide truth from those who had shown themselves unresponsive. But understanding came to those who had rightly responded to the message of the kingdom preached by Jesus. Jesus interpreted his own parabolic ministry as a kind of judgment on unbelieving Israel.

C. The Interpretation of the Sower (13:18–23)

Jesus' explanation of the parable of the sower reveals three reasons why the Word of the kingdom does not always take root and produce fruit: the interruptive activity of Satan (see Luke 8:12), external opposition that comes from the pressures of peers and persecutions of those who oppose the message of the gospel, and internal distractions that come from desiring wealth and other interests that tend to choke off the desired effects of the Word in one's life.

D. The Seven Other Parables (13:24–52)

The parable of the weeds (13:24–30). This parable was spoken beside the sea but Jesus gave the interpretation of it to the disciples after they went into a house. This parable and the dragnet parable (13:47–50) both speak of the consummation of the present age when Christ will send His angels to separate the wicked from the righteous. Weeds ("tares," NASB; the botanical term is *Zizania*) and wheat look much the same except at the time of the harvest when the weeds, also known as darnel, have a rotten center, a fitting image for the heart difference between the righteous and the wicked. This parable points out hypocritical religiosity, which is all too often confused with genuine Christianity. Both Christ and Satan have planted their "sons" in the world, which have opposite characters. Satan seeks to counterfeit the genuine kingdom of God for his selfish purposes, but Jesus has "planted" His disciples in the world as His representatives. At the end of the age the wicked will be separated from the righteous. The righteous will enter the earthly phase of the kingdom that follows the judgment at the second advent of Christ.

Two parables of growth (13:31–35). The parable of the mustard seed tells of the international growth that will occur in the present age between Jesus' first and second comings. While rejected by the majority in Israel, the kingdom, though starting small with only a remnant, will grow to international proportions. The imagery of the birds of the air nesting in branches was taken from the Old Testament (Ezek. 17:22–23; 31:6; Dan. 4:12) to depict gentile participation in various kingdom settings.

The leavening process speaks of permeation, which may be bad or good. Leaven or yeast is often used of evil (Exod. 12:8, 15–20; Matt. 16:6; Mark 8:15; 1 Cor. 5:6; Gal. 5:9). Yeast was not to be used in foods eaten on the Feasts of Passover and Unleavened Bread (Exod. 23:18; 34:25). But in thank offerings (Lev. 7:13; see also Amos 4:5) and the wave offerings on the Feast of Pentecost (Lev. 23:17) leaven was required.

In Matthew 13:33 and Luke 13:20–21 leaven is used of the permeating growth of the kingdom of God. To take it negatively in these passages in the Gospels would imply that the phrase "until it worked all through the dough" means that the kingdom of God will be totally corrupted with evil. Instead, God's kingdom is characterized by righteousness and will succeed until the kingdoms of this world become the kingdom of His Son, Jesus Christ (see Rev. 11:15).

The parable of the weeds explained (13:36–43). Jesus and Satan have competing plans, as seen in the people they "plant" in the world. Jesus explained that the harvest is the judgment at the end of the age and that angels will carry out that judgment. Harvesting was a common Old Testament symbol for divine judgment (Jer. 51:33; Hos. 6:11; Joel 3:13). All that is wicked will be removed so that the millennial kingdom established by Jesus will include none but the righteous. The wicked will be separated from the righteous and sent into judgment, and "the righteous will shine like the sun in the kingdom of the Father." Shining as the sun may reflect Daniel 12:3 and Malachi 4:2, where those who enter the kingdom are said to be identified with the character of Him who judged them worthy of such entrance. The kingdom of God the Father and the kingdom of the Son are essentially the same.

The parables of the hidden treasure and of the pearl (13:44–46). These two parables speak of the value of the kingdom. Whether one is looking for the kingdom (as in the pearl) or not (as in the hidden treasure), the kingdom is so valuable that it is portrayed as worth everything. Since these parables were spoken to only the disciples, the parables were intended to challenge the disciples to make God's kingdom their top priority. Because God's kingdom program is so important, nothing should stand in the way of a wholehearted commitment to it. No sacrifice is too great, for what one gains will far outshadow anything relinquished.

The parables of the dragnet and of the householder (13:47–52). These two parables speak of the responsibilities of believers in the present age. The dragnet parable teaches that evangelism is to be done without racial or national discrimination. The net illustrates how far the kingdom message should be spread and that many are invited to respond. Jesus is the Judge, and His standard of good or evil will be based on character alone. The parable of the householder (13:52) illustrates the need to teach both new and old truths of the kingdom. The old treasures are those truths taught in the Old Testament and in the early period of the life of Christ. The new treasures are the mysteries of the kingdom revealed in the parables of Jesus, which reveal what He is now doing in the present age.

Major Truths Taught in Matthew 13

1. Not everyone will respond to the message of the kingdom, and not all who do respond are equally fruitful.
2. Satan is personally active in seeking to keep people from receiving the message of God's kingdom.
3. Both external pressures and internal distractions hinder the proper appropriation of the Word of God.
4. God desires that we hear, understand, and apply the truth of His Word if we are to be fruitful for Him.
5. Those who hear the Word are responsible to live in accord with its truths.
6. Satan sends his representatives into the world to masquerade as sons of the kingdom to interrupt the work of Christ.
7. Believers need to be realistic about the presence of hypocrites, but must leave the judging to Jesus.
8. Servants of the Lord need to wait patiently for Jesus to judge and to separate the wicked from the righteous.
9. In light of the impending judgment, people should decide to follow Christ.
10. God has promised the righteous will reign with the Son and the Father in the future phase of the kingdom.
11. The work of God cannot be fully evaluated as to its success until the coming judgment.
12. God intends that people from all nations respond to the kingdom message.
13. Messiah has come in humility and will one day reign in sovereignty.
14. What Jesus is doing is significant for God's kingdom designs.
15. The work of the Holy Spirit authenticates the ministry of Jesus Christ.
16. Believers must depend on the invisible yet powerfully transforming work of the Holy Spirit.
17. The kingdom of heaven should be the highest priority of anyone who finds it.

18. No sacrifice is too great in light of the value of the kingdom.
19. The joy of participating in God's work repays any sacrifices made for it.
20. Discipleship calls for a wholehearted dedication to God's kingdom purposes.
21. No one should allow anything to stand in the way of participating in the kingdom.
22. Jesus places a high priority on evangelism to all classes and cultures.
23. Participation in God's kingdom is not restricted to one particular race of humanity.
24. The need to evangelize the world is motivated by the fact that judgment is coming.
25. God's future judgment will be based on individuals' inner character, not their cultural backgrounds.

VI. THE PROGRESSIVE REJECTION OF THE KING (13:53–18:35)

A. A Series of Reactions to Jesus (13:53–16:12)

The conflict at Nazareth (13:53–58). The people in Nazareth were both amazed and offended at the wisdom and power of Jesus. They could not comprehend that He was more than just a carpenter, the son of Mary and Joseph, and the sibling of His brothers and sisters. Jesus led a perfect life and still had family members and friends who struggled to believe. Sometimes those most difficult to reach are those who know us best.

Herod's beheading of John the Baptist (14:1–12). Matthew 14–16 includes five episodes from the life of Peter not found in any of the other Gospels (14:28–31; 15:5; 16:17–19; 17:24–27; 18:21). At times the emphasis is on his success and other times on his failures. Thus he serves as a model to imitate as well as to shun, depending on the episode.

The people of Nazareth misunderstood Jesus, but so did Herod Antipas. He governed Galilee and Perea from 4 B.C. to A.D. 39. Because of the reports of Jesus' miracles, he thought Jesus was John the Baptist who had come back from the dead. Along with the account of John's death this shows how the rejection of John paralleled that of Jesus. John had pointed a righteous finger at the unrighteousness of Herod Antipas in taking Herodius from his half brother Philip. Both Matthew and Mark noted the conflicting emotions of the governor in ordering the death of John.

The feeding of the five thousand (14:13–21). The miraculous provision for the five thousand is the only miracle other than Jesus' resurrection that is recorded in all four Gospels. Quite a contrast is seen between the compassion of Jesus for the crowds and the attitude of the disciples. Jesus' challenge to the disciples to give the crowds what they needed was intended to test the disciples' faith and resourcefulness. Their confined thinking was set in bold relief against Jesus' miracle-working power. For whatever reason, Jesus was and still is far too often the last option of consideration for those who are called on to meet the needs of the multitudes. Just as the miraculous provision of food in Elijah's and Elisha's ministries demonstrated God's power (1 Kings 17:9–16; 2 Kings 4:42–44), so this miracle demonstrates Jesus' divine power in the presence of the people. This is a powerful argument by Matthew that Jesus is indeed the Messiah of God.

Jesus' withdrawal avoided premature conflict with the political authorities and further shows that Jesus was fully aware of the timing of His own death.

Walking on the water (14:22–33). Jesus needed to pray, and the disciples needed to exercise faith. So Jesus dismissed the crowds and sent the disciples out in a boat. The lake of Galilee was a place of danger, and several times storms were occasions for Jesus to test and teach the disciples. Twenty–five to thirty stadia would equal between three and four miles. The fourth watch of the night was between three and six o'clock in the morning. Several important lessons can be learned from this account. (a) Courage comes from knowing that Jesus is present. (b) The answer to fear is faith, and faith is best placed in the One who is identified as the "I Am." (c) Doubt is an evidence of a divided mind. (d) Confessing Jesus' divine sonship is evidence of faith. (The final statement about the continuing miracles of Jesus [14:34–36] verified the truth of the disciples' confession that He is the Son of God.)

> The "walk of faith" is achieved by keeping one's focus on Jesus instead of on the circumstances.

The "unclean" leaders (15:1–20). The conflicts recorded in this section came from the leaders who traveled from Jerusalem to Galilee. They attacked the disciples about the issue of washing hands before meals. Jesus took up this issue of cleanliness, but first He dealt with a more serious issue. As recorded in verses 3, 6, and 9, Jesus revealed three downward and dangerous steps one takes when traditions become more important than divine revelation. The first is to transgress God's commands by simple disobedience. The second is to invalidate the Word of God as if it did not apply. The third and most blatant is to substitute the traditions of men for the Word of God.

The classic illustration with which Jesus argued His case was the practice the Pharisees called "Corban." According to their tradition people could dedicate everything to God and then be exempt from sharing their wealth or helping the needy. As a result, even elderly parents were being ignored. Jesus charged that the Pharisees' traditions had caused them to disobey the command to honor their parents (Exod. 20:12; Deut. 5:16). By quoting Isaiah 29:13 (recorded in Matt. 15:4) He warned that they were candidates for the capital crime of cursing their parents (Exod. 21:17; Lev. 20:9). This quotation from Isaiah exposed their hypocritical legalism as a sin that invalidates genuine worship.

Matthew 15:10–20 returns to the issue of cleanliness in which Jesus stated that cleanliness is more a matter of the heart than the hand. The spiritual condition of the heart is the source of evil or righteousness. Jesus set aside Mosaic dietary laws (Mark 7:19) in anticipation of what He would fulfill through the Cross. What makes a person spiritually unclean in the sight of God is sin in the heart.

The faith of the Canaanite woman (15:21–28). Having distanced Himself ideologically from the Jewish leaders, Jesus now distanced Himself geographically as He journeyed to the region of Tyre and Sidon. These two cities were the chief seaports of Phoenicia and were representative of Israel's enemies throughout her history (see, for example, Isa. 23; Ezek.

26–28; Amos 1:9–10). Mark said this woman was a Greek (Mark 7:26), but Matthew called her a Canaanite, which to the Jews was as derogatory a term as being a Greek.

> The tragedy of traditionalism is that it tends to substitute the opinions of people for the Word of God.

The account of this woman and the healing of her demonized daughter serves as a turning point in the earthly ministry of Christ. Jesus had hinted that Israel's violent rejection of Him would pave the way for an ordained mission to the Gentiles (Matt. 12:18; see also Isa. 42:1–4). For national, cultural, gender-related, and spiritual reasons, the woman should normally have been shunned. The disciples' treatment of her seems to model the expected treatment from the nation of Israel.

However, the woman's affirmations of Jesus as Lord and the Son of David show a faith that was lacking in Israel. Her insight is also commendable because she realized that the "bread" that Israel was rejecting was to be made available to the Gentiles. Her statement is highly significant. Jesus' ministry, which had been concentrated on Israel, was now intentionally expanding to the Gentiles. Israel's rejection of Jesus justified His turning to the Gentiles.

The feeding of the four thousand (15:29–39). The feeding of the five thousand (14:13–21) took place in Jewish territory, whereas the feeding of the four thousand occurred in gentile territory. Having gone "along the Sea of Galilee," Jesus then went up into the hills (15:29). Mark stated this was in Decapolis (Mark 7:31; 8:1), the region east of the Jordan River. Though the Canaanite woman had faith in the Lord, the disciples flunked Jesus' test when He asked them to feed the multitudes. She understood that He was available for her, but the disciples had yet to figure out that He was also available for the multitudes.

The "yeast" of the Pharisees and Sadducees (16:1–12). Jesus rebuked the leaders' continual demand for a sign because they had failed to discern the "sign of the times" (16:3), a phrase used in the Bible of only the first coming of Christ. The Jews had missed the message of Jesus' miracles and so they failed to respond to Jesus as their King. The only answer for a wicked and adulterous people is the gospel. No sign will ever be good enough or convincing enough before one believes the gospel. Jesus' resurrection depicted by Jonah was the supreme proof that He is both the Son of David and the Son of God (see Rom. 1:4).

The conversation with the disciples across the lake also showed their struggle as well with all that God was doing through His Son. They misunderstood His remarks about the religious leaders' yeast. His five questions were designed to convict them of their lack of faith and to warn them against the Pharisees and Sadducees' false teachings.

B. A Series of Revelations by Jesus (16:13–18:35)

Peter's confession (16:13–20). Caesarea Philippi served as the perfect background for the interchange between Jesus and His followers about His identity. Carved into the sides of the bedrock of Mount Hermon are niches with inscriptions celebrating the worship of the pagan god named Pan, dating back to days before the time of Jesus Christ. This nature god was revered in this region because of the massive mountain from which flows a key tributary for the Jordan River.

Peter's confession, in response to Jesus' questions about who the crowd thought He was, came not from human intuition but from revelation by the Father in heaven. This revelation that Jesus is the Messiah and the Son of the living God (as opposed to the superstitions about Pan) was and still is the supreme confession of faith. The play on the words for rock, *petros* and *petra*, revealed that Peter was one stone (*petros*) and on a large rock (*petra*) Jesus would build His church. Ephesians 2:18–20 and 1 Peter 2:6–7 state that the foundation of the church is the apostles and prophets, with Jesus Himself the Cornerstone. Peter was one stone, but he was not the only foundation of the church.

The phrase "keys of the kingdom of heaven" indicates that the authority to act on Jesus' behalf had been passed to the disciples as the representatives of heaven on earth. That authority also has been extended to others in the church, as can be seen in Matthew 18:18–19. This authority from God is especially represented when His message is preached. Binding and loosing in heaven refer to the affirmations and warnings that come as the result of people responding to or rejecting the message.

Jesus' initial accouncement of the Cross (16:21–28). Verse 21 repeats the phrase in 4:17, "from that time on," and the major theme was now the need for the Cross rather than the imminent declaration of the kingdom. Now that the national leaders had rejected Jesus, and knowing that the people would later reject Him, Jesus began announcing events that would lead Him to the cross. In this section He said His death, resurrection, and second coming would occur according to the Lord's ordained timetable.

Peter modeled the view of so many who struggle with the idea that the Messiah would have to die by crucifixion. But Jesus addressed Peter as Satan because he had in mind not the things of God "but the things of men" (16:23). Almost every time Jesus announced His going to the cross, He also challenged His hearers to follow Him in committed discipleship. To exchange one's life without Christ for life with Christ is to find life as God intends it to be. To live life without Christ is to forfeit one's soul. Verses 27–28 form a transition to the Transfiguration account in chapter 17. Jesus announced that He would come again with the glory of the Father accompanied by the angels to judge and reward humanity. In light of His rejection such a message might have seemed strange to the disciples. Therefore Jesus promised that some of His disciples would see that glory before they died. The Transfiguration fulfilled that prediction.

Jesus' transfiguration and kingly glory (17:1–13). The mountain on which the Transfiguration occurred was most likely Mount Hermon. The Greek word for "transfigured" means to take on the outward form of what is true in one's nature. Jesus appeared in the glory He shared with the Father as a confirmation of His deity and of His right to rule. This would have greatly encouraged the disciples who were with Him on the mountain. The presence of Moses and Elijah along with the Lord prompted Peter to suggest building three booths. His statement reveals his belief that since Moses and Elijah, representatives of the saints of the ages, and the Messiah were present, the kingdom must have been present. Zechariah 14 had prophesied that the Feast of Tabernacles would be celebrated when the Messiah rules as King of the whole earth. The Father's affirmation of Jesus Christ (Matt. 17:5) confirmed the identity of the Messiah, as prophesied in Psalm 2:7.

In answering the three disciples' question about Elijah, Jesus affirmed that John the Baptist was the Elijah for those who could accept Him, but that another Elijah would come before the great and terrible day of the Lord, as stated in Malachi 4:5–6. At that time there will be a great restoration. This refers to the restoration of the kingdom to Israel, spoken of as a renewal in Matthew 19:28. The Transfiguration was an apocalyptic vision (17:9), which Jesus asked to be kept secret until after His resurrection. His suffering had to be understood before His glory could be realized.

The disciples' need for faith and prayer (17:14–23). Jesus' healing the demonized boy shows that God's power is not available by a formula or any set procedure to be called on whenever desired. Prayer is encouraged as the demonstration of faith. If we do not pray, either we do not believe God wants to be called on for help or we believe He is not powerful enough to solve a given problem. Both are an evidence of unbelief. Prayer demonstrates faith in God, who acts according to His sovereign will. The supernatural power that will one day defeat Satan is available for deliverance from Satan now. This paragraph ends with another announcement of the Lord's betrayal, death, and resurrection.

> *Prayer is the demonstration of faith in God who acts with power.*

The temple-tax confirmation of Jesus' kingship (17:24–27). The miracle of the coin found in the fish's mouth was designed to teach the disciples and especially Peter that just as the sons of kings were exempt from civil taxes so was the Son of God exempt from the temple tax (as are all those who are related to Him by faith). Jesus' instructions demonstrated His omniscience and thus His deity. The coin miracle hinted again of the transition from temple worship that would come as a result of His death and resurrection. A new era in the economy of God was about to begin. Since His death would be delayed for a short time, the temple tax was to be paid to avoid undue offense against the religious leaders, though exemption could have been claimed. The four-drachma coin was enough for the tax owed by both Peter and Jesus.

The need for humility (18:1–14). Jesus used children as His example of greatness because greatness, He said, results from a heart of humility. Humility is necessary for the kind of saving faith that qualifies one for entrance into the kingdom of heaven. Looking down on (that is, belittling or despising) children, the "little ones" of the family of faith, is so serious an offense that it warrants drastic action. In fact, any sin calls for serious self-discipline. Jesus illustrated His concern for children by comparing them to lost sheep.

The need for discipline (18:15–20). Too often church discipline begins and ends with the question of excommunication. If the church followed Jesus' teachings more carefully, that step would rarely have to be faced. Four distinguishable steps are noted, with each being dependent on the former. Each successive step brings more of the church into the problem-solving process. Interpersonal sins are best confessed and forgiven when kept between the involved parties. If the truthfulness of the issue is at stake, confirmation comes at the testimony of two or three witnesses as prescribed in the Mosaic Law (Deut. 19:15).

> *Biblical church discipline should always have restoration as its motivation.*

The reference to binding and loosing is best interpreted in light of Matthew 16:19: With the confirming testimony of two or three witnesses the church acts on behalf of God with the authority of heaven on earth (18:18). The agreement of two or three witnesses refers to church discipline, not to agreement in prayer. God is not hammerlocked into submitting to our desires by a prayer of "agreement." For believers to be heard by God the Father, Jesus has already instructed that getting alone by oneself in a closet is all that is necessary, assuming one's heart is right before God (6:6). While God appreciates corporate prayer, having more people pray is not a necessity for Him to be persuaded to answer us. Treating a sinning Christian like a tax collector or a Gentile meant separating from him or her for the purpose of arresting that person's attention and encouraging repentance.

The need for forgiveness (18:21–35). Peter went beyond the religious leaders' limit of forgiving an offense three times by suggesting one could be forgiven seven times. Jesus raised the level to "seventy times seventy," a hyperbole meaning no limits. In the parable of the unforgiving servant He suggested a series of principles that can help shape a forgiving heart. From the contrasting amounts of the debts in the narrative, believers are to realize that they have offended God infinitely more than they have ever

> *Bitterness is a serious sin which imprisons the soul and tortures the heart.*

been offended by another person. Based on the response of the king to the first servant, forgiveness can be understood as an act of compassion whereby one releases the offender by canceling any expectation of repayment. From the negative example of the unforgiving servant, one can see that forgiveness is generated by the will that determines to extend mercy simply when asked. The failure to forgive will result in the failure to be forgiven. This passage assumes the family relationship of those involved, and therefore the lack of forgiveness in this context does not mean a loss of salvation. What is in view is God's discipline for a Christian who regards iniquity within his or her heart by failing to forgive a brother or sister in the family of faith.

VII. THE PRESENTATION OF THE KING (CHAPTERS 19–25)

A. Teachings en Route to Jerusalem (chapters 19–20)

Questions about divorce and remarriage (19:1–15). From Galilee Jesus traveled to Perea across the Jordan River from Judea. The question asked by the Pharisees was an attempt to involve Jesus in the rivalry between the rabbinical schools of Hillel and Shammai. The former was more liberal, allowing divorce and remarriage for almost "any and every reason." The latter was more stringent in allowing divorce and remarriage only for the "cause of indecency."

Jesus employed a typical rabbinic argument by appealing to a more original source of authority. Jesus cited both Genesis 1:27 and 2:24 to show that God's original purpose for marriage was a oneness that only death would separate. His response to the presumed exception for divorce (Deut. 24:1–4) revealed that (other than divinely designated exceptions) all divorce promotes adultery and therefore is classified as sinful. Any divorce reflects the hardness of the heart of at least one of the partners. The reality that laws were instituted to deal with sin did not mean that sin was therefore permissible. God hates divorce because of the damage it brings to the marital relationship (Mal. 2:15–16).

The disciples thought Jesus' teachings about divorce were so strict that they concluded it would be better not to get married at all. The term "eunuch" described three different kinds of singleness: those born with inabilities to carry on a marital relationship; those who were surgically altered, as was the custom of many of the court officials who worked in the palace that housed the king's harem; and more generally applicable, those who answered God's call to devote themselves fully to His service. Twice Jesus said not everyone could handle this arrangement. The implication is that not too many are called to stay single for ministry purposes. Because of the disciples' insensitivity to children, Jesus again (see Matt. 18:1–3) emphasized the value of children and their example of faith.

Salvation and rewards in the kingdom (19:16–30). The principle taught in this account is that neither poverty or wealth guarantees eternal life. The rich young man is a prime example of those who adopt a relative standard of righteousness, which allows them to justify themselves in relation to others. The selections from the Law that Jesus used to convict the young man of his sin included Exodus 20:12–16; Deuteronomy 5:16–20; and Leviticus 19:18–19. To break the Law at all is to break all the Law (James 2:10).

The man failed to understand that no one is righteous apart from his or her response of faith in Jesus Christ. Self-righteousness disqualifies one from both salvation and rewards. To follow Christ in faith is the requirement for salvation; to give away one's wealth in obedience to Christ would lead to rewards in heaven. In Jesus' day many Jews believed that wealth was an indication of God's favor. However, what guarantees eternal life is following Christ (in faith), and what guarantees eternal rewards is living according to His commands (obedience). Salvation is received by faith, and obedience guarantees rewards.

What the rich young man rejected, the disciples also misunderstood. Salvation is difficult for the rich because of their self-sufficiency. In reality it is impossible for either the rich or the poor to save themselves, because salvation comes only by the grace of God. The phrase "with God all things are possible" echoes the explanation for the birth of Isaac (Gen. 18:14) and the virgin birth of Christ (Luke 1:37). Quite fitting therefore is the conclusion that salvation is also impossible without the work of God. All three are the life-giving work of God's Spirit.

Peter ventured to ask what many have thought: What rewards will God give those who have sacrificed to follow Jesus? In Jesus' answer He promised that the twelve disciples will have a special blessing and then He stated a general principle applicable to all who follow Him. The first is specific: A time is coming when the Son of man will reign from His glorious throne with the twelve disciples reigning on twelve thrones over the nation of Israel. This is called the "renewal" or "regeneration," which speaks of the restoration of Israel as the people of God over whom Messiah will reign in kingly power.

A more general promise of gracious reward for personal faithfulness ends the chapter. No disciple who sacrifices earthly possessions and relationships for the sake of Christ will fail to be more than compensated, whether in the present life or the future kingdom. Jesus' final caution to Peter (Matt. 19:30) alerted him to eliminate the mercenary attitudes of being presumptuous in anticipating rewards. There will be major surprises when it will be seen who will be most rewarded in heaven.

The parable of the vineyard (20:1–16). This parable carries forward the theme of humble service. The story is built from the daily routine of the migrant day workers of the Middle East and was designed by Jesus to lead His followers away from the "acid of legalism" that can too easily eat away at one's soul. Peter's question of what he would get for his sacrificial life (19:27) prompted the parable. In the parable the response of the king to the complaining servant illustrated three attributes of God that form the foundation planks of His reward program. First, like the landowner, God is just; He will never fail to keep His promises. Second, God is sovereign; He has the right to do whatever He wishes with what is His. As Lord, He has the right to call His own workers, assign their responsibilities, and pay or reward them as He pleases. All belongs to Him and can be used as He wills. Third, like the landowner, God is generous; since God initiates the calls and assigns the tasks, He can show His grace to those who have had limited opportunities or have come lately into His kingdom. The repetition of the proverb in 20:16 (with the wording reversed from what is stated in 19:30) reinforces the need to be humble, faithful, and obedient, but not proud or presumptuous in the service of the King.

Another prediction of His passion (20:17–19). The third announcement of Jesus' death and resurrection was made to the disciples on the way up to Jerusalem from the Jordan Valley. Both Jews and Gentiles were implicated in His prediction of their vicious treatment of Him. He continued to Jerusalem, all the while knowing what lay ahead for Him. Death by crucifixion was again predicted, as was His resurrection on the third day.

> *Believers should be grateful for the privilege of ministering on behalf of God, who is just, sovereign, and gracious.*

The desire for greatness (20:20–28). When the mother of the Zebedee brothers asked Jesus if her sons could have the favored positions in the kingdom, she may have had in mind Jesus' words in 19:28 about the disciples being seated on thrones. Jesus challenged the two with the willingness to suffer, and He challenged all the disciples with the need for a servant's heart. This is Jesus' definition of true greatness. Craving positions of power is worldly and is the exact opposite of the self-sacrificing model of Jesus. A major difference is that His death was the price needed to purchase the redemption of humanity.

The blind who see (20:24–34). In recording the story of Jesus healing the blind at Jericho, Matthew and Mark said Jesus was leaving Jericho (Matt. 20:29; Mark 10:46), but Luke said He was entering the city (Luke 18:35). Also Mark and Luke mentioned one blind man, whereas Matthew referred to two blind men at the scene. Mark wrote that the blind man's name was Bartimaeus. No doubt two blind men were there, but Mark and Luke referred to one for the purpose of emphasis. The location of the healing is explained by understanding that there were two Jerichos—the ancient site of Jericho and the Herodian Jericho built by Herod a few kilometers south of the ancient site. (This newer city straddled the Wadi Qilt to better facilitate the acquisition of the water supply.) If Jesus were between the two sites moving south toward the ancient travel route known as the Ascent Adummim, He could have been going out of old Jericho

> *Faithful discipleship should always be the response to the grace and mercy of God and His Son.*

(Matthew and Mark) and into new Jericho (Luke). Luke and his gentile audience, familiar with Roman history, would have been aware of the Herodian Jericho, and Matthew would have been assuming his Jewish readers would think of the older city.

The insight of the blind men is again ironic (see 9:27). They acknowledged that Jesus is the "Lord, Son of David" and the Source of mercy (20:30). Jesus' miraculous cure confirmed their confession and in their response they followed Him.

B. Controversies in Jerusalem (chapters 21–22)

The Triumphal Entry (21:1–11). The first time Jesus called Himself "Lord" was on the day He entered Jerusalem from the small village of Bethphage on the Mount of Olives. In quoting from Zechariah 9:9 Matthew apparently intentionally changed the words "Rejoice, O daughter of Jerusalem" to "say to the daughter of Jerusalem" because of the nation's rejection of Him. No joy could be experienced without accepting the Messiah. The humble entrance on a donkey was in keeping with the prophetic expectations for the king of Israel. The accolades of the crowd included the cries of "Hosanna," a quotation from Psalm 118:26, and their affirmation that Jesus is a prophet. "Hosanna" is a Hebrew expression meaning "God save!" which became an acclamation of praise. Their call was for the Son of David to come and deliver them. They did not comprehend that He was actually there presenting Himself as the Lord, the Messiah of Israel. Amazingly, these words of praise by the crowd at the beginning of the Passion Week turned to cries for crucifixion by the end of the week.

This "triumphal event" foreshadowed the irony revealed by the ministry of Jesus during the last week of His earthly life. The Jews celebrated a religion without having a real relationship with the God whom they claimed to worship. Unfortunately they missed the Messiah they had expected would someday arrive.

The cleansing of the temple (21:12–17). Twice Jesus cleansed the temple. The first incident is recorded by John, and in it Jesus cleared the money changers out of the temple, charging them with doing business in His Father's house (John 2:16). Here in Matthew, as in Mark and Luke, Jesus condemned them for turning what was supposed to be a house of prayer into a "den of robbers" (see Jer. 7:11). The Jewish conduct at the temple had gone from bad to worse; from business to robbery. By contrast, those viewed as unacceptable to the religious leaders were the objects of Jesus' compassionate healing. Children, often marginalized by others, were defended by Jesus as they shouted praise. In defending the children He cited Psalm 8:2, an indirect claim by Jesus that He is worthy of praise that is rightly directed to God.

> *Personal prejudice can blind people to the realities of Christ and the gospel.*

Jesus' custom was to spend His evenings at the house of Mary and Martha in Bethany, a village east of Mount of Olives less than two miles from Jerusalem.

The cursing of the fig tree (21:18–22). Matthew telescoped his account of this incident by combining two days of events into one unit without specific time references. Taken with the previous account of the temple cleansing, the cursing of the fig tree represents judgment on unbelieving Israel for their failure to produce the fruit of repentance (see Luke 3:8). This was the only destructive miracle Jesus performed. Because the tree did not have figs, it lost the opportunity to bear any figs at all. One of the Old Testament images of God's judgment on Israel was the picture of the land being unable to bear figs (Jer. 8:13; Mic. 7:1–6). Therefore because of the spiritual bankruptcy of the religion of Israel at the time of Christ, the cursing of the fig tree symbolized the judgment that would come on Israel for rejecting the Messiah and the kingdom message He preached. The destruction of Jerusalem and the temple as its central sanctuary of worship in A.D. 70 initially fulfilled this symbolic act and the accompanying pronouncement by Jesus.

The reference to "this mountain" (Matt. 21:21) may be the link between Jesus' announcement of judgment and the faith of the disciples.

They would witness God's judgment on Mount Zion where the temple was built, and they would need to respond in faith. Just as Jesus had power to perform great deeds, the disciples' faith would produce extraordinary results. When they would see the destruction of Jerusalem, they would need to have faith to understand the plan of God as well as to forgive those whom God would use in carrying out that judgment.

The question of authority (21:23–27). The literary structure of Matthew is symmetrical here. Two incidents about authority (21:23–27 and 22:41–46) serve as "bookends" to three parables (21:28–22:14) and three controversial dialogues with the Pharisees and Herodians, the Sadducees, and the Pharisees (22:15–40). The three parables chronicle the salvation history of John the Baptist, the rejection of Jesus as the Son of God, and the extension of the kingdom to the Gentiles. The three dialogues surfaced the rebellious responses of the leaders.

When the leaders questioned Jesus about the source of His authority, He "out-questioned" them with His query as to the source of John's authority. Because the people viewed John as a great prophet, to say he did not minister at the direction of God would have pitted the leaders against the people. So the questioners refused to answer Jesus' counterquestions.

The parable of the two sons (21:28–32). Obedience is the righteous result of faith. Israel professed a righteousness that lacked genuine obedience because it was not rooted in faith. They failed to believe in the message preached by John the Baptist even after God sought to provoke them to jealousy through the saving faith of outcasts, who before their conversion were among the blatant rejecters of God. Their repentance and belief became an object lesson for Israel, convicting the Jews of continuing hardness of heart.

The parable of the wicked tenants (21:33–46). This parable, one of the most overlooked in the Gospels, exposed the blatant rejection of the Son of God by those to whom He was sent. Israel had a history of persecuting and killing the messengers God sent to it, and it would do the same with Jesus. The parable and the quotation of Psalm 118:22–23 (see also Isa. 28:16) show that Jesus, the rejected Stone, will become the foundation of another structure (the church). The church would temporarily replace Israel as the responsible custodian of the kingdom in this current phase of God's program.

Matthew 21:43 could be the key verse in the entire argument of Matthew. The transference of kingdom representation to the church was justified by the rejection of Jesus as the Son of the Vineyard Owner (God). The rejected Stone will be the very Agent of judgment (21:44). Ephesians 2:18–20 and 1 Peter 2:4–8 verify that the church is the new agency of God's activity on the earth.

The chapter closes with the mention of the leaders' desire to arrest Him and their fear of the crowd. No doubt they understood that He claimed to be the Son of God and thus believed He was guilty of blasphemy and therefore worthy of death.

> *All excuses to reject the gracious invitation of Christ and His provision for entering the kingdom are illegitimate and rooted in self-interest.*

The parable of the wedding feast (22:1–14). The final parable of this triad of prophetic parables explains that the kingdom is extended to the outcasts and Gentiles. This was because Israel rejected the Messiah by giving illegitimate and selfish excuses. God's righteous judgment is reserved for those who by their rejection show themselves unworthy of the kingdom (22:8). "Worthy" is Matthew's term for those who respond in faith to the message of the kingdom as recipients of God's grace and mercy provided through Christ.

The Pharisees' and Herodians' question about taxes (22:15–22). The Jews resented the taxation practices of the Romans, and so the Pharisees, intending to trap Jesus, wanted to see if He would agree with them or side with the Romans. The Pharisees viewed taxes paid to Rome as money taken from the righteous and given to the wicked. The Herodians, a Jewish sect, were loyal to the Herodian family appointed by Rome to govern the region. The Pharisees' and Herodians' feigned praise of Jesus' character and their crafty question on whether the payment of tribute taxes to Rome was right were intended to entrap Him. To answer in favor of one party would make Him an enemy of the other. Wise to the entrapment, Jesus stepped outside the line. Using the tribute coin and the imprinted image and inscription, Jesus taught that people can be loyal to the state and God at the same time.

> *To withhold either worship or taxes is to be in sinful disobedience to Jesus Christ.*

God is sovereign and deserves all worship. Human government has also been ordained by God and therefore also has legitimate authority because of what it was designed to provide (see Rom. 13:1–7).

The Sadducees' question about the Resurrection (22:23–33). The Sadducees accepted only the first five books of Moses as their "Old Testament." The levirate command stipulated that an unmarried brother was responsible for marrying the widow of his deceased brother in order to provide for her and to protect the family property within Israel's tribal system. Their question with the extreme example of a woman with seven dead husbands showed a scoffing attitude and a malicious spirit. Their appeal was loosely based on Genesis 38:8 and Deuteronomy 25:5. Jesus rebuked them for not knowing the Pentateuch and for assuming they understood what only God Himself knows—the nature of the afterlife. Ironically Jesus was charging that they didn't really know either the Law or God, two objects they claimed to know.

Jesus appealed to Exodus 3:6 to prove that in order for the patriarchs to inherit the kingdom in fulfillment of the Abrahamic Covenant, the resurrection is a logical necessity. And then He stated that God has the power to so transform the human body that it will be fit to join the angels for an eternal existence. Sexual reproduction will be impossible because no fallen humanity can be procreated in the absolutely righteous environment of heaven. Another mention of the astonished crowds ends the account (Matt. 22:33).

The Pharisees' question about the priority command (22:34–40). When the Sadducees were silenced, the Pharisees rallied with a question. One of them sought to test Jesus with a question about which law He believed was the most important. This question revealed the Pharisees' attempts to rank the laws of God. Jesus responded with not one but two commands that summarize the entire Law. No part of the Law was unimportant to God.

In quoting Deuteronomy 6:5, Jesus changed "strength" to "understanding," thus speaking directly to the error of playing mind games with biblical application. He added a second quotation (from Lev. 19:18) and asserted its "equal" importance. The first passage speaks of wholehearted devotion to God and the second speaks of the implications of that commitment in one's interpersonal relationships.

Leviticus 19:2–37 teaches that a person has obligations to his family, the worship community, employers, neighbors, and governing authorities. None can be ignored. To love God is to keep His commands in every area of responsibility. The believer has a circle of priorities which cannot be relegated to the lower end of the ladder of man-made obligations of legalism.

Jesus' question about messianic identity (22:41–46). Now it was Jesus' turn to ask a difficult question. Jesus led the Pharisees into a logical trap with reference to the father of the Messiah. He asked them about the Messiah's ancestry, to which they rightly responded (according to 2 Sam. 7:13–17), that the Messiah was to come from the family of David. Jesus then asked, If the Messiah was to be a descendant of David, why would David address His own son as Lord, as in Psalm 110:1? How could it be that the highest office of the land would show submission to another besides God?

Jesus' question silenced them, and so from that time on they didn't dare question Him further. The implication of Jesus' question is that He is not just the Son of David; He is also the Son of God, to whom the Father has bequeathed the earthly kingdom. (No wonder Ps. 110:1–4 is the portion of the Old Testament that is quoted most often in the New Testament—in Acts 2:34–35; Heb. 1:13; 5:6, 10; 7:17, 21). Jesus Christ is the Co-regent of the Father, who will sit at the Father's right hand until the entire kingdom of God is placed under His feet. According to Revelation 10–11, that phase of the kingdom will commence at the return of Christ to the earth when the kingdoms of this world will become the kingdom of the Lord Jesus Christ (Rev. 11:15). When that millennial kingdom is finalized and all rule and authority, including death, have been conquered, Jesus will hand the kingdom back to the Father so that God can be seen to be God over all (1 Cor. 15:24–28).

C. Further Denunciations of Israel's Leaders (chapter 23)

The warnings for the multitudes (23:1–12). Jesus condemned the Pharisees for their practice, their pride, and their positioning. Matthew's original readers were thus encouraged not to make the same mistake as the Jewish leaders, who were allowing their traditional legalism to blind them to the claims of Jesus as the Messiah. Though the leaders had a legitimate role, they violated their sacred trust by not practicing the very things they were teaching. What they did was for the praise of men rather than God. Jesus exposed their pride as the basic reason for their style of dress, their manipulation to have the best seats at dinner, and their insistence that they be called "Rabbi." Such arrogance, Jesus asserted, replaces the reverence we are to have for God the Father and His Son Jesus Christ (23:8–10). Jesus again affirmed that true greatness comes from humble servanthood.

> *God will judge the proud and exalt the humble.*

The woes against hypocritical leaders (23:13–36). In a series of seven "woes" Jesus denounced the religious leaders and justified the predicted judgments that will come on the nation. (These judgments were then expounded in the Olivet Discourse in Matt. 24–25.)

> *Woes of Judgment on Religious Leaders in Matthew 23*
> 1. Obstructing the way of salvation (23:13–14)
> 2. Belittling the proselytes (23:15)
> 3. Creating escape valves to avoid personal commitments (23:16–22)
> 4. Being picky with minor legal matters and missing major moral issues (23:23–24)
> 5. Emphasizing externals but neglecting heart attitudes (23:25–26)
> 6. Putting on the appearance of righteousness (23:27–28)
> 7. Failing to identify with the sins of the past (23:29–32)

Jesus condemned the people of his day for being guilty of bloodshed from the time of Abel until the time of Zechariah (23:33–36), the entire Old Testament period. Having rejected Jesus, they joined their forefathers in persecuting the righteous messengers whom the Lord had sent to the nation.

The departure of the Messiah and the delay of the earthly kingdom (23:37–39). This is one of the most significant passages for a proper understanding of Matthew and his presentation of the kingdom, and especially for the Olivet Discourse, which immediately follows this announcement. Jesus' lament over Jerusalem revealed that He made a legitimate offer of the kingdom to Israel and that it was His desired will that they would respond. As a result of their having rejected such a contingent offer, their house was destroyed. Here the word *house* can refer to the temple, to Jerusalem, or to the nation. The city and temple were destroyed in A.D. 70. As a nation, Israel then came under the disciplining judgment of God and lost the privilege of being the custodian of the kingdom message and God's representative in the present age. Furthermore Jesus announced that He, the Messiah, was leaving and would not come back until the nation repented and recognized Him as the legitimate Messiah, who would come "in the name of the Lord" (Ps. 118:26). This time of Jesus' absence sets the stage for the events outlined in the Olivet Discourse. The time from His rejection to His return is the "mystery" phase of the kingdom, as described in Matthew 13. The final period of that phase is outlined in chapters 24–25.

D. The Olivet Discourse (chapters 24–25)

The questions of the disciples (24:1–3). The disciples' questions in 24:3 must be understood in light of the five preceding verses (23:37–24:2). Jesus had just told them He would be leaving and that He would not come back until the nation was ready to receive Him. In 24:1–2 Jesus predicted the fall of the temple (implying also the fall of Jerusalem). The words "Not one stone upon another" suggest complete destruction. The disciples wondered about two issues: When would the events just announced take place? What would be the sign of the end of the age when the Lord will return? Jesus refused to reveal the answer to the question as to when these events would happen. But in answering their second question, Jesus gave many details in the Olivet Discourse (24:4–25:46) about events related to the Tribulation and the Second Coming.

The overview of the Tribulation (24:4–14). Verses 4–8 of this chapter describe the first half of the Tribulation, and verses 9–14 describe the second half. While the conditions described in these verses may sound familiar in the international political climate of today, a comparison with Revelation 6 shows that these correlate with the seal judgments that will occur at the beginning of the Tribulation. These future deceptions and destructions are the "beginning" and "not the end" of the Tribulation (24:4–8). "Birth pains" is a common metaphor from the Old Testament prophets to depict terrible human suffering (Isa. 21:3; 42:14; 66:7; Jer. 22:23; Hos. 13:13). Matthew 24:9–14 describes the second half of the Tribulation, which will extend to the end of the age just prior to the beginning of the millennial kingdom. Persecution of the righteous, defection from faith and families, and the rise of false prophets will surface the need for standing firm to the end while trusting in the Lord's promised deliverance (24:13). Jesus guaranteed that the gospel of the kingdom would have worldwide coverage before the end of the Tribulation would come (24:14). In the Tribulation God will reach the world with the gospel before the world is judged at Christ's second coming.

The highlights of the second half of the Tribulation (24:15–28). The reference to the abomination of desolation in verse 15 and the reference back to Daniel 9:27 pinpoints the middle of the Tribulation. According to Daniel's prophecy of the seventieth week (of years), in which the plans for Israel as a people and the city of Jerusalem will be completed, the greatest tribulation in history will take place in the last three and a half years of that seven-year period. Judea and Jerusalem will be the focus of satanic fury as well as of God's refining judgments. The distress to be experienced will be unparalleled—a strong statement in view of the Jewish Holocaust of the twentieth century. The times will be so deceptive that even believers will be tempted to follow the heresies of the false prophets and fake messiahs. Their manipulating signs will lead many astray. The end of the Tribulation will witness the sudden and unexpected judgment associated with the Second Coming that will leave the carcasses of humanity to be eaten by the birds.

The Second Coming (24:29–31). Jesus then highlighted specific events that will occur at the Second Coming. Cosmic signs will be associated with the return of the Lord to the earth "after the distress of those days" (24:29). The darkening of the sun and the moon and the falling of the stars were prophesied as indicators of the Messiah's coming (Joel 2:30–31). The Second Coming will have a universal audience and nations will mourn (Zech. 12:10–14). The Messiah will appear in the clouds in all His splendor. The previous section of the discourse ended by referring to the judgment associated with the Lord's return (Matt. 24:27–29), but this section ends with reference to the salvation and gathering of the elect from all over the world (24:31).

Applications for the generation alive at the Second Coming (24:32–51). The lessons of imminency, urgency, preparedness, and faithfulness are to be applied in light of the Lord's return to the earth. While the primary interpretation and intention of these verses was meant for those who will witness the signs of the tribulation (24:34), these verses may apply to those expecting the arrival of the Son to rapture the church. If the arrival of the Messiah with all the signs described in this chapter can come so suddenly and unexpectedly at the end of such a stated timetable, how much more important it is for people to be prepared for the unannounced and "sign-less" resurrection and rapture of the church (1 Cor. 15:52; 1 Thess. 4:13–14).

> *Because the event of the Lord's return is certain and yet the time is unknown, everyone should be prepared and live faithfully now.*

Though the time of the Lord's return is unknown, the fact of His coming is certain. The repeated references to the day and the hour (Matt. 24:36, 44, 50) stress the need for proper preparation to avoid the sudden judgment that will precede the coming of the kingdom. The fact that the leaves of a fig tree are a sign that summer is near shows that the signs of the Tribulation will be intended to awaken the world to the fact that the coming of the Lord and the establishment of the earthly phase of the messianic kingdom will be "near, right at the door" (24:33; see also Luke 21:31).

The word *generation* in Matthew 24:34 does not mean a period of forty or more years, as some prophecy teachers suggest. As Matthew used the word throughout his book, the term refers to a group of people who will be present at that time. The "generation" that will see all the events of the Tribulation along with the accompanying cosmic signs in the sky is also the generation of people who will see the coming of the Messiah and the establishment of the kingdom. The promises of God for Israel's future and the coming kingdom are as secure as heaven and earth itself. No part of those prophecies will be left unfulfilled. Those alive at the coming of the Lord to the earth will not pass away until they see the kingdom established. Daniel 12:5–13 predicts that the transition will take no more than seventy-five days.

The sudden and unexpected arrival of the Flood in Noah's day underscores the need for preparation. And the need for alertness (including faith) is the point of the parable of the returning landowner (24:42–44). The need for wise service (including faithfulness) is the lesson to be learned from the parable of the wise and wicked servants (24:45–51). Faith will be evidenced by being alert and faithfully awaiting the Lord's coming. And faithfulness is symbolized by obedient service, while disobedient defiance evidences the lack of faith. Misunderstanding the nature of the gracious Master, who is coming to reward, will result in being judged by that Master.

The parable of the ten virgins (25:1–13). This parable emphasizes the need to be properly prepared in light of the unknown time of the Lord's return. A bridegroom taking his bride back to his house as part of the marriage ceremony was the cultural background for the parable. Here, as in chapter 24, alertness and preparation, in light of the unknown time of arrival, are used to picture genuine faith in the Messiah. The lack of alertness and proper preparation, symbolized by five unprepared virgins, means a lack of faith. As a result these girls were excluded from the wedding banquet. Hoping to get in, they were denied access: "I tell you the truth, I don't know you."

The parable of the talents (25:14–30). As the parable of the ten virgins shows the need for the preparation of faith, so the parable of the talents stresses the need for faithfulness. The first speaks of salvation; this one has reward and judgment as its major themes. This parable is to be compared with that of the minas in Luke 19:1–11. A talent was a unit of currency that approximates $2,500 in today's economy. Here the entrustments varied and yet the reward was the same. In Luke 19:1–11, however, the entrustments were the same, and the rewards were proportional. Some aspects of stewardship are given in proportion to ability (25:15). Not all have the same intellect, gifts, opportunities, or levels of responsibilities. God will not expect the same from us all, but we can all receive the same commendation from Him for a life of goodness and faithfulness, and receive equal rewards. The parable of the minas (see comments on Luke 19:1–11), on the other hand, discusses the varying degrees of faithfulness to equal opportunities. Both principles must be maintained in order to understand God's reward program.

> *Faithful service is a demonstration of genuine faith and will be graciously rewarded at the return of the Lord.*

The rewards include not only the commendation of the king but also expanded responsibilities in the future kingdom. The first two servants show that faithfulness will be graciously rewarded. The third servant illustrates the principle that to squander one's responsibility is to show lack of both faith and faithfulness, and that it brings with it the loss of privileged service. Good stewardship brings reward, while poor stewardship results in loss.

The separation of the sheep and the goats (25:31–46). Matthew 24:1–25:30 focused on the judgment on Israel; now the judgment of the Gentiles is in view. The throne on which Christ is seated in the present age is in heaven, but His glorious throne in 25:31 will be on earth in preparation for His messianic kingdom. The timing of this judgment is the Second Coming of Christ at the end of the Great Tribulation. The basis of the judgment is the righteous works done to those who represent Christ.

As elsewhere in the New Testament, Christ treats others in response to the way they treated those who represent Him to the world (12:30; John 15:20). Righteous works are an evidence of righteousness (1 John 3:7–10), which comes by faith. Genuine faith will result in righteous works. The lack of faith, evidenced by a lack of response, will result in eternal punishment. Righteous works, which demonstrate a righteous heart of faith, result in eternal life. In this passage inheriting the kingdom and entering eternal life are interchangeable concepts.

The background of separating sheep from goats may be Ezekiel 34:17–19. The right hand is a position of honor and so it is appropriate that Jesus said the "sheep," representing the righteous, would be on His right. Sheep and goats of the Middle East tend to look much more alike than they do elsewhere. This judgment relates specifically to the way Gentiles will have treated the believing remnant of Israel during the tumultuous events of the Tribulation.

VIII. THE PASSION OF THE KING
(CHAPTERS 26–28)

A. The Preparation for the Passover (26:1–16)

The plot against Christ (26:1–5). Jesus and the Jewish leaders had conflicting agendas. He continued to predict His own death along with its timing in association with the coming Passover. And the chief priests and elders plotted in Caiaphas's palace to arrest and kill Him. However, the priests and elders wanted to wait until after the Feast of Passover before carrying out their plans. The fact that Jesus masterminded the timing of His own death proved the sacrificial and self-initiated nature of the Atonement (see John 10:18).

The anointing of Jesus and the bribe for Judas (26:6–16). Jesus explained that the woman's anointing of His head with expensive perfume foreshadowed His burial (John noted that the woman was Mary, Lazarus's sister; John 12:1–8.) The displeasure of the disciples (John specified Judas; 12:4–6) at the apparent waste of money showed their lack of spiritual understanding as they neared the time of Jesus' death. Ironically the betrayal payment for Judas was arranged immediately after the anointing by Mary. Thirty pieces of silver was the betrayal price (26:15). If these coins were shekels, then the total amount would equal about four months' pay for the average day laborer.

B. The Inauguration of the Lord's Supper (26:17–30)

Jesus was soon to become the true Passover Lamb (see Exodus 12) through His death the day after He celebrated the Passover meal with His disciples. The Feast of Passover was also called the Feast of Unleavened Bread because no leaven (yeast) was allowed in the food or even in the homes of the

Jews. Jesus said that His appointed time was near (26:18), indicating that in His omniscience He knew that His death was soon to take place. Jesus also knew of the man who would allow them to use his house for the last Passover meal (26:17). Mark gave a much more detailed description of how the man would be identified and the size of the room where they met (Mark 14:13–15). Whether by careful planning or supernatural insight, as with the request for the donkeys in Matthew 21:1–3, Jesus foreknew and orchestrated the events leading to His death.

At the Passover table Jesus revealed who the betrayer was (26:20–25). The table was probably a typical three-sided table (*triclinium*) made in the shape of a "U," since they reclined as they ate (26:20). Earlier Jesus had predicted His betrayal (20:18), but now He identified the betrayer. The disciples, possibly suspicious that Jesus knew it might be one of them, began asking who it would be while at the same time vowing they would not do such a thing. Jesus identified the betrayer as one who shared His bowl, and He pronounced a judgment woe on that disciple. To Judas's dismay, he was identified by Jesus.

The Lord's Supper, as it has come to be called, was initiated when Jesus took the bread to show what would happen to His body and the cup to illustrate what He would do through the shedding of His blood. The provision of the New Covenant included the forgiveness of sin (Jer. 31:31–34). While the word *new* with *covenant* is absent here in Matthew, the allusion to Jeremiah 31 would have been clear to a Jewish audience. (The word *new* is included in Luke 22:20.) The blood has Exodus 24:8 as its background. The idea of forgiveness echoes the predictions of the value of the Messiah's death in Isaiah 53:4, 10, 12.

The use of the term *cup* heralds back to Matthew 20:22–23 and ahead to 26:39, indicating the suffering that He would endure. While the New Covenant in its entirety awaits the judgment and restoration of Israel, the New Testament makes it clear that all who trust in the blood of Christ have come under certain provisions of the New Covenant. Some aspects of the covenant are yet to be enacted with the redeemed remnant of Israel, but the present provisions for believers include the indwelling work of the Spirit and the forgiveness of sins.

This meal is called the "Last" Supper because of Jesus' statement that He would not eat this special meal with them again until they were all together in the kingdom. Here was another hint of His departure and future return. This is the means by which all believers since that night in the Upper Room are to remember their Lord. Believers look back, commemorating the death of the Lord, and they look forward, anticipating the kingdom to be experienced at His return to the earth (see 1 Cor. 11:17–33).

C. Gethsemane and the Arrest of Jesus (26:31–56)

Jesus' prediction of Peter's denials (26:31–35). The accounts of both Judas and Peter in their failures are alarming and humbling. One would have expected that simply to identify Jesus to the enemies, as Judas did, was not as serious as denying Him before others, as Peter did. One might have expected Peter to have gone his own way and Judas to be reinstated. But this shows the danger of both prejudging someone's life and doubting whether God can restore a fallen sinner.

Jesus predicted that the disciples would "fall away," which comes from a Greek word meaning "to be tripped up" or "to stumble." The disciples' flight was prophesied in Zechariah 13:7, "the sheep will be scattered." God the Father was ultimately responsible for Jesus' suffering, for He said, "I will strike the shepherd." Jesus also affirmed that after He was stricken, His followers were scattered, and He was resurrected, He would meet them in Galilee (Matt. 26:32). Peter objected to these words of Jesus and affirmed an unqualified loyalty, failing, though, to believe that he could ever be the one who would "fall away." Jesus countered that Peter would deny and disown Him three times, not just once. For a second time Peter refused to believe the Lord's word, as did the other disciples.

Jesus' agony in Gethsemane (26:36–46). Since the word *Gethsemane* means "oil press," this garden probably had an olive orchard with presses for procuring oil from the olives. The thought of bearing the judgment for the sins of the world sent Him into a level of unprecedented emotional and spiritual distress: "My soul is overwhelmed with sorrow." In His anguish He perspired, and, as Luke wrote, His "sweat was like drops of blood falling to the ground" (Luke 22:44).

We see again here how Jesus was both truly man and truly God. Knowing as the Son of God what would occur on the following day, His human emotions surfaced as He contemplated the significance of being separated from the Father by bearing the sins of the world. His humanity was seen in the several prayers about the possibility of "the cup" being removed, and His deity was affirmed in His commitment to the Father's will.

> *Spiritual warfare demands supernatural weaponry that supersedes the inadequate will of the flesh.*

Jesus' prayer to the Father was answered, even though God did not rescue Him from the cross. As Hebrews 5:7 states, God the Father saved Him from death, that is, the Father delivered Him out of death by the resurrection. Sometimes God answers prayers in ways that differ from what we expect. Also to be learned from this passage is the fact that not all grief has sinful roots. Extreme agony and sorrow may be part of God's plan for the righteous suffering of Christians.

When the Lord needed His disciples the most, they were at their worst. Jesus' persistence in going "farther" with each round of interaction is contrasted with the repeated failures of the disciples who had said they were committed to die with Him (Matt. 26:35). This threefold failure of the disciples to stay awake may foreshadow the threefold failure of Peter. Their frailty was exposed in that they could not stay alert to pray for even one hour. When Jesus said, "The hour is near," He meant the time of His Passion, which began with the betrayal and ended with His death (and possibly includes even the glory of the Resurrection and the Ascension). John made much more of the "hour" theme (John 2:4; 7:30; 8:20; 12:23; 13:1; 16:4; 17:1).

Jesus' arrest (26:47–56). Judas betrayed Jesus with the prearranged signal of a kiss. The weapons mentioned imply the presence of soldiers (see John 18:12). Matthew referred to Judas as simply "the betrayer" (Matt. 26:48). Matthew, Mark, and Luke did not name Peter as the one who attempted to defend Jesus with a sword, but John did (John 18:10). Possibly John did so because of the timing. John wrote his fourth Gospel much later (around A.D. 85–90) after the destruction of the temple in A.D. 70. The likelihood of recrimination against Peter by the temple officials would have been much

> *Even the best of Christian leaders may struggle to be bold in the face of intimidating opposition.*

less then, compared with what it might have been soon after the incident. Luke recorded that Jesus healed the man's ear (Luke 22:51), and John named the victim as Malchus (John 18:10). Unique to Matthew is the section that explains His relationship with the Father, the availability of the twelve legions of angels (appropriate for a Jewish audience with twelve tribes), and the need for Scripture to be fulfilled. Jesus' voluntary submission to His Father in going to the cross is again highlighted.

D. The Trials (26:57–27:26)

The trial before the Sanhedrin (26:57–67). This trial took place at the house of Caiaphas. Determined to kill Jesus, the leaders invented charges to justify their accusations. Matthew documented the charges as "false" (26:59). Jesus affirmed that He is the Messiah, the Son of God, and then announced that He will descend to earth in the clouds from the right-hand position of power and privilege by the Father, "the Mighty One" (26:64). The leaders accused Jesus of blasphemy because He had claimed that God is His Father. The sentence of death was passed, and Jesus was then subjected to physical abuse: spit, blows, and mockery.

The denials of Peter (26:69–75). From a distance Peter had followed the procession to the house of Caiaphas (26:58). The three denials escalated in their intensity as the emotions of Peter grew. Jesus' prediction (26:34) was fulfilled as Peter "disowned" the Lord. When the rooster crowed, Peter remembered and went outside to weep in bitter remorse. Again a contrast is intended by Matthew as He put Jesus' bold confession side by side with Peter's terrified denials. The faithfulness of Jesus contrasts with the faithlessness of Peter. God remains faithful even when His people are faithless (2 Tim. 2:13).

The death of Judas (27:1–10). With the sentence of death on Jesus, the religious leaders delivered Him over to Pilate, the Roman governor. This was because the Jews did not have the right to execute their own prisoners (John 18:31). Pilate, one of the procurators, ruled in Israel from A.D.

26 to 36. Judas felt great remorse, and, declaring Jesus' innocence, he tried to return the betrayal silver to the leaders, but the chief priests and elders refused it. For His Jewish audience Matthew argued that even the trail of custody of the silver was an evidence that Jesus is indeed the promised Messiah for Israel. Judas' throwing the money into the temple and the leaders' using it to buy a potter's field for a cemetery fulfilled Jeremiah 19:1–13 and Zechariah 11:12–13. Joining two quotations from two Old Testament books and assigning them to one (in this case, Jeremiah) was also done in Mark 1:2–3, in which Isaiah 40:3 and Malachi 3:1 are quoted but are assigned to Isaiah. This follows the custom of mentioning the more notable prophet first.

Matthew 27:9 is another example of Matthew's typological use of Old Testament texts. He has strung these texts together like pearls on a string to argue for the messianic identification of Jesus to a Jewish audience familiar with the Old Testament. What Jeremiah, Zechariah, and Jesus have in common is that all were rejected by their respective communities even though they were God's appointed representatives. Tradition associates the potter's field with the Valley of Hinnom, south of Jerusalem (Jer. 19:7). Judas's regret, which was not genuine repentance, led him to feel irrational despair and to take his life by hanging. Knowing that death by hanging was a curse (Deut. 21:23), perhaps Judas anticipated his spiritual fate and took his life accordingly.

The civil trial (27:11–26). Pilate was concerned not about the religious squabbles but whether Jesus had violated any Roman law. When Pilate asked Jesus if He was the King of the Jews, He echoed Pilate's statement to the leaders and in essence said, "It is as you have said," thereby affirming the truthfulness of His claim. Jesus employed His characteristic style of quiet self-control (see 12:17–21). Pilate sought to pit Jesus against the notorious Barabbas in hopes that the people would see the difference and let the innocent one be released. Mark 15:7 contains a more complete description of the crimes of Barabbas. Ironically a "son of the father" (the meaning of "Barabbas") was released by retaining for death "the Son of the Father." Some manuscripts even record Barabbas's surname as "Jesus." The guilty was released at the expense of the innocent!

Only Matthew recorded the message sent to Pilate by his wife. She had a troubling but revealing dream and warned him that Jesus was innocent. That God may occasionally reveal Himself through unbelievers' dreams is seen in Nebuchadnezzar's dream (Daniel 2), but this may be rare. The persistence of the chief priests and elders in calling for the execution of Jesus contrasts with that of the reluctance of the Roman governor. Pilate, who was intimidated by the crowd's demand for Jesus' crucifixion, washed his hands, wanting to absolve himself while advocating the innocence of Jesus. The people's self-condemning words, "Let his blood be on us and our children!" was a chilling cry, which has and will continue to have prophetic ramifications. Israel faced judgment for its rejection of Jesus Christ and will continue to do so. This does not justify, however, an anti-Semitic spirit. Vengeance belongs to the Lord.

Both the Romans and Jews participated in the death of Jesus. In another sense the whole world cost Jesus His life as the Sin-Bearer for all. The people's rejection of Jesus reached its zenith at the trial before Pilate. The crowd followed the leaders and thus the whole nation was implicated. Pilate released Barabbas, had Jesus flogged, and then handed Him over to the soldiers to be crucified. The scourging was done with a *flagellum,* a whip made of leather thongs with sharp imbedded metal pieces to rip open the flesh of the victim. Evidently Pilate was hoping that the suffering from a beating would be enough to satisfy the angry crowd. But it was not!

E. The Crucifixion (27:27–56)

On the way to the cross (27:27–32). The *praetorium* was the official residence of the Roman governor. The blatant inhumanity of the soldiers was shown by their brutality against Christ. He became the sport of the "company," which numbered some six hundred strong, a tenth of a legion. He was victimized and mocked with the royal paraphernalia of a robe, a crown of thorns, a reed scepter, and the feigned ascription of Him as the King of the Jews (27:29). The priests and elders had spit on Jesus and hit Him and slapped Him (26:67), and now the soldiers did it.

Wearing a robe to the site of crucifixion was unusual; normally victims of crucifixion were led naked to the site. Perhaps this was a concession by the Romans because of His innocence, or it may have been in defer-ence to the Jewish laws of decency. The custom of being made to carry one's own cross was a symbol of the humiliation of submitting to the authority of Rome. Because Jesus was voluntarily laying down His life, the Father saw fit for Simon of Cyrene to carry the cross. Cyrene was located in what is now Libya.

The crucifixion of Jesus the Messiah (27:32–56). Of the four Gospels the Book of Matthew has the briefest description of what Jesus personally suffered on the cross. His purpose seems to be to show how all the others acted in those hours, thereby depicting the total rejection of the King. *Golgotha* means "the Place of the Skull," a name probably given because of the deaths that took place there. The first three hours Jesus suffered at the hands of men in full daylight. The offer of the wine mixed with gall was a kind of anesthesia, but Jesus refused it. The soldiers' gambling by casting lots for Jesus' clothing fulfilled Psalm 22:18.

Crucifixion was a gruesome way to die. The process could take days. Death usually came by asphyxiation because the victim was too weak to facilitate breathing by pushing up with his legs or pulling up with his arms. The title that was put on the cross above Jesus' head was ironically both the charge against Him and the truth about Him, "This is Jesus, the King of the Jews." The complete phrase can be deduced by combining the wording from all four Gospels: "This is Jesus of Nazareth, the King of the Jews."

Even the scene of the crucifixion was meaningful. Jesus was crucified *for sinners* in the midst of sinners, although that was not understood by those who crucified Him. The divided opinion about Him was modeled by the two thieves; one believed in Him and the other mocked Him. Even their taunts were truer than they realized: "He saved others, but He can-not save Himself." The fact that He could not save Himself was not because of a lack of power, but because of the resolve of His purpose.

The last three hours Jesus suffered at the hand of God in total darkness. The eternal transaction between the Son and the Father for the sins of the world was too sacred for any human being to watch. The darkness lasted from the sixth hour to the ninth hour, that is, from noon until three in the afternoon. The only "word" recorded by Matthew of the "seven last words" of Jesus was His statement about being forsaken by God (27:46). The words

"Eloi, Eloi, lama sabachthani" reflected Psalm 22:1. A wine-vinegar sponge was offered to Him and He cried out and died. The words "gave up His spirit" were an idiom for dying. Death was signaled by the cessation of breathing. Matthew's record shows that even in His death Jesus was in charge of His own destiny.

Two more supernatural events marked the occasion: an earthquake and the tearing of the temple veil from top to bottom. The rending of the veil was a sovereign act of God that brought to an end the era of the Law (see Heb. 7:12) as well as a hint that the judgment predicted by Jesus would indeed come on the house of Israel and her temple. The veil's rending also portrays the direct access believers have to God, access made possible through the death of Jesus on the cross (4:16; 9:1–8; 10:19–22). The resurrection of a number of saints must have taken place after the resurrection of Jesus since He was the firstfruits of the dead (1 Cor. 15:20). This event was recorded here to anticipate through the death and resurrection of Jesus the hope for the believing dead as well as the living who will die. The references to "many holy people" and "the holy city" anticipated a future for both the city and the believing remnant (Matt. 27:52–53). Matthew took note of two responses: A fearful centurion at the foot of the cross confessed Jesus as the Son of God, and a group of women who had been with Jesus watched the events of the cross from a distance.

F. The Burial (21:57–66)

Jesus was buried in the tomb of Joseph from Arimathea, a town about twenty miles from Jerusalem, now identified with Ramathaim, the birthplace of Samuel (1 Sam. 1:1). Joseph had asked for the body in order to bury it before sundown so as to keep from defiling the Sabbath by leaving the body on the cross until the next day (Deut. 21:22–23). A member of the Sanhedrin, he had not yet publicly followed Jesus, but he did so after His death. Matthew may have offered the Jewish readers a model for their faith. Would they too be willing to identify with the crucified Christ? Isaiah 53:9 here also comes to mind, "He was assigned a grave with the wicked and with the rich in his death." He was laid in the tomb and a stone was rolled into place. The "Preparation Day" was the Friday before the Sabbath. The religious leaders asked Pilate that a guard be stationed at the gravesite and that the grave be secured for three days. They feared that the disciples would steal the body and propagate a myth that He had been resurrected. Guards were dispatched and the tomb was sealed with clay pressed with a Roman seal attached to a rope or leather cords.

G. The Resurrection and the Great Commission (chapter 28)

The Resurrection (28:1–10). Jesus' resurrection is the obvious crowning climax of the book. No other event in the history of the world better attests to the divine sonship of Jesus than His resurrection (Rom. 1:1–4). No wonder it is the core of Christian theology as developed within the Scriptures (Acts 2:22–36; 1 Cor. 15:1–12; 1 Thess. 4:13–18; Heb. 1:1–4). If the Resurrection did not happen, then the Christian faith is worthless (1 Cor. 15:19). This section highlights the witnesses to the Resurrection, which ironically included both friends and foes of the gospel.

The uniform testimony of the Gospels is that Jesus arose early on Sunday, the first day of the week. By the time the women came at "dawn" to anoint the body with spices, He was no longer there. The record of female testimony in the culture of that day is actually an argument for the integrity of the event. Had it been contrived, the authors of the plot would have claimed male witnesses in order to give greater credibility to their assertion. This second earthquake pointed to the divine significance of the event. In the angels' testimony of the Resurrection they gave two invitations: "come and see" and "go and tell."

The report of the guard (28:11–15). The elders bribed the soldiers to fabricate a story about a theft of the body during the night. The elders promised to satisfy the displeasure of the governor in order to protect the soldiers. This arrangement and the money must have been enough to risk the death penalty for falling asleep while on guard. The "stolen body theory," invented to explain away Jesus' resurrection, has an early origin.

The Great Commission (28:16–20). The eleven disciples went to the appointed mountain in Galilee to wait for Jesus. Both worship and doubt continued to be the divided opinion among Jesus' men. The Great Commission is one of the most famous and favorite passages in the Book of

Matthew. Each phrase is full of meaning and implication. Jesus' authority in making such a command is said to be universal in scope. The imperative is always personal for those receiving it. The primary command in the passage is to "make disciples." Discipleship is intended to extend to an international audience, which includes all people groups. The core curriculum for discipleship is the life and teachings of Jesus. The need is not just for truth to be taught but for transformation to take place in the life of every disciple. The focus of the Trinitarian baptismal confession is faith in Jesus, who deserves His rightful place along with God the Father and God the Spirit. The promise of the abiding presence of the Son's ministry throughout the present age lends comforting assurance for such a daunting task as a worldwide mission.

MARK
Jesus, Model of Faithful Service

AUTHOR

*A*lthough the author is not named in the book, several facts indicate that he was Mark. This is the only Gospel that records the incident of the young man who fled from Gethsemane (Mark 14:51–52). The detailed description of the "guest room" in 14:12–16 (compare Matt. 26:17–19; John 13:1–12) suggests that Mark was writing about his own house.

Knowledge of Aramaic and of local customs fits Mark, who was a Palestinian Jew (Acts 12:17). A close connection between Mark and Peter (1 Pet. 5:13) is noted when the content of the Gospel is compared with Peter's sermon in Acts 10:36–41. Also Eusebius quoted Papias as saying that Mark wrote down what Peter had remembered of the things Jesus said and did. Mark's name appears nine times in the New Testament (Acts 12:12, 25; 13:5, 13; 15:37–39; Col. 4:10; 2 Tim. 4:11; Philem. 23–24; 1 Pet. 5:13). John was his Jewish name and Mark was his Roman name. He was the son of a Jerusalem widow, whose spacious home was a meeting place for the believers during the early days of the church. Because he left Barnabas and Paul when they were on their first missionary journey, Paul did not want to take him with them on this next journey. So Barnabas took Mark, his cousin. Later, however, Paul was apparently reconciled to Mark, because the apostle spoke well of him (2 Tim. 4:11).

DATE

Some scholars say the Gospel of Mark was the first of the four Gospels to be written. They date it as early as A.D. 45. Others, who say Matthew is the first Gospel, date the writing of Mark near the time of Peter's martyrdom and before the destruction of Jerusalem, that is, around A.D. 67 or 68. A date later than A.D. 70 is out of the question because the fall of Jerusalem (which occurred that year) was prophesied in Mark 13:2. Therefore a date of sometime beteen A.D. 65 and 67 seems most probable for the writing of the Book of Mark.

HISTORICAL BACKGROUND

According to the testimony of the second-century church father Clement of Alexandria, the Gospel of Mark was written in Rome at the request of the Roman Christians and was delivered to them on its completion. Mark's presence with Peter in Rome is confirmed in 1 Peter 5:13, if "Babylon" refers to Rome.

The earliest testimony in support of a Roman readership is found in the Anti-Marcionite Prologue, which is attached to the Gospel accounts in many Old Latin manuscripts (around A.D. 160–180). Evidence in the book itself favors a gentile rather than a Jewish audience. For example, Mark quoted the Old Testament only once, used a number of Latin phrases, explained Aramaic expressions and Jewish customs, and recorded that Jesus said the temple is to be a house of prayer for all nations (Mark 11:17). The reference to Simon as the father of Alexander and Rufus (15:21), certain technical Latin terms, and several unusual Greek constructions all point to gentile readers as the addressees.

When Mark was written, believers were suffering at the hands of the Roman emperor Nero. The Christians were blamed for a fire that swept the city in A.D. 64, and life became precarious for them.

PURPOSE

As revealed by the twofold title for Jesus in Mark 1:1 ("Jesus Christ, the Son of God") and the two climactic confessions in the book (8:29; 15:39), the Book of Mark was written to show that Jesus is in fact "the Christ, the Son of God." Not written to present a comprehensive life of Christ, Mark is both evangelistic and edifying in its presentation of Jesus as the suffering yet powerful Servant, who not only must die but who is also the Savior of mankind. As the Savior, He is the Son of God for all, especially the Roman world. As the Servant, He is the Model and Motivator for discipleship.

CHARACTERISTICS

Several features are unique to the Gospel of Mark.

First, Mark stressed the element of secrecy imposed by Jesus in connection with many of His miracles (1:44; 5:43; 7:36; 8:26), exorcisms (1:25, 34; 3:12), Peter's confession of Jesus' messiahship (8:30), and the Transfiguration (9:9).

Second, Mark repeatedly noted the presence of the masses around Jesus.

Third, the Greek word for "immediately" occurs forty-two times in the book. This is the gospel of action.

Fourth, Jesus' emotions are noted in the book, more so than in the other three Gospels.

Fifth, special attention is given to Jesus' preparation of the disciples for future ministry (chapters 8–10).

Sixth, more than two-fifths of the entire book deals with the last week of Christ's life, thus placing major emphasis on His suffering.

Seventh, the Gospel of Mark emphasizes the deity of Christ.

Eighth, the miracle narratives are prominent in Mark's Gospel, and many of them include more details than the other Gospels.

Ninth, Mark emphasized Jesus' power over Satan, as seen in several exorcisms.

OUTLINE

I. The Servant to the Multitudes (1:1–8:26)
  A. The Preparation and Initial Ministry of Jesus (1:1–20)
  B. The Miracles of Authenticity (1:21–2:12)
  C. The Contrasting Responses to Jesus (2:13–8:26)
II. The Servant to the Disciples (8:27–10:52)
  A. The Confession of Peter (8:27–30)
  B. The First Announcement of Jesus' Death (8:31–38)
  C. The Transfiguration of Jesus (9:1–13)
  D. The Manifestation of Jesus' Power (9:14–29)
  E. The Second Announcement of Jesus' Death (9:30–32)
  F. The Instructions to the Disciples (9:33–10:52)
III. The Sacrifice for the World (chapters 11–16)
  A. The Controversies in Jerusalem (chapters 11–12)
  B. The Discourse from Olivet (chapter 13)
  C. The Betrayal and Denials of Jesus (14:1–42)
  D. The Arrest and Trials of Jesus (14:43–15:20)
  E. The Crucifixion and Burial of Jesus (15:21–47)
  F. The Resurrection of Jesus (chapter 16)

I. THE SERVANT TO THE MULTITUDES (1:1–8:26)

A. The Preparation and Initial Ministry of Jesus (1:1–20)

Jesus' preparation (1:1–8). The title of the book, given in the opening verse is, "The beginning of the gospel about Jesus Christ, the Son of God." This title is developed in two major sections of the book, each climaxing with a portion of the title confessed. Peter confessed that Jesus is the Christ in Mark 8:29, and the centurion confessed that He is the Son of God in 15:39. Each half of the book builds to a climactic confession. The gospel focuses on Jesus, who is the Messiah and the Son of God. The deity of the Servant is stressed from the beginning, thus showing that His servanthood and His divine sonship are intimately connected.

John's ministry as the forerunner of Christ is linked to Malachi 3:1 and Isaiah 40:3. His ministry was one of preparation for the coming of the Lord, the Messiah of Israel. The location of the wilderness and the call for repentance show the Lord's approach to Israel from outside the religious community, which had lost its moorings and perverted the message of salvation. John's clothing was reminiscent of Elijah's attire, as was his message of repentance. John's baptism, symbolizing repentance of heart and confession of sins, was needed by all who had not yet made that decision. The contrast between John and Jesus was stated by the Baptizer himself, who distinguished his preparatory ministry from that of the Messiah, who had both the authority and the power to send the Holy Spirit from God.

Jesus' baptism (1:9–11). Jesus, the sinless One, identified Himself through baptism with the righteous remnant whom He came to deliver from their sins. The descent of the Spirit and the voice from the heavens call to mind Psalm 2:7; Isaiah 42:1; and 61:1. The book's emphases on Jesus' divine sonship and His role as suffering Servant are therefore authenticated and paradoxically linked through this introduction. This paradox is noted throughout the book.

Jesus' temptations (1:12–13). Unlike Matthew and Luke, Mark wrote that Jesus was sent by the Holy Spirit to the desert to be tempted, that wild animals were there, and that angels ministered to Him. His victory in the midst of conflict shows that He is qualified to be a ransom for many (10:45). The image of victory over Satan foreshadowed the other exorcisms, a major part of Jesus' work recorded in this Gospel.

Jesus' preaching (1:14–15). Matthew reported that John and Jesus preached the same message of repentance in light of the coming kingdom (Matt. 3:2; 4:17). Mark recorded a slightly longer message given by Jesus: Repentance was to be linked with belief in the good news of Jesus Christ. The gospel needed to be believed in light of the coming kingdom. Mark highlighted the uniqueness of the timing with the presence of the Messiah on earth as a fulfillment of Old Testament expectations. Jesus embodied the fulfillment of the Old Testament prophets and the message of the imminency of the kingdom that He would establish. The proper preparation for entrance into the kingdom was to repent of trusting in oneself or one's works and to place faith in the only adequate provision for salvation, Jesus Christ Himself.

> *Repentance and belief in the good news of Jesus is the proper preparation for the coming kingdom.*

Jesus' call of the disciples (1:16–20). Jesus called Simon and Andrew from their occupation of fishing to a new ministry of fishing for men. They responded immediately, as did James and John, sons of Zebedee, who likewise followed Christ. In light of John 1:35–42, which seems to indicate they had already believed in Jesus Christ, Mark 1:16–20 indicates that Jesus was calling them to a life of discipleship and a ministry of evangelism. The disciples were chosen to commit themselves to the Lord and His ministry. The imagery of fishing for men may allude to Jeremiah 16:16, in which God said "fishermen" would call Israel back to Himself for judgment and restoration.

B. The Miracles of Authenticity (1:21–2:12)

Jesus' authority over demons (1:21–28). Two recurring themes repeated in the first two chapters of Mark are Jesus' teaching and healing ministries. Together these fulfilled the Old Testament expectations of Isaiah 29:18; 35:5; and 42:7. It is noteworthy that Jesus' first act of ministry recorded in Mark was an exorcism and that it occurred in the place of worship, the synagogue in Capernaum. His teaching had inherent authority in contrast to the derived authority of the scribes. Jesus taught and acted with authority, and such power caused His reputation to spread throughout all of Galilee (1:28). The demons recognized that Jesus of Nazareth is "the Holy One of God," a title Isaiah used of the coming Messiah. Ironically, though the demons recognized Jesus, the leaders of Israel did not. This was a sad commentary on the religious community in His day. Sometimes in Mark these agents of Satan are called demons and other times, as here, they are called "evil [literally, 'unclean'] spirits."

Jesus' authority over sickness (1:29–39). Jesus healed Peter's mother-in-law and restored her to complete strength. A summary passage in 1:32–34 points up Jesus' ability to heal all who were demon-possessed and afflicted with various diseases. In the midst of such a popular ministry Jesus prioritized His time and modeled the need for solitude and prayer. The crowds never controlled His calendar, and He followed the purpose of God to take His Word to smaller venues than even the disciples expected.

> *Prayer is a key to maintaining proper priorities in our lives and ministries.*

Jesus' authority over defilement (1:40–45). By curing a leper, Jesus showed that He had the power to cleanse from defilement without becoming defiled Himself. Mark was unique in mentioning Jesus' compassion as He reached out to touch and heal the leper. Leprosy seemed to symbolize the defilement of sin. Like sin, leprosy was incurable apart from God. Any healing could be validated only by the declaration of a priest who recognized that God had acted to heal a leper. Only after healing could a leprous person be accepted back into the community. Similarly righteousness is provided only by God, is declared and imputed to the sinner, and thus makes the sinner acceptable to serve Him. The failure of the leper to obey the Lord totally showed how disobedience can thwart one's desired ministry for God.

Jesus' healing of the paralytic (2:1–12). This miracle showed that Jesus has the authority to forgive sins. His healing of the man's visible paralysis shows that He had the ability to heal the invisible defilement of sin. The faith of the man and his stretcher-bearers was a catalyst for the miracle and for forgiveness of his sin. Throughout the Gospels Jesus' title "the Son of man" emphasizes three ministry periods in His life: His incarnation and earthly ministry, His death and resurrection, and His second coming. Although the term can be used of normal humanity, as in the Book of Ezekiel, Jesus adopted and filled out the phrase, so that it became an identification that relates uniquely to Him, the Messiah.

C. The Contrasting Responses to Jesus' Ministry (2:13–8:26)

The calling of Matthew (2:13–22). Tax collectors were despised because of their association with Rome and their reputation for collecting taxes dishonestly. Jesus provided an atmosphere in which sinners could approach Him, but this produced a hostile response among the religious leaders. Jesus' response through a proverb ("It is not the healthy who need a doctor, but

> *The recognition of sin is a prerequisite for accepting the Savior.*

the sick") and a pronouncement ("I have not come to call the righteous, but sinners") showed that His mission was to reach sinners and save them. By their very attitude the self-righteous denied themselves the possibility of being helped.

In response to the question of why His disciples didn't fast, Jesus likened Himself to a Bridegroom and predicted that there would be a hostile response to Him in that role. The imagery of the bridegroom is rooted in the Old Testament (Jer. 3:1–14; Ezek. 16:1–62). Fasting is not necessary when one is in the presence of the Messiah. But when He would be rejected and crucified, the disciples would mourn and fast.

The illustrations of the patch on the old garment and of the old wineskin reveal that Israel was unable to accept Jesus' ministry because of its allegiance to its traditions. Jesus did not come to repair an old system but to create a new one.

The Sabbath controversy (2:23–28). In Jesus' day the Jewish leaders had made Sabbath observance a test of one's allegiance to the Law. The Pharisees' challenge to the disciples was not that they were eating grain from the fields; the poor and the hungry were allowed to do that (Lev. 19:9–10). The Pharisees' complaint was that the disciples, they assumed, were working by preparing a meal on the Sabbath ("They began to pick heads of grain"). Jesus refuted the Pharisees' objections by an appeal to the time when David and his group of men ate the consecrated bread in the tabernacle (1 Sam. 21:1–6). David's breach of the religious legal rule was necessitated by the urgency of his situation. Jesus claimed that His ministry, along with that of His disciples, was an equally urgent mission. The Sabbath, He said, was not made for people to obey but for people to be helped by it. And as the Lord of the Sabbath He could help people on the Sabbath. He had the right to determine the day as well as govern its legalities. This identity was what the leaders of Israel failed to recognize.

Jesus' healing of a man's shriveled hand (3:1–6). The leaders tried to trap Jesus into disobeying the traditional teaching about Sabbath observance. The rabbis had restricted healing on the Sabbath to life-and-death issues. Jesus did not avoid the trap, but instead asked a question to get to the heart of the issue. His question showed that to do good on the Sabbath was as important as saving a life from death. The Pharisees could not respond without condemning themselves, so they refused to answer. Mark recorded Jesus' anger and grief at the stubbornness of their hearts. This is one of the infrequent references to the righteous anger of Jesus. This event served as the catalyst for the Pharisees and the Herodians to join forces in plotting to kill Jesus.

Religious intolerance and political correctness sometimes join forces against the Savior and His message.

Jesus' popularity (3:7–12). Sometimes the populace is not as blind as the religious leaders. People came from great distances to hear Him and to be healed by Him. Such popularity caused Jesus to use a boat as a makeshift pulpit in order to minister to the crowds. Mark again mentioned Jesus' exorcism ministry. Ironically the demons recognized Jesus as the Son of God while some humans, particularly the Jewish leaders continued to struggle with such an identification.

Jesus' appointment of the Twelve (3:13–19). Jesus spent much time in prayer with God the Father before choosing His disciples. If the Son of God needed that time alone, how much more do those who call themselves His disciples. He chose them to do two things—to spend time with Him and to go forth in ministry. His invitation to communion with Him precedes His imperative of commission for Him. Those chosen to be mentored were to be the missionaries. No one can make disciples unless he or she is willing to continue becoming a disciple of Jesus. The lists of the disciples in the New Testament always contain the same three units of four names each and were always headed by the same three: Simon, Philip, and James, son of Alphaeus (see Acts 1:13). This suggests that there may have been some early organization and small-group accountability in the ranks of the disciples. Their driving out demons would demonstrate the truth of their message of the kingdom, which was appropriate in Jesus' offer of the kingdom to Israel during His earthly ministry.

The blasphemy of the Spirit (3:20–30). The leaders from Jerusalem not only thought Jesus was crazy (3:21); they also accused Him of being demon-possessed (3:30). Jesus refuted their charges by a series of logical arguments.

First, he stated that Satan casting out Satan would be self-destructive. Second, the expulsion of demons would be a defeat and not a victory for Satan. Third, such willful and deliberate refusal of the Spirit's testimony was a sin that could never be forgiven. Such blasphemy of the Holy Spirit, which has become known as "the unpardonable sin," is attributing to Satan the works of the Holy Spirit demonstrated in Jesus' ministry. Having rejected the testimony of the Father, the Son, and now the Spirit's miraculous authentication, nothing more could be done for the salvation of those religious leaders. To come to such a conclusion about Jesus, after all of the evidence to the contrary, was unpardonable. If on the other hand, Jesus was strong enough to defeat Satan, then He could deal with sin and the devil (13:27–28) because He is the Savior and the Son of God.

> Only God can defeat the supernatural forces that stand against Him.

The true family of God (3:31–35). Jesus' true family members are those who are related to Him spiritually because of a common faith. Doing the will of God begins by believing in the message of His Son whom He has sent to be His representative to humanity. Family loyalty is demonstrated by obedience. Spiritual ties are stronger than physical ties. God's family has a more binding connection than any earthly family could ever have.

The parable of the sower and the soils (4:1–20). Mark recorded only two of the parables Matthew recorded in Matthew 13—the sower and the soils (Mark 4:1–20) and the mustard seed (4:30–34). The parable of the sower and the soils addressed the response of people to the message of the kingdom of God (4:9). Various conditions of the heart cause differing degrees of receptivity. Only one ground was seen as good enough to produce fruit. The other three soils all illustrate why the Word of God is not well received. The birds on the path illustrate satanic opposition that preempts faith and keeps a person from becoming a Christian (4:4, 15). The rocky soil symbolizes affliction and persecution, which cause some people to turn away quickly from the Word of God (4:5, 17). The thorny soil depicts the internal distractions of worry, riches, and desires which choke out the intended effect of the Word of God in a person's life (4:7, 19). The good soil represents the receptive heart, which has been prepared to accept the message of the kingdom. These people hear and accept the Word, and various levels of fruitfulness are the result (4:8, 20).

The parable of the lamp (4:21–25). Just as lamps are intended to bring light, so the parables were intended to communicate the truth of the kingdom that will one day become reality. The need "to hear" was repeated in the passage to call again for an obedience to the truth. Those to whom much has been revealed are called to be responsible stewards of that truth. Jesus' principle, "For whoever has, to him more will be given; but whoever does not have, even what he has will be taken away from him" (4:25), reinforced the dual purposes of the parables: to reveal truth and to conceal truth related to the kingdom of God.

The parable of the seed growing of itself (4:26–29). The present mysterious and invisible phase of the kingdom will one day become visible. The gradual but persistent growth of the kingdom was pictured in this analogy. By its very nature the kingdom will succeed because God alone is responsible for its success. In contrast with other parables that stressed either the beginning or the consummation of the kingdom, this parable highlights the active though invisible growth of the kingdom.

The parable of the mustard seed (4:30–34). This last parable of the chapter has the most intricate introduction. The parable contrasts the seemingly insignificant beginnings of the present phase of the kingdom and the international extension of the kingdom throughout the gentile world. The birds nesting in the branches is an Old Testament image of the presence of Gentiles in the kingdom of God (Ezek. 17:22–23; 31:6; Dan. 4:12). Though many may have been tempted to disregard Jesus in His earthly ministry, the integrity of His life and message are being demonstrated by the kingdom's extension. Though the parables were told in public, it was Jesus' practice to explain them to the disciples in private.

The confirmation by means of a miracle (4:35–41). Mark recorded Jesus' miracle of the stilling of the storm to show that Jesus has the power to establish the kingdom because He shares the power of His Father in controlling the world of nature. The dual nature of the Son was seen in His fatigue on the one hand and the miraculous stilling of the storm on the other. The Psalms refer often to God's power over the seas (Pss. 65:7; 89:9; 106:9; 107:23–32). Thus Jesus' stilling of the storm demonstrates

God may lead different people to witness for Him in differing ways.

His divine power and authority. His challenge to the disciples about their lack of faith is a familiar theme in the Gospel of Mark (2:5; 4:40; 5:34, 36; 9:23; 10:52; 11:22).

Jesus' curing of the demoniac (5:1–20). On the other side of the Sea of Galilee Jesus landed at a site which Mark called the region of the Gerasenes. With slightly different spellings Matthew called the region the Gadarenes (Matt. 8:28), while Luke mentioned the Gerasenes (Luke 8:26). The general territory was the region known as the Decapolis, the ten city-states of the Greeks. The significance of the title "Most High God," by which the demoniac addressed Jesus, had its precedent in the Old Testament when Gentiles confessed faith in God (Gen. 14:17–24; Num. 24:16; Ps. 97:9; Dan. 4:17; 7:18, 22, 25, 27). The name "Legion" pointed out the extent of demonic opposition to Jesus (a legion consisted of about six thousand soldiers). The reaction of the crowd illustrates the parable of the soils in Mark 4:1–20 that the message of Jesus was rejected because of the unwillingness of the people to suffer material loss. Jesus' command to the healed demoniac to tell the story in gentile territories contrasted with the commands to silence that Jesus gave in the Jewish regions.

Jesus' healing of a dead girl and a sick woman (5:21–43). Jesus' power over death is the greatest demonstration of His power recorded so far in the Gospel of Mark. The Gospels record two others whom Jesus restored to life from the dead: the boy at Nain (Luke 7:11–17) and Lazarus of Bethany (John 11:1–44). Later both Peter and Paul also raised people from the dead (Acts 9:41; 20:10). The first resurrection with an eternal body was that of Jesus, "the firstfruits of those who have fallen asleep" (1 Cor. 15:20). These others who were resurrected eventually died again.

The healing of Jairus's daughter shows that Jesus is the Lord of life, and the healing of the woman with the problem of persistent bleeding shows that He is the Lord of health. The story of the raising of the girl from the dead is sandwiched around the miracle of the sick woman. Interestingly the daughter was twelve years of age, and the woman had been sick for twelve years. Jairus believed that the touch of Jesus was necessary, and the woman believed that by touching Jesus, she would be healed. In both cases further teaching was needed beyond the individuals' faith in the touch of Jesus. Both showed the need for faith above superstition. Jesus' miracle of healing the woman underscored her faith, but the raising of the twelve-year-old exposed the unbelief of the multitudes who laughed at Jesus.

The rejection in Nazareth (6:1–6). Signs by themselves are never a cure for unbelief. People with spiritual blindness are also blind to supernatural power. Perhaps this explains why most of Jesus' miracles occurred in the opening chapters of Mark. People in His hometown of Nazareth could not get past His human connection, even though they were astonished at the wisdom and power with which He was ministering. The unbelief in Nazareth limited the demonstration of His power. Of course, the power of God is never diminished, but He does not waste His work on those who persist in their unbelief. Jesus was amazed at the unbelief of rejecting hearts. The proverb that "a prophet is not without honor except at home" proved true even with Jesus, the Son of God.

> *Unbelief stifles the otherwise powerful ministry of God.*

Jesus' commissioning of the Twelve (6:7–13). This was the second time the disciples had been sent on a mission (see 3:15). The disciples were sent out with the authority to represent Jesus and to convey the message of the kingdom, with the ability to perform kingdom miracles. Power to counter disease, death, and demons was delegated to them. How people received the messenger indicated their response to the message. Shaking dust from one's feet symbolically announced God's judgment against unholiness.

The death of John the Baptist (6:14–29). John was a forerunner of Jesus in his birth, ministry, and death. Also the way people identified John the Baptist was as varied as the way they identified Jesus. Some confused John with Elijah, or another prophet, or even Jesus. Herod Antipas, son of Herod the Great, was fascinated with John and liked to listen to his preaching. However, he eventually exchanged John's life for his own pleasure and reputation. By contrast, John's loyalty in the face of death provides a model of committed discipleship even in times of suffering.

> *God wants His followers to be faithful disciples regardless of the opposition they may face.*

Jesus' feeding of the five thousand (6:30–44). Jesus' compassion for the hungry multitude contrasts with the disciples' frustration. His challenge to His disciples to meet the needs of the multitude was designed to expose both their inability and His ability. In testing their resourcefulness, Jesus pushed them to wrestle with what they had in comparison with Him. Who can meet the needs of the multitudes? Everything the crowd needed was available in Christ. The leftovers showed that Jesus has more than enough power and provision to meet people's needs.

Jesus' walking on the water (6:45–52). The name Bethsaida means "the house of the fisher." The town was located near the north shore of the Sea of Galilee. Jesus' walking on the lake was His second "sea miracle" (see 4:35–41). By doing what only God can do, Jesus demonstrated His deity. The Old Testament refers to God having the power to tread on the water (Job 9:8; Ps. 77:10). Jesus showed His ability to do the same. The disciples' amazement at this miracle exposed their hardheartedness. They lacked faith and were afraid because they misunderstood Jesus' miracle of multiplying the loaves and fish.

Jesus' healings around Gennesaret (6:53–56). Even though the disciples, like others, failed to grasp what Jesus was all about (6:52), He still demonstrated His healing power toward those for whom He had compassion in the region surrounding the village of Gennesaret. The power of the King validated the potential of the kingdom.

The terrible trend of traditionalism (7:1–23). The Pharisees' question about clean and unclean hands related to their traditions and not to explicit commands of Scripture. Jesus, however, exposed their traditionalism by noting that it was selective, it fostered a spirit of elitism, and it was placed above Scripture. Isaiah's statement about people honoring God by their words but having faraway hearts (Isa. 29:18) was quite descriptive of Israel in his day as well as in Jesus' day. Mark 7:6 is the only reference in Mark to Jesus' charge of hypocrisy against the religious leaders. "Corban" (7:11) referred to the practice of dedicating to God what would have been used for something else (Num. 30:1–16; Deut. 23:21–23). To excuse oneself by such a practice from helping even one's parents was shown to be a misuse of tradition and a clear violation of the Scriptures.

Jesus then explained, first to the crowd and then privately to the disciples, that impurity is sourced not in external matters but in the heart. While Jesus set aside the Mosaic dietary laws (7:19), He affirmed the need for internal righteousness as preached by the prophets (Isa. 1:10–20; Amos 5:21–27). Righteous or wicked conduct is really a revelation of the heart.

> *It is dangerous to substitute human traditions for the Word of God.*

The faith of the Syrian Phoenician woman (7:24–30). This was the only time in Jesus' ministry when He traveled beyond the borders of Israel. Early gentile Christians would have been encouraged by this account of a Canaanite woman whose faith was extolled by Jesus. What this woman believed about Jesus was what God wanted Israel to understand. The purpose of the narrative was to show that in light of Israel's rejection of the message, the gospel had been extended by God's gracious compassion to the Gentiles. Jesus' initial mission was to present the kingdom message to Israel. But because of their unbelief, blessing was extended to the Gentiles, a theme Paul developed in Romans 9–11. Regardless of ethnic and religious backgrounds, anyone can come to faith in Jesus Christ and find the satisfaction that only He can bring. While the "bread" is being taken to the Gentiles, the "children" (Israel) are encouraged to eat all they want. Individual Israelites can always come to the Savior even though God's program in this present church age is focused on the Gentiles.

Jesus' healing of the man with a hearing-and-speech impairment (7:31–37). Mark 7:24–37 may have been an extended allusion to Isaiah 35, which mentioned Lebanon (35:2), where Tyre and Sidon were located, as well as the confirming miracles of the coming Messiah (35:5–6), including healing those who can't hear and those whose speech is impaired. A rare word for speech impediment is used in Mark 7:32. To create faith in the man, Jesus touched his ears and tongue to signal what His healing word would bring about. "Ephphatha" is an Aramaic expression that means "be opened." Even though Jesus told the people not to tell what He had done, they kept talking about it.

Their acclamation that He did all things well was a fitting compliment to His works, but an incomplete confession of faith in His person.

Jesus' feeding of the four thousand (8:1–9). Again Jesus had concern for the crowd. The sufficiency of the miracle was again seen in the amounts that were left over. The first miracle of multiplying loaves and fishes was in a Jewish setting (6:30–44), but this may have taken place among the Gentiles (see 7:31). The "bread" that was offered to the Jews was now offered to the Gentiles. Comparing Jesus' prayers offered before these two feeding miracles shows that the first included the Jewish blessing of looking toward heaven (6:41), whereas the second was a simple thanksgiving (8:6). The baskets used in the second miracle were larger than in the first. These larger baskets were the same kind Paul used when he escaped over the wall of Damascus (Acts 9:25).

Jesus can enable His disciples to meet the needs of the multitudes.

Opposition from the Pharisees (8:10–21). Dalmanutha is identified as Magdala on the northwest shore of the Sea of Galilee. Magdala is the region from which Mary Magdalene came (Luke 8:2). The Pharisees' call for a sign was an attempt to test Jesus. Their continued perpetual refusal to believe in Jesus caused Him to sigh deeply in His spirit. This sigh of weariness and grief plagued His soul. Mark recorded that Jesus refused to give them any sign, but Matthew added that Jesus said they already had a miraculous sign, namely, Jonah (Matt. 12:39–40). Jesus' death and resurrection, pictured by Jonah's being in the fish's belly and then expelled from it, were the ultimate signs that demonstrated Jesus' identity as the Son of God (Rom. 1:3–4). The term *generation* referred to a group of people with evil motives, namely, the Pharisees.

Jesus then warned the disciples about the yeast of both the Pharisees and Herod. The Pharisees' yeast was the hypocrisy of their self-righteous traditionalism, and Herod's yeast was the spirit of imperial pride. Jesus' eight questions in Mark 8:17–21 were His strongest rebuke of the disciples, a rebuke in which He used words normally addressed to unbelieving Israelites. The disciples struggled to understand the significance of the feeding of the five thousand and of the four thousand. His point was that if He could meet the needs of the multitudes, He could meet their needs as well. And if He could meet the needs of the Jews, He could also meet the needs of Gentiles.

Jesus' healing of the blind man (8:22–26). This was the only one of Jesus' miracles that He did not do immediately. This account was probably intended as a visual aid to expose the disciples' lack of spiritual perception, already noted in 8:17–21. The man would see physically, but the disciples failed to see spiritually. Jesus told the man not to go into the village, probably to avoid his causing excessive public commotion. This miracle served as a fitting introduction to the extended section on discipleship development recorded in 8:27–10:52.

II. THE SERVANT TO THE DISCIPLES (8:27–10:52)

A. The Confession of Peter (8:27–30)

This event took place in the region of Caesarea Philippi near the foot of Mount Hermon in the territory of Philip the Tetrarch. Peter acted as the spokesman for the disciples in his confession that Jesus is the Christ. While Matthew recorded the confession with two statements about Jesus—that He is both the Christ and the Son of God (Matt. 16:16)—Mark included only the first acclamation: "You are the Christ." Perhaps Mark was intentionally showing the "partial sight" of the disciples, illustrated by the previous miracle in two stages (8:22–26). Peter understood that Jesus is the Messiah (Christ), but he struggled with the fact that He is the suffering Savior. The command for silence as to His identity related in some measure to the sovereign timing of the future establishment of the messianic kingdom.

Satan used one of Jesus' closest followers to oppose the message of the gospel. Peter stumbled because he could not harmonize Jesus' crucifixion with His being the Messiah. A violent death did not mesh well with the concept of messianic authority. By having in mind "the things of men," Peter's thinking was dominated by a humanistic viewpoint.

> *The message of the Cross is a call to identification with and dedication to Christ.*

B. The First Announcement of Jesus' Death (8:31–38)

Following Peter's confession, Jesus gave three announcements of His death and resurrection (8:31; 9:30–32; 10:32–34). The three predictions indicted the Jews and Gentiles, both of whom were involved in the crucifixion. With each announcement Jesus gave a call to committed discipleship (8:34–38; 9:35–37; 10:43–45).

C. The Transfiguration of Jesus (9:1–13)

The Transfiguration was recorded by Mark to document the revelation of Jesus as the King and to bolster the faith of the disciples during the time before the kingdom will be established. This vision of the kingdom was a foreshadowing of Jesus' earthly messianic kingdom. The term *transfiguration* comes from the Greek verb *metamorphō*, from which we get the word "metamorphosis." This connotes a change in outward appearance in keeping with one's inner nature. The appearance is similar to the theophanies (appearances of God) in the Old Testament (for example, Dan. 7:9).

Moses and Elijah both left the world by unusual circumstances. Their appearance on this occasion may have been intended to represent the believers in the periods of the Law and the prophets, believers who will be present with New Testament believers when the kingdom is established. Luke wrote that the conversation revolved around Jesus' departure (literally, "exodus") that He would experience in Jerusalem (Luke 9:31), which may refer to either His death or, more likely, His ascension. When Jesus said, "Elijah has come" (Mark 9:13), He referred to John the Baptist, who came "in the spirit and power of Elijah" (Luke 1:17). But Jesus also spoke of the fact that Elijah himself must return and restore all things (Mark 9:12; see also Matt. 17:11). This Elijah will come just before the Messiah returns at His second advent (Mal. 4:5–6). Like John the Baptist, he will prepare people for the coming King.

Jesus commanded that the three disciples not tell anyone about the Transfiguration (Mark 9:9). Perhaps this was to convey that before the messianic kingdom could be established in the future He had to die and be resurrected. After His resurrection, the disciples would understand for sure who Jesus is and what His ministry was about. The disciples' wonderment about the meaning of "rising from the dead" revealed their need for more discipleship development.

D. The Manifestation of Jesus' Power (9:14–29)

When Jesus came down from the mountain, He saw confusion in the crowd. This is similar to Israel's disarray that Moses saw when he came down the mountain (Exod. 32). The power of the demons was seen in the incredible suffering they caused the boy. Both the impatient father and the powerless disciples needed to learn a lesson of faith. The faith of the man needed to be directed toward the Lord, and the faith of the disciples needed to be exercised through prayer. Only God can defeat the enemy and enable His followers to minister. Different kinds of demons evidently possessed varying degrees of power (Mark 9:28). The disciples' unbelief, revealed in their prayerlessness, resulted in their spiritual ineffectiveness.

> As Ruler of the world, Jesus will establish His messianic kingdom when He returns to earth.

E. The Second Announcement of Jesus' Death (9:30–32)

Jesus told the disciples not to reveal where they were because His progressive self-revelation of Himself was still being carried out. He told them again about His coming betrayal, death, and resurrection. But still they didn't understand and therefore were fearful of what the announcement would mean for Him and for them.

F. The Instructions to the Disciples (9:33–10:52)

The danger of causing offenses (9:33–50). Jesus' instructions here focused on the family relationships of fellow believers. While Jesus was teaching the disciples about His death and resurrection (9:31), their minds were occupied with thoughts of personal greatness and positions of power and superiority. Jesus warned against the spirit of elitism that can exist within a ministry team and between ministry teams. The answer to elitism from within is to have a servant's heart, and the answer to elitism toward outsiders is to recognize the unity of the family of God that transcends smaller groups of ministry.

The illustration of the child taught that people were to be accepted because of their relationship to Him and not because of any external standard of greatness. Servanthood is the highest priority of a committed disciple, and a servant's heart is to be rooted in personal humility. In fact, the humble heart of a servant is the hallmark of true greatness in the sight of Jesus Christ. Having observed other exorcists, the disciples may have been trying to change the subject (9:38), but Jesus continued the lesson. Fellowship is based on one's attitude toward Jesus Christ rather than the personal styles or philosophies of ministry among those who would seek to serve Him. All service done in the name of the Lord and for the glory of God will be rewarded.

> *Servanthood is the highest priority of a committed disciple.*

Jesus then warned against causing "little ones" to sin (9:42–50). Physical death is to be preferred to the discipline or judgment Jesus will execute on the offenders. Any stimulus that could cause offense should be removed. Those who cause stumbling blocks are unbelievers who will suffer eternal judgment in hell. Jesus used such expressions as "where the fire never goes out," "their worm does not die," and "the fire is not quenched" to speak about the punishment and permanence of hell. While some may not think hell is real, Jesus certainly did.

The questions about marriage and divorce (10:1–12). Perea, ruled by Herod Antipas, was the territory east of the Jordan River which extended from the region of the Decapolis in the north to the Dead Sea in the south. In asking Jesus whether divorce was lawful, the Pharisees may have been attempting to put Jesus at odds with Herod and the Herodians in forcing Him to take a stand similar to that of John the Baptist (see 6:18). Could this have been the springing of the trap mentioned in 3:6?

Three differences exist between Mark's and Matthew's versions of this account. First, Matthew recorded Jesus' "exception" clause ("except for marital unfaithfulness," Matt. 19:9), which Mark did not include. Second, Mark included Jesus' reference to a wife divorcing her husband; this would not have been tolerated in Judaism, and so Matthew omitted it. Third, the phrase "against her" (Mark 10:11) is not included in Matthew.

> *Hell is a real place of eternal punishment and therefore a place to be feared and from which to be delivered by Jesus.*

The Pharisees' question centered around Deuteronomy 24:1–4, a legal passage that protected the rights of the wife against the practice of divorce on frivolous grounds. Any law that governed the results of sin was necessary because of the hardness of the heart that gave birth to that sin. The law in Deuteronomy 24 was therefore not to be viewed as an excuse to sin but as a restraint on sin; it was intended to regulate divorce with a view to discouraging its practice. God's plan for marriage is permanent monogamy (Gen. 1:27; 2:24). Jesus raised the status of women by condemning unbiblical divorce, a sin that could be committed more easily against them.

Children and childlike faith (10:13–16). Mark recorded eight times when Jesus touched someone, and each occasion had beneficial effects (1:41; 3:10; 5:28, 41; 6:56; 7:32; 8:22; 10:13). Not surprisingly, people brought children to Jesus for Him to touch them. This again gave Jesus opportunity to illustrate the humility required of those who desire to enter the kingdom. All that is required to be saved is a childlike faith in Christ alone. Receiving the kingdom is the same as receiving eternal life, and faith is the only stated condition.

Salvation and rewards (10:17–27). Riches create obstacles in the road of one who would come to faith in Jesus. What the young man did not understand was the nature of goodness. Good is absolute righteousness, which no one but God possesses. Jesus referred to six of the Ten Commandments in an attempt to expose the man's sinfulness to which he was apparently blind. The man refused Jesus' loving invitation to faith and obedient stewardship because of his unwillingness to allow Jesus to command his finances.

Many wealthy people find it difficult to come to Christ because of their self-sufficiency. Putting a camel, the largest animal known to that culture, through the small opening of a sewing needle is easier than for the rich to be saved. Great wealth and sincere religion are not sufficient to secure eternal life. Only faith in Christ enables one to enter the kingdom. Benevolence with one's finances will be rewarded with true treasure in heaven.

Rewards for faithfulness (10:28–31). Jesus affirmed that sacrificial obedience will be generously rewarded. The mention of "persecutions" (10:30), which the other Synoptic writers did not include in this statement by Jesus, was appropriate for the Roman believers, who were being challenged through this book to be faithful in the face of persecution. Their source of comfort rested in the knowledge that God would reward them both in this life and in the life to come. Whatever possessions or relationships were sacrificed for Jesus' sake would be more than repaid. The proverb about the first and the last was a word of caution against presuming on one's rewards and comparing oneself with others. Jesus can be trusted to reward faithfulness generously.

The third annoucement of Jesus' death (10:32–45). This third announcement about the Cross and the Resurrection was intended to surface in the disciples their need to commit themselves to sacrificial service. Both their amazement and their fear were observable as they journeyed to Jerusalem. For the first time Jesus spoke of Gentiles and their inhumane treatment of Him at His trials. The request of James and John for special positions in the kingdom was answered with another lesson on servanthood. The cup was a familiar image of judgment in the Old Testament (for example, Ps. 75:8; Isa. 51:17–22; Jer. 25:15–28; 49:12; 51:7; Lam. 4:21; Ezek. 23:31–34). The judgment Jesus would face in His crucifixion would be for the sins of the world.

The "baptism" Jesus mentioned referred to His death by which He would identify with sinners. This statement may have inspired Paul to use baptism as an illustration of the death and resurrection of Christ. The death of Christ became both the means of salvation and a model for discipleship. The word "ransom" means the price paid to free a slave. Jesus was the price paid by God the Father, which provides for freedom from and forgiveness of sin. Many people think of Mark 10:45 as the key verse of this book. Jesus' self-sacrifice is the model of humble service that will protect disciples from attitudes of superiority.

> *Jesus is the ultimate example of servant-hearted leadership.*

Jesus' healing of the blind man (10:46–52). This second account of the blind being healed (see 8:22–26 for the first account) concludes this central section of Mark (8:27–10:52) and serves as "bookends" of this section. Recorded as they were and where they were may be suggestive of the trouble the spiritually blind disciples were having in grasping the need for the death of Christ and the need for faithfulness in taking a stand for Christ in the midst of opposition.

This passage is the only place in Mark where someone called Jesus "Son of David." That Jesus accepted this title and healed the man is evidence that He affirmed the truth that He is indeed the Messiah. The Greek word rendered "healed" also means "saved." Jesus was the Lord who could extend mercy and heal from both physical and spiritual defilement. Of the two blind men who were healed (Matt. 20:29–34), Bartimaeus was the one whom Mark chose to highlight. The man then responded to Jesus by following Him along the way.

III. THE SACRIFICE FOR THE WORLD (CHAPTERS 11–16)

A. The Controversies in Jerusalem (chapters 11–12)

The entrance into Jerusalem (11:1–11). Jesus' entry into Jerusalem was His official presentation of Himself to Israel's capital city. His riding on a donkey never before ridden may reflect the practice of using a previously unused animal in religious ceremonies (Num. 19:2; Deut. 21:3; 1 Sam. 6:7). While the approach was a humble one, donkeys were ridden by royalty. Placing garments on the colt and in Jesus' path was a gesture of respect reserved for dignitaries. The word *Hosanna* is Hebrew for "Save now!" The crowd's welcoming words in Mark 11:9–10 are from Psalm 118:26 in the Septuagint, the Greek translation of the Old Testament. Psalm 118 is one of the *Hallel* (praise) psalms (Pss. 113–118), which were sung when the

Passover was celebrated. Psalm 118:26 anticipated the coming Messiah and His kingdom. Little did people realize that the one they honored was to be the rightful King.

The cursing and the cleansing (11:12–26). The sandwiching of the cleansing of the temple (11:15–19) within the account of the cursing of the fig tree (11:12–14, 20–26) illustrates the judgment pronounced on the nation of Israel because of the unclean state of her central sanctuary, the temple. What was true of the tree was true of the whole religious system of Israel. Though ripe figs were not expected until June, smaller "pre-figs" would appear with the leaves in March or April. Jesus was looking for those indicators that genuine fruit would one day result. Since they were absent, Jesus knew the tree was not good for fruit. Like leaves on a fig tree, Israel had all the appearance of life in her temple rituals, but was missing the real evidence of the life of God. The cursing of the fig tree was a prophetic announcement of judgment, based on Old Testament imagery (Isa. 20:1–6; 19:1–13; Ezek. 4:1–15).

> *Profession of life without the appropriate fruitfulness of life is self-deceiving.*

This second cleansing of the temple (the first cleansing is recorded in John 2:12–25) shows that the materialistic outlook of the Jewish leaders had not changed at all throughout His ministry. The temple was being used for personal gain and not as an international house of prayer (Mark 11:17; see Isa. 56:7). The need for moneychangers was due to the Jewish system of temple taxation in the Roman economy. Exchange centers were set up to convert common Roman coinage into Jewish shekels.

The disciples, amazed at the withered fig tree, needed to exercise faith in Him. Even though He would execute judgment on Israel for her lack of righteousness, the disciples needed to exercise faith in prayer. And to cope with the events that would unfold in the coming days, the disciples needed forgiving hearts.

The question of authority (11:27–33). Jesus' cleansing of the temple prompted religious leaders to question the source of His authority. This question was raised because the Jews believed that only a member of the Sanhedrin, a prophet, or the Messiah could cleanse the temple. Jesus "out-questioned" them by countering with a question about John's authority, a question that put the questioners on the horns of a dilemma.

The parable of the vineyard workers (12:1–12). This is the second of three parables Jesus delivered that same day (Matt. 21:28–22:14). The wording in Mark 12 is appropriately taken from Isaiah 5:1–7, which depicted Israel as a vineyard. Israel was as unresponsive in Jesus' day as she had been in Isaiah's day. In spite of the repeated appeals for appropriate response to God, Israel had rejected Him, including His beloved Son. As a result, the custodial privilege would be taken from the nation and given to those more responsive. The imagery of Christ as the rejected Stone (Mark 12:10–11) is taken from Psalm 118:22–23. Though rejected by Israel and her leaders, Jesus would become the Capstone or Cornerstone for the church in the present age (1 Pet. 2:4–10). The death of the tenants in the parable depicted the death of Jerusalemites when the temple was demolished by the Romans in A.D. 70. Israel's leaders rejected Him because of their greed (Mark 12:7).

The controversies with the leaders (12:13–34). The Jews abhorred the image of Caesar on Roman coins and the worship that the emperor demanded the people give him. In answer to the Herodians' question about money given to Rome, Jesus taught that people are to be subject to earthly as well as heavenly authorities (12:13–17). Treason even to an ungodly national power is never an option for the righteous. At the same time, idolatry is prohibited because honor is to be given to God, who is supreme over all human governments.

The challenge of the Sadducees about the resurrection (12:18–27) was ironic since they did not even believe in it. Their question related to the law of levirate marriages, which provided for the preservation of the land and inheritance of a family by having the nearest relative to the deceased marry the new widow (Deut. 25:5–10). Jesus condemned them for not knowing the Scriptures or the power of God. The presence of the patriarchs in the kingdom demanded a transformed body. If God's covenant promises are to be fulfilled, those to whom the promises were made centuries earlier needed to have a future existence. Jesus' reference to the angels may have been a humorous insult to the Sadducees, who didn't believe in angels either (see Acts 23:8).

Jesus answered the question about the most important command of the Law (Mark 12:28–34) by appealing to two summary commands that balance one's responsibility to God and neighbor. Jesus quoted Deuteronomy 6:5; 11:13–21; and Leviticus 19:18 to show this dual responsibility, which summarizes the whole Law. The rabbis argued among themselves about which command was most significant, to the exclusion of the other commands. But Jesus stated that the internal condition of the heart is more important than external obedience to temple rituals.

The question of sonship (12:35–37). Jesus turned the tables against the religious teachers as He went on the offensive. The Old Testament is filled with statements about the expectation of the Davidic Messiah (for example, Isa. 9:6–7; 16:5; Jer. 23:5; 30:8–9; Ezek. 34:23–24; Hos. 4:5; Amos 9:11). The Jews had long recognized that Psalm 110:1 refers to the Messiah. So, quoting that verse, Jesus posed the question as to how the Messiah could be both the Son of David and the Lord of David. Though the Jewish leaders did not respond to Jesus (Matt. 22:46), the real answer is that only the Messiah fulfills Psalm 110:1 because He is both the physical Son of David and the divine Son of God. Only through the Virgin Birth does Jesus possess the dual nature that allows Him to be both David's Son and David's Lord.

> The amount of a gift to God is not as important as the attitude with which it is given.

The pronouncements of Jesus (12:38–44). This section of conflicts in chapters 11–12 concludes with a condemnation and a commendation by Jesus. The warning (12:38–40) addressed the pride and oppression of unrighteous leaders who would be severely judged by God. A widow, on the other hand, was complimented because of her sacrificial giving (12:41–44). Godly disciples humbly serve with a sacrificial attitude.

B. The Discourse from Olivet (chapter 13)

The interest of the disciples (13:1–4). The discourse from the Mount of Olives should be interpreted in light of Jesus' cleansing of the temple and His cursing of the fig tree (11:12–26). He predicted the destruction of the temple (which occurred in A.D. 70) long before the temple was completed in

A.D. 64. The disciples asked Jesus about the timing and the signs of the fulfillment (13:4). While the following descriptions related primarily to the events of the yet-future Tribulation, the near-view fulfillment in the first century served as a foreshadowing of the end times.

The first half of the Tribulation (13:5–8). Rather than being preoccupied with when the Lord will return, Jesus' followers should be concerned with being properly prepared for that return. Certain unnerving events must take place before the end-time fulfillment. In light of coming end-time events the disciples were not to be misled or afraid. Early military conflicts and natural disasters are merely the "beginning of birth pains" (13:8).

The second half of the Tribulation (13:9–23). Persecution of believers because of their stand for Christ will characterize the last half of the Tribulation. Jesus guaranteed that the world will be reached with the gospel before the final judgment. Dependency on the Holy Spirit is the secret of an effective confession in the midst of suffering. Family hatred as well as political and religious persecution will be common. A faithful and persevering testimony in the face of great persecution will be the primary marks of faithfulness in the end times.

"The abomination that causes desolation" refers to Daniel 9:27 (see also 11:31; 12:11). The word "abomination" refers to something idolatrous or defiling (Ezek. 8:9–10, 15–16). About 167 B.C. Antiochus Epiphanes erected an altar in the temple to Zeus (1 Macc. 1:54, 59), and the Romans destroyed the temple in A.D. 70—both of which foreshadowed the abomination by the Antichrist that Daniel prophesied would take place at the midpoint of the seven-year Tribulation. Because of the unexpected speed with which these events would happen, those unable to move quickly would be the most vulnerable. The unparalleled judgment makes the phrase "the Great Tribulation" very appropriate.

The salvation of the elect will be accomplished in spite of the intensity of their suffering. Jews would understand the word *elect* (Mark 13:20, 22, 27) to refer to their nation (for example, 1 Chron. 16:13; Ps. 105:43; Isa. 65:9, 15). In most of the New Testament, however, the word usually refers to the church (Rom. 8:33; Col. 3:12; 2 Tim. 2:10; 1 Pet. 1:2). In the Tribulation the word *elect* may refer to both Jewish and gentile believers. God will preserve the righteous remnant for His purposes.

In the Tribulation false Christs and false prophets will rise. The arrival of the Antichrist and his prophet in the midst of such claims will make it all the more difficult to identify him before he is publicly revealed. Hasty judgments and identifications are discouraged. If such cautions will be appropriate then, how much more should believers be wary of false teachers today?

The second coming of Christ (13:24–27). The personal, bodily return of the Son of God to the earth at the end of the Tribulation will be preceded by certain cosmic signs, predicted in Isaiah 13:10 and 34:4. The picture of "the Son of Man coming in the clouds" is taken from Daniel 7:13. Jesus had identified Himself by the title "Son of man," which He now linked with His return as the Messiah from heaven. That the Son of man has the authority to reflect God's glory and to send angels is a claim to Jesus' deity and His sovereignty. The suffering Servant is the saving Sovereign who will come to gather the elect from the whole world.

The parables of preparation (13:28–37). Jesus' parable of the fig tree teaches that watchfulness is needed in light of the uncertain and imminent timing of the Lord's return. When the events of the Tribulation take place, His return to earth will soon occur. The certainty of the event is authenticated with the certainty of the Scriptures ("My words will never pass away"). One can trust the Scriptures, and they speak of the prophetic future. Both are certain!

The parable of the steward reveals the need for alertness. Alertness is another way of speaking of faith. Responsibility is enjoined in light of the certainty of the Lord's return, and readiness is encouraged in view of the unannounced and sudden nature of that return. Just as a wise and faithful steward prepares for the return of the house's owner, so believers in the Tribulation should be prepared for the return of Christ. If this is true for the generation that will see the return of Christ at the end of the Tribulation, how much more important it is for those awaiting the rapture of the church before the Tribulation.

C. The Betrayal and Denials of Jesus (14:1–42)

The symbolic preparations for the Passover (14:1–11). The treacherous schemes of the chief priests and the scribes were renewed two days before the Feast of Passover and Unleavened Bread. Jesus often stayed with Lazarus in Bethany on His way to and from Jerusalem. Judas was concerned with hoarding money to use for selfish purposes, but the woman was willing to pour out lavishly the vessel of perfume in worship and humble adoration of Jesus.

At times our lavish worship of Christ must outweigh all other concerns.

Nard was an expensive aromatic oil extracted from a root that grew best in India. The cost was equivalent to almost a year's wages for the average day laborer. It is difficult to be sure if the woman knew the significance of her act. Jesus said her anointing helped prepare for His burial and will be remembered as an anticipation of the events that would be the basis for the gospel message. The benevolent donations to the poor must be balanced with the lavish worship of God through sacrificial giving. When done with a holy heart, both are righteous, God-pleasing activities. Because of Judas's materialism he easily responded to the bribery of the high priests with whom he conspired to betray Jesus.

The actual preparations for the Passover (14:12–25). According to Jewish tradition the Passover meal was to be eaten in Jerusalem. Jesus' detailed instructions about preparing for the Passover meal may have been given in light of the betrayal plot. These intricate predictions were further evidence that He was sovereignly setting the stage for His own voluntary suffering as the Servant of the Lord (14:12–16). Mark 14:18 alludes to Psalm 41:9, whereas John included the actual quotation (John 13:18). Jesus predicted that His betrayal would come from within the ranks of His disciples. No help from any of His friends was anticipated (Mark 14:17–21).

The last Passover became the first Lord's Supper. The bread is a metaphor for the Lord's body, and His blood is symbolized by the cup. Through His death on the cross, provisions for the New Covenant were established. A new arrangement of relating to God was grounded in the death of Jesus Christ. Whereas the Passover looked back to the Exodus as foundational to the old Mosaic Covenant, the bread and cup looked forward to the events of the Crucifixion as foundational to the New Covenant. Both were based on substitutionary sacrifice. The reference to blood being poured out was a

Hebrew way of speaking of a violent death (Gen. 4:10–11; 9:6; Deut. 19:10; 2 Kings 21:16). Jesus' promise that the disciples would one day observe this supper in the kingdom shows that the supper was a foretaste of the messianic banquet in the kingdom of God.

The prediction of the denials (14:26–31). Jesus quoted Zechariah 13:7, which speaks of the smitten shepherd and the scattered sheep. In spite of the failure of the disciples and His own death, Jesus anticipated meeting them in Galilee after His resurrection. This was later rehearsed by the angel who told the disciples to meet Jesus in Galilee, "just as he said" (Mark 16:7, NASB; see also Matt. 28:16). The journey to the Garden of Gethsemane on the Mount of Olives and the three rounds of prayer show the loneliness of the suffering Servant and the negligence of the disciples. While the other Gospels recorded the crowing of the cock, Mark added the detail that before the cock would crow twice, Peter would deny the Lord three times. Peter repeatedly objected and pledged full commitment in spite of Jesus' announcement.

For the Roman readers, Jesus is seen as the model of faithfulness in the face of intense trial.

> *Prayer is a resource of strength in times of testing and temptation.*

The agony in Gethsemane (14:32–42). The extent of the suffering is noted by Jesus through His allusion to Psalm 42:6. The familiar "Abba" is Aramaic for "Father" and reveals the intimacy of His approach to God (see Rom. 8:15; Gal. 4:6). The "hour" was the hour of Jesus' suffering and death. The "cup" referred to the suffering that God asked Jesus to "drink" on behalf of the world. The suffering rightly feared by Jesus was His being spiritually separated from the Father. While not *wanting* to drink of the cup, He was *willing* to drink it because it was the Father's will. When the disciples were asleep when they should have been praying, the betrayal was transpiring (14:42). The weakness of the flesh and the willingness of the spirit alludes to Psalm 51:12. In contrast to David who sinned, Jesus did not sin in the face of temptation.

D. The Arrest and Trials of Jesus (14:43–15:20)

The arrest of Jesus (14:43–52). The mob was led by Judas. The record of betrayal, which began in 14:10–11, is continued here. Judas's sign to the authorities was a kiss, as was his use of the title "Rabbi." Though not named here, Peter was the one who drew his sword in his effort to defend Jesus. Jesus rebuked the mob for the untimely arrest. The desertion of the disciples was anticipated in the Old Testament (Isa. 53:8–9, 12; Zech. 13:7). Many believe the "streaker" was Mark's veiled reference to himself, the author of this Gospel. Even Mark fled in the face of suffering. This, too, would be a negative example for the Roman Christians not to imitate.

The religious trials of Jesus (14:53–72). The major charge against Christ at His religious trials was blasphemy. This section contains the denunciation of the priests (14:53–65) and the denials of Peter (14:66–72). Both His opponents and His closest friends rejected Him in this hour of trial. A contrast exists between Jesus' unwavering stand before the dignitaries and Peter's faltering denial before their lowly servants. Jesus withstood intense persecution, and Peter failed in even responding to a spoken question. Before the Sanhedrin, Jesus assented to the title of the Messiah (14:62). Coupled with His claim to be the Son of God, the charge of blasphemy and the sentence of death were sure. Israel had rejected her King!

All four Gospels record three denials by Peter. The accounts are not easily harmonized, and this has led some to ponder the possibility of six denials, because Jesus gave two predictions. One was in the Upper Room that Peter would deny the Lord three times before the cock crowed, and one was in Gethsemane when Jesus warned Peter that he would deny Him three times before the cock would crow a second time. However, all four Gospels record only three denials. What is unique is Mark's record of the cock crowing twice (14:30, 72). Mark's honesty in dealing with the failure of such a noted leader as Peter testifies to the veracity of the Scriptures in revealing the failures and not just the successes of the early saints. Peter even resorted to profanity in trying to distance himself from Jesus.

The trial before Pilate (15:1–20). The major charge against Jesus at His political trial was treason. Jesus was delivered to the Romans because at that time the Jews were prohibited from exercising capital punishment.

Jesus was sent to Pilate, Judea's procurator. After Pilate questioned Jesus (15:1–5), he debated with the religious leaders about releasing Barabbas (15:6–11). The Crucifixion was evidence that the early church did not invent Jesus' claim to be the Messiah. Even His enemies understood the core claims of His message. Six times in this chapter He is referred to as "the king of Israel" or "the king of the Jews" (15:2, 9, 12, 18, 26, 32). While the charges against Him were false, the reality is that Jesus is indeed the King. Jesus claimed that His authority exceeded that of Rome.

The practice of releasing a prisoner at the Passover is noted here. Pilate baited the crowd and may have manipulated the call for Jesus' crucifixion, which allowed him to "wash his hands" of the matter. The Son of the Father from heaven was delivered over to death so that Barabbas, whose name means "a son of the father" (!), could go free. The story is one of ironic substitution. Both the Jews and the Gentiles were guilty of His execution because both the priests and Pilate handed Him over to be crucified (15:10, 15).

The crowd was satisfied by the exchange of prisoners (15:12–15). Politics and not righteousness ruled the day then, as it so often does now. The soldiers' mocking and brutal treatment of Jesus (15:16–20) shows the tremendous injustice He suffered at their hands. This degrading treatment would no doubt strike a chord in the hearts of suffering Roman believers, who would be reminded of what Jesus had endured for them. The crown of thorns, the purple robe, and the faked hailing of Him as the King of the Jews were a bitter mockery of the One who really is the King. Jesus' response to His suffering is a model for all who would suffer for Him (see 1 Pet. 2:21).

E. The Crucifixion and Burial of Jesus (15:21–47)

The Crucifixion (15:21–41). For the first three of Jesus' six hours on the cross He suffered in daylight at the hands of humans (15:21–32). In the darkness of the second three hours He suffered at the hands of God. Usually a condemned person was compelled to carry the cross as a symbol of submission to the Roman authorities. Jesus began the procession, carrying His own cross (John 19:17). He must have been weakened by the excessive flogging and on the way, Simon of Cyrene was compelled to help. Golgotha, which means "the Place of the Skull," was where executions took place outside the city, in all likelihood at a major crossroad for everyone to see. Wine mixed with myrrh was a narcotic to help deaden the pain, but Jesus refused to lessen His suffering. The criminal's clothes were often a reward for the executioners, who in this case gambled for the pieces.

Apparently Mark counted the hours differently from the way John did (see John 19:14). The trial before Pilate was at the sixth hour, which according to Roman time would have been six in the morning. The Jewish method placed the Crucifixion at the third hour, or 9:00 A.M.

The placard that was nailed on the cross identified Jesus as the King of the Jews. The crucifixion of two criminals on either side of Jesus fulfilled Isaiah 53:12. The people's cries of "save yourself" (Mark 15:30) and the other jeers prove conclusively that Jesus claimed to be the Messiah and the Son of God. And yet what they did was blasphemous (15:29–30). The darkness could not have been a natural daytime eclipse because Passover came at the time of a full moon. The darkness therefore was supernatural.

Jesus' cry, "Eloi, Eloi, lama sabachthani," was spoken in Aramaic and was from Psalm 22:1. This prayer, in which He asked the Father why He had forsaken the Son, provides a glimpse into the inner suffering of Christ. While on the cross the Son experienced the displeasure of the Father as He bore the sins of the world. He became "sin for us" (2 Cor. 5:21). Vinegar was thought to quench one's thirst better than water. Jesus accepted it (John 19:29–30), perhaps to have the strength to make His final victorious cry before surrendering His life when He "breathed His last" (Mark 15:37).

> Christians can best endure their suffering for Christ when they remember how much He suffered for them.

The rending of the temple veil from top to bottom was the miraculous symbol that Jesus then became the Mediator between mankind and the Father. Sacrifices according to the Law of Moses have been superseded by Jesus. The centurion's confession that Jesus is the Son of God (15:39) probably stated more than what he understood, but it communicated the truth about who Jesus really is. In contrast to the fleeing disciples the women stayed on through the suffering. They became the eyewitness link of both the death and resurrection of Christ (15:40–41).

The burial (15:42–47). Normally the body of a crucified criminal would be left on the cross to be eaten by scavengers. The desire to bury the body before the Sabbath and Passover motivated Joseph and Nicodemus to ask for Jesus' body in order to bury it before sundown on Friday, the day of preparation for the Sabbath. Righteousness is defined by a faith that is willing to identify with Jesus at all costs in anticipation of the coming kingdom of God.

Faithful followers remain when all others desert the Savior.

F. The Resurrection of Jesus (chapter 16)

Most scholars believe the Book of Mark ends abruptly with verse 8 of chapter 16. This is because two of the most ancient Greek manuscripts, Vaticanus and Sinaiticus, end there. But the majority of Greek manuscripts include verses 9–20, even though the style in those verses differs considerably from the rest of the book. The events recorded in verses 9–20 generally agree with events included in the Book of Acts and thus their truth should not be in question even if verses 9–20 were not a part of the original. Perhaps a writer other than Mark wrote Mark 16:9–20 (under the inspiration of the Holy Spirit), and God intended those verses to be an authentic part of the New Testament.

The Resurrection (16:1–8). The resurrection of Jesus authenticates that He, the suffering Servant, is indeed the Christ, the Son of God. This is the crowning moment of the book and the central tenet of the gospel message. Christianity hinges on the truthfulness of the events of the death and resurrection of Jesus. When the women went to Jesus' tomb early Sunday morning, they took liquid spices to perfume the dead body to offset the odor of decay. To their surprise, the stone had already been rolled away from the entrance. An angel attired in white announced what must be seen as the climax of the book: "He is risen! He is not here" (16:6). His words gave the divine interpretation of the events and removed all suspicion as to what happened to the body of Jesus. The angel's instruction for the women to meet Jesus in Galilee recalled His prediction in Mark 14:28 and confirmed that Jesus was alive. The women's paralyzing fear provided a provocative and "unfinished ending" to the book if the book ends with verse 8. Their response raises the question, What would a committed disciple do with the message?

The postresurrection appearances (16:9–20). These events generally agree with Luke 24:13–35 and John 20:11–18. Three separate appearances by Jesus are noted, and in all three the disciples' unbelief is highlighted (Mark 16:11–14). In Jesus' commission to preach the gospel in all the world (16:15–16), belief is outwardly confessed through baptism, and unbelief leaves a person condemned in the sight of God. The confirming signs of the apostles were evident in their early ministries, as recorded in the Book of Acts (except the drinking of poison, which is nowhere exhorted or modeled). The bodily ascension of the Lord and His exalted position at God's right hand (16:19–20) confirm that Jesus is all He claimed to be. Because He is the Lord, the message needs to be preached to everyone.

LUKE
Jesus, Perfect and Innocent Savior

AUTHOR

*L*uke wrote two books of the New Testament, the Gospel of Luke and the Book of Acts, both addressed to the same person, Theophilus (Luke 1:3–4; Acts 1:1–2). The material in Acts perfectly supplements what is presented in Luke (1:1–2). The emphasis on the person and work of the Holy Spirit is similar in both Luke and Acts, and the vocabulary, style, and language of both books are closely connected.

The "we" sections of Acts (16:10–40; 20:5–21; 21:18; 27:1–28:16) point to an author who was with Paul in some of his travels and in his Roman imprisonment. The medical language in both Luke and Acts suggest the author was a physician, which corresponds with the fact that Paul referred to Luke as the "beloved physician" (Col. 4:14).

DATE

Because Luke 21:20–24 predicts the fall of Jerusalem, the book must be dated before A.D. 70. Because of the abrupt ending of the Book of Acts, it seems likely that Luke concluded writing it at the end of Paul's two years of imprisonment in Rome. The introduction of Acts (1:1) indicates Luke was written before Acts. Therefore this would place the writing of Luke before A.D. 62, the end of Paul's Roman imprisonment. Evidently Luke gathered his material during his ten-year service with Paul, and then before leaving Palestine with Paul on the journey to Rome, he sent the Book of Luke from Caesarea to his friend Theophilus. It is reasonable to conclude that Luke wrote his Gospel during Paul's two-year imprisonment at Caesarea, and this would date the book to A.D. 58–59.

HISTORICAL BACKGROUND

As stated above, the Book of Luke was possibly written in Caesarea, where Luke was with Paul while he was imprisoned there for two years. But other possible places where Luke may have written the book are Rome, Arabia, Asia Minor, and Alexandria. Theophilus, to whom the book was addressed, was probably a Gentile of high standing. Nothing is known of him except the allusions in Luke 1:3 and Acts 1:1. The material contained within the book was intended not only for him but also for the whole Christian community and the Greek-speaking world. Luke's references to Palestinian geography and the fact that he did not use certain Semitic terms (such as "rabbi" and "hosanna") suggest he had a Greek audience in view. When philosophical views such as Stoicism and Epicureanism flourished, the need for a presentation of the historical truths of the Christian faith was great.

PURPOSE

Luke stated that his purpose in writing the book was to give Theophilus a comprehensive, accurate, and historical account of the matters concerning Christianity so that he would be assured of the reality of the things he had been taught (Luke 1:1–4). Another purpose was to convey these truths to gentile readers to awaken and deepen their faith in Jesus as the divine Son of man, the Savior of the world.

CHARACTERISTICS

Several features are unique to the Book of Luke.

First, Luke is the most literary of the four Gospels. The author was a master of the classical Greek language.

Second, between eighteen and twenty of Jesus' parables are unique to the Gospel of Luke.

Third, Luke often mentioned the ministry of the Holy Spirit (1:15, 35; 3:22: 4:1, 18; 10:21).

Fourth, Luke's more than twenty references to angels highlight the deity of the Son of man.

Fifth, Luke emphasized the redemptive mission of Christ, with a number of references to Isaiah 53 and 40–66 (Luke 22:37; 24:27, 44, 46).

Sixth, only Luke related certain events in Jesus' life to secular history (2:1–2; 3:1).

Seventh, the book has a special section (9:51–18:14) which focuses on Jesus' geographical movement to Jerusalem. This is known as the "travelogue" of Luke. Jesus is pictured as absolutely determined to go to Jerusalem.

Eighth, Luke emphasized Jesus' ministry to women and children.

Ninth, Luke highlighted the fact that Gentiles are included in God's plan of salvation.

OUTLINE

I. The Prologue (1:1–4)
II. Jesus' Preparation for Public Ministry (1:5–4:13)
    A. The Annunciations of John and Jesus (1:5–56)
    B. The Births of John and Jesus (1:57–2:52)
    C. The Ministries of John and Jesus (3:1–4:13)
III. Jesus' Galilean Ministry (4:14–9:50)
    A. Jesus' Rejection Foreshadowed at Nazareth (4:14–30)
    B. Jesus Authentication through Miracles and Discipleship (4:31–6:16)
    C. Jesus' Sermon on the "Level Place" (6:17–49)
    D. Jesus' Assertions of His Identity and Authority (chapters 7–8)
    E. The Transitions toward the Cross (9:1–50)
IV. Jesus' Journey to Jerusalem (9:51–19:27)
V. Jesus' Entrance into Jerusalem (19:28–21:38)
    A. Jesus' Triumphal Entry and Cleansing of the Temple (19:28–48)
    B. Jesus' Confrontations with Israel's Leaders (20:1–21:4)

    C. Jesus' Olivet Discourse (21:5–38)

VI. The Passion Narrative (Chapters 22–24)

    A. The Celebration of the Passover Meal (22:1–38)

    B. The Agony and Arrest in the Garden of Gethsemane (22:39–53)

    C. The Trials of Jesus (22:54–23:25)

    D. The Crucifixion of Jesus (23:26–56)

    E. The Resurrection and Commissioning of Jesus (chapter 24)

I. THE PROLOGUE (1:1–4)

The prologue of Luke includes his purposes: to provide for gentile readers (Theophilus in particular) an orderly account of the life and ministry of Jesus Christ, and to certify that He who was the promised Messiah for Israel is indeed the Son of God who became the Son of man, and that His ministry provided the way for Gentiles as well as Jews to enter the kingdom of God. Luke mentioned his use of written and oral sources in order to establish the credibility of his record. Traditional accounts, eyewitnesses, and other servants of the Word all contributed to the process by which the Spirit of God led Luke the physician to become a historian and theologian of the faith. The book gave Theophilus, and by extension, the rest of the church, assurance about their faith in Jesus Christ. Luke's emphasis on the sources he consulted lends credibility and certainty to his Gospel record.

II. JESUS' PREPARATION FOR PUBLIC MINISTRY (1:5–4:13)

A. The Annunciations of John and Jesus (1:5–56)

The announcement to Zechariah (1:5–25). The infancy narratives of both John and Jesus were recorded to show how they fulfilled the Old Testament and to preview the ministries they would fulfill by their lives and deaths. The announcements to Zechariah (1:5–25) and to Mary (1:26–56) introduced John the Baptist and Jesus, respectively, to Luke's readers. The announcement to Zechariah concerning the birth of John the Baptist was made in Jerusalem. The section records the identity of John the Baptist's parents (1:5–7), the incident of the angelic announcement, in which Zechariah was unable to speak for nine months because of his unbelief (1:8–23), and Elizabeth's response of praise to the Lord in the time of her pregnancy (1:24–25).

Both Zechariah and Elizabeth were from a priestly line. Unlike many of the religious leaders in and around Jerusalem, they were righteous in their walk with God. Barrenness on the part of Elizabeth and the age of the couple portrayed their hopelessness of ever having children. Gabriel's announcement to Zechariah in the temple most likely occurred at the time of the midafternoon sacrifice, when prayers were offered for national deliverance. The answer to the elderly couple's prayers included not only the birth of a child (1:13) but also hope for the nation (1:16). Their son would be the one to introduce the Messiah and Savior of Israel (1:17). Born miraculously, the son of Zechariah and Elizabeth would be filled with the Holy Spirit. In his ministry he would preach repentance, to prepare the people for the coming of the Lord. His message, his living and preaching in the desert, and his attire were all reminiscent of Elijah (1:80; 3:2–3; Matt. 3:2–4), in whose spirit John came to minister.

The announcement to Mary (1:26–56). The angel Gabriel's announcement to Mary about the birth of Jesus Christ took place in Nazareth about six months after the angel's announcement to Zechariah about the birth of John. Mary was told that she would have a son whose name would be Jesus, that He would be the Son of God, and that He would fulfill the Davidic Covenant promises, as predicted in 2 Samuel 7:13–17. He would sit on the throne of His father David. He would reign forever over the house of Israel and thus His kingdom would have no end.

Mary did not ask whether this birth could happen; she asked how God might bring it about. Therefore her faith contrasts with the doubts of Zechariah, for she said, "May it be to me as you have said" (1:38). The angel confirmed this announcement to Mary by telling her that her elderly relative Elizabeth was also pregnant. The classic statement "For nothing is impossible with God" (1:37) recalls the miraculous prediction of Isaac's birth to Abraham and Sarah (Gen. 18:14). The God who miraculously provided a son for Abraham and Sarah and for Zechariah and

Elizabeth is the same God who miraculously sent forth His Son from a virgin womb.

Jesus Christ was conceived as an act of the Holy Spirit within Mary's womb, and through the miracle of the Incarnation, God became man in the person of Jesus Christ, the Son of God. When Mary visited Elizabeth in Judah (1:39–56), the baby in Elizabeth's womb leaped for joy at the prospect of being near the Son of God. Both Elizabeth's blessing on Mary (1:39–45) and Mary's song of praise (1:46–56) extol the grace and mercy of God, who stepped in through this process to fulfill His promises to Israel and to provide redemption for all mankind. The themes of God's judgment against the proud and His elevating people of humble faith which are introduced here in Luke, are developed later in the book.

B. The Births of John and Jesus (1:57–2:52)

The birth of John the Baptist (1:57–80). The births of John the Baptist (1:57–80) and of Jesus (2:1–52) were recorded in orderly fashion, again to show comparisons and contrasts between the two. At his birth John was named by Zechariah, and God's judgment of silence on the father was lifted (1:57–66). The words of Zechariah (1:67–79) are a carefully crafted poem or hymn to emphasize the fact that what God was doing in both John and Jesus was in fulfillment of Old Testament covenant promises. Several statements in the first part of Zechariah's words parallel statements in the latter half.

Zechariah's tying together Old Testament texts and their New Testament fulfillments is a masterpiece of literary genius and artistry. The Incarnation is viewed as a visitation of God to earth and of the entrance of light into darkness (1:68, 78–79; see also Zech. 3:8; Mal. 3:2). The Savior would be a King from the house of David (1 Chron. 17:9) and salvation through Him would include the forgiveness of sins (Luke 1:69, 77). These themes were spoken by the prophets of old (1:70) and were now made specific by John the Baptist, "a prophet of the Most High" (1:76), who would prepare the way for the Lord to come (see Isa. 40:1–3). The theme of rest and deliverance from enemies is also cited in both portions of Zechariah's discourse (1:71, 74–75). Such deliverance should result in serving God without fear and with a holy and righteous heart.

The center of Zechariah's poem focuses on the fulfillment of the Abrahamic Covenant (1:72–73). By His covenant and His oath God had bound Himself to fulfill His promises. How fitting, therefore, that Zechariah's and Elizabeth's names mean "God remembers" and "God's Covenant." John's name means "God is gracious." Thus God was faithful to *remember* His *covenant* and was *gracious* in providing John to prepare the people for His Son, the Savior. Jesus Christ will fulfill all God's covenants of promise in His first and second comings. The final statement about John's growth (1:80) highlights his spiritual and physical development.

The nativity (2:1–7). The event of Jesus' birth was linked to the decree of Caesar Augustus and Quirinius the governor of Syria. Caesar Augustus was the first emperor of Rome; he reigned from 27 B.C. to A.D. 14. Possibly his decree was issued a few years before it actually was implemented in Israel. Because both Mary and Joseph were descendants of David, Bethlehem, David's birthplace, was where they were required to register. (Also a portion of Jerusalem was designated the city of David because he had reigned there as king.) Luke noted that Jesus' birth took place before Joseph and Mary's marriage was consummated.

The visit of the shepherds (2:8–14). The heavenly glory that shone with the angels who appeared to the shepherds was in keeping with the way God often gave divine revelation in Old Testament times (Exod. 16:10; 20:18; 40:34; 2 Chron. 7:1; Ezek. 1:27–28). The "good news of great joy for all people" was the message that Jesus, who was born as a baby in Bethlehem, was identified as the Savior, Messiah, and Lord (Luke 2:11). Historical records reveal that these shepherds were probably hired by the temple priests to tend sheep that were destined for sacrifice in Jerusalem. That these shepherds would see a baby wrapped in a style normally reserved for burial ("in strips of cloth"; compare 23:53) would indeed be a significant sign. This may account for the unique combination of the shepherds' wonder, worship, and witness. Jesus' circumcision on the eighth day fulfilled the requirements of Leviticus 12:3 and shows that His parents kept the Mosaic Law faithfully.

The presentation of Jesus at the temple (2:22–38). This visitation to the temple fulfilled two Old Testament requirements. Every male child not born in the tribe of Levi was required to be redeemed from priestly service (Exod. 13:2, 12–15), and every woman was to be purified by offering appropriate offerings at the end of her period of ceremonial uncleanness (Lev. 12:6–8). Because Joseph and Mary were not from wealthy parents, they could bring two doves or two pigeons.

Simeon's and Anna's adorations of Jesus include two important revelations for that moment of history. Simeon's speech revealed that Jesus would be a light to the Gentiles as well as a glory to Israel (see Isa. 49:6). Luke 2:34 contains a hint of rejection: Accepting Him would bring great blessing, but rejecting Him would bring great judgment. Such opposition would cause deep grief to Mary, but would be the means by which the hearts of all would be judged (2:35). Anna's adoration of Jesus highlighted the redemption that Christ could provide for Jerusalem and the rest of the nation. Jesus Christ is both the revelation of the Father and the means of redemption for all humanity.

The growth of Jesus (2:39–52). The references to Jesus' physical and spiritual growth in 2:40 and 2:52 serve as "bookends" to His visit to Jerusalem at age twelve. At this young age Jesus knew that He was the Son of God and that His life would be spent pursuing the interests of His Father. This section is a fitting conclusion to the narratives about His birth and early life, as it reinforces the dual nature of Jesus as both the son of Mary and the Son of God. He was responsible and obedient to His human parents, but He affirmed His loyalty to His heavenly Father.

C. The Ministries of John and Jesus (3:1–4:13)

The ministry of John the Baptist (3:1–20). The ministry of John was an intregal part of the historical hinge between two major eras of history: the old age of the Law and the new age of Jesus' ministry. The ministry of John began in the fifteenth year of Tiberias, who reigned from A.D. 14 to 37. His fifteenth year would have been A.D. 27–28 or 28–29. Differing methods of dating, however, make it difficult to know the exact year when John the Baptist began his ministry.

Pilate governed Judea from A.D. 26 to 36. And Annas and Caiaphas served together in the politically appointed office of the Jewish high priesthood. John's ministry as an Old Testament prophet is linked to Isaiah

40:3–5, which points to him as the herald of the
Messiah. The phrase, "And all mankind will see God's
salvation" (Luke 3:6), not recorded in the other three
Gospels, illustrates Luke's emphasis on the inclusion
of Gentiles in God's plan of redemption.

> *Bringing
> people to
> repentant
> faith in Christ
> is the best way
> to bring
> renewal to a
> society.*

John preached a message of repentance that
was visualized through the rite of baptism. In cas-
tigating the Jewish leaders, he was showing that
they were unqualified for the kingdom of God if
they refused to repent and believe that the One
he was introducing was the Messiah. Being Jewish was not enough to qualify one for the kingdom.
Judgment is imminent for unbelievers, just as surely as the kingdom is
imminent for believers. Examples of the fruits (results) of repentance were
generosity, honesty, and fairness. These were respectively applied to the
crowd, tax-collectors, and soldiers.

In answering the question of whether John was the Messiah, he taught
that his baptizing in water was only a prelude to Jesus' "baptism" by the
ministry of the Holy Spirit, and in judgment ("fire"). Those who believe
will be baptized with the Spirit, whereas those who refuse will suffer the
fire of judgment (3:17). This is referred to as the "good news" of John's
preaching. People can avoid the judgment of Christ by repenting and
believing that Jesus is the Messiah, who has the right to both redeem and
judge the world. This section on John's ministry concludes with mention
of his arrest for having preached against Herod's infidelity with his sister-
in-law Herodias.

The baptism of Jesus (3:21–22). At Jesus' baptism He was praying when
the Spirit descended on Him in the form of a dove. The voice from heaven
combined themes from Psalm 2:7 and Isaiah 42:1 to speak of Jesus' divine
Sonship and His sovereign right to rule by the Holy Spirit's power. The
dove symbolized His spiritual anointing and enabling for His coming
ministry. Through the Father's declaration Jesus was authenticated as the
One to represent the Father on earth.

The genealogy of Jesus (3:23–37). Jesus was thought of as the physical son
of Joseph but in actuality He descended from Mary's line. Jesus' genealogy

was traced back from David to Adam to show His genuine humanity. Matthew, however, traced Jesus' line forward from Abraham and David to show His right to sit on the throne of David as Israel's King.

The temptations of Jesus (4:1–13). The presence of the Spirit does not exempt one from the temptations of the enemy. The period of forty days is a common length of time for trials and temptations (see Gen. 7:4; Exod. 24:18; 1 Kings 19:8). Jesus' turning stones into bread would have meant following His own physical desires rather than the leading of the Spirit. The answer Jesus gave emphasized the need to find in the Scriptures God's directions for life (Deut. 8:3).

> *Material gratification is no substitute for spiritual satisfaction.*

The second temptation was Satan's attempt to get Jesus to accept a relative position of authority from him. For Jesus to have accepted the kingdom from Satan without first conquering him at the cross would have betrayed the will of God for His life. The kingdom will not be established by giving in to Satan; instead it will be established by Jesus' victory over Satan. The establishment of a God-designed kingdom leaves no room for other competitive loyalties (Deut 6:13).

In Satan's third effort he tempted Jesus to put God the Father to the test by saving His life as He jumped off the temple pinnacle. The devil omitted a phrase from Psalm 91:11–12 when he quoted this passage. The phrase left out, "to guard you in all your ways," when rightly understood, would keep people from doing the very thing Satan was asking of Jesus. Jesus' quotation of Deuteronomy 6:16 answered the temptation to gain an instant reputation by putting the testimony of God on the spot. The Israelites often tested God throughout their history, especially when they showed dissatisfaction with what God had planned for them.

These three temptations parallel the areas in which Satan tempts believers today: the lust (desires) of the flesh, the lust of the eyes, the pride of life (1 John 2:16, KJV).

III. JESUS' GALILEAN MINISTRY (4:14–9:50)

A. Jesus' Rejection Foreshadowed at Nazareth (4:14–30)

This introductory summary of the ministry of Jesus in Galilee and Nazareth foreshadows the themes of Israel's rejection of the Messiah and His turning to the Gentiles. All this was prophesied in the Old Testament. His popularity in Galilee was mentioned before the specific account in the synagogue in Nazareth. The spiritual blindness of the religious leaders stands in contrast to the anointed ministry of Jesus, the Messiah and the Son of God. When Jesus read from the scroll in the Nazareth synagogue, He quoted from Isaiah 61:1–2a. He did not read Isaiah's words in 61:2b about God's "day of vengeance" because He wanted to focus on the salvation through the forgiveness of sins, the theme of His first coming. The "year of the Lord's favor" (Luke 4:19) brings to mind Israel's year of Jubilee when people were to forgive debts owed to them and to release prisoners.

The hearers' initial response was positive until Jesus applied the message by pointing out Israel's lack of response (4:24–27). His quotation of the proverb "Physician, heal yourself" anticipated that rejection, in which others would accuse Him of being guilty of the very sins they themselves would commit. What the leaders of Israel did not understand was that Jesus did not need what He could provide for them. He is sinless and they were sinful. He could cure their spiritual blindness because he is the Messiah. Jesus cited the Old Testament illustrations of the Zarepheth widow and of Naaman, the Syrian, both of whom were Gentiles, to convict them. These two—and other Gentiles—were more responsive to God than were the Jews. The Jews' attempt to kill Jesus by throwing Him down a cliff validated His predictions of their rejection of Him.

B. Jesus' Authentication through Miracles and Discipleship (4:31–6:16)

Jesus taught and healed with authority (4:31–44). In Capernaum Jesus healed many people. Even the demons recognized Jesus' authority and right of judgment. They confessed that He is "the Holy One of God," a title amazingly similar to Isaiah's often-used title of God, "The Holy One of Israel." Many missed the irony that if the demons know Jesus has the right to judge them, He also has the power to judge people. The word "rebuked" in verses 35 (NASB), 39, and 41 shows that Jesus had divinely authoritative power. When Peter's mother-in-law was healed of a high fever, she immediately responded by serving others. The summary statement in 4:41 shows that the demons acknowledged that Jesus is the Son of God (as well as the Holy One of God). Jesus told them to be silent in order to protect His plan of progressively revealing Himself throughout His life. Jesus maintained His priorities in the face of popularity, and He moved about to make the gospel known.

Jesus' commissioning of the disciples (5:1–11). Cleaning fishing nets was a necessary daily activity following a night of fishing. The miraculous catch of fish in the Lake of Gennesaret, another name for the Sea of Galilee, provided the backdrop for Jesus' commission of three disciples, Peter, James, and John. The size of the catch was so large that it began to break the nets. Seeing that Jesus possessed divine power, Peter confessed His own sinfulness. Jesus promised the three that they would be successful evangelists, for from that time on they would be "catching" people. Fishermen caught live fish to kill them, but the disciples would be catching people who were dead to give them life. The Greek word for "catch" (5:10) means "to take alive."

Jesus' healing of the leper (5:12–16). This Gospel, written by Luke, a physician, gives more medical information than the other Gospel writers. This case of leprosy was in an advanced stage. The Law required lepers to live away from the rest of the community (Lev. 13:45–46). Leprosy could be declared healed only if a priest so confirmed it (14:1–32). Jesus wanted the man to go through the proper procedure so that he would be accepted back into the community legally. Yet Jesus did not want the man to tell others; He was not trying to gain popularity. So He withdrew to more remote places for prayer (Luke 5:16). The fact that Jesus could touch the leper and heal him without defiling Himself argues for His messianic identity (see Isa. 35:5–6).

Jesus' healing of the paralytic (5:17–26). Hearing of Jesus' miracles, representatives came to Him from as far away as Jerusalem. The style of the homes in those days allowed access to the roof by a set of outside stairs and the tiles in the roof were removable. Jesus pronounced the man forgiven on the basis of his faith and that of those who carried his stretcher. Because of Jesus' claim to forgive sins, the Pharisees charged Him with blasphemy. To this charge Jesus asked the logical question, "Which is easier: to say, 'Your sins are forgiven,' or to say, 'Get up and walk'?" Jesus did the apparently more difficult thing (healed the man) to prove that He can do the apparently easier (to say the man's sins were forgiven).

Jesus' calling of Levi (5:27–39). Levi, also known as Matthew (Matt. 9:9), was evidently a man of great means as indicated by the size of the banquet he held. Jesus justified His presence with the outcasts much the same as a doctor ministers to those who are sick. While none is righteous in himself, Jesus can save only those who recognize they have a need for the Savior. Jesus has come so all can repent of their self-righteousness and believe in Him for their salvation.

In response to a question about fasting, Jesus said He is the Bridegroom, an Old Testament image for the Messiah. Fasting would again be appropriate when the Bridegroom would no longer be with them. The phrase "taken from them" (Luke 5:35) indicates a rejection motif which was fulfilled when Jesus died and departed from the earth. The parables of the patch and the wineskins illustrate the Jewish leaders' rejection of Jesus. Being inflexible like an old garment and an old wineskin, the Pharisees were unable to receive the new ministry of Jesus. Their ties to their traditionalized religion kept them from accepting the Messiah.

> *Jesus has come to offer a new way of life, not to fix up the old one.*

Jesus as Lord of the Sabbath (6:1–11). While traversing a field, travelers were allowed to pluck ears of corn or stalks of wheat by hand. They were not allowed to use a tool of harvest, however (Deut. 23:24–25). When Jesus was criticized for picking some heads of grain on the Sabbath, He referred His audience back to David's eating the consecrated bread from the tabernacle, food to be eaten only by the priests (1 Sam. 21:1–6). Jesus then explained that as the Son of man He also had the prerogative of lordship over the Sabbath. He has authority to forgive sins (Luke 5:24), and now He stated that He has the authority of the Creator and Lawgiver.

In another conflict on another Sabbath, the Pharisees and teachers of the Law attempted to trap Jesus by seeing if on the Sabbath He would heal a man with a withered hand. After healing the man, Jesus asked His critics a question. In this way He showed that His desire to heal stood in stark contrast to their audacity to plot His death on the sacred day. Man was not made for the Sabbath; instead that day was set aside for the needs of humanity. Therefore to do what would minister to the needs of individuals was not against the intent of the Sabbath law.

Jesus' calling of the Twelve (6:12–16). Of the four Gospel writers only Luke mentioned that Jesus had prayed all night before calling the disciples. He called them "apostles" to define the purpose for which they were chosen (Mark 3:14). They would be sent forth to represent Him in Israel and then later to the whole world. "Apostle" means "one sent with authority." Bartholomew was probably the same as Nathanael (John 1:45–51). Matthew and Levi are two names for the same person (5:27), and Judas the brother of James is probably another name for Thaddaeus. "Iscariot" in Judas Iscariot's name means "man from Kerioth," a town in Moab.

C. Jesus' Sermon on the "Level Place" (6:17–49)

The level place where Jesus gave this sermon could have been on the side of a hill. This may be Luke's version of the Sermon on the Mount (see Matthew 5–7) without the more Jewish-oriented references, or this message may have been given on a different occasion. The fact that both Luke 6:17–49 and Matthew 5–7 are followed by the incident of the centurion and his commendable faith argues for the view that these were not two separate messages. However, there are several differences in Luke's record. Four blessings and four woes (Luke 6:20–22, 24–26) are mentioned in balanced statements here, whereas Matthew has nine opening beatitudes (Matt. 5:3–11). Luke did not include Jesus' discussion of the Law (see Matt. 5:17–42) and some of Matthew's emphasis on Jewish religious practices. The message in Luke is more geared to believing disciples; Luke left the multitudes even more in the background than Matthew did.

The people who are blessed in God's sight are those whom the unbelieving community despises because of their identification with Jesus as the Son of man. The kingdom and its rewards are promised to them, just as it was to the prophets of old who were likewise mistreated for taking their stand for righteousness. The woes are pronounced against the unrighteous, who think they are well off but whose future is bleak because of God's coming judgment.

Application of the Word of God produces stability in times of testing.

Luke 6:31, 36, and 38 serve as the backbone of principles that govern the righteous behavior preached by Jesus. Treating others as one wants to be treated tempers the natural desires for revenge and retaliation (6:27–31). Extending the mercy of the Father into our relationships transforms human behavior into a supernatural testimony. Mercy and grace are godly character qualities that distinguish believers as genuine children of God (6:32–36). Withholding unjust judgments and forgiving offenses allow a believer to heap grace on his fellow human beings in ways that are very Godlike (6:37–38).

Israel's leaders, like blind people, were leading their people astray (6:39). Jesus contrasted Himself with them to show the need for people to follow Him. Hypocritical self-righteousness causes a person to be insensitive to his own need for help. Whether fruit is good or bad depends on the nature of the tree. Similarly the conduct of one's life is determined by the nature of his or her heart. The closing illustration of the two ways of building a house was a call to follow Jesus. Not listening to and obeying Jesus' teaching can lead to disastrous results. Matthew called obedience the wise way of life and disobedience the foolish lifestyle (Matt. 7:24–27).

D. Jesus' Assertions of His Identity and Authority (chapters 7–8)

Jesus' healing of the centurion's servant (7:1–10). It is quite fitting that Jesus' message on His lordship is followed by an account of the recognition of that authority, especially by a Roman centurion. Viewing himself as one who held a relative position of authority, the soldier realized he was unworthy for Jesus even to come to his home. Such a humble approach to Jesus demonstrated a model of faith that was missing in Israel. His own people often thought of Him as only the son of Joseph.

> *God has committed all authority to the Son so that He can offer salvation and execute judgment.*

Jesus' raising of the widow's son at Nain (7:11–17). Nain was about ten miles southeast of Nazareth on the northern slopes of the Hill of Moreh. The graveyard was located outside the city. Tradition dictated that if a person encountered a funeral procession, he or she should join it. Jesus and a large crowd of followers were moving into the city. As these two "parades" collided, the Prince of Life met the procession of death. Like the prophet Elijah, who restored a woman's dead son to life (1 Kings 17:17–24), so Jesus brought a woman's son back to life. Thus the report that "a great prophet has appeared among us" was not surprising. God had visited His people in His Son, but unfortunately they recognized Him as only a prophet, not as the Son of God.

Jesus and John the Baptist (7:18–35). Jesus clarified who John the Baptist was, and He condemned Israel for rejecting both of their ministries. Luke included these two points in order to warn his readers of the danger of missing the messages of salvation and judgment. Jesus was evidently not establishing the kingdom as quickly as John had expected. In response to an inquiry from John the Baptist, Jesus quoted from Isaiah 35:5–6 to confirm His identity as the Messiah. Jesus then explained that John was a transitional figure, ending one era and introducing the new era that came with Christ. John's role as the forerunner set him apart as a unique prophet (Luke 7:27; Mal. 3:1).

The comparison of John as greatest among those born of women and the least of those born into the kingdom of God has been explained in two ways. Some say that because John did not live to see the new era begin, the lowest individuals in the new phase of God's kingdom are greater than John. This is an emphasis on the privilege of being in the kingdom in the present age. Another view is that two spheres are being contrasted— the sphere of humanity and the sphere of the kingdom family of God. Being in the kingdom is not to be compared with greatness in the realm of humanity. Whichever interpretation is followed, the advantage of a right relationship with Christ and participating in His kingdom is more valuable than any position of greatness on this earth. Nothing should deter a person from securing through faith such a privileged place with Christ.

When Jesus compared Israel to children playing in the marketplace (7:29–35), He wanted to provoke a right response to John's and His messages. The Pharisees and the scribes were correct in linking John and Jesus, but they rejected both, and in so doing they rejected God's purpose for themselves. Like children whose dance music and funeral dirge were both rejected, the leaders rejected both John and Jesus, even though John's and Jesus' lifestyles and message differed. John's message, like a funeral dirge, was one of judgment, and Jesus' message, like joyful flute music, was one of grace. Failing to believe John, the religious leaders missed Jesus' message as well. John and Jesus delivered contrasting but complementary messages. If one does not respond to the warning of judgment or the wooing of grace, there is no other message.

Simon and the sinful woman (7:36–50). A custom of the day allowed people to congregate around the outside of an open courtyard while the guests reclined together at the table. This accounts for the sinful woman's presence in the house of Simon the Pharisee and her access to the feet of Jesus. Simon's self-righteousness blinded him to the true identity of Jesus and his own need. Simon's doubting of Jesus' prophetic abilities was countered by the fact that Jesus read his very thoughts.

Jesus' parable of the two debtors and His comments to Simon and the woman teach a number of lessons: (a) Salvation is the result of God's gracious work received by faith. (b) God graciously forgives the debt of sin that no one can repay. (c) Peace with God is possible because of the forgiveness of sins. (d) The more one understands forgiveness, the more love he will have for Christ. (e) Humble service stems from a heart of gratitude for God's grace.

> *Being least in the kingdom is better than being the best anywhere else.*

The support for Jesus' ministry (8:1–3). Luke mentioned a number of women who traveled with Jesus and supported His ministry. The previous account of Simon, the self-righteous Pharisee, and the sinful but forgiven woman (7:36–50) is surrounded by two passages that illustrate these two responses to Jesus. The first "bookend" is 7:30–35, which speaks of Pharisees who, like Simon, refused to believe in Jesus because of their self-righteousness. The second "bookend" is 8:1–3, which speaks of women who, like the sinful woman at Jesus' feet, were of questionable or unknown backgrounds but who served Jesus humbly out of gratitude for His work in their lives.

The parable of the sower and the soils (8:4–15). This parable describes four soils on which seed was sown. Each soil yielded a different crop. Jesus explained that the parable (8:11–15) speaks of the different ways people hear and respond to the Word of God. The pathway soil represents those who experience the satanic theft of the Word from the heart, which prevents them from believing. The seed in the rocky soil represents the temporary reception of the Word that tends to fade in the face of testing. The thorny soil stands for those who are consumed with the internal distractions of the heart and thus fail to mature. Worries, riches, and pleasures choke out the life of the Word that would have resulted in growth had there been a better response. The good soil pictures those who hear and respond to the Word with a good heart, retain it, and through perseverance produce a good crop.

The lamp on a stand (8:16–18). Just as a lamp is to yield light, so similarly the life of a disciple is meant to be a good testimony. Truth will one day be revealed. Therefore to keep secret what God wants to be shared is meaningless. The exhortation to be careful to listen follows from the previous parable. Spiritual apathy can result in losing ministry possibilities. This was true of the nation of Israel, and it was also true of the disciples whom Jesus warned about the danger of losing the privilege of being used by God for eternal purposes.

> *To whom much is given much is required.*

A new standard of relationships (8:19–21). Jesus noted that true family relationships are based on a right response to the Word of God rather than physical descent. Brothers and sisters in Christ form an eternal relationship that far outlasts family ties on this earth.

Jesus' calming of the storm (8:22–25). Both the humanity and the deity of Jesus are seen in this event. That Jesus was tired was an indication of His humanity; that He could calm the stormy sea was a revelation of His deity. He followed His rebuke of the storm with a rebuke of the disciples for their lack of faith. If Jesus has power over nature, then He has the right to direct people's lives.

> *Jesus has the power to free people from the powers of darkness.*

Jesus' healing of the demoniac (8:26–38). The exact location of this miracle is difficult to determine because of the spelling differences in the manuscripts. Gergesenes, Gerasenes, and Gadarenes are all used. Gergesa has been identified with the site of Kursi on the eastern edge of the Sea of Galilee. Geresa has been identified with the site of Jerash; and the city of Gadera was one of the ten Greek city-states known as the Decapolis. All three sites have some manuscript support. The geography seems to argue best for Gergesa, because caves and cliffs are not far from Kursi on the eastern edge of the lake. The extremes of demonic control were experienced by the men (Matt. 8:28–34 speaks of two such men, but Mark 5:1–20 and Luke 8:26–38 focus on one). The name of one was "Legion," which suggests that he was under the control of numerous demons (a Roman legion was made up of about six thousand soldiers). The demons begged Jesus not to send them to the Abyss, the prison for those demons now held captive for final judgment (Rev. 9:1–11). The healing was total and the response of the crowds was fear. That fear and the loss of their herd of swine caused them to ask that Jesus leave. Fear of the unknown and materialism could have been two reasons for their response.

Jesus' raising of Jairus's daughter and healing of a woman (8:40–56). Jesus returned to the Capernaum synagogue. The two healings in this passage are linked by the number twelve. The woman had been plagued by bleeding for twelve years; the daughter of Jairus was twelve years of age. Both disease and death were defiling. The journey to Jairus's house was interrupted by the encounter with the woman. Jesus corrected the superstitious faith of the woman by telling her that her faith rather than her touch of His garment, was the cause of her healing (8:48). During the delay Jairus's daughter died. But Jesus promised that she would be raised on the basis of faith (her father's faith, not hers). Because the custom was

> *Everything believers need for ministering to the masses is provided by Christ Himself.*

to bury a person the same day he died, funeral arrangements were already being made, and mourners were already present at Jairus's house. Jesus' announcement that she was only sleeping should not be taken to mean she had not died. He meant He could raise her from the dead as easily as He could arouse someone from sleep. Jesus raised her from the dead and proved the miracle by having her eat. A fully functioning body was the testimony of a genuine miracle.

E. The Transitions toward the Cross (9:1–50)

The commissioning of the Twelve (9:1–9). Jesus delegated to His disciples His authority to preach and heal. Their simple lifestyle was to help picture the response to the gospel. Those responsive to the message of the kingdom would take care of them and those who opposed their message would not. Shaking the dust from their feet was a sign of judgment for those who were unresponsive. To reject the message of Jesus as preached by His messengers made one liable for the judgment of God. Luke recorded that people confused Jesus with John the Baptist, Elijah, or another prophet. Even Herod feared that John the Baptist had returned from the dead, and so Herod wanted to see Jesus to distinguish Him from John.

The feeding of the five thousand (9:10–17). Bethsaida, the hometown of Andrew, Peter, and Philip (John 1:44), was a fishing village on the north shore of the Sea of Galilee where Jesus sought to retreat with His disciples. Only Luke mentioned the physical need of the people for lodging. Jesus challenged the Twelve to feed the multitude to make them wrestle with the fact that their resources were inadequate and that He alone could meet their needs. The leftovers revealed the gracious abundance of Jesus' provision for the people.

The confession of Peter (9:18–27). This event took place at Caesarea Philippi, where the Greeks revered Pan, a nature god. In response to Jesus' questions about His identity, the same three options were given. Some thought He was John the Baptist, Elijah, or another one of the prophets.

When Peter was addressed personally, he spoke up and said, "The Christ of God" (9:20). Jesus' command for secrecy (9:21) affirmed Peter's answer and showed that Jesus was conducting His ministry on a planned schedule that allowed for the events of rejection and suffering (9:22) before giving a full-blown disclosure of His identity. The Cross and the kingdom were both part of God's plan for His Son. In light of His coming death and resurrection Jesus called on others to identify with His sufferings through a commitment to discipleship even in the face of intimidating opposition. The paradox of losing one's life to find it reinforces the new value system Jesus was advocating. The loss of everything in order to experience all that Christ has to offer is actually no loss at all.

What is gained in Christ far outweighs all that is lost for Christ.

The Transfiguration (9:28–36). Of the three Synoptic Gospel writers only Luke mentioned that Jesus prayed on the Mount of Transfiguration. (Also only Luke mentioned that Jesus prayed at His baptism; see 3:21). Jesus' transfiguration allowed what He is by nature to be shown publicly for the first time in His earthly life. As with Jesus' baptism, God the Father verbally affirmed Jesus' identity as His Son (3:22; 9:35).

The presence of Moses and Elijah with Him anticipated the presence of the Old Testament saints, who will be raised to be with Christ in the future millennial kingdom. Their discussion centered on the theme of Jesus' departure (literally, His "exodus") in Jerusalem. This may refer to the Cross, but more likely it speaks of the Ascension, which Luke mentioned later (9:51).

Peter suggested that they build three booths probably because of the prophecy in Zechariah 14:16 that the Feast of Tabernacles (Booths) would be celebrated when Christ reigns on the earth. Apparently Peter thought that with Moses, Elijah, the three disciples, and Christ all present, this must be the beginning of the earthly kingdom. But the facts that Moses and Elijah disappeared and that Jesus did not stay in His glorified appearance revealed that the kingdom had not yet come. The Transfiguration served as a prophetic foreshadowing (Matthew called it a vision; Matt. 17:9) that some day Jesus will reign with His saints on the earth. The

> *Knowing that Christ and His kingdom will come should motivate all saints to serve Him courageously now.*

Transfiguration was intended to encourage the restricted audience of the three disciples that in spite of the cross Jesus would wear a crown. They should serve Him faithfully with that anticipation of the future.

Jesus' rebuke of unbelief (9:37–45). The remainder of the chapter includes instructions the disciples needed as they anticipated the journey of Christ to Jerusalem. The disciples who had not been with Christ on the mountain found themselves unable to heal a demonized boy with epileptic-type seizures. Such seizures are not often brought on by demonic influence, but in this case they were. Jesus rebuked the faithlessness and perversity of His generation because of their lack of faith in God's power. Jesus' healing of the boy testified to the great power of Christ, who can defeat the powers of the evil one. Since Jesus has this kind of power, whatever happens to Him as the Son of man in His suffering must be seen as voluntary and therefore necessary for the purposes God has for Him.

Jesus' lessons on humility (9:46–50). The need for humility is seen in two erroneous tendencies—seeking positions of status (9:46) and promoting sectarian elitism (9:49). The disciples' arguing about who was the greatest revealed their failure to understand the suffering Servant and His model of humility. His lesson still stands: "For he who is least among you all—he is the greatest." Humility, as seen in a little child, is the answer to selfish ambition, just as Christ is the answer to a divisive spirit. He countered their sectarian attitude by telling them whoever was for them (and thus for Him) was not part of the competition.

IV. JESUS' JOURNEY TO JERUSALEM (9:51–19:27)

The many events in Luke's travelogue may be viewed as arranged in a chiasm, as seen in the diagram on the next page.

Inverted Parallelism (Chiasm) in the Lucan Travelogue (9:51–19:27)

A Jerusalem and Ascension (9:51)

  B Samaritans and Salvation (9:52–56) (Purpose for His Coming)

    C Discipleship and Following (9:57–62)

      D Message of the Kingdom (Rejection) (10:1–24)

        E A Lawyer and Eternal Life (10:25–42) (Service and Rewards)

          F Prayer (11:1–13) (Children)

            G Blasphemy of Pharisees (11:14–28)

              H Sign of Jonah (11:29–36) (Resurrection)

                I Woes on the Pharisees (11:37–54)

                  J Discipleship Taught (12:1–34) (Money and Faithfulness)

                    K Parables of Readiness (12:35–48) (Faithfulness)

                      L Discipleship (12:49–53) (Division)

                        M Hypocrites (12:54–59) (Poor Judgment)

                          N Parable of Grace (13:1–9) (Repentance)

                            O Healing on the Sabbath (13:10–17)

                              P Growth of the Kingdom (13:18–21)

                              (Universal Inclusion)

                              P' Judgment on Israel (13:22–35)

                              (Jerusalem Rejection)

                            O' Healing on the Sabbath (14:1–6)

                          N' Parables of Invitation (14:7–15)

                          (Humility)

                        M' Rejection (14:15–24) (Poor Judgment)

                    L' Discipleship (14:25–35) (Dedication)

                  K' Parables of the Lost (chapter 15) (Reconciliation)

                J' Parable of the Unjust Steward (16:1–13)

                (Faithfulness and Money)

              I' Condemnation on the Pharisees (16:14–18)

            H' The Rich Man and Lazarus (16:19–31) (Resurrection)

           G' Judgment at the Second Advent (chapter 17)

         F' Prayer (18:1–17) (Children)

        E' A Rich Young Ruler and Eternal Life (18:18–30) (Service and Rewards)

      D' Announcement of Jerusalem (Rejection) (18:31–34)

    C' Bartimaeus and Following Jesus (18:35–43)

  B' Zacchaeus and Salvation (19:1–10) (Purpose for His Coming)

A' The Parable of the Pounds (19:11–27) (Delay of the Messianic Kingdom)

> *Vengeance blinds one to the gracious salvation message.*

To Jerusalem: The Ascension anticipated (9:51). Everything in the "travelogue" in 9:51–19:27 is to be understood in light of Jesus' pending "departure" in Jerusalem. The major purpose of these events was to prepare the disciples for life and ministry after Jesus returned to heaven. In Luke, Jerusalem was the goal toward which Jesus was moving (9:51; 13:22; 17:11), where His death and resurrection would become the focus of the gospel. In Acts, however, Jerusalem was the launching pad for the church, who took that message to the world.

The Samaritans and salvation (9:52–56). The Jews hated the Samaritans because of their mixed bloodlines and unorthodox religious beliefs. When the Samaritans didn't respond to Jesus, the disciples were incensed. The mission statement, "For the Son of man did not come to destroy men's lives but to save them," is not found in some of the better manuscripts (see NIV margin on v. 55), but nevertheless the sentiment (see 19:10) , "For the Son of man came to seek and to save what was lost") is true because of the Lord's rebuke to James and John, who wanted to call down fire from heaven and consume the Samaritans.

Following Christ wholeheartedly (9:57–62). By their negative example three kinds of men whom Christ could not use reveal the kind of heart He desires in true discipleship. By His response to each one, Jesus exposed their error and expressed the attitude He longs to see in a committed disciple. The first man (whom Matthew said was a teacher of the law; Matt. 8:19) was too interested in the comforts of this life. He didn't understand that a life identified with Jesus would not be easy. Jesus had no permanent home in His earthly ministry. On earth Jesus had even less than the birds and animals He created.

The second man was hesitant to commit himself because of his concern for his father. Because people were buried the day they died, the man's father was probably still living. So this was a strange excuse. The man placed responsibilities to his family above his commitment to Christ. Jesus answered that the spiritually dead can wait for physical death by themselves, and that the spiritually sensitive should follow Him. Nothing should delay immediate obedience to the call of Christ on one's life.

On the surface the third excuse seems more reasonable—just saying good-bye to one's family. But the man was too homesick to follow the Lord. The man's words may allude to Elisha's comment to Elijah about saying good-bye to his family (1 Kings 19:20). Jesus' illustration of plowing a crooked row because of looking back is a fitting reminder that one cannot live in two worlds. Kingdom life and ministry are to supersede all other commitments.

The seventy-two and the message of the kingdom (10:1–24). Of the Gospel writers only Luke recorded this ministry of the seventy-two disciples. (Some Greek manuscripts read "seventy.") Sending them out by twos meant the messengers had companionship. Their message was a final appeal for response to Jesus as He prepared for His departure (9:31). Picturing evangelists as workers in a harvest was a topic often mentioned by Jesus (Matt. 9:37; 13:30, 39; John 4:35–36). Jesus' instruction that the seventy-two not take luggage and provisions with them highlighted the brevity of the mission as well as the urgency of the message. People's reactions to the disciples indicated whether they were responding positively or negatively to the Messiah and His message of the kingdom (Luke 10:16). The message that the kingdom was near (10:9, 11) was the same message John and Jesus had been preaching. Jesus delegated miraculous power to the disciples (10:19–20) for the mission that authenticated the presence of the Messiah and His offer of the kingdom.

> *The way one treats the messengers of Christ is an indication of his or her response to Christ Himself.*

Three cities of Jesus' ministry were condemned for their lack of response, despite their having experienced a more than gracious portion of the Lord's ministry. As a result, Korazin, Bethsaida, and Capernaum will all be held more accountable in the day of judgment than Tyre and Sidon (10:13–15). Because of their unique privilege of being exposed to Jesus' ministry, the generation that rejected Jesus will experience a more severe condemnation than Tyre and Sidon experienced.

The victories the disciples would experience on their mission pointed to the dramatic defeat of Satan at the cross. The supernatural powers given

> *True love sacrificially reaches beyond the zones of comfort to meet the genuine needs of others.*

to the disciples were tempered by Jesus' caution that eternal destinies are more important than earthly demonstrations of power (10:21). Spiritual insight is reserved for the humble of heart, and therefore the disciples were entrusted with the mysteries of the kingdom that were hidden from others (10:23–24; Matt. 13:10–11).

Eternal life and humble service (10:25–42). The two great commandments, loving God and loving others as oneself, became a means by which Luke framed the accounts of the Good Samaritan (10:30–37) and the conversation at the home of Mary and Martha (10:38–42). The question the legal expert asked Jesus reflects the self-justifying motives of many today. Confusing merit for mercy and grace for works is unfortunately too common. If works were the basis of our approval with God, then it would be necessary to keep all of the commands of God in order to be saved. Holiness and perfection have always been the standard, since the basis of evaluation has always been God's righteousness (Lev. 11:44–45; 19:2; Matt. 5:48). The motive and manner of a works-based salvation is always self-justification.

Apparently the man wanted to set a limit on the circle of people he was obligated to love as his neighbors. So through the parable Jesus turned around his question "Who is my neighbor?" by focusing not on the object of those loved but on the subject of the one loving. The issue is not who is to be loved as one's neighbor but how a person himself can be a loving neighbor.

The parable of the Good Samaritan reflects the culture and geography of Jesus' day. A number of priests who served the temple in Jerusalem lived in Jericho. The road from Jericho to Jerusalem was called the Ascent Addumim (the "Ascent of Blood") because of the frequent robberies that took place on that winding path. Just as the priest and the Levite in the story did not take care of the injured man, so the Jewish leaders had failed to meet an elementary obligation given in the Law, which was to love one's neighbor as himself (Lev. 19:18). On the other hand, the Samaritan, being in a hostile, cross-cultural, uncomfortable, and even dangerous environment, was vulnerable as he reached out in love and sacrificially met the needs of the hurting Jew. That was the kind of love that reflected the character of God and fulfilled the law of God.

The parable of the Good Samaritan illustrates the second great command to truly love one's neighbor, and the account of Mary and Martha pictures the first and greatest command to love the Lord fully. Jesus taught the sisters that true love for Him is better shown by a full devotion to Him than by being obsessed about fulfilling duties for Him. Worshiping Christ is a higher priority than working for Christ.

Persistent prayer (11:1–13). When the disciples asked Jesus how to pray, He taught them a model prayer. Then in the parable of the pestering neighbor, He encouraged them to be persistent in prayer. In the culture of that day hospitality was a higher priority than convenience and family comfort. The man was reluctant to answer the door, probably because of the way his family's sleeping mats were arranged. One could not get up and step over the children without waking several family members. If the man would get up and give his friend what he needs, certainly God, who is greater, will meet our needs. In fact, God is better than a friend next door; He is a loving heavenly Father who knows just what to give His children to meet their needs. Our greatest need for living life as God desires it is the presence and ministry of the Holy Spirit.

Blasphemy of the Holy Spirit (11:14–28). "Beelzebub" is the Greek transliteration of a Hebrew word that means "lord of the flies." This title, given to one of the Philistine deities, was brought into Judaism as a derogatory reference to Satan as the prince of the demonic hosts. Jesus' Jewish opponents could not accept the truth that He is God or that He had been sent by God the Father. So they said His work was empowered by Satan.

Jesus answered that accusation by stating that divided kingdoms or homes cannot continue to exist. Satan would not drive himself out in defeat of himself; therefore Jesus was not in league with the prince of demons. Jesus then challenged the leaders to articulate how one distinguishes the powers of exorcism. He knew they couldn't answer His questions because in doing so they would contradict themselves. If Jesus is who He claimed to be, then His exorcisms were a sign of the imminent presence of God's kingdom. And if Jesus were actually casting out demons, then He had proven Himself stronger than satanic forces, thereby proving His divine identity.

Failure to identify with Christ is to oppose all that He is (10:23). Exorcising evil spirits without the person having God's presence within opens up that individual to even worse satanic influences. When a woman blessed Mary for having given birth to Jesus, He turned her comment into a word about obedience.

The sign of Jonah (11:29–36). Jesus said He is greater than both Jonah and Solomon. Jesus' words about Jonah show that He believed in the historicity of the Book of Jonah. Jonah was a miraculous sign to the people of Nineveh through his encounter with the great fish, and similarly through His resurrection Jesus was a sign to His and following generations. Solomon proclaimed God's wisdom, and the Queen of Sheba came to listen to him. But Christ and His message are far superior to either Jonah or Solomon. Therefore both the Ninevites and the Queen of the South will rise at the resurrection and condemn those in Jesus' day who rejected His superior message. The message of Christ is to be believed and shared, not hidden, much as a lamp is to give off light and is not hidden. The spiritual perception one has affects his entire life.

> *Jesus' view of the Scriptures sets the pattern of faith for all others.*

Woes to the Pharisees (11:37–54). Jesus pronounced a series of judgmental "woes" on the Pharisees for their hypocritical religious practices. Though they were concerned about having clean dishes, inwardly they themselves were contaminated (11:37–41). They were more interested in outward appearance than in the condition of their hearts. They disregarded the true essence of the Law, for while they tithed to the nth degree, they failed to practice the basic principles of justice and love (11:42). They loved prominent places of status and respectability within the culture, thereby feeding their self-righteousness. In reality, they were spiritually dead and therefore deadly in their influence on others (11:43–44). They burdened people with legalistic requirements they themselves did not obey (11:45–46).

Jesus said the Pharisees approved what their forefathers did in killing the prophets. Therefore the Pharisees, because of their flagrant sin, would be held responsible for all the bloodshed since Creation, represented by the first and last murders (of Abel and Zechariah) in Old Testament history (Gen. 4:8; 2 Chron. 24:20–22). The tragedy was that these "experts" of the Law not only did not use the key of knowledge to enter the kingdom of God, but also by distorting the truth they kept others from entering the kingdom as well.

> *Self-righteousness blinds one from the truths of genuine Christianity.*

Wholehearted discipleship (12:1–34). In the atmosphere of opposition from the Pharisees, Jesus preached a message to the overflowing crowds. The message included a mixture of themes including warnings against the hypocritical teachings ("yeast") of the Pharisees and the need to be prepared to testify for Christ in the face of persecution. The coming judgment and the need for proper preparation are the threads that tie all of chapter 12 together. God is to be feared beyond humans (12:4–5, 11) since it is God who determines the eternal destiny beyond the life-and-death experiences of this world. Blaspheming against the Holy Spirit meant saying that Jesus performed His miracles by satanic power. For such flagrant rejection of Christ, there is no forgiveness.

Jesus gave the parable of the rich fool (12:16–21) in response to a man who was concerned about getting all the inheritance he thought he deserved (12:13). Jesus exposed the sin of covetousness that can take at least two forms. The encounter with the young man surfaced the kind of covetousness that comes from thinking that getting more of this world's wealth will bring greater satisfaction (12:15). And the parable of the rich fool showed another form of greed—all that one can get will never satisfy the real needs of the heart. Both forms of greed are the result of an inadequate understanding of life.

The man in the story was called a fool for confusing time with eternity, his body for his soul, and what was his for what was God's. Verses 22–34 amplify the principle highlighted earlier in 12:4–7. Worry about food or clothing (like that of the rich fool) is inconsistent with the knowledge of our heavenly Father, who knows and cares for His children far

> *Life is not to be defined by the quantity of one's possessions, but by the quality of one's relationship with God.*

more than He takes care of ravens and lilies. God can be trusted to provide for His own. His kingdom is to remain the highest priority (12:32–34).

Jesus' parables of readiness (12:34–48). While the return of the Lord to the earth is certain, the timing is unknown. The statements in verses 37 and 43 highlight two important preparations in light of the Lord's return—the need to be ready and the importance of being faithful. Through the parable of the expectant servant, Jesus stressed the need to be alert in order to be prepared for His coming. Alertness is a metaphor for faith that prepares one to be ready for the unexpected time of the Lord's return. Two Near Eastern cultural examples of readiness were being properly dressed and having burning lamps (12:35).

The parable of the faithful manager (12:42–46) highlights the need for the servant who was alert to also be "doing" his assigned tasks. "Doing" was Jesus' metaphor for faithfulness. Being "faithful and wise" in serving the Lord will result in reward when He comes again. Rewards will take the form of extended privileged responsibilities in the kingdom established by the Son of God. Jesus warned that the one who was not ready and who was also unfaithful would face severe judgment. Both judgment and rewards will be proportionately meted out by Christ at His coming. The principle of proportionate responsibility for proportionate privilege is emphasized in 12:48, as in Matthew 13:12 and 25:29.

Committed discipleship (12:49–53). Judgment ("fire") is decreed for all who reject the Son. However, Jesus' initial purpose and desired will at His first advent was salvation, not judgment (John 3:17). But to provide salvation He needed to die, and His death ("baptism"; see Mark 10:38) had to occur before He will judge. A person's faith in Christ and disciplined commitment to Him may cause a division in his or her family. The divided opinions mentioned in Luke 12:53 recall the family divisions among the Jews at the time of the Babylonian Captivity.

Hypocrites and their poor judgment (12:54–59). Though Jesus' contemporaries knew how to predict certain weather patterns, they didn't understand the significance of His presence on earth nor the urgent need for them to place their faith in Him in order to avoid judgment. Their attempts to settle their civil affairs out of court should have been matched with an equal effort to "settle up" with God to avoid the consequences of divine judgment that are sure to come.

A parable of grace (13:1–9). Jesus referred to two catastrophes in His day to illustrate the need to repent in order to escape divine judgment. These calamities were Pilate's harsh sacrilegious treatment of the Galileans in reaction to their resistance to Roman intrusion, and the collapse of the Siloam tower that killed eighteen people. Whether people are killed in conflicts or in natural disasters does not indicate degrees of sinfulness. However, repentance is necessary for everyone who hopes to escape the judgment of God.

Jesus then told the parable of the fig tree to explain why judgment had not yet come. The fig tree was a common Old Testament symbol for the nation of Israel (for example, Isa. 5:2). The owner had every right to expect figs on a fig tree. Lack of fruit warranted the destruction of the tree. The three-year time frame parallels the time Jesus had been ministering in Israel. The worker suggested they wait an extra year, in hopes of finding fruit on the tree. If no fruit resulted, then the tree would be cut down. Similarly God extends His grace, but if people still reject it, judgment is inevitable. This is similar to the message of John the Baptist, which he preached near the beginning of Jesus' ministry (Luke 3:8–9).

Healing on the Sabbath (13:10–17). The healing of the crippled woman (13:10–13) and of the man with dropsy (14:1–6) were miracles on the Sabbath, both of which revealed the basic error of the Jews' rejection of their Messiah. The illustration of the beast of burden (13:15) was appropriate to the woman's burdenlike posture that resulted from demonic activity. Demonic activity can manifest itself in physical infirmity with even violent results (8:29). When Jesus healed the woman who had been bound by Satan for eighteen years, the reaction by the religious leaders and Jesus' rebuke of them exposed their hypocrisy. They valued their animals above people and were willing to suspend Sabbath law for personal gain.

The international growth of the kingdom (13:18–21). Jesus told the two parables of the mustard seed and of the leavening process to teach the growth of the kingdom between His first and second comings. The first parable—the large tree that grew from the small mustard seed—speaks of the extension of growth to include Gentiles from all over the world. The imagery of birds nesting in the branches alludes to Ezekiel 17:22–23; 31:6; and Daniel 4:1–12, where Gentiles from other countries are included. Yeast usually symbolizes evil, but here it suggests that righteousness has a permeating effect (see also Lev. 7:13; 23:17). The growth of the kingdom is spiritual in nature and not organizationally driven. The work of the Spirit is what causes the growth of God's kingdom in the present age (see Rom. 14:17).

The judgment on Israel (13:22–35). The theme of the journey to Jerusalem is appropriately mentioned again (see 9:51) along with Jesus' discussion of the unbelief and impending judgments that will befall Israel. The problem of unbelief was introduced when someone asked Jesus if only a few people would be saved. Jesus taught that many would not be saved because they will fail to come the right way or will delay until it is too late. Any claims based on Jewish ancestry will be dismissed as illegitimate. In fact, the presence of Gentiles in the kingdom (from all directions of the globe) and the exclusion of some Jews from the kingdom support the truth that salvation is by faith and is not attainable by familial or national inheritance. The comment that the "last will be first, and [the] first will be last" indicates that we may be surprised to see who will be in the kingdom.

Herod's threat to kill Jesus was actually no threat to Him because what He did and when He did it was scheduled by no one else but Himself. The theme of rejection and death that dominated much of the travelogue is repeated here when He said, "I will reach my goal." Jesus knew that His final rejection and death would happen in Jerusalem in line with the many prophets who had been rejected throughout Israel's history (13:33). Like a "fox" (13:32), Herod was clever and destructive.

Four major truths are given in the indictment in 13:34–35. First, Jesus had wanted the people of Jerusalem, the capital of Israel, to accept His offer of Himself as the Messiah and to believe the message of the kingdom. Second, judgment would fall on the "house" of Israel and it would become "desolate," because they rejected Him. The term "house" can refer to the temple, Jerusalem, or the nation. This prophecy was initially fulfilled in the destruction of the temple and Jerusalem in A.D. 70 with the Roman invasion by Titus. A final fulfillment will take place during the latter half of the Tribulation. Third, the Messiah would leave for an undefined period of time before He returns. Fourth, the Messiah would not return to the nation until they repented and thus would be ready to welcome Him properly (see Matt. 24:29–31). Only then would they experience the national hope expressed in Psalm 118:26, "Blessed is he who comes in the name of the Lord."

Another healing on the Sabbath (14:1–6). This incident and the healing of the crippled woman in 13:10–13 have numerous parallels. In each case the main character was physically afflicted through demonization. One was a woman doubled over with a spinal dysfunction, and the other was a man who had dropsy (a disease stemming from bodily swelling because of water retention). Both were healed on the Sabbath. Both led to questions about appropriate Sabbath activity. Through both incidents Jesus asserted His right to interpret the Law properly. In both, Jesus indicted the leaders with being willing to save their own animals while ignoring the hurting people of their own community.

Through these two incidents Jesus exposed the error of Judaism by showing that the people were violating the very Law they thought they were protecting. When animals become more important than people, the values of the culture are inverted and all kinds of perversions result. By misunderstanding and misapplying the Mosaic Law, the nation rejected Jesus. Ironically in the Law God chose to substitute an animal for the nation as an atoning sacrifice. The generation at the time of Christ had lost sight of the very imagery that best instructed them as to the reason why Jesus came.

Genuine religion expresses compassion for the needs of people.

Jesus' parables of humility (14:7–14) Having been invited to dinner at a Pharisee's home (14:1; see also 11:37), Jesus saw that the guests clambered for the best seats. He addressed the guests first (14:8–11) and then the host (14:12–14). Jesus said that when guests attend a wedding banquet, they

> *Only those who humbly respond to Jesus' gracious invitation will be present to enjoy the kingdom of God.*

shouldn't seek "the place of honor," for they will be rebuked for their pride. Humility, however, will result in their receiving appropriate honor. The elevated "better place" (14:10) was a raised platform on one end of the banquet hall reserved for recognized guests of honor.

Then He said that for a host to invite people to dinner and then expect them to reciprocate the invitation was to act with a self-serving attitude. "The poor, the crippled, the lame, and the blind" were the disenfranchised of the community, who were normally neglected by others. They are the ones who should be graciously invited since they have no means for repayment. Kingdom rewards await that kind of generosity.

The dangers of rejecting the invitation to the kingdom (14:15–24). Jesus' reference to rewards in verse 14 prompted one of the dinner guests to quote a beatitude about eating in the kingdom of God. Jesus took this opportunity to use the imagery of a banquet to illustrate truths relative to God's kingdom program. In the ancient Near East two invitations were usually given for formal dinners. The first was a general announcement that there would be a banquet. The second was given when the meal was ready to be eaten. Being invited to a banquet pictured calling people to the kingdom of God.

However, three men gave lame, selfishly motivated excuses for refusing to accept the invitation. Each one referred to a decision he had made that could not be reversed. To buy a field unseen would be foolish. To wait to test oxen until the next day would not have canceled the sale. Marriage was permanent and therefore a celebration was even more in order. Not surprisingly this disrespect to the host angered and disappointed him. Because Eastern banquets were not to begin until all the places at the tables were filled, the "poor, the crippled, the lame and the blind" (compare 14:13) were outcasts invited to replace those originally invited. Because Jesus' message of the kingdom was rejected by those to whom it was initially offered, it was extended to outcasts, including Gentiles.

The need for committed discipleship (14:25–35). Jesus invited all who were following Him to a life of committed discipleship. Jesus stressed two key characteristics of what it meant to be a committed disciple. One must love Christ with a supreme and incomparable love, and one must be willing to recognize the true ownership of his or her possessions. The illustrations of building a tower and going to battle portray the need to follow, fully aware of the cost to oneself and one's family. To give up all of one's possessions means to relinquish the rights of ownership in favor of stewardship. The salt metaphor that closes the chapter may at first seem misplaced. However, the point is that a disciple loses his or her influence or testimony when personal possessions are held above loyalty to Christ.

The parables of the lost (chapter 15). The three stories in this chapter were viewed as one parable (15:3). Jesus told these parables in answer to the Pharisees and scribes' question as to why Jesus welcomed sinners and ate with them. Jesus shared His Father's heart in rejoicing over the recovery of even one sinner. Shepherds (15:3–7), unmarried maidens (15:8–10), and rebellious sons (15:11–32) were examples of disenfranchised people who were usually excluded by the religious establishment of Jesus' day.

The literary art and message of the three stories are beautifully intertwined. The ratio of ninety-nine sheep to one, nine coins to one, and one son to one focuses in each case on the one recovered. Rejoicing occurs in each case. In the first story those who rejoice are all in heaven. In the second, rejoicing is found in the company of the angels. In the third, the father is the leader of the party, celebrating the return of his wayward son. The lost sheep was located, of course, outside the house; the woman's coin was lost inside the house; and the younger son was lost outside the house.

At the end of the third story, the younger son was back in the house and the older brother was left outside. This reversal connoted the hypocritical self-righteous judgment of the religious leaders who misunderstood what the Father was doing through His Son Jesus. Viewing themselves as having no need of repentance, they did not understand the Lord's joy in seeing the recovery of the lost.

The unjust steward (16:1–13). A word that connects the previous chapter with this one is the Greek word translated "squandering" in 15:13 and "wasting" in 16:2. The stories recorded in Luke 15 were addressed to the

> *Christians are to use money wisely, converting earthly finances into heavenly friendships.*

Jewish leaders, whereas this parable of the unjust steward as manager was addressed to the disciples. The manager planned to use his finances to make friends for the future. Strangely, the owner praised the unrighteous manager. This is probably explained by the fact that illegal interest had been written into the contracts. Interest secretly charged on wheat amounted to 25 percent, and interest on olive oil was as high as 100 percent. The master could not punish the manager for reducing the bills because it was illegal in the first place to charge such interest. The owner praised his manager's shrewdness for beating him within the system.

The parable teaches that believers as "people of the light" (16:8) are to be as shrewd in their kingdom investments for God as unbelievers are in their circles of business. "Mammon" (KJV) is an Aramaic word for money or treasures. When Christians lead their friends to Christ by wise financial investments toward eternal dividends, they will find that these friends will welcome them in heaven (16:9).

Jesus said money is a minor issue in life, but it is loaded with implications. How a person handles money indicates whether he or she will be faithful or unfaithful in other areas of life (16:10). Faithfulness in this life with the money of this world will merit the rewards of true riches in heaven. Trustworthy stewardship here will be exchanged in heaven for genuine ownership (16:11–12). The worship of God and the worship of gold are mutually exclusive since they demand opposite loyalties. If one worships gold, the motivation will be to accumulate it; if one worships God, the motivation will be to give money to those things that matter most to Him. A disciple should learn to handle finances with faithfulness.

Transitional illustrations of self-righteousness (16:14–18). These transitional verses between the two parables in this chapter bring into bold relief the dangerous practice of self-justification so prevalent among the religious leaders of Jesus' day. Though they valued money and the applause of people, these things are hated by God, who knows what people are really like. To be "forcing" one's way into the kingdom is to think there is another way of salvation other than by faith. To assume one can be righteous apart from God's provision in Christ shows that that person is not dealing properly with his or her sinful condition. In their superficial righteousness the religious leaders justified their love of money and their setting aside the true intent of the Law of Moses. One example was their disregard for the marriage laws. Some of them thought divorce could be justified for almost any reason. Not much has changed in modern times. (For Jesus' teachings on divorce and remarriage, see comments on Matt. 5:32 and 19:1–11.)

The rich man and Lazarus (16:19–31). Whether this passage should be viewed as a parable or not does not change Jesus' teaching on the afterlife. The realities of bliss and torment after death are here affirmed by the Lord. The narrative points up the contrast between the earthly lot and the eternal destiny of the two leading characters. The rich man enjoyed the luxuries of life in both his dress and his diet, and the poor man was an example of destitute need and inability. When they died, the rich man was buried and angels escorted the poor man to "Abraham's side (NIV)." The side (or "bosom," KJV, NASB) of Abraham refers to the Near Eastern dining custom in which each person would recline near the chest of the person just behind him, usually to his left.

The dialogues from the afterlife in this passage reveal a series of vital truths that serve as correctives to some modern erroneous doctrines. (1) There is immediate consciousness after death; therefore soul sleep is not taught in the Bible. (2) Post-death destinies are irreversible; therefore there is no purgatory or second chance of salvation after death. (3) No one can lose or gain salvation after death. The decisions of this life are final and determinative. (4) The judgments that determine the eternal destinies of either torment or blessing are just. (5) Signs should never be sought as a substitute for the Word of God. The Word of God is the only adequate basis for faith (16:29; see Rom. 10:17).

The humble heart of a servant (17:1–10). Jesus warned about the seriousness of offending those younger in the faith. Offenses are best removed through repentance and forgiveness. Believers are never to set limits on the frequency of their forgiveness. Maybe it was this last command that caused the disciples to ask for an increase of faith. Jesus said that even the smallest amount of faith, like a tiny mustard seed, the smallest of the garden-variety seeds, would produce extraordinary results. The parable of the servant in 17:7–10 teaches that everything done for God should be carried out in humility. Using three rhetorical questions, Jesus taught that even the work a servant does should be viewed as a privileged response to the grace that allowed his work to count for God.

> *One should not expect extra reward for expected service.*

The thankful Samaritan (17:11–19). As in 9:51 and 13:22, the reader is here again told that Jesus was on the way to Jerusalem (17:11). The thought of thanksgiving for the undeserved grace of God links this section with the previous one. Nine lepers were cleansed but only one went back, and, amazingly, he was a Samaritan. Thankfulness is the right heart-response of those touched by God. There may be a hint here of Israel's lack of response to God's grace in contrast to those considered outcasts, like the Samaritans. This continues Luke's emphasis on Gentiles being included in God's program because of Israel's rejection. The Law required a cured leper to appear before a priest to be declared cured, as well as to offer the appropriate sacrifices (Lev. 13:12–32; Luke 5:14).

Signs of the kingdom and coming judgment (17:20–37). The fact that the kingdom was "in your midst" (NASB) means that it was present through the person and work of Jesus. The fact that He was speaking to the Pharisees argues against the idea that the kingdom was in their hearts. Through His death many would come to believe in Him, thereby becoming members of His eternal, invisible kingdom (John 3:3; Col. 1:13). In addition, the future manifestation of God's kingdom rule will come when the Messiah returns and reigns over the earth. Jesus told His disciples that the Messiah's return and reign would be postponed. This postponement was justified in part because the present generation of Jews rejected Him as their Messiah (see also 7:30).

When the earthly kingdom does come, it will come with judgment. So people need to be ready now since the kingdom will come when it is least expected, as illustrated by the destruction in the days of Noah and Lot. Those taken are taken away to judgment. No mention is made here of the Rapture of the church from the earth. The return of Jesus to the earth in judgment at the end of the age is what is in view when Jesus as the Son of man will be revealed from heaven. The reference to vultures relates to the great bird supper of Revelation 19:21.

Persistence in prayer is a demonstration of faith in God who is always on time and righteous in His answers.

Jesus' parable of the unjust judge and the widow (18:1–8). References to the coming of the Son of man connect this chapter with the previous one (17:30; 18:8). The two parables that open this chapter both pertain to prayer. Believers need to be persistent but not proud in the pursuit of prayer. Jesus told the first parable because too often people give up too quickly in their habit of prayer. The parable teaches by reversal that, unlike the unjust judge who finally had to give in to the demand of the widow, believers can always trust the character of God as well as His timing when He does answer. He will always act in justice; and though from a human perspective He may delay, when He does act He will do so speedily and in righteousness. While awaiting the judgments of the Son of man, believers should continue to persist in their prayers. Such persistence is a sign of their faith.

The Pharisee and the tax collector (18:9–17). Jesus told this parable to expose the delusionary danger of self-righteousness and its judgmental spirit. The fact that both the Pharisee and the tax collector went to the temple to pray and yet only one went away justified shows that religiosity is no guarantee of spirituality. On the one hand, the Pharisee shows that righteousness is not the result of what one does or does not do, and on the other hand, the tax collector teaches that justification is that act of God in which He extends mercy and grace to repentant sinners who come to Him in faith. Specifically, that faith is the belief that God has done everything necessary to accept such an individual. The prayer "Have mercy on me, a sinner" reveals that kind of humble faith. Humility allows God to exalt the individual, while pride must be disciplined. Even the disciples were guilty of falling into a judgmental spirit, as seen in their attitude toward children. Jesus used this occasion to reaffirm the point that simple childlike faith is all that is necessary to enter the kingdom of heaven.

Inheriting eternal life (18:18–30). This account of a wealthy religious ruler is an example of the self-justification exposed in the previous parable. Jesus stated that goodness is a quality only God possesses in its fullness. A person can be accepted by God only because of what God does in and for him. Jesus referred to five of the Ten Commandments to show that even this religious leader had not fully kept what he thought would be the grounds of his own justification, namely, the Law! Jesus taught that following Him would result in eternal life, and benevolence would be rewarded in heaven.

Riches tend to make a person independent, and self-sufficiency based on one's wealth makes it difficult for a person to sense the need for salvation. The camel was the largest animal of that culture, while the eye of a sewing needle was an unusually small opening. What is "impossible with men" but "possible with God" is the creation of life. Three times the Bible uses this statement about the impossible/possible: referring to the birth of Isaac to Abraham and Sarah (Gen. 18:14), the birth of Jesus through the Virgin Mary (Luke 1:37), and the salvation of sinners (18:27). All three were miraculous provisions by God that were impossible for any human to do on his or her own. When Peter affirmed that the disciples had committed everything to Him in the manner He had asked for from the ruler, Jesus announced there would be rewards both on earth and in heaven for any who make sacrifices for Him.

Jesus' prediction of His death (18:31–34). This passage records Jesus' third prediction of His death and resurrection (see 9:22, 44). Jesus said His Passion was in fulfillment of the Old Testament Scriptures. The Gentiles are here shown to be culpable for the death of Christ, along with the Jews. For His sovereign purposes God did not allow the disciples to grasp fully what would happen to Jesus. Had they fully understood, perhaps they would have forsaken Him or would have vigorously tried to prevent His death.

Jesus' healing of the blind man (18:35–43). Luke recorded that Jesus performed this miracle as He was "approaching" Jericho, but Matthew and Mark said that Jesus was leaving Jericho. The most plausible explanation is that both are true: Jesus was leaving the Old Testament location of Jericho and was approaching the Herodian New Testament site of Jericho, which was about a mile south of the original site. Matthew mentioned two men, while Mark and Luke focused on one whom Mark said was Bartimeaus. Only Luke mentioned the praise of both the man and the crowds in reaction to the miracle of his restored sight (18:43). The blind man identified Jesus as the Son of David and the Lord (18:39, 41). This man's healing was attributed to his faith, and his following after Jesus modeled the right response of those who are delivered by Him.

The salvation of Zacchaeus (19:1–10). The phrase "chief tax collector" is unique here, as it is not found in any other ancient Greek literature. Zacchaeus may have been involved in the Roman system of taxation that had been corrupted in provinces such as Judea. Even today there are large sycamore-fig trees in Jericho—the kind Zacchaeus would have climbed in order to get a better view of Jesus. Like the blind man (18:39, 41), Zacchaeus too recognized that Jesus is the Lord (19:8).

This account describes how a sinner becomes a son. Zacchaeus behaved as one with a heart touched by God. His faith was demonstrated in his repentance and his restitution of funds according to the Law, which demanded repayment plus 20 percent (Lev. 6:5; Num. 5:7). Righteous obedience is an evidence of saving faith. Jesus called him "a son of Abraham" to affirm that, like Abraham, Zacchaeus was a man of faith. Luke 19:10 fittingly states the theme of the Book of Luke: "For the Son of Man came to seek and to save what was lost." This account of the salvation of wealthy Zacchaeus shows that, as Jesus said to the wealthy ruler, it *is* possible with God for a rich man to be saved.

Jesus' parable of the minas (19:11–27). Jesus related this parable because the people thought the kingdom would come immediately. What the parable portrayed has been fulfilled. Jesus went away and has promised to return at some unknown point in the future. Jesus also wanted His disciples to know that whatever rejection or violence would happen in Jerusalem would not mean the kingdom would not come.

The parable has historical background in an incident in 4 B.C. when, on Herod's death, his son Archelaus went to Rome to ask for the privilege of reigning in Judea. A group of Jews went to Rome where they and others appealed to Caesar not to allow Archelaus to be appointed. But Archelaus was made governor over Judea, and when he returned home

Rewards and punishment will be proportionately distributed when the Lord returns from heaven.

from Rome he put down the resistance in Jerusalem in order to confirm his right to rule.

Jesus has made His followers responsible for proclaiming the kingdom. In contrast to unequal entrustments in the parable of the talents (Matt. 25:1–14), here each was entrusted with the same amount. A mina is roughly equivalent to three months' wages. The citizens who rejected the delegation (Luke 19:14) were of the nobleman's country and therefore they illustrate Jesus' very own people rejecting Him. Rewards for faithful stewardship take the form of rulership over cities in the kingdom (19:17–18). Rewards will be given in proportion to one's faithfulness. The third man's wicked criticism of the master and his lack of faithfulness illustrate the lack of faith. The more blatant the rejection, the more severe will be the punishment. Withdrawing privileged responsibilities and reassigning them were meant by Jesus to be a warning against the Jewish leaders.

V. JESUS' ENTRANCE INTO JERUSALEM (19:28–21:38)

A. Jesus' Triumphal Entry and Cleansing of the Temple (19:28–48)

The entrance into Jerusalem (19:28–44). Jesus approached Jerusalem by coming across the Mount of Olives through a small town known as Bethphage, which means "the house of unripe figs." This is the first time Jesus directly called Himself "Lord." His entry into Jerusalem on a colt, which Matthew identified as a donkey (Matt. 21:2), fulfilled Zechariah 9:9, which predicted the humble entrance of the King into Jerusalem. Laying clothes on the road was an ancient way of welcoming royalty (see 2 Kings 9:13). Of the four Gospel writers, only Luke mentioned the attempt of the Pharisees to quiet the praise of the crowd.

Psalm 118:26, which the crowd shouted in welcoming Jesus into Jerusalem, was sung every year at Passover as one of the "psalms of ascent" the people sang as they climbed the hills to Jerusalem. Most of the people probably spoke more than they knew, for the Messiah was actually present on this particular year. "Peace in heaven and glory in the highest!" is Luke's rendition of the Hosanna praise (see Matt. 21:9). These themes would recall for the reader of Luke the angelic announcements at night to the shepherds (Luke 2:8–14).

Jesus' grief over the city shows that He really did want the city of Jerusalem (and therefore the nation as a whole) to respond positively to His ministry. The offer of Himself and the kingdom was a legitimate offer, and the nation was held responsible for rejecting it. Jesus assumed they should have known about the day that would bring them peace. But because they failed to recognize the day God visited them through Jesus, they would be judicially blinded (19:42), and their people killed and buildings destroyed. The immediate fulfillment of these words took place with the Romans' destruction of Jerusalem in A.D. 70.

The cleansing of the temple (19:45–48). Jesus quoted from Isaiah 56:7 and Jeremiah 7:11 to show His identification with His Father and the zeal He shared for the true purpose of the temple as a place for prayer. Sacrificial animals and money changing had become a dishonest trade. What was wrongful business in the temple at the beginning of Jesus' ministry (John 2:14–16) had now become even worse—robbery (Luke 19:46). The ritual practices associated with the temple had degenerated during Jesus' life and showed no signs of reversal. One prime example was the leaders' desire to kill Jesus.

B. Jesus' Confrontations with Israel's Leaders (20:1–21:4)

The question of authority (20:1–8). The Sanhedrin was composed of members from the three groups mentioned here: chief priests, teachers of the Law, and elders. The Sanhedrin, with its seventy members, was chaired by the chief priest. As the highest governing body of the land, the Sanhedrin members questioned Jesus about the source of His authority. In His response He answered their question with a question of His own about the authority of John the Baptist. If they showed disrespect for John, they would have found themselves at odds with the people. But if they sided with John, Jesus would ask why they had rejected his announcement that He was the Messiah and that they needed to repent. Trapped, they refused to answer, showing that they were not willing to submit to divine authority even when they themselves recognized it.

> *Unbelief blinds people even to the rebellion in their own hearts.*

Jesus' parable of the wicked tenants (20:9–19). This parable recalls the words of Isaiah in Isaiah 5:1–7, in which a vineyard represents Israel. The rebellion of the tenants in the parable portrays the rebellion of Israel's leaders. They continually rejected the messengers, a reference to the prophets sent by God. The son of the landowner represents Jesus. The Jewish leaders rejected Him because of their desire to control what rightly belongs to Christ in His kingdom, the position of rulership. Luke took note of Jesus' direct look at the people when He quoted Psalm 118:22 to explain that their rejection of Him was like builders tossing aside an unwanted stone. The "stone" (Christ) the builders rejected became the "capstone" or cornerstone of a new building (the church). Those who reject Christ will find themselves judged by Him (Luke 20:18). Even though the leaders knew this parable described them, they continued to plan to arrest Him.

Challenges by the Jewish leaders (20:19–21:4). Matthew's account of the Pharisees who tested Jesus about which command of the Mosaic Law is most significant was not viewed as important for Luke's gentile audience. But the Jewish leaders (along with the Herodians, Matt. 22:16) tried to trap Jesus with reference to tribute money (Luke 20:19–26). They attempted to force Him to choose between Israel and Rome over the issue of the hated poll tax that Rome had imposed on the resentful Jews. By asking for a coin, Jesus showed them they used Caesar's coinage themselves. The silver denarius bore the image of Caesar's head on one side and the goddess of peace on the other. Jesus silenced the Herodians by affirming that they owed allegiance to both government and God.

Then the Sadducees sought to trap Jesus in reference to the doctrine of the resurrection (20:27–40). They were a fairly conservative sect, basing their theology on the Pentateuch, the first five books of Moses. They denied the resurrection and the existence of angels (Acts 23:8). Their question was therefore less than genuine when they asked about a woman who had seven husbands, all of whom died. The levirate marriage laws required the brother of the deceased to marry the widow (Gen. 38:8; Deut. 25:5–6). What would life after death mean for a woman with her history? Jesus exposed their ignorance of even their own Scriptures by pointing out that our heavenly existence will be different from our earthly relationships. He then stated that since God is the God of the patriarchs, this suggests that Old Testament leaders who died have an ongoing relationship with Him centuries after their physical death. The fact that He is the Lord "of the living" points to the reality of the resurrection.

> *Christ has ordained that His people obey both their earthly leaders and God, their divine leader.*

In Luke 20:41–44 the Lord challenged the leaders about the identity and nature of the Messiah from Psalm 110:1. If the Messiah was to be the Son of David, how could David call Him his Lord? The implication is that the Messiah must be more than simply a physical son of David; He must also be the Son of God. Jesus left the leaders with a question that challenged them to think about His identity.

The Lord further challenged the leaders about their self-righteous pride (Luke 20:45–21:4). Jesus warned the disciples about the pompous attitudes and practices of the scribes, who will be punished with severity for their hypocrisy. By contrasting the sacrifice with which a poor widow contributed to the temple treasury with that of the rich, Jesus taught that one's heart is more important than the amount one gives.

C. Jesus' Olivet Discourse (21:5–38)

When Jesus told His disciples Jerusalem would be destroyed, they responded by asking when this and related events would occur. In His answers Jesus outlined the Tribulation and events that would precede and follow it. This Olivet Discourse (see Matt. 24:3) was given to challenge the disciples (and those who would later respond to Jesus) to be prepared for His return and how they are to live in the meantime. Jesus noted that in the Tribulation, there will be false Christs, catastrophic climactic events, and international conflicts, all of which will happen before the Lord returns to the earth (Luke 21:8–11).

He warned the disciples that they would suffer persecution before the tribulational events would take place (21:12–19). These events have parallels throughout the Book of Acts and may be typical of persecutions against Christians in the present age. Suffering—including persecution by both religious and civil authorities—will be a platform for personal witness empowered by the Lord. Perseverance under trial will be rewarded; and if some are martyred, resurrection will deliver even them.

The fall of Jerusalem at the hands of the Gentiles in Jesus' day foreshadowed a more distant destruction of the city that will immediately precede the coming of the Lord (21:20–24). These two destructions are set as "bookends" around the present church age. "The times of the Gentiles" refers to the time when the Gentiles are in a position to control the city and temple site of Jerusalem (compare "the fullness of the Gentiles" in Rom. 11:25). "The times of the Gentiles" began with the Babylonian Captivity and will end when the millennial kingdom is established on earth by the Messiah at His second advent.

The second coming of Christ to the earth will take place after the Tribulation (Luke 21:25–28). His return will be accompanied by miraculous signs in the sky. These cosmic events of judgment were predicted by the prophets (see, for example, Joel 2:30–32) and will help prepare the world for the coming of the Lord. His return will be visible to all, and He will come in power and glory (Luke 21:27). When these series of signs take place, the redemption of the nation of Israel and the deliverance of all the righteous will take place.

Jesus spoke of these events to encourage His hearers to be spiritually prepared (21:29–38). His parable of the fig tree taught that the signs of judgment would alert people to His impending return. Fig trees bud in the early spring in Israel and bear fully developed figs in the summer. This means that when the events of the Tribulation occur, the earthly phase of the messianic kingdom will be next (21:31). When Jesus spoke of "this generation," He was referring to the generation of people who will witness the judgments of the Tribulation and the cosmic signs preceding the coming of Christ. They will see fulfilled in their lifetime the messianic expectation of the return of Jesus and the establishment of the earthly kingdom. Jesus' prophecies are even more certain than the heavens and the earth (21:33).

Jesus stressed the need to be watchful, because, though the time of His return is unknown, the event is certain. Jesus' habit of teaching in the temple during the day and returning to the Mount of Olives to stay there overnight was noted by Luke (21:37–38). Perhaps the crowds camped on the slopes of Mount Olivet while visiting Jerusalem for the Feast of Passover and Unleavened Bread.

VI. THE PASSION NARRATIVE (CHAPTERS 22–24)

A. The Celebration of the Passover Meal (22:1–38)

The approach of the Passover (22:1–7). The Passover was the most sacred of the Jewish festivals since it celebrated the release from Egypt. Matthew and Mark both wrote about Jesus' and His disciples' preparations for the Passover (Matt. 26:17–19; Mark 14:12–16). Luke, however, told of the plots of the leaders to kill Him and of Judas to betray Him. Behind these actions was the sinister activity of Satan himself (John 13:2, 27).

The celebration of the Passover meal (22:7–38). The Feast of Passover and Unleavened Bread was originally two separate festivals, but they were joined into one grand festival. The Passover was celebrated on Nisan 14 and 15 (March–April). During the afternoon of Nisan 14, lambs were slaughtered at the temple. The Feast of Unleavened Bread was then celebrated from Nisan 15 to 21. In Luke 22:7, Nisan 14 is referred to as the first day of Unleavened Bread, probably because both feasts ran together and were viewed as one. Luke and Mark both wrote that Jesus celebrated the feast at the appropriate time.

The room for the Passover meal was prepared according to the Lord's instructions. This last Passover of Jesus became the first celebration of the Lord's Supper. The entire meal was linked to Jesus' coming death (22:15) and was eaten in anticipation of the messianic banquet to be enjoyed in the coming kingdom (22:16, 18). The bread was the metaphor for the body of Jesus and the cup symbolized His blood. Recognizing

> *Spiritual failure can happen in the lives of even the most mature followers.*

God's sovereign plan, Jesus pronounced judgment ("woe") on the one who would betray Him. Evidently Jesus gave two predictions of the betrayal. Mark 14:18 records that He made the announcement before the meal, and Luke wrote that it was given after the meal (Luke 22:21–22).

While the Son of man was humbly preparing to give Himself in death to institute the New Covenant (Jer. 31:31–34), the disciples were arguing over positions of greatness. Jesus rebuked their jockeying for positions as worldly. He taught that serving is the hallmark of greatness, service that He Himself modeled. To those who are faithful in following Him He promised the kingdom, and to the Twelve He promised thrones in the kingdom when they will reign with Him over Israel. Here is an indication that Israel will be an identifiable national entity in the kingdom of Christ on earth.

Peter's denials were anticipated by the Lord when He announced Satan's desire to "sift" him (Luke 22:31–34). Wheat was sifted to remove the chaff and the dirt. In spite of Peter's promises to be faithful to the Lord, Jesus predicted he would deny Him three times before the cock would crow. The instructions to buy a sword may have been misunderstood as suggesting preparation for physical conflict as opposed to spiritual warfare. The phrase "that is enough" (22:38) may have been a rebuke for the disciples' failure to understand. If Jesus was referring in verse 36 to a literal sword, it was to prepare for the Garden experience in which one sword would be enough for Jesus' purposes.

B. The Agony and Arrest in the Garden of Gethsemane (22:39–53)

The "last Adam" faced temptation in a garden and rejected it, whereas the "first Adam" faced temptation in a garden and failed. Jesus submitted to the will of His Father even knowing it would cost Him His life. The cup was a symbol of suffering (Isa. 51:22). Only Luke mentioned that an angel appeared to minister to Jesus, and only Luke mentioned that Jesus' sweat was like drops of blood. The latter indicated how extreme the emotional and spiritual suffering actually was for the Savior. Since the place where Jesus was praying was where He often went, Judas knew where to lead the mob who would arrest Jesus (Luke 22:40). Jesus initiated His own betrayal (22:48). When Peter cut off the right ear of Malchus, the high priest's servant (John 18:10), Jesus squelched that violent resistance and healed the man's ear. Jesus called the sequence of events initiated by His arrest "your hour and power of darkness" (literal translation).

C. The Trials of Jesus (22:54–23:25)

In the religious trials Jesus was charged with blasphemy (22:54–71). The denials of Peter (22:54–65), beatings by the soldiers (22:63–65), and His appearance before the Sanhedrin (22:66–71) marked this trial. Caiaphas was the legally appointed high priest, but his father-in-law, Annas, was also consulted on larger affairs in the territory. That explains why Matthew mentioned that Jesus was taken to Caiaphas's house (Matt. 26:57) and why John mentioned Annas's house (John 18:13).

Roosters crowed at about three o'clock in the morning. Peter denied the Lord three times just as Jesus had predicted, and His look at Peter was all that was needed to remind the apostle how serious were his actions. The soldiers' physical mistreatment of Jesus at the instigation of the Sanhedrin was illegal, unjust, and cruel. And according to Jewish regulations the Sanhedrin could not convene at night.

The religious judges could rule in both civil and religious issues, but the death penalty could be carried out only by Rome. The Sanhedrin questioned Jesus as to whether He is the Messiah and the Son of God (Luke 22:67, 70). In response to the question about His messiahship (22:66–71), Jesus affirmed His deity (22:69–71). He said He is the Son of man, who would sit in the place of honor at God's right hand. Here is a prediction of Jesus' ascension and an affirmation of His lordship.

In the civil trials Jesus was accused of treason (23:1–25). Jesus appeared before Pilate (23:1–5), Herod (23:6–12), and then Pilate again (23:13–25). The force of the Greek construction in verse 3 shows that Pilate was astonished at Jesus' claim to be the King of the Jews. Jesus affirmed the claim as phrased. Three times Pilate affirmed Jesus' innocence

(23:4, 14, 22). This underscores the sinless sacrifice of the Son of Man, a key theme in the Book of Luke. Pilate normally resided in the administrative capital of Rome at Caesarea, but he visited Jerusalem at Passover, as was also the custom of Herod.

Pilate sent Jesus across the city to Herod (23:6–12), who was fascinated by Jesus and hoped He would perform a miracle in front of him. To such insolence Jesus remained silent as if to rebuke the very spirit of the inquiry. Having mocked Him with a royal robe, Herod sent Jesus back to Pilate (23:13–25). Pilate proved weak, being threatened by the people who demanded the death of Jesus. They warned that Pilate would be disloyal to Rome if he did not sentence Jesus to death. Barabbas was an insurrectionist and murderer whom the people wanted released. The scourging (23:22) normally preceded crucifixion (see Mark 15:15).

Though absolutely innocent, Jesus died for the absolutely guilty.

D. The Crucifixion and Burial of Jesus (23:26–56)

The crucifixion of Jesus (23:26–49). Forcing a person to carry his own cross was the Roman way of showing that the criminal was being forced to submit to their authority. Ironically Jesus had to show no such submission since He would lay down His life by His own authority (John 10:15). Luke's concern for women is again seen by his noting the presence of the wailing women. Jesus countered with a wail for Jerusalem and a warning of future remorse (Luke 23:27–31). Two criminals were crucified on either side of Jesus at the site known as Golgotha, "the Place of the Skull." This name was probably taken from the fact that this was the place where people were killed in public execution rather than from the skull-like appearance on the side of the hill on which He was crucified.

Jesus' first recorded words on the cross were a prayer of forgiveness for those who were His executioners (23:34). The first three hours on the cross were in daylight while Jesus suffered at the hands of men. During this time Jesus suffered the mocking of the crowds while He continued to minister to the outcasts at His sides. One criminal responded positively and one rejected His message; such was the tenor of His whole life. The last three hours were spent in a supernatural darkness, in which Jesus suffered at the hands of God.

The supernatural activities during his last three hours on the cross signaled God's work on earth to provide salvation through the Savior. The torn veil signaled the access to God which would be available because of the death of Christ. Jesus surrendered His spirit to the Father in the words of Psalm 31:5. The centurion at the foot of the cross may have confessed more than he realized when he said Jesus is a righteous man. Here, as throughout Luke's version of the Passion, the innocence of Jesus is highlighted.

The burial of Jesus (23:50–56). Bodies of crucifixion victims were usually buried in mass graves. However, recent archeological finds have yielded evidence of some private burials of crucified individuals. After Joseph of Arimathea wrapped Jesus' body, he buried Him in his own tomb, which had yet not been used by any members of his family. The day of Jesus' crucifixion and burial was Friday, the day of preparation before the Sabbath. The women from Galilee followed to see the burial and then waited to come back until after the Sabbath to anoint the body with burial spices and perfumes.

E. The Resurrection and Commissioning of Jesus (chapter 24)

The Resurrection (24:1–12). When the women returned to anoint the body, they were gently rebuked by the angels for expecting the One who had prophesied of His own resurrection to still be in the tomb (9:22; 18:33). Luke's naming of the women lends credibility to the account. All the Gospel accounts agree that the tomb was empty on Sunday morning. Luke mentioned two angels, while Matthew and Mark mentioned only one, probably the one who did the speaking (Matt. 28:2–6; Mark 16:5). The disciples did not believe the women, and so Peter went to the tomb to investigate for himself.

The walk to Emmaus (24:13–35). The report of this incident is not included in the other three Gospels. Emmaus, seven miles north of Jerusalem, is usually identified with the site of el-Qubeibeh. On their walk the two men were prevented from recognizing Jesus. Their questions showed they thought Jesus was a prophet from Nazareth who through word and deed was authenticated by God. They hoped Jesus would be the Redeemer of Israel. Jesus rebuked the men for not having believed the prophets. They should have known that His suffering was necessary before the kingdom could be established. Jesus surveyed the Old Testament to help them understand how it spoke of Him. "Moses and all the Prophets" (24:27) was one way to speak of the entire Old Testament. The two asked Jesus to stay with them for the night. When they finally recognized Jesus at the meal that evening, He disappeared from them. The burning of their hearts during His exposition to them on the road may have come from the convicting work of the Spirit. They immediately went to confirm to the eleven disciples that Jesus had risen from the dead (24:33–35).

Jesus' appearance to the Eleven (24:36–53). Jesus showed the disciples His physical body to prove that He had been bodily resurrected. He also ate with them to prove His body was fully functional.

In His commission He challenged His disciples to preach the message of forgiveness to the gentile world (see Isa. 2:3; 42:6; 49:6; 51:4–5). The basics of the gospel message along with the need for the world to repent are to be the core emphases of their (and our) ministry. The city where He died and arose was the launching pad for the worldwide ministry Luke chronicled in the Book of Acts. The power of the Spirit was promised to those who had witnessed the resurrection. At the beginning of his Gospel, Luke recorded events that occurred earlier than events with which Matthew, Mark, and John began, and here he extended his record all the way to the Ascension (24:50–52).

JOHN

Jesus, the Wonderful Word of Life

AUTHOR

Five men with the name John are mentioned in the New Testament. John the Baptist (John 1:6; 15, 19, 26, 29) was not the author of the fourth Gospel because he was beheaded by Herod long before the events of this Gospel were completed (Mark 6:24–29). John, the father of Peter (John 1:42), is not mentioned in any connection that might suggest he was the author. John Mark (Acts 12:12), was the author of the second Gospel, and the fact that the Gospel of John must have been written by an eyewitness eliminates John Mark as a possibility. John of the Sanhedrin (Acts 4:5–6) is an unlikely candidate because he was an enemy of Christianity. Although his claim is disputed by many critics, John, one of Jesus' twelve disciples, is the most likely candidate for the author of the Gospel of John. John's father was Zebedee, and his brother was James. All three were Galilean fishermen (Matt. 4:21). John referred to himself as "the disciple whom Jesus loved" (John 13:23; 19:26; 21:20).

Although the book does not name the writer, he was a close companion of Peter. The author's use of the Old Testament suggests that he was a Jew (12:14–15, 38, 40; 13:18; 15:25; 19:24, 36–37). And the details he gave about Jesus' life give evidence of his being an eyewitness of the Lord. The author's statement "we have seen his glory" (1:14) must have been the report of one who was at the Transfiguration.

The apostle John also wrote 1, 2, and 3 John and Revelation.

DATE

The discovery in Egypt of fragments of the Gospel of John dating from the early part of the second century A.D. means that the book must have been written in the first century. According to Christian tradition John spent the latter years of his life at Ephesus, where he carried on a ministry of preaching and teaching, as well as writing. He was exiled to the island of Patmos (Rev. 1:9) when Domitian was emperor of the Roman Empire. John's account of the life of Christ seems to presuppose a knowledge of the Synoptic Gospels, and that suggests that John's account was written after the other three Gospels were written. Irenaeus said John wrote the Gospel from Ephesus sometime when he was residing there in the years A.D. 70–98. Most likely, the book was written A.D. 85–90. This would have been long after Peter and Paul's deaths and the destruction of Jerusalem.

HISTORICAL BACKGROUND

The book was probably written in Ephesus, although no mention is made of this in the Gospel. If John went to Ephesus around A.D. 70, then he would have been ministering there for about fifteen or twenty years before he wrote this Gospel. Perhaps some elders of the churches in and around Ephesus asked John to write down the things he had been teaching before he died. With the evidence of the Synoptic Gospels and as one who was an apostle of Jesus, no one was more qualified to present a record of Jesus Christ's ministry as the Son of God.

PURPOSE

In John 20:30–31, John stated that his purpose for writing was to confirm that Jesus is the Christ (the Messiah) and the Son of God and to assure those who believe that they have life in His name. Also he wrote to oppose the false teachings of Docetism, which denied that Jesus had a real physical body, and the teachings of incipient Gnosticism, which believed that material things, which are evil, are in eternal conflict with good, and that God can be known by a select few people through mystical experiences.

CHARACTERISTICS

Several features of the Gospel of John may be noted.

First, this Gospel is both simple and profound in its presentation of Jesus Christ. It is amazingly clear and attractive to the beginning student and awesomely deep to the seasoned scholar.

Second, the Father-Son relationship pervades the book in which the self-revelation of the Son is presented as the reflection of the Father.

Third, the style and vocabulary of the book is simple and generally uncomplicated.

Fourth, the book highlights several of Jesus' personal interviews with others.

Fifth, the book emphasizes future judgment and eternal life.

Sixth, a prominent feature of the Gospel is the editorial comments of the author. Twenty-two such comments are included. Among them is the national blindness of Israel as the major cause and result of their rejection of the Messiah.

Seventh, the prologue (1:1–18) of John is unique. Here Christ's relation to God and to eternity is noted, whereas the Synoptics begin with facts about His genealogy and birth and the ministry of John the Baptist.

Eighth, John recorded seven of Jesus' pre-Cross miracles, seven of Jesus' "I am" statements, and seven witnesses to Jesus, but no parables.

Three Series of Sevens in the Gospel of John

Seven Signs	Seven "I Ams"	Seven Witnesses
1. Water to wine (2:1–11)	1. The Bread of Life (6:35)	1. John the Baptist (1:34)
2. Official's son (4:46–54)	2. The Light of the World (8:12)	2. Nathaniel (1:49)
3. Lame man (5:1–18)	3. The Gate for the Sheep (10:7)	3. Peter (6:69)
4. Feeding the five thousand (6:5–14)	4. The Good Shepherd (10:11,14)	4. Jesus (10:36)
5. Walking on water (6:16–32)	5. The Resurrection and the Life (11:25)	5. Martha (11:27)

Seven Signs	Seven "I Ams"	Seven Witnesses
6. Blind man (9:1–7)	6. The Way, the Truth, the Life (14:6)	6. Thomas (20:28)
7. Raising Lazarus (11:1–45)	7. The True Vine (15:1)	7. John (21:31)

OUTLINE

I. The Prologue (1:1–18)
  A. His Essence as the Word (1:1–5)
  B. His Expression to the World (1:6–13)
  C. His Exposition as the Word (1:14–18)
II. The Presentations of the Son of God to Israel (1:19–12:50)
  A. The Private Presentations (1:19–2:11)
  B. The Public Presentations in Israel's Region (2:12–4:54)
  C. The Public Presentations at Israel's Feasts (chapters 5–12)
III. The Upper Room Discourse (chapters 13–17)
  A. The Discussion around the Table (13:1–30)
  B. The Discourse after Dinner (13:31–16:33)
  C. The High Priestly Prayer of Christ (chapter 17)
IV. The Redemption of the Son of God through Death and Resurrection (chapters 18–20)
  A. The Death of the Son of God (chapters 18–19)
  B. The Resurrection of Christ (chapter 20)
V. The Epilogue (chapter 21)
  A. The Miraculous Catch of Fish (21:1–14)
  B. The Restoration of Peter (21:15–25)

I. THE PROLOGUE (1:1–18)

A. His Essence as the Word (1:1–5)

In relationship to God (1:1–2). These opening lines give a strong affirmation of the deity of Christ. The *Word* (Greek, *logos*) speaks of the personal revelation of the Father through His Son, Jesus Christ. While this word occurs in the Gospel of John only here and in 1:14, the term sets the tone for the entire book. Before taking on human flesh, the Word (Jesus Christ) existed before the universe was created. Whenever the beginning was, the Word already existed. The Word existed as a distinct personality from the Father, but on a par in relationship to the Father. In essence, the Word, Jesus Christ, is God. Whatever attributes the Father possesses, the Son also possesses. Some say that the second part of verse 1 should be rendered "the Word was a god" because in Greek the article "the" does not precede the word "God." However, elsewhere in chapter 1 when God the Father is clearly referred to, the word "God" occurs without the article (1:6, 12–13, 18). To have inserted the article in verse 1 would have destroyed the Trinitarian relationship, making the Father the same as the Son. The Son is God, but God is more than just the Son. The Word "was" God, but God was not (only) the Word.

Thus these opening verses speak of the preexistence of the Son with the Father, the equality of Jesus and the Father ("the Word was with God"), and the essential deity of the Son ("the Word was God"), which He shares with the Father.

> Everyone owes even his or her physical existence to Christ, the divine Creator of all.

In relationship to Creation (1:3). Everything that has ever come into being owes its existence to Jesus. He is the personal Agent of God's creation (see also Rom. 11:36; 1 Cor. 8:6; Col. 1:16). The fact that Jesus, the Son of God, made everything may have been a polemic against the gnostic doctrine that all matter is evil.

In relation to humanity (1:4–5). The themes of light and darkness naturally flow from the creation motif. As Creator, Jesus Christ is the Source of all life, and that creative activity tells us something about His person and work. Light invades and eliminates the darkness. The theme of light has a rich background in the Old Testament expectations of the Messiah (Isa. 9:2; 42:6; 60:1–2). The Greek word rendered "understood" could be translated "overtaken": "the darkness has not overtaken" the light. When the Jews put Jesus to death, they tried to put out the light, but they couldn't extinguish it. It still shines in the darkness! Light will always dispel darkness, but darkness can never defeat light.

B. His Expression to the World (1:6–13)

The witness (1:6–8). John the apostle wrote about John the Baptist's origin, nature, purpose, and message. He was a man "sent from God," and his very name means "God is gracious." The desired result of his ministry was that everyone who heard his witness would believe. He was not the light; he was just a lamp to show the way to the light (see also 5:35). His role was to be a witness about Jesus, the real Source of light and life.

The Word (1:9–13). As the Source of light, Jesus is both Creator and Revealer. The revelation He gives can be trusted, because He is the true light. The phrase "coming into the world" may modify "every man," or it may modify "light." Either one may be true. If it modifies "every man," then the meaning is that everyone is illuminated with enough light about God to make them accountable to Him.

Yet the very people who were created by Christ and to whom He revealed Himself did not recognize Him, even when He came into the world. This theme of revelation ties the ideas of light and life together.

Verses 11–13 could be considered the outline of the life of Jesus as presented by John, with three key ideas—revelation, rejection, and reception. While Jesus' own people should have responded positively to His presence and preaching, they didn't. Others, however, did respond in belief. To those He gave the right and privilege of being called the children of God. Being placed into the family of God is spoken of as a new birth. That "birthright" does not come through racial privilege, physical inheritance, or simply because a parent wants his or her child to be in God's family. Only being born by God qualifies a person to be a member of the Father's family. Eternal life always originates with God in heaven.

> *Receiving Jesus by faith qualifies one to be called a child of God.*

C. His Exposition as the Word (1:14–18)

The Incarnation (1:14–15). These two verses highlight both the humanity and the eternality of the Word. The One who was the Word "became" man! The eternal Son entered time and space through the Incarnation.

This dwelling on earth was temporary; He "lived for a while among us [literally, 'made his dwelling among us']." The verb "lived" means to pitch a tent as a temporary dwelling. The revelation of God came in a person. In a physical and visible manner He displayed His own inherent glory, which equals the glory of the Father in that it was "full of grace and truth." This one and only ("uniquely born") Son of God is the personal revelation of God.

> *The message of the Savior is more important than the servant who proclaims it.*

John the Baptist affirmed through his own testimony his three positions in relationship to the Son. Jesus came "after" John in that John's role was to prepare His way. Jesus was "before" John in that He existed eternally before He became flesh. As a result, He "surpassed" John by being superior to him. Therefore Jesus was to be preferred above John.

The revelation (1:16–17). The "fullness" of Jesus is the source from which grace has been made available, as it had never been before. The phrase "one blessing after another" might better be translated "grace upon grace" or "grace exceeded by grace." Verse 17 explains this phrase. The work of Jesus marked the end of an era known as the Law, which differs from what can be called grace and truth. While there is law in New Testament times and grace and truth are revealed in the Old Testament, these two broad-brushed divisions of time are hinged by the work of Christ. What God did in Christ fulfilled His gracious purposes beyond what He revealed through Moses. There is both continuity and contrast between these two periods of God's economies.

The explanation (1:18). Because God is spirit (4:24) He is invisible to humanity. But Jesus Christ reveals God the Father to us. In the Incarnation, Jesus could reveal God to humanity because He is both God and man. The translation "God the only Son" stresses the nature of Jesus as God. The mention of the Father's "side" (or "bosom," NASB) derives from the dinner custom of reclining next to the chest or side of another person. The imagery is one of presence. Jesus was best qualified to explain God to the world because He shares the nature of the Father and came from the Father's presence in heaven to earth to share the message He Himself would embody.

THE PROLOGUE OF JOHN (1:1–18)

1:1	The Word was in the beginning	The Word was with God	The Word was God
1:14	The Word became flesh	We beheld His glory	The glory of the only begotten Son
1:18	No man has seen God at any time	The only begotten God ... in the bosom of Father	He has made Him known

II. THE PRESENTATIONS OF THE SON OF GOD TO ISRAEL (1:19–12:50)

A. The Private Presentations (1:19–2:11)

The clarifications of John's ministry (1:19–34). These verses clarify both the identity and message of John the Baptist. A series of questions by the Jewish leaders prompted him to explain himself and his role with Jesus (1:19–28). In response to questions as to who he was, John stated that He was not the Messiah, Elijah, or the expected prophet who would be greater than Moses. In answering what he would say about himself, John identified himself with the "voice" in the wilderness (Isa. 40:3), heralding the coming of the Lord. Isaiah wrote that this one would introduce the Messiah, who would provide salvation and establish His kingdom (40:3–5). As to why he baptized, John said his baptism in water was preparatory to the ministry of someone greater.

The message of John centered in Jesus as Lamb and Lord (1:29–34). The lamb of the Passover (Exod. 12) may have been the background for the statement by John the Baptist that Jesus is "the Lamb of God." As a lamb (Isa. 53:7), Jesus was sacrificed for the sins of the world (53:12). John 1:31 repeats the truth about John's position as a witness to Jesus (see 1:15). John did not understand that Jesus is the Messiah until God revealed it to him at Jesus' baptism. The One on whom the Spirit would descend was the expected Messiah (Isa. 11:1; 42:1; 61:1). In recognizing that Jesus is both Christ (the Messiah; see John 1:20, 25) and the Son of God (1:34), John the Baptist was affirming the two identities of Christ mentioned in the book's purpose statement in John 20:31.

> *God delights in using people to introduce others to life in Christ.*

The calling of the first disciples (1:35–51). The purpose of John's Gospel is highlighted in this section too. The first group of disciples, Peter and Andrew, understood that Jesus is the Messiah; the second group, Philip and Nathaniel, confirmed that He is the Son of God. Two of these four came to Jesus by a direct summons and two came through the witness of another. The latter is the more normative means by which people come to Christ.

The "next day" (1:43) is the second in a sequence of days mentioned four times in the first few verses of John's Gospel (1:29, 35, 43; 2:1). John the Baptist had the unique privilege of introducing the first two disciples to Jesus. Their following Jesus (1:38, 40, 43) probably refers to both their literal travel as well as their spiritual journey of faith in Christ. Andrew was instrumental in bringing Simon Peter. In two other references to Andrew, he was leading someone to the Lord (6:4–9; 12:20–22). And Philip called Nathanael. Thus the witness theme continued.

Besides recording the faith of the first disciples, the apostle John identified key titles that were used of Christ: Rabbi, Messiah, Jesus of Nazareth, son of Joseph, Son of God, King of Israel, and Son of man. (The last of these was the title Jesus most often used of Himself.)

Nathanael's question as to whether anything good can come out of Nazareth (1:46) reflected the proverbial humiliation that village suffered. Nazareth was the site of a Roman outpost and was located up on a ridge, removed from the major transportation route in the Esdraelon Valley.

Jesus' reference to angels "ascending and descending on the Son of Man" called to mind the story of Jacob's dream of the ladder (Gen. 28). Just as angels communicated with earth in Israel's dream, so Christ is God's Communication from heaven to earth.

Turning the water into wine (2:1–11). This is the first of seven miracles recorded in John 2–12. John called most of these "signs," a word that means the miracles had significant theological meaning. Cana was most probably located at the site of present-day Khirbet Kana ("ruin of Cana"), nine miles north of Nazareth on a hill overlooking the Bet Netufa Valley.

This miracle reveals a number of key truths important to the argument of the book. When Jesus' mother asked Him to help with the problem of the wedding party having run out of wine, He asserted His authority by the "modestly distancing" question, "Dear woman, why do you involve me?" The claim that His time ("hour") had not yet come was the first of several references to the time of His Passion (7:6, 8, 30; 8:30; 12:23, 27 [twice]; 13:1; 17:1). He was in total control of His own schedule of self-revelation. Not even His mother could rush Him.

By commanding a new use for the purification water from the stone jars used in Jewish ritual traditions, Jesus was claiming to be superior to those traditions. The miracle fits with Jesus' presentation of the kingdom since wine in the millennial kingdom will be abundant (Isa. 25:6; 27:2–6; Jer. 31:12; Hos. 2:22; Joel 2:24; 3:18; Amos 9:13–14). (The facts that the prologue emphasized Jesus' role as Creator [1:3]) and that at Cana he created wine with built-in age may possibly suggest that God would have created the earth with the appearance of age.) Thus the glory of Jesus as the Creator of life and as the One who can bring in the kingdom was displayed. This miracle, as with all His miracles, revealed Jesus' glory as the Son sent into the world to provide salvation for the world.

Faith in Christ is the correct response to the revelation of the glory of the Lord.

The Miracles of Christ

Miracle	Place	Matthew	Mark	Luke	John
1. Turning water into wine	Cana				2:1–11
2. Healing an official's son	Capernaum				4:46–54
3. Delivering a demoniac in the synagogue	Capernaum		1:21–28	4:33–37	
4. Healing Peter's mother-in-law	Capernaum	8:14–15	1:29–31	4:38–39	
5. First miraculous catch of fish	Sea of Galilee			5:1–11	
6. Cleansing a leper	Galilee	8:2–4	1:40–45	5:12–15	
7. Healing a paralytic	Capernaum	9:1–8	2:1–12	5:17–26	
8. Healing a man at Bethesda	Jerusalem				5:1–15

Miracle	Place	Matthew	Mark	Luke	John
9. Healing a withered hand	Galilee	12:9–13	3:1–5	6:6–11	
10. Healing a centurion's servant	Capernaum	8:5–13		7:1–10	
11. Raising a widow's son	Nain			7:11–17	
12. Casting out a blind and mute spirit	Galilee	12:22–32		11:14–26	
13. Stilling the storm	Sea of Galilee	8:23–27	4:35–41	8:22–25	
14. Delivering a demoniac from Gadara	Gadara	8:28–34	5:1–20	8:26–39	
15. Healing a woman with issue of blood	Capernaum	9:20–22	5:25–34	8:43–48	
16. Raising Jairus's daughter	Capernaum	9:18–26	5:22–43	8:41–56	
17. Healing the two blind men	Capernaum	9:27–31			
18. Casting out a dumb spirit	Capernaum	9:32–34			
19. Feeding the five thousand	Bethsaida	14:13–21	6:32–44	9:10–17	6:1–14
20. Jesus walking on the water	Sea of Galilee	14:22–33	6:45–52		6:15–21
21. Exorcising the Syro-phoenician daughter	Phoenicia	15:21–28	7:24–30		
22. Healing a deaf and dumb man	Decapolis		7:31–37		
23. Feeding the four thousand	Decapolis	15:29–38	8:1–9		
24. Healing the blind man at Bethsaida	Bethsaida		8:22–26		
25. Casting a demon out of a lunatic boy	Mount Hermon	17:14–21	9:14–29	9:37–42	
26. The coin in the fish's mouth	Capernaum	17:24–27			
27. Healing the man born blind	Jerusalem				9:1–41
28. Healing a woman crippled for eighteen years	Perea (?)			13:10–17	
29. Healing a man with dropsy	Perea			14:1–6	
30. Raising Lazarus	Bethany				11:1–46
31. Cleansing ten lepers	Samaria			17:11–19	
32. Healing blind Bartimaeus	Jericho	20:29–43	10:46–52	18:35–43	
33. Cursing the fig tree	Jerusalem	21:18–19	11:12–26		
34. Healing Malchus's ear	Jerusalem			22:49–51	
35. Second miraculous catch of fish	Sea of Galilee				21:1–12

B. The Public Presentations in Israel's Region (2:12–4:54)

The cleansing of the temple (2:12–25). After Jesus was rejected in Nazareth (Luke 4:28–30), He centered His ministry in Capernaum. From there He journeyed to Jerusalem for the Feast of Passover. In distinction from the Synoptics, John's record focuses mostly on events in Jesus' life that took place in Jerusalem, and especially at the Passover feasts. Three Passover feasts are mentioned in 6:4; 11:55; 12:1; 13:1; 18:28, 39; and 19:14. (Some scholars believe the feast in 5:1 was also a Passover.) In the last week of His life Jesus cleansed the temple (Matt. 21:12–13; Mark 11:15–17; Luke 19:45–46), but this temple cleansing in John 2:13–17 was at the very beginning of His ministry.

This fulfilled Malachi's prophecy that the Messiah would come suddenly to His temple (Mal. 3:1). Claiming that God is His Father, Jesus said the merchants were abusing the purpose of the temple. Ridding all the merchants from the temple may also have raised messianic expectations, in light of the promise of such cleansing in Zechariah 14:21. In John 2:17 the disciples recalled Psalm 69:9, but Jesus surpassed the psalmist's words since the zeal of Jesus cost Him his life. When Jesus said, "Destroy this temple, and I will raise it up again in three days," the Greek word for "temple" refers to the inner sanctuary of the temple where God was said to dwell, a reference here to Jesus' own body.

The Jews' demand that Jesus perform a miracle to prove His authority was answered with Jesus' promise of His death and resurrection. That series of events became the core of the gospel message (1 Cor. 15:1–4) and the evidence that Jesus is the Son of God (Rom. 1:4). Not until after the Resurrection, however, did the disciples firmly believe (John 2:22). Herod began the refurbishing and enlarging of the temple in 19 B.C., and the Romans finished it in A.D. 64.

The miracles Jesus performed in Jerusalem prompted what could be called a "circumstantial faith." They believed because of the signs and not because of explicit faith in Him and His message. Jesus was not entrusting Himself to them because He could see there was something lacking in their hearts (2:24). This insincere faith is also exposed in chapters 4, 6, and 8. John 2:25 presents a subtle argument for Jesus' deity since He has independent, omniscient insight into the hearts of everyone.

The need for the new birth (3:1–15). The third chapter is connected with the second chapter by the word "man" (see 2:25 and 3:1). Nicodemus is an example of those who were impressed with Jesus' signs but who lacked genuine faith in Him, and therefore still needed to be "born again." John did not state why Nicodemus came at night. This Pharisee may have worked during the day, so that night was the only opportunity he had to visit Jesus. John, on the other hand, may have been pointing to the fact that Nicodemus had not yet come out of spiritual darkness into the light of life from Jesus.

The new birth is needed if one is to enter the kingdom of God. The Greek term for "again" may also mean "from above." Jesus used a number of terms with double meanings as seen especially in the Gospel of John. So He may have been conveying to Nicodemus that this second birth ("born again") would be from heaven ("from above") by the Spirit of God, while one's first birth originates from earth through human parentage. A spiritual birth is necessary if there is to be spiritual life, and that life comes by being born of the Spirit when a person places his or her faith in Christ.

The reference to water in verse 5 has spawned many interpretations. Isaiah 44:3–5 and Ezekiel 37:9–10 refer to both water and wind as illustrations of the Spirit's ministry. Both occur in contexts that suggest the future restoration of Israel just before the establishment of the kingdom. Some suggest that the reference to cleansing in Ezekiel 36:25–27 forms the background of Jesus' words. If that is correct, then the sprinkling of water in Ezekiel 36 symbolizes spiritual cleansing through regeneration.

Another interpretation, based on John 3:4, 6, suggests that water may refer to physical birth (and that by contrast the spiritual or new birth originates from the Spirit of God from above). The fact that water is not mentioned in verse 8 as a requirement may also support this view. Whichever view is taken, the Holy Spirit is the means by which eternal life is provided by Christ. Like the wind, the Spirit is invisible; yet He produces effects that are observable.

Jesus chided Nicodemus, a teacher, for not knowing what God would do on earth through the ministry of the Spirit. Jesus also condemned the people of Israel for rejecting the message that He and John delivered (3:11). How would Nicodemus understand heavenly realities if he and the people were missing what God was doing in Christ through His Spirit? Jesus affirmed again His heavenly origin as the Son of man, "who came from heaven" (3:13).

The experience of Moses and the bronze serpent from Numbers 21 is an illustration of the crucifixion of Jesus. In Moses' day a number of people were bitten by deadly snakes. A symbol of this problem was placed on a bronze pole and whoever looked at it was healed. Similarly Jesus bore the sins of the world in His body on a pole (the cross). Whoever believes in Jesus Christ, whose death provided the answer for the problem of sin, receives the miraculous gift of eternal life. John 3:15 includes the first of many references to "eternal life" in the Gospel of John.

The nature of salvation and condemnation (3:16–21). Christ's provision for the sins of the whole world is nowhere better presented than here. God wants people to be saved, not condemned (see also 1 Tim. 1:4; 2 Pet. 3:9). However, condemnation rests on those who have not trusted Christ as their Savior. Such judgment is viewed as deserved because of the sin of unbelief. One reason some people fail to respond to Jesus as the Light is that they do not want their sin exposed. Many prefer the darkness of sin to the light of the gospel, and they even hate the light. A life lived in truth is identified with the Light, and the good deeds accomplished are credited to God who enables believers to accomplish them.

The early Judean ministry of Jesus (3:22–36). Jesus' disciples and John were both baptizing their converts at the Jordan River. Jesus was overseeing the baptisms (4:2). Aenon and Salim, where John was baptizing, may have been east of Mount Gerizim. Some people were debating with John's disciples about the difference between his baptism and the Jewish purification rites. Various Jewish ceremonies not commanded in the Mosaic Law were introduced with the thought that they would earn merit before God. John's baptism symbolized a repentant faith that trusts in nothing besides the grace of God for the forgiveness of sins. Jesus preached the same message as John, and both were seeing conversions. Some attempted to drive a wedge between John and Jesus over the issues of popularity in their respective ministries. John's model response highlighted the following strategic principles, as stated in 3:27–30.

1. Every ministry is a God-given privilege.

2. A servant's role is to introduce others to the Savior.

3. The joy of fulfilling service comes through serving the Master.

4. A servant should always draw attention to the Lord and not himself.

5. The Lord's servants must humbly recognize the Lord.

Because Jesus is from heaven ("from above"), He has all the prerogatives of deity and lordship. He reveals what He has personally received from the Father, and yet He was not received by the majority of those to whom He ministered. The sweeping overview of rejection (3:32) followed by an exception (3:33) is typical of John's style throughout this fourth Gospel (see 1:11–13). Those exceptional people who do respond in faith find that God is truthful. The unlimited gift of the Spirit is what distinguishes the New Testament era from the Old, the age of Law from the age of grace. The permanent indwelling of the Spirit did not occur until after Jesus was glorified through His death, resurrection, and ascension. Until that time the Holy Spirit came temporarily on individual believers (7:39). To Jesus, God gave all authority, including the authority to speak "the words of God." There is no other way for one to be saved than to believe in Jesus Christ as the Son of God and to accept His word that He is the only way by which one may come to the Father.

The woman at the well (4:1–26). Jews normally avoided traveling the ridge route north of Jerusalem to Samaria. Because of the tensions with the Samaritans, the Jews went east across the Jordan River and north through the Jordan Valley to travel to Galilee. In Jesus' day one of the major debates between the Samaritans and the Jews was about their respective places of worship. The Samaritans believed, for example, that Abraham had offered Isaac as a sacrifice on Mount Gerizim. But Genesis 22 states that it was on Mount Moriah (Jerusalem). The Samaritans also taught that Melchizedek appeared to Abraham at Mount Gerizim, and that when the people arrived in the land, they were to set up an altar of worship at Gerizim (but Deut. 27:4 says it was to be on Mount Ebal). Thus the Samaritan woman regarded Mount Gerizim as the most sacred location in the world and despised and disregarded Jerusalem.

However, God had selected Jerusalem as the place where He would manifest His glory and as the site of the central sanctuary where the Jews were to worship God. About 400 B.C. the Samaritans had erected their own temple on Mount Gerizim and about 130 B.C. the Jews had torn it down. The Samaritans rejected the Old Testament in favor of their version of the Pentateuch. Therefore it is easy to understand the tensions that existed for well over eight hundred years between the Jews and the Samaritans. The city of Sychar, where Jesus sat down by a well, is located in the valley between Mount Gerizim and Mount Ebal in Samaria.

As Jesus began the conversation with the woman of Samaria, He was crossing racial, cultural, gender, and spiritual lines. If John counted days from midnight or noon, as the Romans did, then the "sixth hour" would be 6 P.M. Jesus appropriately referred to water as a metaphor of Himself as the gift of God which, if accepted, would eternally satisfy the thirst of the sinful soul. The well, most likely the one dug by Jacob, is still in existence today, four thousand years after it was dug. What a great picture this is of the fact that Jesus can provide spiritual water that lasts *forever*.

Jesus' instruction to the woman to find her husband was His way of surfacing the sin issue in her life in order to lead her along the path to salvation. Jesus referred to her personal history and the nation's history to lead her to salvation and to give her insights necessary for genuine worship. His knowledge of her past caused the woman to divert the conversation to the Jews' and Samaritans' different ideas on worship. While correcting the erroneous theology of the Samaritans, Jesus at the same time announced a change that would take place in Judaism. With the work Jesus would accomplish at the cross, Jerusalem would no longer be the place of worship. In fact, worship would no longer be confined to any one location. The Father seeks worship that will match His nature of spirit and truth. "Spirit" speaks of the holy character of the believer's heart. The woman's allusion to the Messiah was rooted in the national expectation of the prophet who would be greater than Moses (Deut. 18:15–18). Jesus told her He is that prophet.

The disciples and the priorities of evangelism (4:27–42). The disciples were amazed that Jesus had conversed with this woman, since Jewish rabbis were forbidden to speak to women in public. Jewish religious leaders considered any conversation with a woman a distraction from their study of the Law. The woman became a witness to the Lord among her own people with her leading question, "Could this be the Christ?" In response they began walking toward Him. The disciples were worried that Jesus had spent the day at the well without food. Jesus took the opportunity to teach the disciples a series of principles that underlie the ministry of evangelism (4:34–38).

1. The work of the Lord is the will of God.

2. The ministry of evangelism should never be postponed.

3. Faithful witnessing will bring eternal rewards.

4. Evangelism is a team effort.

Reluctant to trust the woman, the Samaritans trusted the word of Jesus and came to believe that He is "the Savior of the world" (4:42).

Healing the nobleman's son (4:43–54). This was the second miracle performed by Jesus and the second sign in Cana. This incident shows the growth of faith that should have been true among the Jews. The official was an officer in the service of Herod Antipas. The fact that the man went to Jesus on behalf of his sick son demonstrated his belief in the power of Jesus. In Jesus' rebuke (4:48) toward the broader audience, He pointed out that dependence on miracles is inadequate.

Jesus showed that He can give life from a long distance away. This is important in the Book of John, since Jesus later announced His departure to heaven. If Jesus could not heal without being physically present, He would never be able to save from as far away as heaven. The connection between the sign and the gift of eternal life was made with the words, "You may go. Your son will live" (4:50 NIV). So when the official left, he proved his faith in Jesus' promise. The distance between Cana and Capernaum was about twenty miles, so it would have taken almost a full day to get home. When

> *Sometimes sin is the reason for sickness, and if not confessed it can result in further sickness or even death.*

the man returned home and confirmed the miracle and its timing, he and his whole household believed in Jesus. By Roman reckoning of time the seventh hour would have been about seven o'clock in the evening.

C. The Public Presentations at Israel's Feasts (chapters 5–12)

Jesus' healing of the lame man at Bethesda (5:1–18). Excavations in the northeast section of the old city have disclosed a double pool thought to be the pool by the ancient Sheep Gate, a pool with a five-colonnaded construction. The site was originally dedicated to the pagan deities associated with healings. That explains why the multitudes would be gathered there. The spring that fed the supply probably bubbled occasionally, and this may have accounted for the superstition that the one who entered the water first would be healed.

The man by the pool had been lame for thirty-eight years. Jesus' question to him was designed to solicit his faith. Jesus' word to him to take his bed and walk confirmed that he was healed. The Jews took offense at this because the healing took place on the Sabbath. The Jews had developed thirty-nine rules for Sabbath-keeping, the last of which was not to carry one's bed on the Sabbath. Jesus knowingly stood against such traditions by His command to the man and by His response to the leaders.

The later conversation between the man and Jesus at the temple showed that sin was the reason for the man's sickness. John 9:1–3, however, shows that sickness is not always the result of sin. For two reasons the Jews sought to kill Jesus—because He broke the Sabbath and for blasphemy by calling God His Father. Jesus defended His actions in that while God rested from His creative work on the seventh day, He has continued to do His work. Jesus claimed His work was as valid as that of God His Father.

Jesus' claims of deity (5:19–47). In reaction to the charge of blasphemy, Jesus claimed that He, like God the Father, has divine prerogatives in eight areas (5:19–27): (1) Jesus does the same works He sees the Father doing.

(2) The Son shares the Father's knowledge of everything because the Father revealed it to Him. (3) Jesus has the power to give life to whomever He chooses. (4) God has delegated the right and responsibility of judgment to Jesus. (5) Not to honor the Son is to dishonor the Father. (6) Eternal life comes through faith in Christ. Any teachings that suggest salvation is available in any other than Jesus are false. (7) Jesus' voice will resurrect the dead for reward or judgment. (8) Jesus shares the divine attribute of self-existence. Here are some of Jesus' boldest claims of His unity and equality with the Father.

Jesus affirmed that one's works demonstrate the presence or absence of faith (5:29). Annihilation is contradicted here, for both the righteous and the wicked will be raised when Jesus calls them forth from the grave. These prerogatives may be summarized in two statements: Jesus has the right to give life, and He has the right to judge the world.

Besides Jesus' claim of equality with the Father several other witnesses support Jesus' testimony (5:31–37). His personal testimony is free from contradiction and impure motives. An allusion to Deuteronomy 19:15 concludes that one testimony would not be enough even if it were trustworthy, so Jesus pointed out four other witnesses: John the Baptist (who was the lamp but not the light), the works of Christ assigned by His Father, the Father Himself, and the Scriptures. Three times in the Gospels the Father personally testified about the Son: at Jesus' baptism (Matt. 3:17), at the Transfiguration (17:5), and just before He went to the cross (John 12:28).

Jesus condemned the people who rejected His message (5:37–47). The latter part of this chapter presents three ways in which those who rejected Jesus were ignorant: They hadn't heard the voice of God (5:37; compare Moses, Exod. 33:11); they hadn't seen His face (John 5:37; compare Jacob, Gen. 32:30); and they didn't have the Word of God dwelling in them (John 5:38; compare David, Ps. 119:11). The Word of God failed to find an entrance into their hearts because of their lack of faith.

The leaders of Israel thought eternal life was obtained by the study of the Law. Jesus claimed, however, that if they really understood the Scriptures they would have trusted in Him since the Scriptures were designed to lead a person to the Savior. Because they were devoid of the Word, they lacked a love relationship with the Father. They did not receive Him because they wanted the approval of their peers rather than of God. Moses anticipated Jesus, and so by missing Jesus they also missed the true intent of Moses.

Jesus' miracles in Galilee (6:1–15). The miracle of the feeding of the five thousand took place across the Sea of Galilee, here called the Sea of Tiberias (named after a city on the west side of the lake.) This is the only miracle other than Jesus' resurrection which is recorded in all four Gospels. The signs Jesus performed attracted the crowds, who followed Him to the other side of the sea. The phrase "far shore" relates to crossing the political boundary that separated Herod's territory from that of Philip. The former controlled the west side of the lake and the other the east. The dividing line was basically the inlet from the Jordan River.

This miracle took place at the time of the Passover. In asking Philip where they would find bread to feed the huge crowd, Jesus was confronting them with their need to depend on Him. They learned that neither what they had or what could be gathered from anyone else was enough by itself. Jesus then supplied the needs of the crowds in great abundance with the portion of bread and fish given to the disciples. John called this miracle a sign (6:14). In supplying bread for the people, Jesus demonstrated His role as a prophet, for two Old Testament prophets, Moses and Elijah, had been used by God to provide bread miraculously (see Exod. 16:11–16 and 2 Kings 4:38, 41). The people wanted to make Jesus king for only physical reasons, so He withdrew from them.

> *All we need in order to minister to others is found in the Lord, who can use for His glory whatever we give Him.*

Walking on the water (6:16–21). When Jesus left to get away from the crowds, the disciples determined to cross the lake, but the water and wind were against them. Jesus manifested His presence, calmed their fears, and immediately escorted them to the shore.

Jesus' Bread-of-Life discourse (6:22–71). The opening verses of this section explain how those who saw the miracle of the loaves would know to meet Jesus at Capernaum. They were following the disciples back and forth across the lake. Jesus rebuked their pursuit as selfish and superficial in that they were concerned with only physical bread (6:26). So Jesus turned the discussion to His spiritual provisions for eternal life. The theme of continual rejection in the face of God's revelation and provision permeates this discourse. The only "work" (act) that will save is to believe in Jesus, whom God sent from heaven as the true Bread of Life. This Bread is superior to the manna of old since it has been provided for the whole world, not just for one nation. Also the origin of the Bread is heaven, the identity of the Bread is Jesus, and the purpose of the Bread is to provide eternal life for the world.

The Bible often speaks of divine sovereignty and human responsibility in the same context. The sovereign will of God is gracious in its elective choice and purposeful in its certain results (6:36–40). All who come to the Son will have been drawn by the Father, and none who come to the Son will be rejected or lost on the day of judgment.

The Jews grumbled about Jesus' claims to heavenly origins. They couldn't reconcile His divine claims with what they knew of His humble earthly origins (6:19–42). Jesus charged them with being out of step with the work of the Father. Only He had seen the Father and they were trying to tell Jesus what the will of the Father was about. Jesus is superior to the manna in that all who ate it eventually died. But all who believe in Jesus, the Bread of Life, will live forever. Jesus specifically identified the bread as His flesh (6:51), which would be given to provide life for the world. The Bread of Life is superior to the manna in Moses' day because it is available to everyone and because of the lasting results of unity with Christ ("I in him") and eternal life. To the bread Jesus added the idea of His blood as the necessary provisions for eternal life. These two elements anticipated the Last Supper, when Jesus would reveal details about His death. What God sent from heaven Jesus offered on earth for the life of the world.

Jesus' disciples struggled with this discourse too. Some trusted Him and some deserted Him. Even those who trusted Jesus thought His message was difficult to understand. Jesus pointed out that His ascension would be even more difficult to comprehend than His death, and He intimated that it would take the Holy Spirit, who gives life, to understand life. Jesus noted that one of His twelve was an unbeliever and would be a betrayer (6:64). Later John explained in an "aside" that the betrayer was Judas (6:71). When some deserted Him, Jesus questioned the Twelve as to whether they would leave as well. Peter affirmed that Jesus is the only Source for life, "the Holy One of God" (a title also used in Luke 4:34).

Key Theological Principles from the Bread-of-Life Discourse

1. The only act that saves is belief in Christ (6:29).
2. The Father sent the Son from heaven to be the Source of eternal life (6:32–33).
3. Christ gives eternal satisfaction to those who come to Him in faith (6:35).
4. Eternal life is the sovereign work of the grace of God (6:37).
5. God guarantees eternal salvation to those who believe in Him (6:38–40).
6. Salvation is initiated by God and will be consummated at the Resurrection (6:44).
7. Christ is the personal revelation of the Father (6:46).
8. Belief is the only condition for salvation to eternal life (6:47).
9. Christ is the Bread of Heaven, who gives eternal life since He was sacrificed for the world (6:48–51).
10. Personally appropriating Jesus Christ (pictured symbolically as partaking of His flesh and blood) by faith results in eternal life (6:52–58).

The Feast of Tabernacles (chapters 7–8). The Feast of Tabernacles was one of the highest and holiest in Jewish holidays; it originally celebrated the dwelling of God with Israel throughout their wilderness wanderings (Lev. 23:33–43). Jesus' brothers, who had not yet believed in Him, challenged Him to make Himself known at the feast in Jerusalem. He again stated that it was not His time, showing that they, like His mother (John 2:4), did not have the right to control His ministry agenda. Jesus later went to the feast in His own time to confront the anticipating crowd.

One of the themes throughout this record of the feast is the division that Jesus caused among the people and the leaders. Jesus again claimed He was from heaven (7:16) and He reiterated His motive, which was to honor the Father who sent him (7:18). He rebuked the leaders' plan to kill Him (7:1, 19) as a violation of the very law they were seeking to protect. He also rebuked the leaders for condemning Him for restoring life on the Sabbath (7:21–23; see 5:10) when they conducted circumcisions on the Sabbath. Both were evidences of wrong judgment on the part of the leaders (7:24). Proper judgment is based on righteousness, which they were lacking.

Some of the crowd in Jerusalem questioned whether Jesus could be the Christ (Messiah). Their claim to ignorance as to the background of the Messiah was ill-grounded, since Micah 5:2 had predicted that the Messiah's birth would be in Bethlehem, and Isaiah 9:1 had indicated that His ministry would originate from Galilee. Amid further division Jesus spoke of His ascension, and He stated that those who failed to respond to Him could not join Him in heaven (John 7:33–34). The Jews mistakenly thought He was simply going to leave the country to live among the Greeks (7:35–36).

The "greatest day of the Feast" (7:37) was the last day of the feast, when the high priest would lead a procession to the Spring of Gihon, the major water source for the City of David, just south of the temple area. A golden pitcher was filled with water, and the procession of singing pilgrims would make its way to the altar before the temple. There the water was poured as a libation on the altar. This was a reminder of the water from the rock that was provided by God for Israel (Num. 20:8–10). Zechariah had prophesied that water would flow from under the temple in the days of the future messianic kingdom (Zech. 14:8).

On the last day of the Feast, Jesus claimed that *He* is the Source of living water, and He promised that the Holy Spirit would empower believers for the work of evangelism (like streams of water). The Spirit had not yet been given because Jesus had not yet fulfilled His mission on earth. On the Day of Pentecost He would send the Spirit for His fullest ministry yet (John 7:37–39). Again there was divided opinion as to His identity and origin, and though some wanted to seize Him, they were reluctant to do so. Even the temple guards were impressed, for they reported, "No one ever spoke the way this man does" (7:46). The Pharisees showed disdain for the very people to whom they were ministering, but Nicodemus risked his own reputation by urging a hearing before any drastic actions could take place.

John 7:53–8:11 is not found in many early manuscripts or other ancient testimonies. This section may be considered an authentic fragment of history even if it were not part of John's original manuscript. It may have been placed here because it fit the context of Jesus' claims to sinlessness as well as the unjust judgments of Israel's leaders. Within the account the Pharisees tested Jesus in hope of convicting Him of violating either Roman or Jewish law. To release the woman would condone her sin, but to stone her would violate Roman law, which prohibited Jews from carrying out their own executions. The lesson Jesus taught (8:7) was in line with His teaching elsewhere: "Do not judge, or you will be judged" (Matt. 7:1).

Jesus said He is the Light of the world for all who would follow Him (John 8:12). He stated that He and His Father are both valid witnesses to His claims, in contrast to the inadequate judgments made by the Pharisees. Jesus again announced His departure, which the leaders mistakenly understood as a threat of suicide (8:21–22). The death, burial, resurrection, and ascension of Christ validated His claims.

Jesus taught that one of the characteristics of a committed disciple is abiding in the Word (8:31–41), which, along with knowing the Son, gives freedom. Continual sin, on the other hand, brings persistent slavery and shows that one is probably not in the family of God. The Jews claimed to be Abraham's descendants, but Jesus exposed the inconsistency of such pride of origin by showing they had missed the very promise of Abraham.

In answer to their claims that the Jews were God's children, Jesus countered that they were in reality the children of Satan since they did not believe the Father or the Son and their mutual testimony of each other (8:42–45). On the other hand, Jesus claimed His own sinlessness (8:46). In an attempt to dismiss Jesus, they accused Him of being of Samaritan origin and demon-possessed (8:48–53). When Jesus said He existed before Abraham lived, the Jews took this as a claim to deity and hence blasphemy, and so they took up stones to kill Him. The very method by which Jesus escaped through the crowd proved His claims.

Jesus' healing of the blind man (chapter 9). A fascinating progression of faith is seen in this miracle account. The man identified Jesus first as "the man they call Jesus" (9:11). After being questioned again about Jesus, the man replied, "He is a prophet" (9:17). Then after being pressured to degrade Jesus to the level of a blasphemer who was stealing glory from God, the man answered, "Whether He is a sinner or not, I don't know" (9:25). For the reader of the Gospel of John this reinforces the sinlessness of Jesus. The man then contended, "If this man were not from God, he could do nothing" (9:33).

When Jesus asked him if he believed in the Son of man, he indicated his willingness to believe if the Son of man would reveal Himself to him. When Jesus identified Himself as the Son of man, the man responded, "Lord, I believe," and worshiped Jesus (9:38). The combination of all these statements is an impressive affirmation of the theological presentation of Jesus in this book. Jesus took on a human nature in order to be the prophetic voice of the Father. He came from God as the heavenly Son of man, who is also the Son of God. As the Lord, He has the right to be worshiped and obeyed.

Because Jesus healed the man on the Sabbath, the religious leaders again tried to discredit Jesus by putting political and religious pressure on the people to denounce anything He did. The Pharisees were willing to lie in order to lead. Even the "enlightened" man stumped the religious experts and (humorously) invited them to be Jesus' disciples (9:27).

The chapter ends with an insightful twofold purpose statement of Jesus' ministry. He came to heal the blind, and to blind those who claimed they could see (9:39). The blind were those who were willing to recognize their need for His help. Those who claimed they could see were the self-righteous who, because of their refusal to believe, would remain unforgiven and be judged guilty for their sins.

Jesus, the Good Shepherd (10:1–21). The figure of the shepherd and the sheep utilizes a series of metaphors for the relationship of Jesus to His people. The use of shepherds as an imagery for leaders has Old Testament roots (Ezek. 34:11–13; see also Num. 27:15–18). The opening narrative of this chapter utilizes a typical day in the life of a shepherd, who leads his sheep from the fold to the open pasture and then back into the fold at night. Jesus is the true Shepherd in contrast to the false shepherds. A true shepherd knows his sheep and his sheep know him. Sheep will follow only a voice they recognize. This points to the fact that true believers follow Jesus because they recognize and obey His voice found in His Word.

The shepherd would often sleep in the doorway of a sheepfold to function as a "gate." Similarly Jesus functions as the Protector of believers, His "sheep." He is the means of entrance into life and, like a shepherd who leads his sheep into pasture, Jesus provides all that is necessary for growth for His sheep. False leaders, illustrated by thieves and robbers, take advantage of people for selfish gain. Jesus has come to give abundant life. As the Good Shepherd, Jesus laid down His life for His sheep, whereas false leaders abandon their flocks in times of adversity. Jesus was willing to give His life for the security of those He came to save.

The "other sheep that are not of this sheep pen" (John 10:16) refers to Gentiles who would be saved and would join the sheep of Israel in making up a new flock, over which Jesus is the Shepherd. This is John's reference to the church. Jesus is a superior Shepherd for three reasons: He was willing to die for His sheep, He knows His sheep intimately, and He has perfectly obeyed the Father's commands. The security of the sheep is based on Jesus' relationship to His Father. The response of the Jews was divided, as some leveled against Him the charge of demon possession and lunacy.

Jesus at the Feast of Dedication (10:22–39). The Feast of Dedication commemorated the rededication of the temple by Judas Maccabees in 165 B.C. after it had been desecrated in 168 B.C. by Antiochus Epiphanes. The Colonnade of Solomon was the roofed structure supported by pillars on the south end of Herod's temple platform which gave shelter from the winter weather. In answer to the Jews' question about His identity, Jesus affirmed His messiahship in the face of their unbelief (10:24–26). The Lord's sheep are those who believe and receive eternal life that only He can give (10:27–28). They are said to be "eternally secure" in the hand of Jesus and in the hand of His Father, from which no one can remove them.

When the Jews attempted to stone Jesus for what they thought was blasphemy, He appealed to the Old Testament to defend Himself, and in so doing He affirmed the abiding nature of the Scriptures (10:33–35). Jesus quoted Psalm 82:6, which refers to earthly judges as "gods." Since Jewish judges, including even evil ones, could be called "gods," how, Jesus argued, could they accuse Him of blasphemy for identifying Himself as God? Jesus appealed to both His Father and His works to validate His ministry. The Jews again attempted to seize Him (John 7:30, 44), but Jesus departed to the east side of the Jordan, where John had been baptizing. This chapter, like previous ones, records a mixed response of belief in Jesus on the part of some and rejection of Him on the part of others.

The raising of Lazarus (11:1–44). The two references to Mary, who poured perfume on the Lord (11:2; 12:1–8), "frame" the lengthy section on Jesus' claim that He is the Resurrection and the Life. This framing shows that the sign of Lazarus's resurrection would have special reference to the death of Christ. That Jesus could raise the dead proves His earlier claim that He could lay down His life and raise it up again (10:18; compare 5:26). Just as the blindness of the man in chapter 9 was for the purpose of showing God's work, so the sickness of Lazarus resulted in glory to God and His Son.

The purpose of Jesus' delay in getting to Lazarus's home was to instill belief in the disciples. The disciples missed the euphemism of sleep that Jesus used for death. The reference to limited daylight (11:9–11) highlighted the fact that the time to serve the Lord is limited. The fact that Lazarus had been dead for four days is significant, since early rabbinic sources suggested the Jews believed the soul hovered near the body of the deceased for three days (*Leviticus Rabbah* 18.1). Bethany, where Lazarus lived, was located fifteen stadia (about 1.75 miles) from Jerusalem. Such proximity allowed a crowd of comforters to gather to console Mary and Martha. Both Mary and Martha shared the belief that had Jesus been there Lazarus would not have died (John 11:21, 32). Like many, Martha held to good theology but hesitated to apply it to her immediate circumstances.

> *Sometimes the Lord delays His answers to prayer to show more of His glory through much greater works.*

As the Resurrection and the Life, Jesus can bring believers back from the dead and can protect them from the second death, which is eternal. Belief in Christ is what qualifies one for eternal life. Martha's belief that Jesus is the Christ, the Son of God, who came into the world from the Father, anticipated the purpose for the Book of John (20:31). Twice Jesus' love for Lazarus is mentioned in chapter 11 (11:3, 36).

Jesus raised Lazarus from the dead in order to prompt belief and to glorify God. Jesus will glorify God through the resurrection of all believers who die. In contrast to Jesus who was resurrected through His graveclothes, Lazarus was brought back to life needing to be freed from his.

The plot to kill Jesus (11:45–57). The raising of Lazarus resulted in some people believing in Jesus and others rejecting Him. At a meeting of the Sanhedrin the chief priests and Pharisees bemoaned Jesus' popularity and expressed fear in Roman retaliation, which might cost them their place of leadership among the Jews. Caiaphas, the high priest, "prophesied" more than he knew when he said, "It is better for you that one man die for the people than that the whole nation perish" (11:50). Caiaphas could not have known how close his words were to John 3:16. The writer of the Gospel recorded them to show the irony of the fact that Jesus came to die for the nation that would put Him to death in order to save themselves.

Again the leaders plotted to take Jesus' life, so He withdrew to the village of Ephraim, about fifteen miles northeast of Jerusalem. At the Passover the crowds wondered whether Jesus would appear, and the leaders plotted how they might capture Him.

The anointing of Jesus (12:1–11). The anointing of Jesus at Bethany took place at the home of Mary, Martha, and Lazarus six days before the Passover. In contrast to Jewish unbelief, Mary showed great faith when she anointed Jesus with the pint of pure nard. Nard or spikenard is a fragrant oil from the root and spike (stem with flowers) of the nard plant native to northern India. A pint cost three hundred denarii, almost a year's worth of a laborer's wages. By wiping Jesus' feet with her hair, Mary showed devotion and humility. Judas expressed his selfish and devious motives with the flimsy excuse that such an act neglected the poor. In reality, Judas had stolen money from the moneybag, a weakness that showed up again when he sold Jesus for silver at His betrayal. In the parallel accounts in Matthew and Mark, Judas left to make his deal with the Jewish authorities.

> *Selfishness and sordid gain are twin chambers of a greedy heart.*

From this incident Jesus predicted His death, since here and at His burial His body was anointed with perfumed spices. The conclusion of this paragraph, like others in this Gospel, records the attempt of the chief priests to kill Jesus (and on this occasion, Lazarus as well), along with the fact that many Jews were putting their faith in Him.

The Triumphal Entry (12:12–19). The Mosaic Law commanded that palm branches be used to celebrate the Feast of Tabernacles (Lev. 23:40). "Hosanna" means "Save now!" (see Ps. 118:25), the Jewish version of "Hail to the King." Psalm 118 speaks of the rejection (118:22–24) and reception (118:25–26) of the Messiah. This psalm of messianic expectation is the most quoted psalm of the Passion Week in the Gospels. Jesus' riding on a donkey fulfilled Zechariah 9:9, denoting the humble entrance and offer of salvation that the messianic King brought to Jerusalem. Not until after Jesus' resurrection did the disciples understand the significance of these quotations.

Again the response to Jesus varied; some were joyfully spreading the word about Lazarus, whereas the Pharisees were concerned that Jesus was becoming too popular.

The prediction of Jesus' death (12:20–36). As the crowds gathered in Jerusalem for the Passover feast, some Greeks who had come to worship wanted to see Jesus. Philip and Andrew introduced these Gentiles to Him. The quotation of Zechariah 9:9 in John 12:15 was appropriate because Zechariah 9:10–11 records the expectation that the humble King would preach peace to the Gentiles in anticipation of establishing His kingdom. The approach of the Gentiles signaled the coming of the hour when Jesus would lay down His life. The "hour" Jesus had often spoken of throughout His ministry commenced with this event. Jesus' illustration of a kernel of wheat falling to the ground taught that His death was necessary for many people to be saved. By extension, Jesus taught that death to oneself and the world would result in a fruitful life of honor and service to the Father.

At that time God the Father spoke out of heaven for the third time in Jesus' earthly life (see Matt. 3:17; 17:5). The purpose of this heavenly utterance was to authenticate that the death of Christ would be for the glory of both the Father and the Son. Jesus' death was the basis for the defeat of Satan ("the prince of this world") and for human redemption (John 12:31–32). The phrase "lifted up" indicates that Jesus would die by crucifixion. The crowd was confused because they did not understand how the Messiah could rule

> *There is danger in loving the praise of men more than the praise of God.*

forever and still face death, especially crucifixion at the hands of the Romans. Their reference to the Law probably referred to various passages from the Old Testament on which they based their beliefs (Pss. 89:36; 110:4; Isa. 9:6; Ezek. 37:25; Dan. 7:14). Again Jesus spoke of light (see John 3:20–21; 9:4) and the limited time it is available (12:35–36) to encourage belief in Him. Their belief would result in further insight into the seeming contradiction between the Messiah's rejection and His reign.

The concluding summary of rejection (12:37–50). John quoted two Old Testament passages that document Israel's rejection of Jesus. Isaiah 53:1 speaks of the people's lack of response to the power ("arm") of God, evidenced in the miraculous signs He had performed in their presence. As a result of that rejection the nation would suffer disciplinary blindness for rejecting their Messiah, as a further fulfillment of Isaiah 6:10. Jesus applied Isaiah 6 to Himself when He affirmed that the exalted King whom Isaiah saw in his vision was none other than the preincarnate Christ (John 12:41). A mixture of belief and unbelief was again noted. The Pharisees refused to believe Him for fear of being excommunicated from the synagogue, whereas many other leaders did believe. Jesus then reaffirmed the purpose for His coming. He did not come to judge the world but to be the Light of the world (see 1:9) and to save it (12:47). He came to represent His Father in what He said in order to give eternal life to those who would believe (12:48–50).

III. THE UPPER ROOM DISCOURSE (CHAPTERS 13–17)

A. The Discussion around the Table (13:1–30)

Concerning humility and service (13:1–20). The opening words of this section introduce the theological themes that occur throughout the Upper Room Discourse. Jesus gave these instructions to the disciples to prepare them for His absence, and they emphasize for John's readers the priorities by which they are to live as committed disciples under the power of the Holy Spirit. By washing the feet of the disciples Jesus demonstrated humility and service, and also taught the need for daily cleansing of His followers in order for them to be effectively used in such service. There is an interplay of two words for "wash" in verse 10. Peter mistakenly desired total washing, but Jesus insisted it was only Peter's feet that needed to be washed. Jesus' high position of authority was not inconsistent with His model of humble service. His security in who He is allowed Him to serve as He did.

> *Security in one's position in Christ gives freedom to serve others in genuine humility.*

Concerning the betrayal (13:21–30). Having referred to those who were already clean (13:10), Jesus announced that one of them, who was not clean, would betray Him (13:21; see 13:10–11). The betrayal fulfilled Psalm 41:9, which speaks of being betrayed by a familiar friend. In response to John and Peter's efforts to know who would betray Him, Jesus dipped a piece of bread in the dish and gave it to Judas as a sign that he was the one.

Peter and John's positions near Jesus were consistent with the custom of reclining at the meal, using the left arm for support and the right hand for eating. Perhaps Judas was seated to Jesus' left. Matthew 26:25 seems to indicate that Jesus could speak privately to Judas without being heard by the others, and according to John 13:26 he was close enough to be given the morsel dipped in the dish.) To give a piece of bread to someone at a meal was a sign of intimate friendship. How ironic that Jesus in genuine love and humility served Judas, who would soon betray Him. Judas was motivated by Satan himself (13:27). This is the only time in the fourth Gospel where Satan is mentioned by name (in 13:2 he is called the devil).

None of the disciples understood the conversation between Jesus and Judas. When Judas left, they thought he went to buy something for the Passover feast. Possibly John intentionally mentioned that "it was night" (13:30) in order to point up the contrast between Judas's betrayal and the fact that Jesus is the Light. To depart from the presence of the Lord is to walk in darkness. This temporal reference matched the theological inference of the spiritual darkness in Judas's life.

B. The Discourse after Dinner (13:31–16:33)

This final discourse of Jesus to His disciples follows the general literary structure of the farewell speeches of several Old Testament leaders (Gen. 47:29–49:33; Josh. 3:22–24; 1 Chron. 28–29).

The prediction of Peter's denials (13:31–38). Jesus guaranteed that the betrayal, the denials, and His death and resurrection would bring glory to Himself and also to His Father. In anticipation of His departure, Jesus gave the new commandment by which the world would know His disciples. Loving one another, though a theme echoed from the Old Testament (Lev. 19:18), was made new by Jesus' example, who became the model for His disciples. Their love for one another should match His love for them. In response to Peter's pledge that he would lay down his life for Christ, Jesus corrected him by predicting his three denials. Peter's words, "I will lay down my life for you" (13:37), were almost identical to those Jesus used in 10:11, when He spoke of Himself as the Good Shepherd giving His life for the sheep. This is another example of irony in John's Gospel. It would not be Peter who would die for Jesus, but Jesus who would die for Peter. The fulfillment of this prediction about Peter's denials is recorded in 18:15–18, 25–27.

The questions by the disciples (chapter 14). This section of the discourse after dinner is structured around four questions that Jesus answered, each from a different disciple. Peter asked where Jesus was going and why he couldn't follow. Thomas questioned Jesus about the way. Philip asked to be shown the Father. Judas (not Iscariot) asked Jesus why He revealed Himself to the disciples and not to the world. Jesus answered Peter (13:36–14:4) with a promise that He would prepare rooms in the Father's house in heaven and then return to take His own there. This truth may reflect the marriage custom of the bridegroom, who would go to the bride's house and bring her to his father's house, where an apartment would have been built for the new couple. Such a promise was intended to be an encouragement to the disciples during Jesus' absence.

Jesus answered Thomas (14:5–7) by affirming that He is "the way, the truth and the life." God has no other path of salvation besides what He has provided in His Son. Jesus then affirmed that He is God's only provision for the sins of the entire world. In responding to Philip's question (14:8–21), Jesus stated that anyone who has seen Him has seen God the Father, and Jesus and the Father have a mutual relationship in which each is related to the other and each reveals the other (14:11, 20). The greater things that will be done by believers (14:12) will be done through people empowered by the Spirit sent from Christ who will go throughout the world to reach more people in more places than Jesus did in His earthly life. Prayer, obedience, and love are critical for such an endeavor.

The answer Jesus gave to Judas (14:22–31) related the ministry of the Spirit to the life the disciples were asked to live in the world during Jesus' absence. Jesus linked love with obedience and promised a special communion with the Father for those who love and obey Him. The Holy Spirit is called the Counselor, whose ministry includes teaching and illumination. The peace Jesus promised differs from what the world promises. Worldly peace is the absence of conflict; godly peace is the quiet control of the soul regardless of the circumstances. Jesus' death was His ultimate demonstration of obedience to the Father. While Satan sought to defeat Christ, the Father and Son were fulfilling their purposes for much higher ideals.

Priority relationships (chapter 15). In this chapter Jesus outlined three relationships, each with a major responsibility. In relationship to Himself, Christ commanded His disciples to abide in Him and His love. Jesus used the metaphor of the vine and branches to emphasize the need for believers to continue to enjoy the unity that began with their initial belief in Christ. Abiding speaks of the initial relationship established by faith (see 6:56), and abiding also speaks of the ongoing relationship of the believer with the Lord. The statement "I am the Vine" is the last of Jesus' great "I am" sayings in John's Gospel. Several times the Old Testament spoke of the vine as a picture of God's people (Ps. 80:8–16; Isa. 5:1–7; Ezek. 15:1–6; 19:10–14). Jesus said He is the true Vine, by which He was contrasting Himself with unfaithful Israel. The lack of fruit indicated the need for judgment, as seen in the above-listed Old Testament passages and the ministry of John the Baptist (Luke 3:9). Judas is an example of one who would be taken away (John 15:2). The challenge to disciples who are bearing fruit is to bear more fruit.

The casting out in John 15:6 speaks of the disciplinary judgment on a

> *The key to spiritual fruitfulness is abiding in fellowship with Christ.*

believer who because of unfaithfulness is prohibited from any further opportunity of service. Abiding occurs when the Word of Christ is absorbed by the believer and the prayers of the believer are received by Christ. Such a life is one of love, joy, and productivity. The Father's love for the Son serves as the pattern for the love of the Son for His disciples. And the obedience of the Son to the Father serves as an example of the obedience the Lord's followers should have for Christ.

In the believers' relationship with other believers, Christ commanded them to love (15:12–17). The command to love each other in verses 12 and 17 brackets this section. Five characteristics of genuine love are detailed in verses 13–16. True love is sacrificial; it is demonstrated in obedience in Christ; it always communicates truth; it takes the initiative in meeting the legitimate needs of others; and it will always bear fruit with abiding results. Prayer is important in order for these characteristics to be exhibited.

In the relationship that believers have with the world (15:18–27), Christ commissioned His disciples to witness by the power of the Holy Spirit. Believers can expect the world to hate them because the world hated Christ. This hatred for Christ was rooted in the unbelievers' sense of shame because He exposed their sinfulness. If one hates Jesus, he also hates the Father who sent Him. Because of their identification with Christ, Christians can expect to be persecuted by the world. Christ sent the Holy Spirit from the Father to testify about Christ through the ministry and witness of committed disciples. A person's testimony for the Lord is effective only as he or she is abiding in Christ.

Empowerment by the Spirit (16:1–15). Jesus warned the disciples of religious opposition that would come to them under the guise of spiritual activity (see, for example, Acts 9:1–2). To a devout Jew, being put out of the synagogue meant that he had been cut off from his Jewish heritage. This made the ministry of the Spirit even more necessary. Jesus promised that He would send the Spirit to convict the world of sin, righteousness, and judgment. The most problematic sin is that of unbelief. Jesus has made it possible for people to be declared righteous before God because He was accepted back into the presence of His Father. The conviction of judgment came with the statement that Satan, "the prince of this world" (12:31; 14:30), now stands condemned (16:11). While Satan has not yet been imprisoned, he has been sentenced. For those who have failed to believe in God's provision of righteousness through Christ, Satan's fate also awaits them.

Christ predicted that the Holy Spirit's ministry toward believers would include spiritual guidance about the message of Christ, as it has been delegated by the Father. The Spirit does not operate independently from the Father and the Son. His work is to glorify the Son as the Father intends Him to do. These two ministries of guidance and glorification reinforce what God was doing in Christ.

Announcements to the disciples (16:16–24). Jesus acknowledged that there would be sorrow at His death and departure. He likened the present and the future to a woman giving birth to a child. The pain of childbirth is quickly replaced with the joy of the new life of a child in the family. The promise of the return of Christ is a source of joy in the midst of hostility and grief.

> *Joy is permanent when the perspective of a glorious future remains constant.*

The abstract of the discourse (16:25–33). Jesus said that after the Crucifixion and Resurrection He would speak openly to His disciples (Luke 24:44–48). Up to that time He often cloaked His words in figures of speech in order to lay out the plan of His suffering and glory progressively. A summary of Jesus' incarnation and ascension is captured in 16:28: "I came from the Father and entered the world; now I am leaving the world and going back to the Father." This plain statement helped the disciples believe that Jesus had come from God. In an allusion to Zechariah 13:7, Jesus warned that their level of belief would be challenged and they would be scattered because of the hostile activity Jesus would suffer at the hands of His opposition. But they would experience inner peace in the midst of a world of trouble, since He has overcome the world.

> *Tribulation in the world is conquered through confidence in Christ.*

C. The High Priestly Prayer of Christ (chapter 17)

Jesus' prayer for Himself (17:1–5). In this prayer Jesus prayed for Himself, His disciples, and all future believers. The portion of the prayer in which He prayed for Himself is permeated with the theme of glory. The hour of His Passion would become the hour of His glory. Eternal life is defined as knowing the only true God and Jesus Christ whom God sent (17:3). Jesus prayed that God the Father would restore the glory that He shared with the Father before the world began, a prayer that affirmed both His deity and His preexistence.

Jesus' prayer for His disciples (17:6–19). In praying for His disciples Jesus acknowledged certain truths and made several requests. Jesus affirmed the truth that He had revealed to the disciples all that the Father had given Him. Jesus prayed for the security of the disciples, for the fulfillment of their joy, for their protection from Satan, and for their sanctification by the truth.

Disciples are those whom Christ has chosen to be in the world but not of the world, as they represent Christ in much the same way as He represented the Father. Jesus had sanctified Himself in the sense that He had set Himself apart to minister to the disciples as a pattern for their own sanctification for the work of the ministry.

Jesus' prayer for future believers (17:20–26). Jesus also prayed for all future believers who would believe through the message of the disciples. Using the model of His own unity with the Father, Jesus prayed for the oneness of all believers. That oneness should promote spiritual harmony founded on the truth of God's Word.

Jesus also requested of His Father that all believers would be joined to Christ in order to see His glory. Jesus also prayed that the love He shared with the Father would become the experience of all believers. Unity, community, and compassion are Jesus' requests for His church.

IV. THE REDEMPTION OF THE SON OF GOD THROUGH DEATH AND RESURRECTION (CHAPTERS 18–20)

A. The Death of the Son of God (chapters 18–19)

The arrest of Jesus (18:1–11). John did not record Jesus' experience in Gethsemane because that portrays something of the humanity of Jesus, and John's Gospel emphasizes the deity of Christ. The place of the arrest was on the Mount of Olives across the Kidron Valley from Jerusalem. Judas led the soldiers to the familiar meeting place of Jesus and His disciples in an olive grove on the mountain. A "detachment" (18:3) consisted of six hundred men, which included the temple police. The unique mention of the torches, lanterns, and weapons contributes to John's emphasis on the hour of darkness. Jesus' powerful words "I am He" affirmed His claims recorded throughout the rest of this book and caused his arresting audience to fall to the ground. Verse 9 records the fulfillment of Jesus' promises in 6:39 and 17:12 that He would lose none of those given to Him by the Father.

> *Unity among believers is a great testimony that God has sent Christ into the world as the ultimate demonstration of His love.*

John's Gospel is unique in recording the names of Peter and Malchus, whose right ear Peter impulsively cut off. The date when John wrote this book allowed him to mention both names without any fear of reprisal since the temple system of Jerusalem had been destroyed some twenty years earlier. However, John did not record Jesus' miracle of healing the ear of the priest's servant because John selected only those miracles that had theological significance and that reinforced Jesus' discourses. The "cup" of suffering had been appointed by the Father and therefore Jesus submitted to the arrest. John stressed that the Jewish officials were the ones who had arrested Jesus and brought Him to the high priests, Annas and Caiaphas.

The trials of Jesus (18:12–19:16). Jesus was first brought before Annas, Caiaphas's father-in-law. John omitted Jesus' appearance before the Sanhedrin since it was his style to highlight individuals and their conversations with the Lord. The three denials by Peter took place during these religious trials. Peter made his first denial near a charcoal fire. In the presence of servants and officials he told a servant girl, who was the keeper of the door, that he was not one of Jesus' disciples (18:15–18). The second denial also took place at the fire. The third denial was in response to a relative of Malchus who said he saw Peter with Jesus in the Garden. At the very moment Peter made this third denial, a rooster began to crow, just as Jesus had predicted in the Upper Room (13:38).

The trial before Pilate took place in the Roman palace in the early morning. "The sixth hour" (19:14), by Roman reckoning, would have been 6 A.M. The Jews avoided entering the palace to prevent ceremonial contamination during the Passover. John detailed the in-and-out pattern of Pilate throughout this trial. Pilate was outside the palace when he conversed with the accusing Jews (18:29, 38; 19:4, 13), but he went inside the palace with Jesus before the Roman court (18:33; 19:8). The root issue in the trial was the definition of truth (18:38). Ironically the Jews were insistent in their ritual purification while they were inconsistent morally in the way they treated Jesus (18:28–32; 19:12–16). Jesus' claim of heavenly authority does not eliminate the possibility of an earthly kingdom (18:33–38; 19:8–11). Pilate repeatedly asserted Jesus' innocence (18:38; 19:4, 6). In between these assertions, Jesus was scourged and mockingly given a crown of thorns and a purple robe (19:1–3). While the Jews accused Jesus of treason, they committed the ultimate act of blasphemy themselves by saying, "We have no king but Caesar" (19:15).

The crucifixion of Jesus (19:17–37). Jesus' journey to Golgotha outside Jerusalem brings to mind two Old Testament events: Isaac's carrying the wood for the sacrifice of himself (Gen. 22:6) and the high priest's taking the sin offering outside the camp (Lev. 4:12). The Aramaic word "Golgotha" means "the Place of the Skull," which in the Latin version was translated "Calvary." The script on the cross, "Jesus of Nazareth, the King of the Jews," was posted in Greek, Latin, and Aramaic to provide the message for everyone. Against the backdrop of the crowds' opposition, Pilate stood by his statement that Jesus was their King, though he was not fully aware of the significance of the message he nailed to the cross. At the scene of the cross, there was an obvious contrast between the soldiers and the friends of Jesus and their respective conversations. The soldiers argued over who would get His undergarments, which fulfilled Psalm 22:18. Among His family and friends, Mary was entrusted to John. She moved into his home to be cared for there in Jesus' absence.

The final moments of Jesus' earthly life were marked with seven cries from the cross, two of which John recorded: "I am thirsty" (John 19:28) and "It is finished" (19:30). That the Water of Life became thirsty is evidence of the extent to which Jesus went to procure salvation for the world. "It is finished" refers to the completion of His task of obeying the Father and paying the full price for sin.

The Jews asked that the legs of Jesus and the other two be broken in an attempt to hasten their deaths so that their bodies could be removed before the Sabbath. Jesus had already died, having given up His spirit (19:30), which fulfilled His promise that no man would take His life but that He would lay it down of His own accord (10:11, 17–18). The flow of blood and water from His pierced side affirmed the physical reality of Jesus' death. Affirming the truth of what he wrote about Jesus' death, John then encouraged the faith of his readers by quoting Old Testament passages he saw fulfilled in the events of the Cross (Exod. 12:46; Num. 9:12; Ps. 34:20; Zech. 12:10).

The burial of Jesus (19:38–42). Only John recorded the cooperation between Joseph of Arimethea and Nicodemus, who asked Pilate for Jesus' body and buried it with a mixture of myrrh and aloes in accord with Jewish customs. Jesus was buried in a new tomb in a garden near Golgotha. Both the new tomb and the garden reflected Joseph's wealth.

B. The Resurrection of Christ (chapter 20)

The empty tomb (20:1–10). John was highly selective in the events of Jesus' resurrection he chose to record. John singled out Mary Magdalene, whereas Matthew, Mark, and Luke mentioned other women too. John recorded her encounter with Peter and himself and their mistaken conclusion that Jesus' body had been stolen. John, the disciple who outran Peter, wrote his Gospel as an eyewitness to the Resurrection. John specifically noted the exact position of the graveclothes and the folded headcloth separate from the linen. Not until later did Peter and John understand how these events fulfilled Scripture (20:9).

Jesus' appearance to Mary Magdalene (20:11–18). Struggling to believe that Jesus was resurrected, Mary was gently rebuked by the angels. She mistook Jesus for the gardener before He revealed Himself to her. Jesus would not allow her to cling to Him since He had already told her that He must ascend to the Father. Mary told the disciples she had seen the Lord and that He said He would be returning to the Father.

Jesus' appearance to His disciples (20:19–31). That Sunday evening Jesus appeared behind closed doors to His disciples. His risen body with the scars conveyed the proof of His death, and His presence confirmed the proof of His resurrection. Blessing His disciples, He told them they would receive the Holy Spirit, and He gave them authority to proclaim the forgiveness of sins on His behalf. This anticipated the Day of Pentecost and the Spirit-filled preaching of the gospel, in response to which any who believe on Him receive the forgiveness of sins.

The unbelief of Thomas (whose Greek name was Didymus) gave way to belief a week later when he touched the scarred body of the Savior. The confession of Thomas is a climax of faith in this gospel and declares what every reader should conclude: "My Lord and my God!" (20:28). Jesus pronounced a blessing on those who would believe without demanding sight. The purpose statement of the book concludes this chapter. John recorded Jesus' seven sign-miracles before the Cross and the miracle of His resurrection to promote faith in Jesus as the Messiah, the Son of God, who has the power to grant eternal life (20:30–31).

V. THE EPILOGUE (CHAPTER 21)

A. The Miraculous Catch of Fish (21:1–14)

Though some believe this final chapter was written by someone other than the apostle John, both the style and the language agree with previous chapters of the book. Only in John's Gospel is the Sea of Galilee called the Sea of Tiberias (see also 6:1, 23), a popular name used later than when the Synoptic Gospels were written. When the seven fishermen were unable to catch any fish, this gave Jesus a perfect opportunity to restore a fallen disciple and also to reemphasize that He had the power to provide all they need. Though they hadn't caught any fish, He had some on the fire already (21:9)! From the boat John recognized who the Lord was (21:7), just as he had discerned the significance of Jesus' graveclothes (20:8).

B. The Restoration of Peter (21:15–25)

The second mention of the charcoal fire (see 18:18) is appropriate for the scene when Jesus restored Peter. Peter had denied Him three times at the first fire and then affirmed his love for the Lord three times now at the second fire. Too much has been made of the difference in meaning between the two words for love in the conversation between the Lord and Peter. Never rebuking Peter for his replies, Jesus repeatedly commissioned him for the pastoral ministry of God's people. The grace of God had recovered a fallen disciple, one who was later greatly used by God to win many people to Christ (Acts 2–5; 10–11) and who wrote 1 and 2 Peter.

After indicating the kind of death Peter would die, Jesus told him, "Follow Me" (21:19). When Peter compared himself with John, he was rebuffed by a statement that in essence told him to mind his own business.

Jesus told Peter He could keep John alive forever if He so wanted. By the time John wrote this fourth Gospel, a rumor that John would not die needed to be corrected. The final verse emphasizes the selective nature of the Gospel narratives since it would have been virtually impossible to write a total life of Christ.

> We ought not compare ourselves with others since God calls different people to different ministries and destinies.

ACTS
The Beginnings of Christianity

AUTHOR

Passages in the Book of Acts written in the first person plural point to Luke as the writer (Acts 16:10–40; 20:5–21:18; 27:1–28:16). References by early church fathers, comments in early collections of New Testament books, and editorial statements in early notes on certain New Testament books confirm Luke's authorship of Acts. Luke was a Gentile possibly from Antioch of Syria. He also wrote the third Gospel, and he accompanied Paul on his second and third missionary journeys and on his trip to Rome. Paul referred to him as "our dear friend Luke, the doctor" (Col. 4:14).

DATE

The events recorded in Acts cover a period of almost thirty years, beginning with Jesus Christ's ascension in A.D. 33 and concluding with Paul's two-year Roman house arrest that ended about A.D. 62. The date of composition was perhaps A.D. 62 or shortly thereafter.

AUDIENCE

Luke wrote Acts as a follow-up to his Gospel (1:1–3). Both books went originally to Theophilus, an acquaintance of Luke's (Luke 1:1–4). However, Luke undoubtedly intended Acts for a larger audience of Christians and potential Christians.

PURPOSE

One of Luke's purposes was historical: to provide an inspired record of selected events that show the spread of the gospel and the church from Jerusalem, the center of Judaism where the church began, to Rome, the uttermost part of the gentile earth. Luke also had a theological purpose: to show how the sovereign plans and purposes of God were being worked out through history. In particular, he showed how Jesus Christ was faithfully and irresistibly building His church (see Matt. 16:18). This involved clarifying how God's dealings with humankind had taken a different course because of the Jews' rejection of their Messiah. Third, Luke had an apologetic purpose: to defend Christianity before its critics. He frequently pointed out the relationship of the church to the Roman state by referring to many Roman officials, not one of whom opposed Christianity because of its doctrines or practices. This would have made Acts a powerful defensive tool for the early Christians in their struggle to survive in a hostile pagan environment.

THEOLOGICAL EMPHASES

There is a strong note of scriptural continuity in Acts; the book shows that what the Old Testament predicted regarding the rejection of Israel's Messiah and what would follow that rejection had in fact come to pass. God was sovereignly at work, and what was happening was part of what He had planned long ago. Jesus Christ received much attention through the preaching of the apostles, many examples of which appear in Acts as models of addresses to various types of people. The apostles particularly stressed Jesus' death, resurrection, and exaltation. The Holy Spirit was one of Luke's emphases as well, so much so that the book has often been called "The Acts of the Holy Spirit." According to Acts, the Holy Spirit is God's Agent in building the church, and He guides Christians in discerning God's will. He is also a gift to every believer who is a baptized Christian into the body of Christ, the church, He permanently indwells them, and He enables them for service. Luke balanced his emphasis on the sovereignty of God with an equal emphasis on the responsibility of people. While God gave visions to the apostles, people must pray and obey God in order to participate in the building of the church.

Salvation is another major emphasis in Acts. Salvation by grace through faith alone, the problem of gentile salvation (justification and sanctification), and the benefits of salvation (especially forgiveness and the gift of the Holy Spirit) are prominent themes. Also the doctrine of the church is prominent. The relationship between Israel and the church was a source of controversy in early Christianity, which Acts documents and discusses. Gospel preaching and church planting receive much attention. Finally, the note that the church is living in the last days and yet anticipates the eschatological last days is also prominent.

CHARACTERISTICS

Luke structured this book geographically by showing the expansion of Christianity from its birth in Jerusalem to its entrance into the heart of the greatest empire of his time. He also included seven summary statements or progress reports, each of which concludes a major section of material.

SEVEN PROGRESS REPORTS IN ACTS

1. "And the Lord added to their number daily those who were being saved" (2:47).
2. "So the word of God spread. The number of disciples in Jerusalem increased rapidly, and a large number of priests became obedient to the faith" (6:7).
3. "Then the church throughout Judea, Galilee and Samaria enjoyed a time of peace. It was strengthened; and encouraged by the Holy Spirit, it grew in numbers, living in the fear of the Lord" (9:31).
4. "But the word of God continued to increase and spread" (12:24).
5. "So the churches were strengthened in the faith and grew daily in numbers" (16:5).
6. "In this way the word of the Lord spread widely and grew in power" (19:20).
7. "Boldly and without hindrance he preached the kingdom of God and taught about the Lord Jesus Christ" (28:31).

Luke showed similarity and continuity between the ministries of Peter and Paul and that of Jesus; this validated the continuing ministry of the ascended Lord through these major apostles in the church. Luke also deliberately compared the ministry of Peter in the first half of Acts and that of Paul in the last half as a way of validating Paul's controversial ministry to Gentiles. Acts contains twenty-three abbreviated sermons and speeches, most of which present the content of early Christian preaching, the approaches the apostles took to their varied audiences, and the reactions of their hearers.

OUTLINE

I. The Witness in Jerusalem (1:1–6:7)
   A. The Founding of the Church (chapters 1–2)
   B. The Expansion of the Church in Jerusalem (3:1–6:7)
II. The Witness in Judea and Samaria (6:8–9:31)
   A. The Martyrdom of Stephen (6:8–8:1a)
   B. The Ministry of Philip (8:1b–40)
   C. The Mission of Saul (9:1–31)
III. The Witness to the Uttermost Parts of the Earth (9:32–28:31)
   A. The Extension of the Church to Syrian Antioch (9:32–12:24)
   B. The Extension of the Church to Cyprus and Asia Minor (12:25–16:5)
   C. The Extension of the Church to the Aegean Shores (16:6–19:20)
   D. The Extension of the Church to Rome (19:21–28:31)

I. THE WITNESS IN JERUSALEM (1:1–6:7)

The first main part of Acts records the birth and growth of the church of Jesus Christ and other foundational events that transpired in Jerusalem in the church's earliest days.

A. The Founding of the Church (chapters 1–2)

This section includes a preface to the whole book and records preparations for the birth of the church, the account of that birth, and a summary of the early state of the church.

The preface to the book (1:1–5). In his former book (the third Gospel), Luke had recorded what Jesus had begun to do and to teach before His ascension. In this second book he wrote what Jesus continued doing and teaching after His ascension. Theophilus, whose Greek name means "lover of God," was probably a real person, not the personification of all Christians. Before His ascension Jesus had instructed His apostles to remain temporarily in Jerusalem and then to go out into the whole world and herald the good news of salvation to everyone (Luke 24:47–51; Matt. 28:19–20). He had definitely risen from the dead and had appeared to His followers several times during a period of forty days. On one occasion Jesus told His disciples to wait in Jerusalem for the promised baptism with the Holy Spirit, which would come in just a few days (John 14:16, 26; 15:26; 16:7).

The command to witness (1:6–8). The Old Testament associated Spirit baptism with the beginning of the messianic kingdom (Isa. 32:15–20; 44:3–5; Ezek. 39:28–29; Joel 2:28–3:1; Zech. 12:8–10). It was natural, therefore, that the disciples asked if that kingdom was about to begin (Acts 1:6).[1] Jesus did not correct the disciples for believing that the messianic kingdom would come. He only corrected their assumption that they could know when the kingdom would begin and that the kingdom would begin soon. They were not to know yet when the messianic kingdom would begin. Rather, the disciples were to give their attention to worldwide witness. God's Spirit would empower them as they executed their purpose. Starting from Jerusalem the apostles' witness would radiate farther and farther, as ripples do when a stone lands in a placid pool of water.

The ascension of Jesus (1:9–11). Having given this commission, Jesus Christ ascended into heaven. The apostles saw a cloud, the symbol of God's glorious presence, accepting and enveloping Him (see Exod. 40:34; Matt. 17:5; Mark 1:11; 9:7). Two angelic messengers who looked like men (see Matt. 28:3; Luke 24:4; John 20:12) announced that Jesus would return to the earth in a cloud personally, bodily, visibly, and gloriously (see Dan. 7:13; Rev. 1:7).

The appointment of an apostle to replace Judas Iscariot (1:12–26). The disciples returned to Jerusalem to await the coming of the Holy Spirit. They and other disciples gave themselves to prayer for the fulfillment of what Jesus had promised (see Dan. 9:2–3).

> *Divine promises should stimulate prayer, not lead us to abandon it.*

Peter, the leader of these one-hundred and twenty disciples, reminded his brethren that the Hebrew Scriptures had predicted the fate of Judas Iscariot (Ps. 69:25). Part of what it said about him was that someone else should take his place (109:8). Peter encouraged the disciples to choose someone who had witnessed Jesus' entire earthly ministry, from His baptism by John to His ascension. The disciples nominated two men, then prayed for the Lord to make His choice clear, and cast lots (see Prov. 16:33). The lot fell to Matthias, and he became the twelfth apostle.

The birth of the church (2:1–41). The Holy Spirit's descent on the Day of Pentecost inaugurated a new dispensation (governing economy) in God's administration of the human race.

Pentecost was an annual spring feast that took place fifty days after Passover, when Jesus had died. The disciples had assembled on this day indoors. Suddenly a sound like wind, a symbol of the Holy Spirit in Scripture (Ezek. 37:9–14; John 3:8), came from heaven, the place where Jesus had gone, and filled the house. In Scripture fire symbolizes the presence of God (Gen. 15:17; Exod. 3:2–6). The fire separated and rested on each believer. In the past the Spirit of God had hovered over the whole nation of Israel corporately, symbolized by the pillar of fire. Now He came on each believer, as He had on Jesus (Matt. 3:11). Speaking with other tongues (languages; Acts 2:11) was the outward evidence that God had done something to these believers inwardly, namely, filled them with His Spirit (see also 10:46; 19:6).[2]

Jews who lived far away made pilgrimages to celebrate Pentecost in Jerusalem. The sound of the violent wind blowing drew many people in Jerusalem, including foreign pilgrims, to the place where the disciples were meeting. Once there they were bewildered by the languages they heard the disciples speaking. The speakers were Galilean disciples, but they were relating the wonders of God in the native languages of visitors from all over the ancient world. Some observers could not explain this phenomenon, but others said the disciples were drunk.

Peter proceeded to address the assembled crowd of Jews and other visitors to Jerusalem (2:14–41). It was too early in the day for the disciples to be drunk since it was only 9:00 A.M. There was another explanation. What was happening was similar to what Joel predicted would happen in the Day of the Lord (Joel 2:28–32). God had poured out His Spirit on disciples of Jesus, though not on "all people" as He will in the future. Joel referred to deliverance in the Tribulation (2:32), but Peter applied this offer to his audience, before the Tribulation. They needed to call on the name of the Lord Jesus to be saved.

In the next part of his speech (Acts 2:22–36), Peter cited three proofs that Jesus is the Messiah: His miracles (2:22), His resurrection (2:23–32), and His ascension (2:33–35). Jesus' miracles attested to the fact that God had empowered Him (John 3:2), and they led many people who witnessed them to conclude that He is the Son of David (Matt. 12:23). The ultimate cause of Jesus' death was God's plan and foreknowledge, but the secondary cause was the antagonism of godless Jewish and Roman people. God, a higher Judge, reversed the decision of Jesus' human judges by resurrecting and exalting Him in fulfillment of Scripture (Pss. 16:8–11; 110:1). This evidence proves that Jesus is sovereign and is the Messiah.

Peter's sermon convicted his hearers (Acts 2:37–41). They asked him what they should do since they had crucified their Messiah. Peter told them all to repent so they could enjoy the forgiveness of their sins and receive the Spirit. Then he added that each of them should be baptized in water as a testimony to his faith. The promise of the gift of the Holy Spirit was for his hearers, for their children when they trusted in Christ, and for everyone, including dispersed Jews and Gentiles, whom God would call to salvation. By trusting in Jesus, Peter's hearers would be saved from divine judgment that would come on their "corrupt generation" of evil unbelievers (see Matt. 21:41–44; 22:7; 23:34–24:2). In response to Peter's preaching, three thousand more people became Christians that day (see Acts 2:41).

The early state of the church (2:42–47). Luke moved from describing what took place on a particular day to a more general description of the life of the early Jerusalem church shortly after that day (see Acts 4:32–5:11; 6:1–6).

The new converts devoted themselves primarily to two activities: the apostles' teaching and fellowship. The apostles' teaching included the Old Testament Scriptures as well as the teachings of Christ on earth and the revelations He gave to the apostles from heaven. "The fellowship" refers to sharing things with other believers who were all still within Judaism at this time. Two distinctive activities marked the fellowship of the early church. The "breaking of bread" probably included the Lord's Supper as well as a meal in connection with that celebration (see 2:46; 20:7; 1 Cor. 10:16; 11:23–25). In prayer the believers praised and thanked God, and interceded for His glory. The feeling of awe that the obvious working of God in their midst inspired continued among all the people in Jerusalem. Unity marked the believers and extended to their sharing their possessions with each other. They even sold their property and personal possessions to help others in need, thereby demonstrating true Christian love. Daily interaction in the temple courtyards, hospitality, joy, honesty, praise to God, and love toward their unsaved neighbors also marked these earliest Christians. God brought others to salvation and into the fellowship of the church daily.[3]

B. The Expansion of the Church in Jerusalem (3:1–6:7)

This section of Acts documents the continued expansion of the church and identifies the means God used to produce growth. In chapters 3–5 the Christians' witness brought them into conflict with the Jewish leaders.

External opposition (3:1–4:31). Opposition to the Christians' message first came from external sources, particularly the leaders of Judaism. The healing of a lame man resulted in the leaders of the Jews changing their attitude toward the disciples from favorable to antagonistic.

The lame man whom Peter and John saw as they entered the temple was a hopeless case (3:1–5). He lay at the gate called "Beautiful," probably either the Corinthian Gate that led from the Court of the Gentiles into the Women's Court or the Nicanor Gate that led from the Women's Court into the Court of Israel. Peter responded to the crippled beggar's request for money by telling him to look at him and John.

Peter then gave him a gift far better than the one the man expected (3:6–10). When Peter healed this man in the name of Jesus, he was saying that it was Jesus who was ultimately responsible for the healing (see also 9:32–34; 14:8–10; John 5: 9).[4] The healed beggar leaped to his feet and then followed Peter and John, praising God. Many people in Jerusalem would have known this beggar since he had sat so long at the gate. There would have been no doubt about the genuineness of his healing, but how he experienced it puzzled them.

Peter, John, and the healed man moved into the portico of the temple, and a large crowed, amazed by the healing, followed them (Acts 3:11–16). Peter addressed the curious throng from the eastern portion of a covered porch that surrounded the outer temple courtyard. He spoke to his audience as a fellow Jew.[5] First, he denied that it was the power or godliness of himself or John that was responsible for the healing (3:12). Rather it was the God of their fathers who was responsible. He had performed this miracle through the apostles to glorify His Servant Jesus. Peter's hearers had disowned Jesus and put Him to death, preferring that a murderer, Barabbas, be freed. Peter contrasted the Jews' treatment of Jesus with God's (3:13–15). He attributed the lame man's healing to the power of Jesus Christ in whom the man had placed his faith.

Many Jewish rulers and other Israelites did not know that Jesus fulfilled many messianic prophecies in the Old Testament. Peter pointed out that Jesus' sufferings harmonized with those predicted of the Messiah by Israel's prophets (3:18–23). He again called on his hearers to repent (see 2:38), to "turn" to a proper relationship to God that was possible only by accepting Jesus. The results would be forgiveness of their sins and "times of refreshing," the reign of Messiah on earth (see Zech. 12:10–14). Peter explained from Scripture that the Jews needed to obey the prophet whom Moses foretold (see Deut. 18:15–19). By quoting this prophecy, Peter affirmed that Jesus is the Messiah and urged his readers to accept Him or face destruction.

When Samuel announced David's reign, he was also anticipating the coming reign of the Messiah (Acts 3:24). Other prophets had also spoken of David's continuing dynastic rule that was a means to God blessing all humanity (see Gen. 12:1–3). God had called Jesus forth as a prophet to bless the Jews first and then all humanity.

Three separate though related individuals and groups objected to Peter and John addressing the people as they did (Acts 4:1–4; see also Mark 11:27–28; Luke 20:1–2). They were the priests, the commanding officer of the temple police force, and the Sadducees. The Sadducees were the recognized leaders of the Jews, so they objected to the disciples teaching the people. They also did not believe in the resurrection of the body, so they viewed the disciples' witness about Jesus' resurrection as misleading. It was too late in the day to begin a formal hearing of Peter and John (see Luke 22:63–66). So the temple officials arrested them and put them in jail, probably the Antonia Fortress just north of the temple courtyard. In spite of this official opposition, many people who heard Peter's speech believed in Jesus, so the total number of male converts in Jerusalem now reached five thousand.

The next day soldiers brought Peter and John before the Sanhedrin, Israel's supreme court (Acts 4:5–7; see Luke 9:22). Annas had not been the official high priest since A.D. 18, when his son-in-law Caiaphas had succeeded him. However, Annas continued to exert so much influence that many people still regarded him as the high priest (see Luke 3:2; John 18:13; Acts 7:1). "John" may refer to Jonathan, a son of Annas who succeeded Caiaphas as high priest in A.D. 36, and Alexander is presently unknown. The healed lame man was also present (see Acts 4:14). The Sanhedrin wanted to know by what authority Peter and John had healed the lame man.

The Holy Spirit controlled Peter as he served as a witness in obedience to Jesus. Peter explained that the power of Jesus had healed the sick man. Peter laid the guilt for Jesus' death at the Jewish leaders' feet and testified that God had raised Him from the dead. Israel's leaders had rejected Jesus as an unacceptable Messiah, but He would prove to be the most important part of what God was building (Ps. 118:22). Peter was referring to both national deliverance and personal salvation in this address, as he had in the previous one. Apart from Jesus, Peter affirmed, there is no salvation for anyone (see John 14:6; 1 Tim. 2:5).

The Sanhedrin observed in Peter and John what they had seen in Jesus, namely, courage to speak boldly and authoritatively without formal training (see Matt. 7:28–29; Mark 1:22; Luke 20:19–26; John 7:15). They may also have remembered seeing Peter and John with Jesus. The Sanhedrin could not dispute the apostles' claim that Jesus' power had healed the former beggar. After conferring privately, the Sanhedrin ordered the apostles not to speak or teach at all as Jesus' spokesmen (Acts 4:18). This order provided a legal basis for further action should that be necessary (see 5:28). Peter and John could not obey both Jesus and the Sanhedrin because their commands conflicted, so they chose to obey God. Even in the face of open defiance the Sanhedrin could do no more than threaten the apostles again (4:21). By punishing them the rulers would have antagonized the people.

> *Speaking what one has seen and heard (Acts 4:20) is the essence of witnessing.*

After hearing Peter and John's report, the Christians sought their "Sovereign Lord" in prayer (4:23–31). The believers saw a parallel to Jesus' crucifixion in the psalmist's prophecy (Ps. 2:1–2) that Messiah would experience opposition from Gentiles and leaders. They saw God's sovereign hand behind human actions again (Acts 4:28; see also 2:23; 3:18). They voiced a fresh appeal for boldness and miracles since additional opposition and temptations lay ahead of them. Those assembled received assurance from God that He was among them when He shook their meeting place, and the Holy Spirit controlled them and gave them boldness in their witness (4:31).

Internal compromise (4:32–5:11). As was true of Israel when she entered Canaan under Joshua's leadership, failure followed initial success. The source of that failure lay within the company of believers, not their enemies.

The unity of the believers extended beyond spiritual matters to physical, material matters (4:32–36; see 2:44–46). Though they owned personal possessions, they considered them common property, not private possessions. The power in the witness of the believers was their love and grace for one another (see Luke 2:40). The resurrection of Jesus marked their witness because it fulfilled prophecy and identified Jesus as the Messiah (see Acts 2:29–32). Occasionally Christians sold their possessions to make cash available for their brethren (2:45), which the apostles distributed to those in need (6:1–4). Barnabas was one disciple who sold some of his land to provide help.

Another sacrificial act that looked just as generous as Barnabas's arose from a different motive (5:1–4). Ananias presented his gift to the apostles exactly as Barnabas had done. But rather than allowing the Holy Spirit to fill him, Ananias allowed Satan to control his heart (5:3). Peter identified Ananias's sin, but God judged it. Ananias sought to deceive the Christians by trying to gain a reputation for greater generosity than he deserved. By deceiving the church, Ananias was also trying to deceive the Holy Spirit who indwelt the church, and in attempting to deceive the Holy Spirit, he was trying to deceive God.

Ananias and Sapphira's sin resulted in their premature physical death (5:5–10; see 1 Cor. 11:30; 1 John 5:16), and it shocked everyone who heard of it. Immediate burial was common in Palestine at this time. When Annanias's wife, Sapphira, joined the assembled disciples three hours later, Peter gave her an opportunity to tell the truth, but she didn't. Putting the Spirit to the test means seeing how far one can go in disobeying God—in this case lying to Him—before He will judge (see Deut. 6:16; Matt. 4:7). This is very risky business. Peter had been God's agent of blessing in providing healing to people (Acts 3:6), but he was also God's instrument to bring judgment on others, like Jesus Christ. These events produced sobering effects in all who heard about them (5:11).

Intensified external opposition (5:12–42). The Jewish leaders increased their opposition to the apostles, as they had increased their opposition to Jesus, because Jesus' power—manifest through them in blessing (3:1–26) as well as in judgment (5:1–11)—increasingly impacted the residents of Jerusalem.

The apostles were gaining great influence in Jerusalem and in the outlying areas (5:12–16). Now many people were being healed. God was adding multitudes of both men and women to the church continually (see also 1:15; 2:41; 4:4). People wanted to get close to Peter because he was so powerful.

The popularity and effectiveness of the apostles riled the Sadducees just as Jesus' popularity and effectiveness had earlier (5:17–21). They had Peter and other apostles arrested and confined in the public jail. But the Lord secured the apostles' release by means of an angel. The angel instructed the apostles to resist the opposition of the Sanhedrin and to continue preaching the gospel in the temple courtyard. The apostles obeyed and began teaching in the temple again early the next morning.

At the same time, the Sanhedrin assembled to try the apostles, whom they assumed were still in jail, but they soon discovered they were not there (5:21–26). The major concern of the leaders was the public reaction when what had happened became known. Word reached the Sanhedrin that the prisoners were teaching the people in the temple. The apostles were so popular with the people that the captain and his temple police had to be very careful not to create the impression that they were going to harm the apostles.

The apostles accompanied the captain and his officers into the Sanhedrin chambers submissively (5:27–32). They had disobeyed the Sanhedrin's prohibition (see 3:18, 21). The Jewish leaders felt the disciples were unfairly heaping guilt on them for having shed Jesus' blood, but only a few weeks earlier they had said to Pilate, "Let his blood be on us and on our children" (Matt. 27:25). Peter simply repeated their responsibility to obey God rather than men (Acts 5:29; see 4:19). Then he preached Christ to these rulers, stressing the evidence that He is the Messiah.

Peter's words so infuriated the Sadducees that they were about to order the death of the apostles regardless of the public reaction (5:33–40). Gamaliel, a highly respected Pharisee, proved to be God's instrument for preserving the apostles, and perhaps all the Christians in Jerusalem, at this time. Gamaliel warned his brethren privately against doing anything rash. He reminded them of two similar movements that had petered out when their leaders had died. If God was not behind the apostles, in time their efforts would prove futile. If the apostles were of God, the Sanhedrin would find itself in the terrible position of fighting against God. The Sanhedrin decided to settle for flogging the apostles for disobeying their former order to stop preaching, threatened them again, and released them.

The apostles went home rejoicing (5:41). They considered it an honor to suffer disgrace for the sake of Jesus' name. The apostles continued explaining daily, publicly in the temple and privately from house to house, that Jesus is the Messiah.

Internal conflict (6:1–7). The growth of the church made some administrative changes necessary within the church. Two of Satan's favorite methods of assailing the church—methods he has employed throughout history—are internal dissension (6:1–7) and external persecution (6:8–15).

Two types of Jews made up the Jerusalem church. Some were "Grecian

(Hellenistic) Jews" who originally lived outside Palestine and spoke primarily Greek. The others spoke predominantly Aramaic and were native residents of Palestine. Within Judaism frequent tensions between these two groups arose, and this cultural problem carried over into the church. As the church grew, some of the Hellenists charged the Palestinians with discriminating against their widows in the distribution of food. The twelve apostles wisely delegated responsibility for this ministry to other qualified men in the congregation so it would not distract them from their primary duties. All seven men whom the congregation chose had Greek names. The apostles then appointed them to their duties and prayed for them. This solved the problem, and the word of God continued to spread in Jerusalem, resulting in the conversion of even some Jewish priests.

II. THE WITNESS IN JUDEA AND SAMARIA (6:8–9:31)

Three significant events in the life and ministry of the early church centered around three key individuals: the martyrdom of Stephen, the ministry of Philip, and the mission of Saul.

A. The Martyrdom of Stephen (6:8–8:1a)

God used Stephen's martyrdom in Jerusalem to scatter the Christians and the gospel from Jerusalem into Judea, Samaria, and the uttermost parts of the earth.

Stephen's arrest (6:8–15). Stephen, one of the seven men chosen earlier (6:5), was full of grace and power and could perform miracles. The leading men in one of the Jewish synagogues in Jerusalem debated with him about Jesus, but they couldn't prove him wrong. So they falsely accused him of blaspheming Moses and God and brought him to trial before the Sanhedrin. They also charged him with saying things about the temple and the Mosaic Law that were untrue and unpatriotic. But Stephen's submission to the Holy Spirit made him confident, composed, and courageous.

Stephen's address (7:1–8:1a). Stephen's address was not a personal defense designed to secure his acquittal by the Sanhedrin; it was a defense of the new way of worship that Jesus taught and His followers embraced. He reviewed the history of Israel and highlighted elements of that history that supported his contentions. He built this review around outstanding personalities: Abraham, Joseph, Moses, David, and Solomon.

The first section (7:2–16) deals with Israel's patriarchal period and refutes the charge of blaspheming God (6:11). The second major section (7:17–43) deals with Moses and the Law and responds to the charge of blaspheming Moses and speaking against the Law (6:11, 13). The third section (7:44–50) deals with the temple and responds to the charge of speaking against the temple ("the holy place," 6:13) and saying that Jesus would destroy the temple and alter Jewish customs (6:14). Stephen then climaxed his address with an indictment of his hard-hearted hearers (7:51–53). Stephen's purpose was also to show that Jesus experienced the same things Abraham, Joseph, and Moses had experienced as God's anointed servants. As the Sanhedrin recognized these patriarchs as men whom God had anointed for the blessing of Israel and the world, so should they recognize Jesus. The people to whom these three patriarchs went as God's representatives all initially rejected them but later accepted them, which paralleled Jesus' career.

The primary theme of Stephen's speech is that Israel's leaders had failed to recognize that God had told His people ahead of time that they could expect a change. They had falsely concluded that the present state of Judaism was the final stage in God's plan of revelation and redemption.

Stephen's speech caused a revolution in the Jews' attitude toward the disciples of Jesus, and his martyrdom began the first persecution of Christians (7:54–60). The Sanhedrin's response to Stephen's message shows the officials' continuing rejection of Jesus. This response is why the gospel spread as it did and why the Jews responded to it as they did.

Stephen looked up to heaven and saw Jesus standing at God's right hand (7:55–56; see Ps. 110:1), as a Prophet and a Mediator between God and man, and as a Witness. Standing may also imply Jesus welcoming Stephen into His presence as the first Christian martyr. Stephen called Jesus the "Son of Man" (Acts 7:56), a title of Messiah that implied His universal rule (see Dan. 7:13–14). To the Sanhedrin Stephen's identification of Jesus amounted to blasphemy for which stoning was the penalty in Israel (Lev. 24:16; Deut. 17:7). Saul of Tarsus was there and cooperated with the authorities by holding their cloaks while they carried out their wicked business (Acts 7:58). Stephen died as Jesus did, with prayers for his murderers being his last words (see Luke 23:34, 46), though Stephen prayed to Jesus whereas Jesus prayed to His Father. Saul's active approval of Stephen's execution reveals his commitment to the extermination of Jesus' disciples, which he proceeded to implement zealously (Acts 8:1a).[6]

B. The Ministry of Philip (8:1b–40)

Philip took the gospel into Samaria and then indirectly to Ethiopia, one of the more remote parts of the earth (see 1:8).

The evangelization of Samaria (8:1b–25). The first part of Philip's important ministry took place in Samaria. Luke recorded the cause of Philip's ministry there (8:1b–3), its nature (8:4–8), and its effects (8:9–24).

Stephen's execution ignited the first popular persecution of Christian Jews by non-Christian Jews (8:1b–3). This hostility resulted in many of the believers leaving Jerusalem to live in more secure places. This persecution was hard on the Christians, but it was beneficial because it resulted in widening evangelization. There were still Jews in Jerusalem who were sympathetic with the Christians, and some of them mourned Stephen's death and gave him a decent burial. Stephen's execution heightened the hostility of other unbelieving Jews such as Saul.

Like Stephen, Philip was one of the seven men chosen to assist the apostles (6:5). Traveling north from Jerusalem to Samaria (8:4–8), Philip preached "the Christ" to the Samaritans, who looked for a personal Messiah (see John 4:9), and performed miracles as did Jesus and the apostles. Again, deliverance brought rejoicing (see Acts 2:46–47).

Another person who was doing miracles in Samaria, but by satanic power, was Simon, a sorcerer (8:9–13). His ability had made him very popular, and he had encouraged people to think that he was a great power whom God had sent. But Philip's power proved superior to Simon's, and many Samaritans trusted in Jesus and were baptized in water, including Simon (8:13).

Since the Twelve were the divinely appointed leaders of the Christians (1:12–14), it was proper that they send representatives to investigate the Samaritans' salvation, especially since hostility existed between the Jews and the Samaritans (8:14–17). When Peter and John arrived, they asked God to send His Holy Spirit to baptize the Samaritans as He had baptized the Jews who believed in Jesus (2:41).[2] The Spirit's baptizing the Samaritans in response to the laying on of the apostles' hands undoubtedly impressed both the Samaritans and the Jews in Jerusalem that God accepted both types of people simply by faith in Christ.

Simon desired to buy from Peter and John the ability to precipitate Spirit baptism (8:18–19). Peter's stern response, however, revealed the seriousness of Simon's error. God's gifts are free and He gives them to whom He chooses; people cannot purchase them. Simon's heart was not right with God (8:21) because he wanted to bring glory to himself rather than to God. Peter's rebuke terrified Simon, and he asked for prayer that God would be merciful to him (8:24).

Peter and John preached the gospel in other Samaritan towns (8:25) on their way back to Jerusalem, thus showing that they believed Samaritans could be saved just as Jews could.

Philip's ministry to the Ethiopian eunuch (8:26–40). The Lord also opened the doors of the church to God-fearing Gentiles. The Ethiopian eunuch is the first Gentile whose conversion is reported in Acts.

In the midst of evangelistic success in Samaria, God's angel directed Philip to go south to a road that ran from Jerusalem to Gaza. Philip obediently yielded to the Spirit's control. On the road he met a eunuch who was in charge of the Ethiopian treasury. Interestingly Isaiah had written that eunuchs would worship the Lord (Isa. 56:3–8). This official had made a pilgrimage to Jerusalem to worship the Lord and on the trip home he was reading Isaiah's prophecy. Philip approached his vehicle and recognized that he was reading aloud from Isaiah 53. The official was having difficulty understanding what he read, so he invited Philip into his chariot for some help. Philip responded by explaining how Jesus fulfilled Isaiah's prophecy of the suffering Servant (see Luke 22:37). The road crossed several stream beds, and even though the land was desert, water was not entirely absent certain times of the year. There was enough water for Philip to baptize the Ethiopian, which he did. As the Holy Spirit had directed Philip to the eunuch (Acts 8:29), now He led him away (8:39). Luke stressed the Spirit's leadership in this evangelism of the first gentile convert in Acts. Philip proceeded up the coast north to Caesarea preaching the gospel in all the interlying cities (8:40).

The very first Christians were Jews (2:1–8:4). Then Samaritans became Christians (8:5–25). Now a Gentile who was a Jewish proselyte or near-proselyte became a believer in Christ. Probably all these converts thought of themselves as simply religious Jews who believed Jesus is the Messiah. Only later did they learn that what God was doing was not just creating a group of believers in Jesus within Judaism but a whole new entity, namely, the Christian church (see Eph. 2–3).

C. The Mission of Saul (9:1–31)

Saul of Tarsus became God's primary instrument in the spread of the Christian mission to the Gentiles, and Peter's evangelization of Cornelius (Acts 10) continued to advance that theme.

Saul's conversion and calling (9:1–19a). Since Stephen's martyrdom Saul had been persecuting Jews who had come to believe that Jesus was their Messiah (8:3). Saul obtained letters from the high priest giving him authority to arrest Jesus' Jewish disciples from Palestine who had fled to Damascus because of persecution in Jerusalem. Saul's blinding vision was a revelation of Jesus Christ (9:3–6, 17, 27; 22:14; 26:16; 1 Cor. 9:1; 15:8), who spoke to Saul from heaven (Acts 26:14) and asked him why he was persecuting Him. Jews knew that God had spoken to their forefathers from heaven in the past, but Jesus' self-revelation totally shocked Saul, who until then had regarded Jesus as a blasphemous pretender to Israel's messianic throne. Saul now discovered that Jesus is God, or at least was with God in heaven, and yet He was also present in His followers whom Saul was persecuting. Jesus told Saul to enter Damascus and to wait for further directions. Saul learned that Jesus had a mission for him, though he did not know what it would be. The light of the vision he had seen had blinded Saul temporarily, so his companions had to lead him off into Damascus where he waited for three days for further instructions, blind, fasting, and praying.

In Damascus a Jewish Christian named Ananias also received a vision of the Lord Jesus. Jesus gave Ananias specific directions to another house in Damascus where he would find Saul (9:10–12). Ananias wanted to make sure he had heard the Lord correctly since Saul had become infamous for harming believers in Jesus. To bolster Ananias's courage God told Ananias His plans for Saul. The inquisitor, a proud Pharisee, was to become Jesus' chosen instrument, His apostle to Gentiles, kings, and Jews. Ananias found the house, communicated his Christian love to his new Christian brother, and explained his purpose for coming to Saul. God then restored Saul's sight. The first thing Saul did was identify with Christ and the disciples of Christ by water baptism even before breaking his fast of three days (9:18–19a).

Saul's initial conflicts (9:19b–31). The radical changes that took place in Saul proved the genuineness of his conversion and prepared him for later ministry.

As soon as Saul became a Christian, he began to proclaim in the Damascus synagogue that Jesus is the Son of God and the Messiah (9:19b–22). Understandably his conduct bewildered the Jews there. He quickly grew more powerful. Many days later the Jews tried to kill Saul, but his disciples lowered him in a basket through an opening in the city wall and he escaped (9:23–25; see also 2 Cor. 11:32–33). Saul traveled from Damascus to Jerusalem, where the Christians at first feared him. But Barnabas graciously reached out to him in Jerusalem, as Ananias had done in Damascus. Barnabas pointed out to the Christian skeptics why Saul's conversion must be genuine (Acts 9:27).

While Saul was in Jerusalem, he resumed Stephen's work of debating with the Hellenistic Jews. At first he enjoyed freedom in Jerusalem, but soon the unbelieving Jews there tried to kill him too. Evidently Saul continued evangelizing in Jerusalem until it became obvious to the other believers that he must leave immediately or be killed. Saul's concerned Christian brethren escorted him to Caesarea, and from there he departed to Tarsus, his hometown. Saul's departure from Palestine resulted in greater peace for the Christians there (9:31). The church experienced four things: inward strengthening, encouragement provided by the Holy Spirit, numerical growth, and a proper attitude and relationship to God (in contrast to Judaism).

II. THE WITNESS TO THE UTTERMOST PARTS OF THE EARTH (9:32–28:31)

The Ethiopian eunuch took the gospel to Africa, but he had become a Christian in Judea. Now we begin to read of people, especially Gentiles, becoming Christians in places farther from Jerusalem and Judea.

A. The Extension of the Church to Syrian Antioch (9:32–12:24)

As Jerusalem had been the Palestinian center for the evangelization of Jews, Antioch of Syria became the first Hellenistic center for gentile evangelization in Asia Minor and Europe. In this section Luke recorded three important episodes: Peter's ministry in the maritime plain of Palestine (9:32–43), the conversion of Cornelius and his friends in Caesarea (10:1–11:18), and the founding of the Antioch church (11:19–30). An update on what was happening back in Jerusalem (12:1–23) and another summary statement of the church's growth (12:24) conclude this section.

Peter's ministry in Lydda and Joppa (9:32–43). The gospel was being preached effectively in a region of Palestine that both Jews and Gentiles occupied. Peter, the apostle to the Jews, was responsible for its advancing farther into gentile territory (see Eph. 2:11–3:12).

Lydda lay on the Mediterranean coastal plain. While visiting the Christians who lived there, Peter healed Aeneas, another lame man (see Acts 3:6–8). Peter announced that the healing was Jesus Christ's work (9:34), and this miracle resulted in many people in that region believing in Jesus.

Peter also raised a Christian Jewess named Tabitha—her Greek name was Dorcas—from the dead at Joppa near Lydda (9:36–43). Apparently the local believers expected him to raise her back to life, as Jesus had done, since they did not bury her but simply washed her body and laid it in an upper room. The widows mourned her death and showed Peter the garments she had made. Peter's bringing Tabitha back to life resulted from Jesus having given the Twelve the power to raise the dead (Matt. 10:8). Many people became believers because of the news of this miracle too (Acts 9:42; see also v. 35).

The conversion of Cornelius (10:1–11:18). The Jewish Christians initially resisted the idea of evangelizing Gentiles and accepting them into the church apart from any relationship to Judaism (10:14, 28; 11:2–3, 8). God Himself led the way in gentile evangelism and acceptance, and He showed His approval of Gentiles (10:3, 11–16, 19–20, 22b, 30–33, 44–46; 11:5–10, 13, 15–17). Interestingly God used Peter, the Jewish leader of the Jerusalem apostles, rather than Paul to open the door of the church to Gentiles (10:23, 34–43, 47–48; 11:15–17). The Jerusalem church accepted the conversion of Gentiles apart from their becoming proselytes to Judaism because God had validated this in Cornelius's case (11:18).

> God often uses what seem at first to be incidental occurrences to open up great ministries. Luke illustrated this divine method repeatedly in Acts.

Caesarea, the capital of the province of Judea, stood on the Mediterranean coast and was the base of Cornelius, a Roman centurion who was a God-fearing Gentile much respected by the Jews in his community. One day in the middle of the afternoon God gave him a vision in which he saw an angel who commended him for his piety and commanded him to send for Peter.[8] Cornelius immediately sent some servants to Joppa to find Peter (10:1–8).

God also gave Peter a vision the next day (10:9–16). Peter went up on the flat housetop about noon to pray. Feeling hungry he fell into a trance, and in a vision (10:10–11; 11:5) he saw a sheet-like container descending from heaven full of all kinds of clean and unclean animals (11:6). A voice commanded him to get up, kill the animals, and eat them. Peter strongly resisted the command to eat unclean food (see Ezek. 4:14; Mark 7:14–19; Rom. 14:14). The issue of unclean food was the basic one that separated Jews like Peter from Gentiles. Peter's Jewish cultural prejudices were overriding the teaching of Jesus on this subject (Mark 7:18–20). For this reason God repeated the vision two more times so Peter would be sure he was understanding God's command correctly.[9]

Just then Cornelius's messengers arrived with their invitation for Peter (Acts 10:17–22). The Holy Spirit convinced Peter that God wanted him to accompany them to Cornelius's house. Peter invited them inside to be his guests. This was most unusual because Jews normally did not provide hospitality for Gentiles. Immediately Peter applied the lesson of the vision to his relationship with these Gentiles.

Peter wisely took six other Jewish Christians with him when he went to visit Cornelius the next day (10:23; 11:12). Cornelius was so sure Peter would come that even before the apostle arrived he gathered a group of his relatives and friends to listen to him. Cornelius gave Peter unwarranted veneration, which the apostle refused (see also 14:11–15; Rev. 19:10; 22:8–9). Explaining why he was willing to associate with and visit Gentiles—which was taboo among the Jews—Peter asked Cornelius why he had sent for him. Cornelius then told Peter the vision he had seen and what he had done in response to it and invited Peter to tell him and his guests what God wanted him to say to them (10:30–33).

The apostle then delivered his message to Cornelius, the first sermon in Acts addressed to a gentile audience (10:34–43). Peter confessed that he now understood something God had already revealed throughout the Old Testament (Amos 9:7; Mic. 6:8), but which most Jews had not grasped because of centuries of ill-founded pride: The Lord accepts people from every nation, not just Israel. While Cornelius was a man of piety (10:2), he was not saved till he believed in Jesus Christ (10:43; 11:14). Since God does not show partiality (Deut. 10:17; 2 Chron. 19:7; Job 34:19), certainly Christians should not do so either. Peter then outlined Jesus of Nazareth's career for his listeners, assuming some knowledge that was common but adding details. These points included the fulfillment of Isaiah 61:1 (Acts 10:38; see Luke 4:14–30) and the eyewitness of the apostles (Acts 10:39–41; see 1:8), including Jesus' postresurrection eating and drinking with them (10:41; see Luke 24:41–43). Peter stressed that Jesus Christ will one day judge all people as forgiven or not forgiven (Acts 10:42; see 17:31). To be forgiven one must "believe in Him" (10:43; see 5:14; 9:42; 11:17), as all the Old Testament prophets taught (Isa. 53:11; Jer. 31:34; Ezek. 36:25–26).

God interrupted Peter's sermon by giving the Holy Spirit to these Gentiles who, when they heard the gospel, believed on Jesus (Acts 10:44–45). Immediately the Holy Spirit fell on them, filling them (10:47; 11:15; see 2:4) and baptizing them (11:16; see 1:5). The outward evidence that God had given His Spirit to these gentile believers was that they spoke in tongues (that is, they miraculously spoke foreign languages without having learned them) and praised God (10:46; see 11:15–16). This amazed Peter's Jewish companions because it showed that God did not require Gentiles to become Jewish proselytes before He accepted them. There was no reason to withhold water baptism from these converts since they had believed in Jesus Christ and had experienced Spirit baptism just as Jewish believers in Jesus had. Baptism with the Spirit was Jesus' sign of His acceptance of them, and baptism with water was their sign of their acceptance of Him.

Peter's actions in Caesarea drew criticism from conservative Jews back in Jerusalem (11:1–3). When he related to them what had happened (11:4–17), they had no further objections but praised God that He had accepted Gentiles who turned to Him for eternal life (11:18).

The initiatives of the Antioch church (11:19–30). The persecution resulting from Stephen's martyrdom had resulted in Christians going as far from Jerusalem as Phoenicia, Cyprus, and Antioch of Syria. They shared the gospel with fellow Jews, but some believers from Cyprus and Cyrene in North Africa also presented it to Gentiles. God blessed both efforts and many people came to the Lord from both ethnic groups. Luke's reference back to the persecution resulting from Stephen's martyrdom (7:60) suggests that he was now beginning to record another mission of the Christians that ran parallel logically and chronologically to the one he had just described in 8:4–11:18. Antioch was the capital of the Roman province of Syro-Cilicia, north of Phoenicia, and it became the sending city for major missions to the Gentiles that followed.

As the apostles had done previously when they heard of the Samaritans' salvation (8:14–15), they investigated when word of the salvation of Gentiles in Antioch reached Jerusalem (11:22). Godly Barnabas (4:36–37) was an excellent man for this mission since he was from Cyprus. He rejoiced when he observed God's grace at work in Antioch, and, true to his name (which means "son of encouragement"), he encouraged the new converts to remain faithful to the Lord. Even more people became believers there (11:24).[10]

As the church in Antioch continued to grow, Barnabas and others sensed the need for Saul's help, so Barnabas set out to track him down in Tarsus (see 9:30). Saul was an ideal choice for this work since God had specifically appointed him to evangelize Gentiles (22:21), and by this time he had considerable experience in ministry. Barnabas had earlier sponsored Saul in Jerusalem (9:27), and now he brought Saul to Antioch, where together they taught and led the church for a year. For the first time people now distinguished the Christians from religious Jews as well as from pagan Gentiles (see 1 Cor. 10:32).[11]

In the reign of Emperor Claudius (A.D. 41–54) a series of severe famines and poor harvests occurred in various parts of the Roman Empire including Judea, which Agabus, a Christian prophet, had predicted. The Christians in Antioch demonstrated love for and unity with their Jewish brethren in Jerusalem by sending them some relief money by Barnabas and Saul. As the Jerusalem church had ministered to the church in Antioch by providing leadership and teaching, the Antioch church now was able to minister to the Jerusalem church with financial aid.

The persecution of the Jerusalem church (12:1–24). The saints in Jerusalem not only suffered as a result of the famine; they also suffered because Jewish and Roman governmental opposition against them intensified as time passed. Nevertheless God supernaturally protected and blessed His church.

One such incident involved Peter's release from prison (12:1–19). The Feast of Unleavened Bread was a seven-day celebration that began the day after Passover each spring. This was one of the three yearly feasts in Jerusalem that the Mosaic Law required all Jewish males to attend. As on the Day of Pentecost (chapter 2), the city would have been swarming with patriotic Jews when Herod made his grandstand political move of arresting Peter (see also 4:3; 5:18). These Jews knew Peter as the leading apostle among the Christians and as a Jew who fraternized with Gentiles (chapter 10). Sixteen soldiers (four squads of four soldiers) guarded Peter in six-hour shifts so he would not escape as he had done previously (5:19–24). His captors probably imprisoned Peter in the Roman Fortress of Antonia. The Christians prayed fervently about Peter's fate, believing that God could effect his release again.

The night before Peter's trial and probable execution he lay sound asleep in his cell (12:6). Peter was chained by both hands to a guard on either side of him. Again an angel of the Lord visited him in prison (see

5:19; 8:26; 12:23), and a light illuminated his cell. The angel instructed him to get up quickly, and when he did his chains fell from his wrists. The angel urged Peter to get dressed and to follow him out of the prison. Peter was so groggy he did not realize he was really being set free (12:9), but God was orchestrating Peter's release.

Once outside the prison and left alone by his angelic guide, Peter realized that his freedom was genuine. He went directly to a home where he probably knew that Christians would be praying for him. Rhoda's joy at finding Peter at the gate overpowered her common sense. Instead of letting him in she ran inside the house and announced his arrival. The believers could not believe that God had answered their prayers so directly and dramatically. Peter meanwhile stood outside, still trying to get in. Finally they let him in, hardly able to believe that he really was Peter. Assuring them that it was he, the apostle asked them to notify James, Jesus' half brother, who had become the foremost leader of the Jerusalem church after Peter's departure (see 15:13; 21:18; Gal. 1:19; 2:9, 12; James 1:1).

Herod evidently concluded that the guards had cooperated with Peter's escape or at least had been negligent, so he executed them (Acts 12:19). Herod then left Judea (the old Jewish name for the area around Jerusalem) and returned to Caesarea, the official capital of the Roman province of Judea. Even a Roman authority could not prevent the church from growing!

King Herod had become displeased with his subjects who lived in Tyre and Sidon (12:20). Because the people of these towns depended on Galilee, part of King Herod's country, for their food supply, they were eager to get on his good side again. Josephus, first-century Jewish historian, recorded this incident in more detail than Luke did, adding that Herod appeared in the outdoor theater at Caesarea. He stood before the officials from Tyre, Sidon, and his other provinces on a festival day dressed in a silver robe. When the sun shone brilliantly on his shiny robe, some flatterers in the theater began to acclaim him as a god. Immediately severe stomach pains attacked him. Attendants had to carry him out of the theater, and five days later he died. Doctor Luke saw Herod's attack as a judgment from God and gave a more medical explanation of his death than did Josephus. More important than the effect was the cause, namely, Herod's pride (12:23).

In spite of Herod's opposition, the gospel continued to grow and multiply through God's supernatural blessing. Therefore the church continued to flourish in Jewish territory as well as among the Gentiles. Acts 12:24 is another of Luke's progress reports that concludes a section of his history (see 2:47; 6:7; 9:31). Nothing seemed capable of stopping the expansion of the church.

B. The Extension of the Church to Cyprus and Asia Minor (12:25–16:5)

As the Christian mission to the Gentiles unfolded, it paralleled the mission to the Jews. Luke drew attention to this by relating many things the missionaries to the Gentiles did that were similar to what the missionaries to the Jews did. This demonstrates that God was indeed behind both missions and that they are really two aspects of His worldwide plan to bring the gospel to all people and to build a global church. But Acts 12:25–16:5 does more than just present the geographical expansion of the church into Asia Minor (modern western Turkey). It also shows the legitimacy of Christians dealing with Gentiles as Gentiles, rather than through Judaism. The church and Judaism are two separate entities. God was not just refreshing the remnant in Israel with Gentiles who believed in Jesus. He was also creating a new body, the church. This section culminates in the Jerusalem Council (chapter 15) in which the issue of the Gentiles' relationship to the church came to a head.

The divine appointment of Barnabas and Saul (12:25–13:3). After delivering the Antiochian Christians' gift to the church in Jerusalem (11:27–30), Barnabas and Saul returned to Antioch, taking with them John Mark (12:25), Barnabas's cousin (Col. 4:10), who later wrote the Second Gospel. Acts 12:25 connects what follows with the earlier account of the virile Antioch church (11:19–30). The reference to John Mark here also connects the preceding section about the Jerusalem church (12:1–24) with what follows. Luke's purpose in these "connections" was to help readers see that what follows had a solid basis in both the gentile Antiochian church and the Jewish Jerusalem church.

There were five prominent prophets and teachers in the church at Antioch at that time. Barnabas, Simeon, and Lucius were prophets (forthtellers and

perhaps foretellers), and Manaen and Saul were teachers (Scripture expositors). [12] This church was cosmopolitan, and God gifted it with several speakers.
It was while these men were serving that God directed them.

> God usually uses His servants who are already serving Him, as
> they have opportunity, rather than those who are just sitting by idly
> waiting for direction. And God leads His people though a variety of
> means that His disciples who are walking with Him can identify as
> His leading.

The mission to Cyprus (13:4–12). The events of Paul's first missionary
journey, which began here, document the extension of the church into
new territory and illustrate the principles and methods by which the
church grew. They also show God's supernatural blessing on the witness
of Barnabas and Saul.

Peter had encountered Simon, a sorcerer, when the Jerusalem church
initiated its first major outreach in Samaria (8:9–24). Now Barnabas and
Saul met Bar-Jesus, a false prophet and sorcerer, when the Antioch church
conducted its first major outreach to Gentiles.

The missionaries departed from Seleucia, the port of Antioch. Salamis,
the largest town in eastern Cyprus, lay on the coast, and there were enough
Jews there to warrant more than one synagogue. Barnabas and Saul habitually visited the Jewish synagogues when they preached the gospel
because that was where people who were God-fearing anticipators of the
Messiah assembled, including both Jews and Gentiles.

Barnabas and Saul traveled west across Cyprus, coming eventually to
Paphos, the provincial capital of the island. Word reached Sergius Paulus
of the missionaries' preaching, and he ordered them to meet with him so
he could hear their message personally. He was a proconsul, the highest
Roman government official on the island. Evidently Bar-Jesus (literally,
"son of a savior") was a Jewish false prophet in the sense that he claimed
to be a prophet of God but was not. He was only a magician who may
have had some satanic power. "Elymas" seems to have been a nickname
since it means "sorcerer." Luke now introduced Saul's Greek name, Paul
(13:9), by which he referred to him from now on in Acts. Here Paul's

extensive ministry to the Gentiles was launched (see 22:21). Instead of being full of wisdom, Paul said, Elymas was full of deceit and a fraud (13:10). Instead of being the son of a savior, Bar-Jesus was a son of the devil. Instead of being the promoter of righteousness, this magician was making the straight way of the Lord crooked. Paul's show of superior power convinced Sergius Paulus (13:7) of the truth of the gospel, and he believed it (see also 14:1; 17:34; 19:18).

At Paphos Paul assumed the leadership among the missionaries. The missionary journey also became more gentile-oriented. Jewish response continued to be rejection, symbolized by Elymas's blindness. Furthermore this was the first appearance of Christianity before Roman aristocracy and high authority, a new benchmark for the advance of the mission.

The mission to Asia Minor (13:13–14:25). Having evangelized in Barnabas's homeland, the missionaries next moved into Paul's native territory of southern Asia Minor. Pamphylia was a Roman province that lay west of the kingdom of Antiochus, which was west of Cilicia, Paul's home province. Perga lay ten miles inland from the major seaport of Attalia. In Perga, John Mark left Paul and Barnabas to return to Jerusalem. Paul did not approve of his decision (15:38), and we can only guess Mark's motives.

Paul and Barnabas proceeded north about a hundred miles to Antioch of Pisidia, where they ministered next (13:14–52). The road took them from sea level to 3,600 feet elevation through bandit-infested territory to a lake-filled plateau. Antioch of Pisidia was a Roman colony, one of many such colonies situated at strategic places in the empire along frequently traveled roads. Antioch, therefore, was a good place to plant a church, for it was the chief military and political center in the southern part of the Roman province of Galatia.

Paul and Barnabas attended the Sabbath service in a local synagogue (13:14–15). The synagogue leaders invited Paul and Barnabas to give an address if they had some encouraging word to share. In every town with a sizable Jewish population that he visited, the apostle first preached in the synagogue to Jews and God-fearing Gentiles. When the Jews refused to listen further, he went directly to the Gentiles with the gospel.

Luke recorded three of Paul's evangelistic messages to unbelievers: here in Pisidian Antioch (13:16–41), in Lystra (14:15–17), and in Athens

(17:22–31). This is the longest of the three, though Luke probably condensed all of them.[13] This one illustrates how Paul preached to people who knew the Old Testament.

Paul reviewed God's preparation for Israel's redemption from Abraham through David (see 7:2–50; Matt. 1:2–17). He highlighted five important points the Jews often stressed in their confessions (Acts 13:17–22). He then announced that the promised Messiah had come and that He is Jesus. He narrated the rejection, crucifixion, and resurrection of Jesus, all fulfillments of Old Testament predictions. Paul stressed Jesus' resurrection as God's vindication of Him (13:30) as well as the apostles' personal witness of His resurrection (13:31; see also 2:32; 3:15; 5:32; 10:39–41). He supported his claims by quoting three Old Testament messianic passages (Ps. 2:7; Isa. 55:3; Ps. 16:10). Then the apostle concluded by applying Habakkuk's warning to all who reject the good news about Jesus Christ (Hab. 1:5). God's working in their day (by providing the Messiah) was something they could not afford to disbelieve and scoff at, or they would perish.

Paul's message created great interest in many people who listened to him (Acts 13:42–47). He and Barnabas continued clarifying the gospel for their inquirers during the following week. One reason for the unsaved Jews' antagonism was the large crowd that Paul's message attracted. Jealousy, rather than the Holy Spirit, filled and controlled these unbelieving Jews and again led to persecution (see 5:17). Another reason for the Jews' hostility was the content of Paul's message. Like other Jews elsewhere, most of the Jews in Antioch did not believe that Jesus is the Messiah. As the apostles in Jerusalem had done (see 4:29), Paul and Barnabas responded to the opposition with bold words. It was necessary for the gospel to go to the Jews before the Gentiles not only because Jewish acceptance of Jesus is a prerequisite to the messianic kingdom (see 3:26) but also because Jesus is the Jewish Messiah, by whom God promised He would deliver His chosen people. By rejecting Jesus these Jews were really, though not consciously, judging themselves unworthy of salvation. Paul quoted the Servant's commission in Isaiah 49:6 because the apostle was addressing Jews (Acts 13:47). The Jews were to be "a light for the Gentiles," but they had failed this responsibility. So Jesus Christ, the perfect Servant of the Lord, became the ultimate Light to the Gentiles, who would bring salvation to the ends of the earth (see Luke 2:28–32).

Luke again stressed that the results of the preaching of the gospel were due to God's work (Acts 13:48–49). Good news spreads fast, and the good news of the gospel spread through that entire region. The Jews secured Paul and Barnabas's expulsion from their district through influential local residents who brought persecution on the missionaries. Some of these people were devout women, evidently God-fearers (like Cornelius, 10:2) whom the unbelieving Jews turned against Paul and Barnabas. Shaking the dust off one's feet was a graphic way by which Jews illustrated separation from unbelievers (Matt. 10:14; Luke 9:5; 10:11). The missionaries moved on to Iconium, about eighty-five miles to the southeast of Antioch, also in Phrygian Galatia. Fullness of joy and fullness of the Holy Spirit marked these disciples (Acts 13:52).

Iconium, the next venue of the apostles' ministry (14:1–7), was a Greek city. There Paul and Barnabas followed the same method of evangelizing that they had used in Antioch of Pisidia (13:14); they visited the synagogue first. They also experienced the same results: many conversions among both Jews and Gentiles but also rejection by some of the Jews (see 13:43). These unbelieving Jews stirred up unbelieving Gentiles who joined them in opposing the missionaries (see 13:50). Because God was saving many people, the missionaries stayed on in Iconium a long time in spite of opposition that evidently increased gradually. They testified boldly and relied on the Lord Jesus for their success. They did many miracles there too, thus confirming their message (see 2:43; 4:30; 5:12; 6:8; 8:6, 13; 15:12; Gal. 3:5; 2 Cor. 12:12; Heb. 2:3–4). Some of the Gentiles and the Jews, including their rulers, took the initiative to persecute the evangelists (Acts 14:5). The attempt to stone them was apparently an act of mob violence rather than a formal Jewish attempt at execution. Consequently Paul and Barnabas moved south into the geographical region of Lyconia, which was also in the Roman province of Galatia.

Like Antioch of Pisidia, Lystra was a Roman colony, and it was about twenty miles south of Iconium (14:8). There Paul and Barnabas encountered a hopeless lame man (see also 3:1–10; 9:33–35). This man believed God could heal him (14:9), and He did through Paul. Archaeologists have turned up evidence of a legend in Lystra that Zeus and Hermes once visited an elderly couple who lived there years before Paul and Barnabas arrived. Apparently the locals concluded that these gods had returned. Zeus was the chief god in the Greek pantheon, and Hermes was his herald. The residents of Lystra identified Barnabas with Zeus (whom the Romans called Jupiter), and they called Paul Hermes (the Roman Mercury) because he was the chief speaker. They prepared to worship the missionaries as gods because of this healing.

By recording the substance of what Barnabas and Paul said here (14:15–18), Luke preserved a sample of their preaching to pagan audiences (see also 13:16–41; 17:22–31). This was the first time Luke recorded the preaching of the gospel to a group that was predominantly, if not exclusively, gentile. In earlier times, they said, God had manifested the knowledge of Himself to Gentiles, mainly through creation (see Rom. 1:18–20). Now He was giving them more revelation through the missionaries. The hostile Jews from Antioch and Iconium turned the tide of popular sentiment against Barnabas and Paul, convincing the fickle residents of Lystra that the missionaries were deceivers rather than deities and deserved to die. Luke's description of Paul's speedy recovery (Acts 14:20) stresses God's powerful hand in restoring His servant.

Paul and Barnabas next moved about sixty miles farther to the southeast to Derbe on the eastern border of the Galatian province (14:20). Many more people became believers and disciples there. Luke did not record what the apostles experienced there, but this was the hometown of Gaius, one of Paul's later companions (20:4).

The missionaries then began their return trip to Syrian Antioch (14:21–28). They confined their labors to the Galatian province on this trip, retracing their steps to encourage, instruct, and organize the new converts (just as Paul did later; 18:23). The missionaries warned the converts that they too should expect persecution. The elders (plural) in every church (singular) that the apostles appointed must have been the more mature Christians in each congregation. They also committed their new converts to the Lord Jesus, the Head of the church, in whom they had believed.

Paul and Barnabas's return to Antioch of Syria (14:26–28). Leaving

Attalia, the seaport ten miles south of Perga, the apostles sailed directly for Syrian Antioch. Paul and Barnabas had accomplished a wonderful work (14:26), but they were careful to give God the credit for it (14:27–28). Now large numbers of gentile converts were entering the church without first becoming Jewish proselytes. This situation formed the occasion for the Jerusalem Council.

The Jerusalem Council (15:1–35). The increasing number of Gentiles who were becoming Christians raised another problem within the church. What was the relationship of the church to Judaism? Some Christians, especially the more conservative Jewish believers, argued that Christianity was a party within Judaism, the party of true believers. They assumed that gentile Christians, therefore, needed to become Jewish proselytes, which involved their being circumcised and obeying the Mosaic Law. The more broad-minded Jewish believers and the gentile converts saw no need for these restrictions. They viewed the church not as a party within Judaism but as a distinct group separate from Judaism that incorporated both believing Jews and believing Gentiles. This difference of viewpoint led to the meeting that Luke recorded in this section.

The men from Judea who came down to Antioch (15:1) seem to have been Jewish Christians who believed a person could not become a Christian without first becoming a Jew, which included circumcision. This was essentially a denial of the sufficiency of faith in Christ for salvation. They evidently claimed that James, the Lord's half brother and the leader of the Jerusalem church, endorsed their position (see Gal. 2:12). Hot debate of this important issue ensued among the Christians. It ended with a decision to move the discussion to Jerusalem and to place the whole matter before the apostles and elders there for a decision. Men from Antioch accompanied Paul and Barnabas as witnesses. On the way to Jerusalem, the missionaries recounted to the Christians in Phoenicia and Samaria what God had done in Cyprus and Asia Minor. These believers rejoiced because they saw a continuation of what had happened to them. When Paul's party arrived in Jerusalem, the leaders there received them and listened to their missionary report.

Some in the meeting were converted Pharisees who had a high view of the Mosaic Law. They repeated the same objection Paul and Barnabas had encountered in Antioch (15:5; see v. 1). After much discussion, Peter reminded those assembled that several years earlier God had chosen him as the person from whom Gentiles (Cornelius and his friends) should hear the gospel. God had given them His Spirit as soon as they believed in Jesus Christ. This was the same thing that had taken place among the Jews on the Day of Pentecost (15:8). When a Gentile became a Jewish proselyte, the Jew in charge of the ceremony said the Gentile now took up the yoke of the kingdom of heaven (see Matt. 23:4; Gal. 5:1). Peter said this yoke, the Mosaic Covenant, was a burden that was both unbearable and improper for Christians. By referring to the Jews being saved in the same manner as the Gentiles, Peter even repudiated Jewish superiority in the church (Acts 15:11).

The next main speakers were Barnabas and Paul (15:12). They emphasized the signs and wonders God had performed through them because these should have persuaded the Jews that God had validated their ministry to Gentiles (see 1 Cor. 1:22).

Finally James gave his opinion (Acts 15:13–21). James reminded his hearers that the Old Testament prophets supported the salvation of Gentiles apart from Judaism (Amos 9:11–12). Amos predicted the (second) advent of Messiah after "these things" (Acts 15:17), that is, after the Tribulation (Amos 9:8–10). Messiah would set up His kingdom on the earth and restore the nation Israel (during the Millennium) under which the Gentiles would seek the Lord. The present inclusion of Gentiles in the church is consistent, James pointed out, with God's promise to Israel through Amos. Isaiah 45:21 (Acts 15:18b in some manuscripts) supports James's interpretation of the prophecy in Amos 9. James was not in favor of making it difficult for the Gentiles by imposing the requirements of Jewish proselytes on them. But to help gentile converts not put a stumbling block in the path of Jews, he recommended that Christian teachers encourage their disciples to be careful to avoid things associated with idolatry and all kinds of sexual aberrations. If gentile Christians disregarded the convictions of Jews, they would only alienate those they hoped to bring to faith in Jesus Christ or to growth in Christ (see 1 Cor. 8:13).

An official formulation of the group's decision followed (Acts 15:22–29). The Jerusalem leaders chose two witnesses to return to Antioch with Paul and Barnabas to confirm verbally the decision of this council. These men represented both racial segments of the Jerusalem church. They also sent a letter stating that the men who had come to Antioch from Jerusalem advocating circumcision (15:1) had no authorization from the Jerusalem church to do so. The apostles presented Barnabas and Paul as men the Jerusalem saints held in the highest regard (15:25–26). All the leaders had sensed the Holy Spirit's control in the decision they had reached. When the response in Antioch to this decision was positive (15:30–35), another problem had been solved.

The strengthening of the gentile churches (15:36–16:5). After some ministry in Antioch, Paul and Barnabas desired to return to the churches they had planted in Cyprus and Asia Minor and strengthen them. But this trip, Paul's second missionary journey, began after a disagreement with Barnabas (15:36–41). The Holy Spirit evidently led both men to arrive at their respective conclusions regarding the wisdom of taking John Mark with them. Based on 1 Corinthians 9:6; Colossians 4:10; 2 Timothy 4:11; and Philemon 24, their separation was probably friendly. Barnabas's desire to offer John Mark another opportunity was certainly commendable and godly, even though Paul viewed it as unwise. Barnabas took John Mark with him to Cyprus, and Paul and Silas traveled by land north through Syria and Cilicia.

Paul and Silas then strengthened the churches that Paul and Barnabas had planted in Galatia (Acts 16:1–5). At Lystra a young believer named Timothy impressed Paul (1 Cor. 4:17; 2 Tim. 1:5; 3:15). Paul circumcised Timothy because this was necessary for effective evangelistic ministry among the Jews (see 1 Cor. 9:20–22), and he joined Paul and Silas on their travels. Part of Paul and Silas's ministry included acquainting the churches in Galatia with the directives formulated at the Jerusalem Council (Acts 16:4).

A fifth progress report in 16:5 concludes the section on the church's expansion into Asia Minor (12:25–16:5). In this phase of its expansion the church changed from being predominantly Jewish to being predominantly gentile.

C. The Extension of the Church to the Aegean Shores (16:6–19:20)

The missionary outreach narrated in this section of the book took place in major cities along the Aegean coastline, cities connected by major Roman roads.

The call to Macedonia (16:6–19). Probably Paul and his companions intended to follow the Via Sebaste westward to Ephesus, the capital of the Roman province of Asia, but the Holy Spirit closed that door. Again the Holy Spirit prevented them from entering the province of Bithynia to the north, so they traveled northwest to the city of Troas. Luke joined Paul and his associates there in Troas.[14] While Paul was in Troas, God gave positive direction to him in a vision. A Macedonian man appeared to him, urging him to enter the province of Macedonia and help the residents there. Luke recorded Paul's vision of the Macedonian man to explain God's initiative in encouraging Paul and his companions to carry the gospel farther west into Europe. Three names stress the fact that the triune God was leading these apostles: the Holy Spirit (16:6), the Spirit of Jesus (16:7), and God (16:10).

> We should not concern ourselves mainly with the methods God uses to guide people. These varied in Acts and were not Luke's primary concern. We should, however, concentrate on where we can be of most use as the Lord's instruments. This was Paul's dominant concern.

The ministry in Macedonia (16:11–17:15). Luke devoted more space to Paul's evangelizing in Philippi than he did to the apostle's activities in any other city on his second and third journeys, even though Paul was there only briefly (16:11–40).

Traveling by sea from Troas, the apostolic band made its way to the island of Samothrace and from there to Neapolis, the port of Philippi in Macedonia (16:12). Philippi was located ten miles northwest inland at the eastern end of another major Roman highway that connected the Adriatic and Aegean Seas, the Via Egnatia. As a Roman colony, Philippi enjoyed special privileges for having rendered some outstanding service to the empire. All its free citizens enjoyed the rights of Roman citizens.

The conversion of three very different individuals in Philippi illustrates the broad appeal and power of the gospel. Lacking a synagogue, God-fearers in Philippi met beside the Gangites River to pray (16:13, 16). Paul preached the gospel to the women who assembled there, one of whom was a businesswoman, Lydia, and she trusted Christ. God opened her heart to the gospel (16:14; see 2 Cor. 4:4) and the hearts of those in her household. Water baptism followed her conversion immediately. She opened her large home to Paul and his companions while they remained in Philippi.

A demon-possessed slave girl met the missionaries on their way to the place of prayer (16:16). She was a tool of her masters who used her to make money through fortunetelling. The demon within her knew of Paul and announced through her who he was and what he was doing (compare the demons' knowledge in Jesus' day: Mark 1:24; 3:11; 5:7; Luke 4:34; 8:28). She seems to have appointed herself as the apostles' herald, announcing them wherever they went. Paul did not want her to continue doing this, however. Jesus, working through Paul, cast the demon out (Acts 16:18). The girl's masters wanted to get even with Paul for causing them financial loss. It was contrary to Roman law for local people to try to change the religion of Roman citizens. The girl's masters assumed that Paul and Silas were proselytizing for Judaism since the customs Paul proclaimed included worship of Jesus, a Jew, rather than the emperor or local gods. The crowd supported the missionaries' accusers (16:22). The charges against them seemed so clear the magistrates evidently did not even investigate them but proceeded to beat and imprison Paul and Silas as if they were dangerous criminals.

We can see that Paul and Silas were full of the Spirit by the way they reacted to the pain resulting from their beating and from being locked in stocks (16:25). Again God miraculously freed His servants (see also 5:18–20; 12:3–11). Certain that his prisoners had escaped, the jailer was about to commit suicide, to avoid the shame of his being executed publicly (16:27). Paul and Silas's love for the jailer, in contrast to the hatred they had received from many of the Philippians, transformed the jailer's attitude. Now, because of his brush with death, he humbled himself and asked how he could be saved (16:30). He believed that Jesus had the power to protect and deliver His own, and he saw Him as the One with adequate power and authority to save. Other members of the jailer's household believed and were saved just as he was (see also 16:15). The jailer washed Paul and Silas's wounds (16:33), and then they baptized him. He extended hospitality to them, and his whole family rejoiced in their salvation (16:34).

The police officers returned to the jail the next morning with orders to release Paul and Silas. The Roman government guaranteed its citizens a public trial and freedom from degrading punishment such as beatings. Paul was now able to use his citizenship to advantage, namely, for the progress of the gospel (see Phil. 1:18). Roman officials charged with mistreating Roman citizens faced discipline by their superiors. These magistrates meekly appealed to Paul and Silas not to file a complaint. They also wanted them to leave Philippi because popular opinion was still hostile to them because Paul had healed the slave girl. Furthermore, the local magistrates did not want to have to protect Paul's party of foreigners from irate local residents. Paul did not leave Philippi immediately but first encouraged the Christians, the nucleus of the church in Philippi (see Phil. 1:3; 4:10–16).

Paul and his team left Philippi, headed southwest on the Egnatian Road, and arrived eventually in Thessalonica (Acts 17:1–9), the chief city and capital of Macedonia.[15] As such it was a strategic center for the evangelization of the Balkan Peninsula (see 1 Thess. 1:7–8). Paul evidently spoke in the synagogue only three Sabbath days (Acts 17:2), but he may have stayed longer in Thessalonica (see Phil. 4:15–16; 1 Thess. 2:9; 4:1; 2 Thess. 2:5; 3:7–10). He dealt carefully with his hearers' questions and doubts and showed that the facts of gospel history confirmed what the Scriptures predicted. Paul's reasoning persuaded some in the synagogue services, many of whom were God-fearers and some of whom were Jews. The gospel impacted the leadership level of society in Thessalonica.

The Jews treated Paul harshly here as they had in Galatia (Acts 13:45, 50; 14:2, 19). The Jewish antagonists charged the missionaries with the revolutionary teaching that another king, Jesus, would rule and reign (see 1 Thess. 3:13; 5:1–11; 2 Thess. 1:5–10; 2:14). These Thessalonian Jews also claimed no king but Caesar. The city officials could not find the missionaries to bring them to trial, so they made Jason and his friends, who were supporters of Paul, pay a bond guaranteeing that Paul would cause no further trouble and would leave town. Paul did leave, but the Christians carried on admirably, for which Paul later thanked God (1 Thess. 1:7–10; 2:14–16).

For a second time Paul fled a city under cover of night (Acts 17:10; see 9:25). He and Silas left the Via Egnatia at Thessalonica and took the eastern coastal road toward Athens, arriving next in Berea about fifty

miles southwest of Thessalonica. In spite of continued Jewish antagonism Paul and Silas again launched their ministry in this town by visiting
the synagogue (17:10–15). The Jews in Berea did not react out of jealousy (17:5) but listened carefully to what Paul preached and compared
it to the teachings of their Hebrew Scriptures. Many of these noble skeptics believed because Paul's teaching about Jesus harmonized with the
Old Testament.

Hearing of Paul's presence in Berea, the unbelieving Jews of Thessalonica
followed him there (17:13). In forcing Paul out of Berea they evidently
adopted the same tactics they had used in Thessalonica (17:5, 9). Paul
reached Athens safely and sent instructions back with the Berean brethren who had accompanied him that Silas and Timothy, who had remained
in Berea, should join him soon.

The ministry in Achaia (17:16–18:17). In the province of Achaia Paul
ministered first in the city of Athens (17:16–34). Athens had reached its
political prime five hundred years before Paul visited it, but it was still the
cultural and intellectual center of the Greek world. Paul observed many
of the temples and statues that still stand there today, but in Paul's day
they were idols and places of worship the Greeks regarded as holy. Paul
continued his ministry to Jews and God-fearing Greeks in the synagogue,
but he also discussed the gospel with any who wanted to do so in the
marketplace. These people were probably not God-fearing Gentiles but
simply pagan Gentiles.

Paul's hearers implied that he had put together a philosophy of life
simply by picking up scraps of ideas from various sources. (The Greek
word for "babbler" in 17:18 is literally "seed-picker," suggesting someone
who, like birds picking seeds, gathered ideas from here and there.) Others
accused him of proclaiming new gods, though his critics seem to have
misunderstood his words about the resurrection as references not to an
event but to a person, perhaps a female counterpart to Jesus. The Council
of the Areopagus had authority over religion, morals, and education in
Athens. Its members wanted to know what Paul was advocating. This interest of theirs gave Paul an opportunity to preach the gospel.

Paul's address (17:22–31) is a sample of his preaching to intellectual
pagans. In this speech Paul began with God as Creator and then spoke of

God as Judge. The apostle was not flattering his audience by calling them "very religious"; they were firm in their reverence for their gods. The apostle again followed his policy of adapting to the people he was seeking to evangelize and meeting them where they were in their thinking (1 Cor. 9:22). Beginning with the Athenians' interest in gods and their confessed ignorance about at least one god, he proceeded to explain what the Lord had revealed about Himself. The true God created and sustains all things. He is immanent as well as transcendent. The Greeks, and especially the Athenians, prided themselves on being racially superior to all other people, but Paul told them that they, like all others, had descended from one source, Adam. God also is sovereign over the political and military affairs of nations, though the Greeks liked to think they determined their own destiny. God's purpose in regulating times and boundaries was that people would realize His sovereignty and seek Him (Acts 17:27). God, Paul said, is not far from human contact. The apostle cited lines from two Greek writers (Epimenides and Aratus) who expressed ideas that were consistent with divine revelation.

Paul's conclusion was that idolatry is illogical (17:29). If God created people, God cannot be an image or an idol. Before the Incarnation people died as unbelievers and were lost, but now there is more light. Consequently people's guilt is greater since Jesus came. God previously took the relative lack of understanding about Himself into consideration as He dealt with people (17:30). But now that Christ has come, He expects more from people. The resurrected Jesus is God's Agent of judgment. Paul stressed that Jesus is a human being, not an idol or a mythological character such as a Greek god. The proof of Jesus' qualification to judge humanity is His resurrection (see John 5:25–29).

The response of the Athenians to Paul's preaching was typical: Some mocked, others procrastinated, and a few believed (Acts 17:32–34).

Paul then proceeded southwest from Athens to Corinth (18:1–17). Shortly after arriving there, he met Aquila and Priscilla, Jews who had recently left Rome under official compulsion. Paul evidently had a financial need, so he went to work practicing his trade of leatherworking while he preached (see 20:34; 1 Cor. 4:12; 9:1–18; 2 Cor. 11:9). Having felt he had fulfilled his responsibility to deliver the gospel to Jews, Paul turned to evangelizing the Gentiles, as he had done before (Acts 13:7–11, 46; 14:2–6; 17:5). Many of the gentile Corinthians believed the gospel when they heard it from Paul amid considerable opposition. Another vision quieted Paul's fears, and so he stayed a year and a half ministering in Corinth (18:11).

Paul's ministry in Corinth included an appearance before Gallio, the Roman provincial governor (18:12–17). The Corinthian Jews' charge against Paul was the same as the one the Philippian and Thessalonian Jews had raised (16:21; 17:6–7, 13). They claimed he was proselytizing among Roman citizens for a new religion. To Gallio the accusations of these Jews seemed to involve matters of religious controversy that entailed no violation of Roman law. Consequently he declined to hear the case and ordered the Jews to settle it themselves. Gallio's decision resulted in the official toleration of Christianity that continued in the empire until A.D. 64 when Nero blamed the Christians for burning Rome.

The beginning of ministry in Asia (18:18–22). Luke recorded Paul's initial contact in Ephesus in this section to set the scene for the apostle's ministry there when he returned from Syrian Antioch (chapter 19).

Paul stayed in Corinth and ministered quite a while after Gallio's decision. After taking a vow (see Num. 6:1–21), he departed by ship for Syria.[16] Priscilla and Aquila accompanied him as far as Ephesus, the capital of the province of Asia. The openness of the Jews to Paul's preaching there encouraged him to return, which he did later. After Paul's ship landed at Caesarea on the coast of Palestine, he went to Jerusalem, greeted the church there, and then went back north to Syrian Antioch, completing his second missionary journey (Acts 15:40–18:22).

The results of ministry in Asia (18:23–19:20). Paul's significant ministry in Asia Minor advanced the gospel and stabilized the church on the eastern Aegean shores.

Leaving Antioch, Paul returned to the province of Galatia and the district of Phrygia to strengthen the churches there (18:23; see 15:41–16:6).

The ministry of Apollos in Ephesus (18:24–28) set the stage for Paul's ministry in Asia. Apollos, who was from Alexandria, the capital of Egypt, was a Christian Hellenistic Jew who had a thorough understanding of the Old Testament, a gift for communicating and defending the faith, and enthusiasm. But he did not know about Christian baptism. Priscilla and Aquila took Apollos aside and privately instructed him in subsequent revelations about the gospel that he did not know. Armed with this new understanding, Apollos proceeded west where he ministered in Achaia, the southern portion of present-day Greece, by defending the faith to Jews.

The first of two incidents taken from Paul's ministry in Ephesus that bracket Luke's description of his general ministry there is the event involving the disciples of John the Baptist (19:1–7). When Paul asked them if they had received the Holy Spirit, they said they did not even know there was a Holy Spirit. Having learned that they had expressed repentance by undergoing John's baptism, Paul explained that John had urged his disciples to believe on Jesus. These disciples of John then did that and submitted to baptism in Jesus' name. As with the new converts in Samaria, these Ephesian disciples received the Holy Spirit when an apostle, this time Paul, laid his hands on them (see 8:17). Here the identification of the coming of the Spirit with Paul authenticated God's giving the Spirit (see John 14:16–18, 26; 15:26). God made the coming of the Spirit obvious until the church generally appreciated the fact that it normally occurred at the time of regeneration.

Paul preached to the unusually tolerant Jews in the synagogue at Ephesus for three months (Acts 19:8–12). Eventually they grew unresponsive and tried to discredit Paul's preaching. The apostle therefore moved his venue to a neutral site where he continued teaching for two years. As a result, the local Christians preached the gospel all over the province of Asia. Jesus continued to work the same supernatural miracles through Paul that He had demonstrated during His own earthly ministry (see Mark 5:27; 6:56) and that he had manifested through Peter (Acts 5:15). God's using Paul's handkerchiefs and workman's aprons was unusual, but not without precedent (see Luke 8:44).

An incident that involved the seven sons of Sceva (Acts 19:13–20) throws light on the spiritual darkness that enveloped Ephesus as well as on the power of Jesus Christ and the gospel. As had been Peter's experience (see 8:18–19), some of Paul's observers tried to duplicate his miracles. They wrongly concluded that the simple vocalization of Jesus' name carried magical power. Sceva's sons participated in an exorcism that backfired. News reports of this event greatly elevated the reputation of Jesus among all the Ephesians, both Jews and Gentiles. Many converts abandoned their former practices to follow the Lord. As a result, the church became purer as well as larger and stronger. Luke gave a progress report (19:20) to mark the end of another section of his book (16:6–19:20).

D. The Extension of the Church to Rome (19:21–28:31)

The statements in 19:21–22 introduce this last major subsection of Acts, and 28:31 provides a concluding summary.

Ministry on the way to Jerusalem (19:21–21:16). At this point Paul began to focus his attention on taking the gospel to Rome. Thus Jesus Christ extended His church to the very center of the Roman (gentile) world.

Having laid a firm foundation in Asia Minor and the Aegean Sea region, Paul sensed that he needed to press on to yet unreached gentile areas (see Rom. 15:23). But first, he wanted to collect money for the poor Judean saints from the more prosperous Christians in the Aegean region and deliver it to them in Jerusalem (Acts 19:21–22; see 24:17; 1 Cor. 16:1–4).

Christianity, "the Way," had such an influence in Ephesian society that the local pagan worship suffered. The silversmiths in Ephesus took Artemis as their patron saint and, among their other wares, made miniature silver shrines containing images of the goddess that they sold to devotees. As Christianity spread, interest in Artemis and the market for her statuettes declined. Demetrius, the leader of the guild that made these trinkets, rallied the support of the businesspeople whose trades were suffering because of Paul's influence. Soon the whole pagan populace was against the Christians and dragged two of Paul's companions into the outdoor theater. Paul wanted to use this occasion to preach the gospel to the assembled throng in the theater, but the other Christians sensed his danger and begged him not to make himself a target of their violence. Apparently Alexander was a leading unbelieving Jew who wanted the crowd to understand that even though Paul was a Jew the local Jewish community did not approve of him (see 18:12–17). However, like Gallio in Corinth, this crowd did not distinguish between Christianity and Judaism because both faiths stood against idolatry. The crowd shouted Alexander down.

The city clerk (mayor) was eager to end this demonstration. He made four points to quiet the mob. First, there was no danger whatsoever that people would conclude that Artemis was a goddess made with hands since everyone knew the image of her in her famous temple had fallen from heaven. Second, Gaius and Aristarchus had done nothing worthy of punishment. Third, if Demetrius and his fellow silversmiths had a complaint against the Christians, they should handle it in the legally authorized way and take their adversaries to court. Fourth, he reminded the citizens that if the provincial authorities concluded there was no good reason for their rioting, the authorities could impose penalties on the city. These arguments proved effective, and the crowd dispersed.

Shortly thereafter Paul left Ephesus to visit Macedonia and Achaia (20:1–6). He traveled north to Troas (2 Cor. 2:12), moved west into Macedonia, where he met Titus returning from Corinth (7:5–8), and proceeded south to "Greece" (Achaia). Paul probably spent most of three months in Corinth (see Rom. 16:23; Acts 18:7). He evidently planned to travel on a ship from Cenchrea to Caesarea and Jerusalem to celebrate one of the spring Jewish feasts there (20:6, 16). However, when he learned of the Jews' plot to kill him on the way, he changed his plans and decided to go to Jerusalem by way of Macedonia. Representatives of the churches in the provinces of Macedonia, Galatia, and Asia accompanied Paul with the gift of money for the Jerusalem church. After a few delays, the apostle rejoined his companions in Troas.

Paul met on Sunday night with the Christians in Troas for fellowship, worship, and instruction. The apostle kept speaking late into the night. The combination of a long message and lack of oxygen in the third-story room where they met caused Eutychus to fall asleep and fall out of the window to his death. Paul raised him back to life. The Christians then returned to their upstairs room and Paul continued speaking until daybreak. The incident shows the miraculous power of Jesus Christ working through His apostle at this time (Peter, too, had been used by God to restore a dead person to life; 9:36–42).

Paul left Troas the next day for Miletus (20:13–17). By taking the land route to Assos Paul was able to stay in Troas a little longer than his companions who traveled by ship. After a few days of travel, Paul reached

Most churches face opposition from people outside and inside their fellowship. Church leaders need to look in both directions to guard against trouble.

Miletus, just south of Ephesus. From there he sent for the elders of the Ephesian church instead of spending more time in Ephesus himself.

In Paul's address to the Ephesian elders (20:17–35), he first reviewed his past three-year ministry among these elders. He emphasized particularly his humble service of the Lord (see Eph. 4:2), his sorrows (see 2 Cor. 2:4), the opposition of enemies of the gospel (see Acts 19:9; 20:1), his faithfulness in proclaiming what they needed to hear (see Rom. 1:16), his ceaseless teaching ministry (see Acts 19:8–10), and his comprehensive evangelistic efforts (see 20:26–27). Next Paul described his plans for the future (20:22–25). He intended to visit Jerusalem in spite of the danger that awaited him there because he believed that was part of the evangelistic ministry God had given him to do.

Paul did not plan to return to Ephesus (see Rom. 15:23–29). He had carried out the mission God had given him in that region. Their responsibility was to guard themselves from the attacks of the adversary and then the lives of those under their care. They could expect enemies to arise from outside and inside the church, so they needed to remain alert.

Paul concluded his address by commending these leaders to God and to the Scriptures, which would equip them to serve with distinction (Acts 20:32). He also reminded them of his way of life and integrity as a model for their own service (20:33–35). Prayer for God's grace and protection bonded these men together in Christian love as Paul departed from Miletus (20:36–38).

After an emotionally difficult departure from Miletus, Paul and his companions sailed on to Tyre (21:1–6). Paul stayed in Tyre for seven days, fellowshipping with the Christians there who, anxious about his safety, urged him not to go to Jerusalem. Convinced that God wanted him to visit Jerusalem, he left Tyre after another difficult farewell.

When Paul's group advanced to Caesarea (21:7–14), Agabus (see

11:26–28) arrived and prophesied that Paul would be arrested in Jerusa-lem. Paul's companions tried to discourage him from proceeding. Unable to dissuade him, they stopped urging him and committed the situation to the Lord.

The journey from Caesarea to Jerusalem was the last leg of Paul's trip (21:15–16). Jerusalem was about sixty-five miles southeast of Caesarea, a long two days of travel.

Ministry in Jerusalem (21:17–23:32). The events that transpired in Jerusalem when Paul visited the city on this occasion proved crucial in spreading the gospel to Rome.

Soon after his arrival, Paul visited James and the elders of the Jerusalem church and reported on what God had done through his ministry since he had seen them last. His report delighted these leaders, and the elders added that thousands of Jews had also become believers. However, these Jewish converts were very zealous for the Mosaic Law, which Paul and they taught no longer governed the lives of Christians (chapter 15). They explained that these Jewish Christians had some misgivings about Paul's ministry because they had heard he was telling Jewish converts not to practice cir-cumcision or to observe the customs of Judaism. This was a false report. Paul did not teach that these customs were evil; he taught that they were unnecessary for justification and sanctification. The elders' plan aimed to prove to the Jewish Christians in Jerusalem, and to all the Jews there, that Paul had not abandoned the customs of the Jews. Four men had taken a temporary Nazirite vow of separation to God, as Paul had done earlier (18:18). At the end of their vows each of them had to bring an offering to the temple. After presenting these to the priest, they would cut off their hair and burn it on the altar (see Num. 6:18). The elders suggested that Paul go with them to the temple, purify himself with them for temple worship, and show his support of the Nazirite custom by paying for their offerings. Paul did accompany the four men into the temple and underwent the rites of purification with them because he was paying the expenses of their vow.

A riot in the temple followed (Acts 21:27–36). Non-Christian Jews from Asia recognized Paul in the temple and stirred up the crowd, as Demetrius had done in Ephesus (19:23–41). They accused him of the same crimes the unbelieving Jews of Jerusalem had accused Stephen of committing (6:11, 13–14) and of bringing Gentiles into one of the temple's restricted areas. The priests had posted notices prohibiting Gentiles from entering the sacred enclosure, the area that included the courts of the women, Israel, and the priests. The rumor of Paul's alleged capital offense traveled quickly throughout Jerusalem, resulting in a mob of zealous Jews swarming into the temple courtyard. The priests dragged Paul out of one of the inner courts into the court of the Gentiles. They then closed the doors that separated the court of the Gentiles from the inner courts to prevent the defiling of the inner courts by the tumult. The Jews proceeded to beat Paul in the court of the Gentiles (21:31).

News of this commotion reached the Roman commander of the Antonia Fortress connected with the temple area on the northwest. He summoned soldiers and ran down the steps of the fortress into the court of the Gentiles. The Jews stopped beating Paul when they saw the commander and the other soldiers.[17] The commander arrested Paul, assuming he was a criminal. When the commander tried to learn who Paul was and what he had done, he received conflicting information. The Jews were trying to tear Paul apart, so the commander ordered Paul brought into the "barracks," the Fortress of Antonia.

On hearing from Paul that he was a Roman citizen and not the Egyptian terrorist that the commander suspected him of being, the commander granted Paul permission to address the crowd in Aramaic from the fortress steps (21:37–40).

Paul then proceeded to speak in his own defense (22:1–21). He needed to defend himself against the charge that he had been disloyal to his people, the Mosaic Law, and the temple (see 21:28). He began by relating his manner of life before his conversion to show his hearers that he was as zealous for his Jewish heritage as any of them (see Gal. 1:14). He next related the events of his conversion and stressed the supernatural revelation God had given him. This revelation accounted for the radical change in his life. As a good Jew, Paul obeyed divine revelation. He described Ananias as a devout Jew who carefully observed the Law and who had a good reputation among his fellow Israelites. Ananias explained to Paul that it was the God of their fathers who had appeared to Paul so he could know His will, see the Righteous One (the Messiah,

Jesus of Nazareth), and receive direct revelation from Him (Acts 22:14). Ananias also said that God had told him that Paul was to be a witness "to all men" of what Paul had seen and heard. This vindicated Paul's ministry to Gentiles. Ananias had also instructed Paul to submit to Christian baptism. God confirmed Paul's mission by special revelation as Paul was praying in the temple following his return from Damascus (22:17; see 9:26–29; Gal. 1:18–19). In this vision the risen and exalted Jesus of Nazareth instructed Paul to leave Jerusalem because the Jews there would not accept his testimony about Jesus (Acts 22:18). Instead, Paul was to go to the Gentiles, God revealed to him. Yet Paul did not believe the Gentiles would receive his witness. Specifically the Lord directed him to go to the Gentiles who were far away, namely, Gentiles who had no relationship to Judaism.

The Jews' response to Paul's defense was violent (22:22) because Paul claimed that Jesus is God and that Jesus commanded him to approach Gentiles directly with the gospel without first introducing them to Judaism and its institutions. This was equivalent to placing Gentiles on the same footing before God as Jews, and this was the height of apostasy to traditional Jews.

Paul next had to defend himself before the Roman commander, who could not understand why the Jews reacted as they did (22:23–29). He could not tolerate a riot, so he decided to get the truth from Paul by threatening him and, if necessary, torturing him. By affirming that he was a Roman citizen, Paul avoided a brutal beating.

Since the commander could not discover why the Jews wanted to kill Paul, he turned his prisoner over to the Sanhedrin for questioning (22:30–23:10). (This was at least the sixth time the Sanhedrin evaluated the claims of Christ. See John 11:47–53; Matt. 26:57–69; Acts 4:5–22; 5:21–40; 6:12–7:60; 22:30–23:10). Paul said that nothing he had done was contrary to the will of God revealed in the Old Testament. Specifically, his Christian beliefs and conduct did not compromise his Jewish heritage. Paul's claim to uprightness so incensed the high priest that he ordered a soldier to strike Paul on the mouth (which also had happened to Jesus; John 18:20–23). Paul reacted indignantly and uttered a prophecy of Ananias's judgment that God fulfilled later. For any number of reasons Paul may not have known that the person who commanded the soldier to strike him was the high priest. His quotation from Exodus 22:28 showed that he was in subjection to God's revealed will.

Paul recognized that he could not get a fair trial in a court that did not even observe the Law it claimed to defend, so he changed his tactics (Acts 23:6–10). By raising the old controversy of whether resurrection is possible, Paul divided his accusers. The Pharisees sided with Paul, and the Sadducees opposed him. Their emotional dispute excluded any possibility of a serious examination of Paul's conduct or even a clarification of the charges against him. So the commander decided to take Paul into protective custody in the fortress.

The next night the Lord appeared to Paul again (23:11) assuring him that he would bear witness in Rome as he had already done in Jerusalem.

The Jews plotted to assassinate Paul since they could not get a guilty verdict against him in court (23:12–24). Their plan was to have the chief priests and elders of Israel ask the Roman commander to return Paul to the Sanhedrin for further questioning. Assassins planned to kill him somewhere on the streets between the Fortress of Antonia and the hall of the Sanhedrin. But Paul's nephew got wind of their plot and informed Paul and the commander. The commander realized that Paul's enemies in Jerusalem would stop at nothing to see him dead, so he prepared to send him to the Roman provincial capital with a heavy guard under cover of night.

The commander, Claudius Lysias, also wrote a letter to Felix, the governor of the Roman province of Syria which included Judea, that contained the background of Paul's case (23:25–30). In the commander's judgment Paul was not guilty of any crime.

Paul's military escort to Caesarea kept the apostle safe from his enemies (23:31–32). His departure from Jerusalem was the first leg of his journey to Rome.

Ministry in Caesarea (23:33–26:32). Paul ministered in Caesarea from prison. Luke devoted about three chapters to Paul's ministry in Caesarea primarily to reemphasize the legality of Christianity as various Roman officials scrutinized it and to stress major themes in Paul's addresses.

After Paul arrived in Caesarea, he had to appear before Felix (23:33–35). Felix inquired concerning Paul's home province because if Paul had come from an area in the empire that had its own ruler in addition to a Roman governor, that local authority had a right to witness the proceedings. Cilicia was not such a place, however, so Felix could deal with Paul himself. Felix kept Paul in the governor's palace, the Praetorium, until his accusers arrived and he could conduct a hearing.

Five days later Paul defended himself before Felix (Acts 24). Tertullus, the Jewish prosecutor, leveled three charges against Paul (24:5–7). First, he was a troublemaker in the Roman Empire, having stirred up Jews wherever he went. Second, Paul was the leader of a cult outside mainstream Judaism. Third, Paul had tried to desecrate the temple by bringing a Gentile into its inner precincts (see 21:28). All of Paul's accusers confirmed Tertullus's charges (24:9). Felix had repeatedly crucified the leaders of uprisings for disturbing the peace of Rome.

In response to Tertullus's first charge, Paul said that since he had been in Jerusalem only twelve days he had not had time to be much of a pest (24:11–13). Paul rebutted the second charge of leading a cult by explaining that his beliefs harmonized with the teachings of the Hebrew Scriptures (24:14–16). In response to the third charge, Paul replied that he had gone to Jerusalem to worship and to bring money to the Jews there, not to stir up political trouble (24:17–18; see Gal. 2:7–9). Paul pointed out that his original accusers were not present at his hearing (Acts 24:19), but they should have been. He said the Sanhedrin was upset with him over the issue of the resurrection, not for some crime against Rome (24:20–21). This put Felix in the awkward position of having to decide a theological issue over which his Jewish subjects disagreed.

Felix sought to preserve the peace by delaying the trial and by separating Paul from his accusers. While Paul waited for Lysias to appear in Caesarea, the apostle continued to enjoy considerable personal freedom as well as Roman protection from his Jewish enemies (24:22–23).

Several days later Felix, along with his current Jewish wife, sent for Paul (24:24–26). Paul's emphases in his interview with Felix and Drusilla were things Jesus had promised the Holy Spirit would convict people of to bring them to faith, namely, sin, righteousness, and judgment (John 16:8–11). Felix became uneasy and postponed making a decision about his relationship to God. He kept Paul in detention in Caesarea for two years to placate the Jews, until Porcius Festus succeeded him (Acts 24:27).

After two years Paul had the opportunity to testify before Felix's successor (25:1–12). The Jews realized that they did not have much hope of doing away with Paul through the Roman courts. Their case against him was too weak. So they urged the new governor, Festus, who was in Jerusalem at the time, to send Paul back from Caesarea to Jerusalem so they could kill him on the way there. Festus did not agree to their request but promised to try Paul in Caesarea if his accusers would go down there (25:1–5).

In the hearing that followed in Caesarea, the Jews from Jerusalem could not prove their charges against Paul and produced no witnesses, so all Paul had to do was deny them categorically (25:6–8). As the new governor, Festus did not want to do anything that would turn the Jewish authorities against him, so he asked Paul if he would consent to a trial in Jerusalem (25:9). Paul's appeal for a trial in Rome was the right of every Roman citizen who believed he was in danger of violent coercion or capital punishment in a lower court (25:10–11). Paul's appeal got Festus off the hook with the Jews, so the governor willingly granted it.

A few days later Paul had the opportunity to testify before yet another magistrate, King Herod Agrippa II (25:13–22). Agrippa and Bernice, who lived about eighty miles northeast in Caesarea Philippi, evidently visited Festus on this occasion to pay their respects to the new governor of their neighboring province. Festus told Agrippa about Paul, and Agrippa, who was part Jewish and had grown up in the Herodian family, asked to hear the apostle. Festus readily agreed.

Paul's defense before Agrippa (25:23–26:32) is the longest of his five defenses in Acts. It centers on the gospel with an evangelistic appeal rather than on the charges against Paul. Festus used this occasion to honor Agrippa and Bernice before the local Caesarean leaders. In reviewing the reasons for conducting this hearing, Festus acknowledged that Paul had done nothing worthy of death (25:25). After explaining his need to clarify the charges against Paul, Festus turned the hearing over to Agrippa.

Paul began his testimony with a customary introduction in which he complimented the king sincerely and urged him to listen patiently (26:1–3).

The essence of the controversy surrounding him, he explained, was the fulfillment of God's promise to Israel, namely, salvation through a Messiah. As a Pharisaic Jew, Paul had strongly opposed the idea that Jesus of Nazareth was the Messiah. But his encounter with Jesus on the Damascus Road changed his mind. Jesus had given him a particular mission in life and the message of salvation. It was for preaching this message and fulfilling this mission that the Jews had opposed Paul. Yet everything he said and did harmonized with what the Old Testament prophets had written.

Festus interrupted Paul to say that he did not understand the significance of these matters (26:24–29). He concluded that Paul was a zealous obscurantist and a bit crazy to risk his life promoting such foolish ideas. Paul replied that what Festus called madness was true and reasonable. Agrippa knew the issues, for Jesus' ministry was well known in Palestine. Furthermore Agrippa believed the prophets. Agrippa was now on the spot (26:28), and so he replied noncommittally. Paul then said he wished that all his hearers, not just Agrippa, might become Christians.

By rising to his feet Agrippa signaled the end of the hearing (26:30–32). In Agrippa's opinion Paul did not even need to be in prison, much less die for what he had done.

Ministry on the way to Rome (27:1–28:15). This stage of the gospel expansion demonstrates God's protection of Paul, illustrates the increasingly gentile nature of gospel outreach, and documents the sovereign Lord's building of His church.

The voyage from Caesarea to Crete provided the venue for the first segment of this stage of Paul's ministry (27:1–12). Luke described Paul's party sailing north from Caesarea and making several stops along the Syrian coast. Since he was a Roman citizen who had appealed to Caesar, Paul enjoyed greater privileges than the other regular prisoners and could visit Christians along the way. The ship then turned west and proceeded along the southern coast of Asia Minor. A northwesterly wind forced Paul's ship southwest to the island of Crete. Paul recommended staying through the winter at Fair Havens, but the centurion had the final word, and he determined to press on to Phoenix.

A storm at sea (27:13–26) provided an unusual opportunity for Paul and validated his ministry. As Paul's ship sailed west along the southern coast of Crete, the wind changed to a violent northeasterly gale. For three days the crew tried to control the ship, but the weather grew worse until everyone despaired of reaching land alive. Paul reminded his fellow travelers of his advice to winter at Fair Havens to encourage them to believe what he was about to tell them. What he had predicted had taken place, and what he was about to predict would also. An angelic visitor had confirmed God's former assurance to Paul that he would see Rome (see 23:11). The angel also now told Paul that all on board would reach land safely, even though the ship would run aground on an island.

Shipwreck followed the storm (27:27–44). For eleven more days the winds and currents carried Paul's ship in a northwesterly direction from the south-central Mediterranean. Sensing that land was near, the ship's crew was about to abandon the passengers and make for land in the lifeboat. Paul warned the centurion of their plan and frustrated it. He also urged all on board to eat to gain strength for the work of getting ashore, and he assured them that they would all survive (see 27:25). Paul's giving thanks to God publicly for the food helped all present to connect their deliverance with God. It was necessary to lighten the ship so it would ride high into shallow water when the sailors beached it. The sailors did not see a mud or sand bar and inadvertently ran the ship aground. It stuck firmly and the waves began to break the ship apart. Normally the centurion would have killed the prisoners to keep them from escaping, but desiring to spare Paul's life he allowed them to try to reach land as best they could. Everyone did so safely.

God also preserved Paul's life on Malta (28:1–6). When the apostle made himself useful by gathering firewood on the beach, he unknowingly picked up a small snake with his wood. It bit him on the hand, and everyone thought this was a sign that he was worthy of death. When he did not die, they changed their minds and said he was a god. God miraculously healed His servant to enable him to fulfill God's purpose that he bear witness in Rome (see 23:11; 27:24).

Besides God healing Paul miraculously, He also enabled Paul to heal the father of the island's leading citizen and many other of its inhabitants (28:7–10). Paul was no god, but he was a messenger of the true God. His ministry to the people of Malta benefited them physically and spiritually, and they expressed their gratitude by honoring him and supplying the needs of his party.

The trip from Malta to Rome also provided a setting for Paul's ministry (28:11–16). Paul and his companions spent the winter on the island of Malta. The centurion was able to secure passage on another Alexandrian ship with the figurehead of twins, Castor and Pollux, two gods thought to guard the safety of sailors. Perhaps Luke mentioned them to contrast God's real protection (as illustrated in the previous chapter and this one) with the protection the pagans superstitiously thought these gods provided. Traveling north, Paul's party finally arrived in Rome. There the apostle was able to live in a house under guard since he was a Roman citizen who had appealed to Caesar.

Ministry in Rome (28:17–31). Paul's ministry in Rome vindicated God's promises to Paul that he would bear witness there (23:11; 27:24). The apostle to the Gentiles was now able to minister in the heart of the gentile world.

Paul began immediately to prepare to witness, and soon he had his first conference with the Roman Jewish leaders (28:17–22). He wanted to see the leaders of the Jewish community soon to preach the gospel to them as Jews first, and he wanted to take the initiative in reaching out to them with an explanation of why he was in Rome. He explained that he had done nothing against the Jews or their customs and that the Roman authorities in Judea had already declared him innocent (28:17–18). He had appealed to Caesar because the Jews in Judea challenged the Romans' verdict, not because Paul had any grievance against the Jews (28:19). His present condition grew out of the promises God had given Israel (concerning her Deliverer and deliverance, 28:20; see 23:6; 24:21; 26:6–8). The Jewish leaders had not received unfavorable reports about Paul, and they were eager to hear more about the Christian "sect," as they regarded it.

Paul had a second conference with even more Jewish leaders shortly thereafter (28:23–28). For a whole day the apostle tried to convince them from the Old Testament that Jesus is the Messiah. Some believed, but others did not. Paul's parting word was a quotation from Isaiah 6:9–10, in which God told the prophet that his Jewish hearers would not believe

God's message through him. Paul saw that this word to Isaiah was as applicable in his own day as it had been in Isaiah's. Having presented the gospel to the Jews in Rome, and having witnessed their rejection of it, Paul now focused his ministry again on the Gentiles (see Acts 13:46–52; 18:6; Rom. 1:16).

Paul lived a relatively comfortable life in Rome for the following two years (A.D. 60–62) and preached the gospel to many who came to see him in his own rented house (28:30–31). Thus the Book of Acts ends with the gospel having free course with Jews and Gentiles and with the apostle to the Gentiles witnessing in the uttermost parts of the earth (1:8).

ROMANS

The Righteousness of God

AUTHOR

Throughout the history of the church, from postapostolic times to the present, most Christians have regarded Romans through Philemon as having been written by the apostle Paul. The Book of Romans includes a claim to Pauline authorship (1:1), and it develops many of the same ideas and uses the same terminology that appear in Paul's earlier writings (for example, Galatians 2; 1 Corinthians 12; 2 Corinthians 8–9).

DATE

On his third missionary journey Paul left Ephesus and traveled by land to Macedonia and continued south, spending the winter of A.D. 56–57 in Corinth. There he wrote the Epistle to the Romans and sent it by Phoebe (16:1–2) to the Roman church.

AUDIENCE

According to Ambrosiaster, a fourth-century church father, the church in Rome was not founded by an apostle, but rather by a group of Jewish Christians. Possibly these Jews became believers in Jerusalem on the Day of Pentecost (Acts 2) or at some other time quite early in the church's history.

Many Jewish and gentile believers lived in Rome when Paul wrote this epistle (see Rom. 16). Many more Christians had contact with Rome because it was the chief city of the Western world in Paul's day. The church in Rome was primarily gentile, but Jews composed part of this church too.

PURPOSE

Paul wrote this epistle because he wanted to prepare the way for his intended visit to the church (Rom. 15:22–24). Another reason was undoubtedly his desire to minister to the spiritual needs of the Christians in Rome (15:14–16). The common problems of all the early churches were dangers to the Roman church as well (15:1–8; 16:17–20). Paul also wrote Romans because he was at a transition point in his ministry, as he mentioned at the end of chapter 15. His ministry in the Aegean region was solid enough that he planned to leave it and move farther west into unevangelized territory. Before he did that, he planned to visit Jerusalem, where he realized he would be in danger. Possibly, therefore, Paul wrote Romans to leave a full exposition of the gospel in good hands if his ministry ended prematurely in Jerusalem.

THEOLOGICAL EMPHASES

The Book of Romans deals with salvation in all of its stages: past, present, and future. It is the fullest exposition of this doctrine in the New Testament and stresses that salvation is by grace alone through faith alone. Another prominent doctrine is the doctrine of God. Romans clarifies the righteousness of God in His dealings with humanity throughout history. The ministry of the Holy Spirit to believers in Jesus Christ is also prominent. Sin receives full treatment in this epistle, and in this connection Romans has much to say about humanity. Eschatology is also prominent, especially the future of Israel. As in all of his epistles, Paul explored some of the practical implications of these and other doctrines. In short, Romans is a very theological epistle.

CHARACTERISTICS

Romans is distinctive among Paul's inspired writings in several respects. It was one of the few letters he wrote to churches he had not visited (Colossians is another such epistle). It is also a formal treatise within a personal letter. Paul expounded the gospel in this treatise. He probably chose to do so in this particular epistle because the church in Rome was at the heart of the Roman Empire. As such it was able to exert great influence in the dissemination of the gospel. For these two reasons Romans is more formal and less personal than most of Paul's other epistles.

OUTLINE

I. Introduction (1:1–17)
   A. Salutation (1:1–7)
   B. Purpose (1:8–15)
   C. Theme (1:16–17)
II. The Need for God's Righteousness (1:18–3:20)
   A. The Need of All People (1:18–32)
   B. The Need of Good People (2:1–3:8)
   C. The Guilt of All Humanity (3:9–20)
III. The Imputation of God's Righteousness (3:21–5:21)
   A. The Description of Justification (3:21–26)
   B. The Defense of Justification by Faith Alone (3:27–31)
   C. The Proof of Justification by Faith from the Law (chapter 4)
   D. The Benefits of Justification (5:1–11)
   E. The Universal Applicability of Justification (5:12–21)
IV. The Impartation of God's Righteousness (chapters 6–8)
   A. The Believer's Relationship to Sin (chapter 6)
   B. The Believer's Relationship to the Law (chapter 7)
   C. The Believer's Relationship to God (chapter 8)
V. The Vindication of God's Righteousness (chapters 9–11)
   A. Israel's Past Election (chapter 9)
   B. Israel's Present Rejection (chapter 10)
   C. Israel's Future Salvation (chapter 11)
VI. The Practice of God's Righteousness (12:1–15:13)

A. Dedication to God (12:1–2)

B. Conduct within the Church (12:3–21)

C. Conduct within the State (chapter 13)

D. Conduct within Christian Liberty (14:1–15:13)

VII. Conclusion (15:14–16:27)

A. Paul's Ministry (15:14–33)

B. Personal Matters (chapter 16)

I. INTRODUCTION (1:1–17)

This great epistle begins with a broad perspective. It looks at the promise of a Savior in the Old Testament, reviews Paul's ministry to date, and surveys the religious history of the gentile world.

A. Salutation (1:1–7)

The salutation, the longest in Paul's epistles, identifies the writer (1:1), introduces the subject of the letter (1:2–5), and greets the original readers (1:6–7). This first sentence (1:1–7) implicitly sets forth the most fundamental facts of Christianity. In particular, it shows that the main facts of the gospel fulfill Old Testament predictions.

The writer (1:1). As in all his epistles, Paul used his Roman name Paul, rather than his Jewish name Saul, since he was the apostle to the Gentiles. In his relationship to Jesus Christ, Paul was a servant. The title "apostle" points up Paul's gift and office in the church. The basis of his authority was God's calling.

The subject of the epistle (1:2–5). Paul next began to exalt the gospel that God had called him to proclaim. He did not preach an unanticipated gospel but one that God had promised through His prophets (see also 4:13–25; 9:4; 15:8).

The original recipients (1:6–7). Paul assured his readers that they were part of the intent of the gospel. God had called them to sainthood, "saint" being a common New Testament term for believers. Paul desired that his readers enjoy a continually deeper and richer experience of spiritual blessing.

B. Purpose (1:8–15)

Since Paul had not met the Christians to whom he wrote, he spent some time sharing his heart with them. The faith of the Roman believers had become well known in the few years since it had come into existence. Paul called God as his witness (1:9) because what he was about to say might be difficult to believe. He claimed to pray for the Romans unceasingly, that is, he never gave up praying for them.

As Paul had prayed often for the Romans, so he had also often planned to visit them for fellowship, that is, the mutual sharing of things profitable. Paul's love for Christian fellowship and his obligation to preach the gospel to all people motivated him to visit Rome (1:14–15). Having received the grace of God himself, he recognized that this placed him in debt to everyone else. He owed them the opportunity to hear the gospel and to receive God's grace.

> *Every Christian is indebted to every non-Christian because we have and can give what can impart life to those who are dead in sin.*

C. Theme (1:16–17)

If anyone thought Paul had not yet visited Rome because he doubted the power of his gospel to work in that sophisticated environment, the apostle now clarified his reason.

Paul not only felt obligated (1:14) and eager (1:15) to proclaim the gospel, but he also felt unashamed to do so (1:16). The reason was that the gospel message has tremendous intrinsic ability to effect change.

The basic outcome of salvation is soundness or wholeness. Salvation restores people to what they cannot experience because of sin. Salvation is a general term; it can describe many aspects of deliverance, including justification, redemption, reconciliation, sanctification, and glorification. The gospel is effective only in those who believe the good news that Jesus is the Christ (the Messiah whom God promised to send) and that He has done everything necessary to save us.

The gospel has a special relevance to Jews. Because God purposed to use Israel as His primary instrument in bringing blessing to the world (Exod. 19:5–6), He gave the Jews first opportunity to receive His Son. Yet the Great Commission makes no distinction between Jews and Gentiles (Matt. 28:19–20).

What makes the gospel powerful is its content. It makes known the righteousness of God, which He imparts to those who believe in His Son. It involves a righteous standing before God, made possible by Christ's atoning sacrifice on the cross.

I. THE NEED FOR GOD'S RIGHTEOUSNESS (1:18–3:20)

Paul began his explanation of the gospel by demonstrating that there is a universal need for it. Every human being needs to trust in Jesus Christ, because everyone lacks the righteousness God requires before He will accept us.

A. The Need of All People (1:18–32)

The reason for human guilt (1:18). Paul explained why Gentiles need to hear the gospel and experience salvation: God has revealed His wrath as well as His righteousness.

The ungodliness of humankind (1:19–27). Natural revelation, discussed in 1:19–20, refers to what everyone knows about God because of what He has revealed about Himself in nature. (What He has revealed about Himself in Scripture is *special revelation.)* The creation bears testimony to its Maker, and every human being "hears" this inaudible witness (Ps. 19:1–4). It is a clear testimony; everyone is aware of it. Everyone can understand it. It has gone out since the creation of the world in every generation, and it is a limited revelation in that it does not reveal everything about God (for example, His love and grace) but only some things (for example, His power and deity, Rom. 1:20). Natural revelation makes people responsible to respond to their Creator in worship and submission, but it does not give sufficient information for them to experience salvation. That is why everyone needs to hear the gospel. Honoring God as God and giving Him thanks (1:21) are our primary duties to God in view of who He is.

The false religions people have devised constitute some of God's judgment on humans for turning from Him. False religion is a judgment from God, and it tends to keep people so distracted that they rarely deal with the true God. God "gave them over" (1:24, 26, 28) by turning them over to the punishment their crime earned, as a judge does to a prisoner. People also reflect their rebellion against God by their impurity in adultery and harlotry (1:24–25). Verses 26–27 describe unnatural acts such as homosexuality.[1] People exchanged the truth of God (1:25) for "a lie" (literally "the lie"), the idea that we should venerate someone or something in place of the true God. Because humankind "exchanged" the truth for the lie, God allowed them to degrade themselves through their passions. The result was that natural human functions were replaced with what is unnatural. The "due penalty" is what people experience as a result of God giving them over and letting them indulge their sinful desires.

The wickedness of humankind (1:28–32). The word "wickedness," used in 1:18, reappears in verse 29 at the head of a long list of sinful practices. It is a general word describing the evil effects in human relations produced by suppressing the knowledge of God. As people disapproved of the idea of retaining God in their thinking, so God gave them over to a disapproved ("depraved") mind (1:28). This letting loose has led to all kinds of illogical and irrational behavior. The final step down in man's degradation is his active promotion of wickedness (1:32).

Paul was viewing humanity historically, but he observed many of these conditions in his own day. He looked at humankind as a whole and did not mean that every individual has followed every aspect of this pattern of departure from God.

B. The Need of Good People (2:1–3:8)

In this section Paul addressed man's failure to respond to special revelation. Since the Jews had more knowledge of this revelation than the Gentiles, they are primarily in view. As in the previous section, specific accusations follow general terms for sin (compare 1:18 with 1:23, 26–32; and 2:1–16 with 2:17–29). Obviously many people could say in Paul's day, and still say in ours, that they are not as bad as the people the apostle described in chapter 1. He dealt with this objection more generally in 2:1–16 and more specifically with Jewish objectors in 2:17–29. Paul's use of "you" in this section shows his use of the literary device called diatribe in which he addressed an imaginary objector.

God's principles of judgment (2:1–16). Paul set forth the principles by which God will judge everyone, and so he warned the self-righteous. He addressed those people who might think they were free from God's wrath because they did not "do" the things Paul had just referred to (1:29–32). Evil motives, as well as evil actions, constitute sin.

God judges righteously (2:2) on the basis of what really exists. Consequently those who have practiced the same sin, though perhaps not in the same way, should not think they will escape judgment (2:3). They should realize that God is simply giving them time to repent (2:4). God will judge them one day when He pours out His wrath on every sinner, the day when people will perceive His judgment as righteous.

God will also judge what every person really did (2:6), not what he or she hoped to do. If a person obeys God perfectly, he will receive eternal life. However, no one *can* obey God perfectly, and so all are under His wrath (3:23–24). The true basis of judgment is not whether one is a Jew or a Greek but what he really does.

Furthermore God will treat everyone evenhandedly (2:11). God gave the Mosaic Law to the Jews, so He will not judge Gentiles by that Law. Justification is a legal verdict that reflects a person's position under the Law. The justified person is one whom God sees as righteous in relation to His Law (see Deut. 25:1). The Law warned that anything short of perfect obedience to it made a person guilty before God (27:26). Even Gentiles who do not have the Mosaic Law know that they should do things that are right and not do things that are wrong (Rom. 2:14), and they have consciences (2:15). All people grow up learning that some things are truly bad and others are truly good. Thus our consciences, while not a completely reliable guide, are helpful as we seek to live life morally.

God's impartial judgment will include people's secret thoughts as well as their acts (2:16). Christ Jesus will be God's Agent of judgment. Throughout this section (2:1–16) the judgment of unbelievers is in view.

> ### Principles by Which God Evaluates People
> - He judges righteously, in terms of reality, not appearances (2:2).
>
> - He judges deeds, both open and secret (2:6).
>
> - He judges impartially, not because of how much or how little privilege they enjoy but how they respond to the truth they have (2:11).

The guilt of the Jews (2:17–29). Even though the Jews had the advantages of the Mosaic Law and circumcision, their boasting and fruitlessness offset these advantages. Divinely revealed religion is no substitute for trust and obedience toward God.

Paul had been speaking of Jews in 2:1–16, but now he identified them by name. The name "Jew" contrasts with "Greek" and calls attention to nationality. The Jews gloried in being members of God's chosen nation (Exod. 19:5–6). They relied on the Mosaic Law because God Himself had given it to Moses on Mount Sinai. They boasted in their knowledge of God which they obtained through that covenant.

Paul first referred to God's gifts to the Jews (Rom. 2:17) and then to the superior capabilities these gifts conferred on them (2:18). Finally he mentioned the role the Jews somewhat pretentiously gloried in. God had called them to enlighten the Gentiles with these gifts and capabilities (2:19–20). With a series of rapier-like interrogations (rhetorical questions) Paul poked holes in the Jews' hypocritical facade. Evidently it was not uncommon for Jews to rob the temples of the pagan Gentiles (2:22). By doing so, they betrayed their own idolatry, which was love of wealth. The Jews' gentile neighbors saw their inconsistency and despised the Lord because of it (2:24).

Next to the Mosaic Law the Jews took great pride in their circumcision. Some of them believed God would not permit any circumcised male to enter perdition. But circumcision would not shield them from God's wrath if they failed to do all He commanded. If a Gentile was completely obedient to God, the absence of circumcision was not of major consequence. Disobedience brings condemnation and perfect obedience theoretically brings salvation, regardless of whether one is a Jew or a Gentile. The person who really praises God is not one who merely wears the label of circumcision but one whose obedience to God is genuine. Such a person has a circumcised heart (see also Deut. 30:6; Jer. 4:4; 9:25–26; Ezek. 44:9).

Answers to objections (3:1–8). God Himself made a distinction between Jews and Gentiles. In Romans 3:1–8, Paul dealt with that apparent inconsistency so there would be no question in the minds of his Jewish readers that they were guilty before God and needed to trust in Jesus Christ. This passage affirms the continuing faithfulness of God to His covenant people but clarifies that His faithfulness in no way precludes His judging sinful Jews.

Paul asked four rhetorical questions in this section, questions that could have been in the mind of a Jewish objector. First, if Jews and Gentiles are both guilty before God, what advantage is there in being a Jew, particularly in being circumcised? There are many advantages, one of which is that the Jews had received "the very words of God" (3:2), that is, His promises. The second question is, Since some of the Israelites proved unfaithful, will God forsake His covenant promises to bless them? No, God brought the whole nation of Israel into Canaan as He had promised, though the unbelieving generation died in the wilderness. God would remain true to His word to bless Israel as He had promised (3:4) even if they all proved unfaithful. The third question is, Since the Jews' failings set off God's righteousness more sharply by contrast, might not God deal more graciously with the Jews in His judgment of them? No, God will not show favoritism to the Jews even though by their unfaithfulness they glorify the faithfulness of God. If He did so, He would be partial and not qualified to sit in judgment on humankind. The fourth question Paul raised was this: If my lying, for example, glorifies God by showing Him to be the only perfectly truthful person, why does God punish me for lying? Answer: God will not overlook sin, though He will overlook uncircumcision (2:26–29). If anyone thinks God should overlook his sinning because, in a sense, it glorifies God, that person deserves condemnation (3:8).

Four Jewish Objections to Paul's Argument

1. "We the Jews are a privileged people" (3:1–2).

2. "God will remain faithful to us Jews despite our unfaithfulness to Him" (3:3–4).

3. "God will be merciful since our failings have magnified God's righteousness" (3:5–6).

4. "God will overlook our sins since they contribute to the glory of God" (3:7–8).

Self-righteous people still raise these objections. Some people assume that because God has blessed them He will not condemn them. Some believe the character of God prohibits His condemning them. Others think that even though they have sinned God will be merciful and not condemn them. Some feel that since everything they do glorifies God in some way, God would be unjust to condemn them.

C. The Guilt of All Humanity (3:9–20)

Having now proved all people, Jews and Gentiles, under God's wrath, Paul drove the final nail in humankind's spiritual coffin by citing scriptural proof.

Jews are not better (or more obedient) than Gentiles even though they have received greater privileges from God. The collection of passages Paul used both affirmed the universality of sin (3:10–12) and showed its pervasive inroads into all areas of individual and corporate life (3:13–18). A statement of the universality of sin opens and closes the passage. Sin has affected human intellect, emotions, and volition.[2] Paul described the words (3:13–14), acts (3:15–17), and attitudes (3:18) of people as tainted by sin. No one seeks God without God prompting and enabling him to do so (see also John 6:44–46). No one will be able to open his mouth in his own defense.

One purpose of the Law was to expose people's inability to merit heaven (Rom. 2:12–13, 23–25). If someone wants to earn God's commendation of being perfectly righteous, he must obey God's Law perfectly (Matt. 5:48). It is impossible, therefore, to earn justification (a righteous verdict) by performing the works that God's Law requires.

> **Summary:** In this first major section of Romans (1:18–3:20), Paul proved the universal sinfulness of humankind. He first showed the need of all people generally (1:18–32). Then he dealt with the sinfulness of self-righteous people particularly (2:1–3:8). He set forth three principles by which God judges (2:1–16), proved the guilt of Jews, God's chosen people (2:17–29), and answered four objections to his argument that Jews could offer (3:1–8). Then he concluded by showing that the Old Testament also taught the total depravity of every human being (3:9–20).

III. THE IMPUTATION OF GOD'S RIGHTEOUSNESS (3:21–5:21)

Paul returned to the major subject of this epistle, the righteousness of God (Rom. 3:21; compare 1:17). He also repeated the need for faith (3:22; compare 1:16) and his point that everyone is guilty before God (3:23; compare 1:18–3:20). This brief recapitulation in 3:21–22 introduces his following explanation of the salvation that God provides for guilty sinners.

A. The Description of Justification (3:21–26)

The "righteousness from God" (3:21) refers to God's method of bringing people into right relationship with Himself, a method apart from Law (3:20). This has taken place through the coming of Jesus Christ. The Old Testament revealed that this would be God's method even before He appeared. God's righteousness becomes a person's possession and begins to operate in his or her life through faith in Jesus Christ (3:28). Faith is the hand of the heart. It does no work to earn salvation but only accepts a gift that someone else provides. All must come to God by faith in Jesus Christ because all have sinned and fallen short of (lack) God's glory, the majesty of His person. Because of sin we lack both the character of God and fellowship with God.

All who believe (3:22) receive justification (3:24). Justification is a forensic (legal) term that means to acquit and to *declare* righteous. God, the Judge, sees the justified sinner in Christ (in terms of his relation to His Son) with whom the Father is well pleased (8:1; see also 1 Cor. 1:30; 2 Cor. 5:21; Phil. 3:8–9). God bestows justification freely as a gift. The basis for His giving it is His own grace, not anything in the sinner. The redemption that came by Christ Jesus is the means God used to bring the gift of justification to humankind. Redemption denotes a deliverance obtained by purchase. Jesus Christ was the sacrifice, but the place where God made atonement was the cross. God has publicly displayed Jesus Christ as a sacrifice of atonement that satisfied God's wrath and removed our sins. His sacrifice brings forgiveness of sins for those who trust in Him.

Another reason God provided a sacrifice of atonement was to justify (declare righteous) His own character, to vindicate Himself. This was necessary because God had not finally dealt with sins committed before Jesus died. The blood of the animal sacrifices of Judaism only covered them temporarily. God accepted those sacrifices as a temporary payment, but the bill came due later, and Jesus Christ paid that off entirely. Jesus Christ's death showed that God is both just in His dealings with sin and the Justifier who provides a righteous standing for the sinner.

B. The Defense of Justification by Faith Alone (3:27–31)

There is no place for human boasting in this plan because God's provision of salvation by faith springs from a different law than salvation by works. This "law" or principle is that salvation becomes ours by faith in Jesus Christ. Faith, not works, is what God requires. If justification is by the Law, God must be the God of the Jews only since God gave the Law only to the Jews. But there are not two ways of salvation, one for Jews, by works, and the other for Gentiles, by faith.

C. The Proof of Justification by Faith from the Law (chapter 4)

Was justification by faith a uniquely Christian revelation as contrasted with Jewish doctrine? No, the apostle showed in this chapter that God has always justified people by faith alone. In particular, he emphasized that God declared that Abraham, the father of the Jewish nation, was righteous because of his faith.

Abraham's justification by faith (4:1–5). Abraham had no grounds for boasting before God, because he received justification by faith, not by works. In Paul's day many of the rabbis taught that Abraham experienced justification because of his obedience rather than because of his faith (1 Macc. 2:51). Consequently the apostle referred to Genesis 15:6 to point out that trust in God's promise is what constitutes faith and results in justification. God credited Abraham's faith to him as righteousness (Rom. 4:3). Work yields wages that the working person deserves, but faith receives a gift that the believing person does not deserve. Incredibly God justifies those who not only fail to deserve justification but who also deserve condemnation because they are "wicked" (4:5; compare 3:24). This is how far God's grace goes (see Deut. 25:1)!

David's testimony to justification by faith (4:6–8). Paul cited another eminent man in Jewish history whose words harmonized with the apostle's. One would assume that David, Israel's greatest king, would have been a strong advocate of the Mosaic Law. He was, but he did not view it as the key to justification. The passage Paul quoted from David's writings (Ps. 32:1–2) stresses that those to whom God "reckons" righteousness (namely, the justified) are "blessed."

The priority of faith to circumcision (4:9–12). When God declared Abraham righteous, the patriarch was uncircumcised. Fourteen years later Abraham underwent circumcision (Gen. 17:24–26). His circumcision was only a sign (label) of what he already possessed.

The priority of faith to the promise concerning headship of many nations (4:13–17). The Jews believed that they had a claim on Abraham that Gentiles did not have. But part of God's promised blessing to Abraham was that he would be the father of many nations. God gave His promise to bless the Gentiles through Abraham long before He gave the Mosaic Law.

So it was wrong for the Jews to think that the blessing of the Gentiles depended on their obedience to the Law. It depended on God's faithfulness to His promise. God gave that promise to Abraham because of his faith, and it even predated his circumcision. To introduce Law-keeping as a condition for the fulfillment of this promise would make faith irrelevant and the promise worthless.

The exemplary value of Abraham's faith (4:18–22). What Abraham did in trusting God is essentially what everyone must do. Abraham's hope rested solely on God's promise. The apostle had proved the point he set out to demonstrate, and he restated Genesis 15:6 in summation.

Conclusions from Abraham's example (4:23–25). God will credit His righteousness to all who believe Him. Jesus underwent crucifixion because of our transgressions of God's Law (compare Isa. 53:11–12). His death secured our justification.

D. The Benefits of Justification (5:1–11)

Is this method of justification certain? Since it is by faith, it may seem unsure. However, this method is reliable, as is clear from the results of justification by faith.

Paul had proved that justification comes to us by faith. The first of the blessings "that came spilling out of the cornucopia of justification," to borrow a phrase, is peace with God (reconciliation). Those who stand justified need not fear God's wrath since Jesus Christ made peace between them and God by His death. The second benefit is access, a continuing relationship with God. The third benefit of justification is joy in sufferings, and the fourth is the indwelling Holy Spirit.

Four terms in this passage that are increasingly uncomplimentary describe those for whom Christ died: "powerless" (5:6), "ungodly" (5:6), "sinners" (5:8), and "enemies" (5:10). Paul contrasted the worth of the life laid down, Jesus Christ's, and the unworthiness of those who benefit from His sacrifice.

So far Paul had referred to four benefits of justification. Still there is "much more" (5:10, 15, 17, 20), many benefits that justified sinners will experience in the future. The first of these is deliverance from the outpouring of God's wrath on the unrighteous (5:9). Jesus Christ's death is responsible for our justification, but His continuing life is responsible for our progressive sanctification and our glorification (5:10). One day in the future we will stand before Him complete (5:11).

Benefits of Justification by Faith in Romans 5:1–11

- Peace with God (5:1)

- Access into the grace of God (5:2)

- Joy in tribulation (5:3–5a)

- The indwelling Holy Spirit (5:5b)

- Deliverance from future condemnation (5:9)

- Present continuing salvation (5:10)

- Union with God (5:11)

E. The Universal Applicability of Justification (5:12–21)

Paul's final argument in support of justification by faith is a development of his previous emphasis on the solidarity that the saved experience with their Savior (5:1–2, 9–10). Just as Adam's sin affected all people, so Jesus Christ's obedience affected all believers.

The apostle viewed Adam and Christ as federal (representative) heads of two groups of people. In this section Paul looked at the one trespass of Adam, namely, the Fall, and the one righteous act of Jesus Christ, namely, His death, and the consequences for those affected by their acts. Adam's act made all of his descendants sinners. Christ's act made all who trust in Him righteous apart from their own works. Adam's sin had a more direct and powerful effect than that of a bad example. Adam was the person in authority over and, therefore, responsible for Eve (Gen. 2:18–23) and for all of his descendants.

Paul compared the manner in which death entered the world—through sin—and the manner in which it spread to everyone—also through sin. Before God gave the Mosaic Law, people died physically because of Adam's sin.

The corporate sinning of all people "in" Adam accounts for the universality of death. Adam was a "pattern" (Rom. 5:14) of one who would follow him, namely, Jesus Christ. Adam's act had universal impact and prefigured Christ's act, which also had universal impact. Each communicated what belonged to him to those he represented. In Adam's case, a single sin by a single individual was sufficient to bring condemnation to the whole human race. In Christ's case, one act of obedience, which the transgressions of many people made necessary, was sufficient to bring justification to all who believe (5:16).

The consequence of Adam's sin was death reigning over humankind, whereas the consequence of Christ's obedience was humankind reigning over death (5:17). Many would become righteous (5:19), both forensically (justified), as they believe, and completely (glorified), in the future. When God provided Jesus Christ, He provided grace (favor) that far exceeded the sin that He exposed when He provided the Law.

Contrasts in Romans 5:12–21

Two men	Adam (5:14)	Christ (5:14)
Two acts	One trespass in the Garden (5:12, 15, 17, 18, 19)	One righteous act on the cross (5:18)
Two results	Condemnation (guilt) and death (5:15, 16, 18, 19)	Justification (life) and kingship (5:17, 18, 19)
Two differences		
In degree	Sin abounds	Grace superabounds
In operation (5:16)	One sin by Adam resulting in condemnation and the reign of death for everyone	Many sins on Christ resulting in justification and reigning in life for believers
Two kings	Sin reigning through death (5:17)	Grace reigning through righteousness (5:21)
Two conditions	Condemned people are slaves of sin by Adam	Justified people reign in life by Christ

Summary: This section (5:12–21) shows that humankind is guilty before God because all of Adam's descendants are sinners as a result of Adam's sin. Earlier Paul wrote that we are all guilty because we have all committed acts of sin (chapters 3–4). Jesus Christ's death has removed both causes for condemnation: guilt for personal sins and guilt for inherited sin. This section helps us understand our union with Christ that Paul explained further in chapter 6.

IV. THE IMPARTATION OF GOD'S RIGHTEOUSNESS (CHAPTERS 6–8)

After discussing why people need salvation (1:18–3:20), what God has done to provide it, and how we can appropriate it (3:21–5:21), Paul then explained that salvation involves more than a right standing before God, which justification affords. God also provides salvation from the present power of sin in the redeemed sinner's daily experience. This is progressive sanctification (chapters 6–8). This process of becoming progressively more righteous (holy) in one's experience is not automatic. It involves growth and requires the believer to cooperate with God to produce holiness in daily life. God leads believers and enables them to follow, but they must choose to do so and to make use of the resources for sanctification that God provides. This progressive sanctification will end at death or the Rapture, whichever occurs first. Then the believer will experience glorification when his experiential condition will finally conform to his legal standing before God. He will then *be* completely righteous as well as having been *declared* righteous. God will then also remove our propensity to sin and will conform our lives fully to His will (8:29).

In chapters 6–8 Paul explained how justified sinners become more holy (godly, righteous) in daily living. We need to understand our relationship as believers to sin (chapter 6), to the Mosaic Law (chapter 7), and to God (chapter 8) to attain that worthy goal.

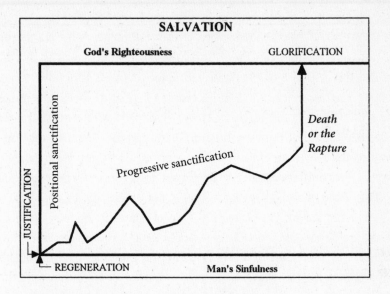

A. The Believer's Relationship to Sin (chapter 6)

This chapter discusses the subject of subduing the present power of sin, which follows from Paul's previous discussion of Adam's sin (5:12–21).

Freedom from sin (6:1–14). Paul began his explanation of the believer's relationship to sin by clarifying the implications of our union with Christ. He had already spoken of this in 5:12–21 regarding justification, but now he showed how that union affects our progressive sanctification.

The apostle referred to Jesus Christ's death, burial, and resurrection. Seen from the viewpoint of His substitute sacrifice, these events did not involve the believer's participation. Jesus Christ alone endured the cross, was buried, and arose from the grave. Nevertheless His work of redemption was not only substitutionary but also representative (5:12–21; 2 Cor. 5:14). It is in this respect that in the following verses Paul described believers as identified with Christ in His death, burial, and resurrection. Sin has no further claim on Christ because He paid the penalty for sin, and sin no longer has a claim on us because He died as our Representative. We are free from sin's domination because of our union with Him.

Paul had just said that grace superabounded where sin increased (Rom. 5:20). Perhaps then believers should not worry about practicing sin since it results in the manifestation of more of God's grace and His greater glory. One expression of this is Voltaire's famous statement, "God will forgive; that is his 'business.'" W. H. Auden voiced similar sentiments: "I like committing crimes. God likes forgiving them. Really the world is admirably arranged."[3]

But the response of Paul's alleged objector in 6:1 is definitely not a proper conclusion (see 3:8). Paul personified sin and described it as having a ruling power and realm (6:2). We died to sin when we experienced conversion. Paul did not say it is impossible to live in sin or that sin is dead to the Christian (that it no longer appeals to us). He meant it is unnecessary and undesirable to live in sin, to practice it habitually.

Our baptism into Jesus Christ (that is, Spirit baptism, 1 Cor. 12:13) resulted in our death to sin (Rom. 6:3–4). Water baptism, on the other hand, joins the believer with Jesus Christ in public profession and represents joining him with Christ in His death. God not only raised Jesus Christ but also imparts new life to believers. Walking in newness of life shows that the believer has received new life. In 6:5 Paul was speaking of the resurrection of the body at a future date rather than the believer's resurrection to a new type of life with Christ at conversion. Our union with Christ in His death and resurrection is the basis for our future resurrection.

As we sinned in Adam, so we died with Christ (6:6; compare Gal. 2:20). It is important that we "know" this because it is crucial to understanding our relationship to sin as believers. Our old "self" refers to the person we were before we experienced justification. That person was crucified with Christ and is now dead. Nevertheless we can adopt his old characteristics if we choose to do so. The believer is not the same person he used to be before justification. The old self, by the way, is not the same as the old nature. The old nature refers to our sinful human nature that every human being possesses so long as he lives. The old nature is the same as the flesh (Rom. 7:5). The sinful flesh is unalterably evil and will war against the Holy Spirit within us until Christ comes. Only the Holy Spirit can subdue the flesh (8:1). Even though our old self has died, our old nature lives on. I am not the same person I was before justification because sin no longer can dominate me, but I still have a sinful human nature. The result of our crucifixion with Christ was that the body no longer needs to be an instrument that we use to sin since we are no longer slaves to sin.

Because of our death with Christ we have no obligation to respond to the dictates of our sinful nature. We may choose to do so, but we do not have to do so, and we should not do so.

The Christian is no longer under the slavery of sin that he used to live under. God has broken the chain that once bound believers to sin, and, happily, we are free of its domination. Unfortunately we will not be free of its enticement until our glorification. Death could not hold Jesus Christ, our Representative, and it cannot hold the believer either. Furthermore neither He nor we will die a second time. When Jesus Christ died, His relationship to sin changed. It was never the same again. Sin now has no power over Him. Because believers are "in Christ," our relationship to sin has also changed.

Since God has united us with Christ we should "count" ourselves as those who are not under the dominating influence of sin any longer (6:11). We must realize that we are free to enjoy our new relationship with God forever. Paul previously stressed the importance of knowing certain facts (6:3, 6, 9). Now he said that we should count on their being true. If we believe sin does not have enslaving power, we will be more apt to resist temptation, to stay clear of sin, and to anticipate death less fearfully.

Next we need to present ourselves to God in a decisive act of self-dedication (6:12–23). We should not let sin reign in our bodies (selves) any longer. Sin is no longer our master so we should stop carrying out its orders. When temptation comes, we do not have to yield. We should "offer" ourselves to God and our members as His tools to fulfill His will (compare 12:1). The believer has a choice: We can present ourselves to sin or to God.

Sin will no longer master the believer. We are not under the Mosaic Law as the authority under which we live but under grace. God has redeemed us, not by the Law but by grace, and we now live under that authority.

Knowing our relationship to sin as Christians and believing it to be true, we need to present ourselves to God for His service and then allow the Holy Spirit to transform our lives by following the revealed will of God, with His help. If the Spirit is not transforming us, we either do not have the Spirit living within us (are unsaved), or He is there but we prefer to live life on our own.

Slavery to righteousness (6:15–23). Christ has broken the bonds of sin that enslave the Christian (6:1–14), but even though we are free we can become enslaved to sin again by yielding to temptation (6:15–23).

A sinful lifestyle and acts of sin are both inappropriate for a believer who is living under God's gracious authority. Obligation always follows dedication, whether the dedication is to sin or to obedience. The outcome of dedication to sin is death (5:12; 8:13), but the outcome of dedication to obedience is righteousness.

For the Christian, dedication to God is voluntary, not automatic (6:13; 12:1). If a believer does not truly dedicate himself to God, he will continue to practice sin (6:16). Progressive sanctification is not totally passive or automatic. It requires some human action, specifically acts of the will.

When the readers had chosen the slavery-to-sin option in the past,[4] they did not become more righteous in their conduct. Shame was the immediate result and death the final fruit. Now, in contrast, they were free from sin's tyranny because of their union with Christ (6:22). If they presented themselves as slaves to God voluntarily, they could anticipate the sweet fruit of progressive sanctification (holiness) and fullness of eternal life (John 10:10; 17:3). Death is the wage a person earns by his working, but eternal life is a gift free to those who rely on the work of another.

Three Steps to Practical Sanctification in Romans 6:3–19

1. We must "know" certain facts about our union with Christ, specifically that sin no longer possesses the dominating power over the believer that it has over the unbeliever (6:3–10).

2. We must "count on" (believe) these facts to be true of us personally (6:11).

3. We must "offer" ourselves to God in dedication as His slaves to perform righteousness (6:12–19).

B. The Believer's Relationship to the Law (chapter 7)

Similarly believers are no longer under obligation to keep the Mosaic Law because of our union with Christ (7:1–6). But we become slaves to our flesh if we put ourselves under the Law (7:7–25). People naturally tend to view law as a means of making progress, so it was important that Paul clarify our relationship to it.

The Law's authority (7:1–6). Paul's Roman readers lived in the capital of the empire where officials debated, enacted, and enforced laws. Of all people they were very familiar with legal matters. They would not have argued Paul's point that law has authority only over living people. The Mosaic Law has not died, but we died with Christ to the Law. The relationship that once existed between the believer and the Law no longer exists. Paul viewed Jesus again as our Representative (as in 5:12–21 and chapter 6) rather than as our Substitute (as in 3:25). Since we died with Christ we no longer have to live according to the Mosaic Law. In 7:5 Paul had preconversion days in mind when he wrote of our having been controlled by our sinful nature.

The Mosaic Law was a unified code that contained moral, religious, and civil regulations governing the life of the Israelites as a nation of God's people (Exod. 20–Num. 10). God terminated the whole code as a regulator of life when Christ came (see Rom. 10:4). Thus believers are released from the Law of Moses. Christians now have received "the Law of Christ" (Gal. 6:2). It contains some of the same commandments as the old Mosaic Code including nine of the Ten Commandments. Nevertheless it is a new code.[5] The Law of Christ consists of the teachings of Jesus Christ that He communicated during His earthly ministry, plus the teachings that He gave through His apostles and prophets following His ascension to heaven.

The Law's activity (7:7–12). The believer is dead to both sin (6:2) and the Mosaic Law (7:4). Are they in some sense the same? No, the Law is not sinful simply because it provides awareness of sin. The Law is similar to a machine in a medical laboratory that reveals a tumor. The machine itself is not bad because it reveals something bad. Likewise the Law is not sinful because it exposes sin.

The apostle probably appealed to his own personal experience in 7:7–12. He broadened this into a more general picture of the struggle that every believer encounters when he tries to serve God by obeying the Law. Every believer feels frustrated by the operation of his sinful human nature (7:13–25).

In his past Paul had lived unaware of the Law's true demands and was therefore self-righteous (Phil. 3:6). His preconversion struggles were mainly intellectual (for example, Was Jesus the Messiah?) rather than moral. When the commandment entered Paul's consciousness, it aroused sin, and he died in the sense that he became aware of his spiritual deadness.

The intent of the Law was to bring people blessing (life) as they obeyed it (Lev. 18:5). Nevertheless because Paul did not obey it, he found that it condemned him. Sin plays the part of the tempter as well as that of the revealer. It deceived Paul and slew him. Paul's sinful nature urged him to do the very thing the commandment forbade.

The Law's inability (7:13–25). The forces of external Law and internal sin (his sinful nature) conflicted in the apostle. In 7:5 Paul addressed the struggle unbelievers have, but in verses 13–25 he was describing his own personal struggle as a Christian to obey the Law and so overcome the promptings of his sinful nature (flesh) to disobey it. However, what he wrote here is not normal or necessary Christian experience. Paul experienced this struggle as a believer before he understood his new relationship to the Law as a believer in Christ.

The responsibility for death belongs to sin, not the Law. In contrast to the good Law, Paul was fleshly (literally, made of flesh), that is, unspiritual. People are essentially different from the Law because we have a sinful nature whereas the Law itself is sinless. Therefore there is a basic antagonism between people and the Law.

Paul did not say that being dead to sin means that sin has lost its appeal for the Christian. It still has a strong appeal to the Christian whose human nature is still sinful (6:15–23). Being dead to sin means that we no longer must follow sin's dictates. In one sense the Christian is not a slave of sin (6:1–14). We have died to it, and it no longer dominates us. Nevertheless in another sense sin still has a strong attraction for us since our basic human nature is still sinful, and we retain that nature throughout our lifetime.

Paul's sinful human nature influenced him to such an extent that he found himself choosing to do (approving) the very things that he despised intellectually (7:15). This caused him to marvel.

The apostle's attitude toward the Law was not the reason for his dilemma (7:16). Rather his problem was traceable to the sin that dwelt within him, namely, his sinful human nature (7:17). Viewed as a whole person he was dead to sin. Nevertheless the source of sin within him was specifically his sinful human nature that was still very much alive.

Sin had thoroughly corrupted his nature. Even though he was a Christian, he was still a totally depraved sinner (3:10–18, 23). He knew what he should do, but he did not always do it. Intellectually Paul argued that he should obey Christ's Law (7:22), but morally he found himself in rebellion against what he knew was right. This natural rebelliousness was something he could not rid himself of. Happily Paul explained in chapter 8 that someone with infinite power can enable us to control our rebelliousness.

What Christian has not felt the guilt and pain of doing things that he or she knows are wrong? We will never escape this battle with temptation in this life. The solution to this dilemma is not escape from temptation but victory over it (7:25).

Some Results of Our Union with Christ in Romans 6 and 7

	Chapter 6	Chapter 7
Subject	The believer's relationship to sin	The believer's relationship to the Law
Our former condition	Enslavement to sin (6:1–11)	Obligation to the Law (7:1–6)
Our present condition	No longer slaves of sin (6:12–14)	No longer obligated to keep the Law (7:7–13)
Our present danger	Becoming slaves to sin by yielding to it (6:15–18)	Becoming incapable of overcoming the flesh by trying to keep the Law (7:14–24)
Our present responsibility	Present ourselves to God and our members as His instruments (6:19–23)	Trust and obey God who alone can enable us to overcome the flesh (7:25)

C. The Believer's Relationship to God (chapter 8)

As the fifth chapter climaxed Paul's revelation concerning the justification of the sinner, so the eighth chapter culminates the truth concerning the sanctification of the saint. Both chapters end by affirming the eternal security of the believer. In chapter 5 our security depends on the Son's life and in chapter 8 on the Spirit's power, both of which rest on the Father's love.[6] This chapter explains the benefits of sanctification made available through the presence and power of God's Holy Spirit who indwells every believer.

Our deliverance from the flesh by the power of the Spirit (8:1–11). Paul first stated (8:1–4) and then explained (8:5–11) the believer's condition.

God will never condemn us to an eternity separate from Himself because of our sins. Why? Because the believer is in Christ Jesus, who suffered the consequences of our sins. The Mosaic Law cannot set us free from sin and death because its only appeal is to the basic nature of man, and it does not provide sufficient power for obedience. Fortunately God sent His own Son out of the depths of His love to deal effectively with sin. God fulfills the Law's requirements in us by His Spirit who indwells and empowers us if and as we walk by the Spirit rather than walking in submission to and dependence on the flesh (see Gal. 5:16).

A mind that is set on following the desires of the flesh ultimately leads to death. But a mind that is set on yielding to the Spirit will experience life and peace with God (reconciliation). A mind that is set on the flesh is essentially hostile toward God. The mark of a true Christian is that God's Spirit indwells him (Rom. 8:9). The same Holy Spirit who raised Jesus will also raise believers (8:11).

Our new relationship to God (8:12–17). The apostle next applied the truth of the believer's condition (8:12–13) and attested it (8:14–17).

Because of what God has done for us (8:1–11), believers have an obligation to respond appropriately and not indulge the flesh. But we can do so only with the Spirit's help. Progressive sanctification is not something the Christian may take or leave. God commanded us to pursue it (2 Pet. 1:3–11). Sin produces death in many forms, for example, spiritual death (separation of the body from the soul), social death (separation of the person from others), or psychological death ("separation" of the person from himself). Conversely believers who continually follow God's will with the enablement of the Holy Spirit will experience abundant life.

The believer who is aware of his secure position will be more effective in mortifying his flesh. The Holy Spirit leads every true child of God (Rom. 8:14; Gal. 5:18), but we can choose to follow or not follow Him (Rom. 8:13). He leads us objectively through the Scriptures and subjectively by His internal promptings (8:16; John 20:31; Gal. 4:6; 1 John 3:24; 5:13). Unlike sin the Spirit does not enslave us by compelling us to do God's will, but He appeals to us to do so as adopted sons of God (Rom. 8:15). God has provided the believer with two witnesses to his salvation, the Holy Spirit and the believer's own human spirit.

Our present sufferings and future glory (8:18–25). In the light of eternity we should view the cost of suffering with Jesus Christ now as insignificant in view of the glory that lies ahead for us (2 Cor. 4:17). Paul personified all creation as leaning forward, eagerly anticipating the great day when God will fully redeem it too (Rom. 8:19). Because of the Fall God subjected the whole creation to "frustration" so at present it never reaches the perfection that He originally intended it to achieve (8:20). The creation acts as though it is going through birth pains in that it is straining to produce its fruit, to achieve its potential. The saints share the sense of groaning and anticipation that Paul said the creation feels, but happily the saints possess the firstfruits of our redemption (the Spirit) now. God's gift of the Spirit at the commencement of the believer's Christian life is His pledge that He will complete the process of salvation. In the meantime we should look forward with hope to what God has promised and patiently endure present sufferings.

Our place in God's sovereign plan (8:26–30). Hope helps us in our sufferings (8:24–25) and so does the Holy Spirit (8:26). We know how to approach God in prayer and we know the general subjects that we should pray about, but we still struggle with exactly how to pray most effectively and with what to pray for. The Holy Spirit comes to our aid by interceding for us with deep compassion. God determined the destiny of the elect before Creation (8:29; Eph. 1:3–4). That destiny is specifically conformity to Jesus Christ's image, much more than just deliverance from sin and death. Paul summarized the steps God Himself takes in bringing His purpose to reality: calling, justification, and glorification (Rom. 8:30).

Our eternal security (8:31–39). The key to the believer's security is that "God is for us" (8:31). What He has done for us through His Son in the past and what He is doing for us through the Spirit in the present should give us confidence. He will certainly complete His work of salvation by glorifying us in the future. Since Jesus made the greatest possible sacrifice for us already, we can know that He will also do whatever else may be necessary to conform us to the image of His Son. God is the only one in a position to charge the believer with guilt since all sin is against Him ultimately, but He will not do so because He is for us. He has provided His Son to pay the penalty for our sins, and He has already declared us righteous. Jesus Christ is God's appointed Judge who will condemn the unrighteous (Acts 17:31), but He will not condemn the elect. Present trials and sufferings, which have always been the portion of the righteous, are no indication that God has withdrawn His love from us. The Cross is the great proof of God's love for us, and it is the basis for our victory (Rom. 8:37). No force of any kind can remove us from His loving care. Nothing in all creation can drive a wedge between the loving, electing God and His redeemed people, not even the redeemed themselves.

> **Summary:** Chapter 6 reveals the believer's new relationship to sin, chapter 7 to the law, and chapter 8 to God. To experience progressive sanctification (spiritual growth) we need to apply these facts to our lives.

In the Holy Spirit, God has provided guidance and all Christians need to overcome temptation. Proper relationship to the Holy Spirit guarantees not only these things but joy and assurance as well.

V. THE VINDICATION OF GOD'S RIGHTEOUSNESS (CHAPTERS 9–11)

A major problem concerning God's righteousness arises out of what Paul just claimed for God: If God is for His elect and will never remove His love from them, why has He set aside His chosen people, the Jews? It certainly looks as though something separated them from His love. If God has turned away from Israel, are Christians really that secure?

In Romans 9–11 the apostle defended the righteousness of God in His dealings with Israel. Having explained how God saves sinners Paul now found it necessary to "justify" God Himself, to prove and declare Him righteous. God's present dealings with Israel do not indicate that He has abandoned the Jews. But God's ways need viewing in the light of His future plans for them. In the future God will glorify Israel. The whole section dealing with Israel culminates in rapturous praise to God (11:33–36), much as the section on individual salvation (3:21–8:39) ends with praise (8:31–39).

A. Israel's Past Election (chapter 9)

God's blessing on Israel (9:1–5). Paul's sorrow and grief over Israel's condition contrast with his joy and exultation over his own condition (8:38–39). The apostle named eight more of the Jews' special blessings (compare 3:2): adoption, glory, covenants, the Law, temple worship, promises, the patriarchs, and Christ.

God's election of Israel (9:6–13). Because God's election of Israel did not depend on natural descent (9:6–10) or human merit (9:11–13), Israel's disobedience cannot nullify God's sovereign purpose for the nation. Paul evidently had in mind God's revelation of His plans for Israel in the Old Testament (Exod. 19:5–6; Isa. 42:6). Even though all the descendants of Israel constitute the nation, God also spoke of Israel in a more restricted sense, namely, believers within Israel (Rom. 9:6; see also 2:28–29).

Moreover, even though God promised to bless Abraham's descendants, He singled out only one branch of his family for special blessing, only Isaac's descendants. Isaac's unusual birth confirmed God's choice of that son as the channel of special blessing. God's special election of one portion of Abraham's descendants for special blessing is also evident in His choice of Isaac's son Jacob rather than Esau. God chose Jacob even though Esau was born before Jacob was. God chose Jacob before he had done any deeds or manifested a character worthy of blessing. The Lord does not wait until He sees how individuals or nations develop and what choices they make before He elects them. He chose Jacob and the nation of Israel for reasons that lay within Himself, not because they merited election (Deut 7:6–8).

God's freedom to elect (9:14–18). The question of fairness arises whenever someone makes a choice to favor one person over another. God cannot be unjust, because He is God. When Israel rebelled against God by worshiping a golden calf (Exodus 32), God took the lives of only three thousand of the rebels. Though this seems unjust, His mercy kept Him from wiping out the entire nation. Pharaoh is another example of God not giving people what they deserve but extending mercy to them instead.

God's mercy toward Israel (9:19–29). Some might wonder, Is it not logical that if God is going to show mercy to whom He will, then human actions really provide no basis for His judging us? Is the basis of judgment really God's will rather than human actions? Paul answered that it is presumptuous for human beings as the objects of divine judgment to sit in judgment on their Judge. Israel had no right to criticize God for shaping her for a particular purpose of His own choosing. Hosea 1:10 and 2:23 in their contexts refer to a reversal of Israel's status. Paul saw an analogy between God's present calling of Gentiles and His future calling of Israel to Himself. Gentiles were not a distinct people as were the Jews. Nevertheless by God's grace believing Gentiles became members of the new people of God, the church. Israel's election as a nation did not preclude God's judgment of the unbelievers in it. His mercy and faithfulness are observable in His sparing a remnant. The remnant of believers among the mass of racial Jews is proof of God's mercy to that nation.

God's mercy toward the Gentiles (9:30–33). Israel struggled hard to obtain the prize of justification but crossed the finish line behind Gentiles who were not running that hard. Israel as a whole hoped to gain justification by doing good works, but believing Gentiles obtained the prize by believing the gospel. Intent on winning in her own effort, Israel as a whole, excluding the believing remnant, failed to recognize the Stone prophesied in Scripture who was to provide salvation for her (Isa. 8:14; 28:16; 1 Pet. 2:6–8). Israel's rejection of Jesus Christ did not make God unfaithful or unrighteous in His dealings with the nation but made it possible for Gentiles to surpass the Jews as the main recipients of salvation.

B. Israel's Present Rejection (chapter 10)

The chapter division signals a shift in Paul's emphasis from God's dealings with Israel in the past, specifically before Christ's death, to His dealings with them in the present.

The reason God set Israel aside (10:1–7). Paul and Israel both had zeal for God, but it was zeal that lacked knowledge because it was knowledge that refused to accept Jesus as the Messiah (1 Tim. 1:13). The Jews were ignorant of the righteousness that comes from God as a gift (Rom. 1:17) so they sought to earn righteousness by keeping the Law. The Mosaic Law ended when Jesus Christ died (10:4). Paul used the Law (Lev. 18:5) to prove that Moses showed that it was futile to trust in Law-keeping for salvation. Positively Moses taught that justification came by faith (Deut. 30:11–14); pleasing God was something beyond their reach.

The remedy for rejection (10:8–15). Belief in Jesus Christ in one's heart results in acceptance by God (justification, imputed righteousness, and positional sanctification). Testimony to one's belief in Jesus Christ normally follows and normally is verbal. The blessing of justification is available to Jew and Gentile alike (Rom. 3:22).

The continuing unbelief of Israel (10:16–21). Even though the door of salvation is open to Jews as well as to Gentiles (10:8–15), the majority within Israel still refuse to believe in Jesus Christ.

Was Israel's rejection of her Messiah due to a failure to get the message to the Jews (10:14)? No, the Jews' response was due to deliberate rejection, not ignorance. Moses and the prophets warned Israel of this attitude repeatedly, but the chosen people persisted in it even after God had provided their Messiah.

C. Israel's Future Salvation (chapter 11)

God's future plans for Israel, when unfolded, will fully vindicate His righteousness. God has a future for ethnic Israel, the racial descendants of Jacob. That future is distinct from the future of the church, which is composed of believers.

Israel's rejection not total (11:1–10). Even now some Jews believe the gospel, so there is hope for Israel's future. God has not rejected the Israelites;

they, on the whole, have rejected Him. The proof of this is that Paul himself was a member of the believing remnant, a Christian Jew. Elijah concluded that he was the only Israelite who had remained faithful to the Lord, but God assured him that He had preserved other Israelites who were a believing remnant within the unfaithful nation. Likewise in Paul's day and today believing Jews are a remnant among Jacob's physical descendants. And all this is because of God's grace, not any works.

Israel's rejection not final (11:11–24). Paul then discussed Israel as a whole. Even while Israel now resists God's plan centered in Messiah, the Lord is at work bringing Gentiles to salvation. Gentile salvation really depends on Israel's covenant relationship with God, as Paul illustrated with the olive tree. The salvation of Gentiles in the present age not only magnifies the grace of God, but it will also provoke Israel to jealousy and lead her ultimately to return to the Lord.

The stumbling of Israel did not result in a hopeless fall (see 9:32–33; 11:9). One reason God now deals with Gentiles on the same basis as Jews regarding their salvation is to make Israel jealous of the Gentiles, so that Israel will be encouraged to turn back to Him. God promised to bless the world through Israel (Gen. 12:1–3). When Israel turns back to God, great blessing will come to the world—even greater than is coming to the world now while she is in rebellion against God! When Israel returns to God and He accepts her, the results for all humankind are comparable to life from the dead (Ezek. 37). God's blessings on humanity now will pale by comparison with what the world will experience then.

The first piece of dough (firstfruits) describes the believing remnant in Israel now (Rom. 11:16). The "batch" refers to the whole nation. The root refers to the Abrahamic Covenant in view of how Paul proceeded to develop this illustration. In the Old Testament the cultivated olive tree was a symbol of the nation Israel (Jer. 11:16–17; Hos. 14:4–6), and the wild olive tree represents the Gentiles. The rich root of the cultivated tree corresponds to the Abrahamic Covenant from which all God's blessings and the very life of the nation sprang.

Gentile believers should not feel superior to Jewish unbelievers, the branches God has broken off (Rom. 11:17, 19). Really it is God's faithfulness in honoring the Abrahamic Covenant that is responsible for that.

The gentile believer who may feel superior to the unbelieving Jew needs to remember that he is saved only because he has simply believed God. If God set Israel aside temporarily because of unbelief, He could do the same with Gentiles because of their boasting. Gentiles can become objects of God's sternness, and Israel can become the object of His kindness, depending on their responses to God. In the illustration the whole trunk of the cultivated olive tree represents Israel and the natural branches are the believing and unbelieving segments of it. If God did the difficult thing, namely, grafting wild branches onto cultivated stock, it should not be difficult to believe that He will do the easier thing, namely, restoring the pruned branches of the cultivated tree to their former position.

Israel's restoration assured (11:25–32). God is not only able to restore Israel, but He will do it. Israel's hardening of heart is only temporary. When all the Gentiles whom God has chosen for salvation during the present age of Israel's rejection have experienced salvation, God will precipitate a revival of faith within Israel as a whole when Messiah will come out of the heavenly Jerusalem. This will be at His second coming (Zech. 12:10). Isaiah 27:9 also predicted a great removal of Israel's sins and connected it with the bestowal of the New Covenant blessings on Israel (see also Jer. 31:31–34). Under the present economy God views Israel's physical descendants as a whole as His enemies because of their unbelief. They are "enemies" of His, however, for the sake of the Gentiles to whom He extends grace in this period of Jewish unbelief. However, from the standpoint of their national election for a special purpose, they are the objects of His love because of the patriarchs. He did not choose Israel for her goodness, and He will not abandon her for her badness.

Gentile believers should beware of becoming critical of God for planning to bless Israel in the future and proud because we are presently the special objects of God's favor. God chose Israel so we Gentiles could enjoy salvation (Gen. 12:1–3). As everyone has been disobedient, Gentiles and Jews alike, so God will show mercy to all as well. This is a great ground of assurance and basis for praise.

Praise for God's wise plan (11:33–36). This doxology corresponds to the one at the end of chapter 8. There the emphasis was on the people of God. Here it is on the plan of God.

God is able to arrange His plan so that it results in the good of all concerned and His own glory, and He is able to complete such a plan. His decisions spring from logic that extends beyond human ability to comprehend. His procedures are so complex that humans cannot discover them without the aid of divine revelation. No one can know God's mind fully. He is so wise that He has no need of counselors. He is the Originator, Sustainer, and Finisher of everything ultimately. In view of all these things (11:33–36), He deserves all glory forever.

Summary: This concludes Paul's theological exposition of how unrighteous human beings can obtain the righteousness of God. What remained was for Paul to explain the implications of having this righteousness. This practical guidance is especially important since the Christian is no longer under the regulations of the Mosaic Law (7:6; 10:4).

Knowing how God will keep His promises to Israel should give believers confidence that He will be faithful to His promises to keep us secure as well. Israel cannot escape entering into all that God has prepared for her, and neither can Christians.

VI. THE PRACTICE OF GOD'S RIGHTEOUSNESS (12:1–15:13)

Chapters 1–11 deal primarily with God's actions for humanity, and chapters 12–16 deal with people's actions in response to God's. God's provision contrasts with the believer's responsibility to behave in a manner consistent with what God has done, is doing, and will do for him. The first part is more teaching for belief, whereas the last part is more exhortation for action. The first part stresses right relations with God, and the last part emphasizes right relations with other people.

Essentially this exhortation deals with behavior within the spheres of life where the believer lives: his relationship to God, to other members of the body of Christ, and to the civil state. Chapters 12–13 give directions for Christian conduct generally, and 14:1–15:13 deals with a specific problem the Roman Christians faced.

A. Dedication to God (12:1–2)

Our relationship to God is foundational and governs all our other conduct. Paul had already called for Christians to present themselves to God (6:13–19), and now he repeated that duty as the Christians' most imperative obligation.

Because of all God has done for us, it is only reasonable to present our lives to Him as living sacrifices for His service. The believer-priest's whole life needs giving over to the Lord. We need to separate our lives from sin to God, which is the essence of holiness (6:19). This kind of sacrifice is acceptable to God and pleases Him. We should make it decisively as often as we desire. The Christian should be continually renewing his mind by returning mentally to the decision to dedicate himself to God and by reaffirming that decision. A daily rededication is none too often. The Holy Spirit is the unidentified transformer that Paul set in contrast to the world (see 8:9–11). Total commitment to the lordship of Jesus Christ is a prerequisite for experiencing God's will.

B. Conduct within the Church (12:3–21)

Every Christian has the same duty toward God, namely, dedication (12:1–2), but the will of God for one Christian will differ from His will for another concerning their life and ministry within the body of Christ (12:3–21).

The diversity of gifts (12:3–8). Christians should not think more highly of ourselves than they should; instead they should use sober judgment in evaluating themselves. The faith in view refers to one's ability to view and use one's gifts as abilities that God has given and trusting in God to work through us to bring blessing to others. Such a view of oneself in relation to his gifts is sound judgment because it is consistent with reality. As members of one another, our work cannot be effective if it is done independently. The list of gifts here is not exhaustive; it is illustrative. It is important that we use our gifts and that we use them in the proper way.

The necessity of love (12:9–21). Verses 9–13 deal with the importance of demonstrating love to fellow believers, and verses 14–21 broaden this responsibility to include wider application to nonbelievers.

Sincere love is of primary importance. Giving recognition and appreciation to those who deserve it is a concrete way of expressing love. We must never lose sight of our hope of things in the future that God has promised us because this will help us persevere in tribulation. Prayer is our great resource whenever we feel stress and strain. We should never be so self-centered that we fail to reach out to others. Believers should share the joys and sorrows of their neighbors, especially fellow believers. Feelings of superiority are neither realistic nor appropriate for those who owe all to God's grace. We should give thought to how we do what is right so our witness may be most effective to believers and unbelievers alike. If hostility erupts, the Christian should not retaliate but should trust God to right the wrong. Being overcome by evil means giving in to the temptation to pay back evil for evil. The general nature of the commands in those verses illustrates the essentially gracious character of the Law of Christ (Gal. 6:2) under which Christians now live.

C. Conduct within the State (chapter 13)

Paul expounded what it means to render to Caesar what belongs to him (Matt. 22:21). This subject has bearing on the spread of the gospel so it is especially appropriate in this epistle. The church is not a nation among other nations as Israel was. Therefore it was important that Paul clarify the duties of Christians to our earthly rulers as well as our duty to our heavenly Ruler.

Conduct toward the government (13:1–7). Subjection or submission involves placing oneself under the authority of another so that he does what the authority requires. Submission involves an attitude of compliance that is not necessarily present in obedience. The Christian may have to disobey his government (Acts 5:29), but in those cases he must still be submissive and bear the consequences of his disobedience (see

Dan. 3:12–17; 6:16–17). Every ruler exercises his authority because God has allowed him to occupy his position. God has established three institutions to control life in the present dispensation: the family (Gen. 2:18–25), civil government (9:1–7), and the church (Acts 2). In each institution there are authorities to whom we need to submit in order for God's will to go forward. Those who resist God's ordained authority can expect to suffer condemnation by the government, which is really the indirect judgment of God (Rom. 13:1). The obedient Christian should also prepare himself to accept the consequences of his actions. God will use government, good and bad, to bring to submissive Christians what is good from His perspective (Rom. 8:28). Believers who are not submissive should fear because government has received its power from God to punish evildoers. A Christian needs to be submissive to his government because the government may punish him if he is not submissive, and God may punish him (13:5). This double duty to government and God should also make the Christian submissive when the bill for his taxes falls due (see Mark 12:14, 17).

Conduct toward unbelievers (13:8–10). There are two kinds of debts: those with the lender's consent and those without his consent. It is the second type to which Paul referred here. We do have a debt that continues forever, namely, our obligation to seek the welfare of fellow human beings (Rom. 8:4).

Conduct in view of our hope (13:11–14). What lies before us as Christians provides essential motivation for practicing these commands. It is important that we follow God's will carefully because the final phase of our salvation (glorification) will take place very soon. We must be ready to meet the Lord and to give an account of our stewardship to Him (Phil. 3:20; 1 Thess. 5:6). When the Lord Jesus calls us to Himself, a new day will begin for us in which we will walk and live in sinless light. In view of this prospect we need to prepare for it by laying aside evil deeds as a garment and putting on deeds of holiness. Paul referred to these new clothes as "armor" because we are still at war with sin and the forces of evil (Eph. 6:11). Our behavior, and especially those things Paul called on his readers to do in Romans 13:1–10, should be distinctively Christian since we live among unbelievers. There must be a deliberate turning away from desires to indulge in sin (Rom. 6; 2 Tim. 2:22; 1 Pet. 2:11).

D. Conduct within Christian Liberty (14:1–15:13)

This section of the book deals with Christian conduct when God does not specify exactly what we should do in every situation (see also 1 Cor. 10). In such cases some Christians will do one thing and others another, both within God's will. The command to accept one another begins (Rom. 14:1) and climaxes this section (15:7). Within it Paul also gave three other "one another" references (14:13, 19; 15:5).

The folly of judging one another (14:1–12). Judging one another was a particular temptation to those Christians who believed that they should refrain from some practices they thought were displeasing to God but which other Christians felt were legitimate. Paul urged the Christian who appreciated the extent of his freedom to accept his weaker, critical brother as an equal. Nevertheless he was not to accept him and then condemn him mentally, much less publicly, for his scruples.

Romans 14:2–3 present a specific case of disagreement. For some reason some Christians believed they would please God more by not eating meat than by eating it. But they were wrong. God has not prohibited any food for Christians (1 Tim. 4:3–4). The person who eats should not view himself as superior, even though he is right, or look down on his extremely sensitive brother. Nor should the weaker brother not judge the more liberal Christian as unacceptable to God. The weaker brother needs to remember to whom the stronger brother is responsible and to leave the judging to God.

Romans 14:5 introduces a second illustration. In this case the weaker brother does something and the stronger does not, the opposite of the situation Paul pictured in the previous illustration. The most important thing is to seek to please the Lord in all that we do. Christians will come to differing conclusions about what this means in practice, but their submission to Jesus Christ's lordship is primary. Jesus Christ also lived, died, and lives again, so He is Lord of both those who have died and those who are still alive. He is the Judge, and we are not. Both the critical weaker brother and the scorning stronger brother are guilty of the same offense, namely, judging prematurely and without warrant. We will not have to answer for our fellow Christians or anyone else, but we will have to account for our own deeds (14:12).

The evil of offending another (14:13–23). The stronger brother's liberty might retard the weaker brother's progress as he walks the Christian path. The Lord Jesus taught that the distinction the Israelites were to observe between ceremonially clean and unclean food had ended (Mark 7:15–23). Yet if one's behavior regarding amoral things is creating spiritual problems for another Christian, his conduct is not loving (Rom. 12:10). The welfare of a brother should obviously take precedence over our liberty to do something amoral (1 Cor. 8:13). The primary issues in the lives of dedicated Christians should not be external amoral practices but the great spiritual qualities the Holy Spirit seeks to produce in them. Acceptance with God for Christians involves the stressing of these great kingdom graces rather than whether we engage in some amoral practice. This emphasis also wins the approval of other people. Paul himself was willing to forego any particular food or drink to avoid causing spiritual growth problems for a brother (1 Cor. 8:13). Certainly we should be willing to do the same.

> We willingly alter our pace of walking while leading a small child by the hand so he will not stumble. How much more should we be willing to change our Christian walk for the benefit of a weaker brother or sister in Christ.

The strong believer can be happy in his private enjoyment of certain activities because he knows that he is neither violating the will of God nor the conscience of a weak brother. The weak brother who eats something he believes he should not eat stands condemned by his own conscience and by God. "Faith" here (Rom. 14:23) refers to what a person believes to be the will of God for him. If a person does what he believes to be wrong, even though it is not wrong in itself, it becomes sin for him because his action has become rebellion against God for him.

The importance of pleasing one another (15:1–6). This section develops the key concept in chapter 14, namely, putting the welfare of others before that of self, which is love.

The strong ought to take the initiative in resolving the tension between the strong and the weak. They need to be willing to limit their Christian liberty if by doing so they can reduce the problems of their brethren. The weak need knowledge, and the strong need love, but all Christians, not just the strong, need to apply this principle of love.

Sacrificing His own preferences for the welfare of others did not make Jesus Christ acceptable to everyone, but it did make Him acceptable to His Father. Christians need to show as strong a commitment to building up God's spiritual house, the church, as David displayed in promoting His physical house, the temple (15:3). The Scriptures give us hope because in them we see God's approval of those who persevered faithfully in spite of opposition and frustration. Endurance and encouragement come to us through the Scriptures as gifts from God. United vocal praise of God in the assembly is an evidence of unity among the strong and the weak.

The importance of accepting one another (15:7–13). It is inconsistent for a Christian to reject someone whom God has accepted because we are to receive one another as Jesus Christ has received us. Typically stronger gentile believers were not to despise their sometimes weaker Jewish brethren. God always purposed to bless the Gentiles, so conservative Jewish believers were not to despise their more liberal gentile brethren either.

Summary: This concludes Paul's exposition of the theme of the righteousness of God that constitutes the heart of this epistle (1:18–15:13). Paul showed man's need of God's righteousness (1:18–3:20), how God imputes it to people who trust in His Son (3:21–5:21), and how He imparts it to those to whom He has imputed it (chapters 6–8). Moreover he demonstrated that God is righteous in doing all this (chapters 9–11). He ended by urging his readers to practice their righteousness in their most important relationships (12:1–15:13).

VII. CONCLUSION (15:14–16:27)

The conclusion of this epistle corresponds to its introduction in that both sections deal with matters of personal interest to Paul related to the gospel and they frame his exposition of the righteousness of God.

A. Paul's Ministry (15:14–33)

The apostle gave information concerning his past labors (15:14–21), explained his present program (15:22–29), and shared his future plans (15:30–33).

Past labors (15:14–21). Paul now balanced his instructions to the strong and the weak by pointing out other strengths in the church. First, he commended the Roman Christians (15:14–15). Paul regarded the Gentiles who were coming to faith and growing through his ministry as his offering to God, but he gave Jesus Christ all the credit for what had happened. Signs and wonders (miracles) had accredited him as a messenger of God and validated the message he proclaimed (Acts 2:22; 5:12). Paul's arena of ministry when he wrote this epistle stretched about fourteen hundred miles from Jerusalem to the Roman province of Illyricum on the east side of the Adriatic Sea opposite Italy. Paul's desire to do pioneer missionary work grew out of his zeal to reach as many unsaved people as possible (Rom. 1:14). He found encouragement to pursue this goal in the prophecy from Isaiah that describes the mission of the Servant of the Lord (Isa. 52:15).

Present program (15:22–29). The apostle felt that the Christians in the areas he had evangelized were in a good position to carry on the propagation of the gospel in their territories. Therefore he believed that he could look to comparatively unreached fields farther to the west in Europe (1:11–12). The purpose of Paul's collection of money from the Macedonian and Achaian churches was to relieve the poverty that existed among the Jewish Christians in Jerusalem and to cement relations between gentile and Jewish believers.

Future plans (15:30–33). Paul drew attention to the great need he felt for his readers' prayers by using the same term he did when appealing for them to dedicate themselves to God (12:1). He exhorted them to pray for his safety from the opposition of hostile Jews and to pray that the Jewish

Christians would receive the monetary gift of their gentile brethren. The granting of these two requests would hopefully contribute to the realization of a third goal: Paul's joyful arrival in Rome in God's will (1:10) and his being refreshed by the fellowship of the Roman saints.

B. Personal Matters (chapter 16)

Paul named thirty-five persons in this chapter, nine of whom were with him, and the rest were in Rome. He identified seventeen men and seven women plus at least two households (16:10–11) and three house churches (16:5, 14–15) along with some other unnamed brethren (16:14) and two other women (16:13, 15). The ministry of women in the Roman church is quite evident in this chapter; Paul referred to nine prominent women.

A commendation (16:1–2). Phoebe was evidently the woman who carried this epistle from Corinth to Rome. She was a "servant" (the same Greek word from which we get "deacon") of the church in her hometown, Cenchrea, the port of Corinth (Acts 18:18; 2 Cor. 1:1).

Various greetings to Christians in Rome (16:3–16). It may seem unusual that Paul knew so many people by name in the church in Rome since he had never visited it, but travel in the Roman Empire was fairly easy during Paul's lifetime. Probably he had met some of these people elsewhere and knew others of them by reputation. Most of the names are Latin or Greek, but some of these people were evidently Jews who, like Paul, also had Greek or Latin names (16:7, 11).

A warning (16:17–20). Paul strongly warned the Roman Christians about false teachers who might enter their fold. He was confident that his readers could handle this threat because they had a reputation for following the apostles' instructions. He wanted his readers to be wise concerning all good and innocent only regarding evil (Matt. 10:16). God desires peace among His people, not the antagonism that some in the church who chose to follow Satan's spokesmen would create. The Roman Christians would frustrate Satan's work among them soon as they rejected false teachers.

Greetings from Paul's companions (16:21–24). The men whom Paul mentioned in 16:21 all seem to have been his fellow missionaries who were working with him in Corinth when he wrote this epistle.

A doxology (16:25–27). The apostle brought together words and ideas from his earlier epistles as well as from this one in this doxology. He was confident that God could do for his readers what they needed (1:11; Eph. 3:20), the gospel being God's chief tool to that end. As the only God, He is the God of both Jews and Gentiles (Rom. 3:29–30). As the wise God, He is the author of the plan of salvation for all humankind that Paul had expounded (11:33).

1 CORINTHIANS

The Spiritual Viewpoint on the Church

AUTHOR

*M*ost New Testament scholars believe the apostle Paul wrote this epistle. Internal evidence as well as the testimony of early church fathers supports this conclusion.

DATE

Paul first arrived in Corinth from Athens during his second missionary journey. There he preached the gospel and planted a church. He ministered in Corinth for eighteen months, probably in A.D. 51 and 52. He then left and proceeded on to Syrian Antioch by way of Caesarea. Returning to Ephesus on his third journey Paul made that city his base of operations for about three years (A.D. 53–56). There he heard disquieting news about immorality in the Corinthian church. He wrote a letter urging the believers not to tolerate such conduct in their midst. Paul referred to this letter as his "former letter" (1 Cor. 5:9). No copies of this letter exist today. He then received a letter from the church in Corinth requesting his guidance in certain matters (7:1). Those who carried this letter and perhaps others also reported other disturbing conditions in the church (1:11; 16:17). These factors led Paul to compose 1 Corinthians. He evidently sent this epistle from Ephesus by trusted messengers in the late winter or early spring of A.D. 56 (see 16:8).

AUDIENCE

The city of Corinth had a long history stretching back into the Bronze Age (before 1200 B.C.). In Paul's day it was a Roman colony and the capital of the province of Achaia. The population consisted of Roman citizens who had migrated from Italy, native Greeks, Jews (Acts 18:4), and other people from various places who chose to settle there. Corinth's strategic location brought commerce and all that goes with it to its populace: wealth, a steady stream of travelers and merchants, and vice. In Paul's day many of the pagan religions included prostitution as part of the worship of their gods and goddesses. Consequently fornication flourished in Corinth. What marked the city also characterized the Christians in Corinth to some extent.

PURPOSE

It seems that a conflict had developed between the Corinthian church and its founder, Paul. There was internal strife in the church, as the epistle makes clear. However, the larger problem seems to have been that some in the Christian community were leading the church into a view of things that was contrary to Paul's teaching. This resulted in a questioning of Paul's authority and his gospel. The key issue between the apostle and the Corinthians was what it means to be "spiritual." Underlying Paul's explanations, exhortations, and pastoral counsel in this letter we can detect this fundamental concern, which surfaces throughout its chapters.

THEOLOGICAL EMPHASES

What concerned Paul in this epistle was the theological implications of the gospel, particularly as these affect theology, ethics, and morals. The doctrine of the church is his primary subject, especially the church in its local manifestation. Paul also corrected wrong views of the Cross, spirituality, the church, and the resurrection.

CHARACTERISTICS

First Corinthians is a very pastoral letter. Paul wrote it to Christians whom he loved greatly but who concerned him greatly too. It is largely a response to situations in Corinth that Paul used to correct aberrations of basic Christian truth in this congregation. Some of his instruction was personal advice, which he distinguished from the Lord's will for these believers.

OUTLINE

I. Introduction (1:1–9)
   A. Salutation (1:1–3)
   B. Thanksgiving (1:4–9)
II. Conditions Reported to Paul (1:10–6:20)
   A. Divisions in the Church (1:10–4:21)
   B. Lack of Discipline in the Church (chapters 5–6)
III. Questions Asked of Paul (7:1–16:12)
   A. Marriage and Related Matters (chapter 7)
   B. Food Offered to Idols (8:1–11:1)
   C. Propriety in Worship (11:2–16)
   D. The Lord's Supper (11:17–34)
   E. Spiritual Gifts and Spiritual People (chapters 12–14)
   F. The Resurrection of Believers (chapter 15)
   G. The Collection for the Jerusalem Believers (16:1–12)
IV. Conclusion (16:13–24)
   A. Final Exhortations (16:13–18)
   B. Final Greetings and Benediction (16:19–24)

I. INTRODUCTION (1:1–9)

A. Salutation (1:1–3)

The apostle Paul began this epistle as he did his others by identifying himself as the writer. He also mentioned Sosthenes, a fellow worker known to the readers. Then he identified and described the recipients of the letter and greeted them with a benediction.

Paul's description of himself as one whom God had "called to be an apostle of Christ Jesus" reminded his original readers of his privilege and authority. Sosthenes was probably the same person who was the ruler of the synagogue in Corinth (Acts 18:17). Paul frequently referred to all the

Christians in a particular locality as "the church of God" in that place. God had set the Corinthian believers apart to be His holy people by uniting them with Him through faith in His Son. They were saints by divine calling, though not very saintly in their conduct, as this letter makes clear. Evidently Paul wanted his readers to remember that they were part of a large body of believers (1 Cor. 12:12), and they needed to fit into the family of God harmoniously rather than being a rebel congregation.

B. Thanksgiving (1:4–9)

Paul followed his salutation with an expression of gratitude for his original readers, as he usually did in his epistles. In this case the focus of his thanksgiving was on God's grace in giving the Corinthians great spiritual gifts.

Paul was grateful that God had poured out His unmerited favor and divine enablement on the Corinthian believers through Christ. By their "speaking" the apostle meant eloquence, the ability to express their "knowledge" fluently and effectively. As we shall see, knowledge and eloquence were two things the Corinthians valued very highly. The Corinthians' reception of these gifts had corroborated the truthfulness of the gospel (1:6). By God's sustaining power Christians will stand free of guilt before Him when He calls us to Himself (1:8; see also Phil. 1:6; Col. 2:7; 1 Thess. 3:13; 5:23). Paul's confidence of this did not rest primarily on the Corinthians' persevering faithfully to the end but on God's ability and promises to preserve them. The apostle's confidence enabled him to deal with the problems in the Corinthian church optimistically and realistically.

II. CONDITIONS REPORTED TO PAUL (1:10–6:20)

The warm introduction to the epistle led Paul to continue with a strong exhortation to unity in which he expressed his reaction to reports of serious problems in this church that had come to his attention.

A. Divisions in the Church (1:10–4:21)

The first major problem Paul dealt with was the divisions that were fragmenting the Corinthian church, which had their roots in warped theology.

The manifestation of the problem (1:10–17). Members of the church were applauding their favorite leaders too much and not appreciating the others enough.

By exhorting his readers "in the name of our Lord Jesus Christ," Paul put what he was about to say on the highest level of authority. He urged them to unite in their thinking. Chloe evidently had a household or business that included servants, some of whom had traveled to Corinth and had returned to Paul in Ephesus, carrying reports of conditions in the Corinthian church. The Corinthians had overdone the natural tendency to appreciate some of God's servants more than others. One thing that made Paul, Apollos, Peter, and Christ attractive to various segments of the Corinthian church was evidently their individual oratorical styles. In addressing his own supporters (1:13), Paul pointed out how foolish it was to elevate him over Christ, since Christ did what was most important.

Some Christians contend that water baptism is essential for salvation. If it is, it would seem natural that Paul would have emphasized its importance by personally baptizing more than just Crispus, Gaius, and the members of Stephanas's family. But Paul deliberately did not baptize his converts so there would be no question as to whose disciples they were. This was one way he kept Christ central in his ministry. Preaching the gospel is more important than baptizing, even though baptizing is part of the Great Commission (Matt. 28:19). Paul placed confidence not in the method of his preaching but in the message of the Cross (1 Cor. 1:18).

The gospel as a contradiction to human wisdom (1:18–2:5). Having pointed up a contrast between cleverness of speech and the Cross in verse 17, the apostle then developed this contrast with a series of arguments. His discourse on the nature of the Cross (1:18–2:16) is one of three key expositions in this letter, the others being the nature of Christian community (12:4–13:13) and the resurrection of the dead (chapter 15). First, he pointed out that the gospel, with its message of a crucified Messiah, does not appeal to human wisdom (1:18–25). Second, believers are not considered wise in the eyes of humanity (1:26–31). Third, though Paul's preaching was not impressive in human wisdom, it bore powerful results (2:1–5).

In 1:18–25 Paul discussed the folly of a crucified Messiah. When people hear the message of the Cross, it produces opposite effects. Those on the way to perdition consider it folly, whereas those on the way to glory recognize it as God's power. It has always been God's method to show up the folly of mere human wisdom (Isa. 29:14). The wisdom of "this age" and of "the world" is natural wisdom in contrast to the wisdom God has revealed, wisdom that centers on the Cross. Human reasoning does not enable people to get to know God nor does it deliver them from their sins. These benefits come only through the "foolishness" (in the eyes of the unsaved) of the gospel message preached (1 Cor. 1:21).

The Jews characteristically asked for signs as demonstrations of God's power (1:22; see Matt. 16:1–4). In contrast, the message of the Cross seemed to them to be a demonstration of weakness, specifically Jesus' inability to save Himself from death. The Greeks, on the other hand, typically respected wisdom, things that were reasonable and made sense, but to them the message of the Cross was illogical. How could anyone believe in and submit to One who was apparently not smart enough to save Himself from execution as a criminal when He was innocent? Furthermore how could anyone look to such a One as a teacher of wisdom? A crucified Messiah was a stumbling block to the Jews because they regarded Messiah as the person on whom God's blessing rested to the greatest degree (Isa. 11:2). However, Jesus' executioners hung Him on a tree, the sure proof, to the Jews, that God had cursed Him (Deut. 21:23).

Christ is the instrument of God's wisdom in solving the problem human reasoning cannot unravel, namely, how people can know God and come to God. The "foolishness" of God, the gospel of the Cross, is wiser than human wisdom, and the "weakness" of God, in the eyes of unbelievers, is stronger than human strength. In these verses (1 Cor. 1:18–25) Paul sought to raise the Corinthians' regard for the gospel message by showing its superiority over anything humans can devise through their reasoning and philosophizing. They should, therefore, value the content of the message more highly than the "wisdom" evident in the styles of those who delivered it.

Next Paul pointed out the folly of the Corinthian believers (1:26–31). They themselves were evidence that God's "foolishness" confounds the wise. Few in the Corinthian assembly came from the higher intellectual and influential levels of their society (1:26). God has chosen this method so the glory might be His and His alone. How wrong it is then to glorify His messengers!

Paul's preaching among the Corinthians was a further illustration of what God's wisdom can do (2:1–5). It was not marked by excellence of rhetorical display or by philosophical subtlety. The reason Paul felt weak, fearful, and trembling was probably his sense of personal inadequacy in the face of the spiritual needs he faced when he entered Corinth (see Acts 18:9–10). Paul did not design his content ("message") or his delivery ("preaching") to impress his hearers with his eloquence or wisdom. Rather he emphasized the message he announced, the message of the Cross. Conviction came as a result of the Holy Spirit's power, not the "wisdom" of the preacher. Paul's reason for this approach was so his converts would recognize that their faith rested not on a natural foundation but on a supernatural one, namely, the enlightening ministry of the Holy Spirit.

> *Instead of emphasizing the Lord's servants and what they have done, we should focus on what the Lord Himself has done in providing wisdom and power in Christ.*

The Spirit's ministry of revealing God's wisdom (2:6–16). Paul's reference to the Holy Spirit's power (2:4–5) led him to elaborate on the Spirit's ministry in enlightening the minds of believers and unbelievers alike. The Corinthians needed to view ministry differently. The key to this change was the Holy Spirit's illumination of their thinking. Paul pointed up three contrasts that overlap slightly. The first contrast is between those who receive God's wisdom and those who do not (2:6–10a), and the second one is between the Spirit of God and the spirit of the world (2:10b–13). The third contrast is between the "natural" person and the "spiritual" person (2:14–16).

Paul's preaching of the gospel was simple and clear, but his message possessed a depth that he did not want the Corinthians to overlook. The deep things of God require a type of wisdom different from secular wisdom. By "spiritual" he probably meant one who has followed God's Spirit for some time, not just one who has His Spirit. He later distinguished the natural (unsaved) person, the spiritual person, and the carnal person (2:14–3:4).

The wisdom Paul proclaimed is wisdom that God had not revealed previously. The message of the Cross is a further unfolding of God's plan and purpose beyond what He had revealed and what people had known before. "The rulers of this age" (2:7–8) were probably the intellectual trendsetters Paul mentioned in 1:20, including those responsible for Christ's death (see Acts 3:17–18; 4:25–28). If they had understood the central place that Jesus Christ occupied in God's plan for humanity, they would not have crucified Him. Many things can be known only by divine revelation. Yet we can understand and appreciate the wonderful mysteries that God has prepared for those who love Him because the indwelling Holy Spirit can enlighten us.

Only humans can understand things pertaining to human life. Likewise it is necessary for someone to have the indwelling Spirit of God to understand the things of God (1 Cor. 2:11). All believers have received the Holy Spirit (12:13; Rom. 8:9), who helps us understand the mind of God and what God has given us. This Spirit is vastly different from the spirit (viewpoint) of the world. Unbelievers cannot understand the things of God as believers can, because they have no one who can help them perceive these supernatural things. Paul and the other apostles spoke the truths that the Holy Spirit had helped them understand (1 Cor. 2:6–7). Spiritual thoughts or truths are concepts the Holy Spirit enables us to understand. Spiritual words are those He guides us to use in expressing these thoughts. In short, the Holy Spirit plays an indispensable role in both our understanding God's revelation and our communicating it.

"The man without the Spirit" (2:14), that is, any unbeliever, has viewpoints and ideas that are only what is natural. He does not *accept* all that God wants him to have. One of these things is eternal life through faith in His Son. Since unbelievers cannot understand or accept spiritual things, they need an interpreter, and that is a ministry that ultimately only the Holy Spirit can perform.

The spiritual person, a believer who has the Holy Spirit dwelling within and follows His leading, stands in contrast to the "natural" person. One of the things the spiritual person is able to do is appraise or make judgments regarding all things. In other words, a spiritual individual looks at everything somewhat differently than unbelievers because he has spiritual perception. So he is a puzzle to the unsaved. A profane person cannot understand holiness, but a holy person can understand the depths of evil. Though others can't fully understand the spiritual person, that is not a problem to the spiritual Christian because his judge is ultimately God, not other people (2:15). To summarize his thought, Paul again cited Isaiah (40:13), who marveled at the wisdom of God.

The basic theological point of tension between Paul and the Corinthians in this epistle was over what it means to be a "spiritual" person. Because of their experience of glossolalia (speaking in tongues) they considered themselves to be as the angels and in need of only shedding their bodies. The sources of this distorted view were popular philosophy tainted with Hellenistic dualism.[1] The result was a false "spirituality" and an alleged "higher wisdom" that had little connection with ethical behavior.

The spiritual yet carnal condition (3:1–4). The Corinthians had not been viewing things from the spiritual point of view; they were exalting one or another of God's servants above the others (1:10–17). So Paul urgently appealed to them to change.

Here the apostle introduced a third category of humanity, namely, the "worldly" (literally, "fleshly") person. As believers, these Corinthians possessed the Holy Spirit, but Paul said he could not speak to them as spiritual people because they were behaving like the unsaved (2:3). Instead he had to address them as babies in Christ. The "fleshly" believer, then, is an immature Christian. When Paul had been with the Corinthians they were new converts ("infants"), so he gave them the "milk" of the Word, the ABCs of the faith. Now when they should have been able to take in more advanced teaching they were not able to do so (see Heb. 5:11–14). Their party spirit was one evidence of spiritual immaturity, lack of growth.

Paul's use of the word "brothers" and of the plural "you" in 3:1–3 indicates that he was addressing the whole church, not just a faction within it. The actions of many in the congregation had defiled the whole body. The reason Paul did not feel he should give them more advanced instruction was that their "flesh," their sinful nature, still dominated them. They had not grown beyond spiritual babyhood, and besides that, they were still carnal, allowing their flesh to control them. All the philosophical schools in Greece had their chief teachers, and there were strong preferences among the students as to who was the best. But this attitude is totally inappropriate when it comes to evaluating the servants of Christ.

The role of God's servants (3:5–17). Paul turned next to explaining how his readers should view him and his fellow workers.

The Corinthians' teachers were fellow workers under God (3:5–9). Paul and Apollos were only servants of Christ, each serving in his own way and sphere of opportunity under the Master's direction. Obviously God deserved more credit for the church in Corinth than either its planter or its nurturer. God's servants are all equal in that they are human laborers with human limitations. Yet the Lord will reward each one at the judgment seat of Christ because of his work.

Christian ministers are similar to builders of God's temple (3:10–15). Paul laid the foundation of the church in Corinth by founding the church, and others added the walls and continued building on that foundation. The quality of the materials and workmanship that go into building the church are very important. Christ Himself is the foundation (Matt. 16:18; see also Rom. 9:33; 1 Pet. 2:6). Basing a church on the work of any other person is improper. Paul laid the foundation for the church in Corinth when he preached Christ there.

Even though the quality of the foundation was the best, the condition of the building also depended on what others built on top of the foundation. Durable materials correspond to those activities that result from reliance on Christ, the foundation. The combustible materials are activities that arise out of human "wisdom" in all its forms. God will expose the work of each of God's servants on the day when believers will stand before God and give an account of the stewardship of their lives at Christ's judgment seat (2 Cor. 5:10; Rev. 22:12). Then the fire of God's judgment will test the quality of each believer's work and his or her workmanship. This judgement will not be for the purpose of determining their salvation, for they will already be in heaven. If the servant of the Lord has made a lasting contribution to the building of the church by emphasizing the gospel, he will receive a reward. If someone has pursued human wisdom, that person will not receive a reward, though he will retain his salvation. The rewards in view seem to be opportunities to glorify God by serving Him in the future (see Matt. 25:14–30; Luke 19:11–27).

Paul concluded this section with a strong warning against destroying the church (1 Cor. 3:16–17). The local congregation was not just any building (3:9) but a sanctuary that God inhabited by His Spirit. If any servant of the Lord tears down the church instead of building it up, God will tear him down (see Acts 9:1–4). In the ancient world destroying a temple was often a capital offense. The church is holy in that God has set it aside to glorify Himself. Paul concluded by stressing the importance of the work that all God's servants were doing in Corinth and the need for unity of viewpoint in the congregation.

Human wisdom and limited blessing (3:18–23). The apostle next combined the threads of his argument, which began in 1:18, and drew a preliminary conclusion. If his readers insisted on taking the natural view of their teachers and continued to form cliques of followers, they would limit God's blessing on themselves needlessly. Rather than their belonging to Paul or someone else, Paul and Apollos and the Corinthians' other ministers belonged to *them* because they were Christ's and Christ is God's.

The Corinthians needed to turn away from attitudes the world regards as wise and to adopt God's viewpoint so they would be truly wise. The best wisdom the natural person can produce is foolishness compared with the wisdom God has revealed in His Word. The reasoning of the unsaved wise of this world regarding the most important issues of life is useless. "So then" (3:21) it is wrong to line up behind one or another of God's servants. In doing so, the Corinthians were not only limiting God's blessing on them but were also rejecting some of God's good gifts to them. The world (universe) belongs to Christians in the sense that we will inherit it and reign over it with Christ one day. Life and all it holds contains much blessing for us. Even death is a good gift because it will usher us into the presence of our Savior. All the Corinthians belonged to Christ, and Christ belongs to God in the sense of being under the authority and protection of the Father (see 8:6; 11:3; 15:28).

The Corinthians' relationship with Paul (4:1–21). The apostle wanted to say more about what it means to be a servant of God, so in this section he clarified the essential features of an acceptable servant of God.

Paul applied the servant model and showed how it relates to the Corinthians' habit of judging God's servants (4:1–5). Christian learners should view their teachers as stewards of God's mysteries rather than as party leaders. Their job was to devote their time, talents, and energy to executing their master's interests, not their own. The most important quality in a steward is that he manage his master's affairs so the desires of his lord are carried out; he must be faithful to his master's trust. For Paul this meant remaining faithful to the gospel as he had received it and preached it.

It mattered little to Paul how well the Corinthians thought he was carrying out his stewardship. His personal evaluations of his own performance were irrelevant too. What did matter to him was God's estimation of his service. As far as Paul knew, he was serving God faithfully, but he realized that only his Master had the insight as well as the authority to judge him. He alone knows the things hidden in the darkness, the unconscious motives of God's servants. Evidently God will find something in every faithful Christian's life for which to praise him on that day (4:5).

Paul next became even more critical and accused his readers of taking pride in the wrong things (4:6–13). They were going beyond the teaching of the Scriptures. In this letter Paul often described attitudes and activities that smacked of human pride rather than godly wisdom and love (see 4:18–19; 5:2; 8:1; 13:4). The Corinthians' attitude was wrong because their outlook was wrong. The apostle reminded them that they were not intrinsically superior to anyone else, an attitude that judging others presupposes. They were behaving as though they had already received their commendation from Christ rather than conducting themselves as faithful stewards. Ironically Paul wished the time for rewards had arrived so he could enjoy reigning with his readers, but, unfortunately, suffering must precede glory. Paul may have had the Roman games in mind, specifically the battles between condemned criminals and wild beasts in the amphitheaters, or of the Roman triumph (see also 2 Cor. 2:14). In either case he seems to have been thinking of the apostles as an ultimately humiliated group. How inappropriate it was for the Corinthians to be living as kings rather than joining in suffering with their teachers. Natural people thought the apostles were fools.

The Corinthians, on the other hand, regarded themselves as prudent in their behavior. To the naturally wise the apostles looked weak, but the Corinthian believers appeared strong. They looked distinguished, while the apostles seemed dishonorable. All these descriptions of the apostles emphasize the depths to which they were willing to stoop to proclaim the gospel.

Paul concluded this section (1 Cor. 1:10–4:21) by reasserting his apostolic authority (4:14–21), which had led to his correcting the Corinthians' shameful conduct and carnal thinking. He now appealed to them as a father to his children and ended by warning them that if they did not respond to his gentle approach he would have to be more severe.

In writing the immediately preceding verses it was not Paul's purpose to humiliate the Corinthians but to admonish them strongly as their father in the faith. They had many "guardians" who sought to bring them along in their growth in grace, but he was their only spiritual father. They should learn from Paul as a son learns from his father.

> Christian leadership involves modeling as well as explaining and exhorting. Paul's example in this section of 1 Corinthians is one that every Christian leader should emulate.

It was the Corinthians and not Paul who had departed from the Christian way that was standard teaching in all the churches (see 1:2; 7:17; 11:16; 14:33, 36). Some of the Corinthians who did not value Paul as highly as they should have had become puffed up in their own estimation of themselves and their ideas. Evidently they felt that Paul would not return to Corinth, and even if he did, they could overcome his influence. However, Paul did plan to return if God allowed him to do so. He knew that all the pretense to superior wisdom in the church resulted from viewing things from a worldly perspective. Real power is the power of the Holy Spirit working through humble messengers. The Corinthians' response to this epistle would determine whether Paul would return to them as a disciplining or as a delighted father.

Summary: The depreciation of some of their teachers resulted in the Corinthians' not deriving benefit from them. It also manifested a serious error in their outlook. They were evaluating God's servants as natural unbelieving people do. This carnal perspective is the main subject of chapters 1–4. The Corinthians had not allowed the Holy Spirit to transform their attitudes.

B. Lack of Discipline in the Church (chapters 5–6)

The second characteristic in the Corinthian church that Paul addressed was lack of discipline. The lack of discipline in the church reflected a crisis of authority in the church (1:10–4:21). The Corinthians were arrogant and valued a worldly concept of power. This carnal attitude had produced the three problems Paul proceeded to deal with next.

Incest in the church (chapter 5). First, the church had manifested a very permissive attitude toward a man in the congregation who was committing incest. Paul explained his own reaction to this situation and demanded that his readers take his view of immorality (5:1–8). Then he spoke to the larger issue of the Christian's relationship to immoral people both within and outside the church (5:9–13).

The apostle began by giving his judgment of this case (5:1–5). The precise offense was a man's continuing sexual relationship with the woman who had married his father. Rather than mourning over this sin and disciplining the offender, the Christians took pride in their broad-minded attitude toward it. The case was so clear that Paul did not need to be present to know the man was guilty of a serious offense that required strong treatment. The apostle wanted the believers to view his ruling as the will of the Lord, and he assured them that God would back it up with His power as they enforced the discipline. Probably he meant that he had delivered the man to Satan for his exclusion from the assembly and physical punishment by Satan (see also 11:30; 1 John 5:16). Paul regarded it best for this sinning Christian, as well as best for the church, that he leave the church and possibly even die prematurely, assuming that he would not repent. This would have been better than his continuing to live in sin.

Using the analogy of the Passover (1 Cor. 5:6–8), Paul argued for the man's discipline. It was primarily for the church's welfare that they should remove him, though also for the man's sake, and the Corinthians were wrong to feel proud of their permissiveness. In Jewish life it was customary to throw away all the leaven (yeast) in the house when the family prepared for the Passover celebration (Exod. 12:15; 13:6–7). They did this so the bread they made for Passover would be completely free of leaven, often a symbol of sin in Israelite life. This is what the Corinthians as a church needed to do regarding sin so they could worship God acceptably. Christ, the final Passover Lamb, had already died, so it was all the more important that the believers clean out the remaining "leaven" immediately.

Paul proceeded to deal with the larger issue of the believers' relationship to fornicators inside and outside the church (1 Cor. 5:9–13). He had written this congregation a previous letter in which he had urged the Corinthians to avoid associating with fornicators. He hastened to clarify that he did not mean a believer should avoid all contact with fornicators or unbelievers outside the church. He had meant that the Corinthian Christians should not associate with such a person if he professed to be a believer. In particular, they were not to dine with such a person. This exclusion was designed to confront the offender with his unacceptable behavior and encourage him to repent. Paul's authority as an apostle did not extend to judging and prescribing discipline on unbelievers for their sins, but he could and did prescribe what the Corinthians should do with a sinning brother.

Litigation in the church (6:1–11). Continuing with the subject of discipline in the church, the apostle pointed out some other glaring inconsistencies that had their roots in the Corinthians' lax view of sin. Rather than looking to unsaved judges outside the church to solve their internal conflicts, they should have exercised discipline among themselves in these cases.

Their conduct had brought shame on the church (6:1–6). The failure of the two men who were suing each other was another evidence that the Corinthian church was not functioning properly; it lacked true wisdom. Christians are generally competent to settle disputes. After all, they have the help and wisdom of the indwelling Holy Spirit available to them. They should do this in the church rather than in the civil courts, and they should select the best qualified people to act as judges, even though they might seem to be fools in the eyes of the world. By going into secular courts to settle their church problems the Corinthians seemed to be saying that there was no one in their church wise enough to arbitrate these matters.

Paul explained his judgment in the matter (6:7–11). He addressed the two men involved in the lawsuit but wrote with the whole church in view. For people who professed to love one another, suing each other was inconsistent. If the Corinthians insisted on going to court, it should be to a court of believers in the church, not unbelievers outside the church. An even more shocking condition was that some of the Christians in Corinth were more than victims of wrong and fraud. They were the perpetrators of these things. God had made the Corinthian Christians saints. Consequently they needed to live like saints.

Prostitution in the church (6:12–20). The apostle also wanted to help his readers realize the seriousness of other sexually permissive sins that marked them as a church. Some men within the Christian community were apparently going to prostitutes and were arguing that this was permissible for "spiritual" people. Paul began by refuting his recipients' false premises regarding Christian freedom and the nature of the physical body (6:12–14). Some of his hearers concluded that he advocated no restraints whatsoever in Christian living because he taught that Christians are not under the Mosaic Law. The apostle restated his general maxim but qualified it (6:12). Legality is not the only test the Christian should apply to his behavior. Is the practice also profitable, and might it gain control over him or her?

Christians may eat anything, both what some regarded as unclean as well as what they considered clean (Mark 7:19). Jesus has not forbidden any foods for spiritual reasons, though there may be physical reasons we may choose not to eat certain things. Both food and the stomach are temporal. Paul referred to food here not because it was an issue but to discuss the issue of the body and sexual immorality. As food is for the stomach, so the body is for the Lord. The body is part of what the Lord saved and sanctified, so it belongs to Him, and we should use it for His glory, not for fornication. Furthermore the Lord has a noble purpose and destiny for our bodies.

Paul developed two good arguments against participating in prostitution (6:15–17). Apparently the Corinthians had not understood the nature of sexual intercourse or the nature of Christian conversion. Our physical bodies are just as much a part of Christ—united with Him in a genuine spiritual union—as we are part of the mystical body of Christ, the church. When a Christian has sexual relations with a prostitute, he takes what belongs to God and gives it to someone else. This is really stealing from God. Taking a member of Christ and uniting it to a harlot also, in a sense, involves the Lord in that immoral act. We should not think of sexual intercourse as simply a physical linking of two people. Intercourse involves the whole person, not just the body. Sexual relations deeply affect the inner lives of the individuals involved (see Gen. 2:24). Consequently it is improper to put sexual relations on the same level of significance as eating food. In contrast to the union that takes place when two people have sex, the person who trusts Christ unites with Him in an even stronger and more pervasive oneness. It is a very serious thing to give to a prostitute what God has so strongly united to Christ.

There are other good reasons why prostitution is wrong (6:18–20). Sexual immorality is wrong because it involves sinning against one's body, which in the case of a believer belongs to the Lord. Believers, therefore, should flee from fornication. This sin is more destructive than some other sins because the people who engage in it cannot undo their act. Moreover, it involves placing the body, which is the Lord's, under the control of another illegitimate partner. The believer's body is a temple in which the Holy Spirit resides (Rom. 8:9). So we have a moral obligation to the Giver of our spiritual life to keep His temple pure. Furthermore God has purchased every Christian with a great price, the blood of Jesus Christ (Rom. 3:24–25; Eph. 1:7). In view of this we should glorify God in our bodies (Rom. 12:1–2) rather than dishonoring Him through fornication.

The solution to the problem of lack of discipline in the church (1 Cor. 5–6) is essentially the same as the solution to the problem of divisions in the church (1:10–4:21). We need to return to the Cross, as Paul did in dealing with these problems (6:20; see 1:23–25).

Summary: Incest was one manifestation of carnality in the church (chapter 5), suing fellow believers in the public courts was another (6:1–11), and going to prostitutes was a third (6:12–20). The underlying problem was a loose view of sin, a view shared by the unbelievers in Corinth. In this attitude, as in their attitude toward wisdom (1:10–4:21), the Corinthian Christians needed to adjust their views.

III. QUESTIONS ASKED OF PAUL (7:1–16:12)

The remainder of the body of this epistle deals with questions the Corinthians had asked Paul in a letter. Paul introduced each of these with the Greek phrase *peri de* ("now about," 7:1, 25; 8:1; 12:1; 16:1, 12). The Corinthians seem to have been asking with the attitude of "Why can't we?"

A. Marriage and Related Matters (chapter 7)

The first subject with which Paul dealt was marriage. He began with some general comments (7:1–7) and then dealt with specific situations. The main principle behind his answers was, Do not seek a change in status. This advice occurs in every subsection (7:2, 8, 10, 11, 12–16, 26–27, 37, 40), though in each case Paul allowed an exception. His advice was more pastoral counsel than apostolic decree in this chapter.[2] He also treated men and women as equals, while advocating male leadership in the family.

Advice to the married or formerly married (7:1–16). "It is good for a man not to touch a woman" (a euphemism for sexual intercourse, 7:1, NIV) was probably a Corinthian slogan. Paul responded to that view in all that follows in this section. Some in the Corinthian church were arguing that it was good for a man not to have any sexual relations with a woman. They viewed this as inappropriate for "spiritual" people. This is the opposite view of those who were going to prostitutes and were justifying their behavior on the grounds of Christian liberty.[3]

Paul first emphasized the importance of sexual relations in marriage (7:1–7). He advised married people not to abstain from normal sexual relations. Evidently some of the "spiritual" Corinthians, who held a negative view of the material world, including the body, wondered if it was not preferable for a Christian man to abstain from sexual relations entirely. The abstinence they were arguing for within marriage was totally wrong. Paul urged married couples to have sexual relations with each another, one reason being the prevalence of temptations to satisfy sexual desire inappropriately. Part of the responsibility of marriage is to meet the various needs of the partner (Gen. 2:18), including sexual needs. In marriage each partner relinquishes certain personal rights, including the exclusive right to his or her own body. Evidently the Corinthians had concluded that since they were spiritual they did not need to continue to have sexual relations as husbands and wives. Paul viewed this as depriving one another of their normal sexual rights and urged them to stop abstaining. There are legitimate reasons for temporary abstinence, but couples should abstain temporarily and only with the agreement of both partners. Paul's concession (1 Cor. 7:6) was allowing temporary abstinence from marital sex. He viewed regular marital relations as the norm. To Paul the single state had certain advantages for a servant of the Lord such as himself. He wished everyone could live as he did, but he realized that most could not. The gift of celibacy is a special ability that God gives only some people that enables them to live free from the need for marriage.

Singleness is a legitimate option (7:8–9). Paul moved from advice to the married regarding sexual abstinence to advice to the unmarried. He advised this group, as he had the former one, to remain in the state in which they found themselves, but he allowed them an exception too. What he said applies to all categories of unmarried people. The unmarried state has some advantages over the married state even though it is better for most people to marry. However, if a single person cannot control his or her passions, it would be better to marry than to experience continual lustful temptation (see 7:2).

Paul next gave advice to two types of married Christians, those married to believers (7:10–11) and those married to unbelievers (7:12–16). He advocated no divorce for Christians whose mates are believers (7:10–11). Christians should not break up their marriages (see also Matt. 19:4–6; Mark 10:7–9). They should remain as they are, but again he allowed an exception. If separation (Paul meant long-term separation, namely, divorce)

> *It is difficult for a Christian husband and wife to provide a model of reconciliation to the world if they cannot be reconciled with each other.*

occurs, they should either remain unmarried (stay as they are) or reconcile with their mate. Paul did not discuss the exception that Jesus Christ allowed on the grounds of fornication (Matt. 5:32; 19:9), for he wanted to reinforce the main teaching of Christ on this subject, namely, that couples should not dissolve their marriages.

Paul also prescribed no divorce for Christians whose mates are unbelievers (1 Cor. 7:12–16). In this situation, too, he granted an exception, but the exception is not the ideal. He also reiterated his principle of staying in the condition in which one finds himself or herself. Until now, Paul had been speaking of the typical married persons in the church, namely, those married to other believers. Now he dealt with mixed marriages between a believer and an unbeliever. Though Jesus had not addressed this situation, the risen Lord had inspired Paul's instructions on this subject so they were every bit as authoritative as the teaching Jesus gave during His earthly ministry.

The Corinthians had apparently asked Paul if a believing partner should divorce an unbelieving mate rather than living mismatched with him or her. In addressing this problem, Paul counseled the believer to go on living with the unbeliever if the unbeliever was willing to do so. Even though an unbeliever might affect his or her spouse negatively, it was still better to keep the marriage together because the believing mate would affect the unbeliever positively. God has set aside the unsaved spouse of a believer for special blessing, some of which comes through his or her mate. Likewise the children in such a marriage would enjoy special care from God rather than being in a worse condition than the children in a Christian home. On the other hand, if the unbeliever in a mixed marriage insisted on breaking up the marriage, the believing partner should allow him or her to do so. The reason for this is that God wants peace to exist in human relationships. It is better to have a peaceful relationship with an unbelieving spouse who has departed than it is to try to hold the marriage together if holding it together will only result in constant antagonism in the home. But the Christian does not have the option of departing (7:10–11). When the unbeliever departs, the Christian is no longer under bondage to hold the marriage together. The Christian can have hope that God may bring the unsaved spouse to salvation while the believer does the Lord's will (7:16).

The basic principle (7:17–24). At this point Paul moved back from specific situations to basic principles his readers needed to keep in mind when thinking about marriage (see 7:1–7). Whatever one's marital state, the Christian should regard his or her condition as the position where God wants him or her to be. Paul taught in all the churches the priority of serving Christ over trying to change one's circumstances.[4] His principle applies to being circumcised as well as to being married. Both conditions are secondary to following the Lord faithfully. God did not command celibacy or marriage, circumcision or uncircumcision; they are matters of personal choice among Christians. If we have the opportunity to improve ourselves for the glory of God, we should do so. If we do not, we should not fret about our state but should "bloom" where God has "planted" us. Did the Corinthian Christian slave view himself primarily as a slave or as a freedman?[5] He was both, a slave of men but a freedman of God. Did the freedman view himself primarily as a freedman or as a slave? He was both, a freedman socially but the Lord's voluntary slave spiritually. God has set us free from the worst kind of slavery, having purchased us with the precious blood of His Son (7:23).[6] How foolish then it would be for us to give up the liberties that enable us to serve Jesus Christ!

Summary: Those who were single when God called them to follow Him should be content to remain single, and those who were married should stay married. Faithfulness to God and effectiveness for God do not require a change.

Advice concerning virgins (7:25–40). The Greek phrase *peri de* ("now about") in verse 25 introduces another subject about which the Corinthians had written Paul, namely, the subject of single women. Obviously this subject relates closely to what immediately precedes. Paul continued to deal with problems related to marriage that the Corinthians' asceticism created.

Paul recognized the advantage of the single state (7:25–28). It seems that the question the Corinthians had asked Paul was whether an engaged girl should get married or remain single. One might understand 7:17–24 as commanding that no unmarried person should change his or her situation and get married (see 7:8), but this was not necessarily what Paul advocated. Probably the virgins were females who were engaged or thinking of becoming engaged, but were experiencing pressure from the "spiritual" people in the church to forgo marriage. As he did in the first part of this chapter, Paul offered some good pastoral advice, but he was not commanding that everyone do exactly the same thing in every situation. Thus to choose not to follow Paul's advice did not amount to sinning. In view of Paul's description of the present distress (7:29–31), it seems that he was speaking of the fact that we live in the last days. If an unbelieving spouse had abandoned his or her Christian spouse, or if he or she had lost his or her spouse to death, a single life would provide greater opportunity for Christian ministry. Nevertheless marrying in such a case is not sinful, though the decision to marry may complicate one's service for the Lord.

Paul developed other reasons for remaining single (7:29–35). He called his readers to take a different view of their relationship to the world since they lived in distressing times and the form of the world was passing away in that the Lord's return was closer every day. The Christian should use the world and everything in it to serve the Lord, but must not get completely wrapped up in the things of this world. Therefore whether a person is single or married, he or she should live with an attitude of detachment from the world. Earthly life is only temporary and is passing away. Paul wanted his readers to be free from concerns about this present life so devotion to the Lord would be consistent (also see Matt. 6:25–34; Phil. 4:11; 1 Pet. 5:7). Comparing two equally committed Christians, an unmarried person can give more concentrated attention to the things of the Lord. Even though for this reason the unmarried state is desirable, it is not intrinsically better (see Gen. 2:18). Paul did not want his readers to regard his preceding comments as an attempt to build too strong a case for celibacy, as ascetics do (see 1 Tim. 4:1–5). He wanted to help his readers appreciate the realities of the single and married states as servants of the Lord.

In conclusion Paul reinforced the legitimacy of marriage (1 Cor. 7:36–40). This section wraps up Paul's entire teaching on marriage in this chapter. Probably the man in view is the fiancé of the virgin who is considering the possibility of marriage. The passage then summarizes what Paul already taught.

Paul urged any man not to feel that he must remain single or that he and his virgin fiancée must forgo sexual fulfillment after marriage (7:1–7). Likewise the man who preferred to take Paul's advice to remain single should feel at peace about his decision. The decision in view is one involving the good and the better for each individual, rather than the right and the wrong.

Women should not separate from their husbands (7:39–40). This concluding reminder is especially important for virgins considering the possibility of marrying. Again Paul referred to marriage as a binding relationship (see 7:15, 27). He expressed his opinion—that a widow would probably be better off to remain unmarried—with a very light touch, one that he used throughout this chapter. This decision, as well as all decisions about whether to marry, pivots on a delicate balance. Paul would have acknowledged that in certain conditions a widow might be better off to marry (1 Tim. 5:14).

Summary: This chapter is one of the central passages on the subject of marriage (see also Deut. 24; Matt. 5; 19; Mark 10). It reveals that Paul was not a hard-nosed bigot or advocate of celibacy for all, as some have accused him of being. He was very careful to distinguish his personal preferences from the Lord's will.

B. Food Offered to Idols (8:1–11:1)

The Corinthians had asked Paul another question, evidently in a combative spirit, judging from the apostle's response. A regular part of worship in antiquity, both Jewish and pagan, involved the eating of cultic meals. These were social as well as religious occasions, and the Corinthians participated in them almost as freely as we eat in a restaurant. However, the food consumed was regarded as a sacrifice to some god that the participants honored as present at the feast. Some of the Corinthian Christians had evidently returned to the practice of attending these cultic meals, even though Paul considered such participation idolatry. This appears to have been another practical manifestation of the view of some in the church that since there is only one true God it doesn't really matter if Christians participate in such feasts. This attitude marked the group that viewed themselves as spiritual. However, eating food sacrificed to idols often involved a specific form of idolatry and so was sinful. In view of Paul's arguments that follow, these Corinthians apparently justified their participation by arguing that idols do not really exist (8:1–4), food is a matter of indifference with God (8:8), Paul's apostolic authority was questionable (9:19–23), and church ordinances guarantee the believer's steadfastness (10:1–4). Paul was evidently responding to the Corinthians' objection to his prohibition of this practice that he had written in his former letter to them (see 8:10; 10:1–22).

The priority of love over knowledge in Christian conduct (chapter 8). The Corinthian Christians valued worldly knowledge too highly (see 1:10–3:23). Paul wrote that the real aim of the faith should be love rather than knowledge.

He began this section by comparing the way of love and the way of knowledge to show their relative importance (8:1–3). In dealing with this issue, Paul began as he customarily did in this epistle by identifying some common ground of belief with his readers (see 6:2; 7:1). All the believers knew that there were no other gods beside the true God. This knowledge had led some of them to think that eating in an idol temple was insignificant. But knowledge of this fact was not the only factor they needed to consider. More important, they needed to consider the welfare of other people.

If anyone thinks he has fully mastered any subject, he can count on the fact that he has not, because there is always more to any subject than any one person ever appreciates. For example, accumulating all the facts about God that one can will not result in the most realistic knowledge of Him. One must also love God. If a person loves God, then God knows (recognizes) him in an intimate way and reveals Himself to him (see 2:10; Matt. 11:27). Consequently it is really more important that God knows us than that we know Him.

Every Christian should know that there is only one true God (Deut. 6:4), and the Corinthians did. Nevertheless the pagans regarded many beings as gods and lords over various areas of life. But there is only one God and one Lord, the one true God.

Paul said the criterion of care for a brother should govern Christian conduct (1 Cor. 8:7–13). He described a Corinthian Christian who would go to a feast in an idol temple. That person might feel guilty because by participating he was tacitly approving the worship and thus the existence of the idol. The person's conscience was weak because even though he *intellectually* believed there was only one God, his *emotions* had not fully assimilated that truth. Foods do not make us more or less pleasing to God, but eating idol food in a pagan temple was something else. The Christians who had returned to the pagan temples for their feasts were disregarding how their participation was affecting other Christians who still viewed such practice as worship of idols.

In 8:10–12 Paul appealed on behalf of the rights of the weak. Undoubtedly some of the believers in Corinth were attending these feasts and were encouraging other Christians to take this "knowledgeable" stand. The knowledgeable Christian had destroyed his brother's relationship (fellowship) with God. Christ died for the weaker brother, so the stronger brother dare not view him and his scruples as unimportant. We sin against God and our brother or sister in Christ when we put a stumbling block before him or her. This is the very opposite of what Jesus has called us to do (see Matt. 22:37–39). Paul was willing to forgo all such eating if by doing so he could avoid creating problems for other Christians in their relationships with God.

> Modern culture promotes individual human rights very strongly, and this emphasis has influenced most Christians. But even more important than our freedom in Christ to exercise our rights is the spiritual welfare of other people.

Paul's apostolic defense (chapter 9). The absence of the key phrase "now about" is the clue that this chapter does not deal with a new subject. It is a continuation of the discussion of eating in idol temples.

Subjecting our freedom for the welfare of other people is not something any of us does naturally. Paul knew his readers would profit from more instruction on this subject. Evidently the Corinthian Christians had misunderstood Paul's policy of limiting the exercise of his activities to help others (8:13). Some in the church had apparently concluded that because he did not exercise his rights he did not have them (for example, his right to financial support; see 2 Cor. 12:13). His apparently vacillating conduct also resulted in some of them questioning his apostolic authority. For example, he ate marketplace food with Gentiles but not with Jews.

Paul first identified the marks of a true apostle (1 Cor. 9:1–2). Certainly Paul enjoyed the liberty that every other believer had, and he possessed the rights and privileges of an apostle. The proof of his apostleship was twofold: He had seen the risen Christ on the Damascus road (Acts 22:14–15; 26:15–18), and he had founded the church in Corinth, which was apostolic work.

Next Paul argued for his full apostolic rights (1 Cor. 9:3–14), specifically his right to their financial support. It was customary for the other apostles and the Lord's physical brothers (for example, James and Jude) to take their wives with them when they traveled to minister. Apparently some of the Corinthian Christians took Paul's working with his hands at his trade as an indication that he did not think himself worthy of support because he was not equal with the other apostles. The Lord's servants are certainly not inferior to field hands, farmers, and even animals, for whom God made special provision in the Mosaic Law (9:7) and thus showed His concern for the maintenance of all who serve others. How much more then should those who benefit from spiritual ministry support physically those who minister to them? Furthermore, as the planter of the Corinthian church Paul had a right to the support of the Corinthians more than any of their other ministers did. Yet he did not insist on his right, even though Jews and pagans who ministered in spiritual matters customarily gained physical support from those they served (see also Luke 10:7).

Having argued vigorously for his right to the Corinthians' support, Paul now proceeded to argue just as strongly for his right to give up this right (1 Cor. 9:15–18), his point from the beginning. He did not want his readers to interpret what he had said on this subject as a veiled request for financial support. He had made his decision to support himself while he preached, and he could take justifiable pride in it, as anyone who makes a sacrifice for others can. He could not take justifiable pride in the fact that he preached the gospel, however, because even though it involved sacrificing for the benefit of others, he had made those sacrifices in obedience to the Lord (Acts 26:16–18). If he preached the gospel willingly, he would receive a reward (pay) from the Lord. If he did so unwillingly, he would not receive that reward but would simply be doing his duty as the Lord's steward.

The extent to which the apostle was willing to lay aside his rights deserves great admiration (1 Cor. 9:19–23). Since Paul chose not to receive pay from the Corinthians for his ministry in Corinth, he was free from the restrictions that patronage might impose, which left him free to become the slave of all. Paul was a free man, but as the Lord's servant he had made himself subject to every other human being so he might win some to Christ.

It was the apostle's custom to follow Jewish ways when he was in the company of Jews to make them receptive to him and his message (see Acts 21:20–26). When Paul was with Gentiles, he behaved as a Gentile, which included eating what they did. Even though Paul did not observe the Mosaic Law when he was with Gentiles, he was still under God's authority. Paul's policy of accommodating himself to other people's scruples led some people to conclude that he was inconsistent, but his supposed inconsistency really manifested a more fundamental consistency. The work of the gospel, the message of the Cross, was the great axis around which everything in Paul's life revolved.

The Isthmian Games took place in a town near Corinth every two or three years and were second only to the Olympic Games in importance in Greece. Paul used these contests to illustrate how we should live the Christian life. Christians should run our race so we will receive a reward from the Judge. To receive the prize of our Lord's "well done" we need to give all our effort and to exercise self-control. We may need to limit our liberty for this higher goal. In view of the comparative value of these rewards, Paul ran the Christian race purposefully, not aimlessly or halfheartedly. He did not shadowbox but sought to make every ministry punch score. In another sense Paul viewed his flesh (his sinful human nature) as his enemy and recognized the need to exercise strict self-discipline, including voluntary curtailment of personal rights and liberties. He had no fear that he would lose his salvation (Rom. 8:29–39), but he could lose a reward.

The sinfulness of idolatry (10:1–22). Paul returned to the subject of going to idol temples to participate in pagan feasts. He warned the Corinthian believer who considered himself strong, who knew there are really no gods but the true God, and who felt free to accept the invitation of a pagan neighbor to dine in a pagan temple (8:10). The apostle cautioned this element in the Corinthian church because, even though there are no other gods, the possibility of participating in idolatry is very real. He drew his lesson from the experiences of Israel during the wilderness wanderings (see Exod. 13–17; Num. 10–15).

Persisting in idolatry has dire consequences (1 Cor. 10:1–5). Both the church and Israel had its own "baptism" and "Lord's Supper." The Corinthians' fathers in the faith, believers in Israel, were also all under the loving, protective influence of God, symbolized by the cloudy pillar, and they all experienced a miraculous deliverance when they crossed the Red Sea. All of them also associated with Moses, who was their leader and God's instrument in their redemption, even as Christians associate with Christ, our Leader and Redeemer. The Israelites expressed their identification with Moses by following him and submitting to his authority. The parallel with water baptism was most vivid when they went under the cloud and crossed the Red Sea, a dry "baptism" for the Israelites. Furthermore all the Israelites ate the manna and drank water from the rock (Exod. 17:1–7; Num. 20:2–13; Deut. 8:2–4). The manna and water were "spiritual" food and drink because God provided them supernaturally and because they have spiritual significance. Both of them pointed to Christ, the real Sustainer of His people (John 6:35, 48–51; 7:37–38). Their eating and drinking of God is similar to the Lord's Supper and anticipated it. In short, the Israelites were the chosen people of God, just as Christians are now the chosen people of God. God accompanied and provided for them faithfully in the past just as He does for all Christians now. But in spite of these blessings, God was not happy with the Israelites.

Idolatry was the cause of Israel's failure and the focus of Paul's warning (1 Cor. 10:6–13), but four other evil characteristics of Israel also seem to have marked the Corinthians. These characteristics resulted in the Israelites' dying in the wilderness. Their baptism and partaking of spiritual food and drink did not protect them from God's discipline when they craved evil things. Participation in baptism and the Lord's Supper will not protect Christians either. First, there is a danger that we may compromise our commitment to God, as the Israelites did, when we participate in pagan celebrations. Second, some Christians have participated in fornication that unbelievers have lured them into. Third, we are in danger of failing to appreciate God's provisions for us in Christ. Fourth, we should not grumble against the Lord. We should be careful that we do not overlook the lessons of history since we live in the times of fulfillment about which the Old Testament prophets spoke. Self-confidence can lead to a spiritual fall, as it did so often in Israel's history. The temptations the Corinthians faced were not unique, but the Lord would give them grace to handle any temptation they might face (10:13).

The apostle proceeded to warn of the danger of idolatry by pointing out the incompatibility of Christianity and idolatry (10:14–22). Christians should avoid any activity that involves or leads to idolatry. The Corinthians were sensible enough to judge for themselves that Paul was right (10:15). They gave thanks to God for the cup because of what it symbolized, namely, their sharing in the benefits of Christ's shed blood (see 11:25). Likewise the bread used at the Christian feast, the Lord's Supper, was a symbol of their participation in the effects of Christ's slain body (11:24). Christians who ate the bread at the Lord's Supper thereby expressed their solidarity with one another and with Christ. Likewise Jews who ate the meat of animals offered in the sacrifices of Judaism expressed their solidarity with one another and with God.

Therefore Christians who ate the meat offered to pagan gods as part of pagan worship were expressing their solidarity with pagans and with the pagan deities, whether they realized it or not. The powers behind pagan religions are demonic (Deut. 32:17; Ps. 106:37). Therefore people who sacrificed to idols expressed solidarity with demonic powers. It was inconsistent for Christians who partook in the Lord's Supper to also take part in pagan religious feasts, because in the former he ate and drank in union with Christ and in the latter he united with demons, who directed the devotees to worship idols.

Summary: The Corinthians were arguing for their right to attend pagan religious meals, but Paul responded that attendance was wrong on two counts: It was unloving, and it was incompatible with life in Christ, which their participation in the Lord's Table symbolized.

The issue of marketplace food (10:23–11:1). As with the issue of marriage, Paul granted that there are some matters connected with idolatry that are not wrong. He gave some help in making the tough choices needed in view of the fact that some practices connected with pagan worship were immoral and some were not. He advocated applying the test of what is edifying. Food formerly offered to idols but sold in the marketplace was all right for Christians to eat at home. He himself had eaten such food (9:19–23), but the Corinthians had challenged him for doing so (10:29–30). More importantly, he also dealt with the Corinthians' misplaced priorities.

Earlier Paul addressed the issue of Christian liberty and said that all things were lawful for him, but all things were not beneficial (6:12). Now he stated that "beneficial" means beneficial for others, not just oneself. It was wise not to ask in the home of a pagan host or in the marketplace if someone had offered the food to an idol (10:25). Not inquiring would prevent the possibility of unnecessary concern arising in the mind of an onlooking scrupulous believer. Yet a pagan host might warn his Christian guest that the food before him had been offered in an idol temple because he did not want his Christian guest to be unaware that he was being served food that the Christian might object to and might want to abstain from eating.

Pagans often associated Christians with Jews at this stage of church history, and many pagans would have assumed that Christians observed the same dietary restrictions as the Jews. In such a situation Paul advocated abstaining, not because such food was out of bounds for believers but for the sake of the pagan's moral consciousness. Specifically, if the Christian ate the meat, the pagan might conclude that his guest was doing something Christians should not do. He would be wrong, of course, but Paul advocated not violating the pagan's understanding of what Christians should or should not do.

Why should a person's scruples determine someone else's liberty? Because spiritual welfare is more important than Christian freedom. Sacrificial meat was off limits for Paul only when it offended the moral consciousness of the pagans he was with (and the weaker believers). Christians can give thanks to God for whatever they eat, but they should limit their own liberty out of consideration for what other people think is proper.

Consideration for the consciences of other people and promotion of their well-being glorifies God. Giving no offense means putting no obstacle in the path of a person, whether he is a Jew (9:20) or a Gentile (9:21), so that he might come to faith in Christ. If he is already a believer, it means putting nothing in his way that would hinder his growth in Christ (9:22). Paul said it is essential that no offense be given to any of the three religious groups in view: Jews, Gentiles, and Christians. He did not permit any of his own attitudes or activities to erect unnecessary barriers between himself and those he sought to help spiritually (see also Rom. 15:1–3). Paul recommended that his readers follow his example of exercising and limiting their Christian liberty, glorifying God, and giving no unnecessary offense.

Summary: All of chapters 8–10, including 11:1, deal with the subject of the Christian's relationship to food sacrificed to idols. Paul forbade going to pagan temples for cultic meals, but he permitted the eating of marketplace meat under normal circumstances. If something is not sinful it is permissible for the believer, but even so it may be better to avoid it for the sake of the spiritual welfare of others.

C. Propriety in Worship (11:2–16)

This section and the next (11:17–34) deal with subjects different from meat offered to idols, but Paul did not introduce them with the phrase "now about." These were additional subjects about which he wanted to give the Corinthians guidance.

The argument from culture (11:2–6). Paul introduced with praise the first of the two subjects he dealt with in this chapter, namely, the Corinthian women's participation in church worship. As in the other sections of this epistle, we can see the influence of Corinthian culture and worldview in this section, particularly in the behavior of the women in the church.

Paul commended his original readers for remembering his teaching and example, but things were not as they should have been (11:3). He reminded the Corinthians again (see 3:23; 8:6) of God's administrative order, the order through which He has chosen to conduct His dealings with human beings. Jesus Christ is the head of every male, and the male is the head of woman, that is, any woman who is in a dependent relationship to a man in her family, such as a wife to her husband or a daughter to her father.[7] God the Father is also the Head of God the Son, which shows that headship exists even within the Godhead. When a Jew prayed with his physical head covered, as was common, he did not thereby dishonor himself. In early Christian worship the men did not wear head coverings.

Paul's reference to praying and prophesying (11:4) sets his instructions in the context of the church at public worship. Praying involves expressing one's thoughts and feelings to God. Prophesying might involve any of three things: foretelling future events (Matt. 11:13; Acts 2:17–18; 21:9), declaring new revelation from God (Matt. 26:68; Mark 14:65; Luke 22:64), or proclaiming a message for God (Luke 1:67; Acts 9:6)—a word of instruction, refutation, reproof, admonition, or comfort for others (1 Cor. 13:9; 14:1, 3–5, 24, 31, 39). The last activity is what seems to be in view in other references to prophesying in this epistle, and it suits the context here as well. Praying and prophesying were two major features of early Christian worship services (Acts 2:42).

In contrast to the men, every woman who had her physical head *uncovered* (did not have an external covering on her head) thereby dishonored her metaphorical head, namely, her husband or father (1 Cor. 11:3). In the church meetings Christian women typically wore a head covering similar to a shawl. In Paul's culture most women, Christians and non-Christians alike, wore such a covering whenever they went out in public. Probably the issue in the Corinthian church that Paul was addressing was that certain "wise," "spiritual," liberated women had stopped wearing this covering in the church meetings. Elsewhere Paul wrote that in Christ males and females are equal before God (Gal. 3:28). This teaching, combined with the Corinthians' carnal tendencies, were evidently the root of the problem.

In the Greco-Roman culture a woman who shaved her head did so to appear as a man. This resulted in the blurring of the relationship between men and women, particularly the sexual distinctions. Men typically wore their hair short, and women wore theirs long. If a woman cut her hair short, it indicated she wanted to take the place of a man. This was also true if she did not cover her head. It was a shameful thing for a woman not to cover her head in the early New Testament churches, because such an act made a statement that she was assuming the position of a man. Paul used the common reaction to women's short hair in his day to urge his female readers to wear a head covering. Since it was shameful for a woman to have short hair, it was also shameful for her to have her head uncovered when she prayed or prophesied in the church meetings.

To correct the Corinthians' practice regarding women's head coverings Paul proceeded with a second supporting argument: the argument from creation (1 Cor. 11:7–12). Men should not cover their heads in Christian worship because they are the image of God and therefore reflect His glory (see Gen. 1:26–28). Woman is the glory of man, first, because she came from him in creation. As Adam glorified God by being the product of His creation, so Eve glorified Adam because she came from him. Second, woman is the glory of man because God created Eve to complete Adam; Adam was incomplete without Eve. Paul concluded that women have freedom to decide how they will pray and prophesy within the constraint that he had imposed, namely, with heads covered.

The head covering, then, symbolized both the woman's subordinate position under the man and the authority that she had to pray and prophesy in public. The Corinthian women also needed to wear a head covering because angels, the guardians of God's created order, view what is taking place among God's people (see 1 Cor. 4:9; Eph. 3:10; 1 Tim. 5:21). For other people to see Christian women without a shawl-like covering on their heads was bad enough because it was a sign of insubordination, but for angels to see it was worse.

Women are not independent of men any more than men are independent of women (1 Cor. 11:11). Even though God created Eve from Adam, now every male comes from a female.

Summary: The apostle's emphasis in this section was on the authority that a woman has in her own right by virtue of creation. She must not leave her divinely appointed place in creation by seeking to function exactly as a man in church worship. Furthermore she should express her submission to this aspect of God's will *in a culturally approved way.* At the same time she must maintain a healthy appreciation for the opposite sex.

The argument from propriety (11:13–16). Paul now appealed to the Corinthians' own judgment and sense of propriety, the nature of things. "Nature" itself distinguishes between the sexes, and a woman's naturally longer hair reinforces the propriety of covering her head in worship.

Women's hair naturally grows longer than men's hair. Paul reasoned from this fact that God intended for women to have more head covering than men. People generally regard the reverse of what is natural as dishonorable. In the man's case this would be long hair and in the woman's case short hair. If any of his readers still did not feel inclined to accept Paul's reasoning, he informed them that the other churches followed what he had just explained (11:16; see also 3:18; 8:2; 14:37).

As with the issues of eating in idol temples and meat offered to idols, Paul dealt with a cultural practice when he dealt with head coverings. As should be clear from his arguments, he did not feel this was a major issue. His point here regarded maintaining a custom, rather than a God-given mandate, and he used shame, propriety, and custom to urge the Corinthians to cooperate. However, important issues lay behind the practices. In the case of head coverings the issue is the position of women in the life of the church, in particular their relationship to the men.

D. The Lord's Supper (11:17–34)

Most of the Corinthians had been following Paul's instructions regarding women's head coverings, so he commended them (11:2), but he could not approve their practice at the Lord's Supper. They needed to make some major changes there. Their actions cut at the heart of both the gospel and the church. In antiquity meals typically accompanied public worship. This was true in the early church, in Judaism, and in the pagan world. The early Christians observed the Lord's Supper as part of such a meal, often called the love feast.

The abuses (11:17–26). The first abuse reflects a problem on the horizontal level, between believers in the church, and the second more serious abuse was vertical, involving the church and its Lord.

One aspect of the first problem involved showing disregard for the poorer members of the church when they assembled (11:17–22). The early believers celebrated the Lord's Supper frequently (see Acts 2:42–46; 20:7). The Corinthians' behavior at the Lord's Supper was so bad that they would have been better off not to observe it. They erred because they did not behave as the church, in which there is no distinction between "Jews or Greeks," "slaves or free" (1 Cor. 12:13). But the distinctions the Corinthians were making were not of this type and were wrong. In Corinth, instead of sharing their food and drinks, each family was bringing its own and eating what it had brought, with the result that the rich had plenty but the poor had little. Furthermore some with plenty of wine to drink were drinking too heavily. If Paul's original readers chose to behave in such a selfish way, they should stay home and eat rather than humiliating their less fortunate brethren.

There was an even more serious dimension to this problem. The Corinthians were sinning against the Lord as well as against each other (11:23–26). What Paul taught here came ultimately from the Lord Jesus Himself and was a very important revelation. By describing the night Jesus instituted the Lord's Supper as the night in which He was betrayed, Paul drew attention to the Savior's great love for His own. When Jesus said, "This is my body," he meant, "This represents my body." When Jesus invited his disciples to take the bread, He gave them a share in His body and invited them to participate in the meaning and benefits of His death. His body was "for" them in the double sense that it secured atonement *on their behalf* (15:3; Rom. 5:6, 8) and it was a body offered *in their place* (2 Cor. 5:21; Gal. 3:13). In the Bible "remembering" includes realizing what was involved in the event being celebrated (see Exod. 13:3; 20:8; Deut. 5:15; 7:18). In celebrating the Lord's Supper Christians bring their memory of Jesus back into fresh view. But it is also a memorial celebration of the salvation He accomplished by His death and resurrection.

When Jesus shed His blood on Calvary, that blood ratified (gave formal sanction to) the New Covenant that Jeremiah had predicted (Jer. 31:31–34; see also Exod. 24:8). The New Covenant replaced the old Mosaic Covenant (Heb. 8:8–13; 9:18–28). Even though the Jews will be the major beneficiaries of the benefits of this covenant in the Millennium, all believers, Jews and Gentiles, began to benefit from the death of Christ when He died. The church thus enters into the blessings of the New Covenant. Specific blessings for Israel (ethnic Jews) will not begin until Christ's appointed time arrives, and that is still in the future.

The correctives (11:27–34). Paul proceeded to urge the Corinthians to change their observance of the Lord's Supper. First, they needed to discern the Lord's body (11:27–32). That is, the Lord's Supper should lead believers to reflect on their relationship to one another as Christians as well as to recall Calvary. An "unworthy manner" (11:27) is any manner that does not reflect proper appreciation for the significance of the body and blood of Christ. The Corinthians had lost the point of the memorial, which involves proclaiming salvation through Christ's death portrayed in ritual. Being guilty of Christ's body and blood means being guilty of treating them inappropriately. The reason for examining oneself is to determine that we are partaking in a loving and unselfish way toward our fellow Christians as well as being appreciative of the significance of the Lord's body and blood. We need to examine ourselves or the Lord will examine and discipline us for failing to participate worthily (11:31). Having conducted this self-examination, the believer should then proceed to participate.

Participation in the Lord's Supper lies at the very root of motivation for living a life that glorifies God. If this observance has lost its value, it may be because those who lead it have failed to give it the preparation, attention, and priority it deserves in church life. The frequent observance of the Lord's Supper in a way that takes us back to the Cross is one of the most powerful and effective motivators for living the Christian life.

In the Corinthian church God was judging some believers with sickness and death because of their unjudged sin of selfish living (11:21) and thoughtless participation in the communion service. If God's people do not judge their own sins themselves, God will judge them. This judgment may involve physical illness or even, in extreme cases, premature physical death (Acts 5; 1 John 5:16). This judgment is not eternal destruction (Rom. 8:1) but premature death and the Lord's displeasure at the judgment seat of Christ (1 Cor. 3:15; 5:5).

The Corinthians needed to put the welfare of others before their own rights (11:33–34). Rather than disregarding the members of the congregation who had little or no food to bring to the love feasts, those who had plenty should share what they had and wait to eat until all had been served. If some of the Corinthian Christians were too hungry to wait to eat, they should eat something before they came to the service. Paul planned to address other related issues that needed attention when he visited Corinth again (11:34).

Summary: Paul dealt with matters related to worship since 8:1. He had forbidden the Corinthians from participating in temple meals but had allowed eating marketplace meat under certain circumstances (8:1–10:22). Then he dealt with two issues involving their own gatherings for worship: head coverings and the Lord's Supper.

E. Spiritual Gifts and Spiritual People (chapters 12–14)

The exercise of spiritual gifts (chapters 12–14) was the third issue involving the Corinthians' own gatherings for worship. This is the most important of the three matters relating to their worship as evidenced by the number of verses Paul devoted to it and by the issue itself. Paul explained that being "spiritual" at present (for the perfect state has not yet come, 13:8–13), means to edify the church in worship. The whole section divides into three parts and structurally follows an A-B-A chiastic pattern, as do other parts of this letter (chapters 1–3; 7:25–40; chapters 8–10). First there is general instruction (chapter 12), then an almost poetic exhortation (chapter 13), and finally specific correction (chapter 14).

The test of Spirit control (12:1–3). The presence of the phrase *peri de* ("Now about") plus the change in subject mark another matter about which the Corinthians had written Paul with a question (see also 7:1; 8:1): the gifts (abilities) the Holy Spirit gives believers.

"Spiritual gifts" is literally "the spirituals."[8] This is a broader term than the gifts themselves, though it includes them. It refers primarily to people who are spiritual (2:15; 3:1). Evidently the Corinthians had questions about the marks of a spiritual Christian. A spiritual Christian is a believer under the control of the Holy Spirit rather than his flesh (Gal. 5:16) or a demonic spirit (1 Cor. 10:20–21).[9] Many of the Corinthian believers had been pagans. Paul reminded them that there are "inspired" utterances that come from sources other than the Holy Spirit. Enthusiasm or ecstasy or "inspired" utterance (any utterance that the speaker claims came from God) does not necessarily indicate spirituality. What a person says indicates whether the Holy Spirit is controlling his speech about Jesus Christ. No one the Holy Spirit motivated would curse Jesus Christ. Likewise no one would sincerely acknowledge that Jesus is Lord unless the Holy Spirit influenced him, regardless of whether the person was speaking in an ecstatic condition or in plain speech.

The need for varieties of spiritual gifts (12:4–31). Diversity, not uniformity, is necessary for a healthy church, and God has seen to it that diversity exists (12:6, 7, 11, 18, 24, 28). In the area of spiritual gifts the Corinthians were doing essentially what they were doing in relation to their teachers (3:4–23), that is, preferring one over others and failing to appreciate them all.

Paul first reminded his readers of the diversity within the Godhead and in the gifts (12:4–11). Whereas there is only one Holy Spirit, He gives many different abilities to different people. "Gifts" are manifestations of God's grace that enable a person to serve and glorify Him.[10] God gives them freely and graciously. Likewise there are different "kinds of service" (opportunities for service) that the one Lord over the church gives. Furthermore there are different "kinds of working" (manifestations of the Spirit's power at work) bestowed by the one God who is responsible for all of them. It is God who is responsible for our abilities, our opportunities for service, and the individual ways in which we minister, including the results. Regardless of his gifts, ministries, and the manner and extent of God's blessing each believer demonstrates the Holy Spirit through his life; and through his gifts each believer makes a unique contribution to the common good (12:12–21; 3:4–10).

Paul mentioned nine representative ways the Spirit manifests Himself through believers (12:8–10). Though these manifestations of the Spirit vary, they all indicate the presence and working of the sovereign Spirit of God (John 3:8). There is a general progression in this list from the more common to the more uncommon and esoteric gifts, which attracted the Corinthians.

The church is similar to a human body (1 Cor. 12:12–14). Diversity among the members is an essential part of a unified body. In Spirit baptism the Holy Spirit baptizes the believer into the body of Christ, thereby making us a part of it, and water baptism illustrates this. The Spirit places the believer into Christ, and the Spirit comes into the Christian.

Even though the feet, hands, ears, and eyes are prominent, important members of the body, they cannot stand alone (12:15–26). They need each other. Different functions as well as different members are necessary in the body. A body composed of only one organ would be a monstrosity.

If all the members of the human body were the same, it would not be able to function as a body. God has constructed bodies, both human and spiritual, so the different members can care for one another. He does not ignore any member but makes provision for each one.

Together Christians make up the body of Christ, and each of us is an individual member in it (12:27–31). Paul advised the Corinthians to seek some gifts more than others because some are more significant in the functioning of the body than others. While the bestowal of gifts is the sovereign prerogative of the Spirit (12:8–11, 18), human desire plays a part in His bestowal (James 4:2). As important as sharpening abilities is, it is even more important that we excel in loving.

The supremacy of love (chapter 13). The *fruit* of the Spirit (Gal. 5:22–23) is a more obvious demonstration of the Spirit's presence in a life and His control over a life than the *gifts* of the Spirit. Love is the most fundamental and prominent of these graces. The love in view is God's love that He has placed in the believer through the indwelling Spirit, and it should overflow to God and others.

Love is superior to the spiritual gifts listed in 1 Corinthians 12. Probably Paul began with tongues because of the Corinthians' fascination with this gift. The tongues of men probably refer to languages humans speak, and the tongues of angels may refer to the more exalted and expressive language with which angels communicate or the tongues of angels may be a hyperbole. Angelic tongues may refer to languages unknown to humans, but throughout this whole discussion of the gift of tongues there is no evidence that Paul regarded tongues as anything but languages. Loving behavior is more important than any of the abilities that these gifts represent.

The apostle next pointed out the qualities of love that make it so important (13:4–7). He described these in relationship to a person's character that love rules. He then pointed out that Christian love characterizes our existence now and forever, but gifts are only for the present (13:8–13). Love never fails in the sense of falling away when the physical, temporal things on which affection rests pass away; it outlasts temporal things. Gifts of the Spirit will pass away because they are temporary provisions, but the fruit of the Spirit will abide. In the light of the context, "perfection" probably refers to the whole truth about God. In contrast to what will pass away—namely, knowledge, tongues, and prophecy—faith, hope, and love will endure. Love is not only superior to the gifts; it is even superior to other virtues.

The need for intelligibility (14:1–25). Paul elaborated on the inferiority of the gift of tongues that the Corinthians elevated; he did this to encourage them to pursue more important gifts. His point was that *intelligible* inspired speech (prophecy) is superior to *unintelligible* inspired speech (tongues) in the assembly. He argued first for intelligible speech for the sake of the believers gathered to worship. In this whole comparison Paul was dealing with the gift of tongues without the gift of the interpretation of tongues.

The apostle began this discussion of tongues by comparing it to the gift of prophecy that the Corinthians also appreciated (14:1–5). He urged the Corinthians to value prophecy above tongues because it can edify and lead to conversion since it involves *intelligible* "inspired" speech. Paul's concern was the edification of the church. In contrast to the foreign speech uttered by tongues-speakers, those present could understand what a prophet spoke in the language of his audience. It benefited the hearers by building them up, encouraging them, and consoling them. Paul acknowledged the value of the gift of tongues even though it also required an interpreter, but he made it clear that the ability to prophesy was more important.

Hearers do not benefit at all from what they do not understand (14:6–12). "Revelation," "knowledge," "prophecy," and "word of instruction" all refer to all intelligible utterances. These words probably refer to a new revelation (see 12:8), an insight into truth, a word of edification, exhortation, or consolation from the Lord, or instruction in the faith. Even the sounds people make using inanimate musical instruments need to be intelligible to profit anyone, especially if they are summoning soldiers to battle. For communicating, the tongues-speaker who did not have an interpreter was no better than an incomprehensible barbarian.

In view of this the Corinthians would be better off pursuing the gifts that would enable them to build up the church. The Corinthians were zealous over a particular manifestation of the Spirit, what they considered the mark of a "spiritual" Christian, namely, the gift of tongues (14:14–15, 32).

Paul next clarified the effect that unintelligible speech has on believers gathered for worship (14:13–19). A Corinthian believer who already had the gift of tongues should ask the Lord for the ability to interpret his utterances so the whole church could benefit from them. Public prayer is in view here as it is in this whole chapter (14:16). Paul advocated praising and praying to God with both the spirit (emotions) and the mind (understanding). Corinthian tongues-enthusiasts could not reject Paul's instruction because he did not have the gift. Nor could they say he did not appreciate its value. He believed in the validity of the gift but did not value it highly.

Uninterpreted tongues did not benefit visiting unbelievers any more than they edified the believers in church meetings (14:20–25). Prophecy, on the other hand, benefited both groups. Claiming that tongues-speaking demonstrates spirituality evidences immaturity (14:20). Isaiah had preached repentance to the Israelites in their own language, but they did not repent (Isa. 28:11–12). Then God brought the invading Assyrians into Israel's land. Still His people did not repent, even though He "spoke" to them of their need to repent by allowing them to hear the foreign language of this enemy (see 1 Cor. 14:21). This speaking of a foreign language, then, was a mark of God's judgment on Israel.

Tongues-speaking in the church led visiting unbelievers to assume that the Christians were mad (14:22–23). Prophecy, on the other hand, signified to the believers that God was present and speaking. So prophecy, not tongues-speaking, would result in the repentance of visiting unbelievers (14:24–25).

Paul painted a picture of the Corinthian church assembled and engaged in a frenzy of unintelligible tongues-speaking (14:23). Two types of individuals walk in: One is a believer untaught in the matter of spiritual gifts, and the other an unbeliever. To both of them the worshipers seem insane rather than intelligently engaged in worship and instruction. If, on the other hand, the church was practicing prophesying and was receiving instruction, both visitors would gain a positive impression from the conduct of the believers. More importantly, what the Christians said would also convict them (14:24–25).

The need for order (14:26–40). The Corinthians' public worship practices not only failed to be edifying and convicting, but they also involved disorderly conduct.

The apostle said tongues are to be regulated by interpretation, and he urged the use of discernment with prophecy (14:26–33). He did not want any one gift to dominate the meetings of this richly gifted church. He laid down three guidelines for the use of tongues in public worship. First, the believers should permit only two (or at the most, three) tongues messages and their interpretations. Second, the speakers should give them consecutively rather than concurrently to minimize confusion. Third, the Christians should not allow tongues without interpretation in the church services. Likewise the prophets should minister in an orderly fashion and limit themselves to two or three messages at a service. The others in the congregation should pay attention to what they said, evaluate carefully and, if need be, reject it if the ministry was not in harmony with Scripture. Prophets were to control themselves when speaking. This gift did not sweep the prophet into a mindless frenzy. Inability to control himself indicated that the prophet was not submitting to God's control because God produces peace, not confusion.

Paul had formerly acknowledged that women could share a word from the Lord in the church meetings (11:4–16). Now he clarified one point about their participation in this context of prophesying (14:34–35). The apostle had just permitted others in the congregation to evaluate the comments a prophet made (14:29). Men could raise questions or make comments, but too much of this could ruin the order of the service and the edifying value of the message. So Paul asked the women to refrain.

Paul concluded his answer to the Corinthians' question concerning spiritual gifts (chapters 12–14) and his teaching on tongues (chapter 14) with a strong call to cooperation (14:36–40). They did not set the standard for how the church meetings should proceed but should submit to the apostle's direction. Failure to recognize the Spirit in Paul's letter would lead to that person's failure to be recognized (acknowledged with approval) by the Lord.

Summary: Paul heartily encouraged the exercise of the gift of prophecy, but he only permitted the gift of speaking in tongues under certain conditions. Paul said his readers were not to forbid speaking in tongues provided they followed the rules he had just explained for the exercise of the gift. The foundational principles that should underlie what takes place in church meetings are these: Christians should do everything in a decent and orderly manner, everything should be edifying (14:26), and a spirit of peace should prevail (14:33).

F. The Resurrection of Believers (chapter 15)

Evidently the Corinthians believed in the resurrection of Jesus Christ, but belief in His resurrection did not necessarily involve believing that God will raise all believers in Christ (15:12, 16, 29, 32). Christ's resurrection gave hope to believers about the future, but that hope did not necessarily involve the believer's resurrection. Paul taught them that their bodily resurrection was part of their hope.

The resurrection of Jesus Christ (15:1–11). Paul began, again, by reaffirming their commonly held belief: Jesus Christ was raised from the dead. The Corinthians and all Christians have their standing in Christ as a result of believing the gospel message, which Paul summarized (15:3–8). He stressed the appearances of the risen Christ because they prove that His resurrection was not to a form of "spiritual" (noncorporeal) existence. By denying the resurrection of the body, the Corinthians were following neither Apollos nor Peter nor Christ. They were pursuing a theology of their own.

The certainty of resurrection (15:12–34). Paul proceeded to show the consequences of rejecting belief in the resurrection of the body. First, he presented the negative alternative (15:12–19). Belief in the resurrection of the body seems to have been difficult for Greeks to have accepted in other places as well as in Corinth (see Acts 17:32; 2 Tim. 2:17). If the resurrection of the body is impossible, then the resurrection of Jesus Christ is fiction, and if He did not rise, the consequences are catastrophic.

Paul turned next to show the positive reality (1 Cor. 15:20–28). The resurrection of Christ makes the resurrection of believers both necessary. and inevitable. Physical resurrection is as inevitable for the sons of Jesus Christ as physical death is for the sons of Adam. Even though Jesus triumphed over death in His resurrection, believers presently still die. Therefore we *must* experience resurrection because we are in Christ and because only in the future will the final enemy, death, be subdued. Jesus' resurrection set in motion a chain of events that will ultimately culminate in the death of death. Then God will resume being what He was before creation, "all in all."

Paul turned from Christ's career to the Christian's experience in his arguments in support of the resurrection (15:29–34). The Corinthians' actions, and his, bordered on absurdity if the dead will not rise. If there is no resurrection, we may as well live only for the present. Paul added an old Greek proverbial saying to warn his readers that if they kept company with people who denied the resurrection their character would eventually suffer. Rather than living for the present, the Corinthian Christians needed to stop sinning and fulfill their present purpose, namely, propagating the gospel.

The resurrection body (15:35–49). Some people say the resurrection of the body is impossible because when a person dies his body decomposes and no one can reassemble it. Paul showed, however, that the resurrection of believers is not simply a resuscitation of human corpses but a resurrection of *glorified* bodies. Paul taught a more glorious future for believers than the present "spiritual" existence that some in Corinth lauded. The apostle proceeded to offer two sets of analogies from nature—seeds (15:36–38) and types of bodies (15:39–41)—that he then applied to the resurrection of the dead (15:42–44). Then he returned to his scriptural analogy between Adam and Christ (15:45–49) to reinforce his argument, which he had brought to a head in verse 44. He concluded by reminding the Corinthians that their bearing the image of the heavenly Adam was still future, and it is certain.

The assurance of victory over death (15:50–58). Paul brought his teaching on the resurrection to a climax by clarifying what all this means for the believer in Christ. He also dealt with the exceptional case of the transformation of living believers at the Rapture. Transformation is absolutely necessary to enter the spiritual mode of future existence.

It is impossible for us in our present physical forms to enter into the heavenly place in the kingdom of God that Christ has prepared for us (John 14:2–3) because the kingdom is of the spiritual order. Living believers translated at the Rapture will also receive spiritual bodies. Because Jesus Christ overcame sin and fulfilled God's law, death cannot hold its prey (Rom. 5:12, 20). Paul concluded with an exhortation for all believers to be faithful in the present (1 Cor. 15:58).

Summary: This chapter began with a review of the gospel message from which some in the church were in danger of departing by denying the resurrection. Rather than living *for* the present (15:32), believers should live *in* the present with the future clearly in view.

Jesus' postresurrection ministry and His testimony through His apostles shows us there is life and bodily resurrection after death. Believers will live that life in a changed body that will be incapable of perishing. It is therefore imperative that we make sure that we and others around us enter that phase of our existence with our sins covered by the sacrifice of Christ.

G. The Collection for the Jerusalem Believers (16:1–12)

This is the last section of 1 Corinthians that begins with the words "now about," and it is the least confrontational one.

Arrangements for the collection (16:1–4). The Corinthian Christians had heard about the collection Paul was accumulating for the poor saints in Jerusalem (16:3) and wanted to make a contribution. Paul did not say how much to set aside except that it was to be as the Lord had blessed them; the amount was totally up to the givers. He planned to send a representative from each of the contributing churches, or groups of churches, to Jerusalem with the gift, guaranteeing that the money would arrive safely and that people would perceive the whole project as honest. The apostle himself might accompany this group (see Acts 20:16, 22; 21:17; 24:17; Rom. 15:25–26).

The travel plans of Paul and his fellow apostles (16:5–12). Paul's plans were tentative to some extent. He sensed the need to spend a good long visit in Corinth, and in view of the problems in the church that he mentioned in this letter we can understand why. Timothy's visit to Corinth from Ephesus was not tentative, however (4:17). Paul advised the Corinthians, who judged by external appearances, to give Timothy the respect he deserved for doing the Lord's work as Paul did.

Summary: The second major section of this epistle (7:1–16:12) includes Paul's responses to six concerns about which the Corinthians had asked him for information. These were marriage and related matters (chapter 7), food offered to idols (8:1–11:1), propriety in worship (11:2–16), the Lord's Supper (11:17–34), spiritual gifts and spiritual people (chapters 12–14), the resurrection of believers (chapter 15), and the collection for the Jerusalem believers (16:1–12).

IV. CONCLUSION (16:13–24)

The apostle concluded this epistle with a series of imperatives, exhortations, and news items.

A. Final Exhortations (16:13–18)

Each section in this epistle concludes with some practical admonition, and these verses constitute a summary exhortation for the whole letter. Above all, love should motivate and mark the readers (chapter 13). The Corinthian church had a special problem with submission to authority, as we have seen. First Corinthians 16:13–18 would have encouraged them to appreciate some less flashy servants of the Lord.

B. Final Greetings and Benediction (16:19–24)

Several churches in the Roman province of Asia had come into existence while Paul used its capital city, Ephesus, as his base of operations (Acts 19:10). Aquila and Prisca (also known as Priscilla) served the Lord as a harmonious husband-and-wife team. Their house in Ephesus became a meeting place for the church (Rom. 16:5). Paul customarily dictated his letters and a secretary wrote them down, but he usually added a word of greeting at the end in his own hand that authenticated his epistles as coming from him. He concluded this strong but loving epistle with a prayerful benediction of God's grace, and he added assurance of his own love for all the believers in Corinth.

2 CORINTHIANS
The Christian Ministry

DATE

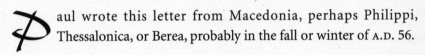

aul wrote this letter from Macedonia, perhaps Philippi, Thessalonica, or Berea, probably in the fall or winter of A.D. 56.

AUDIENCE

This letter originally went to the same group of Christians that received 1 Corinthians, primarily gentile believers along with some Jewish believers.

PURPOSE

First Corinthians did not dispel the problems in the church at Corinth completely. Opposition to the apostle Paul persisted, and Paul's critics continued to speak out against him in the church. The issue was Paul's apostolic authority. His critics were claiming their authority equalled Paul's. This was in effect a claim to apostolic authority on their part and a denial of the full apostolic authority of Paul.

News of continuing problems in Corinth reached Paul in Ephesus during his prolonged stay there during his third missionary journey. He then made a brief visit to Corinth, but his efforts to resolve the conflicts fell through (2 Cor. 2:1; 12:14; 13:1–2). He apparently was insulted and lost face during that "painful visit" (2:5–8; 7:12). He then returned to Ephesus. His next step was to send a "severe letter" from Ephesus by the hand of Titus and another unnamed brother (2:3–4; 7:8–12; 12:18). He apparently directed this letter, now lost, at the party opposed to him and, particularly, its leader. Paul evidently intended to receive Titus's report concerning the effects of this severe letter in Ephesus, but persecution there led Paul to leave that city earlier than he had anticipated (Acts 20:1). He found an open door for the gospel to the north in Troas. Eager to meet Titus, who was taking the land route from Corinth back to Ephesus, Paul moved west into Macedonia (2 Cor. 2:12–13). There Titus met him and gave him an encouraging report (7:6–16).

Most of the church had responded to Paul's directives, and the church had disciplined the troublemakers (2:5–11). Unfortunately some in the congregation still refused to acknowledge Paul's authority over them (10:1–13:10). Paul rejoiced at the repentance of the majority, but his concern for the unrepentant minority and his desire to pick up the money the Corinthians had begun to collect for their poorer brethren in Jerusalem led him to write 2 Corinthians. Along with these primary motives, Paul also felt compelled to refute the charge of fickleness leveled at him by his critics. He had changed his travel plans and had not come to see them as he had said he would.

Paul's purpose in writing this epistle was not mainly to teach doctrine but to answer the criticisms of opponents who were seeking to undermine his ministry, especially in Corinth.

Paul's Corinthian Contacts							
1. Paul's founding visit	2. His "former letter"	3. The Corin-letters to him	4. First Corin-thians	5. Paul's "painful visit"	6. His "severe letter"	7. Second Corin-thians	8. Paul's antici-pated visit

THEOLOGICAL EMPHASES

The situation that Paul faced in Corinth when he penned this epistle gave him an excellent opportunity to clarify the nature of Christian ministry and to explain apostolic authority. He also gave the church the fullest instruction on financial giving that appears in the New Testament (chapters 8–9).

CHARACTERISTICS

Second Corinthians is perhaps the most personal and least formal of all Paul's writings. Like 1 Corinthians, this epistle deals with practical problems in the Corinthian church, but it is more philosophical. It deals more with philosophy of ministry, whereas 1 Corinthians deals more with practice of ministry. Paul opened his heart wide to the Corinthians in this letter and urged them to do the same to him.

OUTLINE

I. Introduction (1:1–11)
   A. Salutation (1:1–2)
   B. Thanksgiving for Comfort in Affliction (1:3–11)
II. Answers to Insinuations about the Sincerity of Paul's Commitment to the Corinthians and to the Ministry (1:12–7:16)
   A. Defense of His Conduct with Regard to His Promised Visit and the Offender (1:12–2:17)
   B. Exposition of Paul's View of the Ministry (3:1–6:10)
   C. Appeal for Restoration of the Corinthians' Confidence in Him (6:11–7:16)
III. Instructions concerning the Collection for the Poor Saints in Judea (chapters 8–9)
   A. The Example of the Macedonians (8:1–7)
   B. The Supreme Motive for Giving (8:8–15)
   C. The Delegates of the Churches (8:16–24)
   D. The Anticipated Visit of Paul (9:1–5)
   E. The Benefits of Generous Giving (9:6–15)
IV. Appeals concerning Paul's Apostolic Authority (chapter 10)
   A. Replies to Charges Made against Paul (10:1–18)
   B. Claims Made by Paul (11:1–12:18)
   C. Exhortations in View of Paul's Approaching Visit (12:19–13:10)
V. Conclusion (13:11–14)
   A. The Exhortation (13:11–12)
   B. The Salutation and Benediction (13:13–14)

I. INTRODUCTION (1:1–11)

The introduction contains a brief salutation and a longer thanksgiving for God's comfort in affliction, which Paul and his readers had experienced.

A. Salutation (1:1–2)

This salutation contains the three elements common in all of Paul's epistles and other popular correspondence of his day: the writer, the addressees, and a greeting.

Paul's use of the term *apostle* so early in his salutation sets the tone for the entire epistle, which is a vindication of his apostleship. Paul claimed that his apostleship came to him "by the will of God." The recipients of this epistle knew Timothy well (1:19; Acts 18:5) since he had visited Corinth as Paul's emissary (1 Cor. 4:17; 16:10). Though the general structure of the salutation was typical of the day, the terms Paul used were uniquely Christian.

B. Thanksgiving for comfort in affliction (1:3–11)

Paul next thanked God for the comfort (1:3–7) and deliverance (1:8–11) he had experienced recently to enable his readers to appreciate what he as an apostle had endured for Christ and the superabounding comfort God supplies to compensate for all afflictions suffered for His sake. Paul's main concern was that his readers learn the *values* of his experiences, not just the facts concerning what had happened to him. He shared the effects of his experiences (1:3–7) and then told them of one experience (1:8–11).

Thanksgiving for comfort (1:3–7). God is the "Father of compassion" in two senses: He is its source, and He is the Father characterized by compassion. "Comfort" is the key word in this section (1:3–7), occurring ten times. It communicates the idea of one person standing alongside another to encourage and support his friend (see John 14:16, 26; 15:26; 16:7). The double designation of God as the "Father of compassion" and the "God of all comfort" was very appropriate to Paul's situation. It sets the tone for the first nine chapters of this epistle.

No matter what variety of affliction we may be experiencing, and no matter what its intensity, God will provide strength and encouragement (comfort) that is more than adequate for our need (2 Cor. 1:4; see 12:9). As God comforts us in all our afflictions, we are to comfort others in any and every one of theirs. Paul personally experienced many afflictions and sorrows, to which he began to refer here (1:5). However, he referred to a particular kind of suffering: the sufferings of Christ, sufferings he experienced because he belonged to Christ and stood up for Christ in a hostile world.

Paul had endured sufferings for the "comfort and salvation" of his brethren in Corinth (1:6). These sufferings enabled him to comfort them better so they would patiently bear up under their afflictions for Christ's sake. The obstinate attitude of the Christians in Corinth could have caused Paul to despair, but he said he was confident that they would continue to function and grow as genuine fruits of God's grace (1:7). The basis for his confidence was the fact that they were suffering for Christ as he was because they were representing Christ in their world. More than that, they would flourish because God's superabounding comfort (strength, encouragement) would cause them to stand and withstand their afflictions.

Thanksgiving for deliverance (1:8–11). Paul's thanksgiving continues, but its focus shifts from the reason for his thanksgiving to the situation that provided the occasion for it.

We cannot identify the precise affliction to which Paul referred. Evidently he wanted the Corinthians and us to focus on the intensity of the affliction. The Corinthians failed to appreciate its severity. It occurred in the Roman province of Asia, and it would have been fatal had God not intervened. Furthermore it was connected somehow with Paul's ministry to the Corinthians (1:6). Paul believed that he was going to die because of this affliction (1:9), but God delivered him from this past hardship, would continue to deliver him from the same or similar afflictions in the future, and would always deliver him.

> Affliction should make us more sympathetic and give us a greater appreciation for God's superabounding comfort and encouragement that He brings to us with the affliction. It should also cause us to trust in God more, and it gives us greater confidence in God's power and greater hope for the future.

Paul believed that his brothers and sisters in Corinth would continue to pray for him (1:11). He painted a word picture of laborers bowed down under some heavy burden that they are working hard to lift, with many faces turned upward toward heaven offering thanks to God for His answers to the united prayers of the apostle and his readers.

II. ANSWERS TO INSINUATIONS ABOUT THE SINCERITY OF PAUL'S COMMITMENT TO THE CORINTHIANS AND TO THE MINISTRY (1:12–7:16)

Paul's primary purpose in writing this epistle was to answer the criticisms of opponents who were seeking to undermine his ministry in Corinth. His strong feelings dictated the flow of his thought in this section more than a list of subjects that he wanted to cover, which is more characteristic of Romans and 1 Corinthians.

A. Defense of His Conduct with Regard to His Promised Visit and the Offender (1:12–2:17)

Paul was addressing a situation in which his own children in the faith were doubting his sincerity and motives. He, too, had doubts about their commitment to Jesus Christ and to himself as the Lord's apostle. He sought to move his doubting readers to a condition of greater faith in this part of the epistle.

The postponement of the intended visit (1:12–2:4). Paul first clarified the motives that led him to change his plans to visit the Corinthians to refute false accusations concerning him that were circulating in Corinth. He wanted to convince the Corinthians that his recent actions arose from sincere motives (1:12–14).

He first claimed, generally, that his actions did not spring from the motives that drive unbelievers, namely, self-serving ambition that seems wise to the carnal mind. He viewed all of life from God's perspective and sought to advance Christ rather than himself. Evidently some in Corinth were saying that to understand Paul's letters they had to read between the lines, that he intended something other than what he had written. Paul claimed that what he had intended was self-evident in his correspondence;

there were no hidden meanings or messages. Even though Paul's correspondence with them had been straightforward, they had not grasped the greatness of his love for them and how proud he was of them (see 1 Cor. 4:14). They had a legitimate right to be proud of Paul as their spiritual father as he had a right to be proud of them as his spiritual children (4:15). They knew him and should have trusted him.

Paul proceeded to help his readers appreciate the fact that his behavior had been consistent with his Spirit-led purposes (2 Cor. 1:15–22). In 1 Corinthians 16:5 Paul had told them that he planned to visit them after he had passed through Macedonia. He was not able to make that trip. Here he explained another plan that he evidently sent the Corinthians after he wrote 1 Corinthians. He says he intended to visit Corinth on his way to Macedonia, probably from Ephesus. He then planned to come back through Corinth as he traveled from Macedonia to Judea. This would have enabled him to see the Corinthians twice. Paul referred to this plan as his original intention. But Paul was in Macedonia, having traveled there from Ephesus by way of Troas, not Corinth. We can see why some in Corinth had concluded that Paul had not followed through with his plans and that they could not count on his word.

Paul found it incredible that anyone in Corinth could really have thought that a change in his plans pointed to a change in his character. He had not deliberately misled the Corinthians any more than God does when He speaks.

God had established Paul and the Corinthians together in Christ. His readers needed to bear their unity in mind when they considered judging Paul inconsistent. He had done everything in harmony with God's will as he knew it at the time and for the welfare of the Corinthians. He cited three evidences of their spiritual unity: their anointing with the Holy Spirit for service, their sealing by the Spirit for security, and their reception of the Spirit as a pledge of future blessings (2 Cor. 1:21–22). These three acts of God uniting believers in Christ build to an emotional climax and reinforce the solidarity that believers have with our consistent God.

The apostle explained why it was desirable that he change his plans. His motivation was love for the Corinthians (1:23–2:4), specifically, to spare them sorrow. He made his decision to postpone his visit because he believed a visit then would not be in the Corinthians' best interests. He took much responsibility for the Corinthians' welfare on himself, but he hastened to clarify that it was as an apostle, not their lord, that he behaved toward them as he did (1:24). Furthermore he recognized that they needed no human lord since they trusted in the Lord Jesus. Paul's visit to Corinth between the writing of 1 and 2 Corinthians seems to be the sorrowful visit that he did not want to repeat (2:1). Paul made up his mind not to come again in sorrow. This is not the language of a vacillator. If he came to them and made them sorrowful again, he himself would be sorrowful since they were his source of joy, so he decided to postpone his visit.

Evidently if Paul had come to them as originally planned he would have had to rebuke them for some situation that existed in the church. Instead of doing this and producing sorrow he decided to wait and give them an opportunity to deal with the problem themselves. Paul evidently wrote this church a severe letter between 1 and 2 Corinthians (2:3). His reference to this former letter strengthens his point that when he came to visit them again he wished to be a source of joy, not sorrow. He wanted them to make him joyful too because of the consequent purity and prosperity of their church. Paul's anguish of heart doubtless arose both from his affliction and the condition of the Corinthian church.

The treatment of the offender and the result of the severe letter (2:5–17). Paul proceeded to explain his perspective on the encouraging and discouraging experiences of his recent ministry to let the Corinthians understand his love for them and to encourage them to adopt his attitude toward ministry.

As a loving pastor, Paul prescribed the treatment of the one who had offended him (2:5–11). The person who caused sorrow to Paul and the Corinthians seems to have done so by insulting Paul either when Paul had been in Corinth last or since then, evidently by challenging his apostolic authority. Paul commended his readers for disciplining the offender, warned them against overreacting, and urged them to convince him of their love for him. A minority apparently held out for more severe discipline of this person (2:6). Paul threw the whole weight of his apostolic authority behind forgiving, as he had previously urged disciplining. By accepting the offender after he repented, the church would be confirming the Lord's forgiveness of him (see also Matt. 16:19; 18:18; Luke 17:3; John 20:23). This action would also show that the church accepted Paul's apostolic authority; it was a test of obedience to him. Paul united in spirit with his forgiving readers. Indeed, he had taken the initiative and forgiven the offending Corinthian before the other Corinthian Christians had.

Paul deliberately understated the seriousness of the offense so no one would imagine that he considered himself virtuous for granting forgiveness readily. He had forgiven the offender in the presence of Christ, that is, with the awareness that Jesus Christ was observing him (2 Cor. 2:10). The apostle had also forgiven the man in order to preserve the unity he enjoyed with this church and to frustrate Satan's desire to create discord in the church and between the church and Paul.

To help his readers appreciate his anxious concern for their welfare, Paul described his recent journey to Macedonia (2:12–13). Paul had left Troas because he had a deep concern for the Corinthians. He had returned to Ephesus from Corinth following his painful visit to the Corinthian church and had then dispatched Titus to Corinth with the severe letter. Paul may have left for Troas because of the riot that Demetrius provoked in Ephesus (Acts 19:23–41). Evidently he had planned to leave Ephesus anyway since he had arranged to meet Titus in Troas or Macedonia. Leaving Troas, Paul moved west into Macedonia because of the situation in Corinth and his concern for Titus (see 2 Cor. 7:5–7).

Paul's recollection of his happy reunion with Titus in Macedonia and the good news his young friend had brought from Corinth precipitated the following "great digression" (2:14–7:4). The Corinthians, Paul learned, had responded favorably to the severe letter. He viewed their response as a divine vindication of his apostleship and a triumph of divine grace in the Corinthians' hearts.

In 2:14–17 he gave thanks for having a share in Christ's triumph. Paul's initial outburst of praise (2:14) sprang from his deep-seated conviction that God's working in and through him, regardless of the appearance of the setback just mentioned, proceeded on triumphantly. This viewpoint is one of the great emphases of this epistle. Jesus Christ is continuing to advance as He builds His church (Matt. 16:18). Because Paul and the Corinthians were in Christ they shared in this triumph.

Paul compared the irresistible advance of the gospel, in spite of temporary setbacks, to a Roman triumph. The wafting of fragrant incense, as the victorious soldiers proceeded through the streets of Rome, resembled God's disseminating the knowledge of Himself through the apostles. Paul also compared the apostles to the aroma of the incense (2:15). Those who preach the gospel are pleasing to God regardless of the response of those who hear it. Many itinerant teachers and philosophers in Paul's day adulterated the Word of God, but Paul claimed absolute sincerity (2:17). His only desire was the glory of God, the advancement of the gospel, and the growth of His people.

> We must grasp Paul's perspective on the unfailing success of God's work in the world today and of those of us who participate in it. We must do this to see life as it really is and to avoid discouragement because of the apparent failure of many of our activities.

B. Exposition of Paul's View of the Ministry (3:1–6:10)

The apostle proceeded to explain his view of Christian ministry further so his readers would appreciate and adopt his viewpoint and not lose heart.

The superiority of Christian ministry to Mosaic ministry (3:1–11). Paul contrasted the ministry of Christians with the ministry of Moses to enable his readers to understand and appreciate the glory of their ministry and its superiority over that of the Mosaic economy. Perhaps Paul developed this contrast because advocates of the Mosaic Law were teaching in Corinth.

He began by referring to testimonial letters (3:1–3). Paul's intention was not to introduce himself to the Corinthians again in a self-commending fashion. Letters written with pen and ink for this purpose were superfluous since they had already received a much better letter of commendation, namely, his life lived among them as an open book. Representatives of the Jewish authorities in Judea carried letters of commendation to the synagogues of the Dispersion (Acts 9:2; 22:5), and the early Christians continued this practice (18:7; Rom. 16:1). Paul contrasted himself with the legalistic teachers of Judaism and early Christianity who believed that observance of the Mosaic Law was essential for justification and sanctification (see Acts 15:5). The Corinthians, too, were such letters that God had written (1 Cor. 3:2).

God's primary method of commending the gospel to others is through the supernatural change that he writes on the lives of believers by His Spirit. The transformation of the Corinthians' lives was the strongest proof of the genuineness of Paul's apostleship. For Paul to have offered other letters written on paper would have been insulting. What God had said about him by blessing his ministry with fruit in Corinth spoke more eloquently than any letter that he could have written. Paul's ministry and the ministry of all Christians consist of being the instruments through whom Christ writes the message of regeneration on the lives of those who believe the gospel.

Next Paul contrasted the Old and New Covenants (2 Cor. 3:4–11). Jesus Christ had given Paul confidence that the changes the gospel had produced in the Corinthians validated his apostolic credentials. That confidence was not merely the product of Paul's imagination. Paul did not want his readers to confuse this confidence with the confidence that comes from feeling adequate or self-sufficient. Christian service is really God working through us rather than us serving Him. God is the one who makes us adequate servants.

Paul identified seven contrasts between the New Covenant under which Christians serve God and the Old Covenant under which pre-Cross Israelites served God. (1) The Old Covenant was essentially an objective, external standard that God revealed for His people Israel without any special enabling grace, but the New Covenant rests on promises that include the indwelling and empowering presence of God's Holy Spirit who enables the believer to obey. (2) The New Covenant is also more general in its demands. (3) The outcomes or results of each covenant differ too. The Old Covenant showed how impossible it was to measure up to God's requirements, and it announced a death sentence on all who fell short. The New Covenant, on the other hand, leads to fullness of life because God's Spirit helps the believer do God's will (3:6).[1]

(4) Another contrast between the two covenants concerns the media God used to carry them to His people: stone tablets for the Old Covenant but His Holy Spirit for the New Covenant. These vehicles represent the

nature of each covenant: hard and unbending compared to personal and loving. (5) A further contrast is the relative glory of the ministries that marked the economies that the covenants created. Both covenants involved ministry to God that resulted in glory for God, but the glory of the New Covenant far surpasses the glory of the Old Covenant. The glory of God (the manifest evidence of His presence) was so strong when Moses reentered the camp that the Israelites could not look at him for very long. How much stronger, Paul argued, will be the manifestation of God's glory in an age when His life-giving Spirit inhabits His people? The New Covenant is also more glorious than the Old in that it manifests the character and purposes of God more fully and finally (see Heb. 1). Greater glory attends the proclamation of the gospel than was true when God gave the Mosaic Law. (6) The purpose of the New Covenant is to produce righteousness, whereas the purpose of the Old Covenant was to show that humans stand condemned because we cannot obey God perfectly. The New Covenant glorifies God so much more than the Old Covenant did that Paul could say the Old Covenant had no glory by comparison. (7) Paul's seventh and last contrast is between the temporary character of the Old Covenant and the permanent character of the New (2 Cor. 3:11). The New will remain, but the Old has passed away. The fading glory on Moses' face resembled the fading glory of the Old Covenant.

Contrasts between the Old and New Covenants in 2 Corinthians 3:6–11			
1. *Ministry*	Old	New	3:6
2. *Type*	letter	spirit	3:6
3. *Results manward*	death	life	3:6
4. *Vehicle*	stone	Spirit	3:7–8
5. *Results Godward*	some glory	greater glory	3:7–8, 10
6. *Purpose*	condemnation	righteousness	3:9
7. *Duration*	temporary	permanent	3:11

The great boldness of New Covenant ministers (3:12–4:6). The superiority of Christian ministry should produce great openness and encourage Christ's ministers. Paul developed these qualities to enable his readers to understand his behavior and to respond the same way in their own ministries.

The apostle began by discussing the openness of Christian ministry (3:12–18). The hope to which he referred was the confidence that he and the other apostles and Christians served God under a covenant that God would not supersede. The boldness to which he referred (3:12) is fearless plainness of speech. Paul could be fearless because of the permanent character of the covenant under which he ministered. Moses, in contrast, could not. Moses ministered with a literal veil over his face much of the time (Exod. 34:29–35), but he removed the veil when he spoke with the people (34:34) and when he spoke with God in the tabernacle. He evidently wore it at other times so that the Israelites would not see the glory of his face fade away. When Moses put the veil over his face, the Israelites could not see the fading of his facial glory.

Christians can behold God's glory more fully in the New Covenant, and it will not fade away. This difference illustrates the superior nature of the New Covenant. Inability to perceive God's revealed glory persists to the present day among the Israelites (see Rom. 11:7). Only when the light of the glory of God from Jesus Christ shines on a person (that is, when the gospel enlightens him) can that individual fully understand that revelation. This applies to all people, but to Jews particularly. Whenever a person comprehends that Jesus Christ fulfilled the Mosaic Law, he or she can then understand that the dispensation of grace has superseded the dispensation of the Law (John 1:17). The Holy Spirit causes a person to understand and believe that Jesus Christ is the fulfillment of the Law.

Believing in Jesus liberates one from sin, death, and the Mosaic Law but not from obligation to respond obediently to God's new revelation in Christ. Even though the Spirit is Lord, His presence liberates the believer rather than enslaving him. All Christians, not just the Israelites' leader, Moses, experience transformation daily as we contemplate the glory of God revealed in His Word (2 Cor. 3:18). The image of God that we see in the Word of God accurately reflects God, though we do not yet see God

Himself. As we observe Christ's glory we advance in Christlikeness and so reflect His glory, not just in our faces but in our characters. This glory will not fade but will increase as we continue to contemplate the Lord. The Holy Spirit is responsible for this gradual transformation too.

Paul now stressed the place of encouragement in Christian ministry (4:1–6). Since we have a ministry in which the Spirit opens people's eyes and transforms their characters we can and should feel encouraged. In view of our inevitable success we do not need to resort to disgraceful subtleties and subterfuge. The reason some people do not immediately understand and appreciate the gospel is that Satan has blinded their minds. Jesus Christ is the image of God that they see in the sense that He visibly and accurately represents the invisible God.

Even though Paul occasionally needed to commend himself to every man's conscience (4:2; 6:4), he never promoted himself. Instead, he proclaimed Jesus Christ as a faithful slave announces his master rather than himself. Paul in his preaching presented Jesus as the sovereign God to whom everyone must submit in faith. He conducted himself as he did because God had dispelled the darkness in his heart by illuminating it with the knowledge of Himself that comes though understanding Jesus Christ. Individual regeneration is a work of God as supernatural and powerful as the creation of the cosmos (Gen. 1:3). Now Paul wanted to share that light with everyone.

The sufferings and supports of a minister of the gospel (4:7–5:10). The nature of Christianity is paradoxical. Second Corinthians explains more of these paradoxes than any other New Testament book. In writing this epistle Paul wanted his readers to realize that his ministry was not faulty, as his critics charged, but that it was solidly within the will of God. To do this he described his own ministry as a projection or extension of Jesus' ministry.

Paul began this section of the epistle by contrasting the message and the messenger of Christ (4:7–15). The treasure that every Christian possesses (4:7) is "the knowledge of the glory of God" (4:6), the gospel. God has deposited this precious gift in every Christian so all may see that the transforming power of the gospel is supernatural and not just human. In four ways the weakness of Paul as a clay jar contrasts with God's power.

(1) Paul had been on the ropes but not trapped in a corner. (2) He was without proper provision but not completely without resources. (3) He was a hunted man but not totally forsaken. (4) He felt beaten down but not destroyed. In these respects his life, representing all believers who herald the gospel, was very much like the Lord's. Paul's numerous escapes from defeat and death were signs of Christ's supernatural power at work in him.[2] Paul was in one sense always dying but in another sense never lifeless. He daily faced threats to his life because of his witness (4:11). Paradoxically the death and the life of Jesus were simultaneously obvious in Paul's experience. Though living, Paul was always in danger of dying, because enemies of Jesus tried to kill him.

However, even though his body was in the process of aging and dying, God kept giving him life—another paradox of the ministry. While Christ's ministers suffer because of their testimony for the Savior, those to whom they minister experience new and greater spiritual life. Paul believed that inner conviction about the truth must result in confession of that truth (4:13). He also believed that physical death was not the end of existence but that the power of God presently at work in him would continue working in him after death and would raise him from the dead. Everything Paul had been experiencing would result in the Corinthians' good and God's glory, so he gladly endured suffering for the gospel. Paul was grateful that he had brought God's grace to Corinth, and now the Corinthians were taking that grace to other people in other places (4:15).

The apostle refused to become discouraged as he served the Lord. In the past he had received a divine commission to proclaim a new and better covenant (4:1). In the future he looked forward to sharing Jesus Christ's resurrection from the dead (4:14). In the present he had the opportunity to promote the Corinthians' spiritual welfare and the glory of God (4:16).

Paul's sufferings, while not fatal, were destroying his body. But even this did not discourage him, for even though he was decaying physically he was still developing spiritually (4:14–18). In another paradox, suffering for Christ now will result in glory later. The apostle could consider the afflictions he had undergone as a servant of Christ as "light" only in comparison with the heavy weight of glory he would receive at Christ's judgment seat (his eternal reward). Another irony is that the physical things

> *The extent to which we view life from Paul's spiritual viewpoint will be the extent to which we do not lose heart in our ministry.*

we see now appear to be permanent, but really the spiritual things that we cannot see are permanent.

By contrasting our present and our future dwellings (5:1–10) Paul continued to give reasons we need not lose heart. First, all Christians will receive an immortal body (5:1). Second, all Christians presently possess the Holy Spirit, God's pledge of our future complete glorification (5:4–5). Third, death begins a new phase of existence for all believers that will be far superior to what we experience now (5:7–8). As we look forward to the realization of these good things, our ambition must be to please God whether we live or die (5:9). We must also bear in mind that we will have to account for our works when we meet the Lord (5:10).

Throughout 4:7–5:10 contrasts between the Spirit-imparted viewpoint on life and the natural viewpoint stand out.

The life of a minister of Christ (5:11–6:10). Paul clarified the driving motive, the divine mission, the dynamic message, and the diverse ministries of the New Covenant to inspire the Corinthians to recognize his ministry as Spirit-led and to follow his example in their ministries.

In 5:11–15 Paul emphasized the constraining love of Christ. Respect for the Lord, since He would be Paul's Judge (5:10), motivated the apostle to carry out his work of persuading people to believe the gospel. Paul tried to persuade them of the truth of the gospel and also the truth about himself. In the previous verses he had bared his soul to the readers not as a way of boasting (3:1) but to give his allies in Corinth ammunition to combat his critics whose judgments about him were wrong. He was simply reminding his readers of things they should have remembered. All of Paul's ministries to and for the Corinthians had been for God's glory and their welfare. The primary reason Paul could not live for himself was God's love for him that extended to Jesus Christ's dying on the cross. Such love merited his complete devotion. All believers died in the person of their representative, Jesus Christ (5:14). Moreover, as Jesus died to His own desires and rose to continue serving us, so we should die to our own selfish interests and live to serve others. Paul modeled what he observed in Jesus' experience and called on his readers to follow Jesus' example.

Paul's emphasis in verses 16–17 shifts to the new creation. Since his conversion, the apostle had stopped making superficial personal judgments based only on external appearances. Whether a person was a believer or a nonbeliever was more important to him than whether one was a Jew or a Gentile. Paul had also formerly concluded that Jesus could not be the divine Messiah in view of His lowly origins, rejection, and humiliating death. Now he recognized Him for who He is and what He had done. Whenever a person experiences conversion, as Paul did, he really becomes a new person. Certain old conditions and relationships no longer exist, and others take their place and continue. The Christian is a new creature (Rom. 6: 4, 6) in this sense (2 Cor. 5:17).

Next Paul developed the ministry of reconciliation (5:18–21). The basis of this total change (new attitudes, 5:16, and new identity, 5:17) is God's gracious provision of reconciliation in sending His Son to die for us. The fact that God has reconciled everyone does not mean that everyone is justified. People still need to respond to the offer of salvation by believing the gospel to receive justification (5:20). God has committed the message of this provision to those who have experienced reconciliation, and our ministry is to present it to all people (Matt. 28:19–20). This makes us God's ambassadors (2 Cor. 5:20), one of the most exalted titles God has given us. Verse 21 explains the "how" of full reconciliation and takes us to the very heart of the atonement. Jesus Christ was the target of God's punishment of sinners; God imputed the sin of all humankind to Him (Rom. 8:3; 1 Cor. 15:3). Now God makes us the targets of His righteousness and imputes that to us (1 Cor. 1:30; Phil. 3:9). He sees us as He sees His righteous Son, fully acceptable to Him.

Paul offered his example as an ambassador of Christ (2 Cor. 6:1–10). Since God appeals to the unsaved through heralds of the gospel (5:20), the herald is a partner with God in His work of bringing people into final reconciliation. As he begged unbelievers to receive God's reconciling grace, Paul also urged his readers to respond quickly and positively to God's grace to them (6:1). The "time of God's favor" (6:2) will not last forever.

Paul tried not to give any cause for others to stumble because of his ministry. Endurance is an extremely important quality in an ambassador of Christ (6:4). The apostle first listed trials of a general nature, then sufferings inflicted by other people, and finally hardships inflicted on himself for the furtherance of the gospel. He then named various graces that God had produced within him mainly in and through these trials, moving from external circumstances to internal qualities (6:6–7a). He described some of the conditions under which he ministered and some of the methods he used. Regardless of people's estimates of him, the great apostle continued to fight the good fight of faith (6:8). Moreover, regardless of how Paul appeared to be doing, in reality God was preserving and blessing him (6:9–10).

C. Appeal for Restoration of the Corinthians' Confidence in Him (6:11–7:16)

Paul now appealed for the Corinthians to reconcile with him in their hearts.

An appeal for large-heartedness and consistency (6:11–7:4). Paul urged his readers to decide to accept him and his ministry so they would continue to experience all the blessings that God wanted them to have.

He began this section by stating his appeal (6:11–13). He had been open with his dear readers, and now they needed to be open to him. They needed to become unrestrained in their affection toward him as he had demonstrated that he was unrestrained in his affection toward them. He could not demand this but only request it, as a parent requests the love of his children.

Then Paul offered a counterbalancing caution (6:14–7:1). He did not want his readers to become dangerously openhearted to all people as well as to himself. He commanded that Christians form no binding interpersonal relationships with non-Christians *that might result in their spiritual defilement.* Paul set forth the folly of ensnaring associations by pointing out five contrasts (6:14–16), all of which clarify the incompatibility and incongruity of Christian discipleship and heathenism. Christians belong to Christ. We already have a binding relationship with Him, and we must not be unfaithful to Him by going after another. Christians should avoid certain probable sources of spiritual contamination, external and internal, in relation to other people and God. Instead we should press on, with the Holy Spirit's help, in our continual struggle against sin (7:1).

Paul concluded this section by restating his appeal (7:2–4). He told the Corinthians he had done no wrong to anyone, had not led anyone astray, nor had he deceived anyone for his own advantage (7:2). Neither death nor the trials of life, including charges against him, would alter his love for this church. There was no reason, therefore, that they should feel restraint in their dealings with him.

The encouraging responses of the Corinthians so far (7:5–16). Paul rejoiced that the Corinthians had recently received Titus and responded favorably to Paul's previous letter. When he had first arrived in Macedonia Paul could not find Titus, and he felt disheartened by several circumstances. But when Titus found him and reported that the Corinthians had responded to his severe letter properly, his distress turned to delight. The Christians loved Paul and wanted to see him again, and they were very sorry that they had been disloyal to him. Moreover they strongly supported Paul against his critics and sought to obey him. His severe letter had led the church into genuine repentance, not excessive discouragement. Several good things had come to his Corinthian readers because they had responded properly (7:11), and their loyalty would fortify them against departing from his teaching in the future.

Titus, who had observed the Corinthians' repentance, had increased Paul's joy further by reporting that to him. Titus appreciated them because of their submissive response to him. Paul was now completely confident that the Corinthians would continue to be obedient to him as their spiritual father and apostle, so he proceeded to appeal to them again (8:1–9:15).

Summary: In answering insinuations about the sincerity of his commitment to the Corinthians and to the ministry, Paul first defended his conduct with regard to his promised visit and the person in Corinth who had offended him (1:12–2:17). He then explained his view of Christian ministry fully (3:1–6:10). Finally he appealed for the Corinthians to restore their confidence in him (6:11–7:16).

III. INSTRUCTIONS CONCERNING THE COLLECTION FOR THE POOR SAINTS IN JUDEA (CHAPTERS 8–9)

Paul was actively collecting money for "the poor among the saints in Jerusalem" (Rom. 15:26) for about five years (A.D. 52–57). He solicited funds from the Christians in Galatia, Macedonia, Achaia, and Asia Minor. The recipients were Hebrew Christians who were poor. Paul devoted much of his time and energy to raising and delivering this collection because he loved these needy Christian brethren. He also believed this gift would honor Jesus Christ and help equalize God's provision for His people's physical needs.

Paul wrote chapters 8–9 to facilitate the collection and to set forth his philosophy of Christian stewardship. This is not the first that the Corinthians had heard about this collection. Evidently they had begun to participate but then dropped the project. Probably the controversy that developed concerning Paul contributed to that decision. However, now that Paul had learned that the Corinthians were responding more positively to him again, he could reintroduce the subject and press for the project's completion.

A. The Example of the Macedonians (8:1–7)

Paul was proud of the Corinthians, but he also rejoiced over the Christians in Macedonia, the Corinthians' neighbors to the north.

These believers were both poor and persecuted, but they demonstrated joy and generosity. Three characteristics marked the giving of these Macedonian brethren. First, they gave sacrificially, beyond their ability (8:3a). Second, they gave on their own initiative, before receiving any suggestion or pressure from others that they should give (8:3b–4). Third, they gave themselves to the Lord and also to Paul for any service he might request of them (8:5). Titus had begun to lead the Corinthians in assembling their gift sometime before his recent visit to Corinth, a year before the time Paul wrote this epistle (8:10). The Corinthians were not facing persecution nor were they facing financial constraints, as the Macedonians were, but they had not yet assembled their offering even though Titus had been with them again recently. Paul now called on them to remember the vastness of their spiritual resources and to make sure liberality marked them as a congregation, as did so many other gifts of God's Spirit (see 1 Cor. 1:5).

B. The Supreme Motive for Giving (8:8–15)

The example of Jesus Christ's gift of Himself for needy humanity should motivate the Corinthians to finish their work of assembling the collection.

Paul did not want them to take his exhortation as an apostolic command since obedience to a command is an inferior motive for giving to others. Rather he hoped that the good example of others, the Macedonians, would motivate them. The incarnation of Jesus Christ is the greatest example of self-sacrificing liberality. Paul strongly urged his readers to complete their collection. They had, after all, both desired to begin a collection and had begun their collection before the Macedonian churches had taken either of those steps. The standard by which God would judge their contribution would be how much they gave in relation to how much they had, not just how much they gave (see Mark 12:41–44). The objective in view was not to make the Judean Christians rich and the Corinthian Christians poor but to establish more equality among them than presently existed.

> God has always wanted His people to share with their brethren who have less than they have. We should implement this principle of relative equality in our giving.

C. The Delegates of the Churches (8:16–24)

Here Paul explained the practical steps he had taken to pick up their gift. He wanted the Corinthians to know what to do and what to expect.

One of Paul's representatives whom he was sending to Corinth to pick up their gift was Titus. It was Titus's desire as well as Paul's that led him back to Corinth. Paul did not identify the other respected brother who would accompany Titus (8:18). The churches of Macedonia, Asia Minor, and

Galatia had chosen this man as a courier. Paul was very conscious of his need to guard his project and the people involved in it from any charge of fiscal mismanagement. He wanted to make sure everyone perceived what he did as honest and aboveboard. Paul had originally thought he would not accompany the delegates who carried the money to Jerusalem (1 Cor. 16:3–4; see Rom. 15:25; 2 Cor. 1:16). He had also insisted that the churches, rather than he, appoint the delegates (1 Cor. 16:3) and that two delegates accompany Titus to Corinth before he arrived (2 Cor. 8:18–19, 22–23).

The third member of the delegation is also unknown to us (8:22). Titus was obviously the man in charge of this project as the special representative of the apostle. Paul concluded his letter of commendation (8:16–24) by warmly encouraging his readers to grant these messengers a reception that would demonstrate to all the other churches the Corinthians' love for Christ, Paul, and the delegates.

D. The Anticipated Visit of Paul (9:1–5)

Paul revealed his plan to visit Corinth soon after Titus and his two companions arrived. He wanted to motivate the Corinthians further to complete their collection and have it ready to go to Judea.

The apostle said he told the Macedonians that the Corinthians had been ready a year ago to start collecting a gift (8:6, 10). Nevertheless it was possible that Paul and his Macedonian companions might find the Corinthians unprepared when they arrived. So Paul mentioned his intention as an added inducement for the Corinthians to complete their collection. He assumed that his readers would collect a substantial sum of money and that generosity rather than covetousness would motivate them.

E. The Benefits of Generous Giving (9:6–15)

Paul concluded his exhortation regarding the collection by reminding his readers of the benefits God inevitably bestows on those who give liberally. Hopefully this would encourage them to follow through with their purpose, believing that God would provide for the need that their sacrifice would create.

One of the great spiritual principles of life is that God blesses people in proportion to their blessing others (see Prov. 11:24–25; 19:17; 22:8–9; Luke 6:38; Gal. 6:7). Paul reminded his readers of this by citing the example of the farmer. If he plants little, he harvests little; but if he plants much, he will harvest much.

Cheerful givers always receive God's loving approval. Such giving need not produce anxiety in the giver even if he is giving away much. God demonstrates His love for cheerful givers by giving them more grace (help) and more opportunity. The righteous person who desires to give to the needs of others will not lack opportunity to do so because God will make this possible for him. What God promised is seed for sowing, the opportunities and resources to make further investments of good works. He did not promise wealth for our own consumption. The context is primarily dealing with righteousness that comes back to the person who sows righteous acts, and God does not assure us we will receive Rolls Royces and Rolex watches.

Another result of the Corinthians' generosity would be that the Jerusalem saints would thank God when the gift came to them—and many others, too, would thank the Lord. Those who received it and heard about it would also reciprocate by interceding for the Corinthians. Only Christ qualifies as an "indescribable" gift (9:15). Reference to Him is appropriate and climactic at the end of this section of the epistle. Paul went back to the primary motivation for Christian giving again (see 8:9) for his final appeal to his readers.

Summary: In this key New Testament passage on giving, Paul appealed to the Corinthians to give to their needy brethren by citing the good example of their neighbor Christians (8:1–7). He then focused on the supreme motive for giving, Jesus Christ's gift of Himself for needy people (8:8–15), and explained the arrangements for collecting and delivering their gift (8:16–24) and his own plans to visit Corinth soon (9:1–5). He concluded by reviewing several benefits of generous giving (9:6–15).

IV. APPEALS CONCERNING PAUL'S
APOSTOLIC AUTHORITY (10:1–13:10)

In this third and last major division of this epistle the apostle Paul defended his apostolic authority in order to silence his critics in Corinth and to confirm the united support of the Christians there. One of Paul's practical purposes in writing this letter was to prepare the way for his next visit. He had just referred to that "anticipated visit" (9:3–4), and he felt compelled to establish his apostolic authority firmly.

A. Replies to Charges Made against Paul (chapter 10)

Paul responded to charges of cowardice, weakness, and intrusion that one or more critics in Corinth had evidently made against him. Failure to submit to apostolic authority could have dangerous consequences, such as disregarding his inspired writings. Paul wrote as he did not out of a sense of wounded pride but to spare his beloved readers from these ill effects.

Reply to the charge of cowardice (10:1–6). Paul gently asked his readers to respond to his appeal to submit to his apostolic authority. He admitted that he walked in the flesh (was only human) but denied that he worked according to the flesh (as carnal Christians and unbelievers do). Carnal weapons like intimidation, manipulation, trickery, double-talk, rumor, and hypocritical behavior are ineffective in spiritual warfare. Reliance on the working of God, however, results in supernatural victories. Paul described the enemy as impersonal. We wage war against invisible, intangible spiritual forces, though obviously Satan is behind these forces. Satan's strategy includes using speculations and incorrect information that contradicts God's revealed truth. Paul claimed to make it his aim to bring all such thoughts and actions into submission to what God has revealed in His Word. He was ready to go to Corinth and punish all disobedience to God's will and his own apostolic authority, but he wanted to do that only after the whole church had made a clean break with the rebels in its midst. If the church would not stand with him in disciplining his unrepentant opponents, his own discipline would not be effective.

Reply to the charge of weakness (10:7–11). Paul also claimed ability to deal forcefully with his critics in person as well as by letter.

The Corinthian Christians tended to evaluate the claims of Paul's critics superficially, so the apostle urged them to look below the surface. At least one critic seems to have been claiming that he had received apostolic authority from Christ that was at least as binding as Paul's. It was unfair for the Corinthians to accept the claim of the critic and to deny Paul's claim. Paul's reference to terrifying his readers (10:9) is ironical, as is clear from verse 10. He evidently was not as showy a speaker as many orators of his day. The power of his influence came from the Holy Spirit's working through his words. For their benefit Paul had restrained his words of exhortation while he was with them. He continued to do that in this letter lest he give substance to the charge that he was only bold and impressive when absent.

Reply to the charge of intrusion (10:12–18). Paul defended his right to preach the gospel in Corinth and denied his critics' claim that they had been responsible for what God had done there to vindicate his former actions and to prepare for future ministry in the regions beyond Corinth.

In irony Paul claimed to be a coward, as his critics accused, when it came to comparing himself with his critics. Evidently Paul's critics were claiming that the apostle had exceeded the proper limits of his ministry by evangelizing in Corinth. He responded that he had not exceeded the territorial limits of his commission by planting the church in gentile Corinth. Paul's ministry had definite divinely prescribed limits; he was to be the apostle to the Gentiles (Acts 9:15; Rom. 1:5; see also Gal. 2:9), and he was to do pioneer missionary work (Rom. 15:20). So he had not overextended his authority by coming to Corinth. His critics were the ones who were overextending themselves by claiming that Corinth was their special domain. Paul was anxious that all the Corinthians acknowledge that he was not doing what his critics were doing, namely, claiming that the spiritual vitality of the Corinthian church was due to their ministry.

Paul could not claim the credit for what his predecessors had done, since he had no predecessors when he planted a new church. He did not want to build on, much less take credit for, the foundational work that any predecessors had done, but to preach the gospel in previously unevangelized areas (Rom. 15:18–21). He did not, however, object to others building on the foundation he had laid or their watering what he had planted (1 Cor. 3:6, 10). He did object to their failing to give credit where credit was due. The only commendation worth anything is the work that God has done through His servants, not their words. This is His commendation of them.

B. Claims Made by Paul (11:1–12:18)

In this section Paul gave further evidence that he possessed apostolic authority. He did this to encourage the whole Corinthian church to continue to respond positively to his ministry.

Paul's reasons for making these claims (11:1–6). The apostle first explained his need to remind the Corinthians of some of the evidences of the Lord's commendation of his ministry. He called this "foolishness" because he should not have had to speak of these things since he and his ministry were well known to his readers.[3] God had jealously guarded His people Israel from the deceitfulness of those who sought to draw their affections away from Himself (see Hos. 2:19–20; 4:12; 6:4; 11:8). Paul felt the same concern for the Corinthians. His jealousy was in that sense "godly," that is, God-like. Paul pictured himself as the father of a virgin bride who desired to keep his daughter, the Corinthian church, pure until she would consummate her marriage to Christ (at the Rapture). The motive of Paul's critics was self-glorification, but Paul's motive was the welfare of his readers.

Besides Paul's critics calling his apostolic authority into question, they were also leading the Corinthians astray. The apostle compared this to the serpent's cunning deception of Eve (Gen. 3:13). The Jesus they were preaching was different enough from the One whom Paul preached that he could say their Jesus was a different person. In listening to the false teachers' message, the church was under the influence of some sort of spirit, but it was not the Holy Spirit. They were in danger of accepting a different gospel. Paul described ironically their accepting it all very graciously and submissively from the false apostles (2 Cor. 11:4). The term "super-apostles" (11:5) probably refers to the false apostles who claimed to be eminent. Even if his critics' charge that he was inferior in speech was true, which it was not, no one could charge Paul with being inferior in knowledge. The Corinthians knew very well his superior knowledge of the revelations of God. Paul was as competent as any of the Twelve or any of his critics in his ability to communicate as well as in his ability to understand God's revelations. He was responding to criticism of himself here (11:6), not conceding inferiority.

Freedom to minister without charge (11:7–15). Paul claimed the freedom to minister in Corinth without receiving financial support from the Corinthians. This illustrated his self-sacrificing love for his readers and his critics' selfishness. He digressed from his "foolish" boasting (11:1–6) to defend his policy regarding his own financial support (11:7–12) and to describe his opponents' true identity (11:13–16).

Paul had previously written that apostles have the right to refrain from working for a living and to live off the gifts of their audience (1 Cor. 9:6, 14). Yet he had made tents in Corinth and had refused to accept gifts from the Corinthians (see Acts 18:3; 1 Cor. 9:4–15). This indicated to some in Corinth that he did not believe he was an apostle. The other apostles normally accepted support from the recipients of their ministries, and these false apostles evidently did so consistently. Paul did not want to burden the people he was currently ministering to, and he knew there were people who would accuse him of preaching to receive payment. He accepted financial help from other churches while not ministering to them directly ("robbed" them) so he could serve the Corinthians without taxing them.[4]

Paul had practiced his trade of leather-working when he had first arrived in Corinth (Acts 18:3). But when Silas and Timothy joined him from Macedonia, Paul stopped this work and devoted all his time to preaching and teaching (18:5). He apparently did this because these brothers had brought financial gifts with them from the Macedonian churches. Paul claimed that he had not sinned in behaving as he had (2 Cor. 11:7) nor had he deceived his readers. Rather, as God knew his heart, he had behaved as he had because he loved the Corinthians. By giving up his right to preach the gospel without cost Paul would have been descending to his critics' level and would have enabled them to compare themselves to him favorably. Paul did not want the Corinthians to associate him with these people because they were counterfeit ambassadors of Christ.

Paul's service and sufferings (11:16–33). To answer his critics and prove the extent of his own service and sufferings for Christ, Paul related many of his painful ministry experiences as an apostle. He did so only to prove to the skeptical minority in the church that he had suffered as much as the false apostles, if not even more than they. The false teachers had impressed the "wise" Corinthians with their boasts, so Paul answered these fools according to their folly (Prov. 26:5). However, he stressed that he was not a fool but was only speaking like one to make his point. Paul evidently knew that only such "boasting" would convince the minority of his own genuineness. Straightforward claims would not convince them, so the apostle was most ironical in these verses. The Corinthians considered themselves unusually wise, but they were being unusually foolish by gladly humoring the foolish critics in their midst. They were absurdly tolerant. They submitted to the teaching of the false apostles even though it resulted in their own enslavement. Ironically Paul feigned shame that he had behaved so "weakly" among them. Now he was experiencing abuse for such gentleness, as his Master had.

After repeated warnings that he was going to boast (2 Cor. 10:8; 11:1, 6, 16), Paul finally began. At first he matched each of his critic's claims with the words "So am I." In his upbringing, his citizenship, and his ancestry Paul was not inferior to any of his Jewish critics. The apostle listed general afflictions he had suffered in the service of Christ (11:23) and then cited specific examples (11:24–25). He turned from nationality (11:23) to achievements (11:24–29). Here he claimed superiority to his critics, not just equality with them. He proceeded from speaking as a fool (11:16, 17, 21) to talking like a madman (11:23). Instead of citing successes that he had experienced in his ministry, he listed his apparent defeats. Thus he boasted in his weaknesses (11:30). Everything Paul described here occurred before Acts 20:2. Paul broadened his description from specific hardships to general types of danger (11:26) and privation (11:27) that he had experienced as an apostle. All the trials he enumerated were temporary, but what follows remained with him always. On top of all his external difficulties, he experienced internal pressure (11:28). Specifically, concern for the weak and the moral failures of his converts disturbed him (11:29).

Paul's weaknesses, humiliations, and sufferings would not initially impress others with his qualifications as an apostle, but these afflictions had come on him as he had served others and Christ faithfully. They were evidences that God had supernaturally sustained His servant through countless discouraging circumstances. They were therefore the greatest proof that Paul was an apostle. The final experience he cited (11:32–33) was his suffering for the gospel.

Special revelations Paul received (12:1–10). Here the apostle mentioned the special visions and revelations that God had granted him to further bolster his readers' confidence in his apostolic calling and authority. He again explained that he felt his boasting was necessary to convince the fleshly minded Corinthian minority. It was not profitable for any other reason. Paul's opponents seem to have been claiming paranormal experiences to validate their apostolate. The "man" of whom Paul spoke was himself (see 12:7–9). He probably referred to himself this way out of reluctance to speak of this matter, and he did not want to give the false impression that he was boasting of such a spectacular experience. Paul could not tell (did not know) whether God had transported him physically into the third heaven (God's presence) or whether his experience had been a vision. What he heard there was a personal message, and he never revealed in Scripture what God told him. However, it had the effect of strengthening his faith and hope that the Lord would abundantly reward his sufferings.

Such a revelation could have made Paul quite a Christian celebrity had he publicized it, but he preferred to proclaim his sufferings so that people could more easily see the supernatural working of God through him. Paul did not want his converts to form an opinion of him based on secondhand testimony. Others might live in awe of Paul because of the spectacular revelations they had heard he had received, but Paul himself was in no danger of becoming too impressed with himself. God had given him a "thorn" in his flesh to remind him of his limitations and keep him humble. What Paul's thorn in the flesh was remains a mystery, but Paul regarded it as a messenger that came from Satan to frustrate him (see Job 2:1–10). Nevertheless God had permitted it and even brought good out of it (Rom. 8:28). Like Jesus in Gethsemane, Paul repeated his request for deliverance three times, which showed how intensely he wanted God to remove his affliction. God used his affliction to teach the apostle dependence on Himself and the sufficiency of His grace. Paul realized that when he was naturally weak the Lord would provide the power that he lacked and needed. God enabled Paul to do things he could not have done had he been naturally strong.

> Both natural weakness and supernatural power are constantly at work in us, as they were in Paul and in Jesus. The greater we sense our weakness, the more we can sense God's power. Our success does not depend on our natural abilities but on God's power working in and through us. Human weakness can be a profound blessing if it results in our depending more on God and less on self.

Paul's supernatural miracles and paternal love (12:11–18). Paul concluded his claim of being a genuine apostle by citing the miracles that God had done and the love that He had manifested to the Corinthians through him. Paul did this to dispel any lingering reservations his readers might have had about his apostolic credentials.

He spoke first of his previous conduct in Corinth (12:11–13). Again he reminded his readers that he had spoken of his own qualifications as an apostle the way he did only because the Corinthians required such proof. They knew he was just as qualified as the "super-apostles," but apart from the grace and calling of God he was not superior to any other believer. Supernatural gifts and activities marked the true apostles, including Paul. His perseverance in his apostolic mission in Corinth despite much opposition distinguished him from the false apostles. Again in irony Paul appealed to his readers for forgiveness because he had not demanded his right of support from them.

The apostle next anticipated his proposed conduct in Corinth (12:14–21). He was about to return to Corinth another time, his "anticipated visit." When he came, he planned to continue his same financial policy and remain financially independent of them. More than their money, he wanted their welfare and their affection, their spiritual maturity and their complete devotion to Christ. Generally parents (Paul) sacrifice for their children (the Corinthians), not the other way around, but children do have a responsibility to help their parents. In family life parents sometimes refuse the support of their children, as Paul did that of the Corinthians, if they feel that doing so is in their children's best interests. In return Paul expected at least their love. But even if the Corinthians did not show Paul love, he would continue to sacrifice for them. Some in Corinth had evidently accused him of craftily obtaining money from them indirectly through his agents such as Titus. However, Paul was crafty not in getting money from them but in giving money to them by working to support himself while in Corinth. Titus's visit with another brother may have been the visit when he began to assemble the special collection (8:6).

C. Exhortations in View of Paul's Approaching Visit (12:19–13:10)

Paul looked forward to his return to Corinth. He shared his concerns about what he might experience and warned his readers to make certain changes before his arrival so he would not have to shame or discipline them when he arrived.

Paul's concerns (12:19–21). Paul said what he did, especially in 10:1–12:18, primarily to build up the Corinthian believers in their faith. His self-defense was only a means to that end. He feared that he might see defects in his readers that he did not want to see if they refused to respond to his instructions in this letter, and he feared they might see the disciplinarian in him; he knew also that he would sorrow if he saw continuing carnal conduct in them. Moreover Paul feared that he might suffer humiliation over their failure to repent of the attitude that had embarrassed him on his former painful visit. This situation would cause Paul to mourn over those in the church who had not repented of their former sins.

Paul's warnings (13:1–10). The church should pass judgment and, on the testimony of the witnesses that Jesus Christ prescribed, decide who was right (see Matt. 18:15–20; 1 Cor. 5:3–5). Paul had warned the Corinthians during his second visit. He was now issuing a second warning in anticipation of his return to Corinth. When he came, he would use his apostolic authority to discipline any in the fellowship who required correction. Then his critics would have firsthand proof of his divinely given power. Paul's threatened judgment of the erring would provide the proof that many of them required that the powerful Christ was working through Paul. Jesus experienced crucifixion because He was obedient to His Father's will and therefore did not assert Himself against His enemies. To onlookers He appeared very weak, but His "weakness" was in reality an evidence of great strength, the strength of commitment to His Father's will. The Father rewarded His Son by sustaining Him with supernatural power. Similarly Paul, in submitting to God's will, had appeared weak to some in Corinth. Nevertheless God would sustain him, too, supernaturally.

That supernatural power would be evident to the Corinthians when Paul arrived in Corinth and dealt with them as Jesus Christ will deal with His people when He returns (see 2 Cor. 5:10). In anticipation of Paul's judgment of them he called on his Christian readers to examine themselves to make sure every one of them was walking in the faith.[5] Paul believed that Jesus Christ was working in each one of them unless they failed this test. In that case there was some doubt whether they were responsive to the Lord. Paul himself claimed to be walking in the faith.

> **Summary:** This section (10:1–13:10) begins with accusations against Paul that he was bold and terrifying when absent but weak when present. It concludes with his answer to this charge: If he wrote sharply when absent, it was to avoid the need for acting with sharpness when present. He conducted himself by the principle that his authority had been entrusted to him to be used for constructive, not destructive, ends.

V. CONCLUSION (13:11–14)

Paul concluded this letter with an exhortation, a salutation, and a benediction to draw its emphases together and impress on his readers the basis and importance of their unity with one another and with himself.

A. The Exhortation (13:11–12)

Paul urged his readers to respond to his letter in five ways. First, they were to rejoice because they had the opportunity to judge themselves before

God would judge them. More generally, they could and should rejoice in the Lord. Second, they were to mend their ways and thus experience completion (restoration) as God would bring them to maturity. Specifically they needed to break permanently with all idolatry, to complete their collection, and to change their attitude toward Paul. Third, they were to accept Paul's exhortation that would result in their comfort. Fourth, they were to foster a united outlook by putting first things first, especially to unite in their attitude toward Paul and his authority. Fifth, they were to live at peace with one another and with Paul. These conditions being met, the God who manifests love and peace as the fruit of His Spirit would remain in fellowship with them. The Corinthians could then exchange the holy kiss sincerely.

B. The Salutation and Benediction (13:13–14)

The love of the body of Christ elsewhere reached out to enfold the Corinthians in unity. Paul wished that God's grace demonstrated in the work of Jesus Christ on Calvary might be the atmosphere in which all his readers lived their lives. He hoped that God's love demonstrated in the Father's work in sending Jesus Christ as our Savior might be the motivation for their lives. And he longed that the fellowship that God's Spirit produces among all the saved might unite their lives with one another and with all believers.

GALATIANS
Liberty in Christ

AUDIENCE

$\mathcal{T}$he apostle Paul directed this epistle to the churches of Galatia (Gal. 1:2), and he called its recipients Galatians (3:1). However, who these people were and where they lived have proved difficult to ascertain. The traditional opinion is that the recipients lived in the geographical district of Galatia, located in the northern part of the Roman province called Galatia, in Asia Minor (modern western Turkey). This view holds that Paul founded these churches on his second missionary journey after the Spirit forbade him to preach in the province of Asia (Acts 16:6). The more popular view today, however, is that Paul wrote to the churches located in the Roman province of Galatia, churches that he founded on his first missionary journey (Acts 13:38–39, 46, 48; 14:3, 8–10). In any case the Galatians seem to have been mainly Gentiles, but the house churches included Jews as well.

DATE

According to the so-called North Galatian theory, Paul probably wrote this epistle during his third journey either from Ephesus about A.D. 54 or from Corinth about A.D. 57. If Paul wrote this epistle to the churches of South Galatia, he probably did so either shortly before the Jerusalem Council in A.D. 49 or shortly after it. If he wrote this epistle after the Jerusalem

Council, then Paul's visit referred to in Galatians 4:13 is the same one mentioned in Acts 16:6. Or if he wrote Galatians before the Jerusalem Council, which seems more likely, then Galatians 4:13 refers to the visit mentioned in Acts 14:21. Assuming the earlier date, Paul probably wrote Galatians from Antioch of Syria shortly after his first missionary journey and before the Jerusalem Council.

PURPOSE

Assuming the South Galatian theory and an early date of writing, Paul wrote mainly to stem the tide of the Judaizing heresy to which he referred throughout the letter. In every chapter he mentioned people who opposed him (Gal. 1:6–7; 2:4–5; 3:1; 4:17; 5:7–12; 6:12–13).

THEOLOGICAL EMPHASES

Galatians has been called the Manifesto of Christian Liberty because it is a proclamation concerning the liberty that comes with being a believer in Jesus Christ. The epistle explains that liberty: its nature, its laws, and its enemies. Many of the same doctrinal issues that Paul expounded extensively later in Romans appear in Galatians in embryonic form, making Galatians a seed plot for Romans. Salvation is the main emphasis.

CHARACTERISTICS

The most distinctive impression one receives from this epistle is its severity. Paul wrote it with strong emotion. What he wrote in this letter was of utmost importance to him, for he was dealing with belief as foundational to behavior.

OUTLINE

I. Introduction (1:1–10)
   A. Salutation (1:1–5)
   B. Denunciation (1:6–10)
II. Personal Defense of Paul's Gospel (1:11–2:21)
   A. Independence from Other Apostles (1:11–24)
   B. Interdependence with Other Apostles (2:1–10)
   C. Correction of Another Apostle (2:11–21)
III. Theological Affirmation of Salvation by Faith (chapters 3–4)
   A. Vindication of the Doctrine (chapter 3)
   B. Clarification of the Doctrine (chapter 4)
IV. Practical Application to Christian Living (5:1–6:10)
   A. Balance in the Christian Life (chapter 5)
   B. Responsibilities of the Christian Life (6:1–10)
V. Conclusion (6:11–18)

I. INTRODUCTION (1:1–10)

The introduction to Galatians is rather perfunctory, with no mention of thankfulness. Paul began at once to marvel at his readers' apostasy, that is, their departure from the truth.

A. Salutation (1:1–5)

In introducing himself as the writer, Paul emphasized the divine source of his apostolic commission. He contended that his apostleship did not originate from men, nor did it come to him through men (Peter, James, Ananias, or whomever). Rather Jesus Christ, equal with God the Father, bestowed it on him. This is the only one of Paul's inspired letters that he addressed neither to Christians in one specific town nor to an individual. The greeting Paul wrote in most of his epistles was a combination of the commonly used Greek (*charis*, "grace") and the Jewish (*šālôm*, "peace") salutations. The purpose of the Lord's self-sacrifice, Paul reminded his readers, was that He might deliver us out of the control of this present evil age. This salutation touches on the chief argument of the letter: the controversy between Paul and his Galatian opponents over the significance of Christ and his redemptive work.

B. Denunciation (1:6–10)

Paul rebuked his readers for turning away from the gospel that he had preached to them and for turning toward a different "gospel." In every other one of his epistles Paul commended his readers before launching into the main subject of his letter, but here he recorded no such praise. Its absence stressed the seriousness of his readers' error and the urgency of Paul's appeal. Teachers of false doctrine had followed Paul and were distorting the good news of Christ. Paul consistently referred to the Galatian troublemakers in the third person but addressed his readers in the second person. This suggests that the false teachers originated outside the church rather than from within it. Probably they were Jews who were putting pressure on Gentiles to believe and to live as religious Jews (see 1:6–9; 2:4–5; 3:1; 4:17; 5:10, 12; 6:12–13). Paul warned his readers to reject this teaching even if it had come from angelic messengers sent directly from heaven. By "accursed" Paul meant being under God's judgment. The false teachers evidently charged Paul with preaching to curry the favor of his listeners. However, Paul said he behaved among them in a manner consistent with his commitment to Christ as his Master.

II. PERSONAL DEFENSE OF PAUL'S GOSPEL (1:11–2:21)

The three major sections of the epistle deal with history (1:11–2:21), theology (chapters 3–4), and ethics (5:1–6:10).

A. Independence from Other Apostles (1:11–24)

This first subsection in Paul's autobiographical account, the historical portion of the epistle, relates the apostle's early Christian experience and his first meeting with the church leaders in Jerusalem.

The source of Paul's gospel (1:11–17). Paul clarified the source of his gospel message to convince his readers that the gospel he had preached to them was the true gospel and what the false teachers were presenting was heresy. Both his gospel and his commission to preach it came directly from Jesus Christ on the Damascus Road (1:15–16). He did not receive it from traditional sources (his teachers) nor did he learn it through traditional means (his formal education). Since his calling had been supernatural and abundantly clear, Paul did not need to consult with other people.[1] Instead he went to an undefined area of Arabia, then returned to Damascus rather than Jerusalem, still feeling no need to obtain the blessing of the other apostles but to preach the gospel.[2]

The events of Paul's early ministry (1:18–24). Paul was not dependent on the other apostles for his ministry or his message. Three years after his conversion he finally revisited Jerusalem and met Peter, for the first time, and James. Furthermore he only stayed fifteen days and did not see any of the other apostles. Paul did not even spend time in Judea but went north into Syria and Cilicia. He had so little contact with the churches in Judea that even after several years they could not recognize him by sight. They only knew him by reputation and thanked God for what He was doing through Paul, the opposite reaction of Paul's Judaizing critics. Certainly the Judean Christians would not have been so happy if Paul had preached a gospel different from the one the other apostles had been preaching and they had believed.

B. Interdependence with Other Apostles (2:1–10)

Paul related his meeting with the Jerusalem church leaders to establish that although he was not dependent on anyone but God for his message and ministry, he preached the same gospel the other apostles did.

Barnabas brought Paul back from Cilicia to assist in the ministry in Antioch of Syria (Acts 11:25–26) fourteen years after the apostle's conversion. Paul's private visit to Jerusalem described here was probably his second visit (11:27–30). A divine revelation was one factor that moved Paul to visit Jerusalem then. Evidently Paul thought that if he did not contact the Jerusalem apostles (Peter, James, and John) his critics might undermine his evangelistic work by pointing out that Paul had had no fellowship with the Jerusalem apostles. They might go on to suggest that

> *Different Christians can minister to different segments of humanity. Nevertheless there must be unity in the message we proclaim.*

there was no fellowship because there was a difference of opinion between Paul and the other apostles over the gospel message. He wanted officially to secure the freedom of the Gentiles from the requirements of the Law and their equality of status with Jewish Christians in the one body of Christ. James, Peter, and John agreed with Paul, the proof of which was their willingness to let Titus remain uncircumcised. Circumcision was the rite by which gentile males became Jewish proselytes. As apostles, James, Peter, and John were not superior to Paul. They contributed nothing to his authority or message. They did not seek to change Paul's message but agreed with it. The only point James, Peter, and John stressed was that Paul should not neglect the poor in his ministry, but Paul had already made a commitment to do that.

C. Correction of Another Apostle (2:11–21)

Paul mentioned the incident in which he reproved Peter, the Judaizers' favorite apostle, to establish further his own apostolic authority and to emphasize the truth of his gospel.

Peter had shaken hands with Paul in Jerusalem (2:9), but when Peter was in Antioch, Paul opposed him. Peter had been eating with the Christians at Antioch, who were both Jews and Gentiles, until some Jewish visitors came from Jerusalem (see Acts 10:28; 11:3). They were from the group that believed Gentiles needed to undergo circumcision before they could become Christians. James had not endorsed their views; they were not from James (Gal. 2:9). Perhaps they came from the same church as James. When these men came, they intimidated Peter, who gradually separated from the gentile Christians. The other Jews living in Antioch hypocritically followed Peter's example, as did Barnabas.

Peter's behavior had influenced many other people, so Paul criticized him publicly for inconsistency. By separating from his gentile brothers

Peter had also cast doubt on the truth that God accepts Jews and Gentiles equally. This played into the hands of the Judaizers. In addition, Peter was insulting the gentile Christians and acting contrary to his own convictions. Unsaved Jews regarded Gentiles as "sinners." Paul ironically referred to them in the same way, since Peter was treating them as if they were. Paul then reminded Peter that both of them knew that God does not justify people because they keep the Mosaic Law, part of which involved observing dietary distinctions. Justification comes by believing in Christ—plus nothing else. Obedience to the Law never justified anyone (Rom. 3:20).

Paul refuted the Judaizers' charge that justification by faith led to lawless behavior (Gal. 2:17–18). He said this made Christ, in effect, a promoter of sin, which could never be. If a Christian puts himself back under the Mosaic Law, the Law will show him to be a sinner since no one can keep the Law perfectly. Christians are free from the requirements of the Mosaic Law (Rom. 10:4; Heb. 7:12). Transgression inevitably follows when the Law becomes the authority in the believer's life (Gal. 2:18). The Law thus condemns (kills) everyone (2:19). If someone is dead, he has no more responsibility to what killed him and is in that sense free. From then on he can devote his energy, as a resurrected person, not to pleasing the Law but to pleasing God.

When a person trusts Christ, God identifies him with Christ not only in the present and future but also in the past. The believer did what Christ did. Thus each Christian can say, "When Christ died, I died. When Christ arose from the grave, I arose to newness of life. My old self-centered life died when I died with Christ. His Spirit-directed life began in me when I arose with Christ." Therefore in this sense the Christian's life is really the life of Christ (2:20). Paul concluded by affirming that he did not set aside the grace of God, as Peter had done by implying that it was not enough. If that is true, Christ died needlessly. It is then really obedience that saves, not Christ.

Summary: This review of Paul's conversion and early ministry supports the divine origin of his gospel and his ministry, which his opponents in Galatia were seeking to undermine.

III. THEOLOGICAL AFFIRMATION OF SALVATION BY FAITH (CHAPTERS 3–4)

To establish the truth of salvation by faith alone Paul moved from a historical review to theological arguments. He first vindicated the doctrine of salvation by faith alone (chapter 3) and then clarified it (chapter 4).

A. Vindication of the Doctrine (chapter 3)

Paul explained the meaning of justification and progressive sanctification by faith alone and argued their validity from experience (3:1–5), Scripture (3:6–14), and logic (3:15–29) to dissuade his readers from returning to reliance on the Mosaic Law. In 3:1–18 Paul argued against legalism, the belief that we can make ourselves acceptable to God by keeping rules. In 3:19–4:7 he argued against nomism, the belief that we need to make law the ruling governor of our lives.

The experiential argument (3:1–5). The Galatians were behaving as though they were under some type of spell and not in full use of their rational faculties. Paul had drawn graphic word pictures of Jesus Christ crucified as their Substitute when he had been among them, and they had understood and believed the gospel.

To bring them to their senses, Paul asked four more questions of them (3:2–5). (1) How did you receive the Holy Spirit? It was obviously not by keeping the Law; it was by hearing and believing the gospel. (2) How is God sanctifying you? Their justification had been a work of the Holy Spirit in response to believing faith, and their sanctification was also a work of the Holy Spirit in response to believing faith. (3) Have your experiences been useless? Their experiences as Christians had been useless if they had believed the wrong gospel. (4) What accounts for the miracles you witnessed (see Acts 14:3, 8–10)? The Galatians had not done something special to earn those miracles. God performed them freely in response to their believing the gospel. His readers' own experience of salvation proved that it is by faith alone.

The scriptural argument (3:6–14). In these verses Paul defended salvation by faith alone by appealing to Scripture. It is incorrect to say that only through conformity to the Law could people become sons of Abraham (3:6–9). If the legalists were logically consistent, they would have to admit that the Law places people under a curse, not special blessing (3:10–14).

In emphasizing the Mosaic Law the Judaizers appealed to Moses frequently. Paul took them back further in their history to Abraham, the father of the Jewish nation. Genesis 15:6 proves that God justified Abraham by faith, not because he kept the Law. The spiritual sons of Abraham, Paul contended, are not necessarily his physical descendants but those who believe God, whether they are Jews or Gentiles. Faith, not circumcision, makes a person a true "son" of Abraham.

Living under the Mosaic Law did not bring blessing; it brought a curse. That is because to obtain God's blessing under the Law a person had to keep it perfectly—and no one could. The person who is righteous by faith is the one who truly lives; therefore no one can be justified by works of the Law. Responding to the idea that both Law and faith are necessary for justification, Paul quoted Leviticus 18:5, which shows that they are mutually exclusive. They are two entirely different approaches to God. The Law requires works, but the gospel calls for faith. Christ paid the penalty for our sins and made justification possible for every person (see 2 Cor. 5:21). The blessing of justification that Abraham enjoyed has become available to the Gentiles, as has the blessing of the promised Holy Spirit's ministry to believers (Acts 1:8; 2:33). Obeying the Mosaic Law never results in the justification or sanctification of anyone, Jew or Gentile. Only faith in God does that.

The logical argument (3:15–29). Paul next showed the logical fallacy of relying on the Law. Faith continued after God gave the Law (3:15–18). Even wills and contracts made between human beings remain in force until the fulfillment of their terms. Likewise the covenant God made with Abraham remains in force until God fulfills it completely. The Mosaic Law did not supersede and thereby replace the Abrahamic Covenant.

The Four Seeds of Abraham in Scripture

1. *Natural Seed:* All physical descendants of Abraham. Genesis 12:1–3, 7
2. *Natural–Spiritual Seed:* Believing physical descendants of Abraham. Isaiah 41:8; Romans 9:6, 8; Galatians 6:16

> 3. *Spiritual Seed:* Believing nonphysical descendants of Abraham. Galatians 3:6–9, 29
> 4. *Ultimate Seed:* Jesus Christ. Galatians 3:16; Hebrews 2:16–17

When Paul wrote in Galatians 3:17 that the Mosaic Law was given "four hundred and thirty years later," what did he mean? Later than what? The best of several views seems to be that the four hundred thirty years extended from the final confirmation of the Abrahamic Covenant to Jacob (Gen. 46:1–4). Thus it went from the end of one era (the Age of Promise) to the beginning of another (the Age of Law).

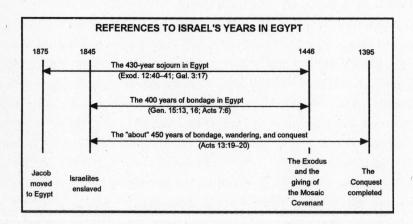

What then is the purpose of the Mosaic Law (Gal. 3:19–22)? God had several purposes in giving it. The Law restrained transgressions, revealed transgressions, and provoked transgressions. It was only a temporary measure designed to function until Christ came. Do the Law and the promises to Abraham contradict each other? Indeed not! God designed them for two different purposes. The purpose of the Law was never to provide justification. It served as a mirror to show people their sinfulness and that they are the slaves of sin. It shows people that their only hope is to accept the salvation God provides.

Paul next discussed the conditions of people under Law and under faith (3:23–29). In Paul's view of salvation history, the coming of faith

(3:23) is synonymous with the coming of Christ. In Paul's day it was common for children between age six and puberty to be under the care of a tutor, who protected them from evil influences and demanded their obedience. The Law did just that for Israel. However, the need for that kind of assistance ended when Christ came. Now all who trust in Christ are adult sons, no longer children. Faith in Christ Jesus makes a person a son of God (3:25). When a Roman boy reached the status of a son, his father gave him a special toga. Paul compared that toga to Christ (3:27). The differences in the house rules that Paul spoke of here reflect different dispensations (literally, "house laws"). Another difference is that under faith all believers share the same privilege and position in their relationship to God.

Those joined to Christ by faith also become spiritual descendants of Abraham and beneficiaries of some of God's promises to him. Ethnic Jews will inherit those promises given to the physical descendants of Abraham. All believers will inherit those given to the spiritual descendants of Abraham. Saved Jews will inherit those given to the physical descendants who are also spiritual descendants.

> Christians live under a new code of behavior compared with Israelites who lived under the Mosaic Law. We must be careful to distinguish our responsibility from theirs. We live under the New Covenant, the law of Christ (6:2). It consists of all that Jesus affirmed directly during His earthly ministry and indirectly through His apostles in the New Testament after He returned to heaven.

B. Clarification of the Doctrine (chapter 4)

In chapter 3 the Jews' preoccupation with the Law of Moses was foremost in Paul's mind. In chapter 4 he reiterated his argument for the benefit of Gentiles for whom religious syncretism and pagan idolatry were primary concerns. Another difference between these chapters is that whereas in chapter 3 Paul dealt mainly with justification (see 3:20), in chapter 4 his emphasis was primarily on progressive sanctification (see 4:3).

The domestic illustration (4:1–11). Continuing his case for faith over the Mosaic Law, Paul cited an illustration from family life to clarify the condition of believers compared with the teaching that Christians must keep the Law.

Paul compared the Law to a trustee appointed to care for a young child and his property, a guardian. The spiritual immaturity of those living under the Mosaic Law before Christ contrasts with the spiritual maturity of those living by faith in Christ. Before a person comes to Christ by faith he is under bondage. God (like the father of the child in the illustration) sent forth Christ when He determined the time was right to free those children held in bondage to the Law. The Messiah was born under the Mosaic Law, which He alone fulfilled by keeping it perfectly (Matt. 5:17). God also sent the Holy Spirit to indwell believers (God's sons and heirs) and to motivate us to approach God as our Father. How foolish it would be then to go back under the bondage of the Law!

The apostle reminded his readers of their former way of life, the transformation that their adoption into God's family had brought about, and his concern that they were in danger of trading their future for a mess of pottage (Gal. 4:8–11). Before conversion Paul's readers (mainly Gentiles but some Jews) were slaves to religious traditions that, in the case of Gentiles, included counterfeit gods. Now free, they were in danger of turning back to the same slavery, a system that lacked power to justify or sanctify, that provided no inheritance, and was elementary. Paul despaired that they were going backward and that much of his labor for them was futile. They were not acting like heirs of God.

The historical illustration (4:12–20). Appealing to his past contacts with the Galatians, Paul called on them to remember his visit to Galatia. He pointed out that he had lived among them as a Gentile, not as one under the Mosaic Law. So he now called on them to live independently of the Law as he did.[3] Paul suffered with some physical ailment when he preached in Galatia (4:13), but the Galatians had put up with that without despising him because they valued the good news he brought them. Now the Galatians were losing their good attitude toward Paul and its accompanying blessing. They had formerly appreciated Paul so much that they would have given him their most precious possessions, but now they were regarding him suspiciously as an enemy. The Judaizers were seeking to pull the Galatians away from Paul's influence so his readers would be dependent on them. But Paul always sought his readers for the right reason, namely, so they would grow in grace. Paul felt as if he were going through labor pains again for them. Their irrational desire to become slaves to the Mosaic system and followers of the false teachers perplexed him.

The biblical illustration (4:21–31). In a figurative way Paul interpreted features of the history of Abraham's two sons Isaac and Ishmael to convince his readers that they were in danger of joining the wrong branch of Abraham's family. His use of Abraham's story was a common rabbinic teaching method the Judaizers probably employed in their teaching.

In recounting the biblical story (4:21–23), Paul challenged his readers, who claimed to value the Law so highly, to consider what it taught. He pointed out two contrasts between Ishmael and Isaac: Ishmael's mother, Hagar, was a slave, but Isaac's mother, Sarah, was free, and Ishmael was born naturally, but Isaac was born supernaturally.

This story, Paul said, illustrates the conflict between advocates of the Law and advocates of grace (4:24–27). The main features in this analogy are as follows.

Hagar is the bondwoman	Sarah is the free woman
Ishmael was born naturally	Isaac was born supernaturally
The Old covenant	The New Covenant
The earthly Jerusalem	The heavenly Jerusalem
Judaism	Christianity

Three applications stem from this analogy (4:28–31). First, Christians are similar to Isaac in that they experience a supernatural birth and are part of the fulfillment of God's promise, so they should not live as enslaved sons. Second, those who advocate following the Law persecute those living in liberty, as Ishmael persecuted Isaac. Third, Christians should exclude lawkeepers from their midst, since lawkeepers have no inheritance with the legitimate sons of God. Paul concluded his argument by reminding his readers of the very basic and drastic difference between himself and the Galatians, who were children of faith, and the legalists and lawkeepers, who were children of the flesh.[4]

Summary: Paul's defense of salvation by faith alone (chapters 3–4) points out strongly the incompatibility of faith and works as methods of obtaining justification and progressive sanctification. The Judaizers were trying to get the Galatians to submit to the Mosaic institutions to merit something from God. This approach is the opposite of grace, which acknowledges that people cannot merit God's favor. They must simply trust in the Lord to deliver what He has promised.

IV. PRACTICAL APPLICATION TO CHRISTIAN LIVING (5:1–6:10)

Paul moved next from theology (chapters 3–4) to ethics, and from instruction to exhortation.

A. Balance in the Christian Life (chapter 5)

Having ruled out the Mosaic Law as a regulatory standard for Christian behavior, Paul proceeded to explain how God does lead us. The apostle discussed two extremes and then the proper middle road.

Living without the Law (5:1–12). These verses emphasize that no one can satisfy the demands of the Mosaic Law by obeying only a few of its commands. Only complete compliance is adequate.

Paul's readers were in danger of returning to the slavery of the Mosaic Law. The false teachers were telling them they needed to submit to circumcision to be truly acceptable to God. However, if the Galatians allowed the false teachers to circumcise them, they would be obligating themselves to obey the entire Mosaic code. Their confidence in circumcision would reveal confidence in their own ability to earn acceptance by obeying the Law. Thus this legal approach to salvation would separate them from Christ since what He did was provide salvation as a gift. They would fall away from the grace method of salvation if they chose the law method.

Paul's approach, and the one he tried to persuade the Galatians to adopt, was simple: to trust God to fulfill His promises, and to anticipate the future because they were now declared righteous (justified). This hope includes our ultimate glorification (see Rom. 8:18–25; 1 Pet. 1:3–4, 13). We do not work for this, but we wait for it. God does not care if a Christian has a circumcised body or not. What does matter is that we trust Him because we love Him.

The false teachers had bumped Paul's readers as they ran the Christian race. God had not led the ones who interfered with them to do so. Paul believed that the Galatians would side with him and that they or God would judge the false teacher or teachers. Paul's gospel was a stumbling block to the false teachers for two reasons: It presented a crucified Messiah, and it advocated a way of salvation apart from circumcision and the Law.

Living without license (5:13–15). Some people might conclude that since it is unnecessary to keep the Law to be saved, it is unnecessary to pay attention to the Law for any reason. However, Paul was not urging his converts to burn their Old Testaments. The Law has values, one of which is to reveal how to express love for God and other people. Under grace we are free to fulfill the Law by loving one another. For the Christian the Mosaic Law has *revelatory* value (2 Tim. 3:16–17) even though it does not have *regulatory* value, controlling our behavior. If his readers insisted on living in slavery, Paul wished they would enslave themselves to love each other. If they wanted to live under Law, let it be the Law of Christ (Gal. 6:2), impelled by the indwelling Spirit. Paul cautioned both sides of the controversy to love one another or they would consume each other.

Living by the Holy Spirit (5:16–26). Paul previously told his readers that they should not live either under the Mosaic Law or licentiously. Here he gave positive direction and explained what the leading of the Holy Spirit means so his readers would know how to live to the glory of God as Christians.

Verses 16–18 emphasize the promise of victory. Walking by the Spirit means living moment by moment by submissively trusting in and obeying the Holy Spirit rather than self. To the extent that we keep on walking by the Spirit we will not carry out our fleshly desires. This is a promise.

We should be trusting in the Lord all the time, but the more we think about our dependence on Him the more consistent we will be in trusting in Him and in walking by the Spirit. The flesh opposes our spirit and the Holy Spirit, and it does so with strong and sometimes evil desires. We experience conflict whether we side with the Spirit against the flesh or with the flesh against the Spirit.

Since we are led by the Spirit, we are not under the Law. The question is, Will we follow His leading and walk after the Spirit (5:16), or will we walk after the flesh? The Holy Spirit leads us to do the moral will of God primarily through Scripture by helping us understand the will of God as He has revealed it there and by giving us the desire and ability to do it. We can overcome the flesh by siding with the Spirit. The Judaizers were advocating submission to the Law as the way to overcome the flesh, but Paul advocated submission to the Spirit.

Verses 19–21 identify the works of the flesh, which are as evident as fruit on a tree. Behavior normally demonstrates one's nature. Paul identified five categories of sins here: sexual (5:19), religious (5:20), societal (5:20–21), intemperate (5:21), and other (5:21). Typically people who practice such sins will not inherit the kingdom of God because they are unbelievers. Though these vices may mark some Christians, Paul mentioned the fate of these unbelievers so the Galatian Christians would avoid their vices.

Verses 22–23 describe the fruit of the Spirit, the behavior characteristics that become evident when we allow the Holy Spirit, rather than the flesh, to control us. The word "fruit" is singular, which suggests the unified Christlike character that the Holy Spirit produces. Paul identified three types of qualities: mental or Godward (5:22), interpersonal or otherward (5:22), and general or selfward (5:22–23). In contrast to the selfish orientation of the works of the flesh, the fruit of the Spirit is selfless and outgoing. There are laws against the deeds of the flesh because they are destructive, but there are none against the fruit of the Spirit because it is edifying.

Verses 24–26 outline God's provision for victory. The Christian has crucified the flesh in the sense that when he trusted Christ God broke the domination of his sinful nature. While we still have a sinful human nature, it does not dominate us as it did before we trusted in Christ (Rom. 6:6–7). Therefore it is inconsistent for us to return to the flesh. Now since God has given us new life we should keep in step with the Spirit who is God's provision for us to live victoriously. We should not trust in ourselves for our sanctification but in the Holy Spirit. Common evidences of self-confidence are boasting, challenging, and envying (Gal. 5:26).

> **Summary:** Liberty lies between legalism and license. The key to being fruitful as a Christian is being submissive to the Holy Spirit, obediently following His leading, and walking in dependence on Him.
>
> ---
>
> The Holy Spirit leads the Christian as a mountain climber leads others up a narrow mountain path. Our responsibility is to keep following Him. We get in trouble when we try to blaze a trail on our own.

B. Responsibilities of the Christian Life (6:1–10)

Being free from the Mosaic Law does not mean that Christians are free from responsibility. In clarifying the Spirit's leading Paul explained various responsibilities that Christians have to each other. Spirituality is evident in personal relationships (6:1–5) and in one's use of money (6:6–10).

Responsibilities toward sinning Christians (6:1). The situation Paul envisioned here is that of sin overtaking a Christian much as a fast runner overtakes a slower runner. Sin has gotten the better of him in a particular instance. The spiritual Christian should restore the overtaken brother and help him to his feet, gently, carefully, and cautiously. We can avoid a spirit of self-righteousness in dealing with those who stumble by remembering our own personal vulnerability to temptation.

Responsibilities toward burdened Christians (6:2–5). Verse 1 deals with restoration and this section (6:2–5) with prevention. Probably the burden Paul had in mind was an excessive burden of temptation and struggle with the flesh. The "law of Christ" encompasses the whole of Jesus' teaching personally while He was on earth and through His apostles and prophets following His ascension (see Acts 1:1–2). Its essence is to love God wholeheartedly and one's neighbor as oneself (Matt. 22:36–40; John 13:34–35; 15:12; 1 John 3:23). The primary characteristic of the Mosaic Law was its legal character, whereas the primary characteristic of the Law of Christ is its gracious character. He did not mean that there is no law under grace any more than he meant that there was no grace under the Mosaic Law. Every Christian is responsible to carry his own weight, which includes helping others in need.

Responsibilities toward teachers (6:6–9). Here is a specific example of mutual burden-bearing. The concept of voluntary giving out of love for the teacher was new and different in Christianity compared with Judaism and the Greco-Roman culture. While all believers possess eternal life, some experience this life to a greater extent than others do. And in the future some believers will enjoy more rewards than others. Similarly, some living human beings enjoy a better quality of life than others. The condition for this reward is not growing weary. Giving up mentally leads to growing faint spiritually.

Responsibilities toward all people (6:10). Christians have a responsibility to do what is good to all people, including the unsaved, but we have a special responsibility to help other Christians as we have opportunity.

V. CONCLUSION (6:11–18)

Paul summarized some of his more important points and appealed to his readers again to urge them to follow through and to put into practice what he had taught them in view of Judaizers. Evidently Paul wrote the rest of this letter himself, having dictated the former verses to a scribe. The "large letters" (6:11) were probably used for the sake of emphasis and to distinguish Paul's handwriting from his secretary's. Since the false teachers required their converts to undergo circumcision, the Jews would look more favorably on them. "The cross of Christ" (6:12) represents the whole doctrine of justification by faith alone that Paul defended in this epistle. Because of the Cross the world system had lost its appeal to Paul, and he had lost his appeal to the world. Paul wished for God's peace and mercy for all who walked by the rule he had expounded, namely, faith apart from works. Especially he wished this for the "Israel of God," that is, Christian Jews. Paul appealed to his readers to end the controversy in Galatia that had caused him so much trouble and distraction. He cited the scars he had received as the target of persecution, in contrast to circumcision, as his final proof of his devotion to Christ.

EPHESIANS
The Mystery of the Church

AUTHOR

Almost all Christians believed in the Pauline authorship of Ephesians until the nineteenth century, when destructive biblical criticism gained influence and asserted that Paul did not write Ephesians.

DATE

Most conservative New Testament scholars hold that Paul wrote Ephesians, along with Philippians, Colossians, and Philemon, the other "Prison Epistles," during his first Roman imprisonment, A.D. 60–62.

AUDIENCE

Paul knew Ephesus and the church in that city well since he had ministered there for about three years, A.D. 53–56 (Acts 19:1–20:1). This church included mostly gentile converts but also some Jews.

PURPOSE

Paul's frequent references to the church as a mystery, previously unknown but now revealed, identify the apostle's main purpose in writing as having been the exposition of the mystery of the church (1:9; 3:3–4, 9; 5:32; 6:19). Particularly he wanted to facilitate unity among Jews and Gentiles in the church.

THEOLOGICAL EMPHASES

Paul emphasized the church as Christ's body in which both Jewish and gentile believers are one. The emphasis on the importance of love is also strong, which indicates that Paul wanted to promote unity in the church.

CHARACTERISTICS

Ephesians is remarkably similar to Colossians, both epistles dealing mainly with the church as the body of Christ. However, in Ephesians Paul stressed the church as the body of Christ, and in Colossians he emphasized Christ as the Head of that body.

OUTLINE

I. Salutation (1:1–2)
II. The Christian's Calling (1:3–3:21)
   A. Individual Calling (1:3–2:10)
   B. Corporate Calling (2:11–3:19)
   C. Doxology (3:20–21)
III. The Christian's Conduct (4:1–6:20)
   A. Spiritual Walk (4:1–6:9)
   B. Spiritual Warfare (6:10–20)
IV. Conclusion (6:21–24)

I. SALUTATION (1:1–2)

Paul probably intended Ephesians to be an encyclical letter. Since Ephesus was a strategic city in both the Roman Empire and in Paul's ministry, it would have been natural for him to send this letter to that city first. Every believer occupies a location in space, but every Christian also lives within the sphere of God's family because of Jesus Christ's work, which Paul spoke of as being "in Christ," a favorite phrase of his in Ephesians. Much of what follows in chapters 1–3 is an explanation of what it means to be "in Christ."

II. THE CHRISTIAN'S CALLING (1:3–3:21)

Paul began, as usual, by setting forth foundational truth and then applying it to the lives of his readers. The first three chapters deal primarily with doctrine (teaching) and the last three mainly with practice (application).

A. Individual Calling (1:3–2:10)

Paul began the body of his letter by reviewing the spiritual blessings that God has for believers in His Son.

The purpose: glory (1:3–14). The believer's position in Christ is something for which Paul praised God. "In the heavenly realms" refers to the sphere in which these blessings operate, the spiritual sphere in which believers now live. God has united us with Jesus Christ so we are in that sense with Him where He is now.

Paul also praised God for the believer's selection by the Father (1:4–6). Then he rehearsed spiritual blessings that have come to us from all three members of the Trinity. The first blessing is election (1:4). God has sovereignly chosen some people for salvation. God chose us "in Him" (Christ) in the sense that He is our Representative. God has ordained that all the elect should be under Christ's authority. God lovingly did this before He created the world so that we should be "holy" and "blameless." Having predetermined the final destiny of the elect, God chose us. Jesus Christ was the agent who made our adoption by God possible by His death. The ultimate goal of predestination and election is that believers will praise the magnificence of God's undeserved favor, which He has shown toward humankind. The elect did nothing to merit God's grace, and it comes to us through Jesus Christ, the Father's beloved Son. Since God loves His Son, believers who are in Christ can rejoice that we, too, are the objects of God's love.

The sacrifice of the Son (1:7–12) is also part of our individual calling. Jesus Christ has redeemed us from sin. The life blood of the perfect sacrifice had to flow out of Him for this to happen. The immediate result of our liberation is that God has forgiven our sins. God lavished His grace on us in His infinite wisdom. This is part of His plan to bring everything into submission to Jesus Christ in the future (1:10). God chose a plan after deliberating on the wisest course of action to accomplish His purpose. He chose Jews and Gentiles to be believers for the praise of His glory. The work of the Son in salvation was setting the sinner free from his sin and revealing God's plan to head up all things in Christ at the end of the ages.

The seal of the Spirit (1:13–14) is the final aspect of Paul's rejoicing over individual election. Besides Jews, who were the first to hope in Christ (1:12), Gentiles also had come to salvation when Paul wrote this epistle. The vehicle God uses to bring His elect to faith is the message of truth, the gospel message. When the Gentiles heard it, they believed it. This resulted in their salvation and their being sealed by the promised Holy Spirit. This sealing provided a guarantee of their eternal security. God seals the believer by giving him the indwelling Holy Spirit, who keeps the Christian securely in Christ. All the blessings spoken of go to both Jewish and gentile believers. The Holy Spirit's indwelling presence is a down payment of all that God will give us as His children. The fact that we possess Him now assures us that the rest of our salvation will inevitably follow, specifically, release from sin's presence. God's "possession" is the believer whom He has chosen (1:3–6), redeemed (1:7–12), and sealed (1:13–14) to the praise of His glory.

Summary: The spiritual blessings Paul identified in verses 3–14 are election, predestination, adoption, grace, redemption, forgiveness, knowledge, sealing, and inheritance. The recurrence of the phrase "in Christ" and equivalent expressions emphasizes that all these blessings come with our union with our Savior. Likewise the repetition of "His will" and its equivalents stresses that the sovereign God is responsible for all these blessings.

The means: knowledge (1:15–23). Paul prayed that his readers would appreciate and appropriate these good things in their own lives.

Paul first commended his readers for what they were doing well (1:15–16). Their faith expressed their trust in God, and their love evidenced proper relationships with other people. These qualities stimulated Paul to give thanks to God repeatedly for their present condition and to petition Him for their present and future needs.

> *Believers should rejoice in the spiritual riches that are ours because of God's abundant grace.*

Paul also asked God to give his readers a spirit (attitude) of wisdom and revelation (understanding) of Himself through the ministry of the Holy Spirit so they might gain greater knowledge of God (1:17–23). The "eyes of the heart," a vivid mixed metaphor, suggests not just intellectual understanding but full personal apprehension of God. Paul prayed this prayer so his readers would know three things: the hope that was theirs because God had called them to salvation, their identity as an inheritance that God would give them when they went to be with Him, and the great power of God that changes Christians' lives. God manifested this power in Christ in three instances: in His resurrection and exaltation, in the Father's subjecting all things to Christ, and in Christ's appointment as Head over the church. The church is the fullness of Christ in that He fills the church with blessings.

The motive: grace (2:1–10). Verses 1–3 are really preliminary to Paul's main point. He described the Christian's condition as an unbeliever before God justified him: hopeless as a part of the world system, controlled by Satan, indulging the flesh, and destined to experience God's wrath. "But" then God in mercy and love "made us alive" (2:5), "raised us up" (2:6), and "seated us" (2:6) with Christ. God will use the regeneration of believers to demonstrate the wealth and richness of His grace, specifically, His kindness toward believers as displayed in all that we have in Christ. Verses 1–3 describe what we were in the past, verses 4–6 what we are in the present, and verse 7 what we shall be in the future. Verses 8 and 9 explain the surpassing riches of God's grace and expand the parenthetical statement in verse 5. The basis of our salvation is God's grace, unmerited favor, and divine enablement. The instrument by which we receive salvation is faith (trust in Christ). Since salvation is a gift of God, no one can boast that he has done something to earn it. God has not saved us because of our works (2:8–9), but He has saved us to do good works (2:10).

B. Corporate Calling (2:11–3:19)

New spiritual life includes but means more than experiencing regeneration individually. Additionally, God brings every Christian into union with every other Christian. In Christ we have oneness with other believers as well as oneness with God.

Present ministry (2:11–22). The apostle stated the reality of the union of all believers in Christ (2:11–13), explained what this involves (2:14–18), and described the consequences of this union (2:19–22).

Great differences existed between Jewish and gentile believers before the Cross, but in Christ gentile believers are one with Jewish believers (2:11–13). Before the Cross Jewish believers enjoyed five privileges not known by gentile believers. But (2:13) because of Jesus Christ's death God has brought Gentiles near to Himself and to the Jews in a sense never before true.

Gentile believers' union with Jewish believers has great significance (2:14–18). Jesus Christ's death has resulted in peace between gentile believers and Jewish believers and peace between gentile believers and God. A spiritual barrier had separated Jews and Gentiles since Abraham's time. With the death of Jesus Christ, God began dealing with humankind on a different basis than He had in the past. He now stopped working with and through the Jews and Judaism primarily and began dealing with Jews and Gentiles on the same basis, namely, their faith in His Son. He began a new dispensation (administration) in His dealings with humanity. The body of Jesus sacrificed on the cross terminated the enmity between Jews and Gentiles because when He died He fulfilled all the demands of the Mosaic Law and so ended the Mosaic Law as His rule of life for the Jews. The Mosaic Law had been the cause of the enmity between Jews and Gentiles. Its dietary distinctions and laws requiring separation, in particular, created hostility between Jews and Gentiles. Jesus Christ created one "new man," the church, out of the two former ethnic groups, Jews and Gentiles. In the church believing Jews become Christians, and believing Gentiles become Christians. God now deals with both believing Jews and believing Gentiles equally as Christians. Jesus Christ's second purpose for ending Jewish-gentile hostility was to bring Jewish and gentile believers to Himself in one body, the church. Formerly access to God was through Judaism, but now it is through Jesus Christ by the Holy Spirit.

Because of this union gentile believers are no longer strangers and foreigners with respect to Israel (2:19–22). They are fellow citizens with Jewish believers in the church, God's new household (1 Tim. 3:15). Christians are also fellow citizens of heaven with all the other saints of other ages. The church is like a temple (Eph. 2:21) that rests on the foundation of the apostles and prophets and whose cornerstone is Jesus Christ.

Summary: The church is not just a continuation and modernization of Israel; it is a new creation (2:15). In it Jewish and gentile believers stand with equal rights and privileges before God. Membership in this new body is one of the great blessings of believers in the present age along with our individual blessings (2:1–10).

Past ignorance (3:1–13). Paul began to pray for his readers again, but he interrupted himself to tell them more about the church. What he said in this section gives background information concerning the church as a mystery.

Since God has blessed us so greatly, Paul prayed that his readers would comprehend fully the extent of God's love for them (2:14–21). He viewed God as dispensing His grace throughout history through various administrators. Paul's responsibility was to carry God's grace to all people but particularly to the Gentiles. This duty involved the reception of revelation not previously given (a mystery), specifically, that Gentiles and Jews are equal partners in the church. The mystery was unknown before God revealed it to the New Testament apostles and prophets. The mystery is both the equality of saved Jews and Gentiles in one body and that new body itself, the church. Neither the church as a distinct entity nor the equality of Jews and Gentiles in the church was previously revealed. Specifically believing Gentiles and Jews are fellow heirs of God's riches and fellow members of the body of Christ. They are also fellow partakers of the promise concerning Christ in the gospel. Paul considered himself the least worthy of all the saints to have received the privilege of proclaiming this gospel and the mystery of the church (3:8). God's manifold wisdom is apparent in the church's manifold construction, Jews and Gentiles united in one body. Paul's Ephesian readers should not, therefore, view his present imprisonment as a tragedy but simply as part of his ministry.

Future comprehension (3:14–19). Paul now prayed that his Jewish and gentile readers might *experience* the unity that was theirs spiritually. God is not only the Father of the family in which gentile and Jewish believers are one (the church), but He is the prototype Father, the ultimate Father over every family that has a father. Paul asked God to strengthen his readers in the inner man according to His vast resources (3:16). This power comes to us through the indwelling Holy Spirit who strengthens our inner man, that is, our innermost being. He indwells every Christian (1 Cor. 12:13) but is truly "at home" in the lives of those believers who let Him be first in their attitudes and activities (John 15:14). As the believer keeps trusting and obeying, Jesus Christ can continue to occupy first place in his life. Paul was praying that his readers would enjoy intimate fellowship with their Lord (see 1 John 1:1–4).

When believers accept Jesus Christ's revelation of the mystery of the church, they are able to comprehend that God's love is broad enough to embrace both Jews and Gentiles in the church (Eph. 3:18). They can appreciate that it is long enough to stretch from eternity to eternity. They can see that it is high enough to raise both Jews and Gentiles into the heavenly places. And they can understand that it is deep enough to rescue both kinds of people from sin's degradation and from Satan's grip. Paul desired that his readers would apprehend the love of Christ fully, but he acknowledged that full comprehension of that love is impossible because it is greater than mortals can conceive. The ultimate goal of Paul's request was that his readers might be so full of knowledge and appreciation for God that they might allow Christ to control them fully (3:19).

C. Doxology (3:20–21)

Paul praised God for the individual and corporate calling that believers have in Christ. The basis for his confidence that God was able to do far beyond what he had prayed for or could even imagine was the fact that God brought Jews and Gentiles together in one body. Ceaseless praise would come to God in the church for uniting these two previously irreconcilable groups and for enabling them to love and work together as fellow members of the same body.

III. THE CHRISTIAN'S CONDUCT (4:1–6:20)

Practical application (chapters 4–6) now follows doctrinal instruction (chapters 1–3).

A. Spiritual Walk (4:1–6:9)

Paul now identified the marks of a spiritual walk, namely, a life that manifests the Holy Spirit's control. This is the result of what he prayed God would produce in the readers (3:16–19).

Walking in unity (4:1–16). The apostle stressed the importance of walking (living) in unity. God will facilitate unity in answer to prayer, but believers are responsible to obey Him.

Paul first explained the basis of unity (4:1–6). Walking worthily involves harmonizing one's conduct with his calling. "Calling" here refers to God's challenge for believers to live in unity (2:13–16). Three virtues contribute to unity in the church: humility, gentleness, and patience. Believers should practice all these virtues with loving forbearance toward one another. Christians must preserve the unity between believers that God has created in the church. Peace is what keeps potential factions together. Seven elements unite believers in the church, and believers should remember them when tempted to break unity (4:4–6): one body, one Spirit, one hope, one Lord, one faith, one baptism, and one God and Father of all.

Paul next urged the preservation of unity (4:7–16). He explained the means by which we can preserve it, namely, with the gifts that the Holy Spirit gives. Whereas each believer has received grace (divine enablement) from God (3:2),

The church that stresses both truth and love will produce spiritually mature, Christlike believers.

God does not give each Christian the same measure of grace. In Romans 12 and 1 Corinthians 12 Paul spoke of gifts given to people, but now he spoke of people given to the church as gifts.

In His death Jesus Christ gained the victory over sin, and He redeemed those whom He would give as gifts to the church. Paul identified the descended Christ with the ascended Christ who now is in position to rule over all (Eph. 1:23). He fills all things with His fullness. After Jesus Christ ascended, He gave gifts to the church, gifts that enable it to function. This order of events is in harmony with the revelation that the church is a new entity that came into existence after Jesus' ascension. He gave some individuals to be apostles in the church, some prophets, some evangelists, and some pastors and teachers (pastor-teachers).

The purpose of all these gifted leaders is to prepare the rest of the saints to minister and so to build up the body of Christ. The role of these leaders is to minister the Word to the saints in the church so the saints can minister the Word in the world. All the saints, not just the leaders, should participate in service. The end in view is completeness in Christ. As each believer exercises the gifts (abilities God has given him), three things happen: the body enjoys unity (4:3–6), it becomes more spiritually mature (4:15), and it becomes more Christlike (see 1:23; 3:19).

One result of gifted people equipping the saints to serve the Lord and others is that believers may be stable in their faith. Infants are easily swayed and confused, as waves blown by the wind (4:14). False teachers create such winds by their teaching and seek to trick people into following them. Another result is that believers should maintain the truth in love in both their speech and their conduct.

Summary: The church, then, is a diverse body composed of many different people who must give attention to preserving their unity (4:7–16). In this passage Paul's emphasis was on body growth more than on individual growth. Each believer contributes to body growth as he exercises his particular gifts (abilities) in the service of Christ.

Walking in holiness (4:17–32). Paul reminded his readers that they should not walk (live) as they used to walk before their conversion to Christianity (4:17–19). He traced the attitude of typical unsaved Gentiles to its source. Lack of worthy purpose rests on unclear understanding, which in turn results from separation from the life that comes from God. This separation arises from natural ignorance of God that rests on insensitivity to God and His ways. As a result, unsaved Gentiles typically give themselves over to lives of sensual self-indulgence.

In contrast to unsaved Gentiles (4:20–32), Christians' minds are no longer dark, they are no longer aliens from God, and their hearts are no longer hard and impure. They did not learn to follow Christ by the natural mental processes that customarily lead to the degradation of unsaved Gentiles. The Ephesian believers had received teaching about Christ and had learned to live in the sphere of His will.[1] Christians should put their former unsaved manner of life aside and take on a new attitude. This renewing is an ongoing process in the life of the Christian, a process we call progressive sanctification. The new self is the person after he or she experiences regeneration. At that time the believer puts on the new man as he pursues the things of Christ rather than the desires of the flesh. God has created the new self (the Christian) in regeneration after the image of our spiritual parent, God Himself. The practice of the new man (4:25–32) should follow his condition (4:20–24).

Verses 25–32 include five exhortations to Christians regarding our conduct. Each one has three parts: a negative command, a positive command, and the reason for the positive command. First, we should stop deceiving and speak truth because we belong to and must function honestly in the body of Christ. Second, we should also avoid sinning when angry and should deal with sin quickly if it does accompany anger. If we do not do so, Satan will have an opportunity to lead us further into sin. Third, we must refrain from stealing, and we must work so we will have something to share with the needy. Fourth, we must speak good things as well as do good things because we can grieve (bring sorrow or pain to) the Holy Spirit by our speech. Fifth, we should abandon vices and adopt God-pleasing virtues (4:31–32).[2]

Walking in love (5:1–6). In addition to calling us to walk in unity (4:1) and holiness (4:17), Paul urged us to walk in love (5:2). He first advocated love (5:1–2), and then negatively he warned us to abstain from evil (5:3–6).

It is only normal and natural for children to imitate their parents. So, too, should the children of God imitate their heavenly Father, specifically, by loving. The measure and model of our love should be Christ's love for us.

The self-centered practices introduced in verse 3 are the opposite of love. Paul was evidently contrasting unbelievers with believers. Words that teach that living a moral Christian life is unimportant are empty because they contain no truth. If the wrath of God is presently coming on the sons of disobedience, certainly His own sons can expect His discipline when they practice the same things.

Walking in light (5:7–14). These verses include three commands concerning walking in the light, with reasons and explanations to motivate us to obey. It is inconsistent for the objects of God's love to become fellow partakers with the objects of His wrath by joining in selfish, immoral, impure conduct. Rather we should walk as children of light. As we do so, we continually seek to discover the will of God so we can do it and please God. Children of light should also abstain from joining the sons of disobedience in their deeds but should rather expose their deeds because they are unfruitful (5:11). Believers should not even discuss the secret dark deeds of unbelievers in normal conversation since discussing these things will draw attention to them and may make them attractive to the carnal minded. Since God will bring all things into the light, it is important that believers wake up and rise from the deadness of their former unsaved lifestyles. If they do, Christ will shine on them in blessing (5:14).

Walking in wisdom (5:15–6:9). We walk wisely by letting the Holy Spirit control our lives. A basic admonition in 5:15–21 is applied to various groups of Christians (5:22–6:9).

The wise person is one who views and sees things the way God does. We live wisely when we use every opportunity to please and glorify the Lord. The unwise (5:15) simply lack wisdom, but the foolish (5:17) behave contrary to what they know to be right. The Lord's will should be the Christian's primary blueprint since He is the Head of the body. God's will includes allowing Him to control (fill) us, being thankful always, and being subject to one another. Paul identified four of the many results of being filled (controlled) by the Holy Spirit. All four deal with praise, and all are public rather than private activities (5:19–20).

The exhortation about being Spirit-filled is applied to six groups: wives and husbands (5:22–33), children and parents (6:1–4), and slaves and masters (6:5–9). In each of the three pairs the first partner is responsible to be submissive or obedient (5:22; 6:1, 5). However, the second partner is also to show a submissive spirit, and all are to relate to each other as to the Lord (5:21).

Christian wives are to be subject to their husbands as an expression of their submission to the Lord Jesus (5:22–24). The reason for wives' willing submission is that God has placed them in a position of authority under their husbands. Wives have authority in their families, but it is an authority that is under their husbands' authority. Similarly, He has chosen to place Jesus Christ in authority over the church. Submission is the proper response to sovereignly designated authority in the church-Christ relationship and in the wife-husband relationship.

Paul summarized the wife's duty as submission and the husband's duty as love, in which he seeks the highest good for her (5:25–33). Husbands are to love their wives in the same way Christ loved the church, namely, self-sacrificially. He gave Himself up in death to provide salvation for her. The husband should love and treat his wife as carefully as he does his own body. The relationship that exists between a husband and his wife is essentially the same as the one that exists between Christ and His church.

Another human relationship that needs to be affected by the filling of the Spirit is that of children and parents. Children express their submission to the Lord by obeying their parents. Honoring (6:2) is a larger responsibility than obeying (6:1). It involves a proper attitude as well as appropriate behavior. For Israel the fifth commandment, to honor one's parents, would result in the nation enduring in the Promised Land (Exod. 20:12). The principle is also true that normally children who obey their parents avoid the perils that would shorten their lives (Prov. 3:1–2).[3]

The duty of fathers (6:4) comes next because fathers are God's ordained family heads on whom rests the primary responsibility for child training. Essentially this command forbids making unreasonable demands on children in the everyday course of family life and providing direction and encouragement for the children.

The third group Paul addressed was slaves and masters. Most slaves served in the home in Paul's day so this section fits in well with what precedes about other household relationships. Christian slaves owed their earthly masters obedience, which demonstrated their submission to Christ. Seven qualifications describe proper obedience (6:5–7). Paul reminded faithful slaves that they would receive a reward from Jesus Christ in the future whether their masters on earth acknowledged their good service or not. This reward will come at the judgment seat of Christ, if not earlier.

Masters should seek to please the Lord in their dealings with their slaves (6:9), even as slaves should try to please Christ as they serve their masters. Masters should not threaten but should provide gracious, just, and fair treatment. Masters should also remember that their Master in heaven will not show favoritism to them because of their social or economic status but will evaluate them by the same standard they have used to judge others (Matt. 7:1–5).

Only a Spirit-filled believer will be able to fulfill these duties (Eph. 5:15–20). Essentially what Paul urged was humility that expresses itself in submissiveness to others rather than arrogant self-assertiveness.

Summary: How should Christians walk? In unity, in holiness, in love, in light, and in wisdom (4:1–6:9).

B. Spiritual Warfare (6:10–20)

Paul introduced this section differently from the five that precede it, and the emphasis in it is on God's resources. Earlier Paul urged the strengthening and growth of the body of Christ (4:12, 16). Now he explained the need for this: The body is at war with a spiritual enemy. We walk, but we also war.

"Finally" introduces what remains for the readers to do (6:10). We need to allow the Lord to strengthen us and to strengthen ourselves in the Lord. Three Greek words for power in verse 10 remind us that the Lord's might is available to us in our spiritual warfare. To be strong in the Lord and to withstand Satan's attacks the Christian must "put on" the full armor that God supplies. These offensives come to us from a very intelligent and experienced strategist, and they are frequently deceptive. This struggle does not take place on the physical plane primarily, though saying no to certain temptations may involve certain physical behaviors. It is essentially warfare on the spiritual level with an enemy we cannot see. This enemy is Satan and his hosts as well as the philosophies he promotes. Probably the four terms Paul used of our spiritual enemies in verse 12 do not identify four separate kinds of adversaries as much as they point out four characteristics of all of them. They operate in the heavenly realms. The evil day (6:13) is any day in which the evil forces attack.

Our main responsibilities are to "stand" (6:14) and "take" (6:17). Paul described the items Roman infantrymen wore in the order in which they would have put them on. Full truth is the only adequate basis for a defense against Satan. Righteous conduct seems to be in view, as well as the righteousness of Christ. Our grip on the gospel will enable us to hold our ground and even advance when tempted. The faith that provides defense for the Christian is trust in all that God has revealed and active application of that trust at the moment of spiritual attack.

In addition to standing firm we also need to receive and put on two more items (6:16). We receive present salvation (deliverance) as we receive all salvation, namely, by calling on God and requesting it. Deliverance involves a mental choice, namely, trust in God rather than self and obedience to Him. The "word of God" for the Christian is similar to the Roman soldier's short sword. It refers to the words of Scripture that we use to counteract the particular temptation we face, the appropriate Scripture spoken or put to use by the Christian in a given instance of temptation (see Matt. 4:4, 6, 10). The Holy Spirit both gives the word and empowers it as we use it. We should be in constant prayer in preparation for our spiritual battles and as we engage our enemy. In addition to praying for our own needs we should also, as good soldiers, keep alert to the needs of other fellow soldiers, namely, all the saints (Eph. 6:18).

Paul sensed his own great need for the prayer support of his readers (6:19–20). He was in heavenly places, but he was also in an earthly dungeon, and an encounter with spiritual enemies awaited him when he would make his defense before Caesar.

Summary: In view of our calling, our Christian conduct consists of a spiritual walk (4:1–6:9) and spiritual warfare (6:10–20).

IV. CONCLUSION (6:21–24)

Paul's anticipation of his defense before Nero brought him back to his present situation in his thinking. All that remained for him to do in this epistle was to share with the Ephesians some personal information and to pray God's blessing on them.

Tychicus accompanied this letter to Ephesus and probably carried it. His mission included giving the Ephesian Christians further information about Paul and comforting and encouraging them. Peace, love, and faith are all important communal virtues in the Christian life (6:23). As the apostle opened his epistle by referring to God's grace, so he ended it (see 1:2). God's grace was the key to the creation of the church and the calling of the Christian, and it is essential to the conduct of each believer. Paul wished God's grace on all who love Jesus Christ faithfully.

PHILIPPIANS
The Mind of Christ

AUTHOR

The apostle Paul claimed to have written this epistle (Phil. 1:1), and the references to his acquaintances, events in his life, and his way of thinking all confirm him as the writer.

DATE

Paul was a prisoner when he penned this letter (Phil. 1:7, 13, 16). References to the palace guard (1:13) and Caesar's household (4:22) imply that Paul wrote from Rome, probably during his first imprisonment when he was under house arrest there (A.D. 60–62; see Acts 28:30–31).

AUDIENCE

Philippi was the first town in which Paul preached after he entered Europe (Acts 16). At that time (A.D. 50) the city had few Jewish residents, and the first two converts were Lydia, a gentile businesswoman from Asia Minor, and the Philippian jailer. A predominantly gentile congregation that greatly loved Paul developed there.

PURPOSE

Paul's primary purpose in writing this epistle seems to have been to reassure the Philippians. Epaphroditus, whom they had sent with a gift to minister to Paul's needs in prison, had recovered from a serious illness and was about to return to Philippi. Secondary reasons included expressing thanks for the Philippians' gift to Paul in prison (Phil. 4:10–14), announcing Timothy's approaching visit (2:19), explaining Paul's desire to revisit his readers (2:24), and encouraging unity in the congregation (4:2).

THEOLOGICAL EMPHASES

The great theological contribution of Philippians is its revelation of the mind of Christ expressed in His self-humbling incarnation (2:5–11). This emphasis provides the basis for all of what Paul wrote in the epistle regarding Christian conduct, particularly participation in ministry.

CHARACTERISTICS

Philippians is the most consistently positive of Paul's epistles. It reflects a joyful spirit. The apostle did not rebuke this church sharply, nor did he refer to any major problems in it. His frequent references to Jesus Christ also stand out.

OUTLINE

    I. Salutation (1:1–2)
   II. Prologue (1:3–26)
      A. Thanksgiving (1:3–8)
      B. Prayer (1:9–11)
      C. Progress Report (1:12–26)
  III. Partnership in the Gospel (1:27–4:9)
      A. A Worthy Walk (1:27–30)
      B. Unity and Steadfastness (2:1–4:1)
      C. Specific Duties (4:2–9)

IV. Epilogue (4:10–20)
    A. The Recent Gift (4:10–14)
    B. The Previous Gifts (4:15–20)
V. Greetings and Benediction (4:21–23)

I. SALUTATION (1:1–2)

Paul began this epistle by identifying himself and his companion Timothy and by wishing God's richest blessings on his readers. In no other of his epistles did Paul address the elders and deacons of the church specifically in the salutation. This was a well-ordered church, and that may be why Paul gave special recognition to its leaders.

II. PROLOGUE (1:3–26)

The positive and encouraging prologue consists of thanksgiving for the Philippians, prayer for them, and a report of Paul's situation when he wrote this epistle.

A. Thanksgiving (1:3–8)

The apostle expressed his sincere gratitude to God for his friends in Philippi to assure them of God's continuing working for them and his satisfaction with their partnership in the work of the gospel, the main theme of Philippians.

    The Christians in Philippi always caused Paul to give thanks to God whenever he prayed for them. The fellowship in view includes all that he and his readers shared as committed Christians who sought to disseminate the gospel. Paul was confident that God would finish the work of salvation He had begun in his beloved Philippians (1:6). They had not only been in prison with Paul in spirit, but they had also been willing to associate with and minister to him through Epaphroditus, their representative.

B. Prayer (1:9–11)

In response to God's working in the Philippians (1:6), it was imperative that they continue to grow in the virtues identified here, specifically, intelligent, discerning love.

Paul prayed that his readers, by approving excellent things, would be sincere and blameless until the day Christ returns (1:10b). Self-sacrificing love should be the motive behind partnership in the gospel. Such love rests on an intelligent appraisal of reality and spiritual sensitivity to truth as God has revealed it in His Word. This kind of love becomes apparent when a Christian values the things God loves and turns away from situations and influences God hates. Possessing this kind of love would enable the Philippians to pursue things of the greatest value and importance.

> Most of the hard choices a spiritual believer faces are not between morally good and morally evil things but between things of lesser and greater value. The things we choose because we love them reflect how discerning our love really is.

C. Progress Report (1:12–26)

Paul explained his personal circumstances because these were of interest to his readers and profitable for them to understand. In relating them the apostle revealed a spiritual viewpoint that is a model for all believers for all time. He began by relating what had happened because of his imprisonment in the past (1:12–18) and then explained his desire to be free and to visit his readers again (1:19–26).

Paul's present imprisonment (1:12–18). Paul's readers could have concluded that his imprisonment had brought the building of the church of Jesus Christ to a standstill or at least slowed its progress significantly. But this had not happened. Because Paul was imprisoned, many people had heard the gospel who would not otherwise have heard it. Paul had the opportunity to witness to many high-ranking soldiers, and he viewed this as a great blessing. His example of aggressive witness had also inspired the Roman Christians to be more outspoken in sharing the gospel. Some were hoping to advance their own reputations by their activities, but others had a sincere desire to reach the lost and to meet the needs that Paul's confinement had created. Rather than valuing his own comfort, reputation, and freedom, the apostle put the advancement of God's plan first.

Paul's anticipated deliverance (1:19–26). The apostle's prison experiences and the consequent furtherance of the gospel were all part of God's completing the good work that He had begun in him. But two means were necessary for this aspect of his salvation to reach fulfillment. Paul was counting on the prayers of the Philippians and the Lord's enabling through His Spirit. Paul did not want to feel ashamed when he stood before the Lord at His judgment seat (see 1 John 2:28). Regardless of whether he would continue to live or would die, Paul's whole life revolved around Jesus Christ.

III. PARTNERSHIP IN THE GOSPEL (1:27–4:9)

Whether Paul was able to return to his beloved Philippians or not, their duty was the same, namely, to conduct themselves worthily of the Lord.

A. A Worthy Walk (1:27–30)

The Philippians needed to stand firm in one spirit and with one mind, the mind of Christ. Unity in the church is necessary so believers can work together effectively as a team carrying out the will of God. They should not let the opposition of unbelievers frighten or detract them from their mission. In calling his readers to unite and steadfastly endure the antagonism of unbelievers in their area, Paul was not asking them to do something he himself had not done. He was urging them to unite with one another and with him and to view suffering for their faith as a privilege that would glorify Jesus Christ.

B. Unity and Steadfastness (2:1–4:1)

In expounding the importance of unity and steadfastness as essential for partnership in the work of the gospel, Paul dealt first with the importance of walking in unity. He explained the basis for unity and illustrated this with the example of Christ. He then clarified the believers' responsibility and further illustrated with his own example and that of two of his fellow workers.

Walking in unity (chapter 2). Paul advocated humility, that is, concern for the needs of others, not just one's own needs, as the foundation for unity in the church (2:1–4). The first reason the readers should be submissive to God and each other is that Jesus Christ has exhorted them to do so. Second, Paul's love for the Philippians should impel them to respond positively to his request. Third, their participation in the Spirit and the common life that He created for them should also make them submissive. Fourth, the affectionate sympathy of God and Christ toward the Philippians would make unity a reasonable expectation for this congregation. The result would be that Paul's joy because of this congregation, which was already great, would become complete. The readers should (a) maintain love for each other, (b) maintain unity in spirit and purpose, (c) view other people as more important than themselves, and (d) consider the interests and affairs of others, not just their own.

Paul illustrated what he meant with the example of Jesus Christ (2:5–11). The Son of God existed with the full nature of God. His full deity is not something Jesus Christ gave up or laid aside when He became a man at the Incarnation; what changed was the manner in which He existed as God. That is, He laid aside the freedom that His former manner of existence afforded Him and became dependent on the Father in a different sense than He had been formerly. Even though Jesus had a fully human nature, that nature was not sinful. He further humbled Himself by becoming obedient to His Father's will to the point of laying down His life in death, even death by crucifixion, a form of execution that was without equal in its pain and humiliation. Because of the Son's submission, the Father raised Him to the height of exaltation through resurrection, ascension, and glorification in heaven. One day every being will acknowledge Jesus as Lord.

Christ's career has implications for the believer (2:12–16). The Philippian Christians had been obedient to the Lord and to Paul in the past (see 1:27). It was even more important that they purpose to obey with Paul absent, since his presence among them provided a measure of external motivation for them. Specifically, they were to work out their salvation, that is, to progress in Christian maturity. We work out our salvation by keeping in step with the Holy Spirit who leads us in the will of God (see Gal. 5:16). As we do so, we must remember that we serve a holy God, we have a strong and intelligent adversary, and we are weak and must depend on God. Such an awareness will produce the attitude of fear and trembling that Paul advocated. God can provide the desire to do His will when we do not have it, as well as the power when we do.

When we complain and argue (Phil. 2:14), we frustrate God's work of producing unity. The children of God are to be free from defilement and not chargeable with justifiable criticism, even though we live in the midst of a twisted and perverted generation. Paul wanted the Philippians to continue serving the Lord (holding on to "the word of life") so that when he stood before the judgment seat of Christ he would have legitimate cause for justifiable pride in them.

Paul held out his own example as further motivation (2:17–18). Even if Paul would die, he could rejoice that he had made a contribution to the Philippians' sacrificial service to God. He viewed himself and them as priests offering sacrifices to God, namely, themselves and their service. The Philippians should not sorrow over their own trials and Paul's; they should rejoice as they worked out their own salvation, adopting his attitude toward their situation in life.

He also cited the example of Timothy (2:19–24). Paul wanted to send Timothy and Epaphroditus to Philippi because they were his true partners in the gospel. The primary purpose of Timothy's visit was to learn the condition of the Philippian believers and to report that to Paul. Paul had no fellow worker with him then who would do a better job in this assignment than Timothy.

Paul next cited the example of Epaphroditus (2:25–30), who would arrive in Philippi before either Paul or Timothy. Epaphroditus would carry this epistle to its destination. Paul wrote what he did to prepare for a proper reception of its courier and to draw attention to Epaphroditus's humility. Paul decided to send Epaphroditus immediately because word had reached Epaphroditus that his fellow Philippians had learned that he had been ill. Epaphroditus had carried out his mission successfully and

> *True partnership in the work of the gospel requires unity among the workers. The key to achieving unity is for each believer to adopt the humble mind of Christ.*

had ministered to Paul with distinction. So Paul urged the Philippians to regard him highly and to welcome him wholeheartedly.

Walking in steadfastness (3:1–4:1). Paul now turned to the second major quality that he introduced in 1:27–30, namely, steadfastness in the face of opposition to the gospel. There were two main sources of opposition the Philippians faced. Having created joy in his readers by referring to the sterling examples of Timothy and Epaphroditus, Paul warned them about certain other people who professed to be servants of God.

Regardless of circumstances, the Christian can and should always rejoice in the person and work of Jesus Christ (3:1). False teachers can rob Christians of joy. Paul proceeded to deal with this threat in the rest of this chapter. He described the Judaizers that plagued Paul and his converts throughout his ministry. They taught that people could enter the church only through the vestibule of Judaism, and that once inside they needed to submit to the Mosaic Law. They emphasized circumcision because it was the rite that brought a person into Judaism, which they viewed as a prerequisite to salvation (Acts 15:1). The Philippians and Paul, and all true believers, belonged to a different camp, that of the true circumcision, the circumcision of the heart that happens when a person trusts in Jesus Christ.

For the sake of the argument, Paul adopted the Judaizers' attitude of confidence in the flesh (Phil. 3:4b–6) to show that his rejection of Jewish advantages was not because he lacked them. Paul formerly regarded all the things he possessed as contributing to God's acceptance of him. Yet he had come to learn since then that such human "advantages" did not improve his position with God (3:7). He had come to realize that absolutely nothing apart from Jesus Christ's work on the cross was of any value in his gaining God's acceptance (3:8–11). So he regarded them as "rubbish." What he had learned to value was Christ Jesus his Lord, so coming to know Christ more intimately was of primary importance to him.

Paul next stressed his persistent zeal (3:12–14). Progressive sanctification does not come automatically by faith, as justification and glorification do. We must pursue it diligently by following the Lord faithfully, as Paul did. Paul's goal was complete relational knowledge of Christ. He would receive a prize when he reached that goal, and he would reach it only when he entered the Lord's presence and saw Him face to face (see 1 John 3:2–3). Nevertheless he pursued the goal while living on earth because he wanted to get to know the Lord as well as possible before then.

Paul charged his readers to adopt his attitude (Phil. 3:15–17). He also promised that God would enlighten those who think differently about minor matters if their attitude was right.

Another threat to the joy and spiritual development of the Philippians was people who advocated lawless living. This is the opposite extreme from what the Judaizers taught (3:2). Three characteristics mark these people (3:18–19). First, they give free rein to the satisfaction of their sensual appetites and do not restrain sin. Second, they find satisfaction and take pride in things they do that should cause them shame. Third, they involve themselves almost totally in physical and material things, things pertaining to the present enjoyment of life, to the exclusion of spiritual matters.

We should follow Paul's example and not that of these sensualists because as Christians we have a citizenship in heaven as well as one on earth (3:20–21). Our heavenly citizenship and destiny are far more important than our brief earthly sojourn. The prospect of our Lord's return should motivate us to live as citizens of heaven even while we are still on earth.

This section of the epistle concludes with another charge; believers are to stand fast in the Lord (4:1). The apostle did not want his readers to lose their balance and tumble spiritually because of bad influences but to adopt the mind of Christ, as he had, and so continue with him in the partnership of the gospel. Standing firm involves living in harmony with each other (4:2–3), rejoicing on all occasions (4:4–7), and nurturing the quality of sweet reasonableness (4:8–9).

Summary: Paul urged his readers to rejoice in the Lord, and he warned them about false teaching of two kinds that would limit their joy. Judaizers wanted to limit the Philippians' legitimate liberty by persuading them to submit to laws God did not intend for them. Antinomians, on the other hand, were urging the abandonment of legitimate law and were advocating self-indulgence. Paul's example (3:4b–16) provides a path that leads safely between these extremes.

C. Specific Duties (4:2–9)

This last section of the body of the epistle deals with the same two subjects as the preceding two sections—unity and steadfastness—but in more detail. Paul gave his readers specific instructions about what they should do.

Restoring unity (4:2–3). Euodia and Syntyche were evidently two women in the Philippian congregation who needed to establish a harmonious relationship. By using the phrase "in the Lord" Paul reminded them that they were under His authority and had much in common as sisters in Christ. Paul also appealed to another person in the Philippian church to help Euodia and Syntyche restore their fellowship. Euodia and Syntyche had evidently labored for the Lord with Paul. The main theme of the epistle comes out clearly again as partnership in the gospel. Clement had been a partner in the gospel as well.

Maintaining tranquillity (4:4–9). Paul gave his readers five other brief positive exhortations, all of which are vitally important for individual and corporate Christian living. They all result in the maintenance of peace in the body of Christ so the saints can work together effectively as partners in the gospel even in the midst of opposing unbelievers. Rejoicing in Christ is something the apostle had commanded earlier (3:1) and had illustrated abundantly for his readers throughout this epistle. There must have been a great need for this attitude in Philippi. Paul was advocating focusing on the blessings we have in Christ and being grateful for these regardless of how sad we may feel. We should also demonstrate forbearance to everyone. The forbearing person is not spineless but selfless. When

Christ returns, He will right wrongs and vindicate those who have given up their rights for the glory of God and the welfare of others.

Rather than becoming distraught over a particular situation we should take it to the Lord in prayer. Peace in the heart will follow praying about what concerns us. Wholesome conduct (4:9) should follow wholesome thinking (4:8). When we do these things, we will experience God's presence by enjoying the peace that comes when we walk in fellowship with Him. In this section of collected exhortations (4:4–9) Paul urged five things: rejoicing in Christ always, being forbearing with all people, praying about difficult situations, thinking about wholesome subjects, and living out apostolic teaching. These are fundamental revelations of God's will for all Christians that are especially relevant to our calling to proclaim the gospel.

IV. EPILOGUE (4:10–20)

The apostle began this epistle by sharing some personal information about his situation in Rome (1:12–26). He now returned from his concerns for the Philippians (1:27–4:9) to his own circumstances (4:10–20).

A. The Recent Gift (4:10–14)

Paul was glad that the Philippians had again expressed their loving concern for him by sending him a gift. Their failure to do so earlier apparently resulted from some unavoidable circumstance. The apostle understood this and did not chide them for their lack of love. Paul was not rejoicing primarily because their gift had met his need, but because their gift expressed their love and concern for him. He had learned to be content and to rejoice regardless of his physical circumstances. It was Jesus Christ who enabled him to be content (4:13).

B. The Previous Gifts (4:15–20)

The Philippians had been very thoughtful and generous with Paul when he left their town after planting their church. Probably the gift to which he referred here is the one that reached him in Corinth shortly after he left Philippi. Even before Paul arrived in Corinth the Philippians had sent him gifts in Thessalonica, the next town he visited after leaving Philippi. However, the most important thing to Paul was not the gifts themselves but the spiritual reward that would come to the Philippians because of their financial investments in his ministry. He viewed their gift as an offering ultimately made to God that was acceptable to Him. God would continue to supply all the needs of His people (see Prov. 11:25; Matt. 5:7; 6:33). In closing, Paul praised God for His providential care.

V. GREETINGS AND BENEDICTION (4:21–23)

Paul concluded this warm, positive epistle with some greetings and a final benediction to cement good relations with the Philippians and to point them again to the Lord Jesus Christ. The apostle wished that the Philippians would pass his greetings to every individual believer whom they would touch. The brethren with Paul in Rome included Epaphroditus, probably Timothy, and some Roman Christians, especially employees of the imperial government, and they sent their greetings. God's grace would enable the readers to do all that the apostle had exhorted them to do in this letter.

COLOSSIANS
The Supremacy of Christ

DATE

This is one of four Prison Epistles Paul wrote during his first imprisonment in Rome (A.D. 60–62). The others are Ephesians, Philippians, and Philemon.

AUDIENCE

Colosse was a town in the Roman province of Asia about one hundred miles east of Ephesus. Its population, which the church there reflected, was mainly gentile with some Jews. Paul had not visited Colosse when he wrote this epistle (Col. 1:4; 2:1), but he had learned of the spread of the gospel there through Epaphras (1:8) and probably others.

PURPOSE

Paul wanted to express his personal interest in this church, to warn the Colossians of the danger of returning to their former beliefs and practices, and to correct the false teaching that was threatening this congregation. Paul's great purpose was to set forth the absolute supremacy and sole sufficiency of Jesus Christ.

False teachers were not giving the person and work of Christ proper interpretation or emphasis in Colosse. The false teaching also contained a philosophic appeal (2:8), and there were elements of Judaistic ritualism and traditionalism present (2:8, 11, 16; 3:11). There was an emphasis on ascetic self-denial (2:20–23) and apparently the idea that only those with full knowledge of the truth as taught by the false teachers could understand and experience spiritual maturity (1:20, 28; 3:11).

THEOLOGICAL EMPHASES

The two main issues Paul addressed were the doctrine of Christ and how this doctrine affects Christian living. The primary Christological passages (1:14–23; 2:9–15) present Christ as absolutely preeminent and perfectly adequate for the Christian. The Christian life, Paul explained, flows naturally out of this revelation. The Christian life is really the life of the indwelling Christ that God manifests through the believer.

CHARACTERISTICS

Many similarities exist between Ephesians and Colossians. The major distinction between them is that in Ephesians the emphasis is on the church as the body of Christ, and in Colossians the emphasis is on Christ as the Head of the body. Stylistically Colossians is somewhat tense and abrupt, whereas Ephesians is more diffuse and flowing. Colossians tends to be more specific and concrete, while Ephesians is more general and abstract. The mood of Colossians is argumentative and controversial, that of Ephesians calm and peaceful. The former is a letter of discussion; the latter is a letter of reflection.

OUTLINE

I. Introduction (1:1–14)
    A. Salutation (1:1–2)
    B. Thanksgiving (1:3–8)
    C. Prayer (1:9–14)
II. Explanation of the Person and Work of Christ (1:15–29)
    A. The Preeminent Person of Christ (1:15–20)

B. The Reconciling Work of Christ (1:21–29)

III. Warnings against Human Philosophies (chapter 2)

    A. Exhortation to Persevere in the Truth (2:1–7)

    B. The True Doctrine of Christ (2:8–15)

    C. The False Doctrines of Men (2:16–23)

IV. Exhortations to Practical Christian Living (3:1–4:6)

    A. The Basic Principle (3:1–4)

    B. The Proper Method (3:5–17)

    C. The Fundamental Relationships (3:18–4:1)

    D. The Essential Practice (4:2–6)

V. Conclusion (4:7–18)

    A. The Bearers of This Epistle (4:7–9)

    B. Greetings from Paul's Companions (4:10–14)

    C. Greetings to Others (4:15–17)

    D. Paul's Personal Conclusion (4:18)

I. INTRODUCTION (1:1–14)

Paul introduced this epistle with a salutation, a thanksgiving, and a prayer.

A. Salutation (1:1–2)

Timothy joined Paul in sending this letter to the Colossians. Paul was an apostle, but Timothy was a brother in the faith. The Colossian believers were "holy" in their position and "faithful brothers" in their practice. Colosse stood beside the Lycus River in the district of Phrygia. Phrygia was in the Roman province of Asia in western Asia Minor. God's "grace" is His unmerited favor and supernatural enablement, and His "peace" is the inner confidence He gives.

B. Thanksgiving (1:3–8)

Paul frequently gave thanks to God for his readers. He wanted them to appreciate the fact that he knew of their situation and rejoiced in their good testimony. Whenever Paul and Timothy prayed for the Colossians, they thanked God for their continuing demonstration of their trust in Christ, their self-sacrificing love for other Christians, and the blessings ahead for them. The gospel had not come to them exclusively but was spreading throughout the whole world. Paul contrasted the gospel with the exclusive message the false teachers in Colosse were trying to get the Christians to adopt. The gospel also has dynamic power to change lives (1:6). Epaphras had evangelized the Colossians but had come to Rome and was now ministering to the apostle. He had given Paul a good report of the Colossian Christians.

C. Prayer (1:9–14)

Paul told his readers he prayed for their full perception and deepest understanding of God's will for them and for all believers. He reminded them that their understanding must come through the working of God's Spirit in them and that correct understanding is foundational to correct behavior.

Paul and his companions had been praying that God would give his readers full and exact knowledge of all His desires for them. "Knowledge" (*gnōsis*) was a favorite term of the gnostic philosophers, and Paul undoubtedly had them in mind when he prayed for full knowledge (*epignōsis*) for his readers. In the broadest sense the will of God is the whole purpose of God revealed in Christ. This knowledge would come to them only by the illumination of the Holy Spirit; it was "spiritual wisdom." By understanding God's will fully, the Colossians would be able to live one day at a time in a manner that would glorify and please their Lord.

Four characteristics mark this worthy walk (1:10–12a). First, it includes continuously bearing fruit in character and in every type of good work. Second, it includes growing in knowledge of God's will so that one not only bears fruit but also grows in ability to bear fruit, as a fruit tree does. Third, it includes gaining strength, manifested in steadfastness, patience, and joy. Fourth, it includes expressing gratitude to God consistently.

Three causes for thankful gratitude follow (1:12b–13). First, God made us heirs of an inheritance. Second, He delivered us from Satan's domain, and, third, He transferred us to Christ's kingdom of light. Gnosticism made much of the light-darkness contrast in its philosophic system.[1] Redemption is a benefit of union with Christ (1:13).

> The Christian grows more like a fruit tree than a stalk of wheat. We do not simply bear fruit and then die. We continue to grow in our ability to bear more fruit as we increase in the knowledge of God. Each passing year should see both growth in the Christian's spiritual life and an increase in his fruitfulness.

II. EXPLANATION OF THE PERSON AND WORK OF CHRIST (1:15–29)

Paul emphasized the "full knowledge" about Jesus Christ, which the false teachers in Colosse were attacking. By having a fuller knowledge of God's will, his readers would be encouraged to reject the false teaching of those who were demeaning Christ.

A. The Preeminent Person of Christ (1:15–20)

Paul described Jesus Christ' preeminence in three relationships: to deity, to creation, and to the church.[2]

In relation to God the Father (1:15a). "Image" involves likeness, representation, and manifestation.

In relation to all creation (1:15b–17). Christ was before all creation in time, and He is over it in authority. God mediated the life of the entire universe through His Son (see John 1:3, 10). Christ is also the Agent of creation and the Goal of creation. Christ is, moreover, the antecedent of creation and not a creature. He is also the Sustainer of creation.

In relation to the church (1:18–20). Our Lord supplies authority and direction for, the church, His body. He is its Sovereign and its Source of spiritual life. The reason for His preeminence in the new creation is His work of reconciliation. God's ultimate purpose in Christ's work was to reconcile all things to Himself. The Cross made reconciliation possible. Christ's death has dealt with the defilement sin caused as well as with its guilt. He reconciled all things in heaven to Himself in the sense of bringing them into subjection to His will.

B. The Reconciling Work of Christ (1:21–29)

Paul continued his exposition of Christ's superiority with emphasis on His reconciling work to ground his readers further in the full truth of God's revelation so the false teachers would not lead them astray.

As experienced by the Colossians (1:21–23). The church at Colosse was predominantly a gentile congregation, as is evident from Paul's description of his readers' preconversion condition. But Christ by His death had reconciled them to God. Paul assumed his readers would continue in the faith. The gospel had wide circulation, in contrast to the comparatively limited circulation of the false teachers' message.

As ministered by Paul (1:24–29). Paul had been given a unique function in the body of Christ. He ministered the gospel of reconciliation primarily to unevangelized Gentiles (1:25). He explained his ministry to his readers so they would appreciate the reconciling work of God more deeply and be encouraged to press on to maturity.

Paul could rejoice because he knew his imprisonment would benefit his readers through his ministry to them in this letter if in no other way. Furthermore he regarded his sufferings as what any servant of Christ could expect in view of the world's treatment of his Master. When believers suffer, Christ also suffers because He indwells us (see Acts 9:4).

Paul's role in the household of God was that of a servant who fully expounded God's revelation for the benefit of his gentile readers. This revelation included a truth previously unknown but now revealed by God. God had hidden this new revelation from human understanding for ages past. That God would save Gentiles was no new revelation, but that He would deal with them as He did Jews was new. Those who rejected this revelation insisted that Gentiles had to become Jews before they could become Christians (Acts 15:1). Paul proclaimed this new revelation as a completed fact. Negative admonitions and positive teaching presented through wise (appropriate) methods were necessary to bring all people, not just the privileged few, as in Gnosticism, to full maturity in Christ. Paul's goal was not just to get people saved but to lead them to maturity. He had to expend physical, mental, and spiritual energy toiling to this end, but the supernatural power of the indwelling Christ energized him.

III. WARNINGS AGAINST HUMAN PHILOSOPHIES (CHAPTER 2)

Paul now became more explicit about the dangers his readers needed to avoid.

A. Exhortations to Persevere in the Truth (2:1–7)

Paul exhorted his readers to continue to believe and practice the truth of God's revelation. This would help prevent their accepting the erroneous instruction of the false teachers who were seeking to turn them away from God's will.

Paul's concern (2:1–5). Paul used an athletic metaphor to describe his anxieties and deep concerns for his readers and their neighbor Christians. The better a Christian understands God's true revelation concerning the person and work of Jesus Christ, the better he will be able to recognize and refute false doctrine. God has revealed in Christ all that a person needs to know to establish a relationship with God. Paul's description of the Colossian church pictures a company of well-disciplined soldiers standing at attention in straight lines. So far the believers were holding their position against the false teachers, but Paul feared that this condition might change. He did not want the false teachers to talk them into something false by deceptive arguments.

Paul's exhortation (2:6–7). Paul encouraged his readers to continue following Christ in harmony with the sound teaching that had resulted in their conversion. Four characteristics describe the healthy Christian: He stands firmly rooted as a tree, he is being built up as a building, he is becoming increasingly stable in the faith, and he demonstrates the fruit of thankfulness constantly.

B. The True Doctrine of Christ (2:8–15)

Paul reviewed what his readers enjoyed in Christ in order to encourage them to remain faithful to the true revelation they had received and believed. "Philosophy" here (2:8) does not refer to the study of basic questions concerning God, man, and the meaning of life but to speculations and ideas of false teachers not rooted in divine revelation. These ideas had come down by merely human tradition, empty deception based on religious practices the false teachers were promoting. What the Colossian readers had in Christ was completely adequate. As those in Christ, we partake of His fullness. Christ is the Head over all spirit beings, and His sufficiency is evident in three things God has done for us in Him: He has spiritually circumcised us (2:11–12), forgiven our sins (2:13–14), and given us victory over the forces of evil (2:15).

C. The False Doctrines of Men (2:16–23)

One error of the false teachers was legalism. They were encouraging the Colossians to place their Christian freedom under their control. They wanted to limit it by prohibiting certain perfectly legitimate activities. The items mentioned in 2:16 were all part of Judaism, so it is probable that the legalistic false teachers were to some extent Jewish.

A second error was mysticism. Whereas Colossian legalism (2:16–17) was primarily Jewish in origin, Colossian mysticism (2:18–19) seems to have been mainly gnostic and pagan. The false teachers also advocated the worship of angels, probably with the idea that they were the proper mediators of prayer and worship to God.

A third error was asceticism (2:20–23). The ascetic practices referred to seem to have been extensions of the Mosaic Law. The false teachers were in effect forcing the Colossians to live by the world system by placing ascetic requirements on them. However, the things prohibited perish through normal usage, the laws are of human origin, and they do not solve the real problem, namely, the desires of the flesh.

The teachings of these false teachers are still with us today: an emphasis on "higher" knowledge (Gnosticism), reliance on obedience to laws to win God's love (legalism), the view that beings other than Christ must mediate between people and God (mysticism), and an emphasis on abstaining from things to earn merit with God (asceticism).

IV. EXHORTATIONS TO PRACTICAL CHRISTIAN LIVING (3:1–4:6)

These verses spell out some of the implications of the supremacy of Christ for Christian ethics and morality.

A. The Basic Principle (3:1–4)

To encourage his readers to turn away from their false teachers, Paul reminded them of their union with Christ and urged them to continue living in keeping with their position in Christ.

Paul returned to his thought about the believer's union with Christ in His death, burial, and resurrection (see 2:9–15). Believers have two responsibilities: "set your hearts on" (3:1) and "set your minds on" (3:2). Since God raised us with Christ and we are already spiritually seated with Him in heaven, we should keep seeking heavenly things rather than the things that are only physical and temporal.

B. The Proper Method (3:5–17)

Here Paul gave more specific advice about how to practice what he had just commanded.

Things to put off (3:5–11). We have three basic responsibilities: "put to death" (3:5), "rid yourselves" (3:8), and "do not lie" (3:9). There must be a decisive initial act that introduces a settled attitude toward evil practices.[3] There is no national or racial distinction that determines one's acceptability to God, nor is there any religious, cultural, or social distinction. Jesus Christ is all that we need for new birth and growth.

Things to put on (3:12–17). Believers also need to clothe themselves with attitudes and actions that are appropriate in view of who they are. Appreciating who we are as believers affects how we behave. All the features Paul identified deal with interpersonal relationships, areas in which the life of

Christ should be especially visible in us. Love is the supremely important Christian virtue.

Believers should follow four precepts (3:15–17). First, when Christians need to make choices, we should normally choose what will result in peace between us and God, and between us and others. Second, we should "be thankful" because we have so much in Christ. Third, we should let Christ's teachings permeate our whole being so that we make all our decisions and plans in their light. Fourth, when faced with a question about what the Christian should do, we should simply ask ourselves what conduct would be appropriate for one identified with Christ.

C. The Fundamental Relationships (3:18–4:1)

These verses set forth certain principles to guide believers in their most intimate interpersonal relationships, thus helping them understand what behavior is consistent with union with Christ.[4] The apostle grouped six classes of people in three pairs in the following verses (see also Eph. 5:22–6:9). In each pair he first addressed the subordinate member and then the one in authority.

Wives and husbands (3:18–19). Paul did not say all women should be subject to all men; he said wives should be subject to their own husbands. This subjection rests on divinely prescribed authority, not on any inherent inferiority. This is "fitting" in that it is consistent with what God ordained at the creation of the human race (Gen. 2:18).

Husbands have two responsibilities toward their wives: to love them and not to allow a bitter attitude to develop toward them.

Children and parents (3:20–21). Children are to obey both parents. The reason children should please their parents by obeying them is that this behavior pleases the Lord (see Exod. 20:12). The father, as head of the household, has the primary responsibility for his children. The habitual provoking of children by insensitive parents is what Paul forbade.

Slaves and masters (3:22–4:1). Slaves were also to obey their masters with integrity and should do their work primarily for the Lord. This view of work transforms a worker's attitudes and performance. The Lord Himself will reward such service. Masters should remember that they, too, have a Master. This view should influence how they treat their slaves.

The principles in these verses (3:22–4:1) are, of course, applicable to modern employer-employee relationships as well.

D. The Essential Practice (4:2–6)

Paul concluded his exhortations concerning Christian living with instructions pertaining to three essential practices for those in Christ. One exhortation deals with his readers' relationship to God, another with their relationship to other people, and the third with their relationship to themselves.

The most important practice to perpetuate in relation to God is prayer, because in prayer we call on God to work, and we express our faith in Him. Paul's repeated emphasis on thanksgiving makes this epistle one of the most "thankful" books in the New Testament (see 1:3, 12; 2:7; 3:17; 4:2). In relation to others, the Colossians needed to intercede in love for their neighbors. Selfward they needed to pay attention to their talk. The Christian's speech should mirror the gracious character and conduct of his God. "Salty speech" probably describes attractive and wholesome speech.

V. CONCLUSION (4:7–18)

Paul concluded this epistle with personal information and instructions in order to bond his readers more tightly to the body of Christ from which they were in danger of separating themselves because of the influence of false teachers.

A. The Bearers of This Epistle (4:7–9)

Paul sent Tychicus with this letter to provide more information about himself and his present ministry and to encourage the Colossians. Onesimus had been a slave in the household of Philemon and a member of the Colossian church, had run away to Rome, and had become a Christian there. Paul sent him back to Colosse with Tychicus, not in chains but as a beloved brother in Christ who had proved himself faithful (see the Book of Philemon). These men traveled from Rome to Colosse, probably by way of Ephesus and Laodicea, with the Epistle to the Ephesians (Eph. 6:21–22). They probably also carried a letter to the Laodiceans (Col. 4:16) and the Epistle to Philemon (Philem. 23–24).

B. Greetings from Paul's Companions (4:10–14)

Paul mentioned six individuals, five of whom he also named in his letter to Philemon. Aristarchus came from Thessalonica (Acts 20:4), had been with Paul in Ephesus (19:29), and accompanied him to Rome (27:2). John Mark (12:25) had rejoined Paul after their separation during Paul's first missionary journey (13:5, 13). Jesus Justus's name occurs only here in the New Testament. These three men were Jewish Christians, as is clear from their names. The following three fellow workers had gentile backgrounds. Epaphras had evidently been instrumental in the founding of the church at Colosse (Col. 1:7). Paul identified Luke as a physician. Demas later forsook Paul (2 Tim. 4:10), but at this time he was ministering to and with the apostle.

C. Greetings to Others (4:15–17)

In addition to greeting generally the neighboring Laodicean Christians, Paul sent specific greetings to Nympha, possibly the hostess of a Laodicean house church. Paul's letter to the Laodiceans was probably not an inspired one and has been lost. Archippus seems to have been Philemon's son (Philem. 2).

D. Paul's Personal Conclusion (4:18)

Paul requested his readers' prayers for him in his house arrest in Rome and wished that God's continuing unmerited favor would be their portion (see Col. 1:2).

1 THESSALONIANS
The Return of the Lord

DATE

Paul probably wrote this epistle shortly after he arrived in Corinth (1 Thess. 1:7–9; 2:17; 3:1, 6; Acts 18:5, 12), about A.D. 51. If one follows the early dating of Galatians (see the introductory comments on Galatians), this epistle would have been Paul's second inspired writing. Or if Paul penned Galatians *after* his second missionary journey, 1 Thessalonians could have been his first inspired epistle.[1]

AUDIENCE

Thessalonica was an important city in the Roman province of Macedonia with enough Jews to warrant a synagogue. Those who responded to Paul's preaching there during his second missionary journey were Jews and God-fearing proselytes to Judaism. Also some leading women of the city and many idol-worshiping pagans turned to Christ (Acts 17:1–5).

PURPOSE

Paul seems to have had at least three purposes in mind when he wrote this epistle. First, he wanted to encourage the Christians in Thessalonica who were making good progress in their new faith (1 Thess. 1:2–10). Second, he desired to correct misinformation about himself and his fellow missionaries that some of his critics in Thessalonica were circulating (2:1–3:13). Third, he wrote to give additional instruction that would contribute to the Thessalonians' spiritual growth (4:1–5:24).

THEOLOGICAL EMPHASES

The greatest doctrinal contribution of this epistle is its revelation concerning future events (eschatology), particularly the return of Christ for his own (the Rapture). Paul also spelled out some ethical and moral implications of these events.

CHARACTERISTICS

This epistle includes at least one reference in each chapter to the Lord's return. A warm and affectionate tone also marks the epistle. The Thessalonians were doing well in their Christian walk, and Paul wanted to encourage them.

OUTLINE

I. Salutation and Greeting (1:1)
II. Personal Commendations and Explanations (1:2–3:13)
    A. Thanksgiving for the Thessalonians (1:2–10)
    B. Reminders for the Thessalonians (2:1–16)
    C. Concerns for the Thessalonians (2:17–3:13)
III. Practical Instructions and Exhortations (4:1–5:24)
    A. Christian Living (4:1–12)
    B. The Rapture (4:13–18)
    C. Personal Watchfulness (5:1–11)
    D. Church Life (5:12–15)
    E. Individual Behavior (5:16–24)
IV. Conclusion (5:25–28)

I. SALUTATION AND GREETING (1:1)

Paul wrote this first sentence to identify himself, his companions (Silas and Timothy), and his addressees, and to convey his customary formal word of greeting. Paul affirmed Jesus' equality with God the Father. The absence of any reference to Paul's apostleship in any of his inspired writings to the Macedonian churches, namely, those in Thessalonica and Philippi, is noteworthy. Evidently they never questioned Paul's apostleship, unlike the churches elsewhere (for example, in Galatia and Corinth).

II. PERSONAL COMMENDATIONS AND EXPLANATIONS (1:2–3:13)

This section of the epistle is very personal and warm. Paul wrote to commend his readers on their spiritual progress and to explain his own activities to his brethren in Christ.

A. Thanksgiving for the Thessalonians (1:2–10)

Paul reviewed several aspects of the Thessalonians' salvation and gave thanks to God for them to encourage his readers to persevere despite persecution.

Summary statement (1:2–3). The Thessalonians' response to the gospel and their continuance in the faith caused Paul and his companions to thank God for them continually. Three characteristics of these Christians stood out to Paul. First, they had turned to Christ in faith. Second, they had served Him out of love. Third, they had patiently borne up under tribulation because of the hope before them. Each virtue found its object in Jesus Christ as they lived before God. They had exercised faith in the past when they first trusted Christ. They were loving Him in the present, and they were hoping for His return in the future.

Specific reasons (1:4–10). Paul's favorite appellation for the Thessalonians was "brothers," which he used seventeen times in this epistle and seven times in 2 Thessalonians. It emphasizes the equality of Jewish and gentile Christians in the family of God. When Paul had visited Thessalonica he had not persuaded them by clever oratory; instead the power of God through the Holy Spirit's convicting work had brought them to faith in Christ. The lives of the preachers who had behaved consistently with what they taught in Thessalonica had backed up their message.

Paul was also grateful that his readers had demonstrated the fruit of their faith by becoming followers of their teachers and their Lord. They had welcomed the gospel message even though it had meant much suffering for them because of the persecution of unbelieving Jews and Gentiles. News of their good example had circulated not only within their own province of Macedonia but had also reached their neighboring province of Achaia to the south. They were so effective at witnessing that Paul felt his ministry of pioneer evangelism was no longer necessary in that area.

They were also awaiting the return of God's Son "from heaven." This was the evidence of their hope (1:3). If this was the only reference to "the coming wrath" in this epistle (1:10), we might conclude that Paul was referring to the outpouring of God's wrath on unbelievers generally. However, later he spent considerable space writing about the outpouring of God's wrath in the Tribulation (see 5:1–11). Therefore it seems that this is the first reference to that outpouring of wrath in the epistle (see 2:16; 5:9). Other passages teach that believers will not experience any of God's wrath (see John 3:36; 5:24; Rom. 5:1; 8:1, 34). He will protect Christians from it by taking us to heaven before the Tribulation begins (1 Thess. 4:13–18; 5:4–10).

B. Reminders for the Thessalonians (2:1–16)

To encourage his readers to continue following Christ faithfully, Paul reminded them of how the gospel had come to them and how they received it.

How the gospel was delivered (2:1–12). In recalling the events of his ministry among the Thessalonians Paul summarized his motivation and actions. He did this to strengthen their confidence in him in view of questions that had apparently arisen in their minds. Paul appealed to them to remember that his preaching had born fruit in their lives. He had come to them recently, having been persecuted for his preaching in Philippi, and he had received the same treatment in Thessalonica. Nevertheless he continued preaching boldly even though his message was not popular and resulted in public ridicule. He claimed that his message was true, his motives were pure, and his methods were straightforward. He did not preach for the approval of men but for the approval of God, who scrutinizes motives. He abhorred the use of speech that would assure him a positive reception regardless of what he preached, and he denied any desire to get rich from his preaching.

> It is always more effective to appeal to people after praising them for their progress, as Paul did here and elsewhere in his writings.

Having explained his ministry in negative terms (2:1–6), Paul then described it positively (2:7–12). He had been gentle and unselfish, like a nursing mother. Out of love for the Thessalonians Paul had given them himself, not just his message. The measure of his love was the toil and trouble he expended as he worked constantly so he would not be a burden to them. He had behaved as a father who has responsibility to prepare his children for the events that lie ahead of them.

How the gospel was received (2:13–16). Paul thanked God for the way his readers had responded when he had preached the gospel to them. They sensed that it was a divine revelation rather than human philosophy, they believed it, and it had transformed their lives. By believing the gospel the Thessalonians had followed in the train of many others who, when they believed the truth, also found that they attracted enemies. The Thessalonians' opponents seem to have been mainly Jews (2:14) whose actions were not pleasing to God and were not in the best interests of all who needed to hear the gospel. They rejected the gospel themselves and also discouraged others from accepting it. It was only a matter of time before God would pour out His wrath on such people. Paul saw continuity in the pattern of Jewish rejection of God's agents from Old Testament times to his own.

C. Concerns for the Thessalonians (2:17–3:13)

The Thessalonians' present situation made Paul anxious to see them again, but in the meantime he rejoiced over them.

Paul's desire to see them again (2:17–3:5). Paul sincerely wanted to return to Thessalonica to help his readers endure the persecution that had come their way. He and his companions had to leave Thessalonica prematurely, and for Paul the separation was a very sorrowful one. However, even though absent in body, his readers were present in his affections. He had attempted to return to them more than once, but Satan (God's instrumental cause) had hindered him. Their development was what he hoped for, their glorification was what he rejoiced in, and their ultimate victory would be a crown of glory for him. Paul expected his ministry to end with the return of Christ rather than by his own death (2:19). Nothing had to occur before His return.

By the time Paul, Silas, and Timothy had reached Athens, they felt they could not stay away from their young converts in Thessalonica any longer, so they decided that Timothy should return to them. Timothy's mission was to strengthen and encourage them in their faith so the persecution they were experiencing would not discourage them excessively. Timothy reminded them that persecution is a normal experience for believers (see Matt. 5:11–12; 24:9–10), just as Paul had previously done. Had the Thessalonians failed to accept persecution, the ministry expended on them would not have resulted in substantial growth and fruit.

Paul's joy on hearing about them (3:6–13). Paul rejoiced when he heard that the Thessalonians were withstanding persecution, and he shared his reaction to this news with them to encourage them to persevere as their afflictions continued.

When Timothy rejoined Paul in Corinth (3:6; see Acts 18:1), he brought the good news that the Thessalonians continued to trust in God and to love others as well as to remember Paul fondly and to desire to see him again. The apostle and his companions kept praying earnestly that God would give them the opportunity to return to Thessalonica so they could minister to the continuing needs of their spiritual children. These Christians were doing well, but they needed to grow more.

Paul's prayer (1 Thess. 3:11–13) reveals his genuine concern for the Thessalonians, and it bridges the narrative material in chapters 1–3 and the exhortations in chapters 4–5. He asked God his Father and Jesus his Lord to clear the way so he and his fellow missionaries could return to

Thessalonica. He also prayed that the Lord would cause the believers' love to increase and overflow even more among themselves and toward all people. Thus they would be free from any reasonable charge whenever Christ might return. Again, Paul anticipated the judgment seat of Christ (see 2:19; 5:23). The saints who will join the Thessalonians there include all Christians (see 2 Cor. 5:10; 2 Thess. 1:10).

III. PRACTICAL INSTRUCTIONS AND EXHORTATIONS (4:1–5:24)

Taking the opportunity to help his readers grow spiritually, Paul instructed them concerning the Christian life generally, the Rapture and their attitude toward it, and church life and individual behavior.

A. Christian Living (4:1–12)

Paul gave his readers basic instruction concerning Christian living to promote their growth in Christ and to guard them from error.

Continued growth (4:1–2). The Thessalonians needed to continue walking as the missionaries had instructed them, but to do so "more and more." The highest motive is to "please God."

Sexual purity (4:3–8). The will of God for the Christian is sanctification, that is, a life set apart from sin unto God. Negatively it involves abstinence from all kinds of sexual behavior that is outside the prescribed will of God. Rather than participating in these acts the believer should learn how to control his body and its passions, not as Gentiles who lack God's special revelation of His will. Sexual immorality is wrong not only because it transgresses the will of God, but also because it injures the partner by bringing God's eventual judgment on two people, not just one, and it defrauds the partner of God's blessing. Rejecting these exhortations amounts to rejecting God, not just the apostle Paul. God has given His Holy Spirit to all believers to enable us to do His will.

Brotherly love (4:9–12). The previous exhortation to avoid sexual immorality is a negative prohibition, but this one is a positive encouragement. Paul's readers demonstrated brotherly love by reaching out to other needy

Christians who lived in their province. They just needed to continue to do so more and more. Paul gave them three specific suggestions. First, a person who leads a restful rather than a frantic life avoids disturbing the lives of others. Second, one who tends to his own affairs does not meddle in the business of others. Third, the person who works to provide for his own needs and the needs of his family does not put a burden on others to support him. Such behavior meets with the approval and admiration of nonbelievers as well as fellow Christians.

B. The Rapture (4:13–18)

Paul turned to another subject on which his readers needed instruction in view of their newness in Christ. He outlined the immediate hope of his readers to explain that those of their number who had died, or would die, in Christ would share in His glory with those who were living when He returned. In other words, he explained the relationship of dead Christians to Christ's return. The translation of living Christians and the resurrection of dead Christians will take place at the same time, but Paul revealed more than this.

To be uninformed about the future as a Christian is not good (4:13). Knowing the future of believers who have died gives hope in the midst of grief. The Thessalonian believers were grieving for two reasons: Some of their loved ones had died, and they thought the resurrection of dead Christians would take place after the Rapture. They also erroneously thought this resurrection would follow the Tribulation. Specifically it was the fact that their dead fellow Christians might not participate in the Rapture with them that upset them. They apparently thought that one had to be alive to participate in the Rapture.

God will bring the spirits of dead Christians back with Jesus when He returns for the saints still living on earth. This was a revelation from the Lord, not just Paul's personal opinion. Paul expected to be in the company of the living when Christ returned. He believed in an imminent Rapture.[2] The fact that the living will have no advantage over the dead when Christ returns means we need not have excessive sorrow for dead Christians.

A supernatural announcement will precede the Lord Jesus' return for His own (4:16). Then God will catch up the saints alive on the earth into the air and unite us forever with Christ.[3] Saints who have died will be resurrected with immortal bodies, and the bodies of living saints will become immortal. Both kinds of Christians will meet in the air with Christ. The hope of being reunited with saints who have died and, more importantly with Christ, gives believers a hope that we can and should use to comfort one another when loved ones die.

The Pretribulation Rapture

C. *Personal Watchfulness (5:1–11)*

In view of the imminency of Christ's return, the apostle exhorted the Thessalonians to be ready to meet the Lord at any time.

Paul had previously taught this church about "the day of the Lord" (5:2) as Jesus had (see Matt. 24:44; Mark 13; Luke 24). This period begins with the Tribulation (judgment) and continues through the Millennium (blessing; see also Isa. 13:9–11; Joel 2:28–32; Zeph. 1:14–18; 3:14–15). People living on the earth at the time of the Rapture (unbelievers, since Christians will be with the Lord in heaven immediately following the Rapture) will not expect it.[4] They cannot escape it any more than a pregnant woman can escape delivering her child. The

> *Believers can comfort one another when their Christian friends die because those who have died are with the Lord, and we will reunite with them in the future.*

443

Thessalonians were not ignorant of these coming events, so Paul exhorted them to remain alert and self-controlled, not asleep (that is, insensible), since the next event, the Rapture, would indicate that the Day of the Lord was at hand.

As soldiers presently engaged in spiritual warfare, they needed to protect their vital parts with trust in God and love for others. They also needed to protect their thinking from attack by keeping in mind their sure hope of deliverance at Christ's appearing. Deliverance from the judgments of the Day of the Lord (the outpouring of God's wrath in the Tribulation) is certain for Christians because God has not appointed His children to wrath in any form or at any time (1 Thess. 5:9; see also 1:10). Rather He has appointed us to full salvation (4:15–17). Our deliverance is certain because Jesus Christ took all God's wrath against us on Himself. Therefore we can have confidence that we will live together with Christ after the Rapture when He comes for Christians. This sure hope is a sound basis for mutual encouragement and edification among believers. Besides comforting one another when believers die (4:18), we should also strengthen one another while we live.

D. Church Life (5:12–15)

In light of future blessings believers are to give attention to present duties.

Attitudes toward leaders (5:12–13). Paul's readers were to appreciate and love their church leaders for their labors, a few of which he identified. They were to do so because of the contribution they made to other believers. This attitude would enable the Thessalonians to continue to experience peace in their church.

Relationships among themselves (5:14–15). All believers, not just the leaders, are responsible to minister to one another. Those who neglected their daily duties needed stirring up to action. Those who were timid or tended to become discouraged needed extra help. Those who had not yet learned to lean on the Lord for their needs as they should were worthy of special support. Above all, the Thessalonians were to be patient with each other and with everyone. They were not to retaliate but to do good to all others.

E. Individual Behavior (5:16–24)

The preceding exhortations led Paul naturally to focus on other individual responsibilities to enable his readers to perceive their personal Christian duties clearly.

Personal actions and attitudes (5:16–18). It is extremely important for Christians to choose to rejoice.[5] We can always rejoice if we remember what God has given us in Christ. Paul expected his readers to continue praying whenever possible. We need to give thanks about everything, knowing that God is working all things together for good for His people who love Him (Rom. 8:28).

Actions and attitudes in corporate living (5:19–22). Quenching the Spirit is a figurative expression describing the possibility of hindering the Spirit's work in and through the believer, like throwing water on a fire. The proper response is to follow the Spirit's direction and control without resistance (see Gal. 5:16, 25). Paul warned against regarding prophetic utterances as only words from men. His readers should test these statements by comparing what the speaker said with the standard of previously given divine revelation, while retaining the good and rejecting the bad. They should also avoid every form of evil.

Divine enablement (5:23–24). Peace in the assembly was extremely important to Paul. "Spirit, soul, and body" point to the believer's relationships to God, himself, and other people and together picture wholeness. Paul wanted every part of them to remain without fault and that they would continue to mature and live free from legitimate grounds for accusation. He was confident that God would do this work in the Thessalonians through the Holy Spirit, assuming their proper response to Him.

IV. CONCLUSION (5:25–28)

Paul added this final postscript to encourage three more actions and to stress one basic attitude. He believed that intercessory prayer would move God to do things that He would not do otherwise (see James 4:2). The man-to-man and woman-to-woman kiss of brotherly affection in Christ was and is a customary greeting in many parts of the world. Paul recognized the edifying value of this letter, so he firmly charged that someone read it aloud to all the congregation of saints. Finally, he longed that the unmerited favor of God would continue to be his readers' experience and source of joy.

2 THESSALONIANS
The Day of the Lord

DATE

*M*ost conservative scholars believe that Paul wrote 2 Thessalonians from Corinth (2 Thess. 1:1; Acts 18:5). The topics he treated in the second epistle seem to grow out of situations he alluded to in his first epistle to this church. Apparently Paul composed 2 Thessalonians quite soon after 1 Thessalonians, perhaps within twelve months.[1] This would place the date of composition in the early fifties, perhaps A.D. 51, and would make this the third of Paul's canonical writings, assuming Galatians was his first.

AUDIENCE

The recipients of this letter are the same as those of 1 Thessalonians, namely, mainly gentile and some Jewish Christians.

PURPOSE

Three purposes are evident from the contents of this epistle. (1) Paul wrote to encourage the Thessalonian believers to continue to persevere in the face of continuing persecution (2 Thess. 1:3–10). (2) He also wanted to clarify events preceding the Day of the Lord in order to dispel false teaching (2:1–12). (3) He instructed the church how to deal with lazy Christians in their midst (3:6–15).

THEOLOGICAL EMPHASES

As with 1 Thessalonians, the main doctrinal contribution of this epistle is eschatological, with implications for Christian living. Specifically Paul clarified when the Day of the Lord would begin.

CHARACTERISTICS

Second Thessalonians, like 1 Thessalonians, is warm and positive. Paul wrote it to encourage new Christians who were running the Christian race well but who were babies in Christ. However, he also needed to correct a doctrinal error that had misled the believers, and in doing so he stressed the importance of understanding biblical revelation accurately.

OUTLINE

I. Salutation (1:1–2)
II. Commendation for Past Progress (1:3–12)
   A. Thanksgiving for Growth (1:3–4)
   B. Encouragement to Persevere (1:5–10)
   C. Prayer for Success (1:11–12)
III. Correction of Present Error (2:1–12)
   A. The Beginning of the Day of the Lord (2:1–5)
   B. The Mystery of Lawlessness (2:6–12)
IV. Thanksgiving and Prayer (2:13–17)
   A. Thanksgiving for Calling (2:13–15)
   B. Prayer for Strength (2:16–17)
V. Exhortations for Future Growth (3:1–15)
   A. Reciprocal Prayer (3:1–5)
   B. Church Discipline (3:6–15)
VI. Conclusion (3:16–18)

I. SALUTATION (1:1–2)

The apostle Paul opened this epistle by identifying himself and his companions to the recipients. He also wished God's grace and peace for them, and he expressed his continuing goodwill toward his children in the faith. Verses 1 and 2 are almost identical to 1 Thessalonians 1:1.

II. COMMENDATION FOR PAST PROGRESS (1:3–12)

Paul thanked God for the spiritual growth of his readers, encouraged them to persevere in their trials, and assured them of his prayers for them. All this was done to motivate them to continue to endure hardship and thereby develop in their faith.

A. Thanksgiving for Growth (1:3–4)

In his earlier epistle to the Thessalonians, Paul had urged them to grow in faith (1 Thess. 4:10) and to increase in love (3:12). Now he rejoiced that they were doing both of these things (2 Thess. 1:3). The Thessalonians' growth had been unusual. They were a model congregation in this respect. No wonder Paul said he cited the Thessalonians to other churches as an example to follow.

B. Encouragement to Persevere (1:5–10)

Suffering for Christ demonstrates the believer's worthiness to participate in God's kingdom. The fire of trials can separate the Christian from the unsaved and show him to be what he really is by God's grace. In the future God would judge the Thessalonians' persecutors and give rest to his readers as well as to all Christians who suffer affliction for the gospel. This will take place when Jesus Christ returns to the earth in judgment (the Second Coming). These non-Christians will suffer "everlasting destruction" (eternal, conscious separation from the person of Christ and the manifestation of His glory).

Jesus Christ's second coming will be a day of great glory and vindication for Him. Paul's readers would participate in it because they had believed the gospel when he had preached it among them.

C. Prayer for Success (1:11–12)

Paul and his companions "constantly" prayed that the Thessalonians would continue to experience purification through their trials, rather than experience apostasy, and that God would note and approve their worth. They also asked that God by His power would bring to full expression every good purpose of theirs to glorify God and every act motivated by their faith in Him.[2]

III. CORRECTION OF PRESENT ERROR (2:1–12)

A. The Beginning of the Day of the Lord (2:1–5)

Paul urged his readers not to be shaken from their adherence to the truth he had taught them by what they were hearing from others. The issue centered on Paul's instructions concerning the Rapture (1 Thess. 4:13–18). Other teachers were telling the Thessalonians that the Day of the Lord had already begun (2 Thess. 2:2). This seemed to be a distinct possibility since Scripture describes that day as a time of tribulation as well as blessing. The Thessalonians were experiencing intense persecution for their faith. The false message also seems to have gained a hearing because it came from several different sources: alleged prophetic revelation, the teaching of other recognized authorities, and a letter Paul had supposedly written that had arrived in Thessalonica. If the Day of the Lord had begun, how could Paul say the Lord's return for His own would precede that day (1 Thess. 1:10; 5:9)?

The Day of the Lord includes the Tribulation, the Second Coming, the Millennium, and the Great White Throne judgment (see Ps. 2:9; Isa. 11:1–12; 13; Joel 2; Amos 5:18; Zeph. 3:14–20). Paul explained that three events had to take place before the judgments of the Day of the Lord began. These were "the rebellion" (2 Thess. 2:3), the unveiling of "the man of lawlessness" (3:3–4, 8), and the removal of the restrainer of lawlessness (3:6–7). He presented these in logical rather than chronological order in this passage.

The Thessalonians' False Idea

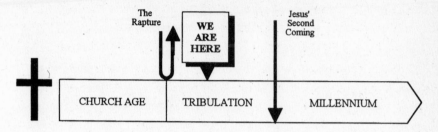

Paul's Correction of Their Error

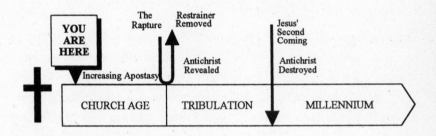

The word *rebellion* (2:3) is a translation of the Greek word *apostasia*. By definition an apostasy is a departure, an abandoning of a position formerly held. It seems that Paul referred here to the same apostasy he and other apostles spoke of elsewhere (1 Tim. 1:18–20; 4:1; 2 Tim. 3:1–5; 4:3–4; James 5:1–8; 2 Peter 2; 3:3–6; Jude), namely, the departure of many professing Christians from the revealed truth of God's Word. Such a departure had begun in Paul's day, but it had not yet reached the proportions predicted to characterize "the rebellion" about which Paul had instructed his readers when he was with them.

Another major event is the unveiling of "the man of lawlessness" (2 Thess. 2:3). This is a person yet to appear who will be completely lawless and whom God will doom to everlasting destruction. The prophet Daniel wrote of such a person who will make a covenant with the Jews but then will break it after three and a half years (Dan. 9:27). The breaking of that covenant seems to be the event that will unmask this individual for who he is, the opponent of Christ. He will eventually seek to make everyone worship himself and will claim to be God (Rev. 13:5–8). Paul reminded his readers that he had told them of these things when he was with them (2 Thess. 2:5). He did not regard prophecy as too deep, unimportant, or controversial for even new Christians.

> Many Christians today play down the importance of prophecy. Paul believed prophetic truth was a vital part of the whole counsel of God and essential to victorious Christian living, so he taught it without hesitation or apology. So should we.

B. The Mystery of Lawlessness (2:6–12)

The period about which Paul spoke would be extremely lawless. When he was with them Paul had told the Thessalonians what was holding back the revelation of the man of lawlessness (the Antichrist). It seems that the Holy Spirit is the restraining influence in view. The Holy Spirit accomplishes His ministry of restraining satanic lawlessness in the world mainly through the influence of Christians whom He indwells, especially through gospel proclamation. At the Rapture the Holy Spirit's restraint of evil through Christians will end as He removes them from the earth. God the Holy Spirit will not entirely abandon the earth, of course, but His ministry of holding back evil through Christians will end.

After the Rapture the lawless one will have greater freedom and will do things that will eventually result in his being identified as the Antichrist. However, the mere breath of the Lord Jesus' mouth will slay him when Christ comes with His saints at the Second Coming (1:10). Satan will empower the lawless one to deceive many people into thinking he is God by doing awe-inspiring, powerful miracles (Rev. 13:2–4; 17:8). Thousands of people, but only a small proportion of the entire population, will place their faith in Jesus Christ during the Tribulation (6:9–11; 7:4, 9–17). Most will refuse "to love the truth and so be saved" (2 Thess. 2:10). Paul could say they "have not believed the truth but have delighted in wickedness" (2:12). These phrases describe all unbelievers, not just those who hear the gospel and willfully reject it before the Rapture.

Summary: Paul's readers could be confident that the day of the Lord had not yet begun. The tribulations they were experiencing were not those of that day. Three events had not yet taken place. These were the departure from the Word of God by many (2:3), the removal of the restrainer at the Rapture (2:7), and then the revelation of the man of lawlessness, the Antichrist (2:3).

IV. THANKSGIVING AND PRAYER (2:13–17)

Paul gave thanks for his readers' salvation and prayed for their steadfastness to help them appreciate their secure position in holding fast to the truth.

A. Thanksgiving for Calling (2:13–15)

Paul was grateful that his readers were not like the wicked unbelievers just referred to in 2:12. He could always give thanks for them because God had chosen them for salvation so they could one day share the splendor and honor that their Lord enjoys. In view of this Paul urged his readers not to abandon what he had taught them in person and by letter.

B. Prayer for Strength (2:16–17)

Paul petitioned God for the encouragement and strength of his dear readers. God's grace is the basis for eternal encouragement in the face of temporary distress. Our hope is beneficial because it motivates us to live in the light of our victorious Savior's return. The Thessalonians needed comforting encouragement in view of their recent anxiety that false teaching had produced, to enable them to stand firm and do everything as to the Lord, and as they continued proclaiming the gospel.

V. EXHORTATIONS FOR FUTURE GROWTH (3:1–15)

Paul again stressed the importance of prayer and warned his readers about idleness, a problem of theirs that had arisen from their mistaken idea concerning the Lord's return.

A. Reciprocal Prayer (3:1–5)

Prayer for the missionaries (3:1–2). Paul exhorted his readers to ask God to facilitate the rapid and wide dissemination of the gospel and thus glorify His Word. His readers had seen God do this in their midst when he and his fellow missionaries first visited their city. The apostle desired that God would grant him and his colleagues deliverance from unreasonable and harmful unbelievers who sought to limit the spread of the gospel.

Prayer for the Thessalonians (3:3–5). Paul was confident that God would provide strength and protection for the Thessalonians in view of His promises to provide for His own. He also believed that his readers, strengthened by the Lord, would continue to follow apostolic instruction as they had in the past. He also prayed that God would give these brothers and sisters a greater appreciation of His love for them and of Christ's steadfastness in the midst of His earthly afflictions so their own love and patient endurance might increase.

B. Church Discipline (3:6–15)

The false teaching that had entered the church had produced inappropriate behavior in some. Paul wrote that the Thessalonians needed to bring their behavior and their beliefs back into conformity with God's will.

General principles respecting disorderly conduct (3:6–10). This command was given with the full authority of the Lord Jesus Christ. The faithful in the church were to separate from the unruly, which would alert the offenders that their behavior was not acceptable and they needed to repent (see 1 Thess. 5:14). Evidently some in the church were not working to support themselves but were living off the charity of their brethren. If anyone refused to work, his brothers and sisters in Christ should not provide for him.

Specific instructions concerning the idle (3:11–13). The teaching that Christ could return at any moment had led some of the believers into idleness. They had quit their jobs and were simply waiting for Him to come. When people are not busy with their own work, they may tend to meddle in the business of others. Paul commanded the idle to settle down and to support themselves (see 1 Thess. 4:11).

> The church should always treat believing offenders as brothers, not as enemies.

Further discipline for the unrepentant (3:14–15). If a believer failed to abandon his idle lifestyle after having received the further warnings in this epistle, increased ostracism should result (see Rom. 16:17; 1 Cor. 5:9, 11; Titus 3:10–11). Hopefully this discipline would embarrass the offenders into changing their ways.

VI. CONCLUSION (3:16–18)

Paul concluded this epistle with an emphasis on unity in the church to motivate his readers to work out their problems and reestablish peaceful conditions that would glorify God. He concluded with two more prayers, his fourth and fifth (2 Thess. 3:16, 18) in this epistle. His main concern was for peace in the church that could take place only as all the Christians obeyed the truth. In view of a forged letter the Thessalonians received (2:2), the apostle felt it necessary to prove that the present one really did come from him. He added a word of greeting in his own hand, as he usually did, to authenticate his epistles for the benefit of recipients. A secretary evidently penned the other parts of the letter. The final benediction is almost identical to the one that ends 1 Thessalonians.

1 TIMOTHY
Effective Church Life

AUTHOR

The authorship of the Pastoral Epistles (1 and 2 Timothy and Titus) is a major critical problem in New Testament studies. Most modern scholars maintain that they are pseudepigraphical, that is, written in Paul's name sometime after the apostle's death. Most today date these three letters around the end of the first century and suggest that the author wanted to revive Pauline teaching for his day or to compose a Pauline-like manual for denouncing heresy in the postapostolic church. But the contents of the epistle as well as affirmations by early church fathers give strong evidence for concluding that the apostle Paul was indeed the writer of these three letters.

DATE

If Paul was released from prison in Rome in the early sixties, which seems most likely, he probably wrote this epistle in the middle sixties, perhaps A.D. 63–66.

AUDIENCE

Paul sent this epistle to his fellow missionary, Timothy, who was at this time serving as the apostle's representative in Ephesus and so had the authority to direct the elders and deacons of the church in Ephesus. Some of what Paul wrote in this epistle was for Timothy's personal benefit, but most of it was to guide Timothy in his work of instructing the leaders of the church.

PURPOSE

Following his trial before Caesar and his acquittal, Paul left Rome and eventually arrived in Ephesus. When Paul departed from Ephesus, he left Timothy in charge as his special representative to continue the work there (1 Tim. 1:3). In this letter Paul instructed Timothy to remain in Ephesus and to continue his needed ministry until Paul would rejoin him there (3:14; 4:13).

First and 2 Timothy and Titus are called "Pastoral Epistles" because Paul wrote them to pastors (shepherds) of churches outlining their pastoral duties. Their main pastoral duties were to defend sound doctrine and to maintain sound discipline.

THEOLOGICAL EMPHASES

The Pastoral Epistles are more practical than theological. They contain more exhortations to defend sound doctrine than explanations and elaborations of what sound doctrine is. The doctrine of the church (ecclesiology) is the primary theological contribution of all three epistles, though there is considerable emphasis on the correct doctrine of Christ as well. First Timothy is more general and deals with life in the church, whereas 2 Timothy and Titus are more focused and deal with special needs within the life of the church.

CHARACTERISTICS

The practicality of the Pastorals distinguishes them among the New Testament epistles. They deal primarily with overriding principles and practices that should characterize all local churches. First Timothy, in particular, is a follow-up letter to what Paul had said to the Ephesian elders when he left them after having ministered among them for over three years (see Acts 20:13–38).

OUTLINE

I. Salutation (1:1–2)

II. Timothy's Mission in Ephesus (1:3–20)
    A. The Task Timothy Faced (1:3–11)
    B. Exhortations to Be Faithful (1:12–20)

III. Instructions concerning the Life of the Local Church (2:1–4:5)
    A. The Priority of Prayer in Church Life (2:1–7)
    B. The Primary Responsibilities of Men and Women in Church Meetings (2:8–15)
    C. The Qualifications for Church Leaders (3:1–13)
    D. The Nature of the Local Church (3:14–16)
    E. The Problem of Apostasy in the Church (4:1–5)

IV. Instructions for Leaders of the Local Church (4:6–5:25)
    A. The Leader's Personal Life and Public Ministry (4:6–16)
    B. Basic Principles of Effective Interpersonal Relationships (5:1–2)
    C. How to Deal with Widows and Elders (5:3–25)

V. Instructions for Groups within the Church (6:1–19)
    A. Slaves (6:1–2)
    B. False Teachers (6:3–10)
    C. Those Committed to Christ (6:11–16)
    D. The Wealthy (6:17–19)

VI. Concluding Charge and Benediction (6:20–21)

I. SALUTATION (1:1–2)

Paul began this very personal letter with a customary salutation to set the tone for what followed. The salutation reveals that this was not just a personal letter, however, as was Paul's epistle to Philemon; it was also official.

As usual (except in 1 and 2 Thessalonians, Philippians, and Philemon), Paul reminded his readers of his authority as an apostle. Timothy would have read this letter publicly in the Ephesian church, and others would have read it in other congregations later as well. Paul's calling came to him by the "command" of God. This strong word is one of many indications that Paul stressed the importance of faithful perseverance in God's calling in this letter. Paul may have led Timothy to faith in Christ personally (see Acts 14:6; 16:1), or Timothy may simply have been Paul's "son in the faith" as his protégé.

II. TIMOTHY'S MISSION IN EPHESUS (1:3–20)

In this chapter Paul charged Timothy to remain faithful to the task with which Paul had entrusted him in Ephesus. He began by reminding his younger friend what that task was and how he should carry out his chief duty. Then he exhorted Timothy to be faithful. Paul reminded him of God's power to transform lives and warned him of the danger of acting contrary to his own spiritually sensitive conscience.

A. The Task Timothy Faced (1:3–11)

Paul penned these opening words to remind Timothy to correct teachers in the Ephesian church who were majoring on minor matters in their Bible teaching. In so doing he reminded Timothy of his own responsibility as a communicator of God's truth.

Paul's geographical movements, to which he referred here, probably took place between his first Roman imprisonment and the writing of this epistle. We cannot fit them into the chronology of Acts. The error of those whom Paul criticized seems to have been more in their emphasis than in their content. "False doctrines" is a general term that contrasts their novel teaching with what is edifying. In particular, these teachers seem to have been emphasizing extrabiblical stories that had become part of the traditions of Judaism that grew out of the Old Testament genealogies. "Myths" and "endless genealogies" evidently describe two aspects of one aberration rather than two separate problems. This kind of emphasis, Paul warned, simply generated questions for which there are no real answers rather than contributing to the spiritual maturation of believers.

The *ultimate* aim of a Bible teacher should not be to generate debate and controversy but to cultivate the lives of his students so they manifest love in their daily living. This love should spring from a pure heart, a conscience void of shame, and a genuine trust in God. Paul probably meant that the false teachers did not understand what they were really saying and not saying by their emphasis. They missed the point of the law (the whole Old Testament including the Mosaic Law).

The law is profitable if one uses it properly, according to its original intention. The primary purpose of all law is not to approve the conduct of righteous people but to expose and condemn the unrighteous. Paul arranged his first six epithets in pairs (1 Tim. 1:9a). The leading attitude in each pair precedes the resulting action. There is a progression in these three couplets from general to specific lawlessness. The first two terms are introductory, and the following sins are violations of the first through the third commandments. The second group of offenders (1:9b–10a) provides examples of individuals who break the fifth through the ninth commandments of the Decalogue. They are sinners arrayed against society. Paul concluded his list (1:10b–11) with a general category of anything contrary to not only the Law of Moses but also the larger gospel that Paul preached, which encompassed the Old Testament. "Sound doctrine" describes not just correct or accurate doctrine but what is healthful and wholesome.

When a person teaches the Scriptures, he should distinguish the teaching of God's Word from speculation that goes beyond what God has revealed. Love should be his primary motive and intent, and the teacher should present a portion of Scripture and explain the purpose for which God intended it. Knowledge of the passage is not enough; a teacher should communicate the spirit of the divine Author as well.

B. Exhortations to Be Faithful (1:12–20)

A positive encouragement (1:12–17). The fact that God changed Paul should enable Timothy to appreciate the fact that God can transform even the worst of sinners and can enable His saints to accomplish supernatural feats. The difficult situation Timothy faced in Ephesus was made more difficult by his personal tendency toward timidity.

God did not save Paul because He foresaw that he would be faithful, but He entrusted him with the ministry he had received at least in part for that reason. Paul believed he was serving God by persecuting Christians. He was mistaken about who Jesus Christ is, and for this reason God had mercy on him.

Seven times in the Pastoral Epistles Paul alluded to statements that had become proverbial in the early church (see 1:15; 2:5–6; 3:16; 2 Tim. 1:9–10; 2:8–13; Titus 2:11–14; 3:3–7). They may have been parts of early Christian hymns or catechisms. Here (1:15) the great truth affirmed is that the purpose of Christ's incarnation was the salvation of sinners. Perhaps the apostle meant that he was the "foremost" sinner in the sense that his sin of aggressively tearing down the work that God was building up was the worst kind of sin. God was unusually merciful to Paul because He desired to make the apostle an example of how God can transform the worst of sinners into the best of saints. Such grace prompted Paul to glorify God in a brief doxology (1:17).

A negative warning (1:18–20). Paul balanced his positive encouragement based on God's dealings with himself (1:12–17) with a negative warning based on God's dealings with two unfaithful ministers. This warning challenged Timothy to remain faithful to God as he discharged his duties.

The command to which Paul referred (1:18) is the one given in 1:3–4. He now returned to the subject he began there. Sometime in the past someone had given prophecies concerning Timothy's effectiveness as a servant of Christ (see 4:14; 2 Tim. 1:6). Paul referred to them to motivate Timothy to carry on. As Timothy fought the good fight, he should continue to trust God and to maintain a good conscience. Paul cited two examples of casualties in ministry with which Timothy was apparently familiar: Hymenaeus and Alexander (see 2 Tim. 4:14, 17). Paul had turned them over to God's discipline because of their determination to continue living contrary to the will of God. This discipline would come on them through the agency of Satan so they would hopefully repent and stop blaspheming God by their lives.

III. INSTRUCTIONS CONCERNING THE LIFE OF THE LOCAL CHURCH (2:1–4:5)

After instructions aimed primarily at Timothy himself, Paul gave him instructions he needed for his pastoral work.

A. The Priority of Prayer in Church Life (2:1–7)

The apostle's first positive instruction to Timothy regarding his leadership of the Ephesian church was that he should encourage believers to pray for everyone. He gave this directive to emphasize its importance, defend its value, and clarify its practice. Every aspect of this prayer touches the church's evangelistic mission.

Though Paul used several synonyms for prayer in urging its practice, the words he chose are not significantly different. By using these synonyms Paul emphasized the importance of prayer more than distinguishing its varieties. Christians must not fail to take advantage of the supernatural resource at their disposal by neglecting prayer. Paul wrote this epistle while Nero was king, an unbeliever for whom Paul specifically told his readers to pray.

Furthermore they should focus their requests not on their own tranquillity but on the king's salvation (2:4). Primarily we should pray for governmental leaders and those in positions of lesser authority under them so we may lead outwardly and inwardly peaceful lives. Thus we can carry out our purpose in the world as Christians, namely, to bring the message of reconciliation to all people and to glorify God in all our relationships. Prayers of this type please God because He delights to rescue sinners from the consequences of their sin. Paul may have cited another common creedal statement in 2:5–6, which is a succinct affirmation of the person and work of Christ. The God-Man is the only Mediator of the

New Covenant between God and humankind, providing salvation for those who believe and facilitating prayer Godward. Jesus Christ died as the substitute for all people. Another reason Paul commanded Timothy to pray for all people was that God had commissioned him to herald the gospel to the gentile world, and he had proclaimed the faith truthfully.

B. The Primary Responsibilities of Men and Women in Church Meetings (2:8–15)

Typically men should take the lead in praying, but women led in prayer occasionally in early church meetings (see 1 Cor. 11:5–16). Those who lead in prayer should do so with inner holiness and outward righteous behavior. When Paul wrote that the men are to lift up holy hands as they prayed, he did not mean they are to pray with upraised hands. Because our hands symbolize what we do, the men are to pray as they practice holiness in their lives; they are to be holy and are to avoid anger and disputes.

The responsibility of women in church meetings needed more explanation. Works that express a godly character should characterize Christian women more than the way they dress and groom themselves. A Christian woman should be remarkable for her Christlike behavior more than for her clothes, hairstyle, and other externals that are of primary importance to many unbelievers (see also 1 Pet. 3:3). Spiritual qualities should always mark a Christian lady, of course, but Paul's concern was that they be outstanding in the church meetings. There the woman's character and conduct would contribute to the orderly and edifying activities rather than detracting from them (see 1 Tim. 3:15). The women were to let the men provide the public instruction and leadership. Typically they should not accept the role of teacher of the congregation or of leader of the whole church.[1]

Some people do not like the idea of "submission" (2:11; see also Eph. 5:21–22; Col. 3:18). The Greek word translated "submission" means being in rank under someone else. In military life, for example, a private who ranks under a colonel is not necessarily of less value or less ability than his superior officer. Rank has to do with order and authority, not personal superiority and inferiority. Another illustration of willing submission is Jesus Christ, who is superior to every other human being yet submitted to other human beings (Phil. 2:5–11). Paul did not want women to teach men or to exercise authority over men in the local church meetings (1 Tim. 3:15). The teaching of the Scriptures is more appropriate to the male's function in the church as a mediator between God and people because it involves interpreting God's Word to the church as an authority figure (see 2:1–2, 8). Paul, however, did approve of women teaching women and children (Titus 2:3–5; 2 Tim. 1:5) and their instructing men privately (Acts 18:26). The Greek word translated "have authority" means to act on one's own authority or to act in an autocratic manner. To exercise authority in this way would be to submit to no higher authority in the church. If a woman exercised some authority in the church (for example, as the leader of a ministry) and she did it in submission to the male leadership, she would not be sinning. What Paul prohibited was a woman taking inappropriate authority on herself. A woman can have authority over others in the church provided she is under the authority of the male leadership of the church. Her silence (quietness) is a concrete expression of the principle of submission that Paul advocated.

Paul gave two reasons why women should conduct themselves in church meetings as he just specified (1 Tim. 2:13–14). First, from Creation it was God's intention that the male should lead the female. God made Adam first and then He made a suitable companion for him in Eve. God made Eve for Adam; He did not make Adam for Eve. God created Adam and Eve equals in that they needed and complemented one another, but God entrusted Adam with leadership responsibility over his wife. Eve was not responsible to God for Adam in the same sense Adam was responsible for Eve. Second (2:14), as part of the judgment on Eve at the Fall God confirmed (made permanent) the leadership of the male over the female (Gen. 3:16). Paul cited God's intention for male-female relationships specifically in marriage, not in general social situations. Christian men and women should bring their proper relationship in marriage over into church life (1 Tim. 3:15) and their families.

God promised women a life of fulfillment as mothers in the home, provided they walk with the Lord, rather than as teachers and leaders in the church (2:15). Certainly a single woman or a married woman who is not a mother can find fulfillment as a woman of God, but usually women find their greatest fulfillment as mothers. Paul was again assuming a typical situation (see 2:11–12).

Summary: Paul exhorted the males in "God's household" (the local church, 3:15) to function as mediators between Jesus Christ, humankind's mediator with God, and His people. They should do this by praying, teaching, and leading the church. The women should concentrate on facilitating godliness in the church family as well as in their homes by cultivating good works and by living godly lives.

C. The Qualifications for Church Leaders (3:1–13)

Paul proceeded from his instructions concerning worship in the church to lay out qualifications for leaders of the church to give Timothy guidance in selecting these important individuals.[2]

Qualifications for elders (3:1–7). Paul cited another well-known saying to introduce and give support to what he was about to teach. "Overseer" is a term that emphasizes this leader's management responsibilities and is evidently synonymous with "elder" (5:17; 1 Pet. 5:1) and "pastor" or "shepherd" (Eph. 4:11). A person can aspire to hold an office out of good or bad motives. The "trustworthy saying" Paul cited assumed good motives: the desire to do a worthy work, not personal glory.

Fifteen characteristics should mark the life of a man who aspired to serve as an elder. Above all, he should be irreproachable, possessing no obvious flaw in his character or conduct. He should also be a faithful husband, assuming he is married. The remaining qualifications are self-evident. Two things were important to Paul. The man should not be guilty of doing something wrong, and other people must perceive his conduct as proper for a Christian. The effective operation of each church depends on its leadership. The New Testament does not legislate the details of church operations, so it is important that the men making these decisions be spiritual men who set a good example and have the respect and confidence of the other church members.

Qualifications for deacons (3:8–13). Paul continued his instructions concerning order in the life of the local church by setting forth qualifications for the deacons to insure Spirit-directed assistants for the elders.

The word "likewise" (3:8) indicates that Paul was describing an office different from that of elder when he spoke of deacons. As time passed, the churches recognized official servants of the churches, and these people held office as deacons. Paul gave a list of twelve qualifications here. Does verse 11 refer to female deacons, the wives of male deacons, or unmarried women who assist the deacons? It is difficult to decide. It probably refers to female deacons since there is nothing about the office as such that would exclude a woman, and it seems unusual that Paul would prescribe qualifications for wives of deacons but not for wives of elders. The apostle cited four special qualifications for these women. Returning to the male deacons, Paul added two more qualifications (3:12–13). The rewards for faithful service as a deacon are two: a good reputation and increased confidence in dealing with other people and with God. Since Paul said nothing about the duties of deacons he evidently did not associate specific tasks with the office. He seems to have intended that deacons should function as official servants of the church in whatever capacity the elders might see a need.

D. The Nature of the Local Church (3:14–16)

In view of the context Paul evidently was thinking of the local church when he spoke of it as a household and as a pillar and foundation for the truth. The local church is a family of believers (see 5:1–2). It should therefore conduct its corporate life as a family rather than as a business, a country club, an entertainment center, a military group, or some other organization. The second figure is of a supporting pillar that upholds something set on top of it.[3] Each local church supports the witness of each believer in it and holds that testimony up before the world. What the believer proclaims is the "truth," the whole truth God has revealed in His Word but especially God's redemptive plan.

The apostle's mention of this message led him to glorify it (3:16). God has made His plan—this great "mystery of godliness"—known to us only

> *To give thanks for a meal or our marriage and then complain about it is inconsistent.*

by special revelation (see Ep. 3:2–11). It is a mystery of "godliness" in that it leads to and results in godliness in those who accept it. It is "great" in its preeminent importance and in its worldwide scope. Three couplets depict Jesus Christ as the essence of this mystery and view His work as completed.

E. The Problem of Apostasy in the Church (4:1–5)

In contrast to the true revelation of God (3:16), false teaching would arise as time passed. Christ had taught that some who held the truth would repudiate it (Matt. 13:21; 24:10–11; Mark 4:17; 13:22; Luke 8:13; see also Acts 20:29; 2 Thess. 2:1–12; 2 Tim. 3:1–13; 2 Pet. 3:1–18). This would happen as a result of their listening to persuasive arguments put forth by God's spiritual enemies and, behind them, demons (1 Tim. 4:1). These apostates had developed hardened consciences by refusing to respond to the truth they knew. Now they called lies the truth, and that is hypocrisy (4:2).

The teaching Paul warned Timothy and the Ephesians to watch out for was asceticism, the idea that abstinence from physical things is essential for spiritual purity. There may be physical reasons for not eating certain foods (allergies, too-high fat content, and others), but there are no spiritual reasons. Likewise there may be physical reasons why marriage in some cases may not be wise or desirable (passing on genetic defects, the demands of a particular ministry, and others), but God has approved the institution of marriage. God created marriage and food for us to enjoy (4:3). Since the coming of Christ, the distinction between clean and unclean foods is one we can eliminate (Mark 7:19; Acts 10:15; 1 Cor. 10:23–33). All God has created is essentially good (Gen. 1:31). What God has created He has set apart for our enjoyment through the Word of God, and we acknowledge that through prayer.

IV. INSTRUCTIONS FOR LEADERS OF THE LOCAL CHURCH (4:6–5:25)

This section discusses the church leader's personal life and public ministry, basic principles of effective interpersonal relationships, and how to deal with select groups in the church.

A. The Leader's Personal Life and Public Ministry (4:6–16)

Paul gave positive directions to enable Timothy to overcome the influences of the ascetic apostates who threatened the church at Ephesus and to remind him of the importance of both his personal life and his public ministry. The apostle selected three essential spiritual priorities.

Timothy was to "point out," a mild approach, the truth about God's good gifts that Paul had just articulated. A faithful servant of Christ must pass along the truth God has revealed without distortion and must continue to nourish himself on the truths of the faith contained in the Bible. He is to abide in the sound teaching he had received from the Lord and His apostles as he had been doing so far. He should not become embroiled in refuting the godless and worthless fables of these false teachers (1:4) that have a certain appeal but are only curiosities. Rather he should train himself in godliness. This requires rigorous self-discipline. Timothy should direct his discipline at the development of spiritual more than physical strength. The reason for this is that we look forward to a genuine hope beyond the grave. That hope rests in the "living" God (3:15) who is the "Savior of all men" (4:10; see 2:2, 4, 6) in that He provided a salvation that is available to all.

Since Timothy was a comparatively young man, he may have felt reluctant to instruct his elders in the Ephesian congregation. Paul promised that no one in the church would discredit his teaching ministry if he backed it up with a godly lifestyle. In his words as well as by his actions, by his love for people and his trust in God, and by his moral cleanness he should provide an example of godliness. He should give attention to his public ministry as well as to his private life. Three duties were crucial. First, he should continue to make sure the church leaders read the Scriptures in the meetings of the church. Second, exhortation should continue to accompany the reading of the Word. Third, systematic instruction in the doctrines of the faith is necessary.

Timothy also needed further encouragement to keep using the abilities God had given him to serve the Lord. He had received ordination for service to God by the laying on of Paul's (2 Tim. 1:6) and some elders' hands. When that happened, a prophet who was present received a revelation from God that Timothy would serve Jesus Christ in a particular way.

Paul called on Timothy to remember that event and the responsibility that was his in view of that special revelation. As Timothy concentrated on these responsibilities (1 Tim. 4:6–16), his personal progress in godliness would become evident to his fellow saints in Ephesus and elsewhere. His rewards would be that he would be delivered from failure and a wasted life (see 2:15; James 1:21) and those to whom he ministered would be delivered from error and retrogression.

B. Basic Principles of Effective Interpersonal Relationships (5:1–2)

Paul turned to the subject of interpersonal relationships to help his son in the faith get along with people effectively and instruct others wisely. One of the greatest failings of people involved in pastoral work is their inability to relate to and work with others effectively. This failure is often traceable to the pastor's attitude toward others, that is, how he views them. Paul wisely prefaced his specific instructions about leadership needs with some fundamental principles designed to facilitate interpersonal relationships. In short, Timothy was to relate to everyone in the church as if they were the members of his own family. Paul had already taught that the local church is a household (1 Tim. 3:15).

Specifically Timothy should deal with older men respectfully and appeal to them gently rather than rebuking them harshly. He could deal with younger men more directly but always as brothers. He should think of and treat the older women in the congregation as he would his own mother. And he should regard the younger women as sisters in the Lord and treat them with the purity one would grant one's actual sister.

C. How to Deal with Widows and Elders (5:3–25)

Paul now dealt with two groups of people in the church that merited special consideration.

Provisions for widows (5:3–16). Widows have been and still are specially vulnerable individuals. As such God has always shown special concern for their protection (see Deut. 10:18; 24:17; Ps. 68:5). Paul distinguished two kinds of widows in the church. First, there were the bereaved who had children or grandchildren who could support them. Second, there were those who had no family to care for them and who were bereft of physical support as well as bereaved. The Christian relatives of the former group should care for the first type (see Mark 7:10–12; Eph. 6:2). The church should care for the latter group and, presumably, widows with nonsupportive family members. The church should honor this second group of widows, the extremely dependent, rather than looking down on them. However, not all in the second category should receive regular financial help. Only those widows without children or supporting relatives who give evidence that they are looking to God for their needs and are seeking to honor Him with their lives qualify. These are "widows indeed." Widows who give themselves to the pursuit of pleasure rather than to the pursuit of God do not qualify for regular support. These women receive in their lives the wages of their sin: spiritual deadness.

Timothy was to teach these things so family members in the church would shoulder their rightful responsibility, and he was to encourage the widows to seek the Lord rather than pursuing lives of wanton pleasure (1 Tim. 5:6). Family members have a universally recognized duty to care for one each other, an obligation that even unbelievers acknowledge. If a Christian fails here, he behaves contrary to the teaching of his faith, and in this particular he is worse than the typical unbeliever who helps his needy relations (see John 19:26–27).

Evidently the Ephesian church had a "list" of widows who received regular support from the congregation. A widow had to meet three qualifications to get her name on this list. She had to be at least sixty years old, she had to have been a one-man woman (see 3:2, 12), and she had to have established a reputation for good works. Paul cited five typical examples of good works: rearing children, being hospitable, serving her Christian brothers and sisters, helping the needy, and devoting herself to good works.

It was not wise to place younger widows on this list because younger widows' sensual desires would be stronger, and these feelings would make it very hard for them to remain committed to serving Christ wholeheartedly as single women. If the church leaders placed them on the list and they wanted to remarry, they would have to set aside this pledge of service to Christ alone. They would thereby incur some form of temporal condemnation.

Placement on the list of supported widows would also not be good for younger widows because it would open them to the temptation of idleness as well as inconsistency. They would normally face temptation to use their energy and time in too much talking and getting into other people's affairs. So Paul encouraged younger widows to remarry and to use their strength to bear children and to care for their families, the primary duties of a typical Christian wife (see Titus 2:5). By doing so, they would not give the enemy (any accuser of believers) an opportunity to criticize them for going back on their pledge to serve Christ. Evidently this had already happened in the Ephesian church (1 Tim. 5:15).

In conclusion, Paul sought to correct a possible misunderstanding. Any financially capable women (who did not have living or believing husbands) should maintain the widows in their families so the church would not have to support them (5:16).

The discipline and selection of elders (5:17–25). The elders Paul referred to in these verses were the church overseers and not just any older men in the congregation. Paul had already given the qualifications for these officers (3:1–7), and now he described them as ruling, preaching, and teaching. The overall duty of the elders was ruling the church in the sense of directing its affairs and giving oversight to all its activities (see 1 Pet. 5:1–4). The single honor that every elder received most likely alludes to the respect that came to the elder for being an elder. The double honor probably involved payment for ministry as well as respect (see 1 Tim. 5:3, 17–18; 2 Cor. 11:8–9; Gal. 6:6).

Not all the elders in the Ephesian church worked hard at preaching and teaching. Probably some elders had more responsibility to preach and teach than others. Paul cited two scriptural authorities to support his instruction to those who serve the church by providing leadership as elders: Moses (Lev. 19:13; Deut. 24:15; 25:4) and Jesus (Luke 10:7). Paul's readers should not entertain accusations against elders unless two or three witnesses agreed to give evidence of wrongdoing (see Deut. 19:15; Matt. 18:16; John 8:17; 2 Cor. 13:1). Following a private rebuke, Timothy should publicly rebuke a persistently erring elder. This procedure would also discourage others from sinning. Paul could hardly have stressed more strongly the importance of absolute objectivity and honesty in dealing with offending leaders (1 Tim. 5:21).

He also urged Timothy to minimize the possibility of elder failure by being extremely careful about whom he appointed in the first place. Laying on hands in this context probably refers to public ordination (see 4:14; 2 Tim. 1:7). Since Timothy occupied the seat of a judge, he needed to stay free from sin himself. Paul may have realized that the process of elder discipline that he imposed on Timothy would have been hard on him physically as well as emotionally. So the apostle prescribed a little wine for Timothy's queasy stomach. Timothy needed to be cautious about choosing church leaders, Paul continued, because sin is not always obvious. However, eventually it will become known. In the same manner good deeds can remain hidden for years.

V. INSTRUCTIONS FOR GROUPS WITHIN THE CHURCH (6:1–19)

In the last major section of this letter Paul called on Timothy to instruct the members of various groups within the church concerning their Christian duties.

A. Slaves (6:1–2)

As he had done previously (1 Tim. 5:1–2), Paul urged the adoption of proper attitudes toward others that would normally make it easier to produce proper actions. Christian slaves were to "consider" their masters as worthy of all honor if for no other reason than that God had placed them in a position of authority over them. Such an attitude would lead to service that would not bring dishonor on the God the slave professed to serve or the faith he professed to follow. Christian slaves who had believing masters had a second reason to give their masters honor and faithful service: They were their spiritual brothers. As such they deserved even greater consideration.[4]

B. False Teachers (6:3–10)

Paul returned to instructions concerning false teachers (see 1:3–11; 4:1–5) to alert Timothy to their underlying attitudes so he could deal with them effectively. False teachers must have been a major concern of Paul's since he framed this whole letter with references to them. The apostle described the actions of the false teachers (6:3), their attitudes (6:4a), the fruits of their ministry (6:4b–5a), and their motivation (6:5b).

The false teachers (a) advocated doctrine that was different from what Scripture and the apostles taught, (b) disagreed with the teachings of the Lord Jesus Christ that fostered spiritual health in those who heard and responded to them, and (c) rejected the doctrine that conforms to and results in godly behavior. Their error was not an innocent one, and it sprang from improper attitudes: the desires to exalt oneself and to hoard money selfishly. Such motivation demonstrated that they really understood nothing that is truly important, and their motives led them to an unhealthy interest in controversies and terminology. This interest produced all kinds of selfish and divisive behavior and attitudes that were not loving and edifying (see 1:5).

Timothy was to remember that real "gain" comes from the acquisition of godliness that includes an attitude of contentment with one's material possessions. Having the basic necessities of life, food, and clothing,[5] we can and should be content (see Heb. 13:5–6). Paul had learned this lesson of healthy detachment from material things in his own life (Phil. 4:10–13), and we must learn it too. In contrast to contentment with the basics of life, greed for more opens the door to temptation that comes in the form of unwise lustful desires that impede one's spiritual progress, much as a trap holds an animal that gets tangled up in it. Eventually the end of such a person is spiritual ruin and personal destruction if he does not escape its grip and turn from it.

Paul then used a second figure to warn against greed (1 Tim. 6:10a). That root attitude bears all kinds of evil fruit in wicked actions. The love of money, not money itself, is the snare. Paul pictured a person wandering from the narrow path of truth as he pursues money. He gets caught in thorns that pierce his skin and cause him great pain (see Matt. 13:22).

> As Christians who live in a materialistic world, we must deliberately cultivate Paul's attitude of contentment. This is a specially difficult task in a society like that of North America. We are constantly hearing through advertising and the media that we "need" all kinds of luxuries. Actually, however, our personal needs as human beings are actually very few. We should seek godliness more diligently than we seek money and the things it can buy.

C. Those Committed to Christ (6:11–16)

Paul continued to appeal to Timothy and all the faithful in Ephesus to pursue spiritual rather than physical goals in life.

In contrast to some who pursued money, Timothy, a man of God by calling and commitment, should flee from this attitude. In following God Timothy should emphasize what the Holy Spirit seeks to produce in the life of a Christian (Gal. 5:22–23) and what is essential for a leader of God's people (1 Tim. 3:1–3). The first two of the goals Paul listed (6:11) are general characteristics that represent one's relationship with God. The second two are specific attitudes that animate the Christian life. The third two are specific actions that define correct ways of relating to a hostile world. Together they draw a silhouette of a "man [person] of God."

Our spiritual enemy opposes the Christian's pursuit of godly ideals, so Paul urged his younger friend to plunge into this conflict. The goal is worth fighting for, and it requires fighting for. Paul's strongest exhortation to Timothy in this letter was to keep God's commandment (the gospel viewed as a rule of life) without shameful inconsistencies or behavior that could elicit justifiable criticism. He reminded Timothy that God, who gives life to all things and who therefore could and would give Timothy fullness of life, was observing him. He also lived under the gaze of God's anointed Servant, Jesus Christ, who had maintained a good testimony in His hour of trial. Paul's doxology (a statement glorifying God) emphasized His sovereignty, immortality, and incomprehensible holiness. To Him belong all honor and rule throughout eternity.

D. The Wealthy (6:17–19)

Paul had not finished all he wanted to say about money, so he returned in these three verses to that subject with a brief word of instruction for the wealthy Ephesian believers. Two attitudes often mislead the rich. One is the idea that one's greater monetary value indicates his greater personal value or worth. The other is that riches guarantee power and security. Paul warned against both of these conclusions. God will determine our future, not our present financial resources, so rich people should put their hope in the Giver rather than in His gifts. Paul urged Timothy to instruct the rich to view their money as God's enablement so they could accomplish good deeds. By doing so, they would be insuring that the Lord would reward them for their faithful stewardship when they stood before Him (6:19).

VI. CONCLUDING CHARGE AND BENEDICTION (6:20–21)

Paul closed this letter with a final exhortation to Timothy to avoid going astray in his ministry so he would finish well. Timothy should guard the truth of the Christian faith that God had committed to his stewardship by proclaiming it accurately and faithfully. Specifically, he should avoid the controversies and false teaching that Paul referred to previously that characterize the world system and are valueless, as well as the opposition of those who claimed superior knowledge. In closing, Paul wished God's grace for Timothy and the other saints in Ephesus.

2 TIMOTHY
Effective Church Leadership

DATE

Following his first Roman imprisonment and subsequent release, Paul ended up in the capital of the empire as a prisoner again (2 Tim. 2:9). He had already had his initial hearing before Caesar and was awaiting trial when he wrote this epistle (4:16). He believed that the Roman authorities would judge him guilty and execute him soon (4:6). Paul probably wrote 2 Timothy in the fall of A.D. 67. According to early church tradition, Paul was executed shortly before Nero committed suicide in June of A.D. 68. Paul penned this last of his canonical epistles fairly near the time of his execution, though before the winter of A.D. 67–68 (4:21).

AUDIENCE

As with 1 Timothy, Paul wrote to his young emissary to encourage and instruct him in his ministry of oversight, probably in Ephesus (1:16–18; 4:14; see also 1 Tim. 1:20; 2 Tim. 4:19). However, Paul knew that this letter would be read to all the believers and that it constituted instruction for Christians as a whole, not just Timothy.

PURPOSE

Ever since Rome had burned in July of A.D. 64 and Nero had blamed the Christians, it had become dangerous to be a Christian and to have contact with leaders of the church such as Paul. Consequently many believers, including some of Paul's coworkers, had chosen to seek a much lower profile and become less aggressive in their ministries. Timothy faced the temptation to do the same. Paul wrote this epistle to urge him to remain faithful to his calling and loyal to his father in the faith.

THEOLOGICAL EMPHASES

Paul continued to deal with the subject of the church in this epistle, as he had in 1 Timothy, but he stressed particularly its leadership. This letter strongly emphasizes the importance of essential qualities that should mark church leaders, particularly Timothy.

CHARACTERISTICS

This is a very personal letter to a son in the faith. Paul believed he would die soon after writing it, so it is a sort of last will and testament. The apostle reviewed his life and ministry and stressed what is most important in the service of Jesus Christ as he anticipated the future condition of the church.

OUTLINE

   I. Salutation (1:1–2)
  II. Thanksgiving for Faithful Fellow Workers (1:3–18)
     A. Timothy's Past Faithfulness (1:3–7)
     B. Charges to Remain Loyal (1:8–14)
     C. Examples of Faithful and Unfaithful Service (1:15–18)
 III. Exhortations to Persevere (chapter 2)
     A. Charge to Endure Hardship (2:1–13)
     B. Charge to Remain Faithful (2:14–26)

IV. Directions concerning the Last Days (3:1–4:8)
   A. Characteristics of the Last Days (3:1–13)
   B. Conduct in the Last Days (3:14–4:5)
   C. Paul's Role in the Last Days (4:6–8)
V. Concluding Personal Instructions and Information (4:9–22)
   A. Fellow Workers and an Opponent (4:9–15)
   B. Paul's Preliminary Hearing in Court (4:16–18)
   C. Additional Greetings and Instructions (4:19–21)
   D. Benediction (4:22)

I. SALUTATION (1:1–2)

As usual, Paul wrote what he did in his salutation to set the tone for his emphasis in the rest of the epistle. There are only three minor particulars in which this salutation differs from the one in 1 Timothy. First, Paul attributed his calling as an apostle to "the will of God" rather than to the command of God. Second, he said his calling as an apostle was because of (in harmony with) "the promise of life in Christ Jesus." Third, Paul referred to Timothy as his "dear son," emphasizing the affection he felt for Timothy and his relationship to him as a spiritual son and protégé whom he had nurtured in the faith.[1]

II. THANKSGIVING FOR FAITHFUL FELLOW WORKERS (1:3–18)

Paul commended Timothy for his past faithfulness, charged him to remain loyal to his father in the faith, and cited examples of faithful and unfaithful servants of the Lord.

A. Timothy's Past Faithfulness (1:3–7)

Paul began his first epistle to Timothy with thanks for his own salvation and ministry (1 Tim. 1:12). In this second epistle he began with thanks for Timothy's salvation and ministry. Throughout this letter Paul looked to the past and ahead to the future, when he would no longer be alive.

Paul regarded his own ministry as part of the continuation of God's great ongoing plan of the ages. He was one of the faithful throughout history who have loyally served God sincerely. Paul had plenty of time to pray for Timothy since he was again in prison (2 Tim. 4:9, 16, 21). Evidently when they had parted last, Timothy had taken their separation very hard. A reunion would encourage Timothy as well as Paul.

The apostle rejoiced over Timothy's genuine faith (1:5). His mother and grandmother had also demonstrated sterling faith in Christ. In view of the quality of Timothy's faith Paul urged his younger friend not to neglect the use of his God-given abilities for the service of Christ. Timothy had received divine enablement to do the work into which God was leading him, but he had apparently held back from some ministry because of timidity. Paul reminded him that such a spirit is not from God, for He makes us spiritually powerful, loving, and self-disciplined.

B. Charges to Remain Loyal (1:8–14)

Paul gave his young protégé exhortations to encourage him further to remain faithful to the Lord.

Exhortation to be courageous (1:8–12). In view of the Holy Spirit's enablement just mentioned, Paul instructed Timothy not to let others intimidate him. Timothy had evidently felt tempted to demonstrate some sign of embarrassment with the gospel and with Paul, perhaps because he was in prison. The apostle reminded Timothy that he was in prison as Christ's prisoner. Timothy should join his mentor in suffering for the gospel by proclaiming it boldly. God would empower him to stand tall by His grace. Paul enlarged on the glory of the gospel to rekindle a fresh appreciation of it in Timothy (1:9–11).[2] Paul proudly acknowledged that God had appointed him, of all people, a herald, an apostle, and a teacher of this good news. He was not ashamed of the gospel or of himself. God would protect him and his work.

Exhortation to guard the gospel (1:13–14). Timothy felt tempted to modify his message as well as to stop preaching it. Paul urged him, therefore, to continue to preach the same message he had heard from Paul and to do so with trust in God and love for people, which Jesus Christ would supply.

C. Examples of Faithful and Unfaithful Service (1:15–18)

To further impress on Timothy the need for him to remain faithful to his calling, Paul cited records of the ministries of other Christians who were mutual acquaintances.

The Christians in Ephesus and in the province of Asia where Ephesus stood had so thoroughly abandoned Paul that he could say all had turned from him. Timothy was the last to maintain his loyalty to and support of Paul among that group, and he was now facing temptation to abandon him. Phygellus and Hermogenes had been strong supporters of the apostle in the past but had eventually turned from him as the rest had done. However, Onesiphorus, who apparently was living in Ephesus when Paul wrote this epistle (4:19), was an exception to the majority. His whole family had diligently and unashamedly sought out Paul and had ministered to him during his current imprisonment. For this, Paul wished the Lord would show him mercy at the judgment seat of Christ (1:12). Onesiphorus's example could encourage Timothy to remain faithful to his calling.

III. EXHORTATIONS TO PERSEVERE (CHAPTER 2)

Paul now became more pointed and charged Timothy to endure hardship and remain faithful.

A. Charge to Endure Hardship (2:1–13)

The apostle continued to encourage Timothy to remain faithful to his calling to motivate him to persevere in his ministry.

Timothy's duty (2:1–7). Paul's charge in verse 1 is general, and specific responsibilities follow. On the basis of what he had already written, Paul urged his son to continue to depend on God. God would then provide strength. As Paul had passed the torch of ministry on to Timothy, so now Timothy should do so to other men who gave evidence that they, too, would be faithful. Paul's long ministry with Timothy had included many hardships, and as Timothy looked forward to training other young men he could expect more of the same. Paul urged him to submit to difficulties as a good soldier.

The apostle used three illustrations to help Timothy appreciate the logical consistency of this exhortation. The first illustration is the soldier, and its point is that Timothy (and all believers) should remain free from entanglement with other lesser goals and activities while serving the Lord. The second illustration, the athlete, emphasizes the need to minister according to the rules God has prescribed. The illustration of the farmer, Paul's third, stressed the toil necessary if one wants to enjoy the fruits of his labors. All three illustrations imply dogged persistence and hold out the prospect of reward for the faithful. Timothy needed to meditate on what Paul had just written, and, as he did so the Lord would help him see the wisdom of his words.

The examples of Jesus and Paul (2:8–10). Paul proceeded to undergird his appeal to suffer hardship with the examples of Jesus (2:8) and himself (2:9–10). He urged Timothy to meditate on the greatest example of suffering hardship for a worthy purpose, namely, Jesus Christ. Paul, too, was willing to suffer hardship for the gospel. He had done so all his Christian life and was presently in prison because of it. Timothy needed to remember that the Word of God was just as powerful to change lives as ever, and even though its champion defender was in chains, Timothy should continue to proclaim it. Because the gospel is the power of God unto salvation, Paul was content to endure anything so long as this message went forth.

A popular saying (2:11–13). To urge Timothy further to endure hardship, Paul cited a commonly accepted and used quotation that encouraged believers to remain faithful to their Christian profession (see also 1:15; 3:1; 4:9; Titus 3:8). It consists of four couplets, two positive and two negative. The first couplet (2 Tim. 2:11) is a comforting reminder that since the believer died with Christ (Col. 3:3), he has also experienced resurrection with Him to newness of life (Rom. 6:2–18). Second, if a believer endures suffering, he will one day reign with Christ (2 Tim. 2:12a). Third, if a believer departs from following Christ faithfully during his life, Christ will deny him at the judgment seat of Christ (2 Tim. 2:12b). He will lose some of his reward (1 Cor. 3:12–15; Luke 19:24–26), not his salvation. (Some say 2 Tim. 2:12b means that if a person professed to be saved but was not a genuine believer, he would be rejected by Christ). Fourth, if a believer is unfaithful to God, Christ will still remain faithful to him (2:13).

Christ's faithfulness to us should motivate us to remain faithful to Him. We should remain faithful to the Lord, and endure hardship if necessary, in view of what Jesus Christ has done and will do.

B. Charge to Remain Faithful (2:14–26)

Paul developed the importance of remaining faithful to the Lord as another motivation for Timothy to persevere.

Faithfulness in public ministry (2:14–18). Timothy was to keep reminding his "reliable men" of the things Paul had just brought back to his own recollection. Furthermore he should warn them against emphasizing hairsplitting controversies in their ministries, since these do more harm than good. Positively, in contrast, Timothy should do his best to make sure that when he stood before God he would receive the Lord's approval and not be ashamed. Most important in gaining this goal was the way he would proclaim God's truth. The way a minister of the gospel presents the Word of God was of primary importance to Paul, and it should be to us. On the other hand, Timothy should turn away from meaningless discussions that characterize the world and that foster ungodliness. Paul cited concrete examples of two men whose verbal speculations were derailing other sincere Christians from the track of God's truth (2:17–18).

Faithfulness in personal life (2:19–21). Even though some in the church were upsetting others and being upset themselves, the church itself had stood and would continue to stand firm. In the church there are individuals who honor the Lord as a result of their dedication to follow His truth, but there are also Christians who because of their lack of commitment to God's truth bring dishonor on Him while they seek to be His instruments of service. If someone avoids the defilement of this second group, he can be a member of the first group.

Summary applications (2:22–26). Paul urged Timothy to run away from the attractive desires that appeal especially to the young: the desire to argue, to develop a unique theology, to make a reputation for oneself by being doctrinally innovative, and sexual passions. In contrast, Timothy should pursue the goals of right behavior, faith in God, love for all people, and peace with his other committed believers. Participating in unwise and immature debates only generates arguments that prove divisive and reveal that the participant is ignorant. Such behavior is inappropriate for a servant of the Lord, who must promote peace and unity among believers. He must also gently correct the erring with a view to their restoration to correct doctrine and correct practice. Thus they may escape the devil's trap and be able to do God's will again.

> **Summary:** In this second chapter, Paul compared the believer-minister to seven things: a son (2:1), a soldier (2:3), an athlete (2:5), a farmer (2:6), a laborer (2:15), a vessel (2:21), and a servant (2:24).

IV. DIRECTIONS CONCERNING THE LAST DAYS
(3:1–4:8)

Focusing on the last days in which Timothy and we serve the Lord, Paul outlined some characteristics, prescribed certain conduct, and explained his plans.

A. Characteristics of the Last Days (3:1–13)

Paul instructed Timothy concerning what God had revealed would take place in the last days to help him realize that he faced no unknown situation in Ephesus and to enable him to combat it intelligently.

Evidences of faithlessness (3:1–7). By the "last days" Paul meant the days preceding the Lord's return for His own, the final days of the present age. He offered a list of nineteen specific characteristics of these days (see also Rom. 1:29–31). Teachers manifesting some of the characteristics he just enumerated made a practice of gaining entrance into households in which the wives were spiritually weak. The false teachers captivated such women with their teaching.

Negative and positive illustrations (3:8–13). Paul mentioned the Egyptian magicians who opposed Moses in the plagues (Exod. 7:11; 9:11) to illustrate the fate of these false teachers. Timothy's past character and conduct stood in stark contrast to that of the false teachers. Timothy needed to realize that when a person determines to live a godly life he will suffer persecution The wickedness of evil people and charlatans will increase as time passes.

B. Conduct in the Last Days (3:14–4:5)

Paul identified two of Timothy's duties in the last days to impress him with what was of highest priority.

Adherence to the truth (3:14–17). In his personal life Timothy should continue living as he had rather than turning aside to follow the example of the evil men Paul had just mentioned. Timothy's convictions had grown stronger because Paul's life had backed up the truth that Timothy had learned from him, and they were consistent with the sacred Scriptures he had known all his life. All Scripture is divinely inspired. This fact in itself should be adequate reason for proclaiming it. Scripture is useful, so Timothy should use it in his ministry. It is profitable for teaching (causing others to understand God's truth) and reproof (bringing conviction of error when there has been deviation from the truth). It is helpful for correction (bringing restoration to the truth when there has been error) and training in righteousness (child-training type guidance in the ways of right living that God's truth reveals). Thus in God's Word, God's servants have all that is essential to fulfill their ministry.

Proclamation of the truth (4:1–5). Paul wanted Timothy to proclaim the truth in his public ministry as well as to adhere to it in his personal life. He reminded Timothy that God was watching him, as was Jesus Christ, who will judge all men and reign eventually. So Timothy needed to herald the Word of God (4:2) and faithfully carry out the ministry God had given him (4:5). This was important because in the future people would not tolerate the truth but would listen only to speakers who told them what they wanted to hear, and they would believe myths rather than the truth. So Timothy needed to keep alert by avoiding false teaching.

C. Paul's Role in the Last Days (4:6–8)

Paul believed that he would die very soon. His life was presently being "poured out" as a sacrifice to God like the daily drink offerings in Judaism,

> *Faithfulness in our walk with the Lord and in our service for Him is the most important quality. It enables us to face death courageously.*

and soon there would be nothing left. He was getting ready to depart this earth, as a traveler leaves one country for another. Paul had run in the most noble race of all, namely, the ministry of the gospel. Because he had been faithful, Paul did not dread dying but looked forward to seeing His Lord. On the day of rewards for Christians Paul was confident that the Lord would give him a reward that was proper. Paul spoke of his death in order to further impress on Timothy the importance of remaining faithful to the Lord.

V. CONCLUDING PERSONAL INSTRUCTIONS AND INFORMATION (4:9–22)

Paul concluded his last inspired epistle by giving Timothy personal instructions and information to enable him to carry out the apostle's last wishes.

A. Fellow Workers and an Opponent (4:9–15)

Paul urged Timothy to join him in Rome soon because he did not expect to live much longer. Demas, Paul's fellow worker, had succumbed to the allurements of the world. Crescens had left Paul and had gone to Galatia and Titus had gone to Dalmatia. Luke was Paul's only companion. Timothy was to pick up Mark (Acts 15:36–40) and bring him with him because Paul believed Mark could be useful to him. Tychicus had gone to Ephesus. Timothy should also bring Paul a certain cloak, perhaps for his comfort as colder weather set in, certain unidentified books, and especially "the parchments," copies of Scripture. Timothy should also beware of Alexander, an enemy of the gospel.

B. Paul's Preliminary Hearing in Court (4:16–18)

It was customary under Roman law for accused prisoners to have a preliminary hearing before their trial. At this hearing, witnesses could speak on behalf of the accused. In Paul's case no one had come to his defense. Paul hoped the Lord would not hold their failure against them. The Lord, however, had not abandoned His faithful servant on that occasion but had strengthened Paul. Evidently Paul was able to give a word of witness at his hearing that furthered his mission to the Gentiles. He had so far escaped death, though he was ready to die and knew he would die a martyr's death (4:6–8), but he saw death as God's vehicle to deliver him from an evil deed (his execution) and to bring him into his Lord's presence. For this prospect he glorified God.

C. Additional Greetings and Instructions (4:19–21)

Paul sent greetings to his old friends and news of other associates to Timothy. Winter severely restricted travel in some parts of the Roman world. Timothy needed to leave Ephesus soon so he could reach Rome without undue difficulty. Paul relayed the greetings of four others, probably local, whom Timothy evidently knew, as well as the greetings of all the local Christians.

D. Benediction (4:22)

In conclusion Paul wished the Lord's ministry of grace on Timothy's spirit (to encourage him to remain faithful) and on all the readers of this epistle.

TITUS
Effective Church Organization

DATE

Paul probably wrote Titus after he wrote 1 Timothy (see Titus 3:12; 1 Tim. 3:14) and before he wrote 2 Timothy, his last inspired epistle. When Paul wrote 2 Timothy, Titus was with him (2 Tim. 4:10, Dalmatia being another name for Illyricum). A date between A.D. 62 and 66 seems a safe estimate for the time of its composition.

AUDIENCE

Paul visited Crete more than once. It seems unlikely that he would have had time to plant a church in Crete on his way to Rome as a prisoner (Acts 27:7–13, 21). Or one may have already been in existence then (2:11). Probably Paul returned to Crete following his release from his first Roman imprisonment. In any case, he had been there and had instructed Titus to remain there when he departed (Titus 1:5). The Cretans had a reputation for being idle and corrupt (1:12). These traits apparently characterized some of the believers as well as the false teachers (3:14). Part of Titus's task consisted of motivating them to change.

PURPOSE

Paul left Titus in Crete to set the church there in order (1:5). The churches on the island of Crete were unorganized, though there seem to have been Christians in several of its cities. Titus's task included dealing with false teachers (1:10–11).

THEOLOGICAL EMPHASES

This epistle, like 1 and 2 Timothy, deals primarily with local-church ministry. This one deals particularly with the order of the local church. In no other of his letters was Paul more forceful in urging pure morality in view of correct doctrine than in this one. The dominant theme is exemplary Christian behavior for the sake of outsiders (2:5, 7, 8, 10, 11; 3:1, 8).

CHARACTERISTICS

Paul had worked closely with Titus, a Gentile, for many years in his pioneer missionary enterprise. This epistle bears the marks of respect, admiration, and confidence for its recipient. Apparently Titus did not have some of the personal needs that characterized Timothy, so Paul's counsel for setting the Cretan church in order is more straightforward and less emotional and personal than we find in 1 and 2 Timothy.

OUTLINE

   I. Salutation (1:1–4)

  II. Instructions for Setting the Church in Order (1:5–3:11)

     A. The Appointment of Elders (1:5–9)

     B. The Correction of False Teachers (1:10–16)

     C. The Conduct of the Saints (2:1–3:11)

  III. Conclusion (3:12–15)

I. SALUTATION (1:1–4)

As usual, Paul began this letter with comments that not only introduced himself and greeted his reader but also introduced ideas that he proceeded to develop. The emphasis in this section is on Paul's duty and the nature of his message rather than his authority. This salutation is remarkably long and heavy for such a short epistle.[1] This fact reflects the seriousness of the matters that Paul addressed in this letter.

The writer introduced himself as a bond-servant of God and an apostle of Jesus Christ, and he explained the ministries each of these titles represented.[2] God intended both prongs of Paul's ministry, evangelism and edification, to bring individuals into the fullness of eternal life, a hope our faithful God had promised from eternity past. In recent times, however, God had revealed the gospel to His apostles, and it concerned that hope. Titus, like Timothy, was Paul's "true son" in the faith.

II. INSTRUCTIONS FOR SETTING THE CHURCH IN ORDER (1:5–3:11)

As in 1 Timothy, Paul plunged into the business of his letter immediately since he was writing to a trusted colleague.

A. The Appointment of Elders (1:5–9)

Titus, like Timothy, served as the agent of an apostle with apostolic authority over the other local Christians. The churches in Crete needed organization. Paul prescribed a general organizational structure but left it flexible. He did not dictate the details but left these open for local leaders to determine. Therefore the quality of the church's leaders was very important.

Paul listed seventeen qualifications for an elder here (see 1 Tim. 3:2–7). The first three are social and domestic qualifications (Titus 1:6). The elder must be blameless, a faithful husband, and he must have his children under control, assuming he is married and has children who are still living at home. Paul divided the elder's personal qualifications into two groups: five vices that must not mark him (1:7) and seven virtues that should (1:8–9). Three doctrinal qualifications complete the list (1:9).

> *The most important consideration when examining potential church leaders is the integrity of their character rather than their spiritual gifts.*

B. The Correction of False Teachers (1:10–16)

Paul emphasized the need to guard the church against false teaching. He said the false teachers are rebellious (against God's truth) and empty talkers (their words were only human opinion rather than God's Word), and deceivers. Titus had to shut their mouths because they were causing great upheaval in the church. Their motive, Paul revealed, was money obtained illegitimately. The Cretan poet whom Paul quoted was Epimenides, who lived in the sixth century B.C. A line from one of his writings had received wide acceptance in the Greek world as being true, and Paul agreed. The Cretans generally tended to be liars, beastly, lazy, and gluttonous. These qualities marked the false teachers especially, so he charged Titus to rebuke them sharply. The false teachers' "commands" (1:14) involved abstaining from certain foods (see also Col. 2:20–22; 1 Tim. 4:1–4). Paul reminded his readers that to the pure in heart all things, including foods, are pure, that is, clean (see Mark 7:15, 20). But the impure in heart spread impurity wherever they go through their words and deeds. The divisive and destructive influence of the false teachers betrayed their inner attitude of impurity regarding God's truth. They were really abominable and disobedient to God as well as disapproved by Him.

C. The Conduct of the Saints (2:1–3:11)

The apostle next reminded Titus and the Cretan Christians what constitutes proper behavior for various groups in the church and for all believers so they would have positive direction in contrast to the teaching of the false teachers.

The behavior of various groups in the church (2:1–15). To establish order in the church, Paul gave Titus instructions concerning the behavior of various groups of Christians that was appropriate for them. He stressed the importance of building up the inner life as the best antidote against error.

In contrast to the false teachers, Titus was to teach conduct that was in harmony with sound (healthy) doctrine. Paul wanted Christians to behave consistently with what they profess to believe. Titus was to remind older men to be temperate, dignified, and sensible—all marks of maturity. They should also be godly, and sound in faith, love, and perseverance. Older women (2:3) should avoid malicious gossip and dependence on enslaving substances such as wine, and should teach what is good by deed as well as by word and encourage the younger women to fulfill their responsibilities. The young women (2:4–5) had seven particular responsibilities. Their proper behavior would guard the Word of God from dishonor by those who would otherwise observe inconsistency between the teaching of Scripture and the conduct of these women.[3]

Young men (2:6–8) should be sensible, carry out good deeds, and maintain purity in teaching God's truth and living it out, be dignified, and speak so that others could not legitimately criticize them. Obedience to these particulars would rob the enemies of the church of any legitimate grounds for criticism. Paul gave slaves a general word of instruction, "be subject to their masters in everything" (2:9), and several specific responsibilities: try to please their masters, not talk back to them, not steal from them, and be trustworthy (2:10). Again, the reason for this kind of behavior is that it is in harmony with and therefore adorns the teaching concerning God our Savior.

Paul's full theological reason for requiring the conduct he specified is that it is the proper response to God's grace (2:11–14). God has manifested His grace in Christ and the gospel, resulting in the possibility of salvation for all and the actual salvation of all who believe in Christ. When the Christian appreciates this grace, it teaches him to deny ungodliness (the root problem) and worldly passions (the manifestation of the root problem). These passions are the desires that unbelievers find so appealing but which are not in harmony with God's character and will, though they are typical of worldly people. God's grace instructs us positively to live sensibly, righteously, and godly in this age.

The blessed hope of our great God and Savior Jesus Christ's appearing in glory at the Rapture also motivates the sensitive Christian to honor God by his behavior now. Waiting for Him should be our characteristic attitude; we should always be ready to welcome our returning Lord. Jesus

Christ's intent in providing salvation for us was to buy our freedom from slavery to sin and wickedness and to purify a people for Himself who are eager to do what is right and good (2:14). In conclusion Paul urged Titus to teach what he had just revealed with full authority since it was divine revelation and to let no one intimidate him, because the truth was at stake.

The behavior of all in the church (3:1–11). Paul broadened the focus of his instructions to clarify the responsibilities of all Christians in view of God's grace. We should be subject to governmental rulers and other authorities by being obedient to them, and we should be ready to do whatever is good. We should slander no one and should be peaceable, gentle, and considerate of everyone. Paul encouraged his readers to comply by reminding them of the way they used to be. They had already come a long way. Each characteristic he mentioned in 3:3 contrasts with one he had urged his readers to adopt earlier in this epistle. The Incarnation constitutes the greatest demonstration of God's kindness and love, and it provides the possibility of Christians conducting themselves as we should. God also poured out His enabling Holy Spirit on believers richly. We owe everything to God's grace. The "trustworthy saying" (3:8; see also 1 Tim. 1:15; 3:1; 4:9; 2 Tim. 2:11) Paul referred to is probably what he had just written in Titus 3:4–7. Titus was to speak about these great truths confidently so that those who had trusted God for salvation would practice good works, works that are essentially excellent as well as profitable for everyone on the practical level.

On the other hand, Titus should shun what was worthless and unprofitable (3:9–11), especially those things the false teachers were promoting (1:14). If a false teacher who engendered faction rather than unity by his teaching refused to change his ways after one or two warnings, Titus should have nothing more to do with him (see Matt. 18:15–17). Such a false teacher is not straight in his thinking, he is sinning, and he is self-condemned.

> God's servants should not spend too much time trying to convince false teachers to change their ways. If they do not respond to correction, we should leave them behind and continue to carry out our duties of evangelizing the lost and edifying believers.

III. CONCLUSION (3:12–15)

Paul closed this epistle by sending Titus instructions concerning fellow workers, a final charge, and greetings to enable him to complete his task of setting the church in order.

Paul evidently intended to send either Artemas or Tychicus (2 Tim. 4:12) to take Titus's place in Crete. The apostle wanted Titus to join him for the coming winter in Nicopolis, probably the one in Illyricum that lay on the Adriatic coast of western Greece opposite northern Italy. Zenas and Apollos were apparently in Crete with Titus and planned to leave Crete for other places of ministry. They may have previously carried this letter from Paul to Titus. Paul urged Titus and the Cretan Christians to help these two brothers by ministering to their needs. He thus gave them a concrete opportunity to put good deeds into practice. Paul gave a final encouragement to the Cretans through Titus to be faithful in providing for their own regular financial responsibilities (see 2 Thess. 3:7–12). Paul sent greetings to the faithful in Crete and closed this epistle with a benediction for them.

PHILEMON
Christian Ethics in Action

DATE

Paul wrote Philemon while he was in prison in Rome during his first imprisonment there. Since Paul evidently sent this letter with the Epistle to the Colossians (as comparison of the two documents suggests), he probably wrote them in Rome at the same time (A.D. 60–62). When Paul sent Tychicus with the Epistles to the Ephesians and Colossians, Onesimus probably went with him, accompanying this letter to Philemon, who lived in Colosse.

AUDIENCE

Apparently Philemon was a comparatively wealthy Colossian who owned slaves, as did most of the rich in his day. He evidently came to faith in Christ as a result of Paul's influence (Philem. 19), perhaps when Paul was residing at Ephesus. Paul addressed the epistle to Apphia, Archippus, and the church meeting in Philemon's house, probably to rally the support of other Christians to encourage Philemon to fulfill his Christian responsibility.

PURPOSE

Onesimus was one of Philemon's slaves and was probably a native Phrygian. He ran away from his master and eventually made his way to

Rome, where he could become lost in the crowd. There he came into contact with Paul and became a Christian (Philem. 10). Following his conversion Onesimus became a valuable helper to the apostle (v. 11). Paul desired to keep Onesimus with him but felt a greater responsibility to return the slave to his Christian master (vv. 13–14). Onesimus had to make things right with Philemon whom he had wronged. Paul and Onesimus both knew the danger the slave faced in returning, since slave owners had absolute authority over their slaves and often treated them as property rather than as people. Paul wrote this brief appeal to pacify Philemon and to affect a reconciliation between the slave and his master.

THEOLOGICAL EMPHASIS

This epistle is primarily an illustration of how the great doctrines of Christianity work out in interpersonal relationships in a culture that is hostile to the gospel.

CHARACTERISTICS

This is one of a few inspired epistles that Paul sent to individuals (the others are 1 and 2 Timothy and Titus), and it is the shortest of these. It is a personal appeal from the apostle to his Christian friend designed to motivate him to respond as a true believer. Paul intended that this letter, along with Tychicus's personal entreaty for Onesimus, would secure the slave's forgiveness and acceptance.

OUTLINE

   I. Greeting (vv. 1–3)
  II. Thanksgiving and Prayer for Philemon (vv. 4–7)
 III. Plea for Onesimus (vv. 8–21)
     A. Paul's Appeal (vv. 8–11)
     B. Paul's Motives (vv. 12–16)
     C. Paul's Request (v. 17)
     D. Paul's Offer (vv. 18–20)

E. Paul's Confidence (v. 21)

IV. Concluding Matters (vv. 22–25)

I. GREETING (VV. 1–3)

Paul began this letter by introducing himself and Timothy, by naming the recipients, and by wishing them God's grace and peace. He did so to clarify these essential matters and to set the tone for his following remarks.

Paul described himself simply as a prisoner of Jesus Christ, that is, he was in prison because he served Christ.[1] The mention of Timothy's name implies that he agreed with Paul concerning what follows in the letter. Apphia was evidently a family member, probably Philemon's wife. Paul may have addressed her specifically because normally the wife had day-to-day responsibility for the household slaves. Archippus may have been their son, Philemon's brother, or his friend. He seems to have been old enough to have been responsible for some kind of ministry (see Col. 4:17). Paul also addressed the letter to the other Christians meeting with Philemon's family in their Colossian home (4:17). Paul's benediction is the same as the one in the Colossian epistle (1:2) except that he added the name of the Lord Jesus Christ here, perhaps to remind the recipients of their union in Christ and God's grace to them in Christ.

II. THANKSGIVING AND PRAYER FOR PHILEMON (VV. 4–7)

Paul commended Philemon for the fruit of the Spirit that Philemon permitted the Spirit to manifest in his life, and he prayed that it would continue to abound. This prayer would have encouraged Philemon to respond to the request that follows in a manner consistent with God's will.

Whenever Paul remembered Philemon in prayer he gave thanks for him. The basis of this thanksgiving was Philemon's love and faith for "all the saints" and "the Lord Jesus" respectively (v. 5). Paul prayed that Philemon's sharing with others, which was an outgrowth of his faith, would become even more energetic. The apostle would give him an opportunity to do that shortly. Paul experienced much joy and comfort as he heard of Philemon's love. Philemon had already demonstrated the kind of behavior that Paul was going to call on him to manifest again. Paul's request would test his response, but Paul was confident of Philemon's cooperation. He appealed to him from the same authority level, as a "brother."

III. PLEA FOR ONESIMUS (VV. 8–21)

Paul appealed to Philemon to receive Onesimus back and to forgive him. He did this to enable Onesimus to fulfill his obligations to Philemon and to encourage Philemon to benefit from Onesimus's conversion rather than to be impeded by it.

A. Paul's Appeal (vv. 8–11)

Paul was confident that if he commanded Philemon to do as he requested, Philemon would do it. Nevertheless Paul declined to act on that basis. Rather he appealed on the basis of love, the love of Christ that bound all the parties involved in this situation together. Paul referred to his aged condition to encourage Philemon further to respond positively. He appealed as a father for his son in the faith. His reference to his present imprisonment also would have encouraged Philemon to accede to his appeal.[2]

"Onesimus" means "useful." Paul mentioned his name here (v. 10) for the first time, having prepared Philemon for the unpleasant memories associated with his formerly unfaithful servant. Paul had led Onesimus to Christ while Paul was in confinement. The apostle sweetened the unpleasantness that the mention of Onesimus's name would have produced by making a pun. Mr. "Useful" had been "useless" to Philemon, but now he was living up to his name. He had proved useful to Paul and he could be useful to Philemon.

B. Paul's Motives (vv. 12–16)

Onesimus had so endeared himself to Paul that his departure was an extremely painful prospect for the apostle. Paul could have justified keeping the slave with him, but he felt that Onesimus's obligation to return to his owner was more important. Furthermore Paul did not really have authority over the slave; that rested with his master. If Paul had kept Onesimus with him, Philemon would have felt obligated by his regard for Paul to let his slave stay with the apostle. Paul wanted Philemon to respond to his slave freely.

> The purpose of Christianity is not to help a person escape his past but to face it and to rise above it.

Paul suggested that God may have permitted the events that had taken place to result in greater good (see Rom. 8:28), and he urged Philemon to view them in that light. The master should now regard his slave not as a slave but as a brother in Christ and to treat him lovingly. In Onesimus, Philemon would receive one with whom he could share the fellowship of Christ and one who would render him more conscientious service than he could expect from a non-Christian.

C. Paul's Request (v. 17)

Finally Paul articulated his request, basing it on his relationship with Philemon as a Christian brother, a partner in union with Christ.

D. Paul's Offer (vv. 18–20)

Paul then hastened to remove a possible obstacle. Pilfering was common among slaves. Paul seemed to be unaware of anything specific that Onesimus owed Philemon, but he offered to pay whatever might be owed if such a condition existed. Paul's offer is a beautiful illustration of God's imputing His grace to those who believe (see Rom. 5:13; 2 Cor. 5:21). Paul personally wrote out his guarantee and reminded Philemon of his own debt to the apostle (Philem. 19). Philemon had become a Christian through Paul's ministry either directly or indirectly. By receiving and forgiving Onesimus, Philemon would be repaying Paul and encouraging him.

E. Paul's Confidence (v. 21)

"Obedience" is a strong word to use to describe acquiescence to a request from a friend. Perhaps by using it Paul indirectly reminded Philemon of his apostolic authority. Doing more than Paul requested probably implied Philemon's wholehearted, enthusiastic acceptance of Onesimus as a forgiven slave rather than just compliance with the letter of Paul's request.

IV. CONCLUDING MATTERS (VV. 22–25)

Paul expected release from his house arrest in Rome soon. This happened, but we have no record of whether Paul fulfilled his desire to visit Philemon. The prospect of this visit would have motivated Philemon further to accept Onesimus. Paul believed the prayers of the Christians in Philemon's church could contribute to his being released. Epaphras was an evangelist of the Lycus Valley and a leading man in the church at Colosse (Col. 1:7). He was probably not in prison with Paul (see 1:8; 4:10) since "fellow prisoner" is more likely a figurative expression referring to the Christian's voluntary servitude to the Lord. In Colossians 4:10 and 14 Paul also mentioned his other four companions.

HEBREWS
The Superiority of Christianity

AUTHOR

As early as Origen, the Alexandrian church father who died about A.D. 255, no one knew for sure who wrote the Epistle to Hebrews. The vocabulary and style of the epistle point to a creative theologian who was also an effective expositor of the Greek Scriptures, probably a Hellenistic Jewish Christian. Commentators have made cases for the writer's being Paul, Apollos, Barnabas, Luke, Peter, Jude, Stephen, Silvanus (Silas), Epaphras (Epaphroditus), Philip the Evangelist, Priscilla,[1] Mary the mother of Jesus, Clement of Rome, Aristion, and others, but none of these suggestions has found enthusiastic general reception. The early Christians originally accepted all the New Testament books as inspired by God because they contained apostolic teaching, so the writer was probably either an apostle or a close associate of at least one of the apostles.

In view of Hebrews 13:24 some scholars say the writer was in Italy when he sent this epistle, perhaps in Rome. However, the expression "from Italy" in that verse probably refers to those living outside Italy, such as Priscilla and Aquila, who were Jews forced to leave Rome by Emperor Claudius's edict (Acts 18:2). This expression suggests that the writer was not in Italy when he wrote.

DATE

The reference to Timothy's release from imprisonment (Heb. 13:23) may mean the book was written when Timothy was middle-aged.[2] The imprisonment of Christians seems to have been a well-known fact of life to this writer (10:34; 13:3). This was true after Nero launched an empire-wide persecution of Christians in A.D. 64. Therefore a writing date near A.D. 68–69 seems most probable. This is also confirmed by the fact that the writer referred to the temple in Jerusalem and sacrifices in it as if it were still standing. (It was destroyed in A.D. 70.)

AUDIENCE

The writer said that he and those to whom he wrote had come to faith in Jesus Christ through the preaching of others who had heard Jesus (2:3–4). Apparently those preachers had died since then (13:7). The original readers had been Christians for an extended period of time (5:12). The title "The Epistle to the Hebrews" implies that they were Jewish Christians. This title is ancient and is probably a safe guide to the identity of the first readers.

References in the epistle also suggest that the original readers were mainly Jewish. The writer assumed that they were quite familiar with the institutions of Judaism. The warnings against turning away from Jesus Christ back to the Old Covenant also imply their Jewishness. Other indications are the emphasis on the superior priesthood of Jesus and the many appeals to the authority of the Hebrew Scriptures. In most of the New Testament churches there was a mixture of Jewish and gentile believers. The appeal of this epistle would certainly have been great to Gentiles tempted to return to paganism, as it would have been to Jews facing temptation to return to Judaism. However, the writer's primary concern seems to have been that his Jewish Christian readers were failing to appreciate that Christianity is the divinely revealed successor to Judaism. He did not want them to abandon their confession of Christ and return to Judaism.

The brand of Judaism in view seems to have been Hellenistic rather than Palestinian. The reference to the generosity of the readers and their helping other believers (6:10) also suggests that the original audience did not live in Palestine. The Palestinian churches had a reputation for needing material assistance rather than for giving it to other Christians (see Rom. 15:25–31; 1 Cor. 16:3). Probably the Jews addressed in Hebrews were Jews of the Diaspora. This conclusion has support in the writer's consistent use of the Septuagint, the Greek translation of the Old Testament. Hellenistic Jews used this translation widely, but Palestinian Jews did not use it as much.

Probably the letter originally went to a house church outside Palestine that had a strong Hellenistic Jewish population. This church may have been in or near Galatia in view of conditions that existed there, as reflected in Paul's Epistle to the Galatians, but they may very well have lived in another area. Many scholars believe that the letter went first to a church in or near Rome.

PURPOSE

Many students of the book have observed that Hebrews is more of a sermon in written form than an epistle in the traditional New Testament sense. The writer even described it as a "word of exhortation" (Heb. 13:22). He urged the original readers to persevere in their faith rather than abandoning Christianity and returning to Judaism. A strong note of urgency and pastoral concern permeates the whole letter. This tone comes through especially strongly in the five warning passages and in the encouragements that follow these warnings. The writer sought to establish the superiority of Christianity over all that went before, particularly the Levitical system of worship. His primary evidence of its supremacy was its finality. Coming to Christ means final access to God.

THEOLOGICAL EMPHASES

The primary theological contribution of the letter is its Christology. The person and work of Christ, especially in relation to earlier revelations and servants of God, receive major exposition. Growing out of this is the strong emphasis on Christianity as the final revelation in contrast to Judaism. There is also a heavy emphasis on the importance of persevering in the faith rather than abandoning their profession and returning to their pre-Christian beliefs, worship, and conduct. Discipleship is a prominent theme.

CHARACTERISTICS

As a sermon, Hebrews is full of warning and encouragement based on the exposition of New and Old Testament revelations. Writing as a pastor, the author urged older and evidently tired believers who were thinking of giving up their Christian commitment and he sought to strengthen them in their faith so they would stand firm. He also warned them that they would incur divine judgment if they failed to go on. He based all this on his understanding of Jesus' significance and sacrifice.

OUTLINE

I. The Culminating Revelation of God (chapters 1–2)
- A. The Agent of God's Final Revelation (1:1–4)
- B. The Superiority of God's Son (1:5–14)
- C. The Danger of Negligence: *The First Warning* (2:1–4)
- D. The Humiliation and Glory of God's Son (2:5–9)
- E. The Solidarity with Humanity of God's Son (2:10–18)

II. The High Priestly Character of the Son (3:1–5:10)
- A. The Faithfulness of the Son (3:1–6)
- B. The Danger of Unbelief: *The Second Warning* (3:7–19)
- C. The Possibility of Rest for God's People (4:1–14)
- D. The Compassion of the Son (4:15–5:10)

III. The High Priestly Office of the Son (5:11–10:39)
- A. The Danger of Immaturity: *The Third Warning* (5:11–6:12)
- B. The Basis for Confidence and Steadfastness (6:13–20)
- C. The Son's High Priestly Ministry (7:1–10:18)
- D. The Danger of Willful Sinning: *The Fourth Warning* (10:19–39)

IV. The Proper Response (11:1–12:13)
- A. Perseverance in Faith (chapter 11)
- B. Demonstrating Necessary Endurance (12:1–13)

V. Life in a Hostile World (12:14–13:25)
  A. The Danger of Unresponsiveness: *The Fifth Warning* (12:14–29)
  B. Life within the Church (chapter 13)

I. THE CULMINATING REVELATION OF GOD (CHAPTERS 1 AND 2)

The writer of Hebrews began each major section of his discourse with a brief statement of that section's theme. The first such statement appears in 1:1–4 and introduces the theme of the culminating revelation of God, which continues through 2:18.

A. The Agent of God's Final Revelation (1:1–4)

These verses contrast God's old revelation with the new, specifically by presenting God's Son as superior to all other previous modes of revelation.

God gave many revelations of Himself to Old Testament believers, "forefathers" being a shortened way of referring to them. He did so in many periods of history by various means (visions, dreams, and face-to-face communication) and in various ways (supernatural events and natural phenomena such as storms, plagues, and other historical events). God's most recent revelation had come through His own Son, Jesus Christ. Seven facts stress the Son's unique greatness and the culminating character of His revelation (1:2b–3). Each one of these seven actions points to the full deity of Christ. The original Jewish audience, faced with the temptation to abandon discipleship of Jesus for return to Judaism, received a strong reminder of His deity at the very outset of this epistle. These seven facts also clearly reveal the Son's superiority to any other of God's messengers, even the angels (1:4).[3]

B. The Superiority of God's Son (1:5–14)

The writer proceeded to explain the exaltation of Jesus Christ to help his readers appreciate the fact that He fulfilled Old Testament prophecy concerning the Son of David. He did this so they would appreciate Jesus properly and not overemphasize the importance of angels.

The writer cited seven Old Testament passages to prove Jesus' superiority over the angels. Probably he used seven facts in 1:2b–3 and seven passages in 1:5–13 to impress completeness on his original Jewish readers. The writer's contrast of Jesus Christ's authority and name with those of the angels suggests that his original readers probably regarded the angels too highly. This was true of certain first-century sects within Judaism, but all the Jews regarded angels highly because God had given the Mosaic Law to them through angelic mediation.

What the writer said about angelic mediators applies to anyone who claims to mediate knowledge concerning God and the afterlife to humankind. It also applies to people who claim to reveal how human beings can find God and secure His acceptance while denying biblical revelation on these subjects.

David referred to Jesus Christ as God's Son in Psalm 2:7, the verse the writer quoted first (Heb. 1:5). The second quotation, from 2 Samuel 7:14 or 1 Chronicles 17:13, ties in with the Davidic Covenant and advances the previous point. Not only is Jesus the Son of God; He is also the promised son of David (see Luke 1:32–33, 68–69; Rom. 1:3). We can see the superiority of the Son also in the third quotation from the Septuagint of Deuteronomy 32:43 in that the angels worship Him as God. Instead of being sovereigns, the angels are servants.

The fourth quotation is from Psalm 104:4. By contrast, the Son's ministry is to rule. His throne is eternal, not created, and immutable. The fifth quotation, from Psalm 45:6–7, describes the final triumph of David's Son, the Messiah, who is God. Psalm 102:25–27, the sixth quotation, also referred to Messiah: The Son is Creator. The seventh quotation in this series is from Psalm 110:1. Angels stand and serve, but the Son sits and rules. The vindication predicted here will take place when Jesus Christ returns at His second coming and at the various judgments of God's enemies that will follow that return.

A primary purpose and ministry of the angels is to assist human beings in reaching their final deliverance over their spiritual enemies, including bringing us to conversion. It also involves protecting and strengthening us so we may one day obtain our full inheritance with Christ in glory. This ministry of service is obviously inferior to Jesus Christ's ministry of ruling. Thus this section closes with a positive encouragement for the readers.

The Son's Superiority to the Angels in Hebrews 1:5–13

1. He is the Son of God (1:5a).
2. He is the promised son of David (1:5b).
3. He is the Sovereign whom angels worship as God (1:6).
4. His ministry is not that of a temporary servant like the angels (1:7).
5. His ministry is that of the eternal Ruler (1:8–9).
6. He is the immutable Creator (1:10–12).
7. He is the Sovereign who will rule as Victor over all His enemies (1:13).

C. The Danger of Negligence: The First Warning (2:1–4)

Having just encouraged his readers with a reminder of God's help for the faithful (1:14), the writer next urged them to be faithful. He warned them of the possibility of retrogressing spiritually and thus losing part of their future spiritual inheritance.

Since Jesus Christ is greater than the angels, we should take the revelation that has come through Him very seriously. If the Israelites received severe punishment whenever they disobeyed the Law that God gave them through angels, the punishment for disregarding what God has given us through His Son will be even more severe. The writer pictured his readers moored at a dock or anchored. If they continued to neglect their attachment to the truth that does not change, the currents of their age might carry them away from it. This is a warning against apostatizing. Bible students differ on the meaning of apostasy but one possible view is that it refers to believers departing from truth they once held.

Under the Old Covenant the connection between sin and punishment was clear and direct. Even more so, the readers could count on the New

Covenant, which had come not through angels but through God's Son, to involve punishment for sinners. Since the writer said, "How shall *we* escape?" it seems clear that genuine Christians are in view in this warning.[4] God testified to His approval of Christ's preaching and the apostles' preaching about Christ by providing authenticating miracles that showed God was with them (see, for example, Acts 2:43; 4:30; 2 Cor. 12:12). These miracles should have bolstered the readers' confidence in the gospel they had received.

D. The Humiliation and Glory of God's Son (2:5–9)

The writer returned to his main argument to develop the destiny of Jesus Christ more fully so his readers would strengthen their commitment to continue following Him. Verses 5–18 present eight reasons for the incarnation of the Son: to fulfill God's purpose for humanity, to taste death for all, to bring many sons to glory, to destroy the devil, to deliver those in bondage, to become a priest for people, to make propitiation for sins, and to provide help for those tested.

The angels administer the present world, but the Son will administer the world to come. The time when all things now under His authority will acknowledge that authority awaits His return to earth at His second advent and the judgments that will follow His coming. Even though believers do not yet see Jesus glorified on earth, we do see Him with the eye of faith glorified in heaven and crowned with glory and honor because He endured death for every person.

E. The Solidarity with Humanity of God's Son (2:10–18)

To heighten his readers' appreciation for Jesus Christ and for their own future with Him, the writer emphasized the future glory the Son will experience. Hopefully this would encourage them to continue to live by faith rather than depart from God's will.

God perfected Jesus by charting His path to glory through suffering, and He does the same for Jesus' followers. By having experienced suffering, Jesus can more perfectly help those of us who are suffering. Jesus will not feel ashamed to call sanctified believers His brothers when He returns and leads us to glory. Jesus Christ broke Satan's power over believers by His death. A believer need not have the same fear of death as an unbeliever. So we need not feel compelled to live for the present as unbelievers do.

Jesus Christ does not give help to angels in the same way He helps Christians. He helps us uniquely as an elder brother and parent (2:11–16). His identification with us makes possible His ministry as High Priest in which He is merciful to us and faithful to God. The basis for this ministry was His making satisfaction for sin by His self-sacrifice. As our priest, Jesus Christ can help us because He has undergone the same trials we experience (in body, mind, emotions) and has emerged victorious.

Summary: The emphasis in this section (2:5–18) is on Jesus Christ's present ministry, whereas that of the first section (1:5–14) is on His future reign. In both sections, however, the writer looks forward to the time when all things will be subject to Him.

II. THE HIGH PRIESTLY CHARACTER OF THE SON (3:1–5:10)

The writer took up the terms "merciful" and "faithful" from 2:17 and proceeded to expound them in reverse order. He spoke of the faithfulness of Jesus (3:1–6, exposition) and the need for his hearers to remain faithful as well (3:7–4:14, exhortation). He then reminded his audience of Jesus' compassion as a merciful High Priest in the service of God (4:15–5:10).

A. The Faithfulness of the Son (3:1–6)

Now the writer turned to Moses, whom the Jews regarded as the greatest of men. He accepted Moses' greatness but showed that as great as he was, Jesus was far greater.

Jesus Christ is now faithful as Moses was in the past. Whereas Moses served faithfully in the system of worship the tabernacle represented, Jesus

Christ designed that system of worship. Moses functioned as a servant preparing something that would serve as a model for a later time. Jesus Christ will not serve; He will reign. He is God's Son, not His servant. As such, He sits. He does not stand like a servant. He is the Possessor of all things, not one who makes preparation for things, as Moses did. God's house presently consists of people, not boards, bars, and curtains.

The readers should follow the example of faithfulness to God that Moses and Jesus set or they could lose their privilege as priests, as the whole nation of Israelites did (Exod. 32). By contrasting Jesus and Moses the writer helped his Jewish readers appreciate Jesus' superiority over Moses. This would discourage them from departing from Christianity and returning to Judaism.

B. The Danger of Unbelief: The Second Warning (3:7–19)

The writer next reminded his readers of the fate of the Israelites when they failed to continue believing God at Kadesh Barnea (Num. 13). His purpose was to help them realize the serious consequences of that behavior and to motivate them to persevere faithfully in the apostles' teaching.

"Today" stresses the urgency of immediate action. The readers were not to become discontented because of their suffering and were not to let discontentment give way to open rebellion, or they, like their forefathers, would lose some of their privileges as believers. He warned against departing from a living, dynamic person, not from some dead doctrine. To reject God's highest revelation is to depart from God, no matter how many preliminary revelations one retains. The writer counseled his readers to encourage each other to avoid the rationalizing that we can get into when we do not confess and forsake our sins. This is especially important since we can become partners with the Messiah by persevering. We see the opposite in Israel's unbelief at Kadesh.

Hebrews 3:16–19 constitute an exposition of the passage just quoted (3:15). The Israelites who died in the wilderness failed to enter into the blessing that could have been theirs because they refused to believe that God would defeat their enemies and bring them into rest. If we fail to believe that Jesus has defeated and will defeat our enemies (1:13–14), we, too, will fail to enter into the blessing that can be ours.

C. The Possibility of Rest for God's People (4:1–14)

In these verses the writer returned again from exhortation to exposition and posed the alternatives of rest and peril that confront Christians, the new people of God.

The writer of Hebrews used the term "rest" as Moses did, as an equivalent to entering into all the inheritance God promised His people. For the Christian this inheritance is everything that God desires to bestow on us when we see Him. None of the original readers had failed to enter their rest (inheritance) because they had missed the Lord's return. However, they might fail to enter their rest (lose part of their inheritance) if they apostatized. As it is possible to receive a greater or a lesser inheritance, it is also possible to enter into more or less rest. These terms refer to blessings that God's people can anticipate in the next stage of their lives. The good news of our inheritance and rest may not profit us if we fail to trust God but turn from Him in unbelief. Christians will receive blessings, even if we fail to obey Him, because we are God's children whom He has saved and keeps by His grace (see Eph. 1:3–14; 1 Pet. 1:3–9). Nevertheless we will not enter into *full* rest or experience *all* we could inherit in the future if we depart from God. It is impossible to enter this rest without faith. Even though God had planned rest for His people when He created the world, His purpose and provision did not guarantee that His people would experience it. This depended also on their faith.

Rest always follows work (Heb. 4:4). The work God called the Israelites in the wilderness to do was trusting and obeying Him. This would have resulted in rest from wandering in the wilderness, rest in the land, if they had continued to trust Him and obey Him. The work He calls us to do is also continuing to trust and obey Him. If we do this, we can look forward to receiving our full inheritance (rest), but if we turn from God we cannot. Every generation of believers needs to continue to trust and obey to enter into our rest (inheritance). The Sabbath rest in view is the rest (inheritance) that every generation of believers and every individual believer enters into when they, like God, faithfully finish their work. That work involves continuing to trust and obey God, namely, walking by faith daily rather than turning from Him. Christians will enter into their rest when they receive their inheritance from Jesus Christ at His judgment seat (2 Cor. 5:10). They will then see what they now only hope for. In the meantime they need to follow Jesus' and Moses' examples of faithfulness to God, continuing to trust and obey rather than turning from Him.

In view of the deceitfulness of sin (Heb. 3:13), we need an objective aid that will point out when we begin to depart from God. The Scriptures are such an aid (4:12). God's Word has power to uphold us as well as all other things in the universe (see 1:3). It can reach to the innermost recesses of our being. The other resource we have is our great High Priest (4:14). He has already proved faithful through suffering and is our example.

D. The Compassion of the Son (4:15–5:10)

Having explored the concept of Jesus as a *faithful* High Priest (3:1–4:14), the writer proceeded next to develop the idea that Jesus is a *merciful* High Priest in the service of God (see 2:17). A high priest must be faithful to God and compassionate with people. This section is entirely exposition, except for 4:16, which is an exhortation to pray. Verses 15 and 16 of chapter 4 announce the perspectives the writer then develops in 5:1–10.

Jesus experienced temptation in every area of His life, as we do. Consequently He can sympathize (feel and suffer) with us when we experience temptation to depart from God's will. Jesus understands us, He sympathizes with us, and He overcame temptation Himself. Since we have such a High Priest to intercede for us with God, we can approach God confidently in prayer.

To qualify for the high priesthood in Israel one had to be a man and to stand between God and people as their representative before Him. A priest's services included presenting gifts (offerings) of worship and sacrifices for sin. He also had to be a compassionate person, which grew out of his own consciousness of being a sinner himself. Also a man could attain the high priesthood only by divine appointment.

The same God who appointed Jesus as His Son also appointed Him High Priest at His ascension. But Jesus' priesthood was different from and superior to the Levitical priesthood. Melchizedek had no successors and thus no "order." Jesus is a Priest of this kind. Jesus' offerings to God included His entire passion ministry. God heard and granted Jesus' prayers, the evidence of which is Jesus' resurrection. Jesus' prayers show His ability to sympathize with those whom He represents.[5] Even though Jesus was the Son of God, He gained experiential knowledge of what being a human involves (also see Luke 2:52). He learned obedience in the sense that He learned to obey His Father's will as a human. Jesus Christ is the source (cause) of our inheritance not only because it comes from Him, but also because as our "file Leader" He has blazed a trail through suffering for us (Heb. 2:10). He is also the source of our inheritance because as our High Priest He provides the help we need to live obediently before God.

III. THE HIGH PRIESTLY OFFICE OF THE SON (5:11–10:39)

The transition from exposition (4:15–5:10) to exhortation (5:11–6:20) marks the beginning of a new division in this sermon. A central theme of Hebrews, redemptive sacrifice, comes into prominence in this section of the text.

A. The Danger of Immaturity: The Third Warning (5:11–6:12)

The writer addressed his immature Christian audience and urged them in irony to stop remaining in a state of spiritual infancy. They had evidently turned aside from following the Lord faithfully because of persecution, but they needed to press on to greater maturity. The writer reminded them of what they had experienced and what they possessed through the gospel.

The readers' condition (5:11–14). Evidently the original readers had begun to let their minds wander as they heard the same teaching repeatedly. They had become mentally and spiritually dull and lazy in their hearing.

Every Christian becomes capable of instructing others when he learns the elementary truths of the faith. When we fail to pass on what we know, we begin to lose what we know. Eventually we may need to relearn the most basic teachings of Scripture. When we stop growing, we start shrinking. We do not just stay the same.

A person becomes a mature Christian not only by gaining information, which is foundational, but also by using that information to make decisions in harmony with God's will. The readers were in danger of not comprehending what the writer had to tell them because they had not put what they did understand into practice in their lives. Instead, they were thinking of departing from the truth.

The needed remedy (6:1–3). Since they needed stretching mentally, they should, with the writer, "go on to maturity," not feeling content with their present condition. These believers did not need more knowledge, but they needed to use the knowledge they possessed. The writer proposed that his readers leave elementary teaching concerning the Messiah in the past, and that they abandon confidence in works for salvation and turn to God in faith. They did not need further instruction in the doctrine of spiritual cleansing, the "laying on of hands" in the sacrificial ritual and commissioning for public office, the resurrection of the dead, or eternal judgment. He wanted them to press on to maturity.

The dreadful alternative (6:4–8). To motivate his readers to pursue spiritual growth diligently, the writer pointed out the consequences of not pressing on to maturity. He described genuine believers as having experienced four essential things (6:4–5). Earlier in this letter the writer warned his Christian readers about drifting away from the truth through negligence (2:1–4), and through failing to keep trusting God and walking by faith (3:7–19). Now he referred to this failure as "falling away" (6:6). Christians departed from the faith in the first century (2 Tim. 2:17–18), and they do so today (see 1 Tim. 4:1). If such Christians persist in their sinful ways, it is impossible to restore such people to repentance.[6] This inability to repent is the result of sin's hardening effect, about which the writer had sounded a warning earlier (Heb. 3:13), and divine judgment (see Exod. 9:12; 10:20, 27; Rom. 1). Even God cannot renew these sinful believers to repentance because He has chosen not to do so. God allows this hard condition because by their repudiating Jesus Christ they dishonor Him. The people in view crucify Him in the sense of passing judgment against Him again, by renouncing Him and His work, as did those who actually crucified Jesus.

In the illustration in Hebrews 6:7–8, the ground represents believers who drink in the water of God's Word and bear fruit as a result. This kind of response leads to God's bestowing a blessing on them who by their fruit-bearing have been a blessing to others. If no good fruit results, however, God will bring judgment on this ground rather than blessing it (see John 15:2, 6). It is "in danger of being cursed," but is not cursed as unbelievers are. This is evidently a judgment God allows on a believer because of his continual refusal to deal with sin in his life (see Isa. 9:18–19; 10:17; John 15:6; Heb. 10:17).

The encouraging prospect (6:9–12). Even though the danger his readers faced was great, the writer believed they could avoid it, so he concluded this warning, as he did the ones in 2:1–4 and 3:1–4:16, with a word of hope to encourage his audience. He obviously expected that his readers would persevere to the end, enter into rest, and obtain many divine blessings (6:10–12). God had taken note of their commendable Christian conduct and would justly reward them for it. Therefore they should persevere in it and not turn aside from it (apostatize). Earlier the writer described his readers as being slow to learn (literally, lazy, 5:11). Now he urged them to be diligent and to stop being lazy (6:12). They needed to remain faithful to God while waiting patiently for Him to fulfill His promises to them regarding their future inheritance.

B. The Basis for Confidence and Steadfastness (6:13–20)

Again the change in approach, this time from exhortation to exposition, signals a new literary unit within the epistle. Here the writer expounded the reliability of God's promise to Christians through Jesus Christ's High Priestly ministry.

The writer offered Abraham as an encouraging and supreme example of one who was strong in faith and patience; he persevered in the face of temptation to stop believing God. The writer was calling his readers to do, in one sense, what God called Abraham to do when He instructed him to go to Mount Moriah. They too needed to continue to trust and obey as they had done in the past, even though it looked as if persever-ance would result in tragedy. God's swearing by Himself signifies that He binds His word to His character (6:13). God gave Abraham double assur-ance that He would indeed deliver what He had promised. In our times of temptation to apostatize, we can flee to the promises of God and take hold of them. When Jesus Christ entered heaven at His ascension, He took our hope of future reward with Him. Our hope of future reward for faithfulness should keep us from drifting away from God (2:1).

C. The Son's High Priestly Ministry (7:1–10:18)

When Christians are tempted to turn from their profession of faith, our great resource is our High Priest, Jesus Christ. The writer therefore wrote a lengthy section expounding His high priesthood.

The person of our High Priest (chapter 7). It would have been axiom-atic for first-century Jews that there was no priesthood other than the Aaronic priesthood, but the writer now showed that the Law itself proves that there is a higher priesthood than that.

Understanding the significance of Melchizedek is foundational to ap-preciating Jesus Christ's High Priestly ministry (7:1–10). Melchizedek was the head of a priestly order. It was not uncommon for one individual to combine the roles of priest and king in antiquity. Aaron was also the head of a priestly order, but he was not a king. Jesus Christ was a member of Melchizedek's order, not Aaron's (6:20). Melchizedek was a prototype of Jesus Christ in two respects. He was both a king and a priest, and what characterized him was righteousness and peace (see Ps. 85:10). The fact that Melchizedek was greater than Abraham is clear from two facts: He blessed Abraham, and Abraham paid tithes to him of all the spoils that he had taken in war (Gen. 14:23–24). Because our knowledge of Melchizedek is limited to what Moses specifically stated in Genesis, no mention is made in Scripture of his parents or children or of his birth or death. In this, too, he represented the eternal Son of God. In the ancient oriental view of things, people regarded a descendant as in one sense participating in the actions of his ancestors (see Gen. 25:23; Mal. 1:2–3; Rom. 9:11–13). Levi had not yet been born, but he was in that sense involved in everything Abraham did.

Having shown the superiority of Melchizedek to Abraham and Levi, the writer then pointed out the superiority of Melchizedek's priesthood and Jesus' priesthood (Heb. 7:11–28) to clarify the inferiority of the Mosaic Covenant and its priesthood. Perfection did not come through the Old Covenant priests but through the Son. Since God promised in Psalm 110:4 that the coming Messiah would be a priest after Melchizedek's order, it is clear that He intended to supersede the Levitical priesthood because it was inadequate. If the Levitical priesthood had been adequate, the Messiah would have functioned as a Levitical priest. The priesthood was such a major part of the whole Mosaic Covenant that this predicted change in the priesthood signaled a change in the whole Old Covenant.

Further confirmation of this change is the prophecy that Messiah would come from the tribe of Judah, not from the priestly tribe of Levi (Gen. 49:10; Isa. 11:1; Mic. 5:2). A third proof that God made a change in the priesthood is that God predicted that Messiah would live forever (Ps. 110:4). This fact shows that Jesus is qualified to be a member of Melchizedek's "order" since the Scriptures gave no record of Melchizedek's death. Jesus is a Priest forever because of His resurrection. God has superseded the Levitical priesthood and the Mosaic Law (Covenant) and has replaced the old system with a system that can do what the old one could not do, namely, bring us into intimate relationship with God. The "better hope" (Heb. 7:19) we have is the assurance that it is now possible for us to experience this relationship, thanks to our great High Priest.

Verses 20–25 of chapter 7 draw out the pastoral implications of this conclusion. Another oath from God (Ps. 110:4) launched Messiah's priesthood. The Levitical priesthood had no such origin, another indication of its inferiority. Because God promised on oath to install Messiah permanently as our Priest, the writer could say that Jesus is the Guarantee of a better covenant. Since the old priesthood was the heart of the Old Covenant and God terminated the Law, a new priesthood must accompany the New Covenant that replaces the Old Covenant. Since the new Priest has come, so must the New Covenant have come (see Luke 22:20).[7] The fact that Christ will not die and will not need to be replaced by another priest means that He can see His work of delivering His people through to the end. Our trials and temptations need not separate us from our inheritance since Jesus Christ can continue to support us by providing mercy and grace (Heb. 4:14–16) all the way to our ultimate reward. In view of His superior ministry, it is only fitting that our High Priest should be a superior person (7:26). Jesus Christ does not need to offer up periodic sacrifices to atone for sin, either for His own sins or for those of His people, as the Aaronic priests did. His one sacrifice of worship and expiation completely satisfied God. No subsequent sacrifices are necessary for that purpose. He will never fail us, and another high priest will never replace Him.

The work of our High Priest (chapters 8–9). The ministry of Jesus Christ as our High Priest involves a particular kind of service that includes a covenant, a sanctuary, and a sacrifice. To help his readers appreciate His adequacy as our High Priest, the writer explained the service that Jesus Christ renders. His discussion of the new sanctuary and the New Covenant in chapter 8 introduces his fuller development of those themes in chapter 9.

The writer again referred to the heavens where God abides and where Jesus Christ now serves in the real tabernacle, the only one that does not imitate something better than itself (8:1–2). In particular, the Most Holy Place is in view. We not only have a High Priest who has taken His seat at God the Father's right hand, but we have One who now ministers as a Priest in the heavenly sanctuary. God had explained to Moses the fact that the tabernacle was a prototype of another temple, the heavenly one (Exod. 25:40). Jesus' priesthood is not an earthly priesthood but one that operates in the realm of heaven. Jesus could have functioned as a priest on earth after the order of Melchizedek, but His real priestly ministry of sacrifice and intercession began when He entered heaven.

The superiority of Jesus' ministry as our High Priest rests also on the superiority of the covenant that forms the basis of that ministry. That covenant in turn rests on superior promises compared with the Mosaic Covenant promises and on a superior Mediator, namely, Jesus Christ, compared with the angels and Moses. As with the priesthood (Heb. 7:11), so it is with the covenant and its promises. Had the first been adequate,

God would not have promised a second. God gave the promise of a New Covenant because the people of Israel had failed Him and because the old Mosaic Covenant did not provide the power to enable them to remain faithful to God. The New Covenant has the power whereby God's people may remain faithful, namely, the presence of God living within the believer. God promised that the New Covenant would enable God's people to do four things: to desire to do God's will (8:10b); to enjoy a privileged, unique relationship with God (8:10c); to know God directly (8:11); and to experience complete forgiveness, not just temporary covering, of their sins (8:12). These are the "better promises" the writer referred to earlier in 8:6. The Mosaic Covenant is now "obsolete" and even as the writer wrote the Book of Hebrews it was also "aging." It virtually disappeared in A.D. 70 when the Romans destroyed the temple, thus removing all Old Covenant ritual and observance.

In 9:1–10 the writer concentrated on the tabernacle and its provisions for cultic worship.[8] He introduced two subjects in the first verse: regulations of divine worship and the earthly sanctuary. He then expounded them in reverse order, as he often did in this homily (see 9:2–5 and 9:6–10). The writer declined to speak of the tabernacle furnishings in more detail (9:5) because his main purpose was to contrast the two rituals and the two covenants. He passed on to the "regulations for worship" (9:1) in the Old Covenant to further show its inferiority (9:6–10). In revealing the limitations of the Levitical system, the Holy Spirit intended to communicate the fact that that system did not provide access for ordinary believers. The Old Covenant system of worship did not meet the deepest need of God's people, namely, intimate personal relationship with God. Its rites and ceremonies extended mainly to external matters until God provided a better system at "the time of the new order" (9:10).

The writer's comparison helps us keep externals in their proper perspective as secondary to inward reality with God. Relationship with God purifies the conscience. It is possible to fulfill all the outward obligations of religion and still have a conscience that is not right with God (9:9). This is one of the tragic inadequacies of religion that does not involve a personal relationship with God.

In 9:11–28 the writer next focused on the issue of sacrifice as a liturgical high priestly act. The lives of innocent animal substitutes were sufficient only to cover sin temporarily. However, the life of Jesus Christ, because He was a perfect human substitute, adequately paid for the redemption of all people forever. Having died "once for all" (7:27; 10:10), Jesus Christ was able to enter God's presence "once for all" (9:12). Old Covenant sacrifices for sin on the Day of Atonement provided only temporary cleansing, but the sacrifice of Jesus Christ provided permanent cleansing. Since we have obtained "eternal redemption" (9:12) through the death of our Mediator and the "eternal Spirit" (9:14), we can have hope in an "eternal inheritance" (9:15). The readers should not feel guilty or disappointed about abstaining from the rituals of the Old Covenant but should appreciate the accomplishments of Jesus Christ's death. They should also turn their attention to obtaining what God had promised them as a future inheritance and should continue to follow the Lord faithfully and patiently in the present (6:12).

In certain respects the covenants God made with humankind are similar to wills (9:16). As is true with all wills, the person who made the will must die before the beneficiaries experience any benefits of the will. The Old Covenant went into effect when the Levitical priests shed the blood of animal substitutes and applied that blood to the covenant beneficiaries. The beneficiaries were the Israelites (Exod. 24:6–8) and the tabernacle (40:9–15). The New Covenant went into effect when Jesus shed His blood and God applied it to its beneficiaries spiritually (see Matt. 26:28). An exception to the need for bloodshed for redemption was God's provision for the poor in Israel. He allowed them to bring a flour offering in place of an animal if they could not afford two doves (Lev. 5:11). But as a principle, God required the shedding of blood for forgiveness under the Mosaic Law. The Israelites saw this most clearly on the Day of Atonement.

The principle expressed is true of the New Covenant as well: Blood is essential for decisive cleansing. Whereas animal blood adequately cleansed the prototype on earth under the Old Covenant, a better sacrifice—Jesus' death—was essential for doing away with sin. Jesus Christ entered the presence of God rather than an earthly tabernacle, He made His offering only once rather than repeatedly, and He put away sins forever rather than covering them only temporarily (9:24–26). Because Jesus Christ died for our sins, we need have no fear of condemnation after death (9:27; see also Rom. 8:1); we can look forward to ultimate deliverance (Heb. 9:28).

The accomplishment of our High Priest (10:1–18). The present section on the superior High Priestly ministry of Christ (7:1–10:18) concludes with an emphasis on the perfecting effect of His sacrifice on New Covenant believers.

The very nature of the Mosaic Law made it impossible to bring believers into intimate relationship with God since it dealt with externals. The Israelites never enjoyed the extent of freedom from sin's guilt that Christians do. The Day of Atonement reminded them yearly that their sins needed covering so they could continue to have fellowship with God. We do not have a yearly reminder since Jesus Christ's sacrifice made us fully acceptable to God.

The writer again clinched his argument by appealing to Scripture. In contrast to some animal that offered its life unthinkingly, Jesus consciously and deliberately offered His life in obedience to God's will. God took away the first Mosaic Covenant and its sacrifices to establish the second New Covenant. Psalm 40 announced the abolition of the old sacrificial system. This was God's will, and it satisfied Him.

The Levitical priests never sat down because they never finished their work, but Jesus Christ sat down beside His Father because His sacrificial work is finished. He now awaits the final destruction of His enemies. The Holy Spirit testified through Jeremiah (Jer. 31:33–34)—and continues to testify, the writer said—that final forgiveness meant the end of sacrifices for sin. God promised this forgiveness in the New Covenant. Therefore no more sacrifices for sin are necessary.

Summary: In Hebrews 7:1–10:18 the writer showed that Jesus is a superior Priest compared with the Levitical priests and that His priesthood supersedes the Levitical priesthood. He also pointed out that Jesus serves under the New Covenant that is superior to the Old Covenant. Furthermore His sacrifice is superior to the animal sacrifices of the Mosaic system. Also Jesus' priesthood brings the believer into full acceptance with God, something the former priesthood could not do. Therefore the readers would be foolish to abandon Christianity and return to Judaism.

D. The Danger of Willful Sinning: The Fourth Warning (10:19–39)

From this point on the writer made application from the great truths concerning Jesus Christ that he had now finished explaining. He followed his exposition of Jesus Christ's superior High Priestly ministry (6:13–10:18) with exhortation, another stern warning against apostatizing, and an encouragement to remain faithful to the Lord (10:19–39). This warning passage is in a sense central to all the hortatory passages in Hebrews. It echoes former warnings (see 2:1–4; 6:4–8; and 10:26–31) and repeats characteristic expressions (see 3:6b and 10:23; and 3:17 and 10:26). Yet it also anticipates what is to come by introducing a triad of Christian virtues, which the writer developed in chapters 11–13. He spoke of faith in 10:22 and developed it in chapter 11, hope in 10:23 and developed it in 12:1–13, and love in 10:24 and developed it in 12:14–13:21.

The threefold admonition (10:19–25). In view of all that Christ has accomplished for us we need to approach God confidently in worship, maintain our Christian confession and hope, and help one another by meeting together regularly for mutual encouragement until the Lord returns. We can have confidence to enter God's presence now and in the future because of what Jesus Christ has done for us (10:22). We should draw near with freedom from guilt and with holy conduct. We should approach God with the assurance that Jesus Christ's death has removed our guilt for sin and has made us acceptable to God. We should exercise faith and also hope (10:23). The admonition to hold fast to our hope is the one the writer emphasized most strongly in this epistle. The third admonition to love (10:24) moves from the vertical to the horizontal dimension of Christian responsibility. The writer was urging mutual accountability since "the Day" that is approaching is the day when we will give an account of ourselves to God.

The warning of judgment (10:26–31). The writer turned from positive admonition to negative warning to highlight the seriousness of departing from the Lord. Willful sin in the context of Hebrews is deliberate apostasy, turning away from God (see 2:1; 3:12; 6:4–8). If an apostate rejects Jesus Christ's sacrifice, there is nothing else that can protect him from God's judgment (see 6:6) at the judgment seat of Christ. This is the judgment of believers (2 Cor. 5:10), not of unbelievers (Rev. 20:11–15). It will result in loss of reward, not loss of salvation. The fire (judgment) that will test believers will also consume unbelievers. Since an Israelite who spurned the Old Covenant suffered a severe penalty, we will suffer a greater penalty if we spurn the superior New Covenant. Continually living in unconfessed sin involves despising the superior blood of Jesus Christ that "sanctified" the believer. Furthermore the apostate insults the Holy Spirit who graciously brought him to faith in Christ. Willful rebels under the Old Covenant lost only their lives (see Deut. 17:2–7; 13:8), but willful rebels under the New Covenant lose an eternal reward. In Deuteronomy 32, which the writer quoted here twice (Deut. 32:35–36, 40–41), Moses warned the Israelites against apostatizing. That was this writer's point here as well. It is a terrifying prospect for a believer who has renounced his profession of faith to fall under God's hand of chastisement.

> *Continuing to grow in knowledge and application of God's Word is the surest way to protect oneself from degeneration, isolation, and consequent failure in the Christian faith.*

The encouragement to persevere (10:32–39). The writer reminded his readers of their former faithfulness. He did this to encourage them to endure their present and future testings (see 4:12–16; 6:9–20). In the past the original readers had proved faithful in severe trials of their faith. They had stood their ground when others had encouraged them to abandon it, had withstood public shame and persecution for their faith, and had unashamedly supported other believers who had undergone persecution in the same way. They had also been willing to suffer material loss because they looked forward to a better inheritance in the future. Moreover they had done this joyfully, not grudgingly. Now was no time to discard that confidence in a better reward (see 3:6; 4:16; 10:19). They needed to persevere, to "keep on keeping on" in their faith. By doing this they would do God's will and eventually receive what He promised, namely, an eternal reward (see 1:14; 3:14; 9:15).[9]

After all, we will not have long to persevere. The Lord's return is near (Rev. 22:20). In the meantime we need to keep walking by faith. If we do not do so, we will not please God. The writer assumed that his readers, along with himself, would not apostatize.

IV. THE PROPER RESPONSE (11:1–12:13)

In this fourth major section of the epistle the writer concentrated on motivating his readers to persevere in their faith with steadfast endurance, thus continuing the idea that he introduced in 10:35–39. Having mentioned the concepts of endurance and faith in 10:39, the writer again developed them in reverse order. He celebrated the character of faith in chapter 11 and then summoned the readers to endurance in 12:1–13. The first of these sections is exposition and the second is exhortation.

A. Perseverance in Faith (chapter 11)

The writer encouraged his readers in chapter 11 by reminding them of the faithful perseverance of selected Old Testament saints. The section is expository in form but its function is to invite readers to emulate the example of the heroes listed. Classical orators and authors frequently used lists of examples to motivate their hearers and readers to strive for virtue. These lists also appear in extrabiblical Jewish and early Christian literature.

Faith in the pre-Flood era (11:1–7). The writer began by stating three facts about faith. These are general observations on the nature of faith and some of its significant features. He then illustrated God's approval of faith with examples from the time before the Flood.

Essentially faith is confidence that things yet future and unseen will happen as God has revealed they will. This is the basic nature of faith. God has approved such confidence, as is clear from His commendations of Old Testament men and women who walked by faith by believing His word. However, faith is a way of viewing all of life, what lies in the past as well as what is in the future. It involves accepting God's viewpoint as He has revealed it in His Word. This extends to understanding how the universe came into being as well as how it will end.

The readers could identify with Abel because he, too, had a better sacrifice. Those who based their hope of God's acceptance on an inferior sacrifice would experience disappointment, as Cain did. Enoch set an example of walking by faith all his life, an example readers would do well to follow. The Lord may return at any time to take modern Enochs into His presence, just as He took that great saint.

Walking by faith involves not only believing that God exists but also believing that He will reward the faithful (11:6). The original readers faced temptation to abandon that hope, as we do. God will reward those who "earnestly seek Him," not believers who stop seeking Him. In almost all the following exemplars of faith there is a clear and direct relationship between faith and reward.

Noah prepared for things to come. He did not live for the present. By continuing to believe the promises of God even when everyone else disbelieved them, Noah inherited a new world after the Flood. The writer had promised the readers "the world to come" (2:5).

Faith in the patriarchal era (11:8–22). Like Abraham, we should look forward to our inheritance in the coming world and should live as strangers and pilgrims in this world (see 1 Pet. 1:1). The city Abraham looked for was a city God would provide for him. A city with foundations offered a permanent, established home in contrast to the transient existence of a tent encampment. Christians look for such a habitation as well, namely, the New Jerusalem (Rev. 21:1, 9–27). Sarah believed God would fulfill His promise and provide something (a child) totally beyond the realm of natural possibility (Heb. 11:11). God wants us, too, to believe He is capable of such miracles. God rewarded her faith far beyond what she imagined, and He will reward ours in the same way.

Verses 13–16 interrupt the recital of Abraham's acts of faith. The writer now decided to preach a little. He emphasized the eschatological perspective that is the point of this entire unit. These patriarchs all continued to live by faith, and they died believing God would fulfill His promises to them eventually. They looked forward to possessing a land that God promised to give them. They did not turn back to what they had left; they did not apostatize. In the same way we should not abandon our hope. God was not ashamed of them because they were not ashamed to believe Him and to remain faithful to Him. Likewise we will not shame Him if we resist the temptation to turn from Him in shame (2 Tim. 2:12). God prepared a heavenly habitation for them, and He has done so for us (John 14:1–3).

In Hebrews 11:17 the writer began to develop the idea that he expressed in verse 3, that faith should be the way the believer looks at all of life and history. Continuance in faith is the only logical and consistent attitude for a believer. Abraham was willing to continue to trust and obey God because He believed God could raise Isaac from the dead to fulfill His promises of an heir (11:19). Similarly we need to continue to trust and obey God even though He may have to raise us from the dead to fulfill His promises to us. Isaac, Jacob, and Joseph all demonstrated confidence in God's word (11:20–22). They believed He would provide for them what He had promised, and we should do the same.

Faith in the Mosaic era (11:23–31). To the Jews, Moses was the second most important person of faith after Abraham, and the central event in both of their lives, for this writer, involved a journey. Faith confronts hostility in a characteristic way that the writer began to emphasize in verse 23. We see the faith of Moses' parents Amram and Jochebed in their placing God's will above Pharaoh's command. Moses had a true appreciation for the promises of God that led him to choose the reward associated with Israel's promised future over the temporary material wealth he could have enjoyed had he stayed in Egypt (11:26). We should also be willing to suffer temporary disgrace, reproach, and loss as we continue to cast our lot with God's faithful disciples. Moses persevered in spite of the king's wrath, and so should we in spite of the wrath we may experience from ungodly opponents. Furthermore as Moses continued to demonstrate confidence in the blood that God provided, so should we. By doing so, Moses avoided God's judgment, which we, too, can avoid by demonstrating confidence in the Lord.

The people of Israel experienced victory over their enemies as they trusted God, and we can too. At the Red Sea the Israelites willingly went forward at God's command rather than turning back. Trust and obedience resulted in their preservation and eventual entrance into their inheritance. Even though Rahab was a gentile sinner, God spared her when he destroyed all those around her. Likewise God will preserve the faithful, not because they are personally worthy but because of their faith in Him.

Faith in subsequent eras (11:32–40). The Old Testament is full of good examples of persevering, lively faith. The writer selected these few for brief mention along with what such faith accomplished.[10] Each individual the writer mentioned was less than perfect, as is every believer. Yet God approved the faith of each one. Joshua conquered kingdoms. Daniel shut the lions' mouths (Dan. 6:17–22), and Samson (Judg. 14:5–6), David (1 Sam. 17:34–37), and Benaiah (1 Chron. 11:22) defeated lions. Shadrach, Meshach, and Abednego escaped fiery deaths (Dan. 3:23–27). David, Elijah, Elisha, and Jeremiah avoided execution. Women even received back their dead sons because they believed God could and would do what He had promised (1 Kings 17:17–24; 2 Kings 4:17–37).

Faith does not result in deliverance in every case, however. Traditionally Isaiah suffered death at King Manasseh's hand by being sawed in two (Heb. 11:37). Sometimes the faithful person's reward comes on the other side of the grave. Some of the readers then and some believers today might have to endure death. Those who accept death without relinquishing their confidence in the Lord are those the world is not worthy of because they do not turn from following God even under the most severe pressure.

Those faithful believers who died in Old Testament and intertestamental times have not yet entered into their inheritances (11:39). This awaits the future. We will have some part in their reward, at least as Christ's companions who will witness their award ceremony. God intended this wonderful chapter to encourage us to continue to trust and obey Him in the midst of temptations to turn away from following Him faithfully.

B. Demonstrating Necessary Endurance (12:1–13)

The writer followed up his scriptural exposition with another final exhortation (chapters 12–13), a pattern he followed consistently throughout this epistle. He first urged his readers to persevere faithfully so they would not lose any reward in heaven.

The example of Jesus (12:1–3). The "cloud of witnesses" refers to the Old Covenant saints whom the writer just mentioned in chapter 11. They are "witnesses" not in the sense of observing us, but in the sense of their lives bearing witness to their faith in God. We have many good examples of people who faithfully trusted God in the past. In view of this encouragement we should lay aside everything that impedes our running the Christian race successfully. The reason for this self-discipline is so we can keep on running the Christian race effectively. As a runner keeps looking toward his goal, so we should keep looking to Jesus, not primarily to the other witnesses (12:1). He should be our primary model when it comes to persevering. He perfected faith in the sense that He successfully finished His course of living by faith. The joy of the prospect of His reward, namely, His victory over death, glorification, inheritance, and reign, motivated Him too (see 1:9, 13–14; 8:1; 10:12). Meditating on Jesus and the Cross encourages Christians to continue to follow God's will faithfully.

The proper view of trials (12:4–11). The writer put his readers' sufferings in perspective so they might not overestimate the difficulty they faced in remaining faithful to God. The original readers had not yet resisted sin to the extent that their enemies were torturing or killing them for their faith, as had been Jesus' experience. We need to remember, too, that God allows us to experience some opposition to make us stronger in the faith (Deut. 8:5; Prov. 3:11–12; James 1:2–5).[11] Another value of divine discipline is that it prepares us to reign with Christ (see Heb. 2:10). God's discipline assures us that we are His sons. The approved sons in view (12:8) in Hebrews are evidently those who persevere through discipline to the end of their lives, whereas the illegitimate children do not persevere. God disciplines all Christians, but when a believer apostatizes, God may let him go his own way without disciplining him further. God disciplines Christians to prepare us for future service, but when we apostatize He may stop preparing us for future service. This is probably true only in extreme cases of departure from God and His truth (see 6:6). As Christians we need to submit to God's discipline in our lives because it will result in fullness of life and greater holiness and righteousness with peace (12:9–11).

> To help us persevere, it is essential that we view our sufferings as the Lord's discipline rather than as an indication of His displeasure, or worse, His hatred (see Deut. 1:26–27). There is a real as well as a linguistic connection between "discipline" and "discipleship."

The need for greater strength (12:12–13). The writer next urged his readers to take specific action that would enhance their continuance in the faith. The original readers were spiritually weak, so the writer urged them to build up their strength so they could work effectively and walk without stumbling. Power comes as we draw on our resources for strength, namely, the Word of God and the ministry of our great High Priest (4:12–16). The readers also needed to level the path of discipleship they trod by removing impediments to their progress.

V. LIFE IN A HOSTILE WORLD (12:14–13:25)

This final major section of the book apparently grew out of the writer's reflection on the Greek text of Proverbs 4:26–27 (Heb. 12:13). He specified how his readers could "make level paths for your feet." The sections of this final division all contain the themes of pilgrimage and covenant privilege and obligation. As in the first division (1:1–2:18), there is much emphasis on God's speaking and the importance of listening to Him.

A. The Danger of Unresponsiveness: The Fifth Warning (12:14–29)

The writer now turned from the hearers' responsibility as they experienced suffering to the peril of rejecting God, who continues to speak to us through His Son by using the Scriptures.

The goal of peace (12:14–17). These verses summarize what the writer said previously about irrevocable loss through disobedience, unbelief, apostasy, and contempt for New Covenant privileges. The fearful warning about Esau brings these earlier cautions to an awesome head.

We need to live peaceably with everyone as much as we can, because peaceful interpersonal relationships foster godliness (James 3:18). Since we will one day see the Lord, and since no sin can abide in His presence, we must pursue holiness in our lives now. Negatively the writer warned against neglecting God's grace (help). God's grace enables us to persevere (see Heb. 3:12), but here "the grace of God" is almost synonymous with the Christian faith (12:15). This neglect would result in unfaithfulness spreading as a poison among God's people (see Deut. 29:17–18). The writer pictured departure from the truth as a root that produces bitter fruit in the Christian community and eventually results in the spiritual defilement of many other believers.

Esau is a historic example of someone who apostatized (Heb. 12:16). He despised his inheritance and forfeited it to satisfy his immediate desires. That is precisely what the writer in this letter warned his readers not to do. Esau could not regain his inheritance later when he wanted it back. His decision had permanent consequences; he could not reverse what had happened (see 4:1; 6:6).[12]

The superiority of the New Covenant (12:18–24). The writer illustrated the superiority of the New Covenant over the Old Covenant by comparing them to two mountains: Sinai and Zion. Sinai and Zion were metaphors to show the difference in quality between a relationship to God under the Old and New Covenants. The emphasis in this comparison is on the holiness of God and the fearful consequences of incurring His displeasure. The giving of the New Covenant and the things associated with it are more impressive because they are the heavenly realities. These realities include the heavenly city and heavenly beings (angels and glorified believers). Everything about this vision encourages us to come boldly into God's presence (4:16).

Jesus's blood is better than Abel's because it did not cry out for justice and retribution as Abel's did. It satisfied God's demands and secured God's acceptance of New Covenant believers (see 9:12, 26; 10:10, 14, 19). It cried out to God for mercy and pardon for those for whom Jesus shed it.

The consequences of apostasy (12:25–29). The writer shifted again from exposition to exhortation. The present warning came from God in heaven and dealt with failure to continue to cleave to His Son (1:1–2; 2:2–3). God's voice shook the earth at Mount Sinai (Exod. 19:18; Judg. 5:4–5; Pss. 68:8; 77:18; 114:4, 7). It will shake the earth and the heavens in the future and will lead to the creation of new heavens and a new earth that will remain (Ps. 95:9–11; Hag. 2:6; Rev. 21:1). Our kingdom is eternal, our motive should be gratitude, our activity should be the service of God, and our attitude toward Him should be reverence and awe in view of His ability to judge the unfaithful.

B. Life within the Church (chapter 13)

The writer concluded his written sermon with specific exhortations, requests, and greetings to enable his readers to continue to worship God acceptably under the New Covenant (Heb. 12:28). The last chapter has two parts: Verses 1–21 develop the idea of thankfulness expressed in service motivated by the fear of God (which the writer introduced in 12:28), and verses 22–25 constitutes a personal note to the readers that lies quite outside the argument of the homily proper.

Pastoral reminders (13:1–21). This section consists of reminders of what the readers already knew or were doing or what they knew they should avoid.

Verses 1–6 record some instructions regarding morality. When love for Jesus Christ falters, love for the brethren normally flags as well. Hospitality (literally, love of strangers) is a concrete expression of Christian love today, as it was in the first century. Abraham received a special blessing because he showed hospitality, and we may too. The prisoners in view (13:3) were evidently Christians who were suffering for their testimonies (see 10:34). The readers might suffer the same fate themselves one day since they were living in a society hostile to Jesus Christ. Christians also need to maintain a high regard for marriage and to remain sexually pure (13:4). God's judgment will follow the sexually impure (see 12:29). Greed has also lured many believers away from a life of faithful discipleship (13:5). We need to cultivate a spirit of contentment so we do not apostatize. We have the Lord, and with Him we have all we need. Furthermore He will never abandon us (Matt. 28:20).

Hebrews 13:7–19 give instructions regarding religious duties. The example of our spiritual leaders is one we should follow. They, as the heroes of faith in chapter 11, set a good pattern. Jesus Christ is the content of the message that the leaders had preached to these hearers. That message and its hero is what this writer had urged his readers not to abandon. As Jesus is always the same, so the readers needed to remain the same in their commitment to God (13:8).

Believers should reject teaching that deviates from apostolic doctrine (13:9). Rather than accepting these ideas we should receive strength by taking in God's grace that comes through His Word (see 4:12–13), from spiritual rather than material food. Jesus' death on the cross is the source of both the saving and sustaining grace of God by which we experience strengthening. Believers under the Old Covenant ate part of what they offered to God as a peace offering (Lev. 7:15–18), but believers under the New Covenant feed spiritually on Jesus Christ, who is our peace offering. Those still under the Old Covenant had no right to partake of Him for spiritual sustenance and fellowship with God since their confidence was still in the Old Covenant. Far from defiling those who associated with Jesus Christ, who is our sin (purification) offering, association with Him leads to holiness (see Lev. 16:27).

Jesus' death outside Jerusalem fulfilled the Day of Atonement ritual in that the high priest burned the remains of the two sacrificial animals outside the precincts of the wilderness camp. It also fulfilled the ritual of that day in that Jesus' execution outside the city involved the shame of exclusion from the sacred precincts. It symbolized His rejection by the Jewish authorities. Christians bear Jesus' reproach when we identify with Him. This was especially true of the original Jewish recipients of this epistle. The city we seek is the heavenly Jerusalem (Heb. 13:14), for our present habitation on earth is only temporary.

Even though God does not require periodic animal and vegetable sacrifices from us, we should continually offer other sacrifices to Him, including praise, good works, and sharing what we have with others. The leaders in view are church elders (pastors, 13:17). These shepherds will have to give account to God one day for their stewardship over us. We should now make their work easier for them by being obedient and submissive to them.

The writer confessed to needing the prayers of his brothers and sisters in the faith (13:18–19). He faced the same pressure to depart from the Lord that they faced, and he longed to return to them again wherever they may have been living.

Verses 20–21 express the writer's final prayerful wish for his readers. It contains another expression of Jesus' superiority over the Mosaic system. The "eternal covenant" is the enduring New Covenant in contrast to the temporary Old Covenant. Jesus' blood was superior to animal blood offered under the Old Covenant. This pastoral prayer brings the sermon to its conclusion.

Personal explanations (13:22–25). These closing verses of Hebrews are an addendum to the body of the homily. The writer added them because he felt concern for his addressees and wanted to add a few additional personal remarks. He urged his readers again to accept the word of exhortation contained in this brief epistle rather than rejecting it. Evidently the writer and Timothy were close associates in the Lord's work. The term "leaders" refers to local church leaders (13:24, NIV). The letter probably went to one house church and from there was circulated widely. "Those from Italy" probably refers to Christians who had left Italy rather than to believers currently living there (see Acts 18:2). If this is true, the writer probably wrote from somewhere other than Italy.

The writer closed with a final benediction and prayer that God's grace would be with his readers in the sense that they would receive strength from it and so persevere faithfully in the Christian faith.

JAMES
Faith at Work

AUTHOR

The writer of this epistle seems to have been the half brother of the Lord Jesus Christ and the brother of Jude, the writer of the epistle that bears his name. This was the opinion of many of the early church fathers.

DATE

Josephus wrote that James died in A.D. 62. It seems that his epistle was the first New Testament book written and that James composed it in the middle or late 40s, perhaps A.D. 45–48. There is no substantial reason to doubt this traditional early date.

AUDIENCE

The recipients of this letter were Jewish Christians of the Diaspora, that is, Jews who lived outside Palestine and had come to faith in Christ (James 1:1). Several Jewish references in the book support the claim that a Jew wrote it to other Jews (1:18; 2:2, 21; 3:6; 5:4, 7). Exactly where this letter went first is uncertain.

THEOLOGICAL EMPHASES

This epistle is famous not for teaching theology but for urging practical application of it. It is the second least theological book in the New Testament after Philemon. The doctrine of God, the doctrine of sin, and eschatology receive the most attention. The Book of James parallels Jesus' Sermon on the Mount, His great ethical discourse, in a number of ways. James explained truths and exhorted his audience to live out Jesus' ethical teachings. Leading themes include perfection, wisdom, and the piety of the poor.

CHARACTERISTICS

James contains no references to specific individuals who were the original recipients, and there is no concluding benediction. There are many imperatives in the letter, about one for every two verses, as well as many figures of speech and analogies. James also alluded to over twenty Old Testament books and referred to many Old Testament characters, including Abraham, Rahab, Job, and Elijah, plus the Ten Commandments and the Law of Moses. The Book of James has many references to nature and many allusions to Jesus' teaching in the Sermon on the Mount. Like Hebrews, James is very sermonic.

OUTLINE

I. Introduction (1:1)
II. Trials and True Religion (1:2–27)
   A. The Value of Trials (1:2–11)
   B. The Options in Trials (1:12–18)
   C. The Proper Response to Trials (1:19–27)
III. Partiality and Vital Faith (chapter 2)
   A. The Problem of Favoritism (2:1–13)
   B. The Importance of Vital Faith (2:14–26)
IV. Speech and Divine Wisdom (chapter 3)
   A. Controlling the Tongue (3:1–12)
   B. Controlling the Mind (3:13–18)

V. Conflicts and Humble Submission (chapter 4)
   A. Interpersonal and Inner Personal Tensions (4:1–10)
   B. Self-Exaltation (4:11–12)
   C. Self-Reliance (4:13–17)
VI. Money and Patient Endurance (5:1–20)
   A. Warnings for the Rich (5:1–6)
   B. The Proper Attitude (5:7–12)
   C. The Proper Action (5:13–18)
VII. The Way Back to Living by Faith (5:19–20)

I. INTRODUCTION (1:1)

The writer was probably the half brother of Jesus Christ, who evidently became a believer after Jesus' resurrection (see John 7:5; 1 Cor. 15:7). He became the leader of the church in Jerusalem early in its history (Acts 15:13–21; Gal. 2:9). But being a servant of God and the Lord Jesus Christ was his preferred self-description. "The twelve tribes scattered abroad" most naturally refers to Jewish Christians of the Diaspora, those who were living outside Palestine.

II. TRIALS AND TRUE RELIGION (1:2–27)

In each of the five chapters of his book, James dealt with a particular aspect of behavior that Jesus had advocated for His disciples. James then broadened his discussion of that behavior to include underlying problems and solutions. In chapter 1 he dealt with trials and what true religion involves.

A. The Value of Trials (1:2–11)

James began his letter, which is in many ways a sermon reduced to writing, by dealing with the problem of trials that all believers encounter. He pointed out the value of trials to encourage his readers to adopt a positive attitude toward them, to endure them, and to view them as God's tools in their lives.

James urged his readers to view the various kinds of trials and tribulations they were encountering as opportunities for growth, as profitable even though unpleasant (1:2). Trials are the means God uses to make Christians the kind of people who bring honor to His name. The character of God within a Christian becomes apparent through trials. These are the "testing of your faith" (1:3) in the sense that our trust in and obedience to God are stretched to the limit by these trials. We should not try to escape from trials but should submit to the maturing process with patient endurance. God will bring every believer who endures trials, rather than running from them, to relative maturity as we persevere in them. The concept of living by faith that James introduced here for the first time is the theme that unites all the parts of this epistle.

What James just explained is divine wisdom, God's view of life. The writer urged that we ask God to enable us to understand and follow His wisdom (1:5). The Christian who repeatedly asks God to do so can count on God's granting his request repeatedly. He will give this wisdom freely and graciously.[1] If a person is not trusting God, he should not think that God will provide what he has asked. Such a person is "double-minded" (1:8), one who trusts and obeys God part of the time but not consistently, one who has a divided opinion or allegiance.

Now James broadened his readers' perspective and encouraged them to adopt God's viewpoint on all their present circumstances (1:9–11). Materially poor believers should derive joy from thinking about their spiritual riches. Likewise the materially rich should remember that riches are temporary and that one's real condition before God is a very humble one. The rich person may fade quickly, like grass and flowers (see Isa. 40:6–8).[2]

B. The Options in Trials (1:12–18)

In these verses James explained the consequences of obedience and disobedience and the source of temptations so his readers could manage their trials effectively.

In view of how God uses trials in our lives, we should persevere in the will of God joyfully (1:12). The Christian who does not yield to temptations to depart from the will of God demonstrates his love for Him, and he will experience life to its fullest potential in the present and in the future. James did not want us to conclude that because God permits us to experience trials He is the source of temptation (1:13–14). God does not try to get us to sin. The only sense in which God is responsible for sin is that He permits other things to tempt us, namely, the world, the flesh, and the devil (see Job 1–2). Rather than blaming God, we need to recognize that we ourselves are responsible when we yield to temptation. James's vivid illustration of the childbearing process (1:15) graphically describes the cause-and-effect relationship of lust, sin, and death.

There is no variation in God's dealings with His creatures (1:16–18). He always does everything for His own glory and His children's good. The greatest of God's gifts is the gift of new life in Christ. God's initiative provided this gift for us, and His special revelation communicated it to us. James believed that eternal life is a gift of God's grace.[3] God's intention for all people, and believers in particular, is always that they be blessed. Rather than viewing temptations to depart from the will of God as heaven-sent, we must see them as the potential enemies of spiritual growth and prepare to endure them, knowing that the effort will make us better this side of the grave, and it will yield a wonderful reward in heaven.

C. The Proper Response to Trials (1:19–27)

Having explained the value of trials and our options in trials, James next exhorted his readers to respond properly to their trials. The Word of God is the key to resisting temptations and responding to trials correctly (see Matt. 4:1–11).

Some Christians respond to trials by complaining about them and becoming angry over them. But an angry response to temptations does not advance the righteousness in character and conduct that God is seeking to produce in believers. The believer should accept submissively what God has revealed and should respond cooperatively to what He commands. The Word of God will then have good soil in which to grow, and it will yield an abundant harvest of righteousness in the believer.

Whereas James 1:19–21 stresses the importance of listening to the Word, verses 22–25 emphasize the necessity of putting the Word into practice, that is, applying it. Doing the Word of God in this context means persevering in God's will when we experience temptation. The law to which James referred (1:25) is the revelation of God's will contained in Scripture. It is perfect because it is the perfect will of a perfect God, and it is a law of liberty because by obeying it we find true liberty from sin and its consequences.

The Jews who were James's original readers typically regarded personal prayer and fasting, regular attendance at worship services, and the observance of holy days and feasts as signs of true spirituality. But a better test of spirituality is God's control of one's tongue (see 3:1–12). Taking care of orphans and widows is a duty that lies close to the heart of God, and personal moral purity is an excellent external indicator of godliness. James argued for reality. He did not want us to deceive ourselves into thinking that we are spiritual if our obedience to God is only superficial.

> We demonstrate behavior that is genuinely religious when we respond appropriately to temptations to depart from God's will, namely, by enduring them and rejoicing in them because we believe God is using them to perfect us for His glory.

III. PARTIALITY AND VITAL FAITH (CHAPTER 2)

A. The Problem of Favoritism (2:1–13)

James's previous reference to hypocritical religiosity (1:26–27) seems to have led him to deal with one form of this problem that existed among his original readers and it is still with us today. It is the problem of inconsistent love for other people that manifests itself in how we treat them.

Personal favoritism or discrimination is inconsistent for a Christian who worships the glorious Lord Jesus Christ to practice it (see Matt. 22:16). The usher in James's illustration made two errors (James 2:2–4). First, he showed favoritism because of what the rich man might do for the church if he received preferential treatment. He should have treated everyone graciously, as God does. This reflects a double-minded attitude, thinking like the world in this case while thinking as God thinks in other respects (see 1:8). Second, the usher, who represents all believers, manifested evil motives in judging where to seat the two visitors. His motive was what the church could obtain from them rather than what it could impart to them. The Christian and the church should seek primarily to serve others rather than getting others to serve them (see Mark 10:45).

Since God has chosen so many of the poor of this world to receive His blessings, it is inconsistent for Christians to withhold blessings from them (James 2:5–7). When a Christian dishonors the poor, he treats them exactly opposite of the way God treats them. The characteristic response of the rich to Christians had been to oppress them and to speak against them, not to favor them. It is inconsistent to give special honor to those who despise the Lord whom believers love and serve. James did not mean Christians should avoid honoring the rich (2:8–9), but that we should love everyone and treat every individual as we would treat ourselves (see Lev. 19:18; Matt. 7:12). This is a primary law of the royal King under whom Christians live, and it expresses conduct worthy of Him. The type of preferential treatment James dealt with here violates God's Law because it treats some as inferior and others as sources of special favor.

Some readers might feel that preferential treatment was not very important, so the writer pointed out that preferring certain individuals makes one a violator of God's Law (James 2:10–11). We become guilty of all God's commands in the sense that we have violated His Law, not that we have violated every commandment in that Law. All sins *are not* equally serious in that the consequences of some sins are greater than others, but all sins *are* equally serious in that any sin is a violation of God's will.

The Law that gives freedom (see also 1:25) is the Law of God that liberates us now, the Law of Christ (Gal. 6:2). As free as we are under the Law of Christ, we need to remember that God will judge us (Rom. 14:10–13; 1 Cor. 3:12–15; 2 Cor. 5:10). We need to speak and act accordingly, that is, without prejudice toward others. God will not judge us with partiality. He will punish the unmerciful unmercifully (James 2:13). We are in no danger of losing our salvation or even experiencing God's wrath, but we will suffer a loss of reward if we sin by practicing unmerciful favoritism (2 Cor. 5:10; see Matt. 5:7; 6:15; 7:1; 18:23–25). On the other hand, if we are merciful in dealing with others, God will be merciful in dealing with us when we stand before Him (see 25:34–40). Mercy triumphs over judgment, just as love triumphs over partiality.

B. The Importance of Vital Faith (2:14–26)

This section of chapter 2 relates to the preceding one in the same way 1:19–27 relates to 1:2–18. It deals with a larger, more basic issue that connects with and underlies the practical problem just discussed. The larger issue underlying favoritism is the whole matter of faith in God. James wrote this section to challenge his readers to examine the vitality of their faith in God. Were they really putting their faith into practice, applying their beliefs to their behavior?

If a person claims to be a Christian but gives no evidence of true faith by the way he lives, there are two possibilities. He may not be saved, or he may be saved, but he is not *living* by faith, trusting and obeying God day by day. Faith is no substitute for obedience (see 1:21–22). Orthodox faith without good works cannot protect the Christian from sin's deadly consequences in this life (a deadening of fellowship with God at least, and perhaps physical death; 5:20; 1 John 5:16). That faith cannot save him from God's discipline of him as a believer. Good works in addition to faith are necessary for that kind of deliverance.[4]

As he did before (James 2:2–4), James provided a hypothetical, though not uncommon, situation to illustrate his point (2:15–16). The situation he described highlights the absurdity of claiming a vital faith but at the same time not obeying the Word of God (see 1 John 3:17–18). A benediction cannot save a starving man from death; only bread can do that. Then James restated his point (James 2:17): If work (obedience to the Word of God) does not accompany faith, it is "dead," that is, inactive, dormant, useless (see 2:14).[5]

The literary form of the diatribe (see Rom. 9:19–20; 1 Cor. 15:35–36) helps us identify that what follows is James's statement of an objector (James 2:18) and James's response to the objector (2:19–23). The NIV and NKJV have the objector saying only the first part of this verse, "You have faith; I have deeds," and James responding in the last part of the verse. The NASB has the objector saying the whole verse. Which is correct? There were no punctuation marks in the Greek text so we have to determine on the basis of what James wrote. The objector seems to be making a point by way of argument rather than making a simple statement (see 2:19–23).

Therefore I prefer the NASB punctuation of this verse. The objector claims that good works are the necessary sign of saving faith. He says, "You cannot prove you have faith unless you have works, but because I have works you can see that I have faith."

James responded to this objection (2:19–23). The demons believe that what God has revealed about Himself is true, but they continue practicing evil works. They understand what their behavior will bring on them, but rather than turning from their evil ways they only shudder as they anticipate their inevitable judgment. James probably selected the demons as an illustration because they are an extreme and clear example of beings whose belief is correct but whose behavior is not. Similarly some Christians persist in rebelling against God's will even though they know they will someday stand before the judgment seat of Christ (2 Cor. 5:10). James thought his objector's argument was foolish. He still asserted that without good works a person's faith in God is "useless," not nonexistent but useless (ineffectual, literally "without work"; see Matt. 20:3, 6).

James then explained what he meant by "useless" (2:21–23). Verse 21 at first seems to contradict other verses that say God declared Abraham righteous when Abraham believed God's promise (Gen. 15:1–6; Rom. 4:1–5). The solution to the problem lies in the meaning of "considered righteous." This Greek word (*dikaioō*) always means to *declare* someone righteous judicially, not to *make* someone righteous practically. Abraham was *declared* righteous more than once. *God* declared Abraham righteous (Gen. 15:6), but about twenty years later Abraham was declared righteous again (22:9–10, 12, 16–18). This time Abraham's *works* declared him righteous. They gave testimony to his faith. Works do not *always* evidence faith (James 2:20), but sometimes they do, namely, whenever a person who has become a believer by faith continues to live by faith. Abraham is a good example of a believer whose good works (continuing trust and obedience to God) bore witness to his righteousness. Abraham's faith was "made complete" by his works in the sense that his works made his faith stronger. Maturity comes as we persevere in the will of God when we encounter trials (see 1:2–4). Continued obedient faith, not just initial saving faith, is what makes a person God's intimate friend (see John 15:14).

James concluded with a final argument (2:24–26). Works declare us righteous in the sense that our works testify to onlookers that we have exercised saving faith. They are the external fruit that bears witness to the eternal life within. Some unbelievers appear to bear the fruit of saving faith, but God will one day expose their "wheat" as "weeds" (see Matt. 13:30). James selected Rahab as an illustration of a person whose physical life was saved precisely because she had works. Thus with the two examples of Abraham and Rahab, James showed the necessity of works for believers regardless of one's background. Faith without works is as dead as a human body without a human spirit. It is of no practical value. Our faith becomes only dead orthodoxy when we stop obeying God. Vital faith then becomes dead faith.

Summary: Good works are not necessary to keep us from going to hell, but they are necessary to keep us from falling under God's disciplinary punishment that may even result in premature physical death. It is possible for a Christian not to *use* his faith, to stop "*walking* by faith." In such a case, his faith is of no practical use here and now. Here and throughout this epistle James was dealing primarily with sanctification, not justification. This is Christian life teaching, not teaching on how to become a Christian.

IV. SPEECH AND DIVINE WISDOM (CHAPTER 3)

A. Controlling the Tongue (3:1–12)

One of the most important aspects of our works, which James had been discussing, is our words. We conduct much of our work with words. James next gave his readers directions concerning their words to help them understand and apply God's will to this area of their lives. Particularly James addressed the misuse of the tongue in Christian worship.

As in the previous two chapters, James introduced a new subject with a command (see James 1:2; 2:1). Every Christian is responsible to teach others what God has revealed in His Word (Matt. 28:19; Heb. 5:12). However, James was evidently speaking of becoming teachers like the rabbis in his day who were "professional" teachers. The Jews regarded teachers (rabbis) with great awe and gave them much honor in James's day (see Matt. 23:8). In the synagogue services men in the congregation could rise and address the rest of the assembly (Acts 13:15). The Christians carried this opportunity over into the meetings of the early church (1 Cor. 14:26–33). As a result, there were many in James's audience who aspired to teach others publicly in order to gain prestige. James warned that God will judge teachers more strictly than others because they presumably know the truth and claim to live by it.

The reason for the warning is that the person who speaks much will err in his speech much (James 3:2). The tongue is the most difficult member of the body to control. No one has been able to master it yet except Jesus Christ. It is the same with horses as it is with humans (3:3). If we can control a horse's tongue by a bit, we can bring the whole animal under control. The controlled tongue can also overcome great obstacles. Though small, the tongue can affect great change out of all proportion to its size. The tongue has as much destructive power as a spark in a forest. Also the tongue is the gate through which the evil influences of hell can spread like fire to inflame all the areas of life that we touch.

Human beings have brought all the major forms of animal life under control, but apart from the Holy Spirit's help no human being has ever been able to tame his own tongue. It is much more dangerous than any deadly animal because it never rests, and it can destroy people's reputations simply with words. We honor God with our words, but then we turn right around and dishonor other people with what we say. This is inconsistent because people are made in the image of God (Gen. 1:27). This phenomenon is contrary to the will of God, and it is also contrary to the natural order of things (James 3:10). Illustrations highlight this natural inconsistency (see Matt. 7:16). One water source can yield only one kind of water. A tree can only produce fruit of its own kind. A salt spring cannot produce fresh water any more than a fallen human nature can naturally produce pure words.

B. Controlling the Mind (3:13–18)

As in the previous chapters James began his discussion of human speech with a practical exhortation and continued to deal with increasingly basic issues. To enable his readers to understand how to control their tongues, he next spoke of the importance of controlling the mind. Wisdom in the mind affects one's use of his tongue.

The essential qualifications of a teacher (3:1) are wisdom (the ability to view life from God's perspective) and understanding (mental percep-tion and comprehension). Look at a person's behavior if you want to see if he is wise (3:13). The wisdom James had in mind did not result so much in what one thinks or says but in what he does. The only way to control the tongue is to place one's mind deliberately under the authority of God and to let Him control it.

"Bitter envy" and "selfish ambition" are motives that must not inhabit the heart of a teacher or he will find himself saying things he should not. The type of so-called wisdom that springs from envy and ambition does not have its source in the fear of the Lord but in the spirit (philosophy) of this world (see 2:1–7) and in Satan. God is not the God of disorder but of order and peace (1 Cor. 14:33). He opposes every evil thing (1 John 1:5). Therefore ungracious envy and selfish ambition are not part of the wis-dom He provides.

In contrast, the wisdom God gives has several characteristics (James 3:17–18): It is free of the defilements mentioned, and it is peace-loving, peace-practicing, and peace-yielding, considerate of others, open to reason and willing to yield to reasonable requests, actively sympathetic to the needy, full of good works, unwaveringly single-minded in its devotion to God, and true to appearances. People committed to preserving peace must teach the Word of God peacefully to reap a harvest of righteousness.

Our words are very important as we seek to carry out the ministry God has called us to fulfill. We cannot control our tongues easily. Therefore we should not be too quick to take on a teaching minis-try. The only one who can control our tongues is God, who can give us wisdom. The marks of the wisdom He provides are humility, graciousness, and peace.

V. CONFLICTS AND HUMBLE SUBMISSION
(CHAPTER 4)

James gave direction to his readers to encourage and enable them to live at peace with God, others, and themselves. This chapter applies the preceding instruction on eliminating strife and loving peace, not just to would-be teachers, but to all believers.

A. Interpersonal and Inner Personal Tensions (4:1–10)

As in the previous chapters James began this one with a clear introduction of a practical problem his readers faced.

Disputes between individuals and tensions within oneself are the enemies of peace (4:1). The satisfaction of desire, which is what pleasure is, is something people spend vast quantities of time, money, and energy to obtain. Our personal desires are part of our human nature, and we will never escape their pull as long as we live in our present bodies. The ultimate end of lust (desire that a person may or may not satisfy) is murder (4:2). Living to satisfy personal desires has serious ultimate consequences. Fights and arguments follow when we do not obtain our desires. The only way to get satisfaction is to ask God to give it. We do not have what God wants us to have because we do not ask Him for these things. Instead we often ask God for things to enable us to satisfy our own selfish desires.

The real issue is, Whom will I love, God or the world? We cannot be on friendly terms with God if we follow the world's philosophy (see Matt. 6:24). God's people who love the world have committed spiritual adultery against Him, but God jealously longs for their love (James 4:4–5).

God has set a high standard of wholehearted love and devotion for His people, but He gives grace that is greater than His rigorous demand (4:6). In view of God's certain supply of this grace, we need to adopt a definite stance toward the people involved in this conflict. Ten imperatives in verses 7–10 demand decisive action and reflect how seriously James viewed double-mindedness. In concluding this section of direct advice, James sounded the same note with which he began: submission to God in humility, putting Him before self. This always results in God lifting the believer up both immediately and eventually.

B. Self-Exaltation (4:11–12)

Having dealt with the source of interpersonal and inner personal conflicts, James dealt next with a different aspect of the same problem to motivate his readers further to forsake the philosophy of the world that puts self first. Criticizing others is dangerous not only because it is a form of selfishness but also because the critic exalts himself even over God when he criticizes.

The speaking in view is speaking disparagingly of another Christian. To criticize another, one must conclude that he is right and the person he is criticizing is wrong. This is passing judgment. We sin against God's Law when we criticize another believer because God has revealed that we should not speak against, or pass judgment on, our Christian brothers or sisters. We should submit to one another (see Gal. 5:13; Eph. 5:21; Phil. 2:3). James was speaking of judging other people without divine authorization to do so. Obviously God has delegated the responsibility of judging some civil acts to human governments, some church conduct to elders, and the behavior of children to their parents.

C. Self-Reliance (4:13–17)

As in the previous chapters, James began with the exposition of a practical problem and moved on to its larger contextual problem, that is, its context in life. Now he pictured a self-centered person living his life to enable his readers to see the root of this problem clearly.

James confronted his audience as the Old Testament prophets did. The person in James's illustration was probably a traveling Jewish merchant. Jewish merchants were common in the culture of James's day, and undoubtedly some of them were Christian Jews. The man's plans were not wrong in themselves. The problem is what the merchant did *not* consider: his complete dependence on God. He should have made his planning in conscious dependence on God, recognizing His sovereign control over all of life. James rebuked those of his readers who were living with this attitude. In conclusion James reminded his readers to put into practice what they knew. They should avoid presumption and self-confidence, and they should submit themselves humbly to God. Failure to do this is sin.[6]

VI. MONEY AND PATIENT ENDURANCE (5:1–20)

The final practical problem James addressed involves money. He wrote these instructions to apprise his readers of a danger, to inform them of the ramifications of the problem, and to exhort them to deal with the situation appropriately.

A. *Warnings for the Rich (5:1–6)*

In a way characteristic of James's well-balanced style, he opened and closed his exhortations (in 2:1–5:6) with references to the rich. There is also a return in this chapter to encouragement to persevere in the will of God when tempted to depart from it (see 1:2–26).

Rich people are usually happy that they have wealth, but James challenged his rich readers to weep and howl in anguish (5:1). Material misery may be just around the corner. The riches that rot are presumably perishable commodities such as food and drink. Garments were one of the most popular forms of wealth in the biblical world. Gold and silver eventually tarnish. Christians should use money, not hoard it. Therefore the presence of rust or corroded gold in the rich man's treasury will bear witness to his unfaithful stewardship of his wealth. The process that destroys gold and silver is the same process that destroys the people who collect these precious metals. Hoarding wealth is a particularly serious sin for Christians since we are living in the last days, the days immediately preceding the Lord's return (5:3). We should be using our money to get the Lord's work done, not to enable us to live lives of luxury and laziness (see Matt. 6:19–24).

Some of James's readers were evidently getting rich by cheating their hired workers out of their fair wages (James 5:4–6). Cries for justice from these oppressed people had entered the ears of the sovereign, omnipotent God, their Defender. The rich are often self-indulgent. In their greedy acquisitiveness the rich fatten themselves figuratively, and sometimes literally, not realizing that they are just preparing themselves for slaughter (judgment) like so many sacrificial animals.

B. The Proper Attitude (5:7–12)

Essentially the attitude of the rich that James condemned was, Get all you can, as fast as you can, any way you can. In the following verses he counseled a different attitude to urge his readers, rich and poor, to practice patience.

Because of the dangers James just expounded and because the Lord's return is near, believers should adopt a patient attitude of self-restraint, (5:7–9). As Christians we are primarily sowing and cultivating in this life, not mainly reaping rewards. When the Lord returns, we will receive our reward at the judgment seat of Christ. It is easy for us to blame one another for our present discomforts. James forbade this because it involves improper judging (see 4:11–12). The writer pictured Jesus poised at the door of heaven ready to step back onto the stage of human history momentarily. The hope of His imminent return should strongly motivate us to live patiently and sacrificially.

One could use just about any one of the Hebrew prophets as an example of patient endurance in suffering (see 1:4). Job was not always patient, but he did determine to endure whatever might befall him as he waited for God to clear up the mystery of his suffering. Job reaped a great reward at the end of his trial. Swearing is an evidence of impatience (5:12). When we become impatient and lose self-control, we tend to say things better left unspoken. The root problem with the improper behavior that often characterizes the rich, as James saw it, is an attitude of impatience that results from rejecting or forgetting divine revelation concerning the future. Knowledge of the future, as God has revealed it in Scripture, has direct application to everyday living. It should affect the way we think about money, among other things.

C. The Proper Action (5:13–18)

James encouraged his readers to pray as well as to be patient to enable them to overcome the temptation to live only for the present and to stop living by faith. This epistle begins and ends with references to trials and also to prayer as the means for managing trials.

Prayer to God, not profanity, is the proper outlet for feelings of sadness caused by suffering as we patiently endure (5:13). The right way to express joy is by praising God, not swearing. It is not surprising to find that James dealt with physical sickness in this epistle. He referred to the fact that departure from the will of God sets the Christian on a course that, unless corrected, will result in his premature physical death (1:15, 21; 5:20). Physical sickness sometimes results from sinful living. It is that kind of sickness that seems to be in view in verses 14–20.

Times of physical sickness are usually occasions in which it is especially difficult to be patient (like Job). Anointing with oil was the equivalent in James's day of taking medicine. People drank oil and rubbed it on as a medication. The Greek term translated "anoint him with oil" refers to medicinal anointing, not religious ceremonial anointing. In times of sickness, sinning Christians should ask their church elders to visit them, to pray for them, and to facilitate needed medical attention. The fact that the sick person was to summon the elders gives a clue that this person's sickness was related to some spiritual condition (see 5:16). Today a skilled physician normally provides the medical attention. The elders need to deal with the spiritual factors affecting the sick person, if any, since they have a responsibility for the spiritual welfare of the flock.

In this context James had a sickness with spiritual roots in mind. Prayer, not the anointing, leads to the healing of the sick person. The Lord will raise him to health if this is His will (see John 14:13; 1 John 5:14). If the sick person has committed some sin that has resulted in his illness, James added, God will forgive this sin. This happens when the sinner confesses it to God (Matt. 6:12; 1 John 1:9). Both sin and sickness must be dealt with when they are linked. In view of the possibility of physical sickness following sin, believers should confess their sins (against one another) to one another (normally privately). Furthermore they should pray for one another so God may heal them (spiritually and physically). To illustrate the power of prayer, James referred to Elijah's experience (James 5:17–18; see 1 Kings 17:1; 18:1, 41–45). In view of the remarkable answers Elijah received, James reminded his audience that the prophet was an ordinary man.

VII. THE WAY BACK TO LIVING BY FAITH (5:19–20)

James concluded this section and his entire epistle by explaining how a brother who had erred could return to fellowship with God and could resume living by faith. Any believer, not just the elders, can help a brother back into the right way. The repentance of the reclaimed sinning believer results in the forgiveness (covering) of his sins.

Summary: This epistle deals with five practical problems that every believer, immature or mature, encounters as he seeks to live by faith and the issues underlying these problems. As a skillful physician, James identified the problems and uncovered their sources, pointed out complicating factors, and prescribed treatment to overcome them with a view to his readers becoming more spiritually mature.

1 PETER
Living as an Alien

AUTHOR

This epistle claims that the apostle Peter wrote it (1 Pet. 1:1). Since there is only one Peter who was an apostle and only one Peter mentioned in the entire New Testament, we may be confident of the identity of the writer. Also the several parallels between this letter and Peter's sermons recorded in Acts point to Peter as the author. Many early church fathers, including Polycarp, Clement of Rome, and Irenaeus, accepted this epistle as genuine.

DATE

Peter died in the mid-sixties, having spent the last decade of his life in Rome, according to reliable tradition. It seems likely that Peter wrote this epistle from Rome about A.D. 64.

AUDIENCE

Peter sent this letter to believers living in the northern regions of Asia Minor (1:1). The locations of these Christians as well as allusions in the epistle indicate that they were mainly Gentiles but also Jews (see 1:14; 2:10).

PURPOSE

Peter stated his reason for writing, namely, to encourage his readers who were facing persecution for their faith to stand firm (5:12). Evidently persecution was widespread among his readers. This condition prevailed after Nero blamed the Christians for burning Rome in A.D. 64. While persecution seems to have been widespread, it may not have been official yet.

THEOLOGICAL EMPHASES

Theologically this epistle deals with living in the end times. Along with its focus on the future there is much emphasis on grace, holiness (personal, social, and communal), hope, salvation, community, relationship to the world, the Trinity, and especially suffering.

CHARACTERISTICS

First Peter deals with basic Christian teaching in contrast to advanced instruction that assumes mastery of the basics, which is more characteristic of Paul's writings. It is similar to James in that both letters are addressed to Christians who were dispersed in various geographical locations, and are similar in length. James was written to scattered messianic Jews and 1 Peter to scattered gentile Christians. Both of these epistles deal with how to manage trials. The tone of 1 Peter is warm, pastoral, and full of encouragement.

OUTLINE

   I. Introduction (1:1–2)
  II. The Identity of Christians (1:3–2:10)
     A. Our Great Salvation (1:3–12)
     B. Our New Way of Life (1:13–25)
     C. Our Priestly Calling (2:1–10)
 III. The Responsibilities of Christians Individually (2:11–4:11)
     A. Our Mission in the World (2:11–12)
     B. Respect for Others (2:13–3:12)

C. Eventual Vindication (3:13–4:6)

D. The Importance of Mutual Love in End-Times Living (4:7–11)

IV. The Responsibilities of Christians Corporately (4:12–5:11)

A. The Fiery Trial (4:12–19)

B. The Church under Trial (5:1–11)

V. Conclusion (5:12–14)

I. INTRODUCTION (1:1–2)

Peter introduced himself and his original readers, and he wished God's blessing on them. He prepared them for dealing with trials by reminding them of who they were, what they had, and where they should be going. Peter called his readers aliens (NIV, "strangers"). In this letter he emphasized that Christians are really citizens of heaven and our sojourn here on earth is only temporary. The particular group of Christians to whom this epistle went first lived in the northern Roman provinces of Asia Minor (modern western Turkey). The Holy Spirit accomplished election when He separated the elect and set them aside to a special calling. God's purpose in election was that we might obey God the Son and that He might sprinkle (cleanse and appropriate) us with His blood (see Eph. 2:10). Peter prayed for God's fullest outpouring of His favor and help on his suffering readers.

II. THE IDENTITY OF CHRISTIANS (1:3–2:10)

Peter reminded his readers of their identity as Christians to enable them to rejoice in the midst of present suffering. They could do this since they would ultimately experience glorification.

A. Our Great Salvation (1:3–12)

Peter gloried in the hope, joy, and witnesses of our salvation as a means of encouraging readers to rejoice in it.

Peter praised God for giving Christians a living hope that rests on the

> *Wherever we look, whether forward, around us, or backward, we find reasons for rejoicing even as we suffer as Christians.*

resurrection of Jesus Christ (1:3–5). As the Israelites anticipated their inheritance, the Promised Land, so Christians should anticipate ours on the other side of the grave. Ours is not subject to destruction from any source, defilement from without, or decay from within. Not only is God protecting our inheritance; He is also protecting us by His power. The salvation ready to be revealed in the last time is the aspect of salvation that we have yet to enjoy, namely, our glorification.[1] We can rejoice greatly in this hope even though we presently must endure trials (1:6–9; see James 1:2). Trials do to faith what fire does to gold. They purify it and show it to be what it really is (see James 1:3). Our trials thus bring praise, glory, and honor to God. Even though we will experience joy when we see the Lord, we can experience joy now, too, because we have hope (1 Pet. 1:3), faith (1:7), and love (1:8). The glory that people will see when God reveals Jesus Christ infuses our present joy. Ultimately we will obtain the full salvation of our souls, namely, glorification.

The Old Testament prophets had predicted that Jesus Christ's life, as their own lives, would include suffering followed by glory (1:10–12). The experience of Christians follows the same pattern. The prophets were not merely religious geniuses but people through whom God spoke (see also 2 Pet. 1:21). At times they knew they did not fully comprehend what they were communicating. At other times they probably thought they understood but did not completely realize the full significance of what they said. The prophets did understand, however, that God would not fulfill all of their inspired revelations in their own days but He will in the future. Even the angels are waiting to see how and exactly when God will fulfill them. Similarly Christians can rejoice in their sufferings even though they cannot see exactly how or when their present trials will end.

B. Our New Way of Life (1:13–25)

Peter wanted his readers to live joyfully in the midst of sufferings, so he outlined their major responsibilities to God, to other believers, and to the world. He presented the believer's duty to God as consisting of three things: a correct perspective, correct behavior, and a correct attitude.

Having focused their thinking on their hope, Peter encouraged his readers to adopt some positive attitudes (1:13–16). They needed to remember that what God would soon give them as a reward for their faithful commitment was worth any sacrifice (see Rom. 8:18). Negatively they needed to stop letting their sinful passions dominate and control them. Positively they were to emulate their holy God who called them to be holy in all their behavior, including thoughts, words, and deeds. Peter reinforced this imperative with an Old Testament quotation (Lev. 11:44–45).[2]

Since the readers had a special relationship to God by virtue of their calling and new birth, it was urgent that they remember who He was and display the reverence He deserved (1:17–21). It is good for us, too, to maintain respect (fear) for God as our judge since He has this power over us. As the death of the Passover lamb liberated the Israelites from bondage in Egypt, so the death of Jesus Christ frees us from the bondage of sin. In speaking of redemption Peter always emphasized our freedom from a previously sinful lifestyle to live a changed life here and now.

Peter next turned his attention to the believer's duty to other Christians (1:22–25). The purification to which he referred occurs at conversion as a result of believing the gospel (John 13:10). This cleansing makes it possible for us to love other Christians. Now we need to do everything out of love for them. The Word of God is the instrument God uses to produce new birth. The quotation from Isaiah 40:6–8 contrasts the transitory character of nature and the eternality of God's Word (see James 1:10–11).

C. Our Priestly Calling (2:1–10)

Peter next wrote about the believer's life in a world of unbelievers. He used four images to describe the Christian life: taking off habits like garments, growing like babies, being built up like a temple, and serving like priests.

Christians need to take off all kinds of evil conduct like so many soiled garments (2:1–3). All the sins mentioned are incompatible with brotherly love. God's Word is spiritual food that all believers instinctively desire, but they must also cultivate a taste for it. Peter's readers had already tasted

God's goodness in their new birth. The more they fed on the Word, the more they would be satisfied and nourished by it.

Besides being the Source of spiritual sustenance for believers, Jesus Christ is also our foundation (2:4–5). Peter changed his metaphor from growth to building and from an individual to a corporate focus. Unlike a piece of rock Jesus Christ is alive and able to impart strength to those who suffer for His sake. Peter saw the church as a living temple, a structure to which God was adding a "stone" with the conversion of each new believer. The "cornerstone" refers to the main stone on which the building rests (2:6). Each believer rests on Christ as a building rests on its foundation and relates to every other believer as the stones of a building under construction relate to one another. Those who reject Christ as the foundation find Him to be a stone over which they trip and fall, the instrument of their destruction. Those who stumble do so because they do not believe. God has not ordained their disobedience, but He has ordained the penalty of their disobedience.

In clarifying the nature of the church Peter explained the duty of Christians in the world (2:9–10). All the figures of the church that Peter chose here originally referred to Israel. But with Israel's rejection of Christ (2:7), God created a new body of people through whom He now seeks to accomplish the same purposes He sought to achieve through Israel, but by different means. Peter highlighted the differences involved in our high calling by contrasting what his readers were and had before conversion with what they were and had after conversion.

III. THE RESPONSIBILITIES OF CHRISTIANS INDIVIDUALLY (2:11–4:11)

Since Christians have a particular vocation in the world, certain conduct is essential. Peter explained what Christian conduct should be negatively (2:11) and positively (2:12). Then he expounded more specifically what it should be positively (2:13–4:11).

A. Our Mission in the World (2:11–12)

Peter again reminded his readers of their identity so they would respond naturally and appropriately. Aliens have no rights in the land where they live, and strangers are only temporary residents. In view of our status we should refuse the desire to indulge in things that are contrary to God's will for us. When we yield to the desires of the flesh that God's Word condemns, we become double-minded, somewhat spiritually schizophrenic. Peter aptly described this as war in the soul. The antagonists are the lusts or will of the flesh and the will of God. Peace in the inner man is necessary for excellent behavior before others. Christians should give their critics no cause for justifiable slander. If they obeyed, their accusers would have to glorify God by giving a good testimony concerning the lives of the believers when they stood before God.

B. Respect for Others (2:13–3:12)

This section of the letter clarifies what it means to function obediently as God's people in a hostile world. It contains one of the lists of household duties in the New Testament (2:13–3:7; see also Eph. 5:21–6:9; Col. 3:18–4:1). This one begins with instructions regarding the Christian's relationship to the state. Peter was concerned particularly with a believer's duties when the government was hostile to Christianity.

Our relationship as Christians to the state and to state officials is quite clear (Rom. 13:1–7; 1 Tim. 2:1–2; Titus 3:1–2). We are to submit to the authority of government rulers by obeying them (1 Pet. 2:13). We should do this not because these individuals are necessarily worthy of our submission, but because by submitting to them we honor God by obeying His Word. Government has a valid and necessary God-appointed purpose. The presence of political corruption should not blind us to the legitimate role of government that God has ordained. Peter believed that there was a proper place for civil disobedience, however (Acts 4:20; 5:29). True, Christians are free spiritually, but they should not use this freedom to sin (1 Pet. 2:16). They are to respect others and to love other believers (2:17).

Peter then addressed the situation of Christians working under the authority of others (2:18–25). The Greek word translated "slaves" means domestic servants, but in that society those people were slaves in that they had some limitations on their personal freedom. In our culture Peter's directions apply to how we behave in relation to those directly over us in society (such as employers, bosses, supervisors, teachers). Again Peter commanded an attitude of respectful submission (see 2:13). The master's personal character or conduct is not the reason for this behavior. This behavior is what God wills. Peter did not want his readers to rest comfortably if they were suffering for their own mistakes. Nevertheless if they were suffering for their testimony, or without having provoked antagonism by improper behavior, they could be confident because God approved their conduct even if other people did not. Part of the Christian's calling includes suffering. Jesus Christ suffered for His righteous conduct at the hands of sinners, and we, too, can expect that our righteous behavior will draw the same response from the ungodly of our day. Peter concluded his citation of Jesus' example by reminding his readers that they, too, like the sheep Isaiah referred to had once wandered from God. Now they had returned to the Good Shepherd, Jesus Christ, who would guard their souls from hostile adversaries. Their enemies might assail their bodies, but the Lord would preserve their souls.

Next Peter addressed wives (3:1–6). This section, like the preceding one, has three parts: an exhortation to defer (3:1–2), an admonition about pleasing God (3:3–4), and a precedent for the recommended attitude or action (3:5–6). As Christ submitted to God the Father (2:21–24), so wives should defer to their own husbands, especially Christian wives with unbelieving husbands. It is simply God's will. Peter did not promise that unbelieving husbands would inevitably become Christians as a result of the behavior he prescribed. That decision lies with the husband. Nevertheless the wife can have confidence that she has been faithful to God if she relates to her husband submissively. Specifically the wife's behavior rather than her speech may be effective in winning an unsaved husband. Giving attention to her physical appearance should not be a wife's total or primary concern. Peter urged the cultivation of the inner person as well. Sarah is a good example of such a woman. She verbally expressed her submission to her husband in a way that was appropriate in her culture.

In Peter's culture a Christian wife married to a pagan husband was in a more vulnerable position than a Christian husband who was married to a pagan wife. The apostle began his counsel to the husbands, too, with a command to think right, to cultivate understanding (3:7). Physically a wife is usually weaker than her husband. In view of this, husbands need to treat their wives with special consideration. The wife is an heir of God's grace just as much as is the husband. Disobeying the will of God regarding how a man should treat his wife hinders the husband's fellowship with God.

Peter concluded this section of instructions concerning respect for others with a discussion of the importance of loving our enemies (3:8–12). Like Jesus and Paul, Peter urged his readers not to take revenge but to return positive good deeds for evil ones. The ground for the Christian's goodwill to others, even our enemies, is the mercy we receive from God. God blessed us when we were His enemies (Rom. 5:10), and He will greatly bless us in the future if we faithfully do His will. Peter again cited an Old Testament passage that clarified and supported what he said (Ps. 34:12–16). This quotation appropriately summarizes all Peter's instructions concerning proper Christian conduct during persecution (2:11–3:12).

C. Eventual Vindication (3:13–4:6)

In these verses Peter emphasized the inner confidence a Christian can have when experiencing persecution for his faith.

If God will punish those who do evil (3:12), who will harm those who do good (3:13–17)? God will not, and under normal circumstances no other person will either. Nevertheless people are perverse and we do sometimes experience suffering for doing good. In such cases we need to focus on the blessing that will come to us for enduring persecution when we do good, as Isaiah did (Isa. 8:12–13). Rather than being fearful we should commit ourselves afresh to Christ our Lord by purposing to live for Him and be ready to explain to others gently and reverently why we behave as we do. A simple explanation of our good conduct may take the wind out of the sails of our critics. We are much better off than the evildoers who oppress us, since God will judge them.

To strengthen the resolve of believers and to assure them of their ultimate triumph in Christ, Peter reminded them of the consequences of Jesus' response to unjustified persecution (1 Pet. 3:18–22). Whereas the previous example of Jesus (2:21–25) stressed the way He suffered while doing good, this passage emphasizes the theme of Jesus' vindication. Jesus died once for all as a substitute sacrifice to bring sinners to God (3:18). He died in His preresurrection condition (following the Incarnation) and now lives in His postresurrection condition (see 4:6). All who trust in Him share that victory. Jesus proclaimed a message to Noah's unbelieving contemporaries in His spirit (His spiritual state of life before the Incarnation) through Noah. Similarly, Jesus Christ was speaking through Peter's readers to their unbelieving persecutors as they bore witness for Him in a hostile world.

Noah faced the same type of opposition in his day that Peter's original readers did in theirs. God would bring Peter's readers safely through their trials just as He brought Noah safely through his trials into a whole new world. Baptism "saves" (that is, delivers) Christians now much as the water that floated Noah's ark saved him and drowned his unbelieving antagonists. Baptism does not save by cleansing a person from defilement, either physically or spiritually, but it announces publicly that the one baptized has placed his or her faith in Jesus Christ. Baptism now delivers us from the consequences of siding with the world. It is a pledge springing from a good conscience, a conscience that is now right with God.

In water baptism Peter's readers had made a public profession of faith in Christ in their community. This had led to persecution. However, by that act of baptism they had also testified to their ultimate victory over their persecutors. Because they had taken a stand for Jesus Christ, they could be sure He would stand with them. Salvation comes, not by baptism, but by faith in Jesus Christ whose resurrection and ascension testify to God's acceptance of and satisfaction with His sacrifice (1 John 2:2).[3] God has subjected all things, even the powers behind our persecutors, to Jesus Christ because of His death and resurrection (1 Pet. 3:22).

Summary: First Peter 3:18 describes the saving work of Jesus Christ. Verses 19 and 20 refer to His ministry of proclaiming good news to those destined for judgment, which ministry we in our day must continue in faithfully, as Noah did in his day. Verse 21 stresses the importance of confessing Christ publicly in baptism by reminding us of what baptism does and does not do. Verse 22 reminds us of our ultimate vindication and destiny.

Since Jesus Christ has gained the victory, Peter urged his readers to rededicate themselves to God's will (4:1–6). He wanted to strengthen their resolve to continue to persevere.

In view of Christ's example of committing Himself to accomplishing God's will, Christians need to commit themselves to the same purpose. The readers had identified themselves with Christ's suffering and death (in water baptism). They should therefore put sin behind them and live a clean life. They had already spent too much time living for themselves in typically unsaved gentile practices. Some of the persecution Peter's readers were experiencing was due to their unwillingness to continue in their old lifestyle with their unsaved friends. Peter reminded them that God would condemn their unsaved friends' behavior, so they should not return to it. The Judge was already "ready" to judge. Because everyone will give account of his life to God (4:5), Christians preach the gospel to enable people to give that account joyfully rather than sorrowfully. In Peter's day Christians had preached to other Christians who later died. Even though these believers had experienced judgment for their sins by dying physically, they lived on in a new spiritual sphere of life since they were believers.

D. The Importance of Mutual Love in End-Times Living (4:7–11)

To prepare his readers to meet the Lord soon, Peter urged them to make the best use of their time, now that they understood what he had written about suffering.

Like the other apostles, Peter believed the return of Jesus Christ was imminent (see Rom. 13:11; Heb. 9:26; James 5:8; 1 John 2:18). This fact should have made a practical difference in the way his readers lived. They were to remain clearheaded and self-controlled so they could pray properly (see Matt. 26:40–41). In relation to their fellow Christians, Peter considered it most important that his readers keep their brotherly love at full strength (4:8), even covering a multitude of the sins of others committed against themselves rather than taking offense or retaliating. Offering hospitality without complaining is one way to demonstrate love for fellow believers (4:9).

God has given every Christian at least one gift that he can and should share with other believers and so serve them. No Christian can claim that he has nothing to offer the church. Those who can share a word from God should do so, by presenting what they say as God's Word, not just as their opinion or as good advice. Those who can serve by providing some other kind of help should do so, realizing that God has made their service possible. The reason for acknowledging one's words and works as from God is that God then gets the credit.

IV. THE RESPONSIBILITIES OF CHRISTIANS CORPORATELY (4:12–5:11)

Peter now broadened his view to specify what Christians should do collectively in times of persecution.

A. *The Fiery Trial (4:12–19)*

Seeing how sufferings fit into God's larger purposes can encourage us to persevere with the proper attitude.

Some Christians feel surprised when other people misunderstand, dislike, insult, and treat them harshly when they seek to carry out God's will. This reaction, however, is not a strange thing; it is normal Christian experience (4:12–14). We can rejoice in these sufferings because when we experience them we share in Christ's sufferings. We experience what He did during His time on earth as He continued being faithful to God's will. God will glorify us just as He will glorify Jesus, so we can rejoice now at that prospect. The indwelling Holy Spirit is already part of our glorification, the firstfruits of our inheritance.

However, we should not take comfort in suffering that we bring on ourselves for sinning. Our suffering should result from our taking a stand with Jesus Christ (4:15–19). Our judgment by unbelievers now is lighter than their judgment by God will be later. It is with difficulty that righteous people pass through this phase of our existence into the next phase because this phase involves suffering for us. Yet it will be even more difficult for godless people to pass from this phase of their lives to the next because they will have to undergo God's judgment. In view of these reasons, we should respond to suffering by entrusting ourselves to the God who created us.

> God allows us to suffer to demonstrate our character (4:12). Those who identify with Jesus Christ will share in the sufferings of our Savior (4:13). In our sufferings God blesses us (4:14). In addition, our suffering will glorify God (4:16).

B. The Church under Trial (5:1–11)

Peter concluded the body of his epistle and this section on encouragement in suffering with specific commands so his readers would understand how to live while suffering for Christ.

Elders are to take care of those under their charge as a good shepherd cares for his sheep. Three contrasts clarify the proper motivation and manner of an elder's ministry: willingly as opposed to grudgingly, zealously and enthusiastically as opposed to selfishly, and by giving an example of godly living that others can follow rather than by driving people forward with authoritarian commands. The Chief Shepherd longs to find his fellow elders faithful when He returns at the Rapture. The crown of glory that does not fade probably refers to glory as a crown that will come to every faithful Christian when Christ returns.

The younger people in the church were and are to take a position under the authority of the older people (5:5). And all Christians, regardless of their age, should put on humility as a garment.

God's almighty hand had permitted affliction to touch Peter's readers. The apostle urged them to submit to God's working in their lives with humility and trust, as to the skillful hand of a surgeon (5:6–7). Eventually they would be better off for their suffering. Humility comes by entrusting oneself and one's troubles to God. We can do this because we have confidence that God has great concern for our welfare.

Christians also need to practice self-control and to keep alert because Satan is on the prowl and seeks to devour us as a lion (5:8–11). Besides forsaking the world and denying the lusts of the flesh, we should resist the devil. Satan's desire is to get Christians to disregard, doubt, deny, and disobey what God has said. Nevertheless God gives sufficient grace so we can resist Satan (2 Cor. 12:9). He will make us complete, establish us, strengthen us for service, and give us peace in His will.

V. CONCLUSION (5:12–14)

To encourage his readers further Peter concluded this epistle with a final exhortation and greetings from those with him and himself.

Silas may have written this epistle as Peter dictated it or in some other way assisted in its composition. Peter wanted to exhort the readers to stand firm in the faith since suffering for the Savior is part of being a recipient of God's grace (5:9). "She" probably refers to the church in the town where Peter was when he wrote this letter (see 2 John 1, 4). "Babylon" probably is a veiled, metaphorical reference to Rome, where Peter spent the last years of his life. Rome was the capital of the pagan world, and Christians had come to think of Rome as Babylon. John Mark was Peter's protégé. In Peter's culture a kiss was a common way to express affection publicly. In the midst of their persecution Peter prayed that his readers might experience God's surpassing peace.

2 PETER
Heresy in the Last Days

AUTHOR

This epistle claims that the apostle Peter wrote it (2 Pet. 1:1). It also claims to follow a former letter by Peter (3:1), apparently a reference to 1 Peter. The author's mention of the fact that Jesus had predicted a certain kind of death for him (1:14) harmonizes with Jesus' statement to Peter recorded in John 21:18. The writings of the church fathers contain fewer references to the Petrine authorship of 2 Peter than to the authorship of any other New Testament book. Regardless of the external evidence, there is strong internal testimony to Peter's authorship of the book. This includes stylistic similarities to 1 Peter, vocabulary similar to Peter's sermons in Acts, and the specific statements already mentioned (2 Pet. 1:1, 14; 3:1). In addition, the writer claimed to have witnessed Jesus' transfiguration (1:16–18) and to have received information about his own death from Jesus (1:13–14).

DATE

Peter's reference to his imminent departure from this life (1:13–15) suggests that the time of composition may have been just before Peter suffered martyrdom. The writings of church fathers place Peter's death in A.D. 67–68 in Rome. Consequently a date of composition about that time seems most likely.[1]

AUDIENCE

Assuming Peter's reference to his former letter (3:1) is to 1 Peter, he sent this epistle to the same general audience. That audience was primarily gentile, but it also included some Jewish Christians living in northern Asia Minor (1 Pet. 1:1). The background of the readers and the situation they faced, as Peter described these, fit such an audience well.

PURPOSE

Peter warned his readers of the awful apostasy that was coming on the church in the last days and, particularly, of the heresy among its teachers.

THEOLOGICAL EMPHASES

Eschatology and Christology are the major doctrines Peter touched on in this letter. Ecclesiology is also prominent in that Peter viewed the church as moving toward increasing apostasy.

CHARACTERISTICS

Second Peter and 2 Timothy are the swan songs of Peter and Paul respectively.[2] Both epistles warn of the apostasy to come. Peter stressed apostasy among the church's teachers and Paul among its general population. There are also similarities between 2 Peter 2 and the Book of Jude, especially Jude 4–18, both of which warn about false teachers.[3] Second Peter is more general and irenic than Jude.

OUTLINE

I. Introduction (1:1–2)
II. The Condition of Christians (1:3–11)
    A. The Believers' Resources (1:3–4)
    B. The Believers' Needs (1:5–9)
    C. The Believers' Adequacy (1:10–11)

III. The Authority for Christians (1:12–21)
   A. The Need for a Reminder (1:12–15)
   B. The Trustworthiness of the Apostles' Witness (1:16–18)
   C. The Divine Origin of Scripture (1:19–21)
IV. The Danger to Christians (chapter 2)
   A. The Characteristics of False Teachers (2:1–3)
   B. The Consequences of False Teaching (2:4–10a)
   C. The Conduct of False Teachers (2:10b–19)
   D. The Condemnation of False Teachers (2:20–22)
 V. The Prospect for Christians (3:1–16)
   A. The Purpose of This Epistle (3:1–2)
   B. Scoffing in the Last Days (3:3–6)
   C. End-Time Events (3:7–10)
   D. Living in View of the Future (3:11–16)
VI. Conclusion (3:17–18)

I. INTRODUCTION (1:1–2)

The writer could hardly have stated his identity more clearly than he did in this verse. He regarded himself first as a servant of Jesus Christ[4] and secondarily as His apostle. Peter referred to his audience in general terms that could apply to all Christians. Every Christian has the same essential faith, including all of its spiritual benefits, as the apostles did. Peter believed Jesus Christ was both God and Savior. In this letter Peter emphasized Jesus' role as Savior because of his readers' need of deliverance (2 Pet. 1:11; 2:20; 3:2, 18). Personal knowledge of God and Jesus is the key to grace and peace. The false teachers could offer nothing better than this.

II. THE CONDITION OF CHRISTIANS (1:3–11)

Peter portrayed the nature of the Christian life with its challenge to spiritual growth and maturity. His readers' spiritual safety lay in their understanding the nature of their new life in Christ and in their spiritual growth and maturity. Appreciating these realities is the best antidote against succumbing to error.

> *Many Christians have forgotten how much God has forgiven them, or they have appreciated His forgiveness only superficially. This appreciation is the key to growth in the Christian life.*

A. The Believers' Resources (1:3–4)

To rekindle an appreciation for the resources God had given his readers, Peter reminded them of God's power and promises.

Grace and peace are possible since God has given all Christians everything they need to lead godly lives. These resources are available through knowing Jesus Christ more personally. To make progress in godliness no believer can get along without God's Spirit and His Word. These become ours as we appropriate His worthy and excellent promises in the Bible that enable us to overcome our temptations.

B. The Believers' Needs (1:5–9)

Having established the believer's basic adequacy through God's power in him and God's promises to him, Peter next reminded his readers of their responsibility to cultivate their own Christian growth. This was to correct any idea they may have had that they needed to do nothing more because they possessed adequate resources.

Since believers have resources that are adequate for a godly life, we should use them diligently to grow in grace. Escaping the corruption of lust takes effort (see 1 Tim. 6:11–12; 2 Tim. 2:2). We must apply all diligence, our most basic responsibility for experiencing Christian growth (2 Pet. 1:10, 15; 3:14). To their faith, as a foundation, believers need to add seven qualities with God's help. Each virtue contributes to the total growth of the saint. Peter arranged the virtues in a random order but presented them so each one receives emphasis. Failure to work on these virtues will make us "ineffective" and "unproductive" as demonstrators of His life (1:8). The absence of these virtues gives evidence of spiritual blindness to the realities connected with relationship with God, in particular, short-sightedness.

C. The Believers' Adequacy (1:10–11)

Simply practicing what Peter had just advocated would prepare his readers adequately for the future. They had no need for the added burdens that false teachers sought to impose on them.

Other people could see the divine nature more clearly in the Christians who added the seven virtues named. This would make God's calling and election of them clearer to everyone. Also by adding them we can walk worthy of the Lord without stumbling along the way. By pursuing Christian growth we give evidence that God really did call and choose us. One of the greatest motivations for purposing to grow in grace is that when we go to be with the Lord He will welcome us warmly.

III. THE AUTHORITY FOR CHRISTIANS (1:12–21)

Peter's readers needed a reminder that rested on apostolic authority that was in harmony with other Scripture.

A. The Need for a Reminder (1:12–15)

Returning to the subject of God's promises (1:4), Peter developed the importance of the Scriptures as the believers' resource. This was designed to enable his readers to appreciate the value of the Scriptures and to motivate them to draw on God's Word so they would grow in grace.

Peter's previous words were a reminder to his readers, not new instruction. Verses 3–11 contain basic truths about the Christian life. Peter apparently believed that he would soon die as a martyr. He said he wrote this epistle so that after his death the exhortation in it would be a permanent reminder to his readers.

B. The Trustworthiness of the Apostles' Witness (1:16–18)

Peter explained that his reminder came from one who was an eyewitness of Jesus Christ during His earthly ministry, which would have heightened respect for his words in his readers' minds. This section begins Peter's defense of the faith that the false teachers were attacking, defense which continues through most of the rest of the letter.

The apostles had not preached myths to their hearers, as the false teachers were doing. They had seen Jesus' power in action as God's anointed Messiah. God had clearly revealed that Jesus is the Christ at His transfiguration when God had announced that Jesus is His beloved Son (1:18).

C. The Divine Origin of Scripture (1:19–21)

The prophetic Old Testament Scriptures confirm the witness of the apostles. That witness is similar to a light shining in a darkened heart and world. Until the Lord returns, we should give attention to the Old Testament and to the apostles' teaching. That is the only real light available to us. What we have in Scripture originated not in the minds of men but in the mind of God (1:21). The prophets did not simply give their interpretation of how things were or would be. They spoke as God's mouthpieces, articulating His thoughts in words that accurately represented those thoughts. The Holy Spirit "carried along" the prophets to do so.

IV. THE DANGER TO CHRISTIANS (CHAPTER 2)

Peter warned his readers of the false teachers who presented a message contradictory to that of the apostles. He wrote of the characteristics of false teachers, the consequences of their teaching, their conduct, and their condemnation.

A. The Characteristics of False Teachers (2:1–3)

False prophets in Old Testament times sought to lead God's people away from the revelations of the true prophets, and false teachers in Peter's time tried to lead God's people away from the teaching of the apostles. The heretics added some of their own false teaching to the orthodox faith, thereby denying the One they professed to submit to as Christians.[5] Their judgment would be sudden. Reckless and hardened immorality would accompany their doctrinal error. False teachers typically desire to satisfy themselves rather than God, which leads them to take advantage of their audiences. God is never late or asleep in executing justice, though He is patient (see 3:9).

B. The Consequences of False Teaching (2:4–10a)

Peter next described the consequences that follow false teaching to help his readers see the importance of avoiding it. He gave three examples of apostates in the past. His first example is the angels who sinned (2:4), an example of how the devil works. His second example is the unbelievers of Noah's day (2:5), an example of the world. The third example (2:6) is the turning of the cities of Sodom and Gomorrah into ashes, an example of the flesh. All three examples show that God will not only punish the wicked, but will also rescue the righteous from the judgment He will send on the ungodly who surround them.[6]

C. The Conduct of False Teachers (2:10b–19)

Peter emphasized the conduct of false teachers in order to motivate his readers to turn away from them. Rather than behaving as good angels do, the false teachers acted like animals. Peter believed the false teachers therefore deserved treatment similar to that of animals. God will give them punishment in keeping with their crimes. Their practices were similar to stains on the clean fabric of the church, blemishes on its countenance, since the practitioners claimed to be Christians. The false teachers sinned without restraint and lured people not firmly committed to Jesus Christ to join them. They were also trying to get the Christians to participate in idolatry and immoral practices. Like the springs and mists Peter described (2:17), the false teachers failed to deliver what they promised and so were hypocrites. They appealed to their audiences with boastful words, promising more than they could deliver. Furthermore they appealed to people who were only just escaping from those who live in error, probably new Christians and/or older carnal ones who were still in the process of making a final break with their pagan practices.

D. The Condemnation of False Teachers (2:20–22)

Peter focused in these verses on the false teachers' final doom to warn his readers of the serious results of following their instruction. The false teachers in view had evidently heard the gospel preached and fully understood the apostles' teaching that Jesus Christ is both Lord and Savior but had rejected it. They only escaped the defilements of the world in the sense that they had understood the gospel, which liberates sinners. But they had thrown away their key to deliverance and had thereby become entangled and overcome again by the defilements of the world. Their first state was also eternal damnation without having heard the gospel, but their final state was eternal damnation for having rejected the gospel.

It would have been better for the false teachers never to have gained full knowledge of God's commandment regarding holy behavior than having gained it to reject it. Dogs return to corruption that comes from within themselves, and pigs return to filth they find outside themselves. False teachers do both things.

V. THE PROSPECT FOR CHRISTIANS (3:1–16)

Peter turned from a negative warning against false teachers to make a positive declaration of the apostles' message in order to help his readers understand why he wrote this letter. His language had been strong and confrontational, but now he spoke with love and encouragement in gentle and endearing terms.

A. The Purpose of This Epistle (3:1–2)

Peter implied that he wrote this letter soon after an earlier one, probably 1 Peter. His purpose was to refresh his readers' memories that were unflawed by evil. He gave his readers credit for not having embraced the teaching of the heretics. Again Peter put the teaching of the apostles, which came from Jesus Christ, on a level of authority equal with the writings of the Old Testament prophets.

B. Scoffing in the Last Days (3:3–6)

The mockers' attitude of intellectual superiority and disdain of scriptural revelation led them into immoral conduct. They denied supernaturalism and believed in uniformitarianism, the view that the world continues in the same uninterrupted patterns. In particular, the scoffers denied the promise of the Lord Jesus that He would return (John 14:1–3; Acts 1:11). God did intervene in the world in the past. When He spoke, the universe came into existence (Gen. 1:6–8; Heb. 11:3). God spoke again and the dry land separated from the waters (Gen. 1:9–10), and He spoke again and the earth flooded (Genesis 7).

C. End-Time Events (3:7–10)

God has indicated that the present heavens and earth will experience another, yet-future judgment. Then God, by His word, will destroy them by fire rather than by water. It does not matter if He gave His promise yesterday or a thousand years ago. He will still remain faithful and fulfill every word. The passage of a thousand years should not lead us to conclude that God will not fulfill what He has promised; He does not forget His promises. God is waiting so people will have time to repent. This holocaust will take place at the end of the Millennium and will result in the destruction of the universe as we know it (see Rev. 21:1).

D. Living in View of the Future (3:11–16)

An understanding of the future should motivate believers to lead holy lives. They are to look forward to the new heavens and new earth, because righteousness will dwell there. Peter again urged his readers to "diligent" action (3:14; see 1:5, 10). He wanted them to be at peace with God, without defect or defilement, and without justifiable cause for reproach.

We should view the apparent delay of the Lord's return as evidence of His long-suffering that leads people to repentance and salvation rather than as an indication that He is never coming back. Perhaps Peter had Romans 2:4 in mind when he said Paul wrote the same thing he had just said. Some people misunderstood and in some cases deliberately misrepresented the meaning of Paul's writings, but this only added to their own guilt before God. Peter regarded Paul's writings as of equal authority with the Old Testament Scriptures (see 1:12–21; 3:2).

VI. CONCLUSION (3:17–18)

Peter concluded his epistle with a summary of what he had said and a doxology to condense his teaching for his readers and to redirect their living to glorify God. Peter's mental picture was of a torrent of false teaching knocking believers off their feet and sweeping them away. The apostle then added a positive exhortation. Rather than being swept away by error, his audience should keep on growing in God's grace by consciously depending on His resources and by growing in the knowledge of Jesus Christ, by getting more intimately acquainted with Him each day (see 1:5–8). The greatest goal for the Christian should be to glorify Jesus Christ, and Peter's final words focused his readers' attention anew on that ultimate priority.

While the Holy Spirit causes growth to take place in the Christian's life, we should never conclude that growth is automatic. Peter commanded his readers to grow. We have a responsibility to appropriate our spiritual resources, or we will not grow as we should.

1 JOHN
Fellowship and Eternal Life

AUTHOR

This epistle does not contain the name of its writer, but from its very early history the church believed the apostle John wrote it. Several ancient writers, including Irenaeus, Clement of Alexandria, and Tertullian, referred to this book as John's writing.

DATE

Many conservative scholars believe John wrote this epistle between about A.D. 85 and 97, when he evidently also wrote the Gospel of John and the Book of Revelation. A date for 1 John in the early 90s seems likely.

AUDIENCE

There is no reference to who the first recipients of this epistle were or where they lived other than that they were Christians (1 John 2:12–14, 21; 5:13). They may have been the leaders of churches (2:20, 27). Some of the original readers were faithful Christians, others were inclined toward Jewish or Hellenistic heresy, and some had seceded from the church. According to early church tradition John ministered in Ephesus, the capital of the Roman province of Asia, for many years after he left Palestine. We know from Revelation 2 and 3 that he knew the churches and Christians in that Roman province well. Perhaps his readers lived in that province.

PURPOSE

The false teachers and teachings to which the writer alluded suggest that he wrote about conditions that existed in Asia: Judaism, Gnosticism, Docetism, and others. John wrote to combat false teaching and to encourage faithful continuance in the faith. Specifically he wanted Christians to enjoy more intimate fellowship with God and greater assurance of their salvation. The internal evidence suggests that John's major concern was that his Christian readers move closer to God (rather than that they come to salvation).

THEOLOGICAL EMPHASES

John stressed a proper understanding of the person of Jesus Christ as the basis for fellowship with God and other believers. Related to this are emphases on salvation, the Holy Spirit, and Christian conduct. First John is concerned essentially with the conditions for true Christian discipleship.

CHARACTERISTICS

This epistle is unique in its black-and-white descriptions of Christian belief and behavior. Writing late in the first century, John assumed much earlier teaching that his readers would have known. This epistle is an exposition of Jesus' teaching in the Upper Room Discourse (John 13–16). Many of the same terms and themes appear in both sections of Scripture. John's literary style is cyclical; he introduced several themes, left them, and then returned to them, often more than once, rather than proceeding in a straight line in his argumentation. Another mark of all John's writings is that he used synonyms frequently.

OUTLINE

I. Introduction: The Purpose of the Epistle (1:1–4)
II. Living in the Light (1:5–2:29)
   A. God as Light (1:5–7)
   B. Conditions for Living in the Light (1:8–2:29)

III. Living as Children of God (3:1–5:13)
    A. God as Father (3:1–3)
    B. Conditions for Living as God's Children (3:4–5:13)
IV. Conclusion: Christian Confidence (5:14–21)
    A. Confidence in Action: Prayer (5:14–17)
    B. Certainty of Knowledge: Assurance (5:18–20)
    C. A Final Warning: Idolatry (5:21)

I. INTRODUCTION: THE PURPOSE OF THE EPISTLE (1:1–4)

This introduction lacks the typical features of other New Testament epistles: the writer, the addressees, and a salutation. Like Hebrews and James, it reads more like a sermon than a letter. John began this epistle by explaining to his audience why he wrote. He said he wrote so his readers would enjoy the fellowship with God that is possible only to those who know Him intimately. This fellowship, he explained, rests on the reality of Jesus Christ's incarnation, and it results in full joy for those who experience it.

The "beginning" to which John referred (1:1) is evidently the beginning of the Christian gospel. He cited personal experience and appealed to empirical evidence to support the humanity of Jesus Christ, which some false teachers were denying. In this epistle John was speaking for others beside himself, and he was seeking to persuade still others of something not all of them had experienced or acknowledged. "Life" is a title of Jesus Christ here (1:2) as "Word" is in John's Gospel (John 1:1). Grace and truth explain the Logos in John's Gospel (1:14), but light and love clarify Life in his epistles. The purpose of the epistle is that "you also may have fellowship with us. And our fellowship is with the Father and with his Son, Jesus Christ" (1 John 1:3). Not only would his readers experience full joy, but so would John as the readers entered into and continued in intimate fellowship with God.

John identified two dangers that are still prevalent in the church today. One is the assumption that Christian fellowship is possible without common belief in Christ. The other is the assumption that a person can have a relationship with God without a relationship with Jesus Christ.

II. LIVING IN THE LIGHT (1:5–2:29)

John began his exposition of how his readers could enjoy fellowship with God by introducing the concept of God as light (1:5–7) and then explaining with four conditions what fellowship with God requires (1:8–2:29).

A. God as Light (1:5–7)

As light, God exposes and condemns sin (darkness).[1] The Christian who claims to have fellowship with God, who is light (that is, holy), but disobeys Him is lying. Two things are true of believers who walk in the light: We enjoy fellowship with God, and we are experiencing cleansing from every sin.

B. Conditions for Living in the Light (1:8–2:29)

John articulated four fundamental principles that underlie fellowship with God to facilitate his readers' experience of that fellowship. To live in the light of God's presence one must renounce sin, obey God, reject worldliness, and keep the faith.

Renouncing sin (1:8–2:2). John continued a structural pattern that he established in the previous section (1:6–7), in which he used pairs of clauses to present a false assertion followed by his correction. This second claim, that we have no guilt for sin, is more serious, and its results are worse: We do not just lie, thereby deceiving others; we deceive *ourselves.* God's truth, as Scripture reveals it, does not have a full hold on us if we make this claim. Acknowledging the sins of which we are aware is the opposite of saying we are not guilty for sinning. If we confess our sins, God will then forgive the sins we confess and will, in addition, cleanse us from all unrighteousness.

The next false claim (1:10) is that what we have done is not really sin. This is the third and most serious charge. It puts God's revelation of sin aside and makes humans the authority for what is and is not sin. This claim says God is wrong in His judgment of humanity and that He therefore is a liar. The claimant dismisses His Word as invalid.

Truth	False claim
God is light (1:5).	We have fellowship with Him (1:6).
Walking in the light is necessary for fellowship with God (1:7).	We have no guilt for sin (1:8).
Confession restores fellowship with God (1:9).	We have not sinned (1:10).

Fellowship with God requires openness to God and full integrity in the light of His Word.

John's preceding comments on the inevitability of sinful behavior (1:6–10) led to his assuring his readers that he did not want them to sin. Avoidance of sin is important even though it is not entirely possible. As our Advocate (our Friend in court, or Defense Attorney), Jesus Christ pleads the cause of the sinning Christian before God the Father. Since Jesus Christ is righteous, He is the perfect Advocate with God. Jesus Christ did not just make satisfaction for the sins of everyone, though He did that. He *is* the satisfaction Himself. Fellowship with God is possible only when we deal with sin in our lives. This is true of believers (1:5–2:1) as well as unbelievers (2:2).

Obeying God (2:3–11). Whereas the first (negative) condition required for intimacy with God is the renunciation of sin (1:8–2:2), the second (positive) condition is obedience, especially to God's law of love (2:3–11). Having fellowship with God, knowing God, and seeing God were virtually synonymous concepts for John. Again John made a categorical statement (2:3) and then stated and refuted three other false claims (2:4–10).

Our personal experiential knowledge of God will affect the way we live, and the way we live, whether obediently or disobediently, will reveal how well we really know God. If a person says he knows God intimately but is not obedient to the revealed will of God, he is a liar, and God's truth does not have a controlling influence over his life (see 1:8, 10). On the other hand, the Christian who is careful to observe all of God's Word (not just His commandments, 2:4) gives evidence that he has come to understand

and appreciate God's love for him. A believer who is abiding in God will obey God just as Jesus Christ abode in God and evidenced that by obeying His Father. When Jesus Christ issued the great commandment anew, He called it a new commandment (John 13:34) even though God had given it previously (see Lev. 19:18). Now it was important in a new sense because He was present with them and because their love was to match His love for them ("as I have loved you," John 13:34; 15:12). Hatred of other Christians is a sure sign that one is not walking with God in fellowship. It places him in darkness outside God's fellowship, it leads to aimless activity in which he is in great spiritual danger and in which there is the possibility of a fall, and it results in mental confusion.

Claim	Condition
"I know Him" (2:4; see John 17:3)	"obeys His word" (2:5)
"[I] live in him" (2:6; see John 15:4)	"walks as Jesus did" (2:6)
"[I am] in the light" (2:9; see John 12:46)	"loves his brother" (2:10)

Rejecting worldliness (2:12–17). To cultivate intimate fellowship with God who is light, Christians also need to reject worldliness.

First John 2:12–14 contrasts the position of the believer who walks in the light with that of the Gnostics who walked in darkness. This pericope contains two series of three sentences. Each sentence begins, "I write to you . . . because." John spoke of three stages of life to describe qualities that ought to characterize all believers. He was writing because the stated condition was true of each group. The apostle mentioned three experiences in their proper experiential sequence in the Christian life. He then proceeded to point out other characteristics of his readers, again using the same three life stages to illustrate their progress. John was not saying that his readers were all immature or all mature. He was acknowledging their spiritual development to encourage them to press on to know the Lord better and to have more intimate fellowship with Him.

Verses 15–17 warn the believer not to fall into the trap of worldliness, as the false teachers did. John again presented three pairs (compare 2:12–14). He said the appeal of the world system is threefold (2:16). Here is a picture of the infernal trinity, the three faces of the world, the three sources of worldly temptation (see also Gen. 3; Matt. 4:1–10). John urged his readers in view of the world's attractiveness to understand the avenues of its temptation and to remember four things (1 John 2:15–17): (1) Love for the world indicates lack of love for God. (2) Love for the world results in consequences that are not what our loving heavenly Father desires for our welfare. (3) The world lasts only a short time. (4) Love for the world precludes intimate fellowship with God.

Keeping the faith (2:18–29). John needed to alert his readers to special deceptions they would encounter to enable them to identify and defend themselves against these temptations. Previously John had been less direct in dealing with false teachers who perverted the truth about intimacy with God. Now he became more pointed and labeled them antichrists (2:18–19). He exposed their method by noting that they lie and deny that Jesus is the Christ (2:21–22). John again used a threefold structure at the beginning of this section. He described three signs or marks: those of the end (2:18–19), of the believer (2:20–23), and of living in the light (2:24–25). Verses 26–27 recapitulate and develop the content of verses 18–25, and verses 28–29 summarize the first major section of 1 John and anticipate the second major section.

III. LIVING AS CHILDREN OF GOD (3:1–5:13)

John now concentrated on the developing spiritual life of his followers. The pattern with which the reader has become familiar continues: John first stated something about God's character (3:1–3; see 1:5–7) and then specified several conditions for living as God's children (3:4–5:13; see 1:2–2:29).

A. God as Father (3:1–3)

This section introduces John's recapitulation and expansion of his exposition of what is necessary for people to have fellowship with God. He changed his figure from God as Light to God as the Father of the believer.

The production of righteous behavior in abiding Christians is evidence of God's great love for us. Unbelievers cannot fully comprehend the children of God because they fail to comprehend God. Approval by the world should be feared, not desired, by Christians. Even though we are presently God's children, we do not yet fully reflect His image as we shall. But when Jesus Christ appears and we see Him, we shall experience full transformation (glorification).[2] Meanwhile we anticipate seeing and knowing Jesus Christ fully, and that anticipation has a purifying effect on us.

B. Conditions for Living as God's Children (3:4–5:13)

Having stated the importance of continuing in Christ, doing what is right and purifying oneself in anticipation of the Lord's coming, John now dealt more particularly with the need for believers to abstain from sin and the possibility of their doing so.

Renouncing sin reaffirmed (3:4–9). Sin stands in opposition to purity, and sin is very serious. Jesus Christ became incarnate to remove sin, and there was no sin in Him. When a Christian walks in close fellowship with God, he does not sin. The Christian who consistently "abides" in a sinless Person does not sin (3:6). If we could abide in Christ without interruption, we would not sin. Unfortunately we cannot do that. Verse 4 sets forth the essential character of sin, verse 5 relates it to the person and work of Christ, and verse 6 relates it to the whole human race. Evidently the false teachers were in danger of deceiving John's readers by telling them the opposite of what the apostle said here.

John could say the Christian is sinless because a sinless "Parent" (God Himself) has begotten the Christian (3:9). The Christian becomes a partaker of God's divine sinless nature when he experiences the new birth. The Christian sins because he also has a sinful human nature. However, in verse 9 John was looking only at the sinless nature of the indwelling Christ that we possess. When a Christian abides in God, he will behave as his heavenly Father, and others will recognize that he is a child of God.

Obeying God reaffirmed (3:10–24). The second condition for living as children of God reemphasizes the importance of obeying God's law, specifically the command to love one another.

The absence or presence of sin in a person's life gives evidence of his relationship to God and Satan (3:10). It shows under whose authority he is living. John divided the world into two classes: those whose parentage is divine and those whose parentage is diabolical. Christians who are abiding in God will produce good works, and others can identify them as Christians by their godly behavior. The absence of righteous behavior in a believer's life indicates the absence of intimacy with God. Likewise the absence of love for one's Christian brother shows that the individual who does not love has little fellowship with God. The message that John and his faithful followers had heard from the beginning was Jesus' command to His disciples to love one another as He had loved them (John 13:34; 15:12).

Cain's murder of Abel evidenced control by Satan rather than by God (1 John 3:12). If we feel loving concern for each other, it should not surprise us if unrighteous people hate us for being more righteous than they are. Love for other Christians shows the presence of new life in us. Murder is the ultimate outward expression of hatred. No Christian whose eternal life (1:2) has control of him and who is walking in fellowship with God, will commit murder.

In contrast to the act of murder by Cain, we see love in Jesus Christ's laying down His life for us (3:16). We may not have the opportunity to save a fellow Christian's life by dying in his place, but we can and should do the next best thing, namely, sustaining his life when he has needs. The evidence of genuine love is not verbal professions but vital performances, deeds rather than words.

Tangible demonstrations of love for other Christians show a believer's true character (3:18). True love demonstrated in deeds of self-sacrifice enables the believer to face Jesus Christ unashamedly when He returns.

Jesus taught the apostles to trust in Him and to love each other (3:23). This summarizes His teaching. Obedience results in mutual abiding, God in the believer, and the believer in God. We know God's Spirit "abides" in us when we manifest faith (4:1–6) and love (4:7–16).

Rejecting worldliness reaffirmed (4:1–6). John previously pointed out that worldly attitudes can be associated with material possessions and ambitions (2:15–16), but here he contrasted God and the world mainly in terms of truth and error.

It is necessary to distinguish the Spirit of God from false spirits (spirits advocating falsehood) because many false prophets have gone out into

The way to distinguish truth from error is to compare it with what the Scriptures teach. Counterfeits become clear when compared with the genuine article.

the world (4:1). False spirits (utterances or persons inspired by a spirit opposed to Christ) result in false teaching. A denial of the doctrine of Christ as the apostles taught it—deviation from orthodox Christology—evidences a spirit opposed to Jesus Christ. John's readers had so far overcome these opponents of Jesus Christ by the Holy Spirit who indwelt them. The antichrists' teachings have an appeal to worldly minds because they come from the world and share the viewpoint of the world. Those believers who know God intimately respond positively to the teaching of the apostles.

Practicing love (4:7–5:4). John spelled out the nature of the love demanded from every believer. We are to love as a response to God's own love and to His loving activity.

Love, as well as faith (acknowledging the true doctrine of Christ, 4:1–6), is a product of God's Spirit (4:7). Absence of love shows that a person does not have intimate fellowship with God. The proof of God's love for people is that He sent His only begotten Son to provide eternal life for us. This was not in response to people's love for Him. Instead God took the initiative in reaching out to us. Jesus Christ became "an atoning sacrifice" for our sins (4:10).

That demonstration of love by God is our model for showing love to others. No one has seen God in His pure essence without some kind of filter. A believer's fellowship with the Lord is demonstrated by love that comes from God's Spirit. The Holy Spirit is the source of the believer's love just as He is the source of our obedience. God's presence is observable when Christians love each other. Confessing that Jesus is God's Son is not the only condition for abiding in God (4:15). It is one evidence that one is abiding. John's readers had seen God in a sense similar to the way in which the apostles had seen Him, that is, in His Son, Jesus Christ. And the readers had seen God in that they had seen Him in His Spirit-indwelt abiding believers. Thus John's readers could bear witness to the truth as the apostles did, and they could enjoy the same intimate fellowship with God the apostles enjoyed.

Our love becomes complete in that we can now have confidence as we anticipate our day of judgment (4:17). We do not need to fear the judgment seat of Christ if we have demonstrated love to others. By loving we become like Jesus Christ, our Judge. Our ability to love and our practice of love come from God's love for us. We need not fear standing before our Judge because we love Him and He loves us. A mere claim to love God is a poor substitute for genuine love of other believers (4:20). Love for the unseen God will find expression in love for our brethren whom we can see.

God commanded us to love Him *and* our brothers, not just Him (4:21). The first part of 5:1 is one of the clearest statements in Scripture of what a person has to believe to be saved. We must believe that Jesus of Nazareth is "the Christ" (the Anointed One whom God promised to provide as a substitute sacrifice for the sins of the world). Genuine love for God will result in obedience to His commandments. The fundamental proof of love for God and people is obedience to the Word of God (5:3). God's commands are not burdensome (oppressive) because every believer has already exercised the faith in God that is essential for obedience and we love Him. Every Christian has overcome the world ultimately by his initial faith in Jesus Christ. To continue to overcome and obey God all we need to do is continue to exercise faith in God.

Keeping the faith reaffirmed (5:5–13). John set out his fifth and final condition for living as children of God. Continuing to overcome the world is not automatic for the Christian. Only those who continue to live by faith (trust and obey God) overcome the world. Furthermore no one can overcome the world unless he believes that Jesus is the Son of God. That trust is the key to overcoming sin. The "water" (John the Baptist's baptism of Jesus in water) and the "blood" (Jesus' death by crucifixion) bear witness to His identity. Actually there are three witnesses to the truth of who Jesus is. These witnesses are the Holy Spirit teaching through the apostles and prophets, the water of Jesus' baptism, and the blood of His crucifixion. God gave His witness concerning His Son in three ways: through the prophets, at Jesus' baptism (Matt. 3:7; John 1:32–34), and at His crucifixion (19:35–37).

Having spoken of the *character* of the divine witness to Jesus (1 John 5:6–9), John discussed the *results* of that witness (5:10–12). The witness is the truth about Jesus Christ that the indwelling Holy Spirit bears. This is the content of God's testimony: Eternal life is inseparable from the person of Jesus Christ. The phrase "these things" (5:13) refers to what John had just written about God's witness (5:9–12). Our assurance of salvation rests on the testimony of God, His promise (5:12).

IV. CONCLUSION: CHRISTIAN CONFIDENCE (5:14–21)

John concluded this epistle by discussing the confidence that a Christian can have if he walks in the light as a child of God.

A. Confidence in Action: Prayer (5:14–17)

Prayer is another expression of the believer's trust in Jesus Christ and confidence toward God (see 3:21). Whenever we need help, but particularly help in obeying God, we can confidently ask for it in prayer. God hears all prayers, of course, because He is omniscient. But He hears them in the sense that He hears them favorably because we are His children asking for help to do His will. He will always grant that kind of request. Prayer should extend to the needs of others.

The general subject of verse 16 is prayer for a sinning Christian. Some sins bring God's swift judgment and result in the premature death of the sinner (see Acts 5:1–11; 1 Cor. 5:5; 11:30). Others do not. In the case of sin leading to death, John revealed that prayer will not avert the consequences. Because some sin does not lead to premature death we should pray for believers when they sin. We do not know if their sin is "to death" or not. Prayer for a sinning Christian is a concrete demonstration of love for that brother or sister (1 John 3:23).

B. Certainty of Knowledge: Assurance (5:18–20)

Faithful, informed Christians knew, and now the readers also knew, what John had written in this epistle. The basic nature of one who has God for his spiritual Parent is not to sin (see 3:9). Furthermore because the believer possesses the sinless nature of the indwelling Christ, John could say that Christ keeps him from sin. In addition, Satan cannot "touch" him in the sense of harming him. Moreover, we are distinct from the world system that Satan controls since we are God's children (5:9–13). Finally, we have spiritual understanding through our anointing with the Holy Spirit (2:20), whom Jesus Christ sent to indwell believers. As a result we can come to know God intimately and can abide in God and in His Son, who is the true God and eternal life.

C. A Final Warning: Idolatry (5:21)

Departure from the true God and His teachings constitutes idolatry. This verse is a New Testament restatement for Christians of the first commandment God gave to the Israelites (Exod. 20:3; Deut. 5:7).

2 JOHN
The Importance of Truth

AUTHOR

The writer of this short epistle identified himself as "the elder" (2 John 1). The early church fathers said he was the apostle John. "Elder" was a more affectionate title than "apostle," and it undoubtedly represented John's role among the churches, unofficially if not officially. He was probably an old man at this time too.

DATE

The conditions existing in the church that John addressed are similar to those he referred to in his first epistle. Therefore the time of composition may have been close to that of 1 John, namely, A.D. 90–95.

AUDIENCE

Probably John personified a particular local church as a lady and the Christians in it as her children. Since John's arena of ministry during his later life was Asia Minor, the probability of this being a church in that Roman province is good.

PURPOSE

John urged his readers to continue to be obedient to God by (a) responding positively to the truth of His revelation and (b) resisting the inroads of false teachers who sought to distort this truth.

THEOLOGICAL EMPHASES

Though this short letter is pastoral and encouraging, its main theological contribution is its emphasis on the importance of revealed truth, bibliology, and its central teaching, Christology.

CHARACTERISTICS

Second John is very similar to 3 John and Philemon in that it is personal and brief. It is a short summary of the teaching of 1 John.

OUTLINE

I. Introduction (vv. 1–3)
II. The Importance of the Truth (vv. 4–11)
   A. Practicing the Truth (vv. 4–6)
   B. Protecting the Truth (vv. 7–11)
III. Conclusion (vv. 12–13)

I. INTRODUCTION (VV. 1–3)

In these opening verses John introduced himself, identified the recipients of this letter, greeted them, and mentioned the major subjects of his concern to prepare his readers for what follows.

The "elder" was evidently the apostle John, the "chosen lady" a local church, and her "children" the believers in that church. The church was "chosen" in that it consisted of elect individuals, Christians. John loved this church and so did other Christians who knew about it. The basis of this love was the truth the Christians there held in common with others. This "truth" refers to God's revelation in Scripture. John wanted his readers to appreciate the importance of guarding divine truth and practicing love for each other. These two things are the basis for grace, mercy, and peace.

II. THE IMPORTANCE OF THE TRUTH (VV. 4–11)

In this central section of his epistle John gave a brief summary of the great contrasts between truth and error, love and hatred, and the church and the world.

A. Practicing the Truth (vv. 4–6)

John had met some of the members of this church who were walking in obedience to God's truth (walking in the light, 1 John 1:7), and this gave him great joy. John's message for this church was a reminder to keep on walking in obedience to God's truth by continuing to love each other (see also 2:7; 4:21). If anyone had a question about what loving each other meant, John explained that it is essentially obeying God's command to love (see 5:2–3a). We love each other best when we obey God's will that His Word reveals.

B. Protecting the Truth (vv. 7–11)

In his second purpose—to encourage his readers to resist the false teachers who were distorting the truth and deceiving some of the believers—John noted that departure from the truth results in a failure of love.

Erroneous teaching was proliferating in the early church. The common error was Christological. The false teachers regarded Jesus as something other than God's Anointed One who had come as fully God and fully man and is now in a glorified human body (see 1 John 5:1). These teachers were deceivers and were opposed to Christ. Compromise with the false teachers could lead to a loss of reward. The picture in John's mind seems to have been that of a Christian who, the false teachers said, did not have the whole truth. It is common even today for false teachers to claim that those who do not agree with them are still in an infantile intellectual or spiritual state. However, John regarded that "infantile" position as proper for the Christian. If his readers advanced beyond it, they would really step out of the truth into error.

So John warned his readers of the danger of apostasy, namely, forsaking truth to embrace error (see 2:23–24). He spoke of a vital personal relationship with God that comes with adherence to the truth, not just dead doctrinal orthodoxy. In the culture of John's day, philosophers and teachers often relied on the people to whom they spoke for lodging and financial assistance (Acts 18:2–3; 21:7). John instructed his readers to refuse to help the false teachers in these ways and not even to give verbal encouragement to these apostates.

> In dealing with such persons ourselves we must also relate to their ministry in one way and to themselves in another. We must not approve or encourage their work but we must show concern for their personal relationship with Jesus Christ.

III. CONCLUSION (VV. 12–13)

John had more to say on this subject that God did not lead him to record in this letter. His readers' joy would be full when they better understood the issue presented here as well as when John visited them (see 1 John 1:4). The Christians in the sister church of which he was a member sent their greetings along with his own to his readers.

3 JOHN
The Importance of Love

AUTHOR

The author of 3 John was evidently the apostle John, who identified himself as "the elder" here (3 John 1) as he did in 2 John 1. The striking similarity in content, style, and terminology in these two epistles confirms the ancient tradition that John wrote both of them.

DATE

Probably John wrote this epistle about the same time he wrote 1 and 2 John, A.D. 90–95.

AUDIENCE

Though there is no internal evidence concerning where Gaius, the gentile Christian recipient, lived, it was probably the Roman province of Asia, the apparent destination of 1 and 2 John.

PURPOSE

John wrote this epistle to stress the importance of putting love into practice. He commended the recipient for his love, warned him of another man's lack of love, and illustrated love with a third person's behavior.

THEOLOGICAL EMPHASIS

As with 2 John, this epistle stresses a subject that John dealt with more fully in 1 John. Here that subject is Christian love. The reciprocal importance of truth and love—revealed truth being the basis for true love—is present in both 2 and 3 John. But whereas the emphasis in 2 John is on the truth, the emphasis in 3 John is on love.

CHARACTERISTICS

Third John is, perhaps, the most personal letter in the New Testament. Most of the epistles originally went to churches or groups of Christians. First and 2 John are both of this type. The Pastoral Epistles, while sent to specific individuals, Timothy and Titus, were obviously written with a wide circulation in mind as well. Philemon, too, gives evidence that Paul intended its recipient to share it with the church that met in his house. Third John also has universal value, and the early Christians recognized that it would benefit the whole Christian church. However, the content of this letter is very personal.

OUTLINE

   I. Introduction (vv. 1–4)
  II. The Importance of Love (vv. 5–12)
     A. Gaius's Love (vv. 5–8)
     B. Diotrephes' Lack of Love (vv. 9–11)
     C. Demetrius's Evidence of Love (v. 12)
 III. Conclusion (vv. 13–14)

I. INTRODUCTION (VV. 1–4)

As in 2 John, the apostle identified himself as "the elder." We do not know exactly who Gaius was. His was a common name in Greek and Latin. He was obviously someone whom John loved as a Christian brother, and who held the truth as the apostles taught it. John prayed that all would go well with Gaius and that he might enjoy good physical health to go along with his good spiritual health. John had heard from others that Gaius's lifestyle was consistent with the truth. He could have been a disciple of John's or simply a younger believer.

II. THE IMPORTANCE OF LOVE (VV. 5–12)

John stressed the importance of genuine Christian love by citing three examples, two positive and one negative.

A. Gaius's Love (vv. 5–8)

John loved Gaius as Gaius loved the Christians to whom he had extended hospitality, and John commended Gaius for his love of them. News that his behavior was consistent with God's truth (see 2 John 1–2) had reached John's church. The elder urged Gaius to continue his commendable treatment of visitors by sending them on their way with adequate provisions and encouragement. The brothers were traveling preachers. To go out in the name of Christ was a great honor because of that name. Early Christian preachers normally received material support from other believers (Acts 20:35; 1 Cor. 9:14; 1 Thess. 3:7–9), or they supported themselves. They did not solicit funds from unbelievers (Matt. 10:8; 2 Cor. 12:14; 1 Thess. 2:9). Giving financial and hospitable aid makes the giver a partner with the receiver in his work.

B. Diotrephes' Lack of Love (vv. 9–11)

Gaius's good example stands out more clearly beside Diotrephes' bad example. John brought Diotrephes into the picture to clarify the responsibility of Gaius and all other readers of this epistle and to give instructions concerning this erring brother.

Diotrephes was guilty of three wrongdoings. First, he had persistently denigrated John in an effort to exalt himself. John promised and warned that whenever he might visit Gaius's congregation he would point out Diotrephes' sinful behavior, assuming it continued. Second and worse than that, Diotrephes was not giving hospitality to visiting preachers, as

Gaius was doing. Third, Diotrephes intimidated others in the church and forced them to stop welcoming these ministers. John's encouragement doubtless strengthened Gaius's resolve to resist Diotrephes. John was not necessarily accusing Diotrephes of being unsaved but of behaving as if he were unsaved. One who knows God intimately (has "seen" God) does not do evil (1 John 3:6).

C. Demetrius's Evidence of Love (v. 12)

Demetrius may have carried this letter from John to Gaius, or he may have visited Gaius later. Demetrius had a good reputation, for he, like Gaius, was "walking in the truth" (see v. 4). His life matched his confession.

> There is a direct connection between a person's adherence to God's truth and his love for others. If we fail to obey God, particularly His command to love our neighbor as ourselves, we will fail to demonstrate love for others, even other Christians.

III. CONCLUSION (VV. 13–14)

John explained the brevity of this epistle and expressed his hope to visit Gaius soon. As friends, Christians should show hospitality to and should support one another, the specific expression of love that John urged in this letter.

JUDE
False Teachers

AUTHOR

Traditionally the writer of this epistle is Jude (also known as Judas), the half brother of Jesus Christ (Matt. 13:55; Mark 6:3) and the brother of James (Jude 1; Acts 15:13). Like James, he was a Hellenized Galilean Jew who wrote with a cultivated Greek style.

DATE

After the Jewish revolts against Rome in A.D. 66–70, Jude probably lived outside Jerusalem and perhaps outside Palestine. References in the text to the false teachers and the apostles (Jude 3–5, 17) suggest a condition in the church some years after the day of Pentecost (Acts 2). Similarities with Peter's writings have led some scholars to date Jude about the time Peter wrote. A date between A.D. 67 and 80 seems reasonable.

AUDIENCE

Jude's many allusions to the Old Testament suggest that his original readers were quite familiar with it. While this could have been true of any Christians, it would have been particularly true of Jewish Christians. The locality of the original recipients is uncertain, but most of them were probably Jewish Christians living in a gentile society.

PURPOSE

Jude stated his purpose clearly: to motivate his readers to contend earnestly for the orthodox Christian faith since false teachers were corrupting it (Jude 3–4).

THEOLOGICAL EMPHASES

Sin and its consequences concerned Jude, as did the importance of persevering in the faith. He warned of apostasy and urged his readers to watch out for a departure from the doctrine of God's grace.

CHARACTERISTICS

Jude is quite similar to 2 Peter in that both epistles warn against false teachers and false teaching. Jude is more emotional in his appeal and more specific in describing the errorists. His epistle contains many illustrations from the Old Testament. It is actually an epistolary sermon. Jude could have delivered what he said in this epistle as a homily if he had been in his readers' presence. Instead he cast it in the form of a letter since he could not address them directly. Other New Testament epistles that are written homilies include Hebrews, James, and 1 John.

OUTLINE

I. Introduction (vv. 1–2)

II. The Purpose of This Epistle (vv. 3–4)

III. Warnings against False Teachers (vv. 5–16)

    A. Previous Failures (vv. 5–7)

    B. Present Failures (vv. 8–16)

IV. Exhortations to the Faithful (vv. 17–23)

    A. The Reminder to Remember the Apostles' Warning (vv. 17–19)

    B. The Positive Instruction of the Readers (vv. 20–23)

V. Conclusion (vv. 24–25)

I. INTRODUCTION (VV. 1–2)

Jude identified himself in a humble way, not as the half brother of Jesus Christ, but simply as His servant and the brother of James, the well-known leader of the Jerusalem church. Jude's threefold description of his readers presents an impression of completeness and well-rounded thought. The readers needed God's mercy, peace, and love in view of the false teachers' influence, which Jude proceeded to discuss.

Doctrinal deviation often accompanies and often seeks to justify ethical and moral sin, as was true of the false teachers Jude described.

II. THE PURPOSE OF THIS EPISTLE (VV. 3–4)

It is enjoyable to talk about salvation and something positive, but occasionally a particular situation compels us to speak about a danger that God's people need to appreciate. The presentation of this subject must sometimes be quite negative, and delivering such a message is not a pleasant task.

The faith delivered to the saints is the special revelation of God that Scripture contains and the apostles preached. Jude's readers needed to struggle to maintain this faith free from corruption. Jude had two major concerns: that the readers would not be led astray by false teachers, and that they would instead take the initiative and contend for the faith. False teachers who advocated immorality and perverted true Christology had wormed their way into the church.

III. WARNINGS AGAINST FALSE TEACHERS (VV. 5–16)

Jude proceeded to denounce libertines and apostates more vehemently than any other New Testament writer.

A. Previous Failures (vv. 5–7)

The writer cited three examples of failure from the past to warn his readers of the danger involved in departing from God's truth. Each one of these illustrations highlights a particular aspect of the false teachers' error. It was a sin of rebellion, it was a proud departure from a position of superior privilege, and it involved immoral behavior.

Jude's first example was certain Israelites (v. 5). After God redeemed Israel and liberated the nation from bondage in Egypt, the people failed to continue to believe God's promises and to trust in His power (Num. 14:11; Deut. 1:32). God judged those who failed by destroying them in the wilderness. The Savior can also be the Destroyer.

Jude's second example was certain angels (Jude 6). A group of angels also did not remain in their privileged position near God but left that sphere and so incurred God's wrath. These rebellious angels are now in bondage and await God's judgment (see 2 Pet. 2:4). These differ from Satan's agents who are at work in the world today, that is, demons who have considerable freedom. The apostates in Jude's day had also abandoned a position of great privilege and blessing, namely, the opportunity to serve and glorify God. God would also judge them severely because of their departure.

Jude's third example was certain pagans (Jude 7). This example shows God's judgment on those who indulge in immorality and sexual perversion, which the false teachers of Jude's day evidently felt free to practice. Apostasy starts with unbelief, leads to rebellion against God, and proceeds to immorality.

B. Present Failures (vv. 8–16)

Jude next expounded the errors of the false teachers in his day to warn his readers even more strongly. Jude referred to certain Old Testament types (vv. 5–7 and 11) and prophecies (vv. 14–15 and 17–18) and then interpreted them as fulfilled by the false teachers (vv. 8–10, 12–13, 16, and 19).

He first exposed the nature of their error (vv. 8–9). Like dreamers living in the fancies of their own imaginations, the apostates substituted an unreal world for the real world of divine truth. Their presumption stands out boldly in comparison with Michael's submission and reverence in dealing with another powerful angel, Satan. Michael could not reject the devil's accusation on his own authority because he was not his judge. All he could do was ask the Lord, who alone is Judge, to condemn Satan for his slander.

Jude next explained the seriousness of the error of the false teachers (vv. 10–13). The things they did not understand but reviled probably refer to aspects of God's revealed will that they chose to reject. What they did understand was the gratification of the flesh, and that would destroy them. Cain's way was the way of godlessness and sensuality, violence and lust, greed and blasphemy, that led to divine judgment (Gen. 4). Balaam's error was compromise with God's enemies and teaching the Israelites they could sin without being punished (Num. 31:16). Korah's rebellion was against God and His appointed leaders, Moses and Aaron (16:1–35). Each of these three examples shows a different aspect of unbelief. Five more illustrations, this time from nature, emphasize the seriousness of the false teachers' error (Jude 12–13).

Jude further warned of the consequences of their error (vv. 14–16). He quoted loosely from a prophecy Enoch gave that is recorded in the apocryphal Book of 1 Enoch. The false teachers would be the objects of God's judgment. Much like the former grumblers, the false teachers in Jude's day grumbled primarily against God. They pursued their lusts for sensuality and gain. Their arrogant words contradicted apostolic revelation. And they flattered people to obtain personal advantage.

IV. EXHORTATIONS TO THE FAITHFUL (VV. 17–23)

Having warned his readers about the failures of false teachers, Jude then exhorted them to persevere faithfully in spite of the danger that faced them.

A. The Reminder to Remember the Apostles' Warning (vv. 17–19)

The apostles had warned that scoffers would arise in the end times who would follow their own ungodly desires. Jude's quotation of the apostles' teaching is a general summary rather than a specific reference. It is the "last times" in relation to Jesus Christ's return to reign on earth. While they may have claimed to be the truly spiritual group, the false teachers were really worldly minded and shared the viewpoint of unbelievers.

B. The Positive Instruction of the Readers (vv. 20–23)

Since believers are God's temples under attack by hostile enemy forces, we need to build ourselves up, to strengthen ourselves spiritually, and to pray for God's help in our warfare. We should also keep ourselves in the sphere of God's love by abiding in Him (John 15:9–10), and we should keep our hope clearly in view since we have only a short time to remain faithful. Too, Christians should tenderly help those of their fellow believers who are struggling and perhaps stumbling under the influence of the false teachers and should attempt to restore those who have fallen into error. In the case of those whom heresy has completely swept away, we should have pity on them rather than condemning them without compassion, fearing God's displeasure and discipline if we embrace their error. We should avoid any contact with these people because of the corrupting influence they can have on us through their words and actions.

V. CONCLUSION (VV. 24–25)

Jude concluded his brief epistle with a formal doxology that included a prayer for his readers. He wanted to assure them of God's ability to help them remain faithful in spite of the apostasy that threatened them. Our confidence rests in *God's* ability to keep us safe and faithful.

REVELATION
The Culmination of History

AUTHOR

The opening verses of this book state that "John" wrote it (Rev. 1:1, 4, 9; see also 22:8). From the ancient times to the present day most conservative scholars have concluded that this means the apostle John.

DATE

Some of the early church fathers wrote that the apostle John was in exile on the island of Patmos during the Roman Emperor Domitian's reign. They wrote that the government allowed John to return to Ephesus after Domitian died in A.D. 96. Thus many interpreters date the writing of this book near A.D. 95 or 96.

AUDIENCE

Jesus Christ gave this revelation to John with instructions to send it to the churches in seven towns in Asia Minor. So the book circulated first among these congregations of mainly gentile and some Jewish Christians.

PURPOSE

The stated purpose of the book is to reveal Jesus Christ (1:1). It reveals His person, His power, and His plan for the future. Specifically it contains revelation from and about Jesus Christ that John had already seen in a vision (chapter 1), about conditions that existed in the churches when he wrote (chapters 2–3), and what would take place in the future (chapters 4–22; see 1:19).

THEOLOGICAL EMPHASES

The Book of Revelation contains many prophecies about the end times and the culmination of history. Also it is the climax of biblical Christology in that it reveals the vindication of Jesus Christ in history. It unfolds the course of events from John's day to the destruction of the present universe and the creation of a new one with emphasis on the judgments coming on the world during Daniel's seventieth "seven" (period of seven years, Dan. 9:25–27), the Tribulation.

CHARACTERISTICS

There are remarkable parallels between this revelation and the Lord Jesus' teaching in the Olivet Discourse (Matt. 24–25; Mark 13; Luke 21). The Book of Revelation clearly builds on that foundation as well as on prophecies previously given to the prophet Daniel (Dan. 7–12). The apocalyptic sections of certain books of the Old Testament—particularly Daniel, Isaiah, Ezekiel, and Psalms—contain former revelation that God gave His prophets about the end times. There are many similarities between Revelation and Daniel. Both books deal with God's sovereign rule over the world. The revelation that Jesus gave in the Olivet Discourse and later to John on Patmos supplements that earlier revelation. Apocalyptic literature is characteristically full of figurative language, and this fullness of imagery marks Revelation.

OUTLINE

I. The Preparation of the Prophet (chapter 1)
  A. The Prologue of the Book (1:1–8)
  B. The Commission of the Prophet (1:9–20)
II. The Letters to the Seven Churches (chapters 2–3)
  A. The Letter to the Church in Ephesus (2:1–7)
  B. The Letter to the Church in Smyrna (2:8–11)
  C. The Letter to the Church in Pergamum (2:12–17)
  D. The Letter to the Church in Thyatira (2:18–29)
  E. The Letter to the Church in Sardis (3:1–6)
  F. The Letter to the Church in Philadelphia (3:7–13)
  G. The Letter to the Church in Laodicea (3:14–22)
III. The Revelation of the Future (4:1–22:5)
  A. Introduction to the Judgments of the Tribulation
     (chapters 4–5)
  B. The First Six Seal Judgments (chapter 6)
  C. Supplementary Revelation of Salvation in the Great
     Tribulation (chapter 7)
  D. The First Six Trumpet Judgments (chapters 8–9)
  E. Supplementary Revelation of John's Preparation for
     Recording the Remaining Judgments in the
     Great Tribulation (chapter 10)
  F. Supplementary Revelation of the Two Witnesses in the
     Great Tribulation (11:1–14)
  G. The Seventh Trumpet Judgment (11:15–19)
  H. Supplementary Revelation of Satan's Activity in the
     Great Tribulation (chapters 12–13)
  I. Supplementary Revelation of Preparations for the Final
     Judgments in the Great Tribulation (chapters 14–15)
  J. The Seven Bowl Judgments (chapter 16)
  K. Supplementary Revelation of the Judgment of
     Ungodly Systems in the Great Tribulation (chapters 17–18)
  L. The Second Coming of Christ (chapter 19)

M. The Millennial Reign of Christ (chapter 20)

N. The New Heavens and New Earth (21:1–22:5)

IV. The Epilogue to the Book (22:6–21)

A. The Testimony of the Angel (22:6–7)

B. The Testimony of John (22:8–11)

C. The Testimony of Jesus and John's Response (22:12–20)

D. The Final Benediction (22:21)

I. THE PREPARATION OF THE PROPHET (CHAPTER 1)

The first chapter contains a prologue to the book, which is similar to the one in John 1:1–18, the prologue to John's Gospel (see also 1 John 1:1–4). It also relates a vision God gave John that prepared him for what follows (see Ezek. 1). This presentation has the effect of showing that Jesus Christ is the culminating figure in human history, and it prepares the reader for the revelation of His future acts that constitutes the bulk of this book.

A. The Prologue of the Book (1:1–8)

This prologue contains a preface, the address and a doxology, and a statement of the theme of the book.

The preface (1:1–3). The apostle John wrote these opening verses to introduce to his readers the main subject dealt with in this book and his purpose for writing it.

Jesus Christ was the giver of this unveiling to His servants, and He is its main subject. He communicated this revelation to an angel who passed it on to John, the Lord's servant. John saw many things and passed this revelation on to the church. Those who read, hear, and apply the lessons of this prophecy to their own lives will receive a special blessing from God. The time when God will fulfill these prophecies was "near" when John wrote this book, relatively near in God's timetable in which a thousand years are as a day (2 Pet. 3:8).

The address and doxology (1:4–6). This mention of the writer, the addressees, and a greeting sets the book off as being like an epistle. John sent in the midst of affliction. John was on the island of Patmos, in the Aegean Sea southwest of Ephesus, as a result of his witness for Christ. There the Holy Spirit caught John up and projected him in his spirit to a future time in a series of visions. This happened on a Sunday. A loud trumpet-like voice instructed John to write down what he saw and to send it to seven churches in Asia Minor.

The source of the commission (1:12–16). When John turned to see the person who spoke to him, he saw a majestic figure clothed in a long robe standing among seven golden lampstands. The man looked like "a son of man," a human being. His clothing was that of a priest and judge. His head, specifically His hair, was very white, suggesting His wisdom and dignity (see Dan. 7:9). His eyes were similar to blazing fire, reflecting His piercing judgment and omniscient understanding. His feet looked like bronze glowing in the reflection of a fire, suggestive of His proven purity. His voice sounded authoritative, powerful, and irresistible, as a mighty river. He held seven stars protectively in His authoritative and powerful right hand. A sharp double-edged sword, the type the Romans used to kill with, proceeded from His mouth. His face shone like the unclouded sun, a picture of pure holiness and righteousness.

The amplification of the commission (1:17–20). John responded to this revelation by prostrating himself before the glorified Christ (see also Dan. 10:7–9). Jesus then comforted His servant and proceeded to give him more information about what He wanted him to do. He identified Himself as the sovereign, eternal, resurrected Jesus, and He repeated His instruction to write down the things He was revealing to him. Some of what John was to record he had already seen, namely, the Man standing among the seven golden lampstands with the seven stars in His hand (Rev. 1:12–16). Some had to do with present conditions in the churches (chapters 2–3). And some had to do with revelations about the times after conditions represented by the seven churches ended (chapters 4–22). Jesus then interpreted the meaning of some of the symbolic things John had seen. The seven stars represented the messengers of the seven churches, their human leaders who acted like angels in mediating between God and His people. The lampstands figuratively supported the corporate witness of the Christians in each church as these believers witnessed in a dark world.

this letter to the seven churches mentioned in Revelation 2 and 3, were in the Roman province of Asia (modern western Turkey). Sir book deals mainly with future events, John described the divine . with emphasis on the continuity of His dealings with humankind and ... was, and ... is to come"). He also added the greeting of th principal angelic messengers ("seven spirits") that serve God and th ing of Jesus Christ. "Faithful witness" (Rev. 1:5) is Jesus Christ's ministry of revealing what follows, "firstborn from the dead" lool culmination of His past ministry when God raised Him to new lit resurrection, and "ruler of the kings of the earth" anticipates Hi ministry following His second coming (see Ps. 89).

John ascribed eternal glory and dominion to Jesus Christ, the of this revelation. He always loves us, He loosed us from the bor our sins by His death, and He has made us a kingdom (corporat priests (individually) to His God and Father. "Amen" signifies the affirmation of the truthfulness of these statements about Jesus (

The theme (1:7–8). These verses contain the first prophetic the book. Verse 7 summarizes the main features of the revelatic low (Christ's return and the response of earth dwellers) and i sense, the key verse in the book (see Dan. 7:13; Zech. 12:10). (firmed the preceding forecast with a solemn affirmation of His s eternity and omnipotence.

B. The Commission of the Prophet (1:9–20)

John next recorded a vision of the glorified Christ that God I him. He related the circumstances of his first commission to w vided a detailed description of the source of that commis: explained more about his commission and the one who gave it

The first commission to write (1:9–11). John now addresse the seven churches to which he sent this epistolary prophec scribed himself to his readers as their brother in Christ and a with them in the religious persecution they were presently e ing because of their faith in Christ, their participation in t kingdom of Christ, and their perseverance as they remained

II. THE LETTERS TO THE SEVEN CHURCHES
(CHAPTERS 2–3)

Each of the seven letters in Revelation 2–3 contains a unique description of the Lord Jesus drawn mainly from 1:12–20 that is appropriate to that church. Each one also contains a word of commendation (except the letter to Laodicea), and each carries some rebuke for the congregation (except those to Smyrna and Philadelphia). Each exhorts its readers to specific action, and each holds out a promise as an incentive for faithful obedience.

A. The Letter to the Church in Ephesus (2:1–7)

> *Service and orthodoxy are important, but Jesus Christ wants our love most of all.*

Jesus Christ told John to write the letter to the church in Ephesus to commend the Ephesian Christians for their labors and perseverance in God's truth, and to exhort them to rekindle their former love for the Savior.

Ephesus was a leading seaport on the Aegean Sea and the capital of the Roman province of Asia. John described Jesus Christ as the One in authority over the church leaders and the One who knew their situation (2:1). This church had remained faithful to Jesus Christ for over forty years, and the Lord approved of the good works of these believers—their toil in His service, their patient endurance of difficult circumstances, and their discipline of evil men and false teachers (2:3–4). They also hated the teaching of the Nicolaitans (2:6), who advocated ethical and moral compromise with paganism.

The Ephesians, however, were serving Jesus Christ and maintaining orthodoxy as a tradition rather than out of fervent love for their Savior (2:4). The corrective for a cold heart that the Lord prescribed was a three-step process. They needed to remember how they used to feel about Him, repent (change their attitude), and return to the love that formerly motivated them (2:5). An invitation preceded the promise, as in all the letters to follow. In addition to the implied promise of the whole church's continuance if obedient, Jesus Christ gave a promise to all the believers in the church (2:7). To motivate the readers to follow Him faithfully in the present, Jesus held out a reminder of what would inevitably be theirs in the future. The Tree of Life in the Garden of Eden, while literal, probably symbolized eternal life. Believers anticipate enjoying eternal life in heaven (see 22:2, 14, 19).

B. The Letter to the Church in Smyrna (2:8–11)

John penned this letter to commend its recipients for their endurance of persecution and poverty for the sake of their Lord and to exhort them to be fearless and faithful even to death. Whereas the Ephesian church needed to return to past conditions, this one needed to persevere in what was characteristic of it then.

Smyrna was also a seaport on the Aegean Sea, about forty miles north of Ephesus. Jesus Christ described Himself to this church as the eternal One who died and experienced resurrection (2:8), a source of hope for persecuted believers. Jesus knew the pressures these Christians were enduring as a result of their testimony for Him, including financial hardship (2:9). Notwithstanding their physical poverty, the Christians in Smyrna were rich spiritually. Some of the persecutors were Jews who slandered the Christians and cursed Jesus Christ. They claimed to be committed to God but were not. They came out of Satan's camp, not God's.

> Believers who suffer for their faith can count on special blessings after death.

Jesus had no rebuke for these saints. In their trials they had remained pure in belief and behavior. They did not need to fear their adversaries or death since they would live forever with Jesus Christ. The devil would incite their foes to imprison some of them shortly (2:10). But they would receive the crown of life, the fullness of eternal life, as a reward for enduring the trials and tests of life even to the point of death without denying Christ. Christians will not in any way suffer injury or harm by the "second death," eternal separation from God (2:11).

C. The Letter to the Church in Pergamum (2:12–17)

The purpose of this letter was to encourage the Christians in Pergamum for their faithfulness to Christ and to urge them to reject the false teaching in their midst.

Pergamum lay about fifty-five miles north of Smyrna, inland a few miles from the Aegean coast. Jesus Christ described Himself to this congregation as the One who judges with His Word (2:12). The Pergamum Christians had held firmly to their commitment to Christ and their witness for Him even though they lived in one of Satan's strongholds. Balaam told Balak that he could overcome the Israelites if he would get them to participate in Moabite religious feasts that included sacred prostitution (Num. 25). This rendered them unfaithful to God and consequently subject to His discipline. Some people in Pergamum were encouraging the Christians to join in their local pagan feasts and the sexual immorality that accompanied them. By participating, some in the church had given tacit approval to Balaam's teaching. The Nicolaitans regarded these sins as acceptable under the pretense of Christian liberty (Rev. 2:15).

If the erring believers would not judge themselves and repent, they could anticipate God's judgment. Christians feed spiritually on Jesus Christ, the Bread of Life (John 6:48–51), who is the real manna hidden from sight now, rather than gaining strength from the idols honored in pagan feasts. Attendees at these pagan meals received white stones with the name of the honored god on them that served as their admission tickets, which some of them saved as amulets. But Christians have a better ticket to a better feast, and the name of Jesus on it truly guards us from danger even though that name is unknown to unbelievers (Rev. 2:17).

D. The Letter to the Church in Thyatira (2:18–29)

Jesus Christ sent this letter to commend some in this church for their service, orthodoxy, and fidelity, and to warn others in it to turn from false teaching and sinful practices.

Compromise with the world draws divine discipline.

Thyatira, the smallest of the seven cities but the one that received the longest letter, lay about forty-five miles to the southeast of Pergamum. Flamelike eyes suggest discerning and severe judgment (1:14). Highly reflective bronze feet picture a warrior with protected legs (1:15; Dan. 10:6). "Son of God" emphasizes Jesus Christ's deity and right to judge (Rev.

2:18). In many particulars some in this church were praiseworthy. They were strong in good deeds, love for others, trust in God, service of their Savior, and patient endurance in trials. Moreover they had become even more zealous recently (2:19).

Evidently a Thyatiran woman who claimed to be a prophetess had been influencing some in this church to participate in the pagan feasts that included immoral acts and the worship of idols. Her behavior reflected that of wicked Queen Jezebel (1 Kings 16–21; 2 Kings 9), who had led Israel into immorality and idolatry by advocating Baal worship (Rev. 2:20). God had not brought judgment on her previously so she might repent, but since she had refused to change her ways, He would judge her and her followers, unless they repented. The other churches would recognize her punishment as coming from God, who knows all people intimately (2:23). Apparently this woman claimed that her teaching was deeper than the apostles' teaching, but it was instead the depths of satanic doctrine. Jesus exhorted the faithful in the church to continue with their present good conduct. He would soon purge the wicked ones from their midst. The prize for faithfulness was the privilege of reigning with Christ in His earthly kingdom (2:26–27). The morning star (the planet Venus) appears in the sky just before the dawning of a new day. Similarly, Jesus Christ will guide faithful believers in the future as the new day of His messianic rule dawns (2:28).

> *Religious teaching that goes beyond Scripture is not more advanced; it is more adulterated.*

E. The Letter to the Church in Sardis (3:1–6)

This letter commended the few faithful Christians in Sardis for their good deeds and challenged the negligent majority to remember what they knew and to obey Him.

Sardis stood about thirty-three miles southeast of Thyatira on a major highway that led all the way to Susa in Mesopotamia. The Lord presented Himself to this congregation as the all-wise God who knew their condition. They were really a dead church, and their good works were not as impressive as they should have been. Only a few of their number were faithful to the

Lord (3:4). These believers needed to awaken from their spiritual slumber, to examine their condition, to realize their needs, and to strengthen the areas of weakness in their church. Like the Ephesians, they needed to remember the spiritual heritage of their church and to return to the attitudes and activities their teachers had taught them. Failure to heed these warnings would result in the Lord sending discipline on the believers that would surprise them. The Christians who were faithful to Jesus Christ could enjoy His intimate fellowship. He would never erase the names of overcomers from the "Book of Life," another metaphor for eternal life (see 2:7). Jesus Christ will also acknowledge all overcomers as His own.

> *A good reputation can lull Christians into a dangerous spirit of complacency.*

F. The Letter to the Church in Philadelphia (3:7–13)

This letter to the church in Philadelphia commended the Christians for their faithfulness in spite of persecution and encouraged them to persevere.

Philadelphia lay about thirty miles southeast of Sardis in central Asia Minor. Jesus Christ presented Himself to these saints as holy, true, and authoritative. He claimed to have God's full administrative authority to distribute or not distribute all God's resources according to His will. The Philadelphia Christians had received an "open door" to opportunity for spiritual blessing that would continue because they had a spiritual power, though they were evidently few in number. They had faithfully obeyed God's Word, and they had maintained a faithful testimony for the Lord in the past.

Jesus gave no rebuke to this church, like Smyrna, but several promises instead. First, their Jewish antagonists would eventually have to acknowledge that the Christians were the true followers of God (see 2:9). Second, they would not go through the Tribulation period (Rev. 6–19). Third, the Lord promised to come soon. Since Jesus Christ's return was imminent, the believers should remain faithful to Him so their detractors would not rob them of the reward that would be theirs for steadfast perseverance. Fourth, God would make them stalwarts in the spiritual temple of God, the New Jerusalem (21:22).

> *Faithfulness to opportunities for Christian service results in rewards all out of proportion to the sacrifice involved.*

Fifth, Jesus would acknowledge them as His own in heaven.

G. The Letter to the Church in Laodicea (3:14–22)

Jesus Christ sent this letter to shake the Laodicean Christians out of their self-sufficient complacency and to exhort them to sacrifice for higher spiritual goals.

The last of the seven cities lay about forty miles southeast of Philadelphia and about ninety miles east of Ephesus. Jesus called Himself the final affirmation of God, the faithful witness to the situation in Laodicea, and the authoritative ruler of God's creation. This church received no commendation, a fact that makes this letter unique compared to the other six. The Laodicean Christians were neither cold nor hot in their love for God but lukewarm, apathetic. The Lord's vomiting these people out of His mouth (3:16) does not mean they would lose their salvation (see 3:19); instead it pictures His intense disgust. He wanted them to be spiritually refreshing and healthful, like cold or hot water, rather than spiritually bland, like lukewarm water.

> *Spiritual riches are more important than physical wealth and are worth making great sacrifices to obtain.*

Since they considered themselves to be rich but were spiritually poor, Jesus urged them to "buy," implying sacrifice, the things they really needed. They should buy "gold refined in the fire," namely, the best spiritual riches. They should buy "white clothes" (3:18) that symbolize righteous conduct (19:8). They should purchase spiritual "salve to put on your eyes," the divine viewpoint that enables people to see life realistically, and they should repent. The Lord invited the indifferent Laodiceans to open their heart's door so He could have intimate fellowship with them. The privilege of reigning with Christ will be the portion of the overcomer.

III. THE REVELATION OF THE FUTURE (4:1–22:5)

John recorded the revelation in this section of the book to unveil the things that would follow Jesus' dealings with the churches just addressed (see 1:19). Jesus' second coming is the true climax of this section of the book (chapter 19), and it is the true climax of history on planet earth.

A. Introduction to the Judgments of the Tribulation (chapters 4–5)

Chapters 4 and 5 prepared John, and they prepare the reader, for the outpouring of judgments on the earth that follow. They reveal the place from which these judgments originate and the Person from whom they come. God gave John this second vision in which He revealed what will take place in heaven following the Rapture to enable the readers to view coming earthly events with this background.[1]

The throne in heaven (chapter 4). After John had received the messages to the seven churches (chapters 2–3), he received a vision of a throne room in a heavenly temple, which Jesus Christ invited him to enter to receive information about future events that must take place. John saw a throne and someone sitting on it, namely, God the Father (see Dan. 7:9–10). John compared His magnificence to precious jewels (Rev. 4:3). A green rainbow, representing His mercy and faithfulness, encircled the throne. Twenty-four holy and honored elders (humans or angels) sat on twenty-four thrones surrounding God's throne. Portents of judgment issued from His throne, and seven other angels prepared to judge.

Four specially wise angels formed an inner circle and surrounded the throne and God (see Ezek. 1:12). Each creature possessed qualities that were appropriate to their service of God. Their movements did not detract from their constant vigilance, and they ascribed holiness to God constantly. Whenever it was appropriate the four living creatures gave praise to the eternal God, glorifying and honoring Him for His perfections and thanking Him for His great works (Rev. 4:8). The twenty-four elders likewise fell down before Him out of reverence. When the crowned elders prostrated themselves before God and symbolically subjected their power to His superior authority, they humbly acknowledged His sovereignty and His right to receive worship. Their verbal praise focused on the wonders of God's creation as the evidence of His glory and power (4:11).

We need to view all that follows in Revelation (chapters 5–22) in the light of God's character manifested in this vision. He is perfectly holy, just, gracious, righteous, pure, omnipotent, eternal, and sovereign. This should help us accept the coming revelation of the outpouring of His wrath in the future.

The Lamb on the throne (chapter 5). In the same vision John also saw that God was holding a scroll that was full of revelation in His right hand. It was sealed with seven seals (see Dan. 12:4, 9). John saw a powerful angel invite anyone to take the scroll and open it, but no one was worthy to do so. John wept because the revelation of God's plans and their execution would apparently remain hidden and postponed, but one of the twenty-four elders comforted him with the news that Messiah would open the scroll (Rev. 5:5).

Then John saw a Lamb who had achieved victory over all God's enemies and therefore had the authority to open the scroll and to reveal its contents. He saw the Lamb in the center of all the creatures gathered around the throne as the central character and most important personage in the entire heavenly scene (5:6). He was standing, ready to complete His work, bearing the marks of His death. The Lamb was assisted by seven powerful and intelligent angels.

Next John saw God the Father on the throne and the Lamb coming and taking the scroll out of His right hand, symbolizing a transfer of authority from the Father to the Son to reveal the future and to execute judgment. This transfer precipitated an outpouring of praise for the Lamb because it signaled that Christ would begin judging in response to the prayers of believers throughout history (5:8). In the ensuing song the Lamb was honored in view of His death, His purchase (redemption) of a people for God, His creation of a kingdom and priests for God, and His blessing of His people by allowing them to rule on the earth (during the Millennium). An innumerable host of angels now joined the four creatures and twenty-four elders in ascribing worth to the Lamb: all power, wealth, wisdom, strength, honor, glory, and praise (5:12). John then saw every creature giving worship to God and to the Lamb, culminating in the four creatures saying "Amen" repeatedly after the vast crowd fell silent and the elders prostrating themselves before God's throne.

B. The First Six Seal Judgments (chapter 6)

After John saw the Lamb break the seals of the scroll, he learned about the judgments that will take place on earth in the future.

The order of events predicted in Revelation 6 is similar to the order Jesus predicted in the Olivet Discourse (Matt. 24–25; Mark 13; Luke 21). Later in the Olivet Discourse Jesus mentioned an event that will occur at the middle of Daniel's seventieth week (Dan. 9:27; Matt. 24:15; Mark 13:14). Consequently the events that He described before the midpoint, namely, those of the first six seals, will probably occur in the first half of the Tribulation. Jesus referred to this three-and-one-half-year period as the "beginning of birth pains" (Matt. 24:8; Mark 13:8).

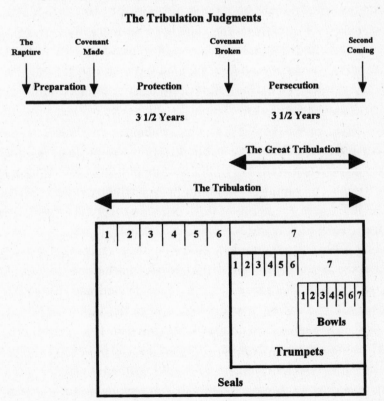

The Tribulation Judgments

The first seal (6:1–2). When the Lamb broke the first of the seven seals on the scroll, one of the four creatures ordered a man mounted on a horse to come forth (see Zech. 1:8; 6:1–8). The horse was white, symbolizing righteousness and holiness. It gave an appearance of purity. The rider carried a bow, symbolizing victory, and he threatened war. He wore an imperial crown, suggesting an authoritative career, and he rode out conquering his enemies and bent on future conquests. Probably the man John saw was the Antichrist who will make a covenant with Israel at the beginning of the Tribulation as a pretense for destroying the Jews (see Dan. 9:27; 1 Thess. 5:3).

The second seal (6:3–4). When the Lamb broke the second seal on the scroll, John heard the second living creature order a second horseman forward. The red horse probably symbolizes bloodshed and war, and his large sword represents the rider's authority to slay people. If we compare Jesus' teaching in the Olivet Discourse, the time when peace ends will probably be before the middle of the Tribulation (see Matt. 24:6–7; Mark 13:7–8; Luke 21:9–10). This is therefore not a reference to the termination of peace with Israel that Antichrist will affect, which will signal the middle of the Tribulation and the beginning of the Great Tribulation (see Matt. 24:15). It will be the beginning of Antichrist's hostility against Israel in the first half of the Tribulation.[2]

The third seal (6:5–6). A black horse symbolizes the ravages of war, that is, famine. Antichrist, the cause of this famine, seems to be the rider of this horse too (see Matt. 24:7). John saw him carrying a pair of balance scales, a symbol of commerce, indicating his control of commodity prices. God announced that the price of food, drink, and fuel will be very high because of strict price controls.

The fourth seal (6:7–8). When the Lamb broke the fourth seal, the fourth living creature called out to the fourth horseman. John saw a pale horse the color of a human corpse. Presumably Antichrist is the rider, since his name is "Death." He is the cause of it. "Hades," which claims people at death, followed on his heels. God gave these enemies authority to take one-fourth of the world's population, evidently the total number that will die as a result of all the catastrophes predicted so far.

The fifth seal (6:9–11). What John saw next took place in heaven. The altar he saw was evidently an altar of incense, and under it were the souls of people who had died for their faith in God and their faithfulness to Him. In death the lives of these martyrs ascended to God like the incense of a sacrifice. The people John described are evidently those who came to faith in Christ after the Rapture (see Matt. 24:9; Luke 21:12). They became believers during the first half of the Tribulation and then suffered martyrdom for their faith.[3] John saw these martyrs calling out to their heavenly Master to punish their murderers. "The inhabitants of the earth" is almost a technical expression in Revelation describing unbelievers who are hostile to God. Each martyr received a long white robe, and God told them to be patient. More people will die as martyrs before it will be God's time for Jesus Christ to return to the earth and judge their living adversaries.

The sixth seal (6:12–17). John next saw something else on the earth. God will send a tremendous earthquake that will rock the whole world (see also Matt. 24:7; Mark 13:8; Luke 21:11). The darkening of the sun, the reddening of the moon, and the falling of the stars (perhaps meteors) to earth are consequences of this judgment. Evidently the sky will appear to split and roll back in two opposite directions. The universe will seem to be coming apart. Earth-dwellers will glimpse the throne room in heaven. God and the Lamb in heaven will be far more terrifying to them than the physical consequences of this judgment. They will realize that the "great day of their wrath" (Rev. 6:17), the outpouring of God's wrath in the Tribulation, has come, and they will run from God in terror.

C. Supplementary Revelation of Salvation in the Great Tribulation (chapter 7)

To explain how God will be merciful during this period of judgment, John recorded what he saw between the opening of the sixth and seventh seals. John received two new visions that corrected the possible conclusion that no one will survive the "beginning of birth pains" (6:17).

God will deliver two groups of people during the first half of the Tribulation. He will preserve 144,000 Jews alive on the earth, and He will take to heaven the spirits of a multitude of people from all nations who will die then. John saw both groups in this chapter, which contrasts the security of believers in Jesus with the panic of unbelievers during the period just described in 6:15–17. It also answers the question posed in 6:17, "Who can stand?"

The sealing of 144,000 Jews (7:1–8). John continued to view things happening on earth, though in a new vision. The general chronological progression of the visions suggests that the events John saw now will happen at the end of the first half of the Tribulation. The winds represent God's judgments coming on the world, specifically those about to follow during the remainder of the Tribulation. An angel instructed four other angels to withhold their judgment on the earth until he had finished sealing God's servants on their foreheads. A seal was a symbol of ownership, authentication, and protection. This seal was probably the name of the Lamb and His Father (7:2). Their sealing marked these believers off as God's redeemed people and guaranteed their protection from divine judgment while they carried out their service for God on the earth during the last half of the Tribulation. Their seals may not protect them from harm that other people inflict on them, but the seal will protect them from the divine judgments sent on unbelievers in the Great Tribulation.[4] Evidently God will give these 144,000 believers special protection in the last half of the Tribulation because the outpouring of God's wrath will be much more severe than in the first half. The references to Israel and the names of the twelve Israelite tribes (minus Dan) clearly indicate that the nation Israel is in view rather than the church. God will deal with Israel as a nation in the future (Rom. 11). Though these believing Jews may not know from which tribe they come, God does, and He will select representatives from each of the twelve tribes.

The deliverance of the great multitude (7:9–17). This vision reveals things happening in heaven at the same time as what John saw happening on earth in Revelation 7:1–8. He saw an innumerable multitude of people, both Gentiles and Jews, in heaven before God's throne. They stood clothed in white robes, symbolic of their righteousness and purity (7:14). These believers had died during the first half of the Tribulation and had joined the angels in the heavenly throne room that John saw previously. Now they held palm branches symbolizing their victory and joy. Together they praised God and the Lamb for their physical deliverance from the Tribulation. The angelic host joined these Tribulation saints in prostrating themselves before God in worship. John did not know the identity of these individuals, so an elder told him who they were (7:14). The elder's description of God spreading His tabernacle over them recalls Old Testament instances of God dwelling among and protecting His people.

There are a number of contrasts between the 144,000 and this great multitude. The number of the first group is not only smaller but definite, whereas the number of the second group is larger and indefinite. People from the twelve tribes of Israel make up the first group, but people from every nation, tribe, people, and language compose the second. God prepares the first group for imminent peril on the earth, but the second group is victorious, secure, and at rest in heaven. Perhaps the 144,000 converted Jews will be messengers of the gospel to the world (Matt. 24:14) as a light to the nations (Isa. 42:6), and the multitudes will be those who come to Christ through the witness of the believers.

D. The First Six Trumpet Judgments (chapters 8–9)

John now received a revelation of more judgments to take place on earth.

The first four trumpet judgments (chapter 8). Chapter 8 introduces additional information about events occurring between the breaking of the sixth and seventh seals. Now the Lamb broke the seventh seal of the scroll. The scene John saw continued in heaven.

When the seventh seal was broken, awesome silence continued as all those assembled around the throne waited to see what God would do next. Then John saw someone give seven trumpets to seven angels standing before the heavenly throne. Another angel acting as a priest came into view and stood before the golden incense altar in heaven. This angel received more incense (prayers) to add to the prayers of the saints already there (8:3). The prayers of the Tribulation saints (6:10) joined those of the rest of God's people in requesting divine justice (see 5:8). The angel offered this incense on the golden incense altar, and the smoke of the incense went up before God, symbolizing His receiving the prayers of His people.

Then the angel took coals from the altar, placed them in his censer, and threw the coals on the earth. These coals of fire, symbolic of judgment, produced portents of catastrophes: thunder, lightning, and earthquake. The whole scene clearly symbolizes God sending judgment on the earth in response to His people's accumulated prayers. The trumpet judgments to follow are what He will send. This appearance of God in a storm introduces the awful calamities that will come in the trumpet and bowl judgments that are ahead. These are the judgments that the angel ascending from the rising of the sun held back until the 144,000 servants of God were sealed on their foreheads (7:3). These judgments are more severe than the first six seal judgments. Their object is to punish hostile unbelievers and to lead them to repentance, though comparatively few will repent (9:20–21).

The scene shifts again, this time from heaven to earth (8:7). The first trumpet blast signaled the beginning of a judgment that involved hail, fire, and blood (see Exod. 9:23–26). This judgment resulted in the fiery destruction of one-third of the earth's land surface. This holocaust consumed a third of earth's trees and all of its grass.[5] These judgments seem to be as literal as the plagues on Egypt were, and they are similar to them.

Following the blowing of the second trumpet, something "like a huge mountain" that was on fire came crashing down from heaven into the waters of one or more of the earth's seas (Rev. 8:8). This resulted in a third of the ocean waters becoming blood (see Exod. 7:20–21). A third of the creatures living in the sea died, and a third of the ships on the seas perished. John was clearly describing supernatural interventions, not natural happenings on the earth.

Next a great fiery star fell from heaven on the fresh water sources on earth (Rev. 8:10). It poisoned a third of the rivers and streams, and many people died from drinking the poisoned water. "Wormwood" was the name of a bitter herb that was fatally poisonous to some people and was an Old Testament symbol of divine punishment (Jer. 3:15; 9:15; 23:15; Lam. 3:15, 19; Amos 5:7).

A fourth trumpet blast announced judgment on a third of the heavenly bodies (Rev. 8:12). Darkness is a common symbol of judgment in the Old Testament, and the Day of the Lord will be a time of darkness (Amos 5:18; Mark 13:24).[6] Evidently God will cut off one-third of the light from the sun, moon, and stars from the earth, perhaps by lessening its intensity (see Exod. 10:21–23). Such a reduction in light will have devastating effects on the earth.

permission to carry out his objective against unbelievers as part of God's outpouring of wrath on earth-dwellers. The fifth, sixth, and seventh trumpet judgments are also the first, second, and third woes (9:12), and they are consecutive, not simultaneous.

When the sixth angel blew the sixth trumpet (9:13), someone near the four horns of the golden altar in heaven commanded the angel who had blown the sixth trumpet to release the four angels who were bound at the Euphrates River, evidently four fallen angels John had not seen before. These angels were ready for a specific assignment at a specific hour in history, namely, to put one-third of those who dwell on the earth to death (see 8:13). This will result in the death of approximately half of those who will be alive at the beginning of the Tribulation.[7] But only the unsaved earth-dwellers, those in rebellion against God, will suffer death as a result of this woe (see 9:20).

John described what these "horses" and their riders looked like (9:17–19). They were swift, terrifying, fierce, and destructive, probably a demonic army. Three distinct plagues will be responsible for the largest death toll in human history so far. But these three severe judgments (fire, smoke, and brimstone) will not move the remaining unbelievers as a whole to repent (just as the plagues on Egypt did not cause Pharaoh to repent). Ironically these unbelievers refuse to stop worshiping demons who are behind idolatry and who are responsible for their misery under this sixth trumpet judgment. These unbelievers will also continue in their sins by murdering, practicing sorcery, committing immorality, and stealing (9:21).

These trumpet judgments, like the seal judgments, will grow more intense as they proceed. Most people living on the earth during these days will be so hard of heart that they will not turn to God in repentance. Nevertheless some will become believers in Jesus Christ (chapter 7). Perhaps the salvation of most of them will take place in the earlier part of the Tribulation before these more severe judgments fall.

> As it was with Pharaoh, so it is with modern man, and so it will be in the Tribulation. If people harden their hearts against the Lord, repentance becomes increasingly difficult for them and eventually they perish in their rebellion.

John next saw, on earth, an eagle (an angel?) interrupt the trumpe blowing angels by flying through the sky and warning those living on th earth to beware of the last three trumpet judgments (Rev. 8:13). Its pos tion in midair and its loud voice reflect the importance of its message. Th last three trumpet judgments, which are also "woes" (9:12; 10:11), will l especially bad because they have people rather than nature as their prima targets. A triple woe announces an extremely bad calamity in Scriptur The objects of these judgments are earth-dwellers, and their judgment w come from God in response to the prayers of the righteous (8:3–5).

The fifth and sixth trumpet judgments (chapter 9). John continued relay the revelation of the trumpet judgments that he had received clarify God's future plans for his readers' benefit. He was still viewi things happening on the earth.

Again John saw a "star" (6:13; 8:10), but this time it was an intellig being, probably a good angel. The "shaft of the Abyss" is the abode Satan (8:11; 20:1–3), some demons (Luke 8:31; 2 Pet. 2:4; Jude 6), a "the beast" (Rev. 11:7; 17:8). It is evidently a preliminary prison, not th final abode, from which this angel was about to release some demo John saw smoke rising from the shaft leading to an underground cha ber, like smoke billowing out of an active volcano. What John s resembled literal locusts (see Exod. 10:12–20), but in view of how Jo described them they were probably demons who assumed some of characteristics of locusts. Their mission was to inflict severe pain on inhabitants of the earth who did not have God's mark of ownership protection on their foreheads (see Rev. 7:3–8). They could not kill peo however, and their terrible tyranny lasted only five months. People seek death to avoid these demons but will not be able to escape their p

Since 4:1 John had been reporting what he saw, but now he sp briefly as a prophet predicting the future (9:7–11). He proceeded to scribe the creatures he saw from head to tail, drawing similarities betw these supernatural beasts and devastating locusts. They were unusi grotesque and frightening in view of their power, intelligence, wildr and invulnerability. Their king is the (leading) angel of the abyss (9: whose name in Hebrew and in Greek means "destroyer." The objectiv all these demons is to destroy people. God granted this lead crea

E. *Supplementary Revelation of John's Preparation for Recording the Remaining Judgments in the Great Tribulation (chapter 10)*

Previously God interrupted the sequence of the seven seal judgments with revelation concerning other events happening at approximately the same time. This took place between the sixth and seventh seals and is recorded in chapter 7. Now He interrupted the sequence of trumpet judgments between the sixth and seventh trumpets with the insertion of other revelation (10:1–11:14). The emphasis shifts temporarily from the outpouring of God's wrath on unbelievers to the consolation and encouragement of believers.

The Literary Structure of Revelation 6–18			
The Seals			
First Six Seals (chapter 6)	Supplementary Revelation (chapter 7)	Seventh Seal (chapters 8–16)	
The Trumpets			
First Six Trumpets (chapters 8–9)	Supplementary Revelation (10:1–11:14)	Seventh Trumpet (11:15–19; chapter 16)	Supplementary Revelation (chapters 12–15)
The Bowls			
First Six Bowls (16:1–16)		Seventh Bowl (16:17–21)	Supplementary Revelation (chapters 17–18)

The appearance of the mighty angel (10:1–4). John saw another strong angel descending from heaven as a messenger of God robed in a cloud, which signified his celestial origin and connection with judgment (10:1). His crown was a rainbow, the symbol of God's faithfulness and mercy. His countenance was radiant, reflecting the glory and majesty of God. His legs were fiery, a manifestation of God's holiness and judgment. The little scroll open in his hand (new revelation from God) was different from the scroll the Lamb unrolled (6:1). This angel's position—standing astride the earth and the sea—pictures his authority over the whole planet. His majestic, loud cry produced seven claps of thunder, an indication of more judgments. An authoritative voice did not permit John to record the judgments these seven thunders revealed. This suggests that God has not revealed in Scripture all the judgments that will take place on the earth during the Great Tribulation.

The announcement of the mighty angel (10:5–7). Lifting one's right hand toward God was and is a customary gesture when making a solemn oath. The angel's oath emphasized the certainty of what he announced, and what was about to happen was extremely important. He appealed to God as the eternal Creator who can cause whatever He pleases to happen. There would be no more delay. The Tribulation martyrs would have to wait no longer for vindication. When the seventh trumpet sounded, God would fully reveal His mystery, previously unrevealed details of His plans for humanity that He was about to make known, specifically what will take place so that the kingdoms of the world become the kingdom of Christ. God had no more to reveal about these kingdom plans beyond what He revealed to John. He had revealed His plans for the future kingdom to His servants the prophets in former times, but only partially.

The instruction of the mighty angel (10:8–11). God the Father (or Christ) then commanded John to take the little book from the strong angel with authority over the whole planet. The angel told John that this revelation would taste sweet at first, but then he would find it bitter. This revelation was pleasant at first (sweetness) because it was a revelation from God, but as John meditated on it and comprehended the fearful judgments (bitterness) that it predicted, he became distressed. John needed to communicate this new revelation contained in the little scroll because it concerned many different peoples, nations, language groups, and kings. What follows would be more burdensome than what John had prophesied so far.

F. Supplementary Revelation of the Two Witnesses in the Great Tribulation (11:1–14)

The temple in Jerusalem (11:1–2). John's first prophetic assignment after receiving his fresh commission (10:9–11) was to provide this information. Again he became an active participant in his vision (see 9:7–11). The person giving John the reed and the instructions was probably the strong angel (10:9–11). John received instruction to perform a symbolic act, as many of his prophetic forerunners had done. The act of measuring probably signifies that the temple is God's possession. One carefully measures what is his own property. The edifice in view is evidently the temple the Jews will build in Jerusalem before or during the first half (three and a half years) of Daniel's seventieth week (the Tribulation; see 11:8; 13:14–15; Dan. 9:26–27; 12:11; Matt. 24:15–16; 2 Thess. 2:4). The "altar" probably refers to the brazen altar of sacrifice outside the sanctuary to which nonpriests will have access. John was to count the worshipers too, namely, believing Jews who will worship God in this Tribulation temple.

The court outside the temple corresponds to the court to which Gentiles had access in the first century, which lay outside the court into which only Jews could come. The Tribulation temple will evidently have similar courtyards. Not measuring this outer court amounts to exclusion from God's favor, just as measuring amounts to enjoying His favor and protection. The nations are the Gentiles, specifically hostile, unbelieving Gentiles who will oppress the holy city, earthly Jerusalem. The forty-two months are the last half of the Tribulation since this will be the time when Gentile hostility to the Jews will be most intense (see Dan. 9:27). The Gentiles will dominate the outer court of the temple and the rest of Jerusalem for forty-two months. Anti-Semitism will peak after the Antichrist breaks his covenant with Israel in the middle of Daniel's seventieth week (Dan. 9:27).

The ministry of the two witnesses (11:3–6). Even though believing Jews will suffer persecution at this time, God will still get the gospel out. Two witnesses will be especially significant. They will probably be individuals alive at that time rather than former prophets brought back to earth for this ministry. Their ministry will last 1,260 days (three and a half years, the last half of Daniel's seventieth week, the Great Tribulation), the focus of John's vision in this chapter. The two witnesses will wear "sackcloth," the dress that in biblical times signified repentance in view of divine judgment. The ministry of these two witnesses resembles that of Zerubbabel and Joshua who sought to restore Israel after her previous (Babylonian) exile. They will be God's anointed servants who bear the light of His truth, are dependent on His Spirit, and speak for Him. They will be able to protect themselves by calling down fire on their enemies who try to harm them, as Elijah did (2 Kings 1:10–14). No one will be able to kill them until God permits this at the very end of their ministry (Rev. 11:7). God will also empower them to do other miracles similar to those Elijah and Moses performed.

The death of the two witnesses (11:7–10). Only when they have finished their ministry will God permit "the beast" to kill the two witnesses. They will not die prematurely. This is the first of thirty-six references in Revelation to the beast, the Antichrist, whose origin is the Abyss (see 9:1). The beast will add insult to injury by allowing the corpses of the two witnesses to lie in the street unburied, a cultural shame worse than death itself in John's day. The city will be similar to Sodom and Egypt in that it will be extremely wicked, morally degraded, antagonistic toward God, and oppressive toward God's people because of Antichrist's influence. The place of Jesus Christ's crucifixion (11:8) identifies this city as Jerusalem. Evidently people from all over the world will be able to view the corpses, probably by television. Earth-dwellers will celebrate because they do not have to listen to the two witnesses' messages from God any longer.

The resurrection of the two witnesses (11:11–13). The breath of life from God will revive the witnesses' dead bodies. Their resurrections will terrify onlookers because these God-haters could do no more to silence their enemies than kill them. The witnesses will hear a voice from heaven calling them home, and their enemies will watch them ascend. Following this ascension an earthquake will destroy 10 percent of Jerusalem and will cause seven thousand people to die. Those who will not die will give glory to God. This does not mean they will become believers, though some might. Instead it means they will acknowledge God's hand in these events.

The end of the second woe (11:14). God interjected the revelations of the mighty angel and the little scroll (10:1–11) and the two witnesses (11:1–13) into the chronological sequence of trumpet judgments to give supplementary, encouraging information. The final woe will follow "soon," on the heels of the second woe.

G. The Seventh Trumpet Judgment (11:15–19)

The scene John saw next was in heaven. The seventh trumpet judgment did not begin immediately, but John received more information preparatory to it (11:15–15:8).

When the seventh angel sounded, loud voices in heaven announced that the long-expected reign of Jesus Christ over the world would begin soon, after the seventh trumpet judgment runs its course. The twenty-four elders' response to this announcement was to prostrate themselves before God. Worship in heaven contrasts with rebellion on earth. The elders thanked God for taking His power in hand and finally reigning. Until now God had allowed powers hostile to His people to control the earth, but soon He will begin to rule directly. The elders continued to anticipate the beginning of Messiah's rule on earth by foreseeing the raging response of unbelieving Gentiles and the outpouring of God's holy wrath (11:18). They also foresaw the judgment of the dead and the rewarding of saints. They further anticipated the destruction of the wicked who have been responsible for the divine judgments that have destroyed the earth.

John then saw the temple in heaven opened (11:19). This event, as the others in this passage, looks ahead and probably pictures the immediate fellowship with God that believers will enjoy following these judgments. The appearance of the ark of the covenant in the vision suggests that God will resume dealing with Israel and will fulfill His covenant promises to that nation. As elsewhere, the storm portrays the manifestation of God's presence and His wrathful judgment. It concludes this part of John's vision which anticipates the end of the Tribulation judgments and the inauguration of God's kingdom on earth.

H. Supplementary Revelation of Satan's Activity in the Great Tribulation (chapters 12–13)

God gave John information about the forces and persons behind the climax of anti-God hostility so he could understand the bowl judgments, which the seventh trumpet judgment contained.

The activity of Satan himself (chapter 12). God gave John a revelation of Satan's activity, especially during the Great Tribulation, to enable his readers to understand better the reasons for and the forces behind the events of this strategic period of history.

As background for the revelation of Satan's activities in the Tribulation, God first gave John information about the devil's long antagonism to Jesus Christ (12:1–6). These verses provide the plot for the drama that unfolds in the rest of the chapter. The great sign John saw was "in heaven." This was the heavenly scene John had already been viewing; this was not the sky. In view of Old Testament imagery the "woman" seems to symbolize the nation of Israel (see Isa. 54:1–6; Jer. 3:20; Ezek. 16:8–14; Hos. 2:19–20). God similarly pictured Israel in one of the nation's early graphic representations (Gen. 37:9–11; see also Isa. 26:17–18; 60:1–3, 20). In the Old Testament there are many figurative references to Israel as a travailing woman who eventually gives birth to Messiah. In John's vision the woman was about to give birth and cried out in labor pains. Probably this pictures Israel's pain before Jesus Christ's appearing at His first advent.

The second "sign" John saw (Rev. 12:3) was the "dragon" whom God later identified as Satan (12:9; 20:2) A dragon is a powerful, aggressive, deadly foe. His red color suggests bloodshed. His seven heads and ten horns represent seven nations and ten rulers (17:12). Ten kings will rule under his authority, but when Antichrist rises to preeminence among them he will subdue three of them, leaving only seven (Dan. 7:7–8, 20, 24; Rev. 13:1). The seven royal crowns picture the political authority of these seven rulers during the Great Tribulation. The "stars" may represent the angels Satan led in rebellion against God, which God cast out of heaven to earth.

Satan proceeded to take out his vengeance against God by trying to prevent the appearance of Messiah at His first advent (12:4; see Matt. 2:13). Satan failed to destroy Jesus at His birth, and because Satan also failed to destroy Him during His life and in His death, Jesus Christ ascended victoriously into heaven. He will yet rule the world with a shepherd's iron rod (Ps. 2:9). The emphases in this whole review of Satan's opposition to God are Jesus' victory and Satan's continuing antagonism. Since Satan could not destroy Jesus, he will turn his attention to Israel. John saw Israel in the Great Tribulation having fled into a wilderness where God protected her 1,260 days (three and a half years), the second half of the Tribulation (Rev. 12:14; see Matt. 24:16; Mark 13:14). Throughout

Scripture a wilderness often represents a place of desolation, safety, discipline, and testing.

In the Great Tribulation God will expel the dragon from heaven (Rev. 12:7–12). Presently Satan has access to God's presence (Job 1–2). Michael the archangel is the leader of God's angelic army and is Israel's special patron (Dan. 10:13, 21; 12:1). He holds high rank among unfallen angels, as Satan does among the fallen. John saw him engaged in battle with Satan and his angels. In John's vision Satan's forces proved weaker, and God threw them out of heaven. Consequently Satan no longer had access to heaven. Satan's expulsion to the earth with his angels will evidently take place at the middle of the Tribulation. During the Great Tribulation there will be unusual satanic activity on earth, including much hardening of heart (Rev. 6–11; 13–18).

John then heard another outburst of praise in heaven, evidently from the Tribulation martyrs (12:10). Their rejoicing anticipated the announced expulsion of Satan. God's salvation (victory), the manifestation of His power, and His kingdom will have come even closer when this happens. Likewise the manifestation of the authority of His Anointed One will be nearer. Believers, whom Satan formerly accused before God, will overcome Satan by Jesus Christ's death and by the word of their testimony. Heaven-dwellers will also rejoice in view of Satan's punishment (12:12) because he will no longer be among them. But everyone living on the earth, especially believers, must beware because he now moves among them more antagonistically than ever. Furthermore he knows that he will have only 1,260 days before Jesus Christ returns to the earth and binds him (see 20:1–2).

In view of his limited time, Satan will concentrate his hatred on the woman, Israel (12:13–17). The Jews will flee from Satan in the future as they fled from Pharaoh in the past (Matt. 24:15–28; Mark 13:14–23). The reason Satan will oppose the Jews is that Christ, his archenemy, came from them, is one of them, and has prepared a glorious future for them. The Jews will receive divine assistance in fleeing from the dragon. God bore the Israelites "on eagles' wings" when He enabled them to escape from Pharaoh (Exod. 19:4; Deut. 32:11; see Isa. 40:31), so the eagle may metaphorically be describing the way God will save them: strongly, swiftly, and safely. Evidently many Jews will flee from Jerusalem into desolate places to escape Satan's persecution (see Zech. 14:1–8; Matt. 24:16; Mark 13:14). God will nourish them in their place of refuge, as He fed the Israelites in the wilderness and Elijah by the brook Kerith.

The reference to a time, times, and half a time (Rev. 12:14) identifies this activity as taking place during the Great Tribulation (see Dan. 7:25; 12:7). A flood is a biblical metaphor for overwhelming evil (Pss. 18:4; 124:2–4; Isa. 43:2), so probably this is a picturesque way of describing Satan's attempt to destroy the Jews who will have congregated in Palestine following the Antichrist's covenant with them. Both water and fire (see Rev. 9:17; 11:5) proceeding from the mouth picture punishment in Scripture. In the past the ground swallowed the Egyptians (Exod. 15:12) and Korah, Dathan, and Abiram (Num. 16:28–33; 26:10; Deut. 11:6; Ps. 106:17). Perhaps God will do similar miracles to preserve the fleeing Jews in the future. Enraged because of his lack of success in completely annihilating all these Jews, Satan will proceed to concentrate his attack on those who believe in Jesus Christ, including the 144,000 (Rev. 7:1–8; 14:1–5).

The activity of Satan's agents (chapter 13). John also received information about Satan's chief human instruments through whom he will pursue his goals during the Tribulation. He recorded this to enable his readers to identify these individuals and to respond properly. This chapter records the continuation of the dragon's activities John described in chapter 12.

John first saw a beast rising out of the sea (13:1–10). He stressed three things about this beast: his conspiracy with the dragon (13:3–4), his success in deceiving the whole world (13:3–4, 8), and his temporary defeat of God's saints (13:6–7). The dragon stood on the seashore watching a beast come out of the sea (see also Dan. 7:3, 7, 8, 19–27). The dragon evidently summoned the beast out of the sea as part of his plan to destroy the rest of the woman's offspring (Rev. 12:17). The ancient world often associated evil with the sea and used the sea as a figure for the Abyss. This figurative use of the sea seems best here since elsewhere John said that the beast came out of the Abyss (11:7; 17:8). The beast had many of the same characteristics as the dragon. They also correspond to the features of the fourth kingdom Daniel saw in his vision (Dan. 7:7–8). In Daniel's vision the ten horns represented ten rulers (7:24). Here the Antichrist has authority over ten rulers. Like the dragon, the beast also had seven heads that apparently represent the remaining seven rulers of nations after three of them disappear (Dan. 7:8). The ten regal crowns are symbols of governmental authority (Rev. 12:3).

The beast is Antichrist, the head of a future empire (13:8, 18; 17:8). He embodies the malevolent forces operative in this empire. This beast will possess characteristic qualities of three animals: a leopard, a bear, and a lion. In Daniel, these animals represented three kingdoms that previously ruled the world: Greece (Dan. 7:6), Medo-Persia (7:5), and Babylon (7:4). The fourth kingdom that Daniel described (7:23) includes the Antichrist's kingdom. The kingdom the beast rules and represents seems to reflect his personal qualities. If the beast's heads represent nations (Rev. 13:1), verse 3 seems to be saying that one of the nations under Satan's authority perished, but then it revived. The apparent resurrection of this nation will be so amazing to the world that many people will give their allegiance and their worship to Antichrist. In so doing they will also submit to Satan who is behind him. Antichrist's ability to revive this nation will make him appear invincible.

The notable abilities of the beast are blasphemy against God and deception of people. These activities also marked Antiochus Epiphanes, the prototype of Antichrist (Dan. 7:8, 11, 20, 25; 12:7). God will give authority to the beast to act as he will during the Great Tribulation. He will blaspheme God by claiming to be God (2 Thess. 2:4). Apparently the beast will share the dragon's antagonism to God and His angels for having cast the dragon out of heaven (Rev. 12:7–9, 12). He will wage war against believers and overcome them and will become a worldwide dictator (Dan. 7:21, 23). No leader has ever been able to rule the entire world. Unbelievers around the world will not only serve Antichrist but will also worship him, but faithful believers will not (Matt. 24:24).

God and John called on the readers of this book to pay attention (Rev. 13:9), particularly those living at this time in the future.[8] God promised the saints that those He has destined for captivity (Antichrist and his followers) will eventually end up as captives, and those who kill others will die (see Matt. 26:52). This assurance that God will execute justice should encourage the saints to persevere steadfastly and to trust God during this period of intense persecution and martyrdom.

John then saw another beast rise to prominence out of the earth (Rev. 13:11–18). His two horns symbolize some power but less power than that of the first beast (13:1). In his external conduct this second beast was peaceful, like a lamb, but his words proved satanic and revealed his true loyalty. The second beast will represent the first beast by acting as his prophet (19:20; 20:10) and will be his agent in directing the persecution of believers. He will lead the worship of the first beast, evidently as the head of a worldwide religious movement, a satanic counterfeit of the Holy Spirit's ministry of pointing people to Christ. Like Pharaoh's magicians, but with greater power, the second beast will have authority to perform supernatural miracles (see Exod. 7:11, 22; 8:7), even calling down fire from heaven (as Elijah did in 1 Kings 18). This power will make many earth-dwellers erroneously conclude that his authority is supreme. He will be able to produce some type of convincing likeness of Antichrist. The second beast will give life to an inanimate object, or he will appear to do so. In either case, he will deceive many people (Rev. 13:14). The image will speak and will put to death those who do not worship the beast. Evidently these events will all take place in Jerusalem and probably in the temple that will stand there at that time.

The second beast will also implement the marking of beast-worshipers from all classes of society. This marking among unbelievers corresponds to the sealing of God's servants in chapter 7. It probably will begin early in the Great Tribulation about the time of the sealing of the 144,000. Those who receive this mark will do so willingly. The mark of the beast is evidently a brandlike mark, similar to a tattoo, that will identify beast-worshipers and will enable them to buy and sell. Those bearing the mark of the beast show by their mark that they are his followers. Many believers, however, will not take the mark of the beast (7:3; 14:1, 9–11), but God will preserve many of them. The interchangeability of the beast's name and the number of his name suggests that the name, written in letters, has a numerical equivalent (13:18). John indicated that it would take wisdom to figure out the number of the beast. By identifying the beast's number believers in the Tribulation will be able to recognize him for who he is. Probably neither the identity of the Antichrist nor the number of his name will be evident until he appears and fulfills prophecy.

Then wise believers will be able to calculate his number as well as identify his person. Until then both aspects of Antichrist's identity will probably remain a mystery.

Chapters 12 and 13 paint a picture of the Great Tribulation in which there is one government, one religion, and one economic system for the entire world. This will be a time of great persecution and martyrdom for believers. Rather than getting better and better, the world will get worse before Jesus Christ's second coming.

As we see world events shaping up for this scenario, they should motivate us to redeem the time before the Rapture or death terminates our ministries here. On the other hand, we should also rejoice that our Savior's second coming is drawing near.

I. Supplementary Revelation of Preparations for the Final Judgments in the Great Tribulation (chapters 14–15)

This section of the book prepares the reader for what will happen toward the very end of the Great Tribulation.

Judgment at the end of the Great Tribulation (chapter 14). The following scenes in John's vision help assure believers of the triumph of Christ and of the judgment of unbelievers at the end of the Tribulation. The sacrifices that believers make to remain faithful to their Lord during this time will not be meaningless. This chapter explains what will become of those who refuse to receive the mark of the beast and are killed (14:1–5), and what will happen to the beast and his servants (14:6–20).

The 144,000 will triumph ultimately (14:1–5). John saw the time at the end of the Great Tribulation when Jesus Christ will return to the earth. His second coming does not take place here but in 19:11–21. John only saw it as happening here in his vision. He saw the Lamb standing on earth, specifically on Mount Zion, with the 144,000 Jewish witnesses whom God had sealed for the Tribulation (7:3). Apparently their sealing will protect them from God's wrath but not from all the antagonism of the dragon and the beasts (12:12, 17). Some of them will evidently die as martyrs (13:15). When Jesus Christ comes back to the earth, they will come back with Him. The seal is the mark of their ultimate victory (22:4). John heard voices singing a new song of praise to God, a song that the 144,000 could appreciate uniquely. They were morally pure, faithful to the Lord, a special gift to God, and people of integrity (14:4–5).

John also heard four climactic announcements that provide incentives for remaining faithful to God and for resisting the beasts (14:6–13). The apostle saw another angel flying in midheaven. He came with good news. He called on earth-dwellers to fear and glorify God because the hour of His judgment had come. This is the very last chance these unbelievers would have to change their allegiance from Satan to God before the final judgments of the Great Tribulation begin (14:6–7). A second angel followed the first with the message that Babylon had fallen (14:8). This is another message anticipating a future event (see chapter 18). Babylon will be like a temptress who gives wine to a man to seduce him to commit fornication. A third angel followed the former two with a third message in this sequence, warning the beast-worshipers of their judgment (14:9–12). The goal of this warning is to alert potential worshipers of the beast to their doom, if they follow the beast, and to encourage believers to remain faithful. Another voice told John to record that it would be a blessing for the believers who live during the Great Tribulation to die as martyrs (14:13). The Holy Spirit added that they would be at rest beyond the grave and God would then reward their faithful deeds.

John then saw a scene on earth that furnishes background information before the revelation of the seven bowl judgments (14:14–20). This description is similar to Daniel's prophecy of Messiah's second coming (Dan. 7:13–14). The person John saw was evidently Jesus Christ. Another angel came out of the opened heavenly temple and announced that the time to judge those living on the earth had arrived. The Judge then judged those on the earth. This judgment will occur at the end of the Tribulation (Rev. 19:17–21).

The fifth angel in this group came out of the heavenly temple ready to execute judgment (14:17). Another angel, the sixth in this chapter, came out from the golden altar of incense in heaven in response to the Tribulation saints' earlier prayers for vengeance (6:9–10). The two reapings seem to describe a single judgment at the end of the Great Tribulation (19:15, 17–21). The vine may represent Jews and the wheat Gentiles. The earth had yielded a "crop" of unbelievers that now, at the end of the Tribulation, would come into judgment. The city in view is Jerusalem. Judgment will take place all over Palestine at this time (14:20).

Preparation for the bowl judgments (chapter 15). This chapter continues the supplementary revelation begun in 12:1 and the emphasis on preparation for the final judgments of the Great Tribulation begun in 14:1.

The "sign" John saw signified God's final judgments on earth-dwellers during the Great Tribulation (15:1). The sign itself was the seven angels who control seven plagues. These angels were now ready to do their duty. The bowl "plagues" that follow have many similarities to the plagues that God sent on Egypt, thereby suggesting that God's purpose in both series of judgments is the same: to punish godless idolaters and to liberate the godly for future blessing and service.

John again saw the sea of glass that was similar to crystal (15:2–4; see also 4:6). The people standing on this sea will apparently be the Tribulation martyrs who will have overcome the beast, his image, and the number of his name. These martyrs sang a song of praise to God that Moses and the Lamb made possible.

John next saw the heavenly temple opened and the angelic agents of judgment (15:5–8), who came out from God's presence to purify the earth. One of the living creatures (see 4:6) gave each angel a bowl full of God's wrath (see 5:8). No one could enter God's presence until He had finished judging the earth-dwellers. This indicates the climactic and intense nature of these judgments.

> **Summary:** Chapter 15 is more of a prelude to chapter 16 than a conclusion to chapters 12–14. Chapters 12–14 record prophetically historical information about the Great Tribulation but not in the chronological sequence of the three sets of seven judgments (seals, trumpets, and bowls). Chapter 15 is similar to 8:1 in that it prepares for the next set of judgments—for the resumption of the chronological progression of events on earth that ended temporarily in 11:19.

J. The Seven Bowl Judgments (chapter 16)

The fact that God told all seven angels to pour out their bowls seems to indicate that these judgments will follow each other in rapid succession (16:1). In the vision the first bowl judgment resulted in ugly and painful sores breaking out on the beast-worshipers (16:2). The outpouring of the second bowl resulted in the destruction of all sea life, not just one-third of it as in the second trumpet judgment (16:3). In the third bowl judgment all the freshwater sources become blood (16:4).

The revelation of these judgments was interrupted as angels and martyrs ascribed praise to God (16:5–7). The angel responsible for the sea and fresh water attributed righteousness to the eternal God for judging. He affirmed that those guilty of slaying the saints and prophets deserve what they get. They took lives contrary to God's will, and now God was taking their lives in exchange. The Tribulation martyrs offered their "amen" from under the altar.

The fourth bowl judgment increased the sun's intensity so it burned many earth-dwellers (16:8–9). But instead of repenting, the beast-worshipers cursed God. The fifth bowl judgment resulted in the darkening of the (first) beast's throne. Since the beast's kingdom is worldwide, this darkening amounts to a global judgment. This judgment of worldwide darkness inflicts excruciating pain on the beast-worshipers also. The earth-dwellers still fail to repent and continue to blaspheme God.

The sixth bowl judgment resulted in war (16:12–16). God dried up the Euphrates River so the kings of the East can cross with their armies (see Dan. 11:44; Isa. 11:15). God earlier dried up the Red Sea so the Israelites could advance toward the Promised Land from the west (Exod. 14:21–22), and He dried up the Jordan River so they could cross over from the east (Josh. 3:13–17; 4:23). Elijah too parted the waters of the Jordan (2 Kings 2:8). These are probably the Oriental armies that will assemble in Israel for the Battle of Armageddon. The drying up of the Euphrates will be an immediate help to these advancing armies, but it will set them up for defeat, as was true of Pharaoh's army. Rulers from all over the earth will join the kings of the East in a final great conflict

(Rev. 16:13–14). Demons will go out to the kings of the earth deceiving them to assemble their armies in Palestine for the Battle of Armageddon.

Jesus Christ Himself evidently gave the parenthetic invitation and warning that John described next (16:15). His second coming will be like a thief in that it will be sudden, and His enemies will not expect it (Matt. 24:43; Luke 12:39; 1 Thess. 5:2). Believers who understand the revelation of this book, on the other hand, will be expecting His return. Jesus Christ urged these faithful believers to be watchful and pure (Matt. 25:1–30).

The seventh bowl judgment (Rev. 16:17–21) has the greatest impact of all since the air into which the angel pours his bowl is what humans breathe. With the outpouring of the final bowl God announced that His series of judgments for this period in history was complete. This statement anticipates the completion of the seventh bowl judgment, which John was yet to describe. Lightning, thunder, and the greatest earthquake this planet has ever experienced will accompany, and to some extent produce, the desolation that follows. A great storm again appears at the end of another series of judgments (see 8:5; 11:19). These are signs of divine judgment, but this earthquake is much larger than any previous one. It heralds the seventh bowl judgment and the end of the seal and trumpet judgments. All three series of judgments end at the same time. A result of this unprecedented earthquake is the splitting of Jerusalem into three parts. Evidently the earthquake will destroy virtually all the cities of the world.

Babylon is the special object of God's judgment, symbolized by the cup of wine she receives. Chapters 17 and 18 describe the fall of Babylon in more detail. The earthquake will also level mountains and cause islands to disappear. The accompanying storm will include huge hailstones that will fall on the earth and crush many people. In spite of all these judgments the hearts of earth-dwellers will remain hard, as Pharaoh's did during the plague of hail in Egypt (Exod. 9:24). They will know that God sent this calamity, but rather than repenting they will shake their fists in God's face.

K. Supplementary Revelation of the Judgment of Ungodly Systems in the Great Tribulation (chapters 17–18)

Before recording the next major event in chronological sequence, God led John to give more revelation concerning the fate of Babylon (see 16:19). Babylon in chapters 17 and 18 represents the head of gentile world power. Chapter 17 focuses on the religious system God identified with Babylon in Scripture, and chapter 18 focuses on the commercial system He identified with it. Babylon is not just the name of a city in the Middle East. It is also a name that epitomizes the chief characteristics of that city throughout history, which have been a certain religious system and a certain commercial system. In a similar way the name "Wall Street" describes a literal street but also a financial system or enterprise, and the name "Hollywood" represents both a city and an industry.

Religion in the Great Tribulation (chapter 17). One of the angels who poured out the bowl judgments served as John's guide as he viewed these events in his vision. The "great prostitute" is Babylon (17:5), the personification of spiritual fornication and idolatry (Isa. 23:15–17; Jer. 2:20–31; 13:27; Ezek. 16:17–19; Hos. 2:5; Nah. 3:4). Evidently the beast and she stood on the shore in John's vision. The "many waters" represent humankind (Rev. 17:15), not a specific geographical site. This fact suggests that it is Babylon as a symbol that is in view here rather than the physical city. Babylon dominates humankind. The "kings of the earth" (17:2) are world leaders who represent their kingdoms (16:14). They committed adultery with Babylon by uniting with the apostate system she symbolizes. This system made all earth-dwellers "intoxicated," that is, it had a controlling influence over them.

The angel carried John away in the Spirit to a wilderness area where he saw the prostitute sitting on a beast (17:3). The description of this animal is exactly the same as the Antichrist in 13:1 except that here it is scarlet. She sat in a position of control over the Antichrist, and he supported her. The woman's clothing was royal and luxurious, and her jewelry made her look like a queen. The cup in her hand contained idolatrous abominations, unclean things connected with her spiritual immorality. She wore expensive, attractive garments and accessories that made her externally appealing, but she is a counterfeit beauty. What is inside her is unclean. It was customary in John's day for Roman prostitutes to wear their names on their headbands. Her name was a "mystery," namely, something not previously revealed but now made clear.

The content of the mystery about this Babylonian system is what John revealed here, especially the new revelation about its evil character and judgment. The harlot represents Babylon, the "mother of prostitutes." Besides being a prostitute herself she is also the fountainhead of many other evil religious systems and everything anti-Christian. This description of Babylonianism probably encompasses all false religions, including perversions of Christianity. This system had destroyed true believers and rejoiced in their deaths, which amazed John. A system purporting to honor God was killing His faithful followers!

The angel promised to interpret these revelations that were so strange to John (17:7). The beast, as we have already seen, is the Antichrist (13:1–3). Here the interpreting angel referred to the resuscitation of one of his nations (see 13:3, 12, 14). Evidently this revival will happen at the middle of the Tribulation. The beast will come out of the Abyss, the home of Satan (11:7) and the hold of his demons (9:1–2, 11), when this revival takes place. This suggests that Satan will give him supernatural powers. The beast's resuscitation of this nation will greatly impress earth-dwellers, who will conclude that he is a divine savior, whereas he will actually be a demonic slaughterer. He will deceive everyone but the elect (see 13:8; Matt. 24:24; Mark 13:22). The beast's seven heads represent seven kings, the leaders of seven nations (Rev. 17:9; Dan. 7:17, 23). The angel also referred to them as "mountains." In the Bible a mountain is often a symbol of a prominent government. The woman sits in authority over the seven rulers and their nations, but she is not one of them.

The seven kings are rulers over seven kingdoms. The prominent one in John's day that "is" was certainly the Roman Empire. The five most prominent world powers preceding Rome that had fallen are probably Egypt, Assyria, Babylon, Persia, and Greece. The seventh kingdom that was yet to come and would remain a little while is the beast's kingdom (Rev. 13:3; 17:8). All these kingdoms have persecuted or will persecute God's people. Evidently the beast is one of the seven in the sense that his initial kingdom is on a par with the seven major empires just mentioned.

He is the eighth in that he will establish an eighth major empire with a worldwide government after he revives a formerly defunct nation. When Jesus Christ returns to the earth, He will destroy the beast and his (eighth) kingdom.

The specific identity of the ten horns (other kings but without kingdoms when John wrote) is not yet clear. They will be allies of the beast and serve under him in his worldwide government during the Great Tribulation (Dan. 7:23–24). They will each rule a kingdom simultaneously and with the beast (7:7, 24). They will have authority to rule "for one hour," that is, only very briefly during the Great Tribulation. Evidently their short, independent rule will immediately precede the return of Jesus Christ to the earth. The beast will give them their authority, but God will permit him to do so. The single purpose of these end-time kingdoms is to oppose the Lamb (Rev. 17:14). The ten rulers will submit to the Antichrist's leadership to achieve this end. He will have to put down three of them who revolt against him (Dan. 7:24; Rev. 12:3; 13:1; 17:3). At the very end of the Tribulation these kings will fight against Jesus Christ as He returns to earth (16:14, 16; 19:19–21). The Lamb will defeat them and will prove to be the Lord of lords and King of kings (19:16), a title Antichrist will seek to claim for himself in his worldwide empire. Those with Christ will accompany Him from heaven.

The angel next helped John understand the judgment of the prostitute (17:15–18). Water is a common biblical symbol representing many people. The harlot will exercise a controlling influence over the population of the world. There will be one religious system that will encompass all nations and peoples during the Tribulation, but the beast and his allies will eventually throw off the harlot and thoroughly destroy her. They will plunder her wealth, expose her corruption, and utterly consume her, as dogs ate Jezebel's flesh. This may occur in the middle of the Tribulation when the Antichrist breaks his covenant with Israel and demands that everyone on earth worship him or die (Dan. 9:27; 11:26–38; Matt. 24:15; 2 Thess. 2:4; Rev. 13:8, 15). The ultimate cause of this action is God's sovereign purpose. The allied kings will submit to the beast's leadership because this will help them achieve their goals of attaining universal power and resisting God. This situation will continue until the end of the age, until all God's words about rebellion against Him in the Tribulation have come to fulfillment. The woman represents "the great city." In the context this undoubtedly refers to Babylon. As a system of apostate religion, which Babylon originated (Gen. 10–11) and symbolizes, it reigned over the leaders and kingdoms of the world. The influence of Jezebel over King Ahab is a striking parallel of religion guiding the decisions of political rulers.

The focus of the revelation in this chapter is an apostate religious system and its relationship to government during the seven-year Tribulation period. During the first half of the Tribulation it will be an ecumenical worldwide body that will stand above government and will be aggressively hostile to true believers in God. In the middle of the Tribulation, the Antichrist will terminate it and demand universal worship of himself.

Commerce in the Great Tribulation (chapter 18). God next led John to reveal the destruction of the commercial and economic system that Babylon also symbolizes. What Babylon symbolizes in this chapter is different from what it symbolizes in chapter 17, but the striking parallels between chapters 17 and 18 point to a unified system represented by a city that rules the world.

Another angel announced the next scene that John saw in his vision (18:1–3). After God judges Babylon, it will be a prison for unclean birds, a biblical figure of desolation. Babylon will become utterly desolate. The political, economic, commercial system originating in Babylon seems to be in view here. Her philosophy will influence all the nations to act immorally and they will grow rich at the expense of and in defiance of others. Babylon's influence will be worldwide. Political self-interest and materialism are its chief sins.

Another voice from heaven instructed God's people to separate themselves from the system that the city symbolizes so they would avoid getting caught in her judgment (18:4). The people addressed are faithful believers living in the Tribulation. Unless they separate from her sins, they will be hurt by the judgment coming on her; but if they do dissociate themselves from her and her sins, they will enjoy deliverance. They should not have the attitude of Lot's wife, who hankered after another worldly city that God destroyed (Gen. 19:26; Luke 17:32). Babylon's sins, like the bricks used to build the tower of Babel (Gen. 11:3–4), will accumulate so they finally reach heaven. She will exhaust God's patience. God will notice and remember her sins, and because He is righteous, He will judge them. Babylon will have persecuted and murdered the saints (Rev. 18:24; 19:2). The cup she will use to seduce others will become the instrument of her own punishment (18:6). This Babylon's claims of superiority and self-sufficiency echo those of ancient Babylon. Babylon and the cities that are the centers for this worldwide network of political and commercial activity will evidently be destroyed in the great earthquake (16:18–19). She will collapse suddenly, not decline gradually. The strength of the Lord God will accomplish this destruction.

Three groups of people mourn Babylon's destruction: kings, merchants, and sea people (18:9–20). World government leaders will mourn when they see the collapse of the system that has sustained them and enabled them to live luxuriously. The merchants also will lament over the destruction of this system. The collapse of economic Babylon results in merchants being unable to buy and sell goods. They sorrow over the loss of customers and profits that its destruction causes. The variety of the goods John listed suggests how extensive trade will be at this time in history. The market is the world. The twenty-eight items listed in 18:12–13 fall into seven categories: precious metals and gems, clothing, furnishings, spices, food, animals and implements, and people. People will even buy and sell other human beings. The merchants will also lose their luxurious possessions. The sea people will stand at a distance, watching the city burn (18:17). Perhaps these sea people are of special interest because they represent distributors of goods in John's day. They will echo the laments and repeat the behavior of the kings and the merchants. In contrast to these earth-dwellers God's people will rejoice when Babylon falls (18:20).

The angel's act of throwing the millstone into the sea (18:21) is symbolic of Babylon's fate. As it is impossible for that huge stone to rise to the surface, so the economic system that has driven this world virtually throughout its history will sink and never rise again. Babylon's destruction will be sudden, violent, and permanent. Many other things will end with the destruction of this system: the rejoicing of unbelievers, the work of producers of goods, the use of their tools, the light their activities produced, and the happiness that resulted. Where there had previously been hustle and bustle, there will then be silence. The angel gave three reasons for this devastation (18:23–24). First, people whom the world regards as great will have enriched themselves and lifted themselves up in pride because of Babylon's influence. Second, Babylon will seduce all nations into thinking that joy, security, honor, and meaning in life come through the accumulation of material wealth. Third, she will kill the saints. Unbelievers have killed many believers, directly and indirectly, in their pursuit of material possessions.

It seems that the Babylon John described in this chapter is the commercial system of buying and selling goods to make excessive profits in a greedy way. This system has become so much a part of life that it is difficult for us to imagine life without it. Self-interest or greed is at the root of this system, which began when people first assembled to make a name for themselves at Babel (Gen. 10–11).

> Whereas believers have always had to live within this system, we have always known that we must not adopt the philosophy that drives it, namely, selfishness. Jesus Christ will destroy this system when He returns at His second coming, and it will exist no longer. Therefore we must be careful to maintain a healthy detachment from the values and ideals that drive this system even though we cannot escape participating in it.

L. The Second Coming of Christ (chapter 19)

John wrote the record of his vision of events surrounding the Lord Jesus' second coming to share the future vindication of Him with his readers. The chapter has two major parts: the rejoicing triggered by Babylon's fall (Rev. 19:1–10) and the events surrounding the Lamb's return to the earth (19:11–21).

The praise of God in heaven (19:1–10). This passage has strong ties to what precedes (16:17–18:24). It is the concluding revelation concerning the fall of Babylon, the latter-day Babel, and the Antichrist, the antitype of Pharaoh of the Exodus. The praise in this section is in response to the angel's invitation for those in heaven to rejoice (18:20). The four songs in verses 1–5 look back to the judgment of Babylon, and the song in verses 6–8 looks forward to the marriage supper of the Lamb. The harlot dies, but the bride begins to enjoy new life.

The first song (19:1–2) praises God for judging the prostitute. A heavenly multitude praises God because of His true and just judgments, especially of the harlot Babylon. Probably both aspects of Babylonianism are in view here, religious and commercial. The essence of the harlot's guilt lies in her corrupting the earth with her immoralities (14:8; 17:2; 18:3). By destroying Babylon God will avenge the blood of believers who died as a result of her influences. A second burst of praise from the same group glorified God for judging Babylon so its influences will never rise again (19:3). This encore heightens the praise in the first song. The twenty-four elders and the four living creatures echoed these sentiments in a third song of praise (19:4). Then an authoritative voice from the throne called for added continuous praise from all God's servants (19:5). The call extends to creatures of all classes.

Together all God's servants in heaven now praised Him for the fact that He reigns (19:6–8). In this statement they look forward to what is about to happen, namely, Jesus Christ's return to earth and the beginning of His messianic reign. This praise is appropriately great since Messiah's earthly reign is the climax of human history. The song continues with an exhortation to rejoice and to glorify God. God deserves praise because He has prepared the bride, the church, for the Lamb. The bride is the Lamb's newly married wife who has been joined to Him in heaven immediately after the Rapture. For the Jews, the wedding figure stressed the intimate relationship that will exist between God and His people in the earthly messianic kingdom.

The person who next spoke to John seems to be the same angel who had been guiding him throughout the revelation concerning Babylon (19:9). He instructed John to write again, this time another beatitude. This blessing gives Tribulation saints additional motivation to remain faithful. Those invited to the Lamb's marriage supper include His friends as well as the bride. This implies the presence of other believers besides church saints at this celebration. These would be Tribulation martyrs and believers who will live through the Tribulation and enter the Millennium alive. They may also include Old Testament saints who will experience resurrection at the beginning of the Millennium (see Isa. 26:19; Dan. 12:2).

The wonder of this revelation and the certainty of its fulfillment overwhelmed John. He fell down to worship the angel who had revealed these things to him, but this was not proper, as the angel explained. Human beings should worship only God. To emphasize the centrality of Jesus Christ in this testimony and to encourage worship of God, the angel said that the spirit of prophecy is the testimony of Jesus (Rev. 19:10). That is, the testimony that Jesus has given is the essence of prophetic proclamation. Jesus is the source of revelation, and angels just communicate it.

The return of Christ to earth (19:11–16). On the one hand, the return of Jesus Christ to the earth is the climax of all that has preceded in Revelation. On the other hand, it is the first of seven final things that John saw and recorded. These things were Christ's return, Satan's defeat, Satan's binding, the Millennium, Satan's final end, the last judgment, and the new heavens and new earth including the New Jerusalem. John recorded these events in chronological sequence. The chronological progression of events on earth resumes from 16:21.

John saw another scene in heaven (19:11). Heaven was now standing open. John saw Christ, rather than the Antichrist (6:2), riding a white horse. John described Him as Faithful (to God) and True (the real Messiah). He came out of heaven to judge the beast and to make war with him on earth. Jesus Christ's eyes suggest His piercing judgment of sin that takes everything into account (19:12). His many diadems symbolize His right to rule the world as King of kings. His name was not known to John or to anyone else at that time, but it may become known when He returns. The blood on His robe is probably the blood of his enemies. The "Word of God" is a familiar title signifying that He is the expression of God's mind and heart, the authoritative declaration that results in the destruction of God's enemies. With Christ, John saw armies mounted on horses. Christ will strike down His enemies with a word that His long, tongue-shaped sword symbolized. He will destroy His enemies with inflexible righteousness pictured by the shepherd's iron rod, and He will execute the fierce wrath of God Almighty that these enemies must drink. He will return as King of kings and Lord of lords.

The destruction of the wicked on earth (19:17–21). An angel standing in the sun cried loudly for all the birds flying in midheaven to assemble (see Matt. 24:28; Luke 17:37). After the Battle of Armageddon, the site will provide a feast for vultures, a great supper God will give to them.

John now saw another scene on earth (Rev. 19:19). The beast at this time will have ten allies (17:12–14). Their armies will represent the world-wide population of earth-dwellers. These armies will unite to oppose Christ (16:13–16). The battle will be over world leadership. When Jesus Christ returns, the beast's allies who will have been fighting each other (Dan. 11:40–44) will unite against Christ (Rev. 16:14). This is a description of the judgment portrayed in 14:14–20. It is surprisingly brief in view of its importance in history. Probably the battle will not last long (see Matt. 24:13–45). Jesus Christ will destroy all who resist Him. The only people left alive will be faithful believers who have not died or suffered martyrdom during the Tribulation. They will enter the Millennium with mortal bodies and will repopulate the earth. The Lord Jesus will then cast the beast and the false prophet alive into the lake of fire (Rev. 19:20), where they will remain forever. The rest of Jesus Christ's enemies, the ten kings and their armies, will die in a moment by His word and will go to Hades. There they will await resurrection and final judgment at the end of the Millennium (20:11–15). So many people will die that the birds will have plenty to eat.

M. The Millennial Reign of Christ (chapter 20)

The binding of Satan (20:1–3). It is predictable that having judged the beast and the false prophet (19:20), Jesus Christ would next deal with Satan. God assigned an angel to bind the devil. This is the end of Satan's time in the Tribulation in which God allowed him to wreak havoc on the earth (12:12). Four titles make the identity of the bound creature certain. There is no reason to take this thousand-year time period as symbolic. God did not reveal the length of the Millennium before now, but neither did He reveal many other details about the future before He gave John these visions. The angel will throw Satan into the Abyss and then shut and seal the opening to it to guarantee that he will not escape (20:3).

During the Millennium Satan will not have access to the earth. The nations in view will be the descendants of mortal believers who will not die during the Great Tribulation and who will live on in the Millennium. God will release Satan to fulfill His plans after the thousand years (20:3).

The resurrection of Tribulation martyrs (20:4–6). In a new scene John saw people sitting on thrones to rule and judge. They are probably the faithful saints who returned with Christ to the earth. They receive authority from God to take charge of the earth, the beast's domain, under Christ's rule. John also saw the souls of some people not yet resurrected. These are Tribulation martyrs who had died because they held steadfastly to the testimony that Jesus bore and the Word of God. They had refused to take the mark of the beast or to worship his image and had died for their faith (13:15). They now experienced bodily resurrection. These martyrs will reign with Christ on earth during the Millennium. The "rest of the dead" evidently refers to the wicked who are physically dead, whom God will raise at the end of the Millennium (see 20:12).

The "first" resurrection refers to the first of the two resurrections John spoke of in the context (20:4–6, 12). It includes the resurrection of the Tribulation martyrs at the second coming of Christ and Old Testament saints resurrected at the same time (Dan. 12:2). The second resurrection is the resurrection of the wicked at the end of the Millennium (Rev. 20:12). Revelation's fifth beatitude (20:6) reveals that those who participate in the first resurrection are blessed and holy. The "second death" is spiritual death beyond physical death, death of the soul as well as the body (Matt. 10:28). Specifically the first resurrection involves deliverance from the lake of fire. Those who participate in the first resurrection are also blessed because they will be priests of God and Christ, and they will reign with Christ for one thousand years.

The final judgment of Satan (20:7–10). At the end of the Millennium God will release Satan from the Abyss. The devil will then resume his former work of deceiving the nations into thinking they will be better off submitting to his authority than to Jesus Christ's. He will eventually gather innumerable soldiers from all parts of the world to fight against Jesus Christ. The people who follow Satan in this rebellion will be those who have not trusted Jesus Christ as their Savior during the Millennium. Even though everyone will know who Jesus Christ is during the Millennium (Jer. 31:33–34), not everyone will trust in Him as Savior. Only believers will enter the Millennium, but everyone born during that time will need to trust Christ to experience eternal salvation. "Gog and Magog" (Rev. 20:8) evidently refers to the world's rulers and nations in rebellion against God. The rebels will occupy Palestine and surround the dwelling place of believers, even the earthly city of Jerusalem, Christ's capital during the Millennium. Nevertheless God will destroy them with fire from heaven. Then He will cast Satan into the lake of fire that He previously prepared for the devil and his angels (Matt. 25:41). The fact that the beast and the false prophet are still there shows that this is a place of conscious torment, not annihilation (Rev. 19:20). Furthermore it is a place of eternal judgment: "day and night forever and ever." This will be Satan's final abode, and this judgment will constitute the ultimate bruising of his head (see Gen. 3:15).

The judgment of the wicked (20:11–15). John viewed another scene in his vision. The "great white throne" is evidently God's throne in heaven. John saw earth and heaven flee from God's presence, which indicates that we have come to the end of His dealings with this earth as we know it. The dead standing before this throne are evidently the unsaved of all ages who are now resurrected and judged. They come from all classes and groups of humanity. The "books" contain a record of their deeds. The "book of life" contains the names of God's elect. God will condemn those raised to face this judgment because of their works, including failure to believe in Jesus Christ (see John 6:29). God will resurrect the bodies of all unbelievers and unite them with their spirits. From this point on there will be no more death. God will cast death and Hades into the lake of fire, which is hell, the place of eternal punishment.

N. The New Heavens and New Earth (21:1–22:5)

John's vision of new heavens and a new earth is a picture of new beginnings, a sharp contrast to the lake of fire, another final end.

The vision of the new heavens and new earth (21:1). John now saw a new scene that elaborated on the passing away of the present earth and heavens to which he had just referred briefly (20:11). The new heavens and earth will come into existence after the Millennium and the Great White Throne judgment. By the first heavens and earth John meant our planet and the heavens above it. The new earth will have no seas, but oceans will exist in the Millennium (see, for example, Ezek. 47:8, 10, 15, 17–20). The sea is the first of seven evils that John said would not exist in the new creation, the others being death, mourning, weeping, pain, the curse, and night (21:4, 25; 22:3, 5). The sea is an evil in that it opposes humankind.

Conditions in the new earth (21:2–8). John saw a city descending from God's presence to the new earth. It was holy in contrast to the former Jerusalem. As Jerusalem was Jesus Christ's capital during the Millennium, so the New Jerusalem will be His capital in the new earth. In the bride-husband metaphor, the city is the bride, and Christ is the husband. This bride of Christ, the New Jerusalem, now evidently encompasses two previous brides of Christ, Israel and the church.

Another loud voice announced that God's tabernacle, the New Jerusalem, was now among men (21:3). Finally the unhindered and unending relationship between God and humankind that God has always desired people to enjoy will become a reality. He will dwell among His cleansed people, and they will experience intimate fellowship with Him. This is the supreme blessing of the New Jerusalem. God will compassionately wipe away all tears at the inception of the new earth, tears caused by life in the old creation. Sorrow, death, and pain will all end, along with the tears, mourning, and crying that result from them. This is a final reversal of the curse (Gen. 3). All these former experiences will be gone forever then.

John turned from the vision of the New Jerusalem briefly to describe some of God's utterances (Rev. 21:5–8). God announced that He will bring a new creation into existence. Evidently an angel then instructed John to write down what God had said because His words were faithful and true. The One sitting on the throne resumed speaking (21:6). The judgments of the Tribulation and the whole old creation stood accomplished. He promised to meet the deepest needs of His people. Anyone, especially believers, can come to God to receive from Him freely what is truly satisfying. Overcoming believers will inherit the new creation. "I will be his

God and he will be My son" is another special honor (21:7). In contrast, the unsaved, whose lives are characteristically marked by sin, will be thrown into the lake of fire.

The description of the New Jerusalem (21:9–22:5). God now provided John with more information about the New Jerusalem. This detail is something of a parenthesis within the larger revelation of the new heavens and new earth. It expands the brief announcement of the holy city coming down out of heaven from God (21:2).

One of the angels with the seven bowls of judgment served as John's guide in this part of his vision (21:9–10). The fact that one of these particular angels helped John understand both the mystery of Babylon and that of the New Jerusalem sets these two cities in stark contrast. Then in a new vision an angel took John to a high vantage point from which he could see the new holy city descending out of heaven from God.

This city obviously appeared extremely impressive to John (21:11–21). The first and most important characteristic that John noted was its radiant glow. It shone with the splendor of God Himself because God was in it. John compared the glory of the city to that of a beautiful gem. The city's secure and inviolable wall with twelve gate towers was what caught John's attention next. Its many gate towers made the city easy to access. The fact that each gate tower bears a name of one of Israel's tribes may indicate that Israel will have a distinctive identity and role in this city as it has had through history. Since there are foundations to the city it will apparently rest on the new earth. Probably each section of the wall, between the gate towers, has its own foundation. Evidently the church, represented by the apostles, will be in the New Jerusalem along with Israel. God has a role for each group and an identity separate from the other in the future as He did in the past and as He does in the present.

The fact that the angel's measuring rod was gold reflects the dignity and importance of the task of measuring this city's gate towers and walls (21:15). John described the shape and then the size of the city. Its base was square, suggesting stability. The dimensions of this city were twelve thousand stadia (approximately fifteen hundred miles) on each of its four sides and fifteen hundred miles high. This description suggests either a cube or a pyramid shape. The city wall was evidently one hundred forty-four cubits (about two hundred sixteen feet or seventy-two yards) thick, the picture of security. The walls appeared to be glistening, overlaid with brilliant material, suggesting further the radiance of the place. The whole city appeared to shine like a mass of pure gold. Perhaps John meant that there was no impurity in the city. The foundation stones were themselves jewels of many different colors, suggesting unusual beauty and worth. Evidently each gate tower resembled one huge pearl, the most precious gem in John's day. Even the streets of the city were made of the most costly and beautiful material. John seems to have been describing the heavenly city with many metaphors rather than giving us a photographic representation of it.

The illumination of the city was of particular interest to John (21:22–27). God will bring people into intimate relationship with Himself in the New Jerusalem. Unlike old Jerusalem, there will be no temple in the new city because God Himself and the Lamb will be there. The whole city will, therefore, be like a temple. Evidently there will be no sun and moon (and stars) in the new heavens because God's glory will illuminate the whole earth. The city will be so bright that it provides light for the whole new creation. The nations may be groups of believers viewed according to their old-creation nationality, which they will retain in the new creation.

The kings (rulers) are probably faithful believers who previously ruled under Christ during His millennial reign. These kings will bring their glory into the city, thus increasing its glory by simply entering it, since they are glorious individuals. In John's day cities closed their gates to keep out enemies, but there will be no enemies in the new earth so the gates will remain open. The gates will admit these leaders who will bring glory and honor to God from their respective groups of followers, signifying worship in the new creation. Only the saved will enter the city. The only way to gain entrance into it is to believe on Jesus Christ, the Lamb of God (21:27).

Essentially what John saw next was Paradise regained (22:1–5). Having viewed the splendor of the New Jerusalem, he now saw what will nourish and enrich the lives of God's people there. The pure river seems to be symbolic of the refreshment and sustenance God provides. This river proceeded from the throne that belongs to God and the Lamb. The

> *The more distinct our vision is of the beauty and glory of the city to which we journey, the less our immediate environment will attract us.*

throne evidently stood at the head of the main street of the city so that looking down this street the throne appeared to John to be in its middle. John also saw the tree of life. When Adam and Eve fell, they lost their access to eternal life in the Garden of Eden. In the New Jerusalem the residents will have access to this literal tree, perhaps symbolizing their eternal life (see 2:7). Perhaps John saw the river dividing and flowing on both sides of the tree. A tree surrounded by water is the epitome of a fruitful tree. This tree was perpetually rather than seasonally in fruit; it produced a new crop of fruit each month of the year.

Evidently the new creation will not have a lunar calendar, since there will be no moon, but another type of calendar will define time.[9] There will no longer be a curse because the tree of life will provide continuous health for the nations. The curse in view is probably the curse God pronounced on the old creation at the Fall. God will have intimate fellowship with His people because this curse will have been lifted. Believers will occupy themselves worshiping and serving God and the Lamb. They will see God's face and enjoy personal, intimate fellowship with Him. They will be able to do this because they will be pure in heart, righteous, and holy then. Moreover they will bear God's name on their foreheads; they will be His and will reflect His divine glory. As His servants they will reign with Him forever. This is the ultimate fulfillment of God's desire and command that mankind should rule over His creation (Gen. 1:26).

The prophecy of things to come (Rev. 1:19), which began in 4:1, closes with a picture of God's servants worshiping around His throne and ruling under His authority.

IV. THE EPILOGUE TO THE BOOK (22:6–21)

John reported concluding information and instructions that God gave him in this final section of the book to comfort and caution his readers. This section consists of verbal exchanges between an angel and John, and between Jesus and John. Three emphases mark this epilogue. First, this prophecy is genuine (22:6–7, 8–9, 16, 18–19). Second, Jesus will return imminently (22:6–7, 10, 12, 20). Third, the unfit should beware, and the faithful should take courage (22:11–12, 15, 17–19). The whole epilogue is similar to the first chapter in many ways.

A. The Testimony of the Angel (22:6–7)

The angel who had been revealing the new creation to John assured him that these things that will happen soon (4:1–22:5) are faithful and true. It was the Lord, the God who inspired the prophets, who had revealed what John had received. God had sent His angel to reveal these things to His servant John, who was one of the prophets. Jesus Christ promised to return soon (22:7). The book closes as it opened, with a special blessing for those who pay attention to what it teaches (see 1:3).

B. The Testimony of John (22:8–11)

John affirmed the angel's words that the prophecy was genuine. He himself had heard and seen the things he had recorded. John reacted by worshiping the angel who revealed them to him. But the angel rebuked John for doing this (see 19:10). People should worship God, not His servants. The specific mention of the prophets as a special group of believers here (22:9) heightens respect for all prophecy and this prophecy in particular. John received instruction from the angel to leave his book open. He was not to close it because the fulfillment of the events predicted was near, and people needed to be aware of them. God had told Daniel to seal his prophecy, evidently because there was more prophecy to come (Dan. 8:26; 12:4, 9–10). As an artist covers his work when it is under construction, so God covered His picture of the future until He finished it. The angel gave John this warning to pass along because the time of fulfillment is near (Rev. 22:10). This is a strong warning not to put off becoming a believer in Jesus Christ. It presents the hopelessness of the final state of unbelievers. But since the time is short, persistence in one's ways, whether evil or good, is all that anyone can reasonably expect (22:11).

C. The Testimony of Jesus and John's Response (22:12–20)

Jesus Christ repeated His promise to return soon (22:12). But instead of promising a blessing, as He did earlier (22:7; 16:5), this time He promised to judge. He will reward both the good and the bad. Jesus Christ offered three titles for Himself that give assurance that He can and will fulfill His former promise to reward. They stress His eternality and sovereignty, that God is the cause and goal of history, and that He finishes what He starts. The final blessing in the book (22:14) announces God's favor on those who cleanse themselves spiritually. People who wash their robes in the blood of the Lamb will have access to the tree of life, that is, they will enjoy eternal life. They will also enter the New Jerusalem by its gates and so enjoy intimate fellowship with God. The opposite of the blessings described in verse 14 is exclusion from the New Jerusalem, namely, eternity in the lake of fire (22:15). Those who will not enter the city are noted for the works that mark their lives of unbelief (22:15).

Jesus Himself had given this revelation to John for the churches, through angelic mediation. David founded old Jerusalem, but David's greatest Son will establish the New Jerusalem. Jesus was the ancestor of David as well as His descendant, the root as well as the offspring of David. He fulfills prophecies concerning David's family. Jesus also called Himself the morning star (22:16). Just as the appearance of the morning star heralds the dawn of a new day, so the Lord's second coming will herald the dawn of a new day in history.

Jesus continued speaking to John (22:17). The "Spirit" is God's Holy Spirit, and the "bride" is probably the church, not the New Jerusalem, since this appeal is to the present bride of Christ (22:16). Jesus quoted both of these entities, reiterating their appeal to Himself to come back to the earth. The one "who hears" the content of this book should likewise pray for the Lord's return. Jesus turned the invitation around. He invited the thirsty to come to Him and take the water of life freely. The one who is thirsty is the person who senses his need. "Whoever wishes" is broad enough to include every individual. This is an unusually winsome gospel invitation. The water of life costs the one who comes for it nothing, but it cost Jesus Christ greatly to give Himself for us.

Adding material to or deleting from the prophecies contained in this book will result in punishment from God. Anyone who perverts the teaching of this book will experience judgment from God similar to the judgments that will come on the earth-dwellers during the Tribulation. Taking away "his share" from the Tree of Life and the New Jerusalem does not necessarily mean he will lose his salvation. If the person who corrupts Revelation is an unbeliever, he will have no part in the blessings of the new creation. If he is a believer, the part lost must be some special privilege in the eternal state, part of his eternal reward.

John now quoted Jesus' promise to come soon (22:20), which was His response to the prayers of the Spirit, the bride, and the faithful hearers (22:17). John added his "amen" to affirm his belief that Jesus will come soon, and to pray that He would do so.

> Since Jesus Christ promised so often in this prophecy to come soon, how can we doubt that He will? Certainly we should live in the light of this revelation as we anticipate our blessed hope.

D. The Final Benediction (22:21)

John's closing benediction wishes God's enabling grace on all God's people. It is a prayer that all the book's hearers and readers may respond appropriately to the revelation in it.

ENDNOTES

ACTS

1. In the Septuagint the term "restoration" (Greek *apokatastasis*) technically refers to God's political restoration of Israel (Ps. 16:5; Jer. 15:19; 16:15; 23:8; Ezek. 16:55; 17:23; Hos. 11:11). Israel (the physical descendants of Jacob) and the church (the spiritual descendants of Abraham) exist simultaneously in Acts. The term Israel appears twenty times and *ekklēsia* ("church") nineteen times. The two groups are always distinct.

2. Spirit filling and Spirit baptism are two distinct ministries of the Holy Spirit. Both occurred on this occasion, though Luke only mentioned filling here (Acts 2:4). Filling by the Spirit results in the Spirit's control of the believer (Eph. 5:18). Spirit baptism always unites a believer to the body of Christ, the church (1 Cor. 12:13). This first occurrence of the baptizing work of the Holy Spirit marked the beginning of the church.

3. This is one of seven progress reports in Acts, each of which concludes a major advance of the church in its worldwide mission (see 6:7; 9:31; 12:24; 16:5; 19:20; 28:31).

4. Jesus Christ gave to the early church the ability to heal instantaneously in order to convince people that He is God and that the message of the Christians had divine authority. He gave it for the benefit of Jewish observers primarily (see 1 Cor. 1:22).

663

5. Luke recorded seven of Peter's addresses in Acts (1:16–22; 2:14–36; 3:12–26; 4:8–12; 10:34–43; 11:4–17; 15:7–11).

6. In the three trials before the Sanhedrin that Luke recorded thus far, the first ended with a warning (Acts 4:17, 21), the second with flogging (5:40), and the third with stoning (7:58–60).

7. Again, as with Saul and Ananias, God prepared two strategic people, one an unbeliever and the other a believer, to get together by giving each of them a vision.

8. We may wonder if Peter remembered Jonah as he thought about the mission God had given him of preaching to the Gentiles. God had also called that prophet to carry a message of salvation to the Gentiles in Nineveh, but Jonah had fled from that very city, Joppa, to escape his calling. Now Peter found himself in the same position.

9. Traditionally Luke came from Antioch, so perhaps he was one of the converts.

10. There are only three occurrences of the name "Christian" in the New Testament (11:26; 26:28; 1 Pet. 4:16), and in each case Christians did not use it of themselves.

11. The Greek particle *te* occurs before Barnabas and before Manaen in this list, thereby dividing the five men into two groups.

12. This is the beginning of the first so-called "we" sections in Acts, the sections in which Luke was traveling with Paul (16:10–40; 20:5–21:18; 27:1–28:16).

13. As a Christian, Paul had freedom to make or not make a vow. He chose to do so on this occasion and to fulfill it according to Jewish custom, not because he was under the Mosaic Law.

14. This is the sixth time in Acts that Paul's ministry had precipitated a public disturbance (14:19; 16:19–22; 17:5–8, 13; 19:25–34; 21:35–36).

ROMANS

1. "Natural" here means in keeping with how God has designed people, and "unnatural" refers to behavior that is contrary to how God has made us.

2. Note the repetition of "none" as well as "all" and "not even one"—all universal terms.

3. W. H. Auden, *For the Time Being* (London: Faber and Faber, 1958), 116.

4. Positionally (in his standing before God) the believer is completely sanctified the moment he trusts in Jesus Christ because he is "in Christ." But practically (in his state among people) he must obey God's will to become progressively more sanctified (holy) in his daily living.

5. The code of laws under which British people live is similar to yet different from the code of laws under which Americans live. For example, it is against the law under both codes to murder someone. But under British law it is illegal to drive on the right side of the highway, whereas under American law it is illegal to drive on the left side. Both codes contain some of the same laws, but there are some differences too. Likewise some of the laws under which the Israelites lived are the same as those under which Christians live, yet the codes are different.

6. This chapter contains the greatest concentration of references to the Holy Spirit in the New Testament, an average of one almost every two verses.

1 CORINTHIANS

1. Hellenistic dualism viewed anything material as evil and anything nonmaterial or "spiritual" as good.

2. Paul's pastoral counsel was every bit as authoritative as everything else he wrote under the inspiration of the Holy Spirit, but it was not as prescriptive as his commands.

3. That both extreme groups were present in the Corinthian church becomes clear again in chapters 8–11.

4. This is the second of four instances where Paul appealed to what was customary in all the churches (see 4:17; 11:16; 14:33). He never did this in any of his other letters. He was reminding this church that its theology, not his, was off track.

5. A freedman was a person who had formerly been a slave but had received his freedom.

6. Paul's thought returned to the Cross again (see 6:20).

7. The context of Paul's discussion of this subject limits the relationships in view to family relationships. They do not apply to all male-female relationships.

8. Paul used *pneumatika* when he wanted to emphasize the Spirit, and he used *charismata* when he wanted to stress the gift.

9. In 2:12–14 Paul described all Christians as "spiritual" (*pneumatikos*, having the Spirit) in contrast to "natural" (unsaved). However, he proceeded immediately to clarify that it is not only possession of the Spirit but also *control* by the Spirit that marks one as truly spiritual (Rom. 8:9–11).

10. The Greek word for "gift" (*charisma*) comes from *charis*, "grace."

2 CORINTHIANS

1. Paul used "Spirit" in this passage in a double sense. On the one hand, he contrasted the letter or exact wording of the Old Covenant with the spirit or true intention of the New Covenant. On the other hand, he contrasted the nonenabling, external words of the Old Covenant with the enabling, internal Holy Spirit of the New Covenant. The second of these senses is more primary.

2. This is the first of several "tribulation lists" in 2 Corinthians: 4:8–9; 6:3–10; 11:23b–33; 12:7–10 (see also 1:5–11; 2:14–17).

3. Some writers have referred to 11:1–12:13 as Paul's "Fool's Speech" because of the recurring "foolishness" terminology in this passage (see 11:1, 16 [twice], 17, 19, 23; 12:11).

4. This is a good policy in church planting, but it is not normative for a settled pastoral ministry (see 1 Cor. 9:14; 1 Tim. 5:17–18).

5. Paul was not questioning the salvation of his readers at this point. He had spoken to them as beloved brethren throughout this letter. He was questioning their obedience to his commands. Would they now walk in the faith by obeying his apostolic instructions?

GALATIANS

1. The term "flesh" (1:16) is important in Galatians. It has several meanings: sinful human nature, the physical body, and here the whole of humanity (see 2:16; Rom. 3:20; 1 Cor. 1:29). It is a figure of speech in which a prominent part stands for the whole or vice versa.
2. Verses 11–17 constitute one of six New Testament passages that describe Paul's conversion and calling (see Acts 9:1–19; 22:6–16; 26:12–16; 1 Cor. 9:1–2; 15:3–11).
3. This is the first imperative (in the Greek text) in Galatians.
4. James's emphasis in his epistle was on the importance of living by faith after God has accepted us (James 2:14–26). Paul's emphasis in Galatians was on what makes us acceptable to God.

EPHESIANS

1. Whenever Paul used the single name of "Jesus" in Ephesians, as here, he drew attention to the death and resurrection of the Savior.
2. These five vices and three virtues are representative of many others.
3. Younger children living at home with their parents are in view here. The household is the context of this whole section, dealing with the responsibilities of members of households to one another.

COLOSSIANS

1. Darkness is also a prominent biblical symbol of ignorance, falsehood, and sin (see John 3:19; Rom. 13:12).
2. Some writers have understood this passage to be an early Christian hymn.
3. Lists of virtues and vices were common in the ethical systems of the ancient world (see Rom. 1:29–32; 1 Cor. 5:9–11; 6:9–10; Gal. 5:19–23; Phil. 4:8; 1 Tim. 3:1–13; Titus 1:5–9; 1 Pet. 4:3), and the imagery of putting off and putting on was also well known .
4. This is one of several "house-rule" lists in the New Testament (see

Eph. 5:22–6:9; 1 Tim. 2:8–15; 6:1–2; Titus 2:1–10; 1 Pet. 2:18–3:7). The writings of some apostolic fathers also contain such lists.

1 THESSALONIANS

1. A few scholars have suggested that Paul wrote 2 Thessalonians before he wrote 1 Thessalonians because of what he wrote in each epistle. This is possible since the traditional basis for the order of Paul's letters in the New Testament is length rather than date. But most scholars do not accept this theory.

2. A comparison of 1 Thessalonians 4:13–18 with John 14:1–3 shows that they refer to the same event, but comparing 1 Thessalonians 4:13–18 with Matthew 24–25 and Revelation 19, which describe the second coming of Christ, shows that the latter three chapters describe a different event.

3. The word in the Latin Vulgate translated "caught up" is *rapturo,* from which we get the word "Rapture."

4. The beginning of the Day of the Lord and the beginning of Daniel's seventieth week are the same (see Dan. 9:27).

5. This is one of approximately seventy New Testament commands to rejoice.

2 THESSALONIANS

1. A few scholars believe that Paul wrote 2 Thessalonians before 1 Thessalonians and that 1 Thessalonians addresses issues that arose out of 2 Thessalonians.

2. This is the first of five prayers for the Thessalonians in this short letter (1:11; 2:16–17; 3:5, 16, 18).

1 TIMOTHY

1. The verbs "teach" and "have authority" are in the present tense in the Greek text, which implies a continuing ministry rather than a single instance of ministry.

2. The Ephesian church already had elders long before Paul wrote this letter (Acts 20:17–35).

3. "Pillar and foundation" is a figure of speech that suggests a "supporting foundation."

4. Other instructions for slaves and masters appear elsewhere in the New Testament (1 Cor. 7:20–24; Gal. 3:28; Eph. 6:5–9; Col. 3:22–25; Philem.; 1 Pet. 2:13–25).

5. Food and clothing represent all the necessities of life.

2 TIMOTHY

1. Paul mentioned Timothy in all of his inspired epistles except Galatians, Ephesians, and Titus.

2. This is one of the seven so-called liturgical passages in the Pastoral Epistles, all of which expound the essentials of salvation (1 Tim. 1:15; 2:5–6; 3:16; 2 Tim. 1:9–11; 2:8–13; Titus 2:11–14; 3:3–7).

TITUS

1. Only Paul's salutation in Romans is longer.

2. Paul usually commented on the source of his apostleship, but here he wrote of its purpose.

3. Paul was addressing himself to the typical young married woman who has children. Other young women would need to make adjustments to their situations in harmony with the principles underlying these directions.

PHILEMON

1. In this letter Paul made six references to himself as a prisoner (vv. 1, 9, 10, 13, 22, 23).

2. Paul was motivating, not manipulating, Philemon. The difference is that in motivation the welfare of the other person is in view, whereas in manipulation selfishness dominates.

HEBREWS

1. The masculine participle *diēgoumenon* ("to tell"), which refers to the writer in 11:32, would seem to rule out a female writer.

2. Almost all scholars believe that the Timothy referred to in Hebrews is the same one named elsewhere in the New Testament.

3. The writer used many comparisons to support his argument that the new Christian order is superior to the old Jewish order.

4. Several other indications that the writer was warning genuine Christians appear in this epistle.

5. The writer of Hebrews said more about Jesus' priestly ministry than any other New Testament writer.

6. Some say Hebrews 6:4–6 refers to a Christian losing his salvation, but this conflicts with other Bible verses on the security of salvation. Others suggest the verses speak of mere profession of faith apart from genuine salvation, but many statements in Hebrews suggest the writer was addressing believers. And some say only a hypothetical situation is being discussed. The context of Hebrews 6 and the thrust of the entire book suggests to me that the writer was warning his Christian readers about the danger of persisting in sin and relinquishing one's profession of Christ, thereby getting to the point where their sin has hardened them against repentance.

7. This is the first mention in the epistle of the word "covenant" (7:22), which plays a major role in the writer's following argument.

8. "Cultic" refers to the rituals involved in religious service.

9. Even though chapter 11 is exposition, it is strongly applicational.

10. If the writer's concern had been the salvation of those readers who were unbelievers, this would have been an opportune time for him to exhort them to believe in Christ. He could have written, "For you have need of regeneration." Instead he exhorted his readers to endure rather than apostatize.

11. This is the only New Testament reference to Gideon, Barak, Samson, and Jephthah. Here the writer employed a rhetorical device in which he suggested that he was not going to mention something but then did so. This technique stresses the suggestiveness of what he has

omitted. In this case the writer suggested that he could have cited many more examples of persevering faith.

12. Hebrews 12:7–11 constitutes an exposition of Proverbs 3:11–12, which the writer quoted in 11:5–6.

13. In Esau's case his inability to repent was not that he became unable to seek mercy from his father, which he did. It was that his father would not respond to his request.

JAMES

1. In Scripture asking in faith always means one of two things, either believing God *will* do what He has promised or, if He has not promised, believing that He *can* do what the person requesting asks (see Matt. 8:1–4; Mark 4:35–41).

2. This introduction to the book (James 1:2–11) is in balance with the conclusion (5:7–20). Both sections talk about the need for patience (1:2–4; 5:7–12) and prayer (1:5–8; 5:13–18), and both end with an emphasis on contrasting circumstances of life (1:9–11; 5:19–20).

3. We need to keep this in mind when we read James's discussion of faith and works that follows in chapter 2.

4. Verse 14 seems to contradict Paul's affirmation that works are *not* a condition for salvation (Rom. 11:6; Eph. 2:8–9). However, Paul and James were talking about different aspects of salvation. This is clear from James's earlier assertion that his Christian readers (1:18) would be able to save their "souls" (*psychas* can mean "lives") if they obeyed God's Word (1:21). Jesus also gave similar warnings that if His disciples did not continue to follow Him they could lose their "souls" (*psychas,* "lives;" see Matt. 16:24–26; Mark 3:4; 8:34–37; Luke 9:23–25). Many commentators believe that James was referring to eschatological salvation (salvation from eternal damnation). However, this interpretation involves bringing works in as some type of condition for that aspect of salvation, which contradicts the clear biblical revelation that salvation is by grace alone.

5. An organ in the human body is dead when it is nonfunctioning, not when it is absent from the body. Similarly a Christian's faith is "dead"

when it is not functioning, when he or she is not trusting and obeying God day by day. James was addressing the issue of Christians who do not put their faith into practice in daily living, not people who have never exercised saving faith in Christ.

6. The verse that concludes each major section of James's epistle, each chapter, is a proverbial statement. It summarizes James's point in the preceding section and states it in a pithy way that is easy to remember.

1 PETER

1. Salvation is the subject of 1:3–2:10. The word "salvation" appears in 1:5, 9, 10, and 2:2. In this epistle Peter referred primarily to the future aspect of our salvation.
2. First Peter contains an unusually high ratio of Old Testament quotations and allusions to its length. Only Revelation contains more.
3. First Corinthians 1:17 clarifies that baptism is not part of the gospel. Acts 10:47 shows that baptism is an important step of obedience for Christians.

2 PETER

1. Most modern scholars date 2 Peter in the early part of the second century and consider it to be the last New Testament book written. They believe an anonymous author claimed Petrine authorship to give his work the authority and tradition of a revered Christian leader.
2. Second Peter bears some of the marks of a last will and testament (1:3–11; 2:1–3; 3:1–4) as well as those of a letter, two different literary genres.
3. It is difficult if not impossible to tell if Peter had Jude in mind when he wrote or if Jude had 2 Peter in mind when he wrote.
4. "Servant of Jesus Christ" is the New Testament equivalent of "servant of the Lord" in the Old Testament.

5. Peter himself had denied Jesus three times, so he did not want others to follow his example.

6. This comparison strongly suggests the pretribulation rapture of the church.

1 JOHN

1. John frequently emphasized his propositions by restating them in a negative form, as he did here (1:5) and elsewhere.

2. John's references to the Lord's return in 2:28 and 3:2 frame his references to the new birth in 2:29 and 3:1.

REVELATION

1. There are several reasons for concluding that the Rapture occurs chronologically before chapter 4 begins. First, there are many scriptural promises that believers will be kept from the Tribulation (1 Cor. 15:51–52; 1 Thess. 1:10; 4:16–17; 5:9; Rev. 3:10). Second, the New Testament writers consistently pictured the return of Christ for His own (the Rapture) as imminent (potentially happening at any moment); they did not picture the Tribulation as imminent (see Dan. 9:25–27; 2 Thess. 2). Third, comparison of passages dealing with the Rapture and the Second Coming indicate that they do not happen at the same time. Fourth, there are no explicit references to the church or to "Christians" in Revelation 4–18; the believers spoken of are described in other terms. Fifth, the Tribulation is presented in the Old Testament as a time when Israel, not the church, will be the focus of God's dealings (Jer. 30:7).

2. Daniel's seventieth week is identical to the "Tribulation." The "Great Tribulation" describes the last half of this seven-year period.

3. Even though all believers in Christ will go to be with the Lord at the Rapture, leaving only unbelievers on the earth, some of these unbelievers will trust in Christ during the Tribulation.

4. Jesus coined the term "the Great Tribulation" (Matt. 24:21) and limited it to the second half of Daniel's seventieth week (24:15–22; Mark 13:14–20; see Dan. 9:27).

5. Grass appears later on the earth in Revelation 9:4, so it will grow again after this judgment.

6. The eschatological Day of the Lord in the Old Testament included a time of judgment (the Tribulation) and a time of blessing (the Millennium).

7. One-fourth will die under the fourth seal judgment (6:7–8), and many more will die as martyrs and for other reasons (see Dan. 12:1–2; Matt. 24:21–22).

8. John made no reference to "the churches" as in similar exhortations in chapters 2 and 3 (2:7, 11, 17, 29; 3:6, 13, 22). This supports the view that Christians (believers living in the church age) will not be present on the earth at this time.

9. The idea that time will cease in the new creation is Platonic rather than biblical. The biblical writers consistently described life in the new creation as "forever and ever" or similar terms that suggest unending existence. While God has a different relationship to time than we do, there will continue to be a succession of events, which time marks.

BIBLIOGRAPHY

MATTHEW

Blomberg, Craig L. *Matthew*. New American Commentary. Nashville: Broadman Press, 1992.

Bruce, F. F. *Matthew*. Scripture Union Bible Study Books. Grand Rapids: Wm. B. Eerdmans Publishing Co., 1970.

Carson, Donald A. *The Sermon on the Mount: An Evangelical Exposition of Matthew 5–7*. Grand Rapids: Baker Book House, 1978.

_____. "Matthew." In *The Expositor's Bible Commentary*, vol. 8. Grand Rapids: Zondervan Publishing House, 1984.

France, R. T. *The Gospel according to Matthew: An Introduction and Commentary*. Tyndale New Testament Commentaries. Downers Grove, Ill: InterVarsity Press, 1985.

_____. "Matthew." In *The New Bible Commentary*. Downers Grove, Ill: InterVarsity Press, 1995.

Hill, David. *The Gospel of Matthew*. New Century Bible Commentary. Grand Rapids: Wm. B. Eerdmans Publishing Co., 1972.

Kent, Homer A., Jr. "Matthew." In *The Wycliffe Bible Commentary*. Chicago: Moody Press, 1962.

MacArthur, John, Jr. *Matthew*. MacArthur New Testament Commentary, 4 vols. Chicago: Moody Press, 1985–90.

Morris, Leon. *The Gospel According to Matthew*. Grand Rapids: Wm. B. Eerdmans Publishing Co., 1992.

Toussaint, Stanley D. *Behold the King: A Study of Matthew*. Portland, Ore.: Multnomah Press, 1980.

MARK

Brooks, James A. *Mark*. The New American Commentary. Nashville: Broadman Press, 1991.

Burdick, Donald W. "Mark." In *The Wycliffe Bible Commentary*. Chicago: Moody Press, 1962.

Cole, Alan. "Mark." In *The New Bible Commentary*. Downers Grove, Ill: InterVarsity Press, 1995.

Cranfield, C. E. B. *The Gospel According to St. Mark*. Cambridge Greek Testament Commentary. New York: Cambridge University Press, 1966.

Grassmick, John D. "Mark." In *The Bible Knowledge Commentary, New Testament*. Edited by John F. Walvoord and Roy B. Zuck. Wheaton, Ill.: Victor Books, 1985.

Hiebert, D. Edmond. *Mark: A Portrait of the Servant*. Chicago: Moody Press, 1974.

Hurtado, L. W. *Mark*. New International Bible Commentary, 2d ed. Peabody, Mass.: Hendrickson Publishers, 1989.

Lane, William L. *Commentary on Mark*. New International Commentaries of the New Testament. Grand Rapids: Wm. B. Eerdmans Publishing Co., 1974.

Wessel, Walter W. "Mark." In *The Expositor's Bible Commentary*, vol. 8. Grand Rapids: Zondervan Publishing House, 1984.

LUKE

Bailey, Kenneth E. *Poet and Peasant*. Grand Rapids: Wm. B. Eerdmans Publishing Co., 1960.

_____. *Through Peasant Eyes: More Lucan Parables, Their Culture and State*. Grand Rapids: Wm. B. Eerdmans Publishing Co., 1981.

Bock, Darrell L. *Luke 1:1–9:50*. Grand Rapids: Baker Book House, 1994.

_____. *Luke 9:51–24:53*. Grand Rapids: Baker Book House, 1996.

Godet, Franz L. *A Commentary on the Gospel of St. Luke*. 2 vols. Edinburgh: T. & T. Clark, 1870.

Liefeld, Walter L. "Luke." In *The Expositor's Bible Commentary*, vol. 8. Grand Rapids: Zondervan Publishing House, 1984.

Marshall, I. Howard. *The Gospel of Luke*. London: Paternoster Press, 1977.

_____. "Luke." In *The New Bible Commentary*. Downers Grove, Ill.: InterVarsity Press, 1995.

Stein, Robert H. *Luke*. The New American Commentary. Nashville: Broadman Press, 1992.

Talbert, Charles H. *Reading Luke: A Literary and Theological Commentary on the Third Gospel*. New York: Crossroad, 1984.

Tenney, Merrill C. "Luke." In *The Wycliffe Bible Commentary*. Chicago: Moody Press, 1962.

JOHN

Beasley-Murray, G. R. *John*. Word Biblical Commentaries. Waco, Tex.: Word Books, 1987.

Blum, Edwin. "John." In *The Bible Knowledge Commentary, New Testament*. Edited by John F. Walvoord and Roy B. Zuck. Wheaton, Ill.: Victor Books, 1985.

Boice, James M. *The Gospel of John: An Evangelical Commentary*. 5 vols. Grand Rapids: Zondervan Publishing House, 1975–1979.

Bruce, F. F. *The Gospel of John: Introduction, Exposition and Notes*. Grand Rapids: Wm. B. Eerdmans Publishing Co., 1983.

Carson, Donald A. *The Gospel According to John*. Grand Rapids: Wm. B. Eerdmans Publishing Co., 1991.

Guthrie, Donald. "John." In *The New Bible Commentary*. Downers Grove, Ill.: InterVarsity Press, 1995.

Harrison, Everett F. "John." In *The Wycliffe Bible Commentary*. Chicago: Moody Press, 1962.

Kent, Homer A., Jr. *Light in the Darkness. Studies in the Gospel of John*. Grand Rapids: Baker Book House, 1974.

Laney, J. Carl. *John*. Moody Gospel Commentary. Chicago: Moody Press, 1992.

Morris, Leon. *Commentary on the Gospel of John*. Grand Rapids: Wm. B. Eerdmans Publishing Co., 1971.

Stott, John R. W. *Christ the Liberator*. Downers Grove, Ill.: InterVarsity Press, 1971.

Tenney, Merrill C. *John: The Gospel of Belief*. Grand Rapids: Wm. B. Eerdmans Publishing Co., 1948.

Westcott, B. F. *The Gospel According to St. John*. Reprint. Grand Rapids: Wm. B. Eerdmans Publishing Co., 1973.

ACTS

Barrett, C. K. *A Critical and Exegetical Commentary on the Acts of the Apostles.* 2 vols. International Critical Commentary. Edinburgh: T. & T. Clark, 1994.

Blaiklock, E. M. *The Acts of the Apostles.* Tyndale New Testament Commentaries. Grand Rapids: Wm. B. Eerdmans Publishing Co., 1979.

Bruce, F. F. *Commentary on The Book of Acts.* New International Commentaries on the New Testament. Rev. ed. Grand Rapids: Wm. B. Eerdmans Publishing Co., 1988.

Haenchen, Ernst. *The Acts of the Apostles.* Translated by R. McL. Wilson. Philadelphia: Westminster Press, 1971.

Harrison, Everett F. *Acts: The Expanding Church.* Chicago: Moody Press, 1975.

Longenecker, Richard N. "The Acts of the Apostles." In *The Expositor's Bible Commentary,* vol. 9. Grand Rapids: Zondervan Publishing House, 1981.

Marshall, I. Howard. *The Acts of the Apostles.* Tyndale New Testament Commentaries. Grand Rapids: Wm. B. Eerdmans Publishing Co., 1984.

Neil, William. *The Acts of the Apostles.* New Century Bible Commentaries. Grand Rapids: Wm. B. Eerdmans Publishing Co., 1981.

Rackham, Richard Belward. *The Acts of the Apostles.* Westminster Commentaries. 9th ed. London: Methuen & Co., 1922.

Stott, John R. W. *The Message of Acts.* The Bible Speaks Today. Downers Grove, Ill.: InterVarsity Press, 1990.

Tannehill, Robert C. *The Acts of the Apostles.* Vol. 2 of *The Narrative Unity of Luke–Acts: A Literary Interpretation.* Minneapolis: Fortress Press, 1990.

Toussaint, Stanley D. "Acts." In *The Bible Knowledge Commentary, New Testament.* Edited by John F. Walvoord and Roy B. Zuck. Wheaton, Ill.: Victor Books, 1983.

Wiersbe, Warren W. *Be Dynamic [Acts 1–12].* Wheaton, Ill.: Victor Books, 1987.

———. *Be Daring [Acts 13–28].* Wheaton, Ill.: Victor Books, 1988.

ROMANS

Barrett, C. K. *A Commentary on the Epistle to the Romans.* Harper's New Testament Commentaries. New York: Harper & Row, 1957.

Bruce, F. F. *The Letter of Paul to the Romans.* Tyndale New Testament Commentaries. Rev. ed. Grand Rapids: Wm. Eerdmans Publishing Co., 1985.

Cranfield, C. E. B. *A Critical and Exegetical Commentary on the Epistle to the Romans.* International Critical Commentaries. 2 vols. Edinburgh: T. & T. Clark, 1975, 1979.

Dunn, J. D. G. *Romans.* Word Biblical Commentaries. 2 vols. Dallas: Word Books, 1988.

McClain, Alva J. *Romans: The Gospel of God's Grace.* Edited by Herman A. Hoyt. Chicago: Moody Press, 1973.

Moo, Douglas J. *The Epistle to the Romans.* New International Commentaries on the New Testament. Grand Rapids: Wm. B. Eerdmans Publishing Co., 1996.

Morris, Leon. *The Epistle to the Romans.* Grand Rapids: Wm. B. Eerdmans Publishing Co., 1988.

Mounce, Robert H. *Romans.* New American Commentaries. Nashville: Broadman & Holman Publishers, 1995.

Murray, John. *The Epistle to the Romans.* New International Commentaries on the New Testament. 2 vols. in 1. Grand Rapids: Wm. B. Eerdmans Publishing Co., 1968.

Sanday, William, and Arthur C. Headlam. *A Critical and Exegetical Commentary on the Epistle to the Romans.* International Critical Commentaries. 5th ed. Edinburgh: T. & T. Clark, 1902.

Wiersbe, Warren W. *Be Right.* Wheaton, Ill.: Victor Books, 1977.

1 CORINTHIANS

Barrett, Charles Kingsley. *A Commentary on the First Epistle to the Corinthians.* Harper's New Testament Commentaries. New York: Harper & Row, 1968.

Bruce, F. F., ed. *1 and 2 Corinthians.* New Century Bible Commentary. Greenwood, S. C.: Attic Press, 1971.

Calvin, John. *The First Epistle of Paul the Apostle to the Corinthians.* Translated by John W. Fraser. Edited by David W. Torrance and Thomas F. Torrance. Calvin's Commentaries. Reprint, Grand Rapids: Wm. B. Eerdmans Publishing Co., 1973.

Fee, Gordon D. *The First Epistle to the Corinthians.* New International Commentaries on the New Testament. Grand Rapids: Wm. B. Eerdmans Publishing Co., 1987.

Godet, F. *Commentary on the First Epistle of St. Paul to the Corinthians.* Translated by A. Cusin. 2 vols. Classic Commentary Library. Edinburgh: T. & T. Clark, 1886; reprint, Grand Rapids: Zondervan Publishing House, 1957.

Gromacki, Robert G. *Called to Be Saints: An Exposition of 1 Corinthians.* Grand Rapids: Baker Book House, 1977.

Mare, W. Harold. "1 Corinthians." In *The Expositor's Bible Commentary,* vol. 10. Grand Rapids: Zondervan Publishing House, 1978.

Morris, Leon. *The First Epistle of Paul to the Corinthians.* Tyndale New Testament Commentaries. Grand Rapids: Wm. B. Eerdmans Publishing Co., 1958.

Robertson, Archibald, and Alfred Plummer. *A Critical and Exegetical Commentary on the First Epistle of St. Paul to the Corinthians.* International Critical Commentaries. 2d ed. Edinburgh: T. & T. Clark, 1963.

Wiersbe, Warren W. *Be Wise.* Wheaton, Ill.: Victor Books, 1983.

2 CORINTHIANS

Barnett, Paul. *The Second Epistle to the Corinthians.* New International Commentaries on the New Testament. Grand Rapids: Wm. B. Eerdmans Publishing Co., 1997.

Barrett, C. K. *A Commentary on the Second Epistle to the Corinthians.* Harper's New Testament Commentaries. New York: Harper & Row, 1973.

Bruce, F. F., ed. *1 and 2 Corinthians.* New Century Bible Commentaries. London: Marshall, Morgan and Scott, Oliphants, 1971.

Gromacki, Robert G. *Stand Firm in the Faith: An Exposition of 2 Corinthians.* Grand Rapids: Baker Book House, 1978.

Harris, Murray J. "2 Corinthians." In *The Expositor's Bible Commentary*, vol. 10. Grand Rapids: Zondervan Publishing House, 1978.

Hughes, Philip Edgcumbe. *Paul's Second Epistle to the Corinthians.* New International Commentaries on the New Testament. Grand Rapids: Wm. B. Eerdmans Publishing Co., 1962.

Martin, Ralph P. *2 Corinthians.* Word Biblical Commentaries. Waco, Tex.: Word Books, 1986.

Plummer, Alfred. *A Critical and Exegetical Commentary on the Second Epistle of St. Paul to the Corinthians.* International Critical Commentary. Reprint, Edinburgh: T. & T. Clark, 1966.

Wiersbe, Warren W. *Be Encouraged.* Wheaton, Ill.: Victor Books, 1984.

GALATIANS

Bruce, F. F. *The Epistle to the Galatians*. New International Greek Testament Commentary. Grand Rapids: Wm. B. Eerdmans Publishing Co., 1982.

Campbell, Donald K. "Galatians." In *The Bible Knowledge Commentary, New Testament*. Edited by John F. Walvoord and Roy B. Zuck. Wheaton, Ill.: Victor Books, 1983.

Fung, Ronald Y. K. *The Epistle to the Galatians*. New International Commentary on the New Testament. Grand Rapids: Wm. B. Eerdmans Publishing Co., 1982.

George, Timothy. *Galatians*. New American Commentaries. Nashville: Broadman & Holman Publishers, 1994.

Longenecker, Richard N. *Galatians*. Word Biblical Commentaries. Dallas: Word Books, 1990.

Morris, Leon. *Galatians: Paul's Charter of Christian Freedom*. Downers Grove, Ill.: InterVarsity Press, 1996.

Tenney, Merrill C. *Galatians: The Charter of Christian Liberty*. Grand Rapids: Wm. B. Eerdmans Publishing Co., 1951.

Wiersbe, Warren W. *Be Free*. Wheaton, Ill.: Victor Books, 1975.

EPHESIANS

Bruce, F. F. *The Epistles to the Colossians, to Philemon and to the Ephesians*. New International Commentaries on the New Testament. Grand Rapids: Wm. B. Eerdmans Publishing Co., 1984.

Hoehner, Harold W. "Ephesians." In *The Bible Knowledge Commentary, New Testament*. Edited by John F. Walvoord and Roy B. Zuck. Wheaton, Ill.: Victor Books, 1983.

Kent, Homer A., Jr. *Ephesians: The Glory of the Church*. Chicago: Moody Press, 1971.

Lincoln, Andrew T. *Ephesians*. Word Biblical Commentaries. Dallas: Word Books, 1990.

Stott, John R. W. *The Message of Ephesians*. The Bible Speaks Today. Downers Grove, Ill.: InterVarsity Press, 1979.

Westcott, Brooks Foss. *Saint Paul's Epistle to the Ephesians*. Reprint, Minneapolis: Klock & Klock Publishers, 1978.

Wiersbe, Warren W. *Be Rich*. Wheaton, Ill.: Victor Books, 1976.

PHILIPPIANS

Fee, Gordon D. *Paul's Letter to the Philippians*. New International Commentaries on the New Testament. Grand Rapids: Wm. B. Eerdmans Publishing Co., 1995.

Getz, Gene A. *Pressing On When You'd Rather Turn Back*. Ventura, Calif.: Regal Books, 1983.

Hawthorne, Gerald F. *Philippians*. Word Biblical Commentaries. Waco, Tex.: Word Books, 1983.

Martin, Ralph P. *Philippians*. New Century Bible Commentary. Grand Rapids: Wm. B. Eerdmans Publishing Co., 1959.

Pentecost, J. Dwight. *The Joy of Living*. Grand Rapids: Zondervan Publishing House, 1973.

Silva, Moisés. *Philippians*. Wycliffe Exegetical Commentary. Chicago: Moody Press, 1988.

Swindoll, Charles R. *Laugh Again*. Dallas: Word Publishing, 1991.

Tenney, Merrill C. *Philippians: The Gospel at Work*. Grand Rapids: Wm. B. Eerdmans Publishing Co., 1956.

Wiersbe, Warren W. *Be Joyful*. Wheaton, Ill.: Victor Books, 1974.

COLOSSIANS

Bruce, F. F. *The Epistles to the Colossians, to Philemon and to the Ephesians.* New International Commentaries on the New Testament. Grand Rapids: Wm. B. Eerdmans Publishing Co., 1984.

Gromacki, Robert G. *Stand Perfect in Wisdom: An Exposition of Colossians and Philemon.* Grand Rapids: Baker Book House, 1981.

Kent, Homer A., Jr. *Treasures of Wisdom: Studies in Colossians and Philemon.* Grand Rapids: Baker Book House, 1978.

Martin, Ralph P. *Colossians and Philemon.* New Century Bible Commentary. London: Marshall, Morgan, and Scott, 1973.

O'Brien, P. T. *Colossians, Philemon.* Word Biblical Commentaries. Waco, Tex.: Word Books, 1982.

Wiersbe, Warren W. *Be Complete*. Wheaton, Ill.: Victor Books, 1981.

1 AND 2 THESSALONIANS

Bruce, F. F. *1 and 2 Thessalonians.* Word Biblical Commentaries. Waco, Tex.: Word Books, 1982.

Constable, Thomas L. "1 Thessalonians." In *The Bible Knowledge Commentary, New Testament.* Edited by John F. Walvoord and Roy B. Zuck. Wheaton, Ill.: Victor Books, 1983.

Getz, Gene A. *Standing Firm When You'd Rather Retreat.* Ventura, Calif.: Regal Books, 1986.

Hiebert, D. Edmond. *The Thessalonian Epistles: A Call to Readiness.* Chicago: Moody Press, 1971.

Morris, Leon. *The First and Second Epistles to the Thessalonians.* New International Commentaries on the New Testament. Grand Rapids: Wm. B. Eerdmans Publishing Co., 1979.

Thomas, Robert L. "1 Thessalonians." In *The Expositor's Bible Commentary,* vol. 11. Grand Rapids: Zondervan Publishing House.

Walvoord, John F. *The Thessalonian Epistles.* Grand Rapids: Zondervan Publishing House, 1967.

Wiersbe, Warren W. *Be Ready.* Wheaton, Ill.: Victor Books, 1979.

1, 2 TIMOTHY AND TITUS

Fee, Gordon D. *1 and 2 Timothy, Titus.* New International Biblical Commentaries. Peabody, Mass.: Hendrickson Publishers, 1995.

Getz, Gene A. *A Profile for a Christian Life Style.* Grand Rapids: Zondervan Publishing House, 1978.

Kelly, J. N. D. *A Commentary on the Pastoral Epistles.* Thornapple Commentaries. London: A. & C. Black, 1963; reprint, Grand Rapids: Baker Book House, 1981.

Kent, Homer A., Jr. *The Pastoral Epistles.* Chicago: Moody Press, 1958.

Lea, Thomas D., and Hayne P. Griffin, Jr. *1, 2 Timothy, Titus.* New American Commentary. Nashville: Broadman Press, 1992.

Towner, Philip H. *1–2 Timothy & Titus.* IVP New Testament Commentaries. Downers Grove, Ill.: InterVarsity Press, 1994.

Wiersbe, Warren W. *Be Faithful.* Wheaton, Ill.: Victor Books, 1981.

PHILEMON

See the bibliography on Colossians.

HEBREWS

Brown, Raymond. *The Message of Hebrews. The Bible Speaks Today.* Downers Grove, Ill.: InterVarsity Press, 1982.

Bruce, F. F. *The Epistle to the Hebrews.* New International Commentaries on the New Testament. Rev. ed. Grand Rapids: Wm. B. Eerdmans Publishing Co., 1990.

Guthrie, Donald. *Hebrews.* Tyndale New Testament Commentaries. Grand Rapids: Wm. B. Eerdmans Publishing Co., 1983.

Hughes, Philip Edgcumbe. *A Commentary on the Epistle to the Hebrews.* Grand Rapids: Wm. B. Eerdmans Publishing Co., 1977.

Lane, William L. *Hebrews 1–8.* Word Biblical Commentaries. Dallas: Word Books, 1991.

———. *Hebrews 9–13.* Word Biblical Commentaries. Dallas: Word Books, 1991.

Moffatt, James. *A Critical and Exegetical Commentary on the Epistle to the Hebrews.* International Critical Commentary. Reprint, Edinburgh: T. & T. Clark, 1963.

Pentecost, Dwight J. *A Faith That Endures.* Grand Rapids: Discovery House Publishers, 1992.

Thomas, W. H. Griffith. *Hebrews: A Devotional Commentary.* Grand Rapids: Wm. B. Eerdmans Publishing Co., 1966.

Westcott, Brooke Foss. *The Epistle to the Hebrews.* Reprint, Grand Rapids: Wm. B. Eerdmans Publishing Co., n.d.

Wiersbe, Warren W. *Be Confident.* Wheaton, Ill.: Victor Books, 1982.

JAMES

Adamson, James B. *James: The Man and His Message.* Grand Rapids: Wm. B. Eerdmans Publishing Co., 1989.

Blue, J. Ronald. "James." In *The Bible Knowledge Commentary, New Testament*. Edited by John F. Walvoord and Roy B. Zuck. Wheaton, Ill.: Victor Books, 1983.

Martin, Ralph P. *James*. Word Biblical Commentaries. Waco, Tex.: Word Books, 1988.

Moo, Douglas J. *The Letter of James*. Tyndale New Testament Commentaries. Grand Rapids: Wm. B. Eerdmans Publishing Co., 1986.

Stulac, George M. *James*. IVP New Testament Commentaries. Downers Grove, Ill.: InterVarsity Press, 1993.

Wiersbe, Warren W. *Be Mature*. Wheaton, Ill.: Victor Books, 1978.

1 PETER

Best, Ernest. *1 Peter*. New Century Bible Commentary. Grand Rapids: Wm. B. Eerdmans Publishing Co., 1971.

Clowney, Edmund. *The Message of 1 Peter*. The Bible Speaks Today. Downers Grove, Ill.: InterVarsity Press, 1988.

Davids, Peter H. *The First Epistle of Peter*. New International Commentaries on the New Testament. Grand Rapids: Wm. B. Eerdmans Publishing Co., 1990.

Goppelt, Leonhard. *A Commentary on I Peter*. Edited by Ferdinand Hahn. Translated and augmented by John E. Alsup. Grand Rapids: Wm. B. Eerdmans Publishing Co., 1993.

Hillyer, Norman. *1 and 2 Peter, Jude*. Peabody, Mass.: Hendrickson Publishers, 1992.

Kelly, J. N. D. *A Commentary on the Epistles of Peter and Jude*. Thornapple Commentaries. Reprint, Grand Rapids: Baker Book House, 1981.

Michaels, J. Ramsey. *1 Peter*. Word Biblical Commentaries. Waco, Tex.: Word Books, 1988.

Swindoll, Charles R. *Hope Again*. Dallas: Word Publishing, 1996.

Wiersbe, Warren W. *Be Hopeful*. Wheaton, Ill.: Victor Books, 1982.

2 PETER

Bauckham, Richard J. *Jude, 2 Peter*. Word Biblical Commentaries. Waco, Tex.: Word Books, 1983.

Hillyer, Norman. *1 and 2 Peter, Jude*. Peabody, Mass.: Hendrickson Publishers, 1992.

Kelly, J. N. D. *A Commentary on the Epistles of Peter and Jude*. Thornapple Commentaries. Reprint, Grand Rapids: Baker Book House, 1981.

Lucas, Dick, and Christopher Green. *The Message of 2 Peter & Jude*. The Bible Speaks Today. Downers Grove, Ill.: InterVarsity Press, 1995.

Moo, Douglas J. *2 Peter and Jude*. NIV Application Commentaries. Grand Rapids: Zondervan Publishing House, 1996.

Wiersbe, Warren. *Be Alert*. Wheaton, Ill.: Victor Books, 1984.

1, 2, AND 3 JOHN

Brown, Raymond. *The Epistles of John*. Anchor Bible. Garden City, N.Y.: Doubleday & Co., 1982.

Bruce, F. F. *The Epistles of John*. Old Tappan, N.J.: Fleming H. Revell Co., 1970.

Burdick, Donald W. *The Epistles of John*. Chicago: Moody Press, 1970.

Hodges, Zane C. "1 John." In *The Bible Knowledge Commentary,* New Testament. Edited by John F. Walvoord and Roy B. Zuck. Wheaton, Ill.: Victor Books, 1983.

Marshall, I. Howard. *The Epistles of John*. New International Commentaries on the New Testament. Reprint, Grand Rapids: Wm. B. Eerdmans Publishing Co., 1984.

Pentecost, J. Dwight. *The Joy of Fellowship: A Study of First John.* Grand Rapids: Zondervan Publishing House, 1977.

Plummer, Alfred. *The Epistles of John.* Thornapple Commentaries. Reprint, Grand Rapids: Baker Book House, 1980.

Smalley, Stephen S. *1, 2, 3 John.* Word Biblical Commentaries. Waco, Tex.: Word Books, 1984.

Westcott, Brooke Foss. *The Epistles of St. John.* 1883. Reprint, Appleford, U.K.: Marcham Manor, 1966.

Wiersbe, Warren W. *Be Real.* Wheaton, Ill.: Victor Books, 1972.

JUDE

See the bibliography on 2 Peter.

REVELATION

Aune, David E. *Revelation 1–5.* Word Biblical Commentaries. Dallas: Word Books, 1997.

———. *Revelation 6–16.* Word Biblical Commentaries. Nashville: Thomas Nelson Publishers, 1998.

———. *Revelation 17–22.* Word Biblical Commentaries. Nashville: Thomas Nelson Publishers, 1998.

Beasley-Murray, George Raymond. *The Book of Revelation.* New Century Bible Commentaries. Rev. ed. London: Morgan & Scott, 1974. Reprint, Grand Rapids: Wm. B. Eerdmans Publishing Co., 1983.

Caird, G. B. *The Revelation of St. John the Divine.* London: A. & C. Black, 1966; reprint, Peabody, Mass.: Hendrickson Publishers, 1993.

Charles, R. H. *A Critical and Exegetical Commentary on the Revelation of St. John.* 2 vols. International Critical Commentary. Edinburgh: T. & T. Clark, 1920.

Johnson, Alan. "Revelation." In *The Expositor's Bible Commentary*, vol. 12. Grand Rapids: Zondervan Publishing House, 1984.

Morris, Leon. *The Book of Revelation.* Rev. ed. Grand Rapids: Wm. B. Eerdmans Publishing Co., 1987.

Mounce, Robert H. *The Book of Revelation.* New International Commentaries on the New Testament. Grand Rapids: Wm. B. Eerdmans Publishing Co., 1983.

Ryrie, Charles R. *Revelation.* Chicago: Moody Press, 1968.

Smith, J. B. *A Revelation of Jesus Christ.* Edited by J. Otis Yoder. Scottdale, Pa.: Herald Press, 1961.

Thomas, Robert L. *Revelation 1–7: An Exegetical Commentary.* Chicago: Moody Press, 1992.

———. *Revelation 8–22: An Exegetical Commentary.* Chicago: Moody Press, 1995.

Walvoord, John F. *The Revelation of Jesus Christ.* Chicago: Moody Press, 1966.

———. "Revelation." In *The Bible Knowledge Commentary, New Testament.* Edited by John F. Walvoord and Roy B. Zuck. Wheaton, Ill.: Victor Books, 1983.

Wiersbe, Warren W. *Be Victorious.* Wheaton, Ill.: Victor Books, 1985.

The
Swindoll Leadership Library

ANGELS, SATAN AND DEMONS
Dr. Robert Lightner

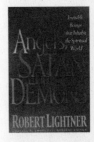

The supernatural world gets a lot of attention these days in books, movies, and television series, but what does the Bible say about these other-worldly beings? Dr. Robert Lightner answers these questions with an in-depth look at the world of the "invisible" as expressed in Scripture.

THE CHURCH
Dr. Ed Hayes

In this indispensable guide, Dr. Ed Hayes explores the labyrinths of the church, delving into her history, doctrines, rituals, and resources to find out what it means to be the Body of Christ on earth. Both passionate and precise, this essential volume offers solid insights on worship, persecution, missions, and morality: a bold call to unity and renewal.

COLOR OUTSIDE THE LINES
Dr. Howard G. Hendricks

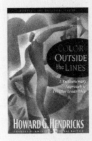

Just as the apostle Paul prodded early Christians "not to be conformed" to the world, Dr. Howard Hendricks vividly—and unexpectedly—extends that biblical theme and charges us to learn the art of living creatively, reflecting the image of the Creator rather than the culture.

EFFECTIVE PASTORING
Dr. Bill Lawrence

In *Effective Pastoring*, Dr. Bill Lawrence examines what it means to be a pastor in the 21st century. Lawrence discusses often overlooked issues, writing transparently about the struggles of the pastor, the purpose and practice of servant leadership, and the roles and relationships crucial to pastoring. In doing so, he offers a revealing look beneath the "how to" to the "how to be" for pastors.

EMPOWERED LEADERS
Dr. Hans Finzel

What is leadership really about? The rewards, excitement, and exhilaration? Or the responsibilities, frustrations, and exhausting nights? Dr. Hans Finzel takes readers on a journey into the lives of the Bible's great leaders, unearthing powerful principles for effective leadership in any situation.

END TIMES
Dr. John F. Walvoord

Long regarded as one of the top prophecy experts, Dr. John F. Walvoord now explores world events in light of biblical prophecy. By examining all of the prophetic passages in the Bible, Walvoord clearly explains the mystery behind confusing verses and conflicting viewpoints. This is the definitive work on prophecy for Bible students.

THE FORGOTTEN BLESSING
Dr. Henry Holloman

For many Christians, the gift of God's grace is central to their faith. But another gift—sanctification—is often overlooked. *The Forgotten Blessing* clarifies this essential doctrine, showing us what it means to be set apart, and how the process of sanctification can forever change our relationship with God.

GOD
Dr. J. Carl Laney

With tenacity and clarity, Dr. J. Carl Laney makes it plain: it's not enough to know *about* God. We can know *God* better. This book presents a practical path to life-changing encounters with the goodness, greatness, and glory of our Creator.

The Holy Spirit
Dr. Robert Gromacki

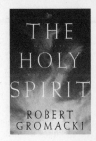

In *The Holy Spirit,* Dr. Robert Gromacki examines the personality, deity, symbols, and gifts of the Holy Spirit, while recapping the ministry of the Spirit throughout the Old Testament, the Gospel Era, the life of Christ, the Book of Acts, and the lives of believers.

Humanity and Sin
Dr. Robert A. Pyne

Sin may seem like an outdated concept these days, but its consequences remain as destructive as ever. Dr. Robert A. Pyne takes a close look at humankind through the pages of Scripture and the lens of modern culture. As never before, readers will understand sin's overarching effect on creation and our world today.

Immanuel
Dr. John A. Witmer

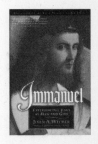

Dr. John A. Witmer presents the almighty Son of God as a living, breathing, incarnate man. He shows us a full picture of the Christ in four distinct phases: the Son of God before He became man, the divine suffering man on Earth, the glorified and ascended Christ, and the reigning King today.

A Life of Prayer
Dr. Paul Cedar

Dr. Paul Cedar explores prayer through three primary concepts, showing us how to consider, cultivate, and continue a lifestyle of prayer. This volume helps readers recognize the unlimited potential and the awesome purpose of prayer.

MINISTERING TO TODAY'S ADULTS
Dr. Kenn Gangel

After 40 years of research and experience, Dr. Kenn Gangel knows what it takes to reach adults. In an easy-to-grasp, easy-to-apply style, Gangel offers proven systematic strategies for building dynamic adult ministries.

MORAL DILEMMAS
J. Kerby Anderson

Should biblically informed Christians be for or against capital punishment? How should we as Christians view abortion, euthanasia, genetic engineering, divorce, and technology? In this comprehensive, cutting-edge book, J. Kerby Anderson challenges us to thoughtfully analyze the dividing issues facing our age, while equipping believers to maneuver through the ethical and moral land mines of our times.

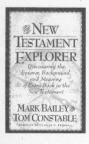

THE NEW TESTAMENT EXPLORER
Mark Bailey and Tom Constable

The New Testament Explorer provides a concise, on-target map for traveling through the New Testament. Mark Bailey and Tom Constable guide the reader paragraph by paragraph through the New Testament, providing an up-close-and-to-the-point examination of the leaders behind the page and the theological implications of the truths revealed. A great tool for teachers and pastors alike, this exploration tool comes equipped with outlines for further study, narrative discussion, and applicable truths for teaching and for living.

SPIRIT-FILLED TEACHING
Dr. Roy B. Zuck

Whether you teach a small Sunday school class or a standing-room-only crowd at a major university, the process of teaching can be demanding and draining. This lively book brings a new understanding of the Holy Spirit's essential role in teaching.

TALE OF THE TARDY OXCART AND 1501 OTHER STORIES
Dr. Charles R. Swindoll

In this rich volume, you'll have access to resourcing Dr. Charles Swindoll's favorite anecdotes on prayer or quotations for grief. In *The Tale of the Tardy Oxcart*, thousands of illustrations are arranged by subjects alphabetically for quick-and-easy access. A perfect resource for all pastors and speakers.

WOMEN AND THE CHURCH
Dr. Lucy Mabery-Foster

Women and the Church provides an overview of the historical, biblical, and cultural perspectives on the unique roles and gifts women bring to the church, while exploring what it takes to minister to women today. Important insight for any leader seeking to understand how to more effectively minister to women and build women's ministries in the local church.